The Impact of EU Free Trade Agreements on Economic Development and Regional Integration in Southern Africa
The Example of EU-SACU Trade Relations

DEVELOPMENT ECONOMICS AND POLICY

Series edited by Franz Heidhues and Joachim von Braun

Vol. 55

PETER LANG

Frankfurt am Main · Berlin · Bern · Bruxelles · New York · Oxford · Wien

The Impact of EU Free Trade Agreements on Economic Development and Regional Integration in Southern Africa

The Example of EU-SACU Trade Relations

Mareike Meyn

PETER LANG
Europäischer Verlag der Wissenschaften

Bibliographic Information published by Die Deutsche Bibliothek
Die Deutsche Bibliothek lists this publication in the Deutsche Nationalbibliografie; detailed bibliographic data is available in the internet at <http://dnb.ddb.de>.

Zugl.: Bremen, Univ., Diss., 2006

D 46
ISSN 0948-1338
ISBN 3-631-55354-4
US-ISBN 0-8204-9921-8

Printed in Germany 1 2 3 4 5 7

www.peterlang.de

Editorial Preface

The study extensively discusses the advantages, possibilities and limitations of free trade agreements as an active development instrument for southern African countries. With the conclusion of a free trade agreement with South Africa in 2000, the EU had built momentum in its trade relations with developing countries. Since then, negotiable, reciprocal trade agreements between industrialised and developing countries are being regarded more and more as a potential development tool, meant to induce consumer benefits, technological spillovers and the inclusion of producers into international trading networks.

Mareike Meyn investigates in her study to what extent these theoretical presumptions fit into the realities of the countries that comprise the Southern African Customs Union (SACU). The study contains three empirical parts based on the findings of field studies undertaken in South Africa, Botswana, Namibia, and Swaziland. With the use of standardised questionnaires and by making use of the framework of the global value chain analysis, M. Meyn develops profiles of the competitiveness and the global value chain position of the South African automotive industry and the Namibian fishing industry and links them to their trade relations with the EU. Both industries are important manufacturing sectors in the respective countries, are highly export-oriented towards the EU market and benefit from significant domestic protection. The author advances the argument that a free trade agreement with the EU is not an adequate instrument to increase sectors' integration into the global value chain and that international linkages and economic successes are determined by other factors including national policy instruments. Consequently, M. Meyn concludes that trade policies need to differentiate between the requirements of the single sectors to promote economic development rather than a 'one size fits all' approach.

Another factor that is often neglected when analysing African countries' potential benefits from free trade agreements with industrialised countries is the challenge posed by a lack of capacity in African countries to participate effectively in these agreements. The challenges of capacity constraints are epitomised in the African context when analysis of the relatively developed SACU countries shows that only South Africa has the capacity to lobby for its interests and to translate them into an effective negotiation strategy.

The study gives the interested reader an all-embracing overview of SACU countries' complex trading environment and the impacts of a challenging trade relationship with the EU. The summary of findings are discussed in detail at the end of every chapter and are combined in a synopsis in the final chapter of the study. Substantial policy recommendations for the single actors in each of the policy fields rounds off the study.

Prof. Dr. Dr. h.c. Franz Heidhues
University of Hohenheim / Stuttgart
Institute for Agricultural Economics and
Social Sciences in the Tropics and Subtropics

Prof. Dr. Joachim von Braun
International Food Policy
Research Institute (IFPRI)
Washington D.C.

Foreword

This study by Dr Mareike Meyn is an important work as it presents a new approach for analysing the recent strategies of the European Union (EU) in its relations with African countries, especially in southern Africa. The author takes stock of the new developments that have emerged after the Lomé and Cotonou Agreements, especially analysing the drive towards new EU strategies and instruments that aim for a more balanced cooperation between the EU and Africa.

The author investigates the following important questions:

- What will be the impact of free trade agreements between the EU and developing countries in terms of economic development, policy formation and regional integration and how can the developmental impacts and results of such agreements be assessed analytically?
- What will be the impact of the EU free trade agreement with South Africa on those countries that are related to South Africa in the regional context of SACU and SADC and what will be the future of SACU and of SADC in the context of these new inter-regional trade agreements?
- What are the options to make the international economic relations between the EU and southern Africa more balanced, results-based and more development-oriented than has been the case in the past?
- How can the EU support development strategies and development paths that strengthen southern African countries economic independence, especially those of the smaller and less developed economies?
- What are the internal and external policy implications of the large differences in SACU countries' development levels?
- How will the new trade and development relations between Africa and the EU impact on African countries' trade and industrialisation strategies and what are the export diversification options associated with these new agreements and strategies?

The study answers most of these questions by combining competently theoretical and empirical analyses. The theoretical work is based on the frame of international production networks what allows it to analyse the degree of internationalisation of specific sectors and enterprises in southern Africa and the international competitiveness of production components, products and services. This theoretical frame also helps to identify specific trade, industry and technology policies that prove to be developmental. Furthermore, the approach is suitable to identify capacity building demands in these areas.

The empirical part, based on intensive field research in the SACU countries, is related to data generation and processing by reviewing national and sectoral data and by analysing the experience of companies in selected industries in qualitative interviews. Empirical research was also extended to chambers of commerce and government offices in the SACU countries so as to get direct information on national policies and development experiences. Further thereto, the author also reviewed and assessed the capacity of governments and the private sector to adequately respond to these new trade agreements.

This combination of analytical and empirical methods in the study provides important results that are of use for researchers, policymakers and for the global development community. Academic scholars will gain new insights into southern African development trends and regional integration perspectives. Development practitioners will get information how EU trade policies impacts African countries. Policymakers and business people can see how trade, industrialisation and regional integration strategies and policies work in Africa, and how these strategies and policies could be reformed in such a way that they become more effective. Moreover, the study gives an interesting picture of the diverse conditions and development trends in southern Africa and presents a critical assessment of the actual influences on international economic relations, especially of the EU, in times of trade liberalisation and globalisation. Overall, the study highlights the actual and potential impacts of the complex new package of trade and development agreements between the EU and the less developed countries in Africa, just in a period when the new Economic Partnership Agreements are discussed and put in place.

Prof. Dr. Karl Wohlmuth
Head, Research Group on African Development Perspectives
Co-ordinating Editor, African Development Perspectives Yearbook
Director, IWIM, Faculty of Economics,
University of Bremen, Faculty of Economics, Germany

Acknowledgements

This study was compiled between April 2002 and October 2005 during my work as a Research Fellow and General Manager at the Institute of World Economics and International Management (IWIM) at the University of Bremen.

Very special thanks go to my supervisor Prof Dr Karl Wohlmuth, who provided me with stimulating discussions, food for thought and innumerable constructive comments not to mention his kind support at all stages of my work. His detailed review process was an essential contributor to the successful finalisation of the study. Special thanks go also to Prof Dr Axel Sell (IWIM) who gave his valuable time in reviewing the study and offering his expert opinion as well as to Prof Dr Hans-Heinrich Bass (University of Applied Sciences, Bremen) and Prof Dr Robert Kappel (German Institute of Global and Area Studies, Hamburg) who were ready to assess my professional knowledge.

I would like to express my deep gratitude to all interview partners in Botswana, Namibia, South Africa and Swaziland for their interest in the topic, their time, openness and for sharing their precious experiences and information with me.

Special thanks go to Clive Williams (NAACAM) and Paul Nichols (FAO) for explaining the intricate functioning of the South African automotive industry and the Namibian fishing industry to me in detail. I am also most indebted to Dr Dirk Hansohm (NEPRU), Dr Kennedy Mbekeani (BIDPA), Dr Afeikhena Jerome (NIEP) and Dr Trudi Hartzenberg (tralac) for accommodating me during my field study and for providing me with important information. Special thanks also go to Ben Bennett (NASSP), Jürgen Hofmann (ATF), Dr Regine Qualmann (SADC), Prof Dr Colin McCarthy (University of Stellenbosch) and Wilhelm Smalberger (DTI) who gave their valuable time and explained and discussed specific issues of my study.

I am furthermore grateful to Dr Anders Isaksson (UNIDO) and James Desai (InWent) for offering me institutional support and to my colleagues and associates, especially Dr Tobias Knedlik (IWIM) and Tenu Avafia (tralac/UNDP), for the thought-provoking discussions and the review process of parts of the study.

The financial support by the German Academic Exchange Service (DAAD) for my 4-months field studies in the SACU region is gratefully acknowledged.

Last but not least I would like to thank my parents and my friends who supported me through various trials and tribulations and who offered their unconditional support for my endeavours.

The views expressed in the thesis as well as any shortcomings remain of course entirely my responsibility.

Bremen, April, 2006

Mareike Meyn

Map of Africa

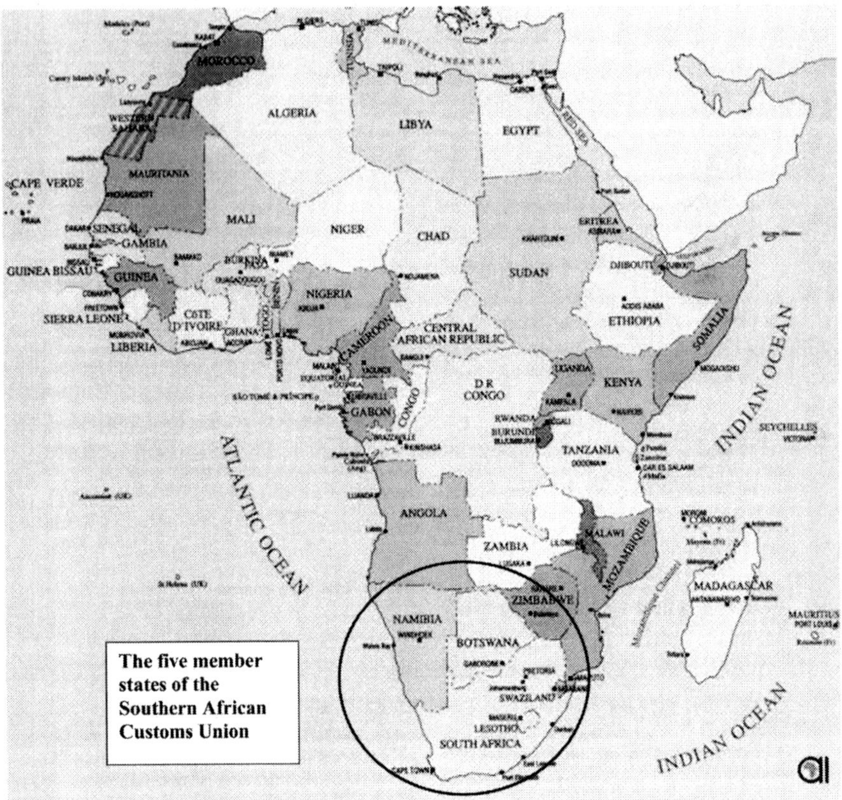

Source: Africa Institute of South Africa.

Maps of the SACU countries

South Africa

Botswana

Lesotho

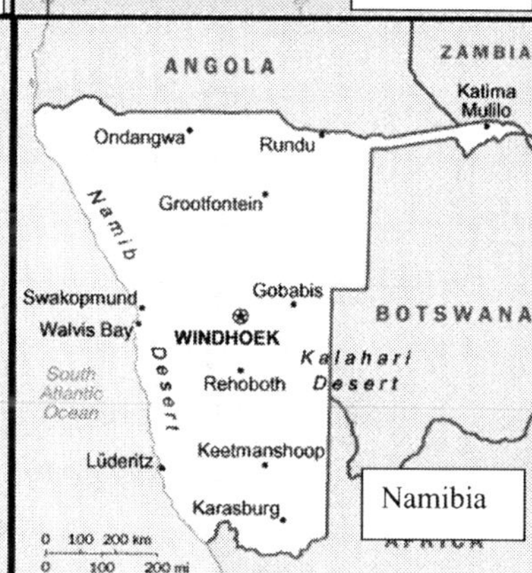

Namibia

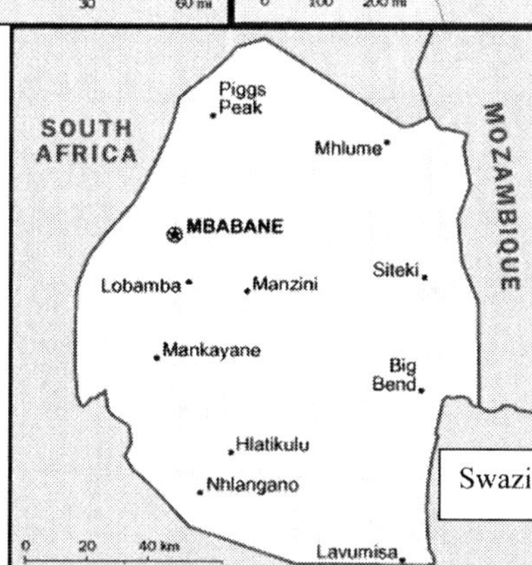

Swaziland

"Africa is being squeezed. Its status as a favored recipient of trade preferences in some markets ... is being eroded rapidly. Increasingly its terms of access to non-regional markets will be on the same basis as its competitors. ... At the same time the region is being asked by some of its traditional trade partners to offer reverse preferences ... These are being presented as supportive of both regional integration and the multilateral system, but it is not certain that the result will be either of these."

African Development Bank 2004:206

"Politics is not judged according to its intentions but according to its results."

Tzvetan Todorocv

Table of Contents

I. List of Abbreviations

ACP	African, Caribbean and Pacific
AfDB	African Development Bank
AGOA	African Growth and Opportunity Act
AIDC	Automotive Industrial Development Council
AIEC	Automotive Industry Export Council
AISA	Africa Institute of South Africa
APEC	Asia-Pacific Economic Cooperation
ASCM	Agreement on Subsidies and Countervailing Measures
ATF	Agricultural Trade Forum
AU	African Union
BIDPA	Botswana Institute for Development and Policy Analysis
BLNS	Botswana, Lesotho, Namibia, Swaziland
BLS	Botswana, Lesotho, Swaziland
BOBS	Botswana Bureau of Standards
BOCCIM	Botswana Confederation of Commerce, Industry and Manpower
BoN	Bank of Namibia
CBI	Cross Border Initiative
CDE	Centre for Development of Enterprises
CEAO	Communaute Economique de l'Afrique de l'Ouest (West African Economic Community)
CEDA	Citizen Entrepreneurial Development Agency
CET	Common External Tariff
c.i.f.	cargo, insurance, freight
CIP	Competitive Industrial Performance
CMA	Common Monetary Area
COMESA	Common Market of Eastern and Southern Africa
CPI	Consumer Price Index
CRP	Common Revenue Pool
CSIR	Council for Scientific and Industrial Research
CSO	Botswana Central Statistic Office
CU	Customs Union
DBSA	Development Bank for Southern Africa
DG	Directorate-General
DTI	Department of Trade and Industry of the Republic of South Africa
EAOB	Exporter's Association of Botswana
EBA	Everything But Arms
ECOWAS	Economic Community Of West African States
EDF	European Development Fund

EEC	European Economic Community
EEZ	Exclusive Economic Zone
EIB	European Investment Bank
EMIA	Export Marketing and Investment Assistance Scheme
EPA	Economic Partnership Agreement
ESA	Eastern and Southern Africa
EU	European Union
FAO	Food and Agriculture Organization of the United Nations
FAS	Foreign Agriculture Service of the US Department of Agriculture
FDI	Foreign Direct Investment
FIGIS	Fisheries Global Information System
fob	free on board
FTA	Free Trade Agreement
GDP	Gross Domestic Product
GEAR	Growth, Employment and Redistribution
GNI	Gross National Income
GoN	Government of Namibia
GSP	Generalised System of Preferences
GVC	Global Value Chain
HDI	Human Development Index
HIPC	Heavily Indebted Poor Countries
HIV/AIDS	Human Immune Deficiency Virus/Acquired Immune Deficiency Syndrome
IDC	Industrial Development Corporation
IEEP	Institute for European Environmental Policy
IMF	International Monetary Fund
IPPR	Institute for Public Private Research
IRCC	Import Rebate Credit Certificate
ITAC	International Trade Administrative Commission
LC	Lomé Convention
LDC	Least Developed Country
LHWDP	Lesotho Highlands Water Development Project
LNDC	Lesotho National Development Corporation
LNS	Lesotho, Namibia, Swaziland
MDG	Millennium Development Goals
MERCOSUR	Mercado Común del Sur (Common Market of the South)
MFA	Multi-Fibre Agreement
MFMR	Ministry for Fisheries and Maritime Resources of the Republic of Namibia
MEY	Maximum Economic Yield
MFN	Most Favoured Nation

MIDP	Motor Industrial Development Programme
MoU	Memorandum of Understanding
MSY	Maximum Sustainable Yield
MVA	Manufacturing Value Added
NAACAM	National Association of Automotive Component and Allied Manufacturers
NAAMSA	National Association of Automobile Manufacturers of South Africa
NAFTA	North American Free Trade Agreement
NAMFI	Namibian Maritime and Fisheries Institute
NCCI	Namibia Chamber of Commerce and Industry
NEDLAC	National Economic Development and Labour Council
NEPRU	Namibian Economic Policy Research Unit
NIC	Newly Industrialised Countries
NIP	National Indicative Programme
NGO	Non-Governmental Organisation
NMA	Namibian Manufacturing Association
NPA	Non-Programmable Aid
NSIQO	Namibia Standards Information and Quality Office
NTB	Non-Tariff Barriers
NUMSA	National Union of Metalworkers of South Africa
OAU	Organization of African Unity
OECD	Organisation for Economic Co-operation and Development
OEM	Original Equipment Manufacturer
OES	Original Equipment Supply
OSY	Optimum Sustainable Yield
PRSP	Poverty Reduction Strategy Paper
PPP	Public Private Partnership
PSSI	Private Sector Support Institution
PTA	Preferential Trade Agreement
R	South African Rand
R&D	Research and Development
RIFF	Regional Integration Facilitation Forum
RMA	Rand Monetary Area
SABTT	South African Board on Tariffs and Trade
SACOB	South African Chamber of Commerce and Business
SACU	Southern African Customs Union
SADC	Southern African Development Community
SADCC	Southern African Development Co-ordination Conference
SAGC	South African-German Chamber of Commerce and Industry
SAP	Structural Adjustment Programmes
SARB	South African Reserve Bank

SCCI	Swaziland Chamber of Commerce and Industry
SDT	Special and Differential Treatment
SIPA	Swaziland Investment Promotion Authority
SMEDP	Small and Medium Enterprise Development Programme
SPS	Sanitary and Phytosanitary Standards
SSA	Swaziland Sugar Association
STABEX	System of the Stabilisation of Export Earnings for Agricultural Exports
SYSMIN	System of Stabilisation of Export Earnings for Mining Exports
TBVC states	Transkei, Bophuthatswana, Venda, Ciskei
TAC	Totally Allowed Catch
TIDP	Trade and Investment Development Programme
TIPS	Trade and Industrial Policy Strategies
TISA	Trade and Investment South Africa (Division of the DTI)
TMA	Trilateral Monetary Agreement
TDCA	Trade, Development and Co-operation Agreement
TRIPS	Agreement on Trade Related Aspects on Intellectual Property Rights
UDEAC	Union Douanière des Etats de l'Afrique Centrale (Central African Customs Union)
UK	United Kingdom
UNAM	University of Namibia
UNIDO	United Nations Industrial Development Organization
USA	United States of America
USAID	United States Agency for International Development
USTR	United States Trade Representatives
VAT	Value Added Tax
WBCG	Walvis Bay Corridor Group
WTO	World Trade Organization

II. List of Tables

III. List of Figures

IV. List of Boxes

V. List of Appendixes

1 Introduction, Objectives and Methodology of the Study

1.1 Introduction

The Southern African Customs Union (SACU) is the oldest customs union in the world and at the time of writing the only fully implemented functioning customs union in Africa. SACU's economic giant, South Africa, has together with Botswana, Lesotho, Namibia and Swaziland (the BLNS countries) formed a unique integration scheme where the motivations for integration can only partly be explained by the general theories of regional integration.

All SACU countries are greatly involved in international trade. In their trade relations with the EU, the most important trading partner for South Africa, and a major trading partner for the BLNS, the SACU countries face severe challenges. In the year 2000, South Africa entered unilaterally into an FTA with the EU, liberalising around 90% of trade flows between the two parties by 2012. The BLNS countries as members of SACU are directly affected by this agreement. Thus, in 2012 most EU imports can circulate free within the SACU market though the BLNS countries are not part of the EU-South Africa FTA but still have a non-reciprocal trade arrangement with the EU. However, BLNS countries' non-reciprocal trade relations with the EU, which have lasted for the past 30 years, also come officially to an end. Thus, the BLNS countries are requested to enter also *de jure* into an FTA with the EU by 2008 if they want to keep their preferential market access to the EU.

The FTA between the EU and South Africa was a paradigm challenge to North-South relations in general and to the EU's trade and development relations with developing countries in particular. For the first time, the EU entered into an FTA with an African country and promoted the instrument of North-South FTAs as development tool. Because unilateral trade preferences vis-à-vis African countries have not fulfilled their high expectations and said to infringe against WTO provisions by discriminating against other developing countries, the instrument of North-South FTAs came on the agenda. North-South FTAs are supposed to improve African countries' access to competitive inputs and consumer goods, assist to create an enabling trading environment, and help to improve the competitiveness of domestic companies by involving them in international networks. Negative effects, such as revenue losses, trade diversion and the break down of uncompetitive domestic industries are supposed to be offset by the exclusion of products from the agreement, safeguard measures, technical assistance and economic growth due to expanded and diversified exports.

Whether these theoretical aspirations are likely to be realised in case of EU-SACU trade relations and what further impacts the EU's approach of North-South FTAs towards the SACU countries imply will be comprehensively discussed in this study. The study contains three empirical parts, based on the findings of field studies undertaken in South Africa, Botswana, Namibia, and Swaziland. The first two empirical parts on the South African automotive and the Namibian fishing industry are found in Chapter 5. These sectors were chosen since they are tremendously important for the overall manufacturing performance of South Africa and Namibia respectively, are highly-export oriented and are an important part of trade relations with the EU. Both industries are relatively protected from competition/foreign access and have successfully adopted national policies to promote industrial development and other national development goals. Another common characteristic of the South African automotive and the Namibian fishing industry is that their main trading partner, the EU, wishes to improve market access in these sectors. The main purpose of the two case studies in Chapter 5 is to investigate whether an FTA with the EU could help the companies in the South African automotive sector and the Namibian fishing industry to increase their integration into the global economy and the global value added chain, which other factors determine international linkages and economic success and how these factors are related to free trade.

The third empirical part of the thesis is found in Chapter 6 where the trade capacity of Botswana's and Namibia's public and private sectors to participate in regional and international trade negotiations is analysed. It is commonly agreed that it is of critical importance for developing countries to build trade capacity if they want to benefit from regional integration and North-South FTAs. Chapter 6 investigates the perception that Botswana and Namibia show only insufficient capacities to be actively involved in their manifold trade relations and lack the capacities to analyse and negotiate their trade interests in a way that allows them to optimise their trade potential.

1.2 Objectives and Scope of the Study

It is the objective of the study to give the reader an extensive overview of SACU countries' complex trade environment and to analyse the impacts of challenging trade relations with the EU on economic development and regional integration. What effects an FTA with the EU has on SACU countries' export performance, their diversification efforts, industrialisation options, and with respect to their efforts for deeper regional integration, are the major questions the study relates to.

To combine the topic of regional integration with the question which impact North-South FTAs have on economic development in southern Africa is not entirely new. BIDPA/IDS (1998) and Goodison (1999) have undertaken detailed studies on the impact of the EU-South Africa FTA on the BLNS countries. These studies have however adopted a quantitative approach to investigate primarily the static effects of the EU-South Africa FTA. Company interviews used for that study were undertaken on an *ad-hoc* basis and were not sector specific. Therefore, the dynamic effects of North-South FTAs, including companies' and public stakeholders' strategies to cope with the challenges arising have not sufficiently been investigated. In this respect, the following study fills a gap in the research on the impact of North-South FTAs on economic development in selected southern African countries. In-depth analyses of the South African automotive and the Namibian fishing industry reveal that the inclusion of sectors into free trade agreements can have very different impacts, depending among others on the sectors' economic performance, domestic policies adopted, and companies' integration into international networks.

The relationship between free trade agreements, in particular North-South FTAs, and economic development is discussed in all Chapters of the thesis. Chapter 2 analyses the special relationship between South Africa and the BLNS countries, their past experiences of regional integration and the costs and benefits for the member countries. Chapter 3 discusses the different trade regimes the SACU countries have with the EU and how these have shifted from a non-reciprocal development-orientated approach to a reciprocal trade approach. Furthermore, the implications of this paradigm change for both economic development and regional integration are elaborated on. Chapter 4 has a closer look at SACU countries' manufacturing activities and performances and investigates the role of trade preferences, domestic incentive schemes and free trade agreements on industrial development in the SACU countries. Thereafter, the positive and negative effects of North-South FTAs for industrial development are explored in detail in Chapter 5 with the examining of the South African automotive and the Namibian fishing industry's trade relationship with the EU. By means of a detailed, empirically backed-up socio-economic analysis of these sectors, investigating their position in the global value chain and their relevance for national development goals, Chapter 5 analyses whether an FTA with the EU can fulfil its theoretical expectations to promote economic development, e.g. by technology transfer and learning effects. Moreover, the question of how the inclusion of the South African automotive industry and the Namibian fishing industry into an FTA with the EU would affect domestic value addition and management processes is investigated. It is the aim of the sector studies to show the complexity of the South African automotive industry and the Namibian fishing industry and how an FTA with the EU influences domestic value addition, export performance, and management tools of the industries.

Chapter 6 deals with another factor that has to be discussed when analysing the relationship between North-South FTAs and economic development, namely trade capacity. Trade capacity, relating to countries' abilities to analyse and lobby for their trade interests, to develop offensive market-access strategies on a regional and multilateral level and to implement existing trade agreements, is crucial for the success of a country's trade strategy. As the discussion shows, the BLNS countries lack to a considerable extent the capacity to trade effectively and are overextended with the manifold trade obligations they have. The lack of trade capacity is therefore one major obstacle for BLNS countries' missing ability to benefit from North-South FTAs.

The broad approach of the study, aiming to give the reader a comprehensive overview of the challenges SACU countries face in a rapid altering trading environment, might sometimes lack a deeper analysis of the single parameters. Thus, the challenges for the SACU countries as a result of the expiration of the WTO Multi-Fibre Agreement, the reform of the EU Common Agricultural Policy, or the implications of the African Growth and Opportunity Act (AGOA) are not discussed in full length. Nevertheless, their socio-economic implications and alternative diversification strategies to meet the challenges of eroding preferences are elaborated on.

1.3 Main Theses and Methodology

It is argued that EU North-South FTAs fail to prove being a successful development tool for the SACU countries since their reality is too complex to allow the theory predicted in terms of which North-South FTAs are a successful development goal *per se* realise itself. As discussed in the Chapters 2 and 3, a North-South FTA is theoretically supposed to help a developing country to a) improve its market access to the developed country; b) to benefit from economies of scale; c) to diversify its exports and to upgrade products and processes by benefiting from competitive inputs and by technology transfer and learning effects as a result of strong cooperation; and d) to optimise production processes by increased competition.

The empirical analyses of the South African automotive industry and the Namibian fishing industry aim to prove these main theses of North-South FTAs by operationalising the assumptions (see section 5.2). It should be elaborated whether an FTA with the EU would really improve exporters' market access in the investigated industries, help to expand their exports, and to strengthen cooperation with their European counterparts. It is furthermore investigated to what extent the companies are already exposed to international competition and whether increased competition would be more likely to have positive or detrimental effects.

Theoretically, North-South FTAs should further help developing countries to promote "open regionalism" by promoting regional integration in a South-South framework, while opening towards international trade. The EU sees regional integration schemes and processes as a "key instrument" for ACP countries' integration into the world economy, which should be "encouraged and supported." (European Commission 2000, Art. 35). However, since the EU's approach in negotiating an FTA with South Africa to the exclusion of the BLNS countries has split-up its trade relations with SACU as a trading block, it is argued that the EU's current trade policy towards the SACU countries does not promote but rather undermines regional integration.

The problems arising from both, incoherent EU trade policies with South Africa on the one hand and the BLNS countries on the other hand, combined with an EU trade policy that is inconsistent with its pronounced development goals, constrains deeper regional integration and economic development in the region. It is therefore argued that the EU needs to apply trade policies more individually and subjectively to make them consistent with SACU countries' trade, development, and regional integration strategies if its trade policy towards SACU countries is supposed to promote economic development and regional integration.

Another shortcoming of the EU's concept of North-South FTAs is the insufficient consideration of capacity constraints in southern African countries. To use international trade as a successful development strategy a country needs to identify its trade interests clearly and translate these interests into policies and negotiation strategies. Furthermore, resources have to be made available to implement trade policies and to define the role of single actors. As the discussion in Chapter 6 shows, South Africa was, despite its transformation process, able to set such an effective trade policy framework into place when negotiating the EU-South Africa FTA in the late 1990s. The BLNS countries however lack capacities at almost every level in their negotiations of an EPA with the EU. Since South Africa was in essence responsible for SACU's trade policy until recently, the BLNS countries are still in the process of developing national capacities to identify their interests and to formulate a consistent trade strategy, taking national development priorities as well as regional and international obligations into account. As the discussion in Chapter 6 and the analysis of interview results from trade-related private and public institutions in Botswana and Namibia reveal, countries' administrative and analytical capacities need to be expanded and paid more attention. By adding findings from selected interviews with government officials from Swaziland and South Africa as well as by referring to the relevant literature, it is furthermore argued that Lesotho and Swaziland are even more capacity constrained than Botswana and Namibia and that South Africa is only partly able to fill this gap. Therefore, the EU needs to take BLNS countries' trade capacity constraints as well as SACU's priority to develop common regional institutions into account before entering into a North-South FTA. Otherwise, the current "hub-and-spoke" trade relationship is likely to aggravate, demoting the BLNS countries to "spokes" supposed to deliver the EU "hub" with raw materials.

Methodology

In studying the South African automotive industry and the Namibian fishing industry as examples for successful industrial policy and in investigating how EU North South FTAs fit into domestic policies, the economic performance of these sectors as well as their position in the global value chain required analyses. For this purpose, standardised questionnaires were developed, using the framework of the global value chain analysis (see Annex I and II).

The global value chain (GVC) analysis has been developed to explain the dynamics of inter-linkage within the productive sector, in particular with respect to their global integration. In this respect it differs from traditional sector analyses, which are static and do not take the dynamic linkages of productive activities into account, such as marketing, logistics and design.

Kaplinsky (2000) and Kaplinsky and Morris (2001) describe three fundamental elements of the GVC approach. The first element is *barriers to entry*, which define the distribution of profits. The higher the barriers to entry, the lower are the number of global producers and the higher are the profits. Thus, markets with high barriers to entry are the most lucrative and attractive ones, which requires that global producers remain continuously innovative and increase their value added activities in order to gain competitive advantage over other producers. The second element is *governance*, which implies a company's responsibility for the coordination and regulation of various activities within the GVC. In other words: if the company governs all parameters from the product's conception, over its production, to the logistics and its final consumption, it is optimally integrated in the GVC. The third element is *systematic efficiency*, which means that the governing party ensures close cooperation between all parties in the chain and assists the participants in the chain to upgrade their products and services. The overall goal is to improve the efficiency of the chain and its position in a global context.

Numerous sectoral studies with respect to the GVC analysis have been undertaken. For the South African automotive industry Barnes (1998, 1999, 2001) and Barnes and Lorentzen (2003) have undertaken some research. For the Namibian fishing industry no according study exists.

The aim of the empirical research was to develop profiles of the competitiveness and the GVC position of the South African automotive industry and the Namibian fishing industry and to link it to companies' trade relations with the EU. The innovative approach of the analysis is that companies' cooperation activities/networks with their European counterparts were investigated, thus elaborating on the question of what extent the companies are part of an EU network and what influence this had on their export performance, their ability to enter the EU market and their position in the value added chain. Assuming that companies' involvement in international networks helps them to improve their position in the GVA (Kaplinksy 2000, Kaplinsky et al. 2002) there is further analysis of how far an FTA with the EU could contribute to this.

For the analysis of the *South African automotive industry*, 25 companies from the Gauteng province in South Africa were interviewed in October 2003. The companies were selected using the National Association of Automotive Component and Allied Manufacturers (NAACAM) 2003 Directory, representing the interests of around 30% of all companies related to the automotive component industry. All interviews were conducted personally by the means of a standardised questionnaire (see Annex I) with the management of the respective company.

The interviews in the *Namibian fishing industry* took place in September 2003 in Walvis Bay in Namibia. 11 companies and grouping of companies were interviewed, representing around three quarters of Namibian fishing companies. The interviews were made personally with the management of the companies, using a standardised questionnaire (see Annex II).

The findings from the South African automotive industry and the Namibian fishing industry were compared with secondary literature as well as with face-to-face interviews with industries' representatives, private sector support institutions and governmental officials.[1] Both case studies do not claim to be representative. However, the findings of the sample of the automotive industry are for the most part in accordance with recent research done in this sector and also reflect the appraisal of the relevant private sector support institutions regarding the current situation in the automotive component industry. The findings from the Namibian fishing industry are likely to mirror the situation in the whole sector since the sample encompasses 75% of all companies with processing plants in the country and are backed-up with relevant studies and expert interviews.

The interviews analysed in Chapter 6 were concluded in September and October 2003 in Windhoek (Namibia) and Gaborone (Botswana). It was the aim of this empirical analysis to investigate the trade capacity in Botswana and Namibia, to identify obstacles to trade negotiations and to get an idea about countries' strategies in regional and international trade relations. For this purpose, a questionnaire was developed (see Annex III), to analyse respondents' knowledge and appraisal of North-South Agreements they are affected by/involved in to determine technical support needed to improve Botswana's and Namibia's participation in international trade negotiations and the implementation of existing trade obligations.

For the analysis in Chapter 6, 34 interviews with public and private organisations in Botswana and Namibia were conducted. The personnel interviews

[1] Detailed information on all interview partners is presented in section 5.4.4.1 (South African automotive industry) and 5.5.5.1 (Namibian fishing industry).

were made with officials from the Ministry of Trade and Industry, the Ministry of Agriculture, the Ministry of Finance, Customs and Excise Departments, domestic research institutions and universities, exporter's association, chambers of commerce and industry and other private sector support institutions, and donor agencies. All interviews were concluded with the management of the respective organisations and/or with experts who were working on the EU-South Africa FTA. Since the interviews comprise a broad selection of all stakeholders involved into trade negotiations, the study allows relevant insights into Botswana's and Namibia's external trade policy, the challenges the countries face from a rapidly altering external trading environment, and their constraints for effective participation in SACU's trade policy.

In total, the empirical data collected comprises 112 personally conducted interviews from Botswana, Namibia, South Africa and Swaziland.[2]

Some readers might argue that the qualitative methodology and the non-representation of findings is a limitation of the study. It is however argued that the broad focus of the study would not have allowed another approach and that the back-up of companies' interview results with interviews from private sector support institutions and research institutions as well as the use of secondary literature, guarantee comprehensive and realistic insights in the two sectors investigated. As the discussion in Chapter 5 shows, the empirical data conducted in the South African automotive and the Namibian fishing industry allows a realistic picture of the two sectors. To guarantee the representation of empirical findings, one had to choose a bigger (and in case of the South African automotive industry) geographical spread sample, which would not have allowed the personal conducting of interviews in the given time frame. It is however believed that the personal conducting of interviews was the decisive factor in successful completion of the study. Results from other researchers show that length and complexity of questionnaires had to be reduced considerably to ensure a certain rate of return of posted questionnaires (see e.g. Matthee et al. 2005, Barnes 1998 and BIDPA/IDS 1998).

[2] 24 interviews were made in Gaborone/Botswana (eight exporting companies from different sectors and 16 public and private institutions), 30 interviews in Windhoek and Walvis Bay/Namibia (13 companies in the fishing industry and 17 public and private institutions), 37 interviews in Johannesburg and Pretoria/South Africa (25 companies in the automotive component and automotive industry and 12 public and private institutions and individual experts), and 21 interviews in Mbabane, Manzini and Matsapha/Swaziland (eight exporting companies from different sectors and 13 public and private institutions).

Furthermore, it would not have been possible to guarantee that the people who answered the questions were also those in charge and that the questions are well understood. Thus, it may have been possible that the quality of answers was reduced significantly, which again would have created the risk of getting a wrong impression about the overall economic situation in the countries studied.[3]

1.4 Organisation of the Study

The study is divided into seven chapters.

Chapter 1 gives the background to the study, introduces to the research problem and to the methodology adopted. The limitations of the study are raised and the arguments to be advanced are outlined.

Chapter 2 introduces the reader to the member states of the Southern African Customs Union (SACU) and SACU's approach to regional integration. The specific history of the SACU in the context of Apartheid and South Africa's economic and political dominance in the region is analysed and linked to the theoretical assumptions of regional integration. Moreover, the economic and political costs and benefits of the SACU 1969 Agreement for South Africa and the BLNS countries and parties' different motivations for re-negotiating the SACU Agreement are discussed. Though the new SACU Agreement was signed in 2002 and ratified by all parties in 2004, it has not been properly implemented to date. Chapter 2 introduces the reader to the democratised decision making processes of the new SACU Agreement but also to the challenges the new Agreement brings to Botswana, Lesotho, Namibia and Swaziland (the BLNS countries). It becomes clear that all parties need to increase their endeavours to bring the new Agreement into life, which is not only crucial for the progress of regional integration and attempts towards deeper regional integration but also for SACU countries' external trade relations. This is of particular importance for SACU countries' trade relations with the EU, which are currently characterised by two different trade regimes – an FTA between South Africa and the EU and non-reciprocal trade relations between the BLNS countries and the EU.

Chapter 3 investigates SACU countries' trade relations with the EU in more detail. The EU is the most important trading partner for South Africa and a major trading partner for Botswana, Namibia and Swaziland. In this context, BLNS long-standing trade relationship with the EU under the Lomé Conven-

[3] The author's experience had shown that some interview partners misunderstood certain questions, which could however easily be clarified during the interviews. Another advantage of personal conducted interviews is that the interviewees do not only "tick" the relevant questions but also elaborate on their answers, thus giving the author relevant insights into the South African automotive industry, the Namibian fishing industry, and into trade related capacities and the challenges Ministries in the region are facing.

tions I-IV and the Cotonou Agreement are explored. The theoretical assumptions of the non-reciprocal Lomé Conventions, their instruments and their experiences within in the BLNS countries, in particular with respect to BLNS agro-based diversification efforts, are discussed and internal and external reasons for the failure of the Lomé Conventions are shown. The switch from a preferential trade regime to reciprocal trade relations is not only an economic paradigm shift but also implies severe challenges for the BLNS countries since they are *de facto* locked-into an FTA with the EU though they officially still have a non-reciprocal trade relationship with the EU under the Cotonou Agreement. The complexity of the situation is made worse because the *de jure* FTA, which the BLNS are meant to conclude with EU by 2008 does not match with the *de facto* FTA they have been part of since 2000. Chapter 3 shows that it is not only southern African countries' approaches towards regional integration that lack consistency but also the EU's approach of North-South FTAs with southern African countries. It is also shown that the current approach of Economic Partnership Agreements (EPAs) does not present a convincing alternative to non-reciprocal trade relations since the internal reasons for the failure of the Lomé Conventions are not sufficiently tackled by the proposed EPAs. In this respect, alternative approaches to a North-South FTA are developed, taking BLNS countries' supply-and demand-side constraints to export to the EU into account and emphasising the development relevance of North-South trade relations.

The implications of an FTA with the EU for SACU countries' industrial development, national and regional industrial policies, and consequently deeper regional integration are discussed in *Chapter 4.* The single industrialisation strategies of the SACU countries and their strong linkages to SACU's trade policy in particular vis-à-vis the EU are elaborated on. Chapter 4 starts with an overview of what industrialisation strategies in developing countries look like by comparing the industrialisation strategies of Eastern Asian countries with those of most African countries and discussing the links between trade and economic development. The Asian countries combined a flexible import-substitution strategy with an active export promotion strategy while most African countries protected all sectors and discriminated against export-oriented sectors. As a result of African countries' failed import-substitution policy, an outward-oriented industrialisation strategy that concentrates on agro-based and simple manufactured exports is proposed. Such a strategy bears however the risk of world-wide oversupply and deteriorating terms of trade since other developing countries have also adopted this strategy. It is therefore emphasised that manufacturing exports cannot judged to be beneficial *per se* but that the value addition to manufacturing activities is important. In this context, Chapter 4 has a look at the development of manufacturing value addition within the SACU countries and discusses SACU countries manufacturing activities and industrialisation policies also with respect to foreign trade preference schemes and domestic export and investment incentives. To date, the SACU countries have not developed a common industrialisation strategy but intend to do so with the implementation of the new 2002 SACU Agreement. Chapter 4 discusses the chances of establishing a common industrialisation policy and to move towards deeper regional integration but also highlights the difficulties arising from countries' different development levels. SACU countries' agreement on common trade-related policies is becoming more and more important since SACU is supposed to have a common trade policy and to negotiate on a bilateral basis as a trading block with "one voice". The fact that SACU has not yet fully implemented its new Agreement reveals however that a common negotiation position does not exist and that SACU's trade policy is still highly dominated by South Africa. South Africa focuses on FTAs with selected developed and developing countries; a trade strategy that is not necessarily in the best interest of the BLNS countries which lack capacities to take optimal advantage of these agreements.

The question of whether free trade agreements can help SACU countries to promote industrial development is investigated in *Chapter 5* by using the example of the South African automotive and the Namibian fishing industry. Both industries are highly export-oriented towards the EU and successful examples of industrial policies. Furthermore, both industries are major contributors to the overall performance of the manufacturing sectors in South Africa and Namibia.

The structure of both case studies in Chapter 5 is similar. The studies start with a detailed overview of the South African automotive and the Namibian fishing industry respectively, investigate their economic performances, domestic policy instruments and their trade relations with the EU. The empirical findings refer to companies' trade relations with the EU, their competition situation, their position in the value chain and their efforts to upgrade activities. After having explored the functioning, management and international position of the South African automotive and the Namibian fishing industry respectively, the impacts of the inclusion of these sectors into free trade agreement with the EU will be conducted. In conclusion, common grounds and differences of the two industries, the factors that have contributed to the economic successes of the South African automotive and the Namibian fishing industry respectively, and the impact of selective openness versus the overall inclusion of the two sectors into an FTA with the EU are discussed.

Since an FTA with the EU does not only imply challenges for SACU countries' industries but also for their institutional capacities to negotiate and implement the agreement effectively, *Chapter 6* highlights the importance of trade capacity building. Chapter 6 starts with an overview on the concept of trade capacity building, focuses on the element of trade policy and elaborates on the relevance of an effective trade policy framework for EU-SACU trade relations and for SACU countries' further trade obligations on a bilateral, regional, and a multilateral level. Thereafter, the capacities of SACU's public institutions, private sector and other civil society actors to participate effectively in international trade are discussed. Special focus is given on trade capacity constraints in Botswana and Namibia, which are the subject of the third case study. Finally, Chapter 6 draws policy recommendations on how BLNS countries' capacities to participate effectively in international trade can be improved and why trade capacity building is of particular importance for making EU trade policy towards SACU countries coherent with expressed development goals.

Chapter 7 concludes with the findings of the thesis referring to the impact EU free trade agreements have on the SACU countries with respect to regional integration, development aspects of trade relations, and options for industrial policies and development. Finally, Chapter 7 tries to develop a scenario on the future of EU-SACU trade relations and formulates open research questions that need further investigation.

2. The Southern African Customs Union (SACU)

2.1 Economic and Socio-Economic Indicators of SACU Member States

The SACU countries are very different relating to their size and number of population but also relating to their level and structure of economic development. In 2001, the combined SACU area of 2674.8 thousand square kilometres contained 51 million people of which 44 million (86.3%) were citizens of South Africa (WTO 2003:1). South Africa is not only by far the biggest and most populated country within SACU but also its economic giant, responsible for almost 93% of SACU's GDP in 2003, as can be obtained from Table 1.

Table 1: Gross Domestic Product, real (in millions US$, constant prices 1995)

	Population (in '000)	GDP	GDP	GDP	GDP	GDP average annual real growth rate	
	2003	1980	1990	2000	2003	1981-1990	1991-2003
Botswana	1,785	1,272	3,574	6,001	6,851	11.2%	5.2%
Lesotho	1,802	500	768	1,076	1,199	3.8%	3.5%
Namibia	1,987	2,432	2,751	4,156	4,533	0.8%	3.9%
South Africa	45,026	127,410	144,736	172,144	187,116	1.2%	2.0%
Swaziland	1,077	640	1,187	1,604	1,731	6.5%	2.9%

Source: African Development Bank 2004.

Economic Activities by Sector

South Africa is by far the most sophisticated economy within SACU. It has huge mineral resources and is the world's largest gold producer and a big producer of diamonds, platinum and chrome. However, South Africa's income from exports, which generated to more than 45% from gold in 1980, has diversified considerably. Today, services are responsible for the bulk of GDP (65% in 2003, see Table 2), while the mining industry contributed only to 7.5% of GDP in 2001 (WTO 2003:A4-273). Core manufacturing activities are the motor industry, textiles and clothing, food processing and beverages, mineral-based industries, machinery and equipment and pulp and paper, contributing to around 30% of GDP. The agricultural sector added only 2.8% to the South African GPD but employed around 11% of the labour force. The agricultural sector is described as dualistic: employment in the sector is created by around 50,000 large-scale farmers, while the large majority of rural people are small-scale farmers that earn their income mainly from livestock production. South Africa's key agricultural products are maize (which contributed to nearly 40% to gross income of all crop production), sugar, wheat, red meat (cattle, sheep, and wildlife), milk products, wool and fishing. Furthermore, wine has become an important agricultural export product (WTO 2003:A4-266-9).

Table 2: Sectoral value addition (in % of GDP)

	Agriculture			Industry			Services		
	1980	**1999**	**2003**	**1980**	**1999**	**2003**	**1980**	**1999**	**2003**
Botswana	10.5	2.8	2.5	49.4	45.8	47.5	40.1	51.4	50.0
Lesotho	29.4	18.0	16.0	30.1	41.0	42.0	40.5	41.0	42.0
Namibia	10.9	11.4	10.0	36.3	27.7	30.9	52.8	60.9	59.1
South Africa	4.9	3.0	2.8	39.5	31.0	31.0	55.6	66.0	65.0
Swaziland	33.0	17.0	11.3	27.8	44.0	47.8	39.2	39.1	40.8

Source: World Bank 2003 and 2004.

Botswana shows together with South Africa the lowest sectoral value addition in the agricultural sector, which is with less than 3% similar to the one in the EU (Lewis *et al.* 2002:3). Economic activities are almost equally contributed to the industrial and the service sector. Botswana is the largest diamond supplier in the world. Diamonds account for around 90% of the country's export earnings and around 50% of total government revenue (WTO 2003:A1-57). Moreover, Botswana has large reserves of low-to-medium-grade coal as well as extensive reserves of platinum, gold, silver, iron, potash, manganese, chromite and uranium (ACP General Secretariat 1995b:15). Price fluctuations, low domestic value addition and the knowledge that the source of diamonds is exhausted one day, foster the endeavours to diversify Botswana's economy. Botswana's beef sector was able to expand substantially due to government's financial support to the ranchers and, most of all, due to preferential access to the EU under the Lomé Convention. Since the early 1990ies Botswana is further diversifying its economy towards low-tech manufacturing (mainly clothing and jewellery), tourism and insurance and banking activities.

Lesotho has only few natural resources, which are water and very few diamonds. Until the mid-1990ies Lesotho's economy was based on subsistence agriculture, livestock, and remittance from mining workers, working in South Africa. However, due to the shrinking gold haulage and restrictive working permits in South Africa this income source has been declined substantially.[1] To-

[1] While around 116,000 Basotho worked in South African mines in 1993, this figure was only 60,000 in 2000. This resulted in a decline of miner's remittance from 60% of GDP in the late 1980ies to 26% in 1999 (ACP General Secretariat 1995c:30, 2002b:72).

day, Lesotho's foreign earnings come mainly from the SACU revenue pool, which constitute some 50% of government revenue, wool, mohair, clothing production as well as from services, mainly the "Lesotho Highland Water Development Project".[2] As can be obtained from Table 2, activities in the secondary and the tertiary sector contribute each to around 40% to Lesotho's GDP. Manufacturing activities are highly concentrated around the garment industry but also include the production of leather, food and beverages and consumer electronics (WTO 2003:A2-143). Income generated from the primary sector is an important feature of the economy and contributes to around 18% of GDP. Two-third of the arable land, which is however only 9% of the total land,[3] is used for the cultivation of maize, the basic food crop, mainly used for the domestic market and exports within SACU (Yedder and Rake 2001:279-280).

Namibia is rich of diamonds, copper and uranium, lead and zinc. It is the leading producer of gem-diamonds and accounts for around one third of the world's output. Mining activities contributes to around 50% of export earnings (BoN 2002:9). Namibia's sectoral contribution to GDP has hardly changed in the past decade: Agricultural production contribute to around 10% of GDP, secondary industries to around 31% of GDP and tertiary industries to more than 59% of the national GDP. Namibia's agricultural base is dominated by stock-farming. 95% of its arable land (or 11% of the total land) is pasture, used for cattle in the northern territory and karakul sheep in southern Namibia (UNIDO 2003b:8). Manufacturing activities are dominated by few large scale companies, mainly operating in the food sector. Other manufacturing activities are in the fields of leather, packaging materials, clothing, furniture, metal components, fish cans and soaps. (UNIDO 2003b:9-10). Third sector activities take mainly place in tourism and government services (BoN 2002:6).

Swaziland does not have mineral resources but is dependent on export earnings from agricultural activities (mainly sugar cane) and agro-processed products. Swaziland's industrial sector accounts for almost 48% of GDP and produces mainly sugar based products (soft-drinks, confectionery), maize products (for human and animal consumption), canned fruits, dairy products, pulp and paper and plastic packages. Since Swaziland has become eligible under the US-initiative AGOA, an increase in the garment and clothing industry has also

---

[2] The "Lesotho Highlands Water Development Project" (LHWDP), sponsored by the EU, the World Bank and the African Development Bank, is the world-largest water transfer project and supplies the South African industrial region around Witwatersrand with water since 1997 (Weed/Urgewald 2002. The LHWDP contributed in average to 25% of GDP in the period 1998-2001 (WTO 2003:A2-139).

[3] Monoculture, excessive use of land, wind and water as well as the fact that little has been spent on its improvement results in land deterioration and soil erosion (ACP General Secretariat 2002b:85).

been noticed.[4] With exception of the garment production, industrial development in Swaziland is based on domestic inputs (WTO 2003:A5-310).

The agricultural sector in Swaziland, which contributes to around 11% of GDP, is heavily dualistic with land divided between the commune (56%) and private property (44%). The private-owned land is much more productive and responsible for 75% of Swaziland's agricultural output (Yedder and Rake 2001:509). The main agricultural crops produced in the formal sector by large-scale firms are sugar cane, maize, meat, dairy products, citrus fruits, avocados, bananas, granadillas, litchis, and guavas. The informal agricultural sector relies on subsistence farming (WTO 2003:A5-335).

Comprising SACU countries economic activities by sectors, it can be stated that income is primarily generated by services (retailing, banking, tourism, government services) and secondary industries (mining, quarrying and manufacturing), while the income obtained from agriculture is comparable low. With exception of Lesotho and Swaziland, all SACU countries are resource-rich countries. Mining and quarrying activities are the main contributors to export earnings and the major source of investment in Botswana and Namibia and do still account for around one third of South Africa's export earnings (DTI 2001:7). The economies in Lesotho and Swaziland whereas are based on export-oriented manufacturing and agro-based activities respectively, namely the garment industry for Lesotho and the sugar industry for Swaziland (see Table 3).

Table 3: Main agricultural and manufacturing products of the SACU economies

	Main agricultural products	**Main manufacturing products**
South Africa	Corn, wheat, wine, bananas, pineapples, citrus fruits, wool, maize, fish, sheep, rice, goats, sugar cane, poultry, tobacco, cattle, tea	Vehicle assembly, metal production, machinery, textile, chemicals, fertilizer, food stuff, fish industry, oil refinery
Botswana	Beef, sheep, maize, citrus, cotton, sorghum, corn millet, pulses, beans, sunflower seeds	Lifestock processing, clothing and garments, semi-assembled vehicles
Lesotho	Wool and mohair, maize, cattle, wheat, corn, pulses, sorghum, barely	Clothing, garments, footwear, furniture, beverages, handicraft, construction
Namibia	Fish, Karakul sheep, cattle, sorghum, millet, maize, peanuts	Fishmeal and fish oil, meat packing, dairy products, semi-assembled vehicles, clothing and garments

[4] The "African Growth and Opportunity Act" (AGOA) and SACU countries' performance under AGOA are discussed in Chapter 4.

	Main agricultural products	Main manufacturing products
Swaziland	Sugar, sugarcane, citrus fruits, forestry, pineapples, maize, sunflowers, tobacco, rice, corn, peanuts, sweet potatoes, sorghum, cattle, cotton, goats, sheep	Fruit canning, wood pulp, soft-drink concentrate, cotton ginning, clothing and garments, electronic products, mining (coal and asbestos)

Sources: SAGC (2001), WTO (2003).

Though the contribution of agriculture to GDP is limited in all SACU economies and has shrunk over the past twenty years, since the countries increased their activities in the services sector and in manufacturing, agricultural activities are crucial for the survival of many people. In Botswana and Namibia around 40% of the workforce earn their income from agriculture and in Lesotho and Swaziland around 70% of the working people depend on income from agriculture. The relevance of agriculture as income source has not significantly changed in the past twenty years (see Table 4). Only in Botswana the number of people working in the agricultural sector has dropped significantly from 70% to around 40%. However, since around 50% of the population live in rural areas, the socio-economic relevance of agricultural is also very high in Botswana (WTO 2003:1).

Table 4: Labour force by sector (in % of total labour force)

	Agriculture			Industry			Services		
	1980	1990	1996	1980	1990	1996	1980	1990	1996
Botswana	70	52	42	13	28	41	17	20	17
Lesotho	86	82	81	4	5	6	10	12	13
Namibia	43	43	40	22	27	37	36	31	23
South Africa	17	14	...	35	32	...	48	54	...
Swaziland	74	67	64	9	12	13	17	21	23

Source: African Development Bank (2004).

Trading Partners and Products

As can be obtained from Table 5, South Africa's exports are much more diversified than those of the BLNS countries regarding both, export products and export partners. South Africa's main trading partner is the EU, followed by the Asian countries (mainly Japan) and the USA. The states of the Southern African Development Community (SADC) (excluding SACU) can be classified as medium-important export market for South Africa, receiving around 10% of its total exports, mainly manufactured goods.[5] The BLNS countries account for around 1% of South Africa's trade.

Table 5: Main exports and export partners of SACU countries

	Main export products (in % of total exports)	Main export products in 2000 (in % of total exports)	Export destinations	Export destinations in 2000
South Africa	1997: Gold, platinum, diamonds, silver, ores and other minerals (30%), other semi-manufactures (20%), machinery and transport equipment (18%), food (11%), iron and steel (7%), vehicles (6%)	Gold, platinum, diamonds, silver ores and other minerals (32.5%), other semi-manufactured (13%), food (9%), iron and steel (8%), minerals and fuels (7.8%), vehicles (5.5%), machinery (5%)	1997: EU (26%), APEC (21%), USA (10%), SADC excl. SACU (16%), SACU (1%)	EU (34%), APEC (30%), USA (11%), SADC excl. SACU (10%), SACU (1%)
Botswana	1994: Diamonds (77%), nickel (11%), meat (4.5%), textiles (3%)	Diamonds (85%), copper nickel (4%), meat (2%), textiles (2%)	1994: EU (81%), SACU (14%)	EU (87%), SACU (7%)
Lesotho	1990: Garments, footwear (59%), food and livestock (15%) other manufactures (11%), crude materials (10%)	Garments, clothing, footwear (74%), machinery + transport (12%), beverages + tobacco 4.5%)	1990: SACU (55%), North America (28%), EU (18%)	N. America (48%), SACU (47%), EU (0.1%)
Namibia	1997: Diamonds (40%), prepared + preserved fish (23%), metal ores (15%), beverages + food (5%)	Diamonds (41%), prepared and preserved fish (24.5%), metal ores (14%), (7%)	1997: EU (41%), South Africa (38%), USA (4.5%)	EU (55%), South Africa (31%), USA (3%)
Swaziland	1997: Sugar cane (21%), machinery and transport equipment (15%), chemicals (11%), soft drinks (10%), agricultural raw materials (9%)	Chemicals (20%), soft drinks (18%), sugar confectionary and glucose (11.5%), sugar cane (11%), machinery + transport equipment (10%), raw materials (11%)	1997: South Africa (68%), EU (17.3%), Mozambique (5%), USA (4%)	South Africa (60%), USA (9%), EU (7%), Mozambique (6%), Asia (2.6%)

Sources: DTI (2001), CSO (2001), CBL (2001), WTO 2003:A3 and A5.

[5] The SADC comprises 14 states, namely the SACU countries plus Angola, DR Congo, Madagascar, Malawi, Mauritius, Mozambique, Tanzania, Zambia and Zimbabwe. SADC aims to establish a free trade area by 2008.

The export structure of the BLNS countries differs considerably from their big neighbour. Botswana and Namibia export mainly mineral products, above all diamonds, which are destined for the EU (mainly the UK). Most of Botswana's and Namibia's manufacturing exports go to South Africa, which received 7% and 31% of their total exports in 2000 respectively.

Lesotho's main export products, namely garments and clothing, used to be destined for South Africa, which received 55% of Lesotho's total exports in 1990. This picture has changed completely due to the AGOA initiative, allowing Lesotho to export its garment and apparel products to preferable conditions to the USA. As a result, the USA is now Lesotho's main export destination.[6]

Swaziland is the only BLNS countries, which does still export most of its goods to South Africa (60% of total exports in 2000), namely agro-based products. Most Swazi garments and apparels go to the USA, which received 9% of Swaziland's total exports in 2000. Swazi sugar cane is mainly destined for the EU where the country receives the best price.

SACU countries' import products show much more similarities than their exports (see Table 6). Electrical and non-electrical machinery, technical appliances, transport equipment, and fuels are SACU countries' main imports. For the BLNS countries, which are all food net importer, foodstuff and basic agricultural crops are also important import commodities.

South Africa receives almost 80% of its imports from the EU and Asian countries (mainly Japan and Taiwan), the BLNS countries receive 70-90% of their total imports from South Africa. BLNS countries′ large trade deficit vis-à-vis South Africa can be explained only limited by South Africa's comparative advantages, such as its proximity to the BLNS countries. Another important reason for BLNS countries' high import share from South Africa is SACU's comparably high common external tariffs for certain manufactured goods (such as textiles, fuels, dairy products, and vehicles and parts thereof), resulting in trade-diverting effects (GoN 2003:18, USTR 2002b). Furthermore, unrecorded imports coming from third countries vis-à-vis South Africa are a problem since the BLNS countries are not able to warrant the supervision of rules of origin within SACU (WTO 2003:A5-312).

[6] However, the figures in the table have to be read with caution since trade statistics in Lesotho are recognised to be unreliable (WTO 2003:A2-115).

Table 6: Main imports and import partners of the SACU economies

	Main import products (in % of total imports)	Main import products in 2000 (in % of total imports)	Import locations	Import locations in 2000
South Africa	1997: Machinery and transport equipment (34%), fuels and crude petroleum (22%), chemicals (11%), office machines (10%), food (5.5%)	Machinery and transport equipment (37%), fuels and crude petroleum (27.5%), office machines (13%), chemicals (12%), food (5%)	1997: EU (37%), APEC (19%), USA (11%), Saudi Arabia (6%), SADC (excl. SACU) (2%)	EU (40%), APEC (37%), USA (12%), Saudi Arabia (7.4%), SADC (excl. SACU) (1.4%)
Botswana	1994: Vehicles and transport equipment (19%), machinery and electrical equipment (16%), food and beverages (16%), metals (9%), chemicals (9%), wood and paper (7%), fuel (5%)	Machinery and electrical equipment (22%), food and beverages (14%), vehicles and transport equipment (12%), chemicals (10%), wood and paper (8%), fuel (5%)	1994: SACU (78%), EU (8.5%), Zimbabwe (6%)	SACU (74%), EU (16.5%), Zimbabwe (3.5%)
Lesotho	Food, building materials, vehicles, machinery, medicine, petroleum products	Food, fuel and energy, vehicles and machinery, medicine	SACU (94%), Asia (2.5%), EU (2.3%)	SACU (88%), Asia (8%), EU (1.5%)
Namibia	1997: Food and beverages (20%), machinery and electrical equipment (16.5%), vehicles + transport equipment (13%), chemicals (12%), fuels (8%)	Machinery and electrical equipment (19%), vehicles and transport equipment (15%), chemicals (15%), food and beverages (13%), fuels (13%)	1997: South Africa (80%), EU (6%)	South Africa (86%), EU (7%)
Swaziland	1997: Machinery (43%), fuels and oils (21%), food (18%), automotives and transport equipment (15.5%)	Machinery (35%), automotives and transport equipment (24%), fuels and oils (21%), food (20%)	1997: South Africa (84%), Asia (6.3%), EU (6%), USA (1%)	South Africa (93%), Asia (3.7%), EU (1%), USA (0.2%)

Sources: DTI (2001), CSO (2001), Central Bank of Lesotho (2001), WTO 2003:A5-351-5.

As can be obtained from the Figures 1 and 2, South Africa and Botswana are the only SACU countries that show trade surpluses while the other SACU countries experienced chronically trade deficits.[7]

Figure 1: South Africa's merchandise trade (in million US$)

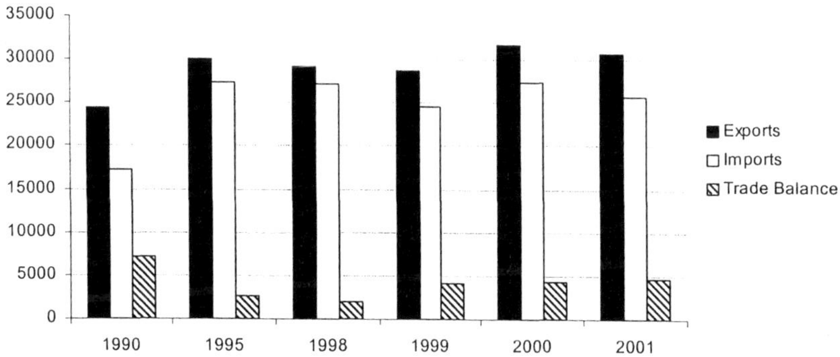

Source: WTO (2003:A4-291).

Figure 2: BLNS countries merchandise trade balance (in million US$)

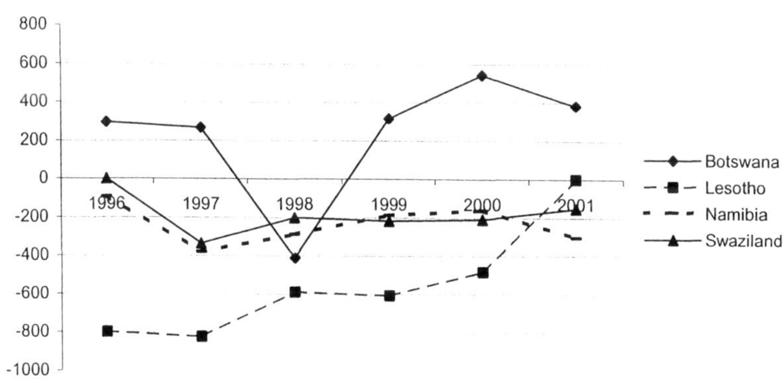

Sources: For Botswana: IMF (2002), for Lesotho, Namibia and Swaziland: WTO (2003).

---

[7] These figures include intra-regional SACU trade. As stated, BLNS import trade is highly screwed towards South Africa, while the EU is their main export destination (with the exception of Lesotho).

Socio-Economic Developments and Poverty

SACU countries population grew by 2.5% p.a. in the period 1991-2003, which is slightly lower than the Sub-Saharan African averages of 2.9% (AfDB 2004:79). Despite an average growth rate of 3.5% of GDP in the same period, the socio-economic conditions have worsened, mainly because of HIV/AIDS. The SACU region shows one of the highest HIV/AIDS infection rates worldwide: The average infection rate was estimated to be 23% in 2002 (UNAIDS 2003). This high level of HIV/AIDS has serious economic impacts on the household level (decreased income and increased expenditures) as well a negative macroeconomic impacts as the illness and death of the working generation implies a loss in economic growth, investment and national savings (AfDB 2002a). The average life expectancy in the SACU region was declining by more than 13 years in the past two decades from 54.8 years in 1980 to 41.2 years in 2003, as can be obtained from Table 7.

SACU countries infant mortality rate is with 79 per 1000 live births as high as the average infant mortality rate for whole Sub-Saharan Africa (AfDB 2002b:107). Concerning the access of the population to basic infrastructure important improvements were achieved in the period 1985-2000. Most SACU countries were able to increase the access to sanitation, safe water and health services considerably (see Table 7).

Table 7: Basic social data I

	Infant mortality rate (per 1000)		Life expectancy at birth (years)		Sanitation		Safe Water		Health Services	
	1980	2002	1980	2002	1985	2000	1985	2000	1985	1992-99
Botswana	71	67	58	36	36	70*	77	70*	...	86*
Lesotho	121	111	53	41	22	92	36	91	50	80
Namibia	91	65	54	44	14	41	52	77	72	59
South Africa	70	59	57	47	...	86	...	87*	....	....
Swaziland	100	92	52	38	...	60*	54	50*	...	55*

* Period 1990-93, later data not available.

Source: African Development Bank (2003).

SACU's illiteracy rate lies below the Sub-Saharan African average and its enrolment rate is much higher than in other African countries. However, there are significant differences among the countries, with Botswana showing the highest illiteracy rate (see Table 8).

According to their GDP per capita South Africa and Botswana are classified as "upper-middle income countries", Namibia and Swaziland are "lower-middle-income countries" and Lesotho is classified as "least developed country". Poverty is widespread within the SACU, with 12% of South Africa's population and 43% of Lesotho's population living on less than 1 US$ per day. If this amount is doubled to 2 US$ per day, one comes to over 60% (BLNS) and 36% (South Africa) of SACU's population that live in absolute poverty (AfDB 2002b:107). Though South Africa has the lowest share of poor people on its total population, it has with around 16.1 million people living on less than US$ 2 per day the highest number of poor people within SACU (OECD 2004:408). In addition to high income inequalities between the SACU members, there are also high inequalities within the countries (see Table 8). Namibia is marked by the highest distribution inequality, with a Gini coefficient index of 67,[8] which is one of the highest levels in the world, followed by Botswana (63) and Swaziland (61).

Table 8: Basic social data II

	GNI per capita (US$, Atlas method)		Human Development Index (HDI) *	Gini coefficient **	Adult illiteracy rate, > 15 years (% population)		Combined labour force participation rate (% population) ***	
	1980	2000	1999	1995	1985	1999	1980	2001
Botswana	1,190	3,300	114	63	37	24	43.6	43.8
Lesotho	490	540	132	56	25	17	42.1	39.8
Namibia	...	2,050	111	67	29	19	41.1	39.6
South Africa	2,540	3,020	94	59.3	21	15	36.8	41.7
Swaziland	970	1,290	113	61	34	21	35.7	37.0

Sources: World Bank (2003), *AISA (2002), **OECD (2004), ***AfDB (2003).

According to the Human Development Index (HDI), which measures a country's achievements in human development concerning the aspects longevity, knowledge and standard of living, South Africa shows the best living conditions within SACU, followed by Namibia and Swaziland. It is remarkable that Botswana shows the worse HDI in SACU despite the highest per capita income. This can be explained by Botswana's high income inequalities and the widespread HIV/AIDS pandemic.

[8] The Gini coefficient is a measure for the income equality in a country. It expresses the relation of the area between the Lorenz curve and the diagonal to the area between the diagonal and the axis. A Gini coefficient of 0 indicates total income equality, a value of 1 total inequality (Baßeler *et al* 1995: 209).

Thus, the life expectancy in Botswana shrank by 22 years in the past twenty years to 36 years in 2002. The incidence of HIV/AIDS is with an infection rate of 39.4% of the adult population the highest in whole Africa (OECD 2004:414).

Summarising the economic and socio-economic overview of the SACU countries it can be stated that the countries are quite different regarding their economic structure and their development level, with South Africa as economic giant and the by far most diversified economy. The BLNS countries are still dependent on few export goods and have only insufficiently diversified their export products and markets yet. Despite their different development levels, all SACU countries face similar socio-economic problems, namely very high unemployment rates, high income inequalities, widespread poverty, and a very high incidence of HIV/AIDS among their population.

What were the motivations for these different five countries to integrate in a customs union? What were and what are the gains and losses of regional integration for the single countries? As we will see in section 2.3, these questions cannot solely be answered by referring to the theoretical assumptions of regional integration that are discussed in section 2.2. The foundation of SACU was historically unique and driven by the dominance of South Africa and the economic dependency of its neighbours so that the theoretic considerations of regional integration are not sufficient when analysing the driving forces and stumbling blocks of SACU's regional integration process. The theoretical assumptions of static and dynamic effects of regional integration are however relevant to explain some of factors that have promoted and constrained regional integration within SACU.

2.2 Costs and Benefits arising from Regional Integration: Static and Dynamic Effects

Classification of regional integration models

According to Viner (1950:4-8) six different regional economic integration forms can be classified. In a *Preferential Trading Arrangement* (PTA), the simplest form of economic integration, the participating countries grant each other preferential access to their markets. The second step of economic integration is the *Free Trade Area* (FTA). Tariffs and quantitative restrictions have been abolished between member countries, allowing complete free movement of goods within the FTA. However, countries still show different external tariffs and have not harmonized their single trade policies. In order to avoid free trade of goods coming from third parties, member countries have to certify that products traded within the FTA are from a member country by a "certificate of origin". This document is superfluous in a *Customs Union* (CU) as member countries have not only agreed on the abolition of internal barriers but also on a mutual trade policy, establishing a common external tariff (CET) on imports from non-member countries.

A more advanced form of regional integration is the *Common Market*, which can be described as a customs union that allows also the free movement of capital and labour among its members. Additionally, trading standards and practises have been harmonised and member countries have a common trade policy towards third parties. The European Community until 1993 can be given as example for a common market.

An even deeper integration form than the common market is the *Economic Union*. The members of an economic union have also harmonized their economic policies. This includes a common co-ordination of monetary and fiscal policies, transportation policies and competition policies. In addition to this, non-economic policies, like security and justice might also be harmonized. An example for an economic union can be given by the European Union after the ratification of the Treaty of Maastricht in 1993.

A *Political Union* is the highest form of integration, where the members of an economic union do also agree on a common policy. The political union has a central monetary system, a common currency (or absolute fixed exchange rates) and a common budget. Decisions over domestic policies are no longer made by member states but by a supranational organisation. The United Kingdom acting as one voice of England, Scotland, Northern Ireland and Wales has the status of a political union.[9]

SACU can be described as customs union that has however some elements of a common market and an economic union. Thus, capital moves free among Lesotho, Namibia, South Africa and Swaziland (which are the members of the Common Monetary Area, see Box 3) and countries are going to establish a common trade policy – both characteristics of a common market. Since the SACU countries have also included excise and sales duties as part of their revenue formula (see section 2.3), a step towards an economic union has been undertaken.

The depth of integration and the longevity of SACU is exceptional within Africa. In all other regions in Sub-Saharan Africa regional integration is still in its infancy, with no effectively implemented FTA or CU in place.[10]

---

[9] However, considering that the United Kingdom is one country, it can be stated that the EU, which covers 25 independent countries, is the most advanced integration scheme in the world.

[10] The Common Market of Eastern and Southern Africa (COMESA) had only established an FTA for nine of its 19 member countries in 2000 and the Eastern African Community (EAC) was at the time of writing busy to fully implement its CU.

The economic reasons for the difficulty to integrate among African countries can be explained by the theoretical framework of regional integration, which shows that regional integration does not only include benefits but also costs for member countries.

Static effects from regional integration

Viner showed in his classic work "The Customs Unions Issue" (1950) that trade flows become altered when entering into a CU, owing to changed conditions of competition. He classified these processes as trade creation and trade diversion (Viner 1950:41-55).[11] *Trade creation* occurs if domestic products are replaced by more competitive regional products. This results in the increased consumption of cheaper substitutes, at the expense of local production. Thus, trade creation has detrimental effects for non-competitive domestic producers that will be displaced by their regional competitors.

Trade diversion means the directional change of trade: products which were formerly imported from the rest of the world are now imported from regional producers as their production costs are lower than those of the rest of the world plus customs duty. Thus, the producer surplus of the regional supplier increases. Viner described trade creation as positive and desirable, as it shifts production towards the more competitive regional producers, resulting in an optimal factor allocation within the region. On the contrary, trade diversion is described as 'welfare decreasing', as it promotes inefficient production. According to these assumptions, whether a CU is globally beneficial or not depends on the dominance of trade creation over trade diversion.

The dominance of trade creation is, according to Viner, more likely the more the countries were trading with each other before entering into a CU. In this case, ineffective domestic producers will be replaced by regional producers (trade creation), and only relatively little trade from the rest of the world can be replaced by regional producers (trade diversion). Furthermore, a substituting production structure should dominate; i.e. the two countries should stand in direct competition to each other. This means that successful economic integration requires a similar level of industrial development, competitive industrial sectors and the potential for complementary development of industrial sectors.

Though Viner's model experienced numerous criticisms,[12] it is still used when explaining the static effects of regional trade integration. However, along-

[11] Trade creation and diversion occur under assumption of perfect competition and functional markets, leading to full employment of all resources. The homogenous factors are mobile within the country but perfectly immobile among national boundaries and the adjustment procedures of factor allocation are costless (Viner 1950:41-55).

[12] E.g. by Gehrels (1956-7, as cited in Kreinin and Plummer 2002:8-9) who demonstrated that trade diversion can also be welfare enhancing, depending on the state of the indifference curve and the level of the intra-regional tariff rate, or by Copper and Massell (1956, as cited

side the static effects of regional integration, there are also several dynamic effects that can occur. In contradiction to static effects, dynamic effects of regional integration regenerate.

Dynamic effects from regional integration

The most obvious dynamic effect from regional integration was formulated by Balassa (1965a) who argued that *economies of scale* do not disappear after the static effects of trade creation and trade diversion are exhausted but are generated due to the enlarged market.[13] Monopolistic distortions would be reduced because of increased competition and companies are able to operate at their optimum capacity level. As a result, production costs decline and the *consumer benefits* from lower prices, which again raise their demand for goods, stimulating economic growth. The increased competition in the national market can further lead to *enhanced efficiency* since companies improve and specialise their products to reduce the pressure of regional competition. Welfare gains will be therefore not only *lower production costs and consumer* prices but also a *higher product quality* (Baldwin and Venables 1994). A further dynamic effect of regional integration is the *stimulation of investment*, both domestic and foreign. This is the case because of three reasons, a) a bigger market size, leading to a higher return on capital (Grossman and Helpman 1991, Krugman 1990), b) lower transaction costs of trade, leading to higher rates of return (Baldwin 1992),[14] and c) the reduction of economic and political uncertainties since the country has entered into a binding agreement, which lowers the risk premium for investors (Collier and Gunning 2000). These factors, which increase the at-

---

in Robson 1998:51-5) who argue for unilateral trade liberalisation, which would allow a country to benefit from trade creation without suffering from trade diversion effects. This thesis was however criticised for not taking a country's individual motivation for discriminating customs reductions into account, such as revenue losses and harmful competition. Though the global welfare maximum might not be reached, a single country can be better off when discriminating against third parties (Goldstein und Quenan 2002:47, Kreinin und Plummer 2002:5).

[13] Economies of scale are reached when total fix costs are distributed to an increasing output so that fix costs per piece are declining. One divides two types of economies of scale: The *internal*, resulting from technological factors, ensuring the optimal size of production and the *external*, which occur if the development of an industry leads to the creation of supplementary services (Baßeler *et al.* 1995:162, 168).

[14] Reduced transaction costs occur not only because of the elimination of tariffs and non-tariff barriers to trade but can further be improved by coordinated export strategies, the establishment of common financial institutions, common use of infrastructure and further trade-related cooperation (Jilberto and Mommen 1999:9). Baldwin (1992) did further argue that lower transaction costs due to economic integration increase the capital stock of a country. Since tradable goods would be generally more capital-intensive than non-tradable goods, this led to an increased demand for capital relative to labour.

tractiveness of a market, can also attract foreign investors. Another reason for foreign companies to invest into an enlarged regional market is the improved market access for regional companies in comparison to companies from third countries: since foreign companies fear to lose out against their regional competitors, they produce in their export destination (Hoeller *et al.* 2000:69). The higher investment level due to regional integration again is supposed to stimulate capital accumulation, which again is an additional source for new investment. Furthermore, the increased level of investment in addition to the effects of trade creation are supposed to create *positive accelerating effects*, which raise the demand for products, increases the demand for labour and thus result in higher economic growth. Economic growth again indicates a booming market and attracts FDI and domestic investment (Hoeller *et al.* 2000:69). Like this, the stimulating growth effects of regional integration renew.[15]

A close cooperation among countries and companies of a region can further help to *increase innovation,* since replications in research and development can be eliminated, resulting in increased efficiency. Moreover, the less developed member countries of a regional integration area have the chance to benefit from *technological spillovers* and learning effects when trading with technological advanced partners (Krugman 1990, Grossman and Helpman 1991). Another optional gain from regional integration is the benefit of *industrial agglomeration*, created by domestic clusters (Puga and Venables 1997). Hence, the investment of companies in a booming regional market can stimulate other companies to follow and to benefit from infrastructure, industrial linkages and internal and external economies of scale.[16]

Additionally to economic dynamics, regional trade agreements might also offer *political dynamics*, such as an advanced relevance in bi- and multilateral trade negotiations due to the bundling of interests. Furthermore, a contractual trading agreement might increase the economic and political reputation of the respective country since trade reforms are "locked in", which increases the security for traders and investors and lowers transaction costs (Padoan 2001, Collier and Gunning 2000). In the case that regional integration leads to the inclusion of hostile neighbouring states, one assumes that this economic integration also

[15] Evans (2000:682) differentiates between full and limited dynamic effects of regional integration. The optimal capacity operation is classified as limited dynamic effect, since the capacity can only be increased to a certain point. The re-investment of initial trade gains whereas and closer political co-operation are fully dynamic as they offer positive accelerating effects.

[16] The standard theory predicts that all member countries of a regional integration scheme benefit from these clusters since raising factor costs in an existing cluster lead to the creation of new clusters. Krugman (1991) whereas argues that an agglomerated industrial location is likely to lead to permanent core-periphery effects since industries tend to cluster in more developed member countries.

helps to stabilise them politically (AfDB 2000:124-5).[17] Moreover, higher income obtained from increased economic activities as a result of economic integration is said to have a civilising influence that promotes the understanding between the countries (Mansfield 1993). This again creates an interdependent relationship between political and economic gains from regional integration, assuming that trust among member countries promotes deeper integration, thus leading to the maximisation of welfare (Schiff and Winters 1998). However, it is important to note that there is no automatism between economic integration and political stability. The justification of regional integration on political grounds needs a confident political approach which again is not possible without regional integration. Moreover, political gains from regional integration are often distributed unevenly among member countries and accrue only later, while the economic costs of regional integration, such as trade diversion, accrue immediately (Konings and Meilink 1999:136).

Box 1: Free trade vs. regional trade agreements

The standard theory of economic convergence assumes that poor countries grow faster than rich ones as they are able to import capital and modern technologies from the advanced economies. Increased volumes of exports and imports lead to increased competition, thus resulting in the allocation of resources according to a country's comparative advantage. The increased import of capital- and technological intensive goods stimulates further the processing of innovations and new technologies through which labour and capital productivity will be increased and economies of scale will be reached. Finally, the income gap between poor and rich economies will close over the time and economic convergence will be reached. This implies that developing countries should open their markets for foreign trade and investment and benefit from imported goods, technology and know-how (Sachs and Warner 1996). However, to date the causality between an open trade regime and economic growth has not been proved empirically. Thus, it is not clear whether countries grow because they export so much or whether are they able to export because they grew (Rodrik 1999).

Continuation on next page.

[17] The prevention of conflicts by economic integration was classically illustrated with the establishment of the European Coal and Steel Community in 1951, which helped to stabilise and integrate the former fascistic countries Germany and Italy (AfDB 2000:124-125). However, on the other hand, political instability of any member of a regional integration scheme is also likely to have negative spill-over effects to other member countries, resulting in increased uncertainty and deterring potential investors (Padoan 2001).

Continuation of Box 1 from previous page.

Furthermore, no consensus has been reached whether regional arrangements are "building" or "stumbling" blocks for free trade. From the (neo-) classical point of view the position is clear: free trade is always superior to regional integration since the imposition of any trade barriers hinders the free flow of trade, thus reducing global welfare. The supporters of regional arrangements again claim that it is much easier to agree on trade liberalisation in a small group of countries than within a multilateral framework (namely the WTO with 149 countries, having very different interests). It is also more likely that political leaders get support for liberalising trade towards selected trading partners than liberalising unilaterally towards the rest of the world, considering the negative adjustment effects of trade liberalisiation (Jilberto and Mommen 1999:9). Like this, regional integration schemes may help to build momentum for liberalisation among regional groupings, finally leading to global liberalisation. Such a regional integration approach has been classified as "cooperative regionalism", which is seen as best choice in a "sub-optimal world", i.e. a world dominated by imperfect markets (Goldstein and Quenan 2002:47, Padoan 2001:40). The EU is often quoted as successful example of complementary regional and multilateral liberalisation (Hoeller *et al.* 2000:79.

Distribution of gains and losses from regional integration

Not only political effects of regional integration can be distributed unevenly among member countries but also economic effects. In a comparative static analysis one supposes equal trading partners, given world market price and total elasticity of supply. In this situation, a "win-win-situation" is the more likely the more the positive effect of trade creation is dominating over the negative effect of trade diversion, which again depends on the production structure of trading partners. Furthermore, the member of a CU can benefit with respect to their terms of trade, since their common external tariff (CET) changes the rate at which their exports exchange for their imports. The more members a customs union has and the greater its area is, the more it is likely that the CU improves its terms of trade towards the rest of the world (Viner 1950:55-6).

However, Viner's considerations of gains and losses of regional integration among consumers and producers of a CU vis-à-vis the rest of the world and within the single countries of a CU did not take all eventualities into account. Thus, a flexible world market price can be assumed for most products since the demand/supply of few big countries and trading blocks influences the world-market prices accordingly. This market power again enables companies from large countries to benefit from over-priced products at the expense of small countries' companies.[18]

For developing countries there are further assumptions of Viner's model, which are not valid. Thus, many African countries show neither functional markets nor a functional infrastructure. Intra-regional trade is little and imbalanced with high transfer costs and manifold barriers.[19] As a result, regional integration does not lead to an optimal factor use, absorption and distribution (Balassa 1965a). Furthermore, one assumes that countries are more successful in regional integration, the closer they are in per capita and absolute income level. This is due to dominance of intra-sectoral trade, which is much more valuable than inter-sectoral trade. Intra-sectoral trade, i.e. the trade within one sector, can be divided between intra-industrial trade (trade within one industry) and inter-industrial trade (trade between different industries). Intra-industrial trade is a feature of trade between countries with similar industrial development, similar per capita income, small differences in market size and similar factor supply. The more advanced a country is, the more intra-industrial trade will occur from both, the demand and the supply side. Thus, the more unequal trading countries are, the less intra-industrial trade will occur (Balassa and Bauwens 1988). Since the bulk of intra-African trade is inter-industrial, it correlates positively with difference in per capita income, which results in high adjustment costs for weaker member countries of a regional integration scheme (de Melo *et al.* 1993:163-4, Foroutan 1993:258-9). So far most regional integration attempts in Africa have resulted in protectionist policies among the "losers" who feared further industrial polarisation (Foroutan 1993:258).

The economic costs and benefits of regional integration also depend on the level of market liberalisation for each country. In the case of a liberalised economy, the costs of regional integration are lower than in a closed economy since the country faces less revenue losses and can better deal with competition so that trade creation is more likely to dominate over trade diversion (Viner 1950:51). Additionally, political costs, such as resistance to change, are also less likely to occur in a liberalised economy (Padoan 2001:48-49).

Because of small economies with low purchasing power, a non-complementary production structure, a low industrialisation degree, and a protective import regime, as well as the missing political and economic will to foster intra-regional trade and investment, regional integration among African

---

[18] John Stuart Mill (1864) formulated the theory of flexible world-market prices first and pointed out that big countries with monopolistic power are in a position to levy taxes and thus, increase their welfare on the costs of the global welfare (Baßeler et al. 1995:524).

[19] It has to be noted that there is an interdependent relationship between infrastructure and regional integration. While a proper infrastructure facilitates intra-regional trade, regional cooperation itself can be an effective instrument to improve the infrastructure of the region (Oshikoya and Hussain 2002:104).

countries was only limited successful to date (AfDB 1993, 2000, Yeats 1998).[20] The limited success of South-South integration in Africa brought North-South regional integration schemes as successful trade and development instrument on the agenda. It is argued that the widespread import-substitution policy[21] among African countries has resulted in inefficient, highly protected industries, which lack of capital and intermediary goods. North-South integration would offer southern countries the options to expand their exports and to diversify since they would benefit from competitive inputs. Furthermore, African countries could benefit from technology and learning effects when strengthening cooperation with industrialised countries (Foroutan 1993:254, Michaely 2004:83-8).

This approach contradicts the classical considerations of Viner (1950:51-3) and Balassa (1965a, 1965 b), arguing that in case of a North-South FTA the detrimental effects of trade diversion are likely to dominate because of a complementary production and trade structure. Foroutan (1993) and other authors (like Piazolo 2001, Collier and Gunning 2000) argue that the different factor endowment does not harm but benefits developing countries when entering into a North-South FTA since it enables them to concentrate on their comparative advantages and export labour-intensive manufactures, thus stimulating the division of labour. Like this, a North-South FTA could act as "engine of growth" for developing countries, radiating positive agglomeration effects. However, this theory neglects some important facts in North-South trade relations, such as the restricted movement of labour, very different capacities and transaction costs, and falling terms of trade for most developing countries' exports.[22] Thus, there is the risk of a polarised development in a North-South FTA, which could manifest the

---

[20] Thus, in 2003 neither SADC nor COMESA was able to reach the level of intra-regional trade flows that existed in 1970 prior the existence of these regional bodies. Since 1990 intra-regional trade stagnates in SADC at around 6% of member countries' total trade. COMESA was able to increase its intra-regional trade level slightly from 7% in 1990 to around 7.5% in 2003 (IMF Direction of Trade Statistics, various issues as cited in Yang and Gupta 2005:17).

[21] Theoretically, import substitution policies are justified by the infant industry argument, which assumes that the industry will be able to become internationally competitive when it has had time to learn the business and to achieve economies of scale under protection. However, the import substitution strategy failed in many developing countries, firstly, on account of the lack of competition, which resulted in inefficient production and high import costs. Secondly, its failure was also a result of the fact that the industries did not build up backward and forward linkages with local suppliers (Todaro and Smith 2002: 562–71).

[22] Another important factor of successful intra-regional trade is seen in the physical distance of trading partners, assuming that the trade volume is higher with neighbouring countries (Padoan 2001:43).

inherited colonial trade pattern between industrialised and developing countries (UNCTAD 2002b, 2000, Padoan 2001, AfDB 2000, El-Agraa 1997b).[23]

Box 2 summarises advantageous and disadvantageous factors for successful regional integration.

Box 2: Factors that advance and constrain regional integration

Factors that advance regional integration	Factors that constrain regional integration
• A similar production structure and a high level of intra-industrial trade among trading partners • Large, prosperous markets • High consumers' purchasing power and a high income equality • High factor mobility: equal distribution of trade benefits • Competitive environment: increased quality of goods and innovation stimuli • Open trading regime: low adjustment costs • Economically and politically stable member countries • Geographical closeness and proper infrastructure: low transaction costs • Cooperation in trade-related areas: facilitation of intra-regional trade • Compensation mechanism: anticipation of regional disparities • Creation of common regional institutions: reduction of political and economic uncertainties • Political will to integrate • Cultural homogeneity and common political values: consensus on common policies	• A different production structure and a high level of inter-industrial trade among trading partners or a very similar factor endowment and a low level of industrialisation among trading partners • Small economies with low purchasing power • High economic disparities among member countries: trade imbalances and dissimilar gains and losses • Low factor mobility and protectionist policies among member countries • Economically and politically unstable member countries • Protectionist trading regime: high adjustment costs (such as fiscal losses) • Geographical disparities and a weak infrastructure: high transaction costs • Lack of intra-regional trade coordination and unclear mandate of regional integration scheme • Missing political will to integrate • Overlapping memberships in different integration schemes with rival goals • Different linguistic and cultural background of the countries: higher costs to agree on common policies

Source: Author's presentation based on sources cited in the text.

[23] According to the hub-and-spoke theory, the European centre ("hub") gains high scale economies due to transaction-intensive activities (industrial production and manufacturing) while the African periphery ("spoke") is only able to deliver primary goods, which reinforces Africa's dependency on European goods (Kennes 2000:112).

It should however not be overlooked that an unequal development in a region can also occur as a result of regional integration among countries with a comparably similar development level. This case is highly evident for regional integration within Africa. Thus, the economically most powerful country of a regional integration framework shows large trade surpluses with its regional partners.[24] Considering the development disparities between South Africa and the BLNS as well as South Africa's economic size in comparison to its neighbours and BLNS countries' economic dependency on South Africa, regional integration in SACU can rather be classified as North-South integration than as South-South integration.

Since it is generally seen as important that all countries of a regional integration scheme benefit from the agreement, there are manifold discussions about compensation mechanism, such as fiscal measures or transfer payment. So far, SACU is the only regional integration scheme in Africa that has implemented such a mechanism successfully.[25]

Before addressing the gains and losses SACU members experienced in regional integration, the historic and economic development of SACU as well as the specific design of the SACU Agreement and its revenue sharing formula, which are both important aspects for regional integration within SACU shall be presented.

2.3 Foundation and Purpose: the SACU Agreement 1969 and the Role of South Africa

The Southern African Customs Union (SACU) is the oldest Customs Union (CU) in the world and still the only full implemented, functioning customs union in Africa. Its common external tariff (CET) and the Common Revenue Pool (CRP) are successfully into force and intra-SACU trade is comparably high, though South Africa's intra-regional exports are dominating. Within the SACU, South Africa, Lesotho, Namibia and Swaziland form the "Common Monetary Area" (CMA), which can be classified a currency board with parity exchange, supposed to reduce transactions and information costs (see Box 3).

---

[24] According to Foroutan (1993:258), Ivory Coast accounted for around 75% of intra-CEAO exports in the late 1980s/early 1990s, Cameroon for 96% of intra-UDEAC exports, Nigeria for 30% of intra-ECOWAS exports and both, Kenya and Zimbabwe for around 30% of intra-PTA exports (today COMESA).

[25] Though SACU's system of transfer payment, as discussed in section 2.3, was not able to equalise economic development within SACU.

Box 3: The Common Monetary Area (CMA)

The CMA aims to achieve monetary stability and better economic and financial cooperation in the SACU region. It exists since 1992 and is the successor of the "Trilateral Monetary Agreement" (TMA), which followed the "Rand Monetary Area" (RMA) (see historic overview). The CMA provides for the free flow of member countries' funds and free access to the South African capital market. Lesotho's, Namibia's, and Swaziland's (LNS) national currencies are fixed towards the South African Rand and are freely convertible within the CMA.[26] LNS Central Banks have the task to regulate credits and can set up interest rates independently. However, since funds move freely in the CMA, the interest rates differentiate only little. Inflation, not only in CMA but also in Botswana, is highly influenced by South Africa's monetary and policy exchange rate policy, which was until 2003 singly destined by the South African Reserve Bank (SARB). The monetary policy of the LNS Central Banks focuses therefore on short-term interest policy and follows in general developments in South Africa and actions of the SARB (Nowak and Ebrill 2003:10, GoN 2003:15). Since 2003 the CMA, which is working to become a monetary union, is administered by a commission, that comprises a representative and appointed advisers of each member country and meets a least once a year, where decisions are made by consensus (WTO 2003:12).

Brief historic overview of the CMA

In 1974 the "Rand Monetary Area" (RMA) was established by South Africa, Botswana, Lesotho and Swaziland. Botswana left the RMA in 1976 but maintained a fixed pegged exchange rate policy with South Africa as it linked its currency, the Pula, to a trade-weighted basket of currencies, dominated by the Rand. Lesotho, Namibia and Swaziland pegged their national currencies at par to the Rand. In 1986, the "Trilateral Monetary Agreement" (TMA) was established as successor of the RMA and became the CMA in 1992, following the accession of Namibia as a formal member. While the formation of TMA (1986) into CMA (1992) was only the extension of the agreement because of a new member country, the difference between RMA (1974) and TMA (1986) was that the new agreement allowed Lesotho and Swaziland to use their currencies not only for internal transactions but also for exchange transactions.

SACU's predecessor was established in 1889 by the Cape of Good Hope and the Orange Free State. One year later, the British colonies Swaziland, Basutoland (today Lesotho) and Bechuanaland (today Botswana) joined. When in 1920, the

[26] The Maloti, the Namibian Dollar, and the Swazi Emalangeni are only convertible within the CMA but not internationally accepted. The South African Rand and the Botswana Pula are the only SACU currencies that are fully convertible.

Republic of South Africa, which was constituted in 1910, got the mandatory over the former German colony South West Africa (Namibia), the SACU in its present size was established.[27] An according agreement was concluded in 1969 and entered into force on 01 March 1970. Namibia became a formalised member after its independency in 1990.

SACU provides duty-free movement of goods and services within its territory and shows a CET as well as common excise and sales duties, common rebates, refunds and drawbacks against third countries. Excise and sales duties are usually not collected within a CU so that SACU's revenue policy is often interpreted as a step towards fiscal integration (McCarthy 1992, 1994).[28]

The primary goal of SACU was and still is to facilitate the cross-border movements of goods and to promote investment and product diversification in its area (Republic of South Africa 1969). However, the SACU Agreement 1969 was not signed between equal partners who wanted to facilitate intra-regional trade but between enemy states, namely Apartheid South Africa on the one hand and Botswana, Lesotho and Swaziland (BLS), which had just become independent, on the other hand. Namibia (at that time South-West Africa) was regarded as *de facto* member and obliged to apply SACU's customs and excise rules under South African legislation (BoN 2003:20).[29] Since BLS were all very poor and highly dependent on the South African economy, the bargaining power was in favour of South Africa. South Africa decided that SACU's CET, the excise and sales duties and the rebates and drawbacks should be those that were valid in South Africa (Republic of South Africa 1969, Art. 4). Furthermore, South Africa set the decision structure within SACU: The South African Board on Tariffs and Trade (SABTT) determined the CET and was able to reject any proposal made by the SACU Customs Union Commission, which met once a year. However, to avoid extreme polarisation of economic development, South Africa also decided to establish a SACU Common Revenue Pool to compensate the BLS from trade displacement, loss of fiscal sovereignty and highly polarised devel-

---

[27] After capitulation of the Germans in 1915, South Africa received the area of South West Africa by the League of Nations as C-mandate, i.e. it was obliged to report to the League of Nations. After Second World War, South Africa refused to sign a convention of trust with the UN and practised its Apartheid politics also in South West Africa. In 1966 the UN withdrew the mandate from South Africa. South West Africa became officially Namibia in 1968 and was - from 1969 on - treated as South Africa's fifth province. In 1971 the International Court of Justice classified South Africa's attendance in Namibia as illegal. The independence movement SWAPO fought for Namibia's independence and succeeded in 1990 (Meyers grosses Taschenlexikon, Band 15, 1995).

[28] A complete harmonized fiscal policy comprises the common coordination of taxation and expenditure as well as the common determination of the relative size of the public sector and the allocation of public sector's responsibilities (El-Agraa 1997a:58-66).

[29] In the following, the term "BLS" will be used prior Namibia's independence and the term "BLNS" for the time after 1990, when Namibia officially joined SACU.

opment in favour of South Africa.[30] South Africa set the CET in favour of the promotion of its import industrialisation strategy, which was often not in the interest of BLS, which had to buy high-priced goods from South Africa, thus increasing their trade deficit (McCarthy 1994:176-177). Though it could be argued that trade deficits are not an adequate instrument for identifying adjustment costs in a CU since a country's total trade is not bi- but multilateral this was not the case for the BLS countries, which imported almost exclusively from South Africa. In addition to its unilateral external policy, South Africa restricted BLS exports to its market in order to protect itself (Republic of South Africa 1969, Art. 7, 11). Since the imposition of quantitative restrictions or other non-tariff barriers to trade are in contradiction to the basic idea of a customs union, BLS countries could not benefit from trade creation but showed increased persistent trade imbalances, which resulted in their further economic marginalisation (McCarthy 1992, 1994).

There are two ways of compensating the weaker member countries of a CU, namely fiscal measures and transfer payments. When applying fiscal measures, the poor countries are allowed to impose limited import duties on certain goods coming from other members of the CU. This should allow weaker economies to protect domestic industries and to stimulate their industrial development. Transfer payments just mean that the richer countries compensate the poorer by the transfer of money. Thus, fiscal measures are an instrument to coordinate industrial development within a CU and to reach a more even industrial development, while transfer payments do not have any guidance effect but are a pure compensation instrument.[31] Since South Africa was not interested in a more equal economic development within SACU but only intended to avoid extreme polarisation, it decided on the instrument of transfer payments (McCarthy 1992:11-14).[32]

The SACU Common Revenue Pool was established on 01 April 1969. Since the trade of landlocked BLS countries was directed through South Africa and Namibia was treated like a South African province, the South African Reserve Bank (SARB) collected all customs, excise and sales duties and distributed it according to a two stage revenue formula among member countries. However,

---

[30] Before the SACU Agreement 1969 entered into force, the BLS got almost no compensation. The revenue distribution was fixed extremely low (between 0.15% and 0.88% of total revenue per country) (McCarthy 1994:168).

[31] Contradictors of fiscal payments argue that such a regulation of market forces, which impedes the free movement of trade, would have a counterproductive effect on gains from regional integration (Foroutan 1993:259-60).

[32] As stated by McCarthy (1992:11): *"Any analysis of SACU must bear in mind, ..., that the history of customs unions in Southern Africa is not one in which the integration schemes were driven by development goals; the customs union was mostly a pragmatic arrangement to distribute revenues among members whose economic integration was a fait accompli."*

the BLS countries claimed that the formula did not compensate sufficiently for their economic costs of SACU membership and that receipts were very unstable. In 1976, the parties agreed to include a stabilisation factor into the revenue formula, which guaranteed BLS a revenue rate between 17 and 23% of imports and excisable consumption. Box 4 explains the calculation of the SACU Common Revenue Pool formula, which was valid until the end of 2004.

Box 4: Calculation of the SACU revenue formula (1969 Agreement)

The CRP contained customs, excise, sales and additional duties collected on goods imported in the SACU. The revenue share of each country was determined by the size of its imports and unaffected by the amount actually collected in the CRP.

1. *Rate of revenue:* In a first step, SACU members received the common revenue in proportion to their annual imports, *plus* the value of production and consumption of dutiable goods (BLS exports to South Africa did not reduce their share to the pool). This basis should have compensated BLS countries roughly from their losses of trade displacement (McCarthy 1992).
2. *Enhancement Rate:* In a second step, this outcome was multiplied with the factor 1.42 in order to recompense costs of economic polarisation and loss of fiscal sovereignty.

   (1) $Y = (i + p)/(I + P) * R * 1.42$

   At which Y is the rate of revenue, calculated by the sum of the value of dutiable imports (i) and excisable production and consumption (p) of a country, divided by the sum of SACU's total dutiable imports (I) and total excisable production and consumption (P), multiplied by the customs revenue pool (R) and the enhancement factor 1.42.

   In order to stabilise the BLS revenue rate between 17% and 23%, the following calculation was applied from 1976 on:

   (2) $Y \geq 0.17\,(m + p)\; and\; Y \leq 0.23\,(m + p)$

   (3) $Y \leq 0.17 + \left(\frac{0.20 - Y}{2}\right) and\; Y \geq 0.23 - \left(\frac{0.20 - Y}{2}\right)$

   If the rate of revenue multiplied by 1.42 times was < 17% (>23%), one half of the difference between 20% and the enhanced rate was added to (subtracted from) the enhanced rate. This was done until the condition stated in formula (2) was fulfilled.

Source: Mayer and Zarenda (1994:14-6).

Though South Africa was ready to guarantee BLS a fixed amount of revenue by including the stabilisation factor into the revenue formula, it refused to re-negotiate the SACU Agreement and to take BLS countries' requests for stronger participation into account. From 1981 on, BLS moved to re-negotiate the SACU Agreement, claiming the following points (WTO 2003:7, Jenkins 2000, Maasdorp 1994):

- The management and institutional aspects of the SACU system needed to be reviewed; in particular the *de facto* unilateral setting of all tariffs by the SABTT.
- Transfers from the CRP were based on two-years-old import data but BLS had to pay into the CRP on a quarterly basis, which was seen as interest free loan to South Africa.[33] Moreover, the high inflation rates reduced BLS income from the CRP considerably.
- BLS claimed that excise duties and sales taxes should be excluded from the revenue formula, as fiscal harmonisation within SACU had not been reached;
- BLS asked for the establishment of a dispute settlement mechanism in order to provide mutually acceptable solutions in case of disputes.

South Africa denied re-negotiation and was even thinking of leaving the arrangement, as it became too costly. Since the CRP was calculated according to BLS imports and affected by the actually collected amount, South Africa's revenues were diminishing over the years. While before the introduction of the stabilisation rate more than 97% of SACU's total revenue accrued to South Africa, this figure declined to 66.4% in 1992 (Mayer and Zarenda 1994:22). In addition to the argument that SACU was already too costly, South Africa also rejected BLS request for a re-negotiation by arguing that the countries would not take their duty-free access to the South African market as well as their guaranteed revenue of at least 17% sufficiently into account. Indeed, the inclusion of the stabilisation rate in 1976 resulted in a substantial increase in BLS countries' share of the CRP total revenue. While BLS share on the CRP was 3.9% in 1969-70, this figure increased to 12.8% in 1984-85 (McCarthy 1992:14). As can be obtained from Figure 3 and Table 9, not only BLS countries' share on total revenue increased significantly but also the total volume of the CRP. Today, income from the CRP is still an important income source for BLNS and accounted for 12.8% of total revenue for Botswana, 30.4% for Namibia and 50% for Lesotho and Swaziland in 2001 (see Table 9).

[33] Due to a lack of statistics the BLS countries received the differences between the initial estimates of revenue amount and the real revenue only two years later (WTO 2003:7).

Figure 3: Distribution of the CRP under the 1969 SACU Agreement

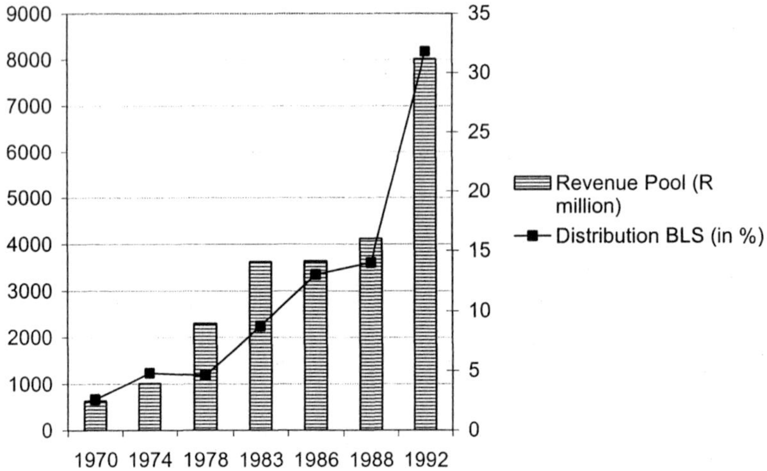

Note: Until 1988 the data apply to BLS. Namibia is included in the 1992 figure.

Source: Report of the Commission of Inquiry into the Tax Structure of the Republic of South Africa, RP 34/1987 and *Hansard*, Parliament of the Republic of South Africa as cited in McCarthy 1994:172.

Table 9: SACU revenue as percentage of current government revenue and GDP

	SACU's revenue as percentage of total government revenue			**SACU's revenue as percentage of GDP**	
	1980	**1991**	**2001***	**1980**	**1991**
South Africa	3.3	8.8	3.9	0.83	2.8
Botswana	39.1	13.4	12.8	14.3	8.5
Lesotho	61.3	51.8	51.0	10.5	13.9
Namibia +	...	37.5	30.4	...	14.7
Swaziland	...	...	54.1	...	...

+ Prior 1981 Namibia received a fixed share of 2.55% of the net CRP according to the "South West Africa Affairs Act 1969". Since 1981, this amount was raised annually (BoN 2003:20).

Sources: World Bank (1993:260), * SACU's Commission Reports as cited in Kirk and Stern (2003:5).

In the 1980ies, the increased revenue share of BLS countries in addition to increasing social expenditure and limited tax income raised South Africa's concern about the 1976 revenue formula. Besides, South Africa faced the problem to include its "independent" homelands into the SACU Agreement, which the BLS countries refused to accept.[34] BLS argued that the homelands are part of South Africa and could not be treated like independent countries. This argument was not only made because of political reasons but also because the inclusion of new states would have reduced BLS income from the CRP (McCarthy 1994:172-174). However, South Africa distributed SACU revenue to its homelands, which rose from 1.7% of total SACU revenue in 1978 to 22.8% in 1992.[35] This policy, as well as South Africa's policy of income diversification, away from tariffs towards indirect taxation, resulted in BLS countries' persistent CRP rate of 17% (McCarthy 1992:14 and 1994:172).

The dispute about SACU's future got new drive in 1994 when the first democratic elections in South Africa have changed the official voice. South Africa started to see SACU as important for itself, for the BLNS countries and for further economic integration in the region. South Africa recognised that the BLNS countries and the wider SADC region are an important sales market for its manufactured products and became interested in building-up a stable region, acknowledging that it cannot survive in a "sea of poverty" (Robson 1997:352-357).

See Figure 4 for a historic overview of SACU.

[34] Which were Transkei, Bophuthatswana, Venda and Ciskei (TBVC states). The Development Bank for Southern Africa (DBSA) was responsible for the development of the so-called homelands, which were forced to become "independent" in 1978, 1979, 1981 and 1983 respectively. From this time on, South Africa treated them as part of the SACU but not as its territory. The "independence" of the homelands was part of South Africa's Apartheid strategy and supposed to dump the unemployed black labour force out of the cities and back to "their countries" (Yedder and Rake 2001:475).

[35] South Africa did also try to promote industrial development in Transkei, Bophuthatswana, Venda and Ciskei, which put obstacles on industrial development in BLS. The Ciskei for instance adopted a complete tax-free system in order to attract foreign investors. Moreover, South Africa tried to lure FDI by offering high rates of return, e.g. by subsidies and preferences. This policy stopped with the start of the post-Apartheid era in 1991 (Ailola 2000:254).

Figure 4: The history of the Southern African Customs Union (SACU)

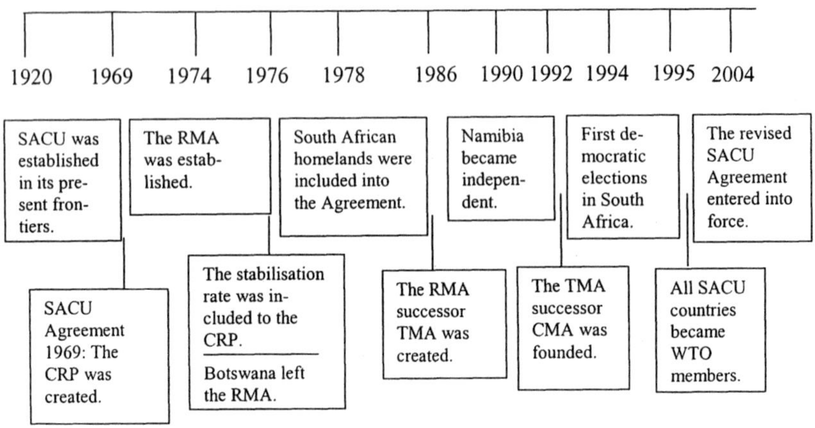

Source: Author's presentation.

However, the BLNS countries did not only win from the political changes in South Africa but also had to accept economic losses. This was mainly the case for Lesotho and Swaziland, which benefited during the Apartheid era from significant development assistance and political support from industrialised countries as well as from investment from South African companies and foreign companies that were seeking to circumvent the sanctions (ACP General Secretariat 1995c:29). The fact that the BLNS countries were differently affected by the political challenge in South Africa also resulted in different positions regarding the re-negotiation process of the SACU Agreement. Though all BLNS acknowledged the importance of re-negotiations in general, their interests diverted: Lesotho, and to a lesser extent Swaziland, were mainly interested to increase their revenue share, which was their main source of income. In return, they were ready to accept the democratic deficit of the SACU agreement. Botswana and Namibia, again, which did not face the same fiscal constraints, were primarily interested in a democratisation of SACU´s decision process, e.g. regarding the setting of the CET in order to develop their industries (ACP General Secretariat 1995c:37).

2. 4 Costs and Benefits of Regional Integration for SACU Members

Though Botswana, Lesotho and Swaziland complained about the revenue formula and the lack of participatory, they considered their SACU membership as important. This was mainly because of their high dependency on the South African economy and the absence of development alternatives. The BLS countries had due to their small population, their narrow markets and their geographical location almost no option to pursue an import-substitution industrialisation strategy. Thus, they had only little to lose from South African competition but a lot to win from improved market access to the biggest market in the region (Maasdorp 1992:20). Furthermore, the guaranteed income from the CRP, South Africa's responsibility for the CET and customs administration, which was initially set in place to eliminate the smuggle problem, was attractive for the BLS countries (Goodison 1999:40).

However, the potential for trade diversion due to the complementary production structure between BLS and South Africa was considerably. While the BLS exported only few primary goods (mining and agricultural products), South Africa showed already in 1969 a comparably well-developed industrial base. Moreover, price-rising effects were predominant because of South Africa's import-substituting industrialisation strategy, which resulted in a high CET against competitive manufactured products from third countries (Platzky 1996, McCarthy 1992:10).[36] A study of Leith (1992) on the costs and benefits of Botswana's membership in SACU found out that the country paid in 1987 R 371 million more for imports from South Africa than world market prices and gained R 30 million through the price raising effects on its exports in the protected SACU market. If one adds the income from the CRP in 1987 to this negative balance, Botswana had a net loss of R 45 million.[37] According to these figures, Botswana might have been better off if it had left the SACU and negotiated an FTA with South Africa (Davis 1994:4). However, considering Botswana's lopsided dependency on the South African market and South Africa's interest to keep Botswana into SACU, it must be regarded as doubtful that South Africa was ready to negotiate an FTA with Botswana. Furthermore, Botswana's costs for building-up institutional and administrative capacities to warrant the rules of origin in a SACU FTA and to collect the customs duties from external trade must also be taken into account when calculating the costs and benefits of its SACU membership.

[36] See Platzky (1996) for a comprehensive overview of South Africa's industrialisation policy prior 1994 and its effects on industrial location within South Africa. Unfortunately, Platzky excludes the effects on the BLNS.

[37] A similar study for Lesotho conducted by Bourne (1989, quoted in Mayer and Zarenda 1994:34) estimated the comparative-static losses in form of trade diversion and loss of consumer surplus due to higher price to be around 145 million Maloti p.a. for Lesotho.

In addition to trade diversion and price raising effects, BLS countries also suffered from non-tariff barriers that protected the South African market. South Africa applied protection clauses, such as quantitative and temporal restrictions, for certain BLS goods within SACU, and offered generous incentives for investing into South African homelands. Furthermore, the SABTT was allowed to apply autonomously for anti-dumping and countervailing duties, which accelerated the price raising effects for BLS imports (WTO 2003:A5-323). In sum, South Africa's external and internal trade policy did rather constrain industrial deepening in the BLS countries and failed to address the causes of unequal development (McCarthy 1994, AfDB 1993:266-70). Thus, the static effects of regional integration were negative for the BLS but positive for South Africa. The BLS countries were not able to benefit fully from trade creation since their market access was restricted. Additionally, they lost their fiscal discretion and had to subsidy the industrial development of South Africa since South Africa practised an import-substitution policy and set the CET in its interest.

South Africa again was able to sell its non-competitive manufactured products above world-market prices and did therefore gain from trade diversion.[38] Moreover, South Africa benefited from its dominance in the SACU institutions and the unilateral tariff settings, which were a constant matter of dispute. Due to its economic and political dominance, South Africa was able to benefit from a regional trade agreement without having to compromise on anything. Moreover, South Africa benefited politically from SACU. The BLNS countries linked South Africa to other African countries during the Apartheid era (McCarthy 1992:19-20).

However, though the static effects from regional integration were negative for the BLS countries, dynamic gains might have outweighed these losses. Benefits from cooperation in the fields of infrastructure, technology, and harmonised economic policies must also be taken into account when judging the effects of regional integration (van Brabant 2001:388). These positive dynamic effects might have, in addition to the protective nature of a CU against the rest of the world, promoted industrial growth in the BLS. In fact, producers in the landlocked BLS countries benefited from using South Africa's infrastructure free of charge and from almost free access to the South African market. BLS consumers benefited from South African retail stores, banks and restaurants that opened in their countries. Furthermore, South Africa's restrictive import-control policy did not only harm BLS consumers and producers by making imports

[38] To what extent South Africa benefited from its exports to BLS is disputed. While some authors state that the economic advantages were very limited since South Africa's exports into BLS accounted only for a small share of its total exports (Margo Commission 1987:359 as cited in Mayer and Zarenda 1994:28), other authors argue that the quality of export products (sophisticated manufacturing goods) contributed significantly to South Africa's growth (Mayer and Zarenda 1994:29, Kirk and Stern 2003:3).

more expensive but also offered BLS producers the chance to build-up industries in a comparably protected market since the BLS countries were not forced to open their markets under international Structural Adjustment Programmes like many other African countries (McCarthy 1992:16-17). On the other hand, it must be taken into account that BLS had only limited options to protect their industries against South African competition and to compete against South Africa's investment incentive schemes. Thus, in a survey undertaken in 1992, covering 283 companies engaged in cross border trade in six SADC countries,[39] the companies named the lack of protection for local industries as main disadvantage of being a SACU member, followed by high competition from South African firms and having to buy South African inputs because of the prohibitive tariff. Still, 73.3% of all companies interviewed regarded SACU as a useful regional grouping that facilitated intra-regional trade. For the CMA area, the consent was even as high as 85.4%. The main reasons the interviewed firms named for favouring a membership in SACU were ease of trade, the availability of competitive goods and services and access to a large market (Maasdorp and Whiteside 1993:43). Membership in the CMA was regarded as useful because of the free mobility of capital, and the fixed exchange rate and thus convertibility of the national currencies in the South African Rand. Collier and Gunning (1999) agree, arguing that the CMA had helped to create a sound macroeconomic environment and to prevent too much economic divergence among member countries. Considering the lack of foreign exchange and the limited number of countries that have convertible currencies in the region, LNS membership of the CMA and Botswana's strong connection to the CMA, can indeed be seen as important factor that helped to flourish intra-regional trade. Thus, SACU has become an economic stable and predictable trading block and is the anchor of economic and political stability in southern Africa. Its members are highly committed to comply with their treaty, which is rather the exemption for regional integration frameworks in Africa. According to Collier and Gunning (1999:82) South Africa had acted as an "agent of restraint", which "locked-in" SACU's trade and customs policy.

Another positive effect of the SACU for the BLS countries was the shift of investment from South Africa. When in the beginning of the 1980ies international sanctions were introduced against the Apartheid regime in South Africa, foreign firms started to produce in Lesotho and Swaziland in order to serve the South African market (Basu and Srinivasanv 2002:26, Robson 1997:359). Moreover, export-oriented South African firms that wanted to avoid the stigma of Apartheid, produced in the BLS (Mayer and Zarenda 1994:42). However, as can be obtained from Figure 5, the quantifiable benefits of increased FDI into

[39] Namely in the BLNS countries, Malawi and Zimbabwe.

BLS during the Apartheid era were limited.[40] Furthermore, the countries lost investment after the end of Apartheid when firms relocated to South Africa.[41]

Figure 5: Stock of FDI inflows to BLNS countries, 1980-2000 (in million US$)

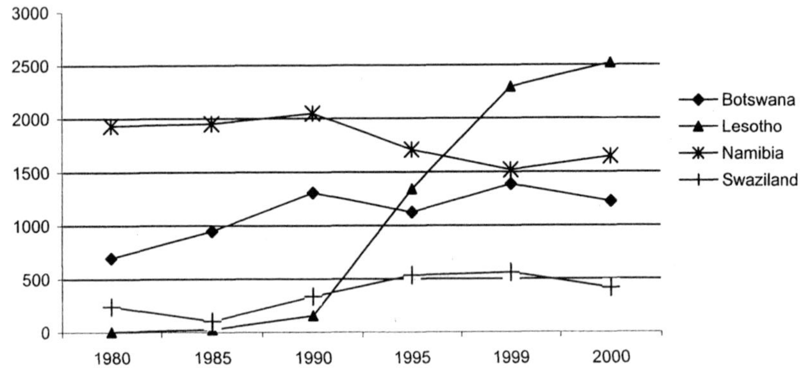

Source: UNCTAD 2002a.

Another benefit for the BLS countries, which is rather related to their proximity to South Africa than to their SACU membership, is the absorption of unskilled BLS labour force by South African gold and coal mines.[42] The remittance from mining workers was from the 1970ies to the 1990ies mainly for Lesotho an important income source. However, because of the shrinking gold haulage and increasingly restrictive working permits in South Africa this income source has declined substantially. While more than 100,000 migrant employees from Lesotho were working in South African mines in the late 1980ies, this figure declined

[40] The sharp increase in Lesotho's foreign investment stock since 1990 can be explained by the creation of the "Highland Water Scheme Project", the largest and most expensive water project in the world that should bring water from the highlands in Lesotho to the Gauteng province in South Africa (WTO 2003:A2-139).

[41] Swaziland e.g. has not received any new large FDI since 1991 and aims primarily to keep foreign investors. Swaziland's reinvestment inflows account for around 90% of total FDI (Basu and Srinivasan 2002:29). Lesotho, again, has lost FDI into its garment industry after the end of Apartheid. However, these losses where outweighed by new FDI due to AGOA. Moreover, Lesotho received huge FDI inflows from the Highland Water Project, which accounted for 90% of its FDI inflows in the period 1999-2002 (WTO 2003:A2-114).

[42] Men from other neighbouring African countries, such as Malawi and Mozambique, were also working in South African mines (Mayer and Zarenda 1994:3).

to less than 60,000 in 2000.[43] As a result miner's remittance decreased from 60% of Lesotho's GDP in the late 1980ies to 26% in 1999 (ACP General Secretariat 1995c:30, 2002b:72).[44]

In sum, it can be concluded that BLS experienced contradicting effects on economic development because of their SACU membership. On the one hand South Africa's hegemony enabled the countries to operate in a relative protected market and to receive a guaranteed share of the total revenue, on the other hand they suffered from trade diversion and South Africa's unilateral external trade decisions that did not take their concerns sufficiently into account.

When linking the theoretical discussion on gains and losses of regional integration to the experience of SACU, the positive and negative effects of regional integration in SACU under the 1969 Agreement can be summarised as follows:

Advantages for South Africa

- The autonomous trade and industrial policy served the interest of most South African producers and protected them against competition from third countries.
- Benefits from trade diversion: non-competitive manufacturing products were sold in the SACU market.
- Economic linkages to other African countries during the Apartheid era because of South Africa's strong binding towards BLS.
- The inclusions of the "independent homelands" into the CRP decreased the total revenue for the BLS countries.

Advantages for the BLNS countries

- Increased market size: the almost free access to the South African market allowed BLNS in some cases to benefit from economies of scale (e.g. with respect to beef production). Furthermore, the BLNS countries were able to reduce their transaction costs by using the South African infrastructure for their imports and exports. Costs for doing business in SACU

---

[43] Botswana and Swaziland had about 14,000 and 16,000 migrant employees respectively working in South African mines in 1991 (Chamber of Mines: Annual Report 1991 as cited in Mayer and Zarenda 1994: 9).

[44] However, some authors argued that the migrant labour was not beneficial for the BLS but increased their dependency on South Africa and impeded economic development. South Africa wanted to broaden its economic and political influence in the region and make the application of international sanctions more difficult to implement. According to this theory, "... *South Africa's involvement in SACU is based on selfish political and strategic motives.*" (Mayer and Zarenda 1994:3).

were also reduced by the free convertibility of the Maloti, the Namibian Dollar and the Emalangeni into the South African Rand.

- Stimulation and attraction of investment: The BLS countries received some FDI from South African and international companies because of their closeness and preferred access to the South African market, which carried by that time the stigma of the Apartheid regime.
- The comparable protected SACU market and the provision for infant industry protection (Art. 8) gave some scope for the development of own industries.[45]
- The guaranteed revenue share of 17-23% of the CRP contributed to a secured and more predictable income for the governments.
- Reduction of country-risk: SACU is regarded as anchor of economic and political stability in southern Africa. Additionally, the CMA membership/the strong connection to the CMA (Botswana) has created a sound economic environment.
- South African mines absorbed many unskilled workers from BLS. The remittance was an important income source for Lesotho and Swaziland and helped to reduce poverty.
- Collection of customs revenue and excise duties by South African authorities exonerated BLS/BLNS authorities.

Disadvantages for South Africa

- Options for trade liberalisation were limited since the BLS/BLNS countries received a guaranteed share from the CRP regardless the actual funds available.
- The guaranteed revenue share for the BLS/BLNS countries resulted in increased expenditures and made SACU less attractive.

Disadvantages for the BLNS countries

- Loss of fiscal sovereignty and over domestic trade policy: trade-related decisions were determined by South Africa.
- Trade diversion due to SACU's comparable high CET that supported South Africa's import substitution policy.
- Non-tariff barriers such as quantitative restrictions for certain BLS/BLNS exports to South Africa.
- Industrial development was constrained by competition from South African companies, South African investment incentives that aimed to channel investment into underdeveloped areas in South Africa, and by the protective CET that made access to competitive inputs expensive.

---

[45] SACU countries' industrialisation strategy and the role of SACU as regional trading block are discussed in Chapter 4.

- Secured income from the CRP reduced BLNS countries' ambitions to diversify income sources and to strengthen their institutional and administrative capacities for customs collection.[46]
- Reduction of revenue by the inclusion of South Africa's "independent homelands" into the CRP.

The fact that none of the countries switched out of SACU can be interpreted in a way that, all in all, the gains from membership outweigh the losses, which is also supported by the fact that Namibia officially joined the SACU after its independence. Considering BLNS countries' high dependency on the CRP, on the South African market and on South Africa's capacities, e.g. with respect to infrastructure and revenue collection, BLNS countries regarded their membership in SACU as advantageous (Maasdorp 1992:20). Still, the BLNS countries complained about their lack of participation in SACU decision processes and the adverse effects on industrial development and location. BLNS urged democratic South Africa to re-negotiate the agreement. South Africa again was interested in restructuring the revenue sharing formula and to limit the amount paid to the BLNS. Attempts to re-negotiate the SACU Agreement started in 1994 but a compromise was very difficult to find. Though all parties agreed that a new SACU dispensation became necessary, member countries interests differed with respect to institutional reforms, decision-making powers and distribution of revenues. Lesotho and Swaziland were less interested in a stronger participation within SACU but wanted to keep their level of revenue, while Botswana and Namibia claimed for a stronger involvement into SACU's decision making process (BoN 2003:22-6). South Africa again wanted to keep the final word over any SACU decision. The parties were only able to reach consensus by the end of 2001, so that the revised SACU Agreement was signed in 2002. However, the new SACU Agreement has left many disputable issues unsolved. The new Agreement entered only into force on 15 July 2004, when the ratification process by national parliaments was finally concluded (Tralac news, 19/07/04).

2. 5 The Revised SACU Agreement: Challenges for the BLNS Countries

Negotiations of the new SACU Agreement took place against the background of a rapid challenging trade environment and increasing obligations by involvement into multilateral and bilateral trade agreements. The new Agreement was therefore also supposed to promote deeper regional integration within the SACU

[46] Kalenga (2000) argued that the guaranteed income from the CRP also discouraged industrialisation within SACU. Since the transfers from the CRP were not targeted at the promotion of efficient production and product diversification they were often used as additional "patronage" for BLS government (Kalenga 2000:8).

and to enable it to enter as block into new trade negotiations (Kirk and Stern 2003:1).

The goals of the SACU Agreement 2002 are formulated in Art. 2, namely,

- the facilitation of intra-regional trade and the creation of common development policies and strategies;
- the creation of effective, transparent and democratic institutions that ensure equitable trade benefits to all members;
- the promotion of fair competition and improved investment options;
- the enhancement of economic development, industrialisation and diversification of member states; and the integration of member countries into the global economy; and
- the facilitation of equitable sharing of the revenues collected by the CRP.

The institutional structure

In the 1969 Agreement, an institutional structure of the SACU barely existed. The only common institution was the Customs Union Commission that met once a year. However, any of its decisions could have been rejected by South Africa.

There were heavy discussions on the new institutional set-up of the SACU and the responsibilities of task among members. Finally, the countries agreed on the following management institutions (SACU 2002, Art. 7-13):

- *Council of Ministers*: The decision making authority of the SACU, consisting out of one Minister of each member state. The Council is responsible for SACU's policy and budget approval and decides by consensus.[47]
- *Customs Union Commission:* Is responsible for the implementation of the Agreement. The Commission consists of member states´ senior officials. They are responsible to report to the Council, to ensure a proper implementation of the SACU Agreement and to supervise the Secretariat.
- *Secretariat:* Is responsible for the day-to-day administration of the SACU, assists the Commission and keeps a record of all transactions into the CRP. The Secretariat is headed by an Executive Secretary from any member state. The Secretariat is based in Windhoek/Namibia where the SACU headquarter has been established.
- *Tariff Board:* Consists out of experts drawn from member states that make recommendations to the Council regarding the level of the CET, anti-dumping, countervailing and safeguard duties on goods imported

[47] Meetings of the Council and the Commission are held at least once a quarter. Next to these institutions, each member state has National Bodies (Art. 14), which investigate effects of tariff changing in the country and give recommendations to the Tariff Board. The CRP finances the Secretariat, the Tariff Board and the Tribunal while the other institutions are financed by the member states directly.

from abroad. Moreover, they give advises concerning refunds or duty drawbacks. The Tariff Board, now called the "International Trade Administration Commission" (ITAC), is an independent institution that replaces the "South African Board on Tariffs and Trade" (SABTT). It is planned that the ITAC serves all SACU countries by common negotiations on tariffs, import and export controls and antidumping measurements and responds quickly to the concerns of firms (Tralac News, 06/08/03).

- *Technical Liaison Committees:* Consists out of four different committees, which advise the Commission in the fields of agriculture policy, customs issues, trade, industry and transport. The Technical Liaison Committees were retained from the 1969 Agreement.
- *Tribunal:* An independent *ad hoc* tribunal, which reports and recommends directly to the Council and assists the Secretary. The Tribunal is responsible for the dispute settlement in the SACU; its determinations are final and binding for all members. It will also play an advisory role on any issue referred to it by the Council. The Tribunal is composed out of three member states that decide by majority.

This new institutional framework should democratise decision processes in the SACU and establish a legal body, able to act as supra-national body in trade negotiations. In fact, the common negotiation of future trade agreements is one goal of the new SACU agreement (SACU 2002, Art. 31).

Common policies

The only policies that have been harmonised under the 1969 Agreement related to tariffs, excise duties, valuation methods, rules of origin and contingency trade remedies. Import duties, customs clearance and import levies (other than import tariffs and excise duties) were not harmonised. To promote economic integration and industrial development in the SACU, the new agreement calls upon member states to facilitate, simplify and harmonise their trade documentation and procedures (Art. 23) and to cooperate in the fields of agricultural and competition policy (Art. 38-40). In the field of competition but also in fields such as standards and technical regulations, BLNS countries' policy still bases on the ones of South Africa though the countries are working on national bills (WTO 2003:x).[48]

The arrangements for marketing of agricultural products have been extended in the new SACU Agreement, allowing each member to impose marketing regula-

[48] In summer 2005, Botswana and Lesotho have created a draft of their national competition bill. Namibia was in progress to implement its competition bill and had appointed five competition commissioners (Hartzenberg 2005).

tions as long as they do not hinder free trade flow (Art. 29).[49] However, the parties have not agreed on a common agricultural policy but work only on harmonised agricultural policies, which are already very difficult to determine (Hoffmann 2003).

Regarding the duty provisions of the new agreement, SACU's Finance Ministers agreed to include not only excise and customs duties but also *ad valorem* excise duties to the new revenue formula.[50] South Africa retains the right to determine and implement duties after consultation with its partners. Furthermore, the countries agreed to apply identical rebates, refunds and drawbacks for all goods produced in SACU, to agree on common customs procedures (Art. 21-23) and to harmonise product standards and technical regulations, including sanitary measurements, in accordance to WTO provisions (Art. 28). However, a common policy on standards and technical regulations is not foreseen. Lesotho and Swaziland have adopted the standards applied by South Africa, while Botswana and Namibia have developed their own standards.[51]

In addition to the democratised structure of the SACU Agreement 2002, the revenue formula has been revised, replacing the 1976 formula (see Box 5). The CRP is managed by South Africa, for the first two years the new Agreement has entered into force. Afterwards, the CRP shall be managed by any member state appointed by the Council of Ministers (Art. 33).

---

[49] Like this, the loophole of the old agreement, where this article was used to protect agricultural production in single member states was addressed (Kirk and Stern 2003:8).

[50] The *ad valorem* excise duty is the calculation basis for customs measurements. The Latin word means "according to the value".

[51] The Botswana Bureau of Standards (BOBS) and the Namibia Standards Information and Quality Office (NSIQO) are responsible to supervise that products made in their countries meet international standards. Moreover, the institutions serve as the countries' focal point on the WTO Agreement on Technical Barriers to Trade. The services provided by the BOBS and NSIQO are product and system certification, testing of health and safety provision, training for laboratories in quality and environment management, trade metrology and standardisation. Both countries have adopted ISO standards so that any company acting in the country can be ISO certified. It is most of all domestic, non-export-oriented companies that ask for assistance to meet the country's health and safety standards (Segomelo and Mbaiwa 2003).

Box 5: The revenue sharing formula of the 2002 Agreement

The new revenue formula, which is only applied since 2005,[52] is designed to stabilise revenue income at the current level and bases on the actual funds available in the Revenue Pool. Thus, the new formula will initially translate any fall/increase in the CRP into reduced/enlarged revenues for any member state. The revised revenue formula is divided into three elements:

1. *Customs component:* The customs component (C_i) is distributed in accordance to its share of intra-SACU imports (c.i.f. value) exclusive re-exports (M_i). Thus, the number of countries (n) that import most from SACU receive the largest share of the customs component. This linkage is supposed to compensate BLNS for the cost-raising and trade divertive effects of being in a CU with South Africa (Ngwenya 2002:28 as cited in McCarthy 2004:8).

$$(1)\ C_i = \left(\frac{M_i}{\sum_{i=1}^{i=n} M_i} \right) * C$$

2. The income from excise duties, which is split into:
   a. *An excise component:* 85% of the excise duties account in accordance to the GDP volume of each country in the current year of calculation (E_i). In the following two years the forecasted excise values will be adjusted to the actual excise revenue collected.

$$(2)\ E_i = \left(\frac{GDP_i}{\sum_{i=1}^{i=n} GDP_i} \right) * E$$

   b. *A development component:* A predetermined share (currently 15%) of total excise duties will form a development component (D_i) and will be distributed in reverse correlation to a country's per capita income. Thus, the poor BLNS countries, Lesotho and Swaziland, which have the lowest per capita income in the SACU, benefit most from the development formula.

Continuation on next page.

[52] The new SACU Agreement was only ratified by all member states in summer 2004. Thus, no experiences about the application of the new revenue sharing formula can be reported but only its expected effects. It has however already become clear that the reconciliation of data to calculate the share from the CRP puts severe strains on the BLNS countries (Erasmus 2005).

Continuation of Box 5 from previous page.

$$(3)\ D_i = [1 - \left(\frac{GDPC_i}{\sum_{i=1}^{i=n} GDPC_i / n} - 1 \right) / 10\ ] * D / n = [11 - \left(\frac{GDPC_i * n}{\sum_{i=1}^{i=n} GDPC_i} \right)\ ] * D / 10n$$

Acronyms

C	=	The customs component: total customs duties collected.
E	=	The excise component: total excise duties collected less D.
D	=	The development component: a predetermined share (currently 15%) of total excise duties collected in SACU.
GDP_i	=	GDP of a specific SACU country.
$GDPC_i$	=	GDP per capita of a specific SACU country.
M	=	total intra-SACU imports of specific SACU country.
n	=	number of SACU member countries (currently 5).

Source: SACU (2002, Art. 32-37), Kirk and Stern 2003:18.

As discussed, South Africa pressured to agree on a new formula to guarantee the sustainability of the CRP. Retaining the old formula, which determines the revenue share of each country according to its imports, unaffected by the actual amount collected in the Pool, SACU payments were expected to increase from R 10 billion in 2002/2003 to R 32 billion in 2011/12. With the new revenue sharing formula SACU payments are "only" expected to increase to R 22 billion by 2011/12 (Stern 2003:4). The revised revenue sharing has considerable implications for the BLNS countries. Positive for them, the time lag between actual trade and distribution of revenue disappears since only the actual funds are taken into account. However, the fact that the share of revenue is now related to the actual funds available results in a lower growth of the CRP. BLNS revenue share is no longer on a guaranteed level of 17-23% and they are affected by the impact of trade liberalisation and the declining share of the customs component on the CRP, which is still the major source of revenue for the BLNS (see Figure 6).

Figure 6: Composition of SACU payment by component – 2002 formula (financial year 2002/03 estimate)

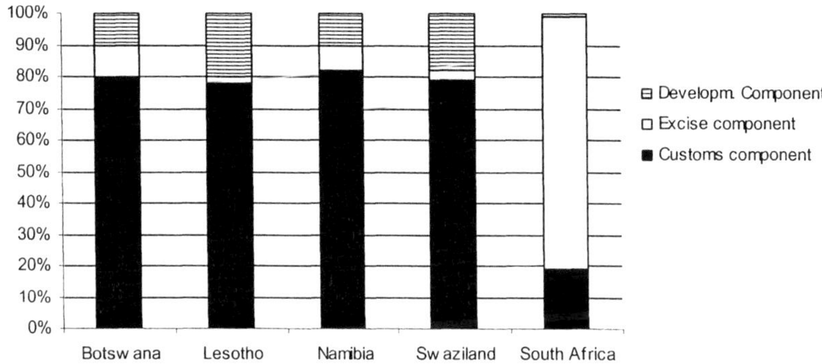

Source: Stern 2003:6.

As can be obtained from Figure 6, customs revenue only contributes to 20% of South Africa's total revenue from the CRP but to around 80% of BLNS total revenue. Thus, South Africa, which distributes around 93% to the excise component of the CRP, can retain around 80% of the total collected excise duties (Kirk and Stern 2003:10). The share of the poorer SACU member countries is further declining with the increasing importance of excise duties. The new revenue formula shares excise duties according to the GDP (where South Africa and Botswana are leading) while customs duties are shared according to SACU imports (where Lesotho and Swaziland are leading). The fact that customs duties are shared according to SACU imports bears the risk of trade diversion. The Bank of Namibia (2003:68) has already recommended *"...to determine to what extent imports may be redirected from extra-SACU source to intra-SACU sources."*

To compensate the weaker SACU members from the decline of the customs component, 15% of the revenue obtained from excise duties is used as development component. The development component is becoming increasingly important the more the customs component is declining.[53] Currently, Lesotho and Swaziland benefit most from the development component. However, due to the increasing relevance of excise duties and the advanced level of trade liberalisation, the development component is not likely to compensate completely for

[53] The initial 15% share of the development component is subject to review but can only be adjusted when all member states agree (SACU 2002, Annex A).

the fiscal losses of BLNS (BoN 2003).[54] In fact, the development of size and growth of revenue share per member country is impossible to predict since the new formula is in contrary to the 1976 formula dynamic and determined by the level and intensity of trade liberalisation, the level of imports per member state, the development of the customs and excise duty share per member state and the economic performance of single member states (affecting the development component). On the other hand, BLNS countries' lower revenue share under the new formula (which is still predicted to result in increasing total revenue for the next ten years) cannot only be judged negatively but might also have positive impulses on their fiscal performance and stimulate the broadening of income sources, i.e. towards VAT. Furthermore, the new SACU Agreement, which is supposed to stimulate deeper economic integration by strengthening cooperation among member states, might have positive effects on intra-regional trade and investment, which outweigh for the fiscal losses. According to McCarthy (2004:9) *"...the effective operation of the custom union in itself represents a move in the direction of fiscal reform."* Another positive effect of the reformed revenue formula is the improved option to enlarge SACU.[55] Under the old formula the accession of new member states would have been too cost-intensive for South Africa due to the guaranteed revenue for BLNS. With the new formula, the share of each member state would decline with the accession of new members. However, considering the fact, that poor countries come to join the SACU, such as Mozambique, this would have a considerable impact on the development component, affecting mainly Lesotho, Swaziland and Namibia (BoN 2003:65).[56]

Table 10 summarises and compares the provisions and decision processes of the SACU Agreement 1969 and 2002 and discusses their practical appliances.

---

[54] It is criticised that the development component is not used for regional development projects but only supposed to compensate weaker member states for revenue losses (Wellmer 2005:33).

[55] According to Art. 6 (SACU 20002), new members may join the SACU following a common decision of the Council.

[56] There is speculation on whether Mozambique is joining SACU. Mozambique has strong trade and investment ties with South Africa and is exploring the benefits and costs of a SACU membership since 2004 (Economist, 19/02/2004). However, considering SACU countries' efforts to move towards deeper regional integration by implementing the new Agreement as well as the many trade negotiations the countries are involved in, it is assumed by the author that SACU's enlargement is currently not on the agenda.

Table 10: The SACU Agreement 1969 and 2002 – official provisions and practical appliances

	Provisions	Practical Appliance / Comments
Supra-national institutions	SACU Agreement 1969 Customs Union Commission (decision making body), SABTT (CET setting) SACU Agreement 2002 Council of Ministers, Commission, Secretariat, Tariff Board, Technical Liaison Committees	An institutional structure was almost non-existent. South Africa was able to decide unilaterally regarding any matter affecting SACU. The BLNS countries are equally involved in SACU's decision-making process and budget approval.
Goods	SACU Agreement 1969 Free movement of goods. SACU Agreement 2002 Free movement of goods	Restrictions for BLNS countries were possible. South Africa was *de facto* able to protect its industries without consulting its partners. The Council decides by consensus whether the free movement of goods should be restricted.
Rebates and refunds / Tax structure	SACU Agreement 1969 No provision. SACU Agreement 2002 Cooperation regarding common rebates, refunds and drawbacks.	SACU members agreed to work towards common rebates and refunds and to harmonise their tax structure, mainly in the field of VAT/sales tax.
CET, customs and excise collection and customs procedure	SACU Agreement 1969 The CET, excise and sales tariff, rebates, refunds and drawbacks were determined by South Africa. SACU Agreement 2002 The Council sets the CET, excise and sales duties on recommendations of ITAC by consensus.	Abolishment of customs between the countries, CET, common excise and sales duties. No agreement on provisions of customs and procedure. Replacement of the SABTT, democratisation of the decision process. Further harmonisation of excise duties and customs procedures is in progress.

	Provisions	Practical Appliance / Comments
Common policies	SACU Agreement 1969 Cooperation in the fields of transport, transit, agriculture and sanitary measurements.	The countries retained single marketing channels for agricultural products. The Agreement did not foresee for a common industrial or agricultural policy. Competition policy was excluded.
	SACU Agreement 2002 Creation of a common industrial policy, harmonisation of agricultural, competition and other trade-related policies.	Member states work towards a common industrial policy and intend to harmonise their agricultural and competition policies. Individual marketing channels for agricultural products are allowed but have to be non-discriminatory. Individual sanitary measures will be applied in accordance to international standards.
Import restrictions	SACU Agreement 1969 BLNS are allowed to restrict the import of goods from third countries in case of economic, social, cultural or other reason.	The SABTT was able to implement unilaterally anti-dumping countervailing and safeguard measures, which posed the risk of abuse.
	SACU Agreement 2002 Same provision as in the 1969 Agreement.	The countries agreed to develop a regional legislation for the imposition of safeguard measures. The Council decides about any import restriction, which limits the abusive application of protectionist measures by one member state.
Protection of industries	SACU Agreement 1969 The protection of BLNS infant industries is allowed up to eight years.	BLNS countries made use of this provision but South Africa was able to claim for the reduction of additional duties.
	SACU Agreement 2002 Same provisions as in the 1969 Agreement.	Claims for infant industry protection have to be applied by the Council, which also supervises terms and conditions of protection.
Dispute Settlement	SACU Agreement 1969 No regulation.	The Customs Union Commission met once a year but any claim from BLNS could have been rejected from South Africa.
	SACU Agreement 2002 Tribunal	Establishment of a common Tribunal, which recommends directly to the Council.

	Provision	Practical Appliance / Comments
Compensation mechanism	SACU Agreement 1969 Establishment of CRP/Inclusion of stabilisation rate (1976) SACU Agreement 2002 Revised revenue formula	Member countries' revenue depended on the size of each country's imports and was unaffected from the total income of the CRP. From 1976 on, the CRP guaranteed the BLNS a revenue rate between 17-23%. Member countries' revenue depends on the actual income of the CRP, inclusion of a development component, enlargement of SACU reduces revenue for each member country.
Monetary Policies	Common Monetary Area (CMA)	Lesotho, Namibia and Swaziland have their own currency but the Rand is legal tender. A common exchange rate policy exists. Botswana linked its currency to a trade-weighted basket currency dominated by the Rand. Free movement of capital within the CMA. The monetary and exchange rate policy is made by the SARB. Steps towards a common monetary union are underway.
Labour	SACU Agreement 1969 No regulation. SACU Agreement 2002 No regulation.	The movement of labour is restricted in the SACU. Since South Africa is the hub for migrant workers not only from the BLNS countries, it fears a worsening of its already very high unemployment rate when allowing labour to move free.
Trade agreements with third countries	SACU Agreement 1969 Only allowed after prior concurrence of all member states. SACU Agreement 2002 Trade negotiations take place through a common mechanism.	Despite the obligation of the 1969 Agreement to receive concurrence when entering into trade negotiations with third countries, South Africa entered into an FTA with the EU in 2000. SACU undertakes currently common trade negotiations with the USA, EFTA and Mercosur. However, a common negotiation mechanism does not exist yet.

Source: Representation of the author as quoted in the text.

All in all, the structure of the SACU has been substantially democratised by the new Agreement and the dominance of South Africa has been reduced, which allows the BLNS countries to improve the application of SACU provisions and the contribution to SACU's policy towards third countries. The independent dispute settlement body will arbitrate in any disputes. Once the foreseen common policies have been implemented, the new SACU Agreement is likely to facilitate cross border trade. However, as will be discussed in the next section, the implementation of the new Agreement is not an easy task and poses many challenges to all member countries. The successful implementation of the new SACU agreement is however crucial for deeper economic integration within SACU and harmonised external trade relations.

2.6 SACU – *Quo Vadis*?

With the ratification of the new SACU Agreement, member states have reformed the CU considerably. The democratised SACU Agreement emphasises member countries' commitment to work towards deeper regional integration and their willingness to establish common institutions that rule in the interest of all member countries and speak with one voice towards third parties. However, to implement the 2002 Agreement effectively, additional annexes have to be developed by the Council (Art. 42). Furthermore, substantive rules regarding technical cooperation, a harmonised agricultural policy, a harmonised competition policy and a common industrial policy have to be developed. Still, the new SACU Agreement has not specified countries' endeavours to work towards common policies but is yet "little more than a framework document" (McCarthy 2004:18) that still needs to be operationalised.

For a proper internal functioning, all new created institutions, namely the Secretariat, the Customs Union Commission, the democratised Tariff Board, the Tribunal and the National Bodies have to be announced and properly equipped and staffed, which has not been the case yet. Furthermore, the tasks and responsibilities of the single institutions still need to be clearly defined.[57] So far, it is only the Secretariat, based in Windhoek, which has been established but still lacks staff (Erasmus 2005).[58] The SACU Secretariat is, together with the single member states, responsible for the development of common policies, which are crucial for a stronger economic cooperation of SACU countries as well as for the formulation of a common negotiation position towards third parties. However, it must be borne in mind that South Africa and BLNS have due to their different economic developments different development strategies, which make the formulation of a common industrial policy very complex. Furthermore, the term "industrial policy" has not been specified in the Agreement so that it is not clear whether industrial policy relates only to the CET or also to coordinated measures, such as tax or investment policies. McCarthy (2004:13-4) emphasises that a balanced industrial development within SACU would require different policy

[57] Regarding the establishment of the Tribunal, Erasmus (2004:2) points out that the rules and procedures still have to be developed. Furthermore, the nature of its jurisdiction has not been clarified yet.

[58] The General Secretary, Mrs. Connie Moremi, the former Permanent Secretary of the Botswana Ministry of Trade, is supposed to hold this post until 2009 (Laletsang 2003).

measures in order to stimulate industrial location in BLNS. However, the new Agreement failed to harmonise SACU countries' different tax systems (see Table 11). This does not only hamper the reduction of transaction costs but also bears the risk of trade distortions and smuggling (WTO 2003:32).[59] Different investment incentives in the single member countries can furthermore lead to a "race to the bottom" for foreign investment.[60]

Table 11: Tax forms and rates in the single SACU countries

Tax Form	Botswana	Lesotho	Namibia	Swaziland	South Africa
Income Tax for Individuals					
< R 20,000	5%	25%	No Tax	No tax	19% (< R 31,000)
< R 40,000	5%	(< R	18%	(< R 13,000)	30% (< R 46,000)
< R 60,000	10%	30,000)	18%		39% (< R 60,00)
< R 80,000	15%		30%	30%	43% (< R70,000)
< R 100,00	20%	35%	30%	(> R 40,000)	44% (< R120,000)
< R 200,000	25%	(> R	35%		45% (> R120,000)
> R 200,000	25%	30,000)	36%		
Corporate Taxes					
Mining	25%	37%	55%		30%
Manufacturing	25%	15%	35%	37.5%	30%

[59] When commodities are transported from one SACU countries to the other, the shipper has to apply for VAT/sales tax refunds from the exporting country and paying the relevant tax to the importing country (WTO 2003:32).

[60] Such an experience was for instance made when southern African countries fought for investment from the Malaysian textile company Ramatex, which Namibia finally won (Namibia Economist, 28/09/2001). SACU countries' incentives to attract FDI and the contribution of FDI to domestic value addition and diversification attempts of SACU countries are discussed in Chapter 4.

Tax Form	Botswana	Lesotho	Namibia	Swaziland	South Africa
Indirect Taxation					
VAT	10%		15%		14%
Sales Tax		5% *			
		10 %		12%	
		15%**		20%	
Excise taxes		various rates +			

* on electricity and telecommunication.

** on alcoholic beverages.

+ on beer, sprits, tobacco, petroleum (products), vehicles and electronic products.

Sources: diverse data as quoted in Iyambo *et al.* 2001:17 (for Namibia and South Africa), IFSC 2003 (for Botswana) and WTO 2003 (for Lesotho and Swaziland).

As can be obtained from Table 11, Botswana has the lowest tax rates within SACU. South Africa shows the highest income tax rates and Namibia the highest corporate tax rate for mining activities as well as the highest VAT rate (15% compared to 14% in South Africa and 10% in Botswana). The tax system in Lesotho and Swaziland is still underdeveloped; the bulk of revenue comes from the CRP. Both countries are busy to replace their sales tax by VAT, which is supposed to follow the South African VAT rate of 14%.

To promote a more equalised industrial development within SACU, it would also be important to form a common labour market. Since the BLNS countries' most important comparative advantage against South Africa is their lower wage level and their less stringent labour market regulations, free movement of labour would be an important part of a common industrial policy in order to upgrade SACU to become a common market. The BLNS countries, mainly Lesotho and Swaziland, could benefit from the free movement of labour, which might compensate for the losses the countries experienced due to the decline in miners' remittance and reduces the pressure of governments to create jobs. Like this, a more equal development in SACU would be conceivable. However, the new SACU Agreement does not contain any provisions regarding the free movement of labour. The discussion of free labour movement in SACU seems to be taboo due to the high unemployment rates in South Africa. Though the net flows of labour migration are likely to be in one direction (from BLNS to South Africa), they are rather unlikely to increase unemployment in South Africa, considering the low population in BLNS. Still, adverse effects of increased unemployment might be possible in border areas, mainly around Lesotho and Swaziland, the main labour-exporting countries. The political acceptance of free labour movement in SACU is therefore critical.

The problem to develop a common industrial policy within SACU aggravates considering countries' different interests with respect to agricultural policies.[61] Since the industries in the BLNS countries produce (with exception of the mining and the garment industry), mainly agro-based products, there are considerable linkages between industrial and agricultural policies. Thus, the development of a common industrial policy without having agreed on a common agricultural policy will be hardly feasible (McCarthy 2004:15).

Another concern raised relates to the democratised decision-making within SACU. Since decisions are made by consensus, the implementation of common policies might be delayed, considering the very different capacities of member states. It is therefore considered as crucial for the BLNS countries to build capacity in the field of customs administration and documentation, statistical compilation, and trade policy analysis and negotiations (Kirk and Stern 2003:9). Improved capacities of the BLNS countries are also relevant with respect to the management of the new Tariff Board. To date, the BLNS have no expertise to conduct tariffs and investigate trade remedies. Doubts about BLNS countries' ability to manage the CRP effectively raise the question whether South Africa will be ready to handover its responsibility accordingly (Kirk and Stern 2003:13).

However, while one could, in view of the democratised decision structure of the SACU Agreement, on the one hand argue that the new Agreement bears the risk to become *"...subject to "hijacking" by entrenched national interests."* (WTO:2003:xi), it can, on the other hand, also be argued that BLNS countries' inability to be involved according to the provision of the new Agreement result in a continuation of South Africa's dominance. In fact, the increased pressure on BLNS countries to involve in bilateral, regional and multilateral trade negotiations poses already a strain on their capacities (Murangi 2001, Mbekeani 2003, Pato 2003).

In summer 2005, SACU finalised FTA negotiations with MERCOSUR and was busy to finalise FTA negotiations with EFTA. The FTA with the USA, which was supposed to be finalised by December 2004 was still in the pipeline. In addition to these FTA negotiations, SACU explores options to negotiate

---

[61] These different interests became obvious during the negotiations of the Doha Round in summer 2003, when South Africa joined the G20+, which focussed on the abolition of industrialised countries' agricultural subsidies and improved market access for developing countries. BLNS again joined the group of African countries, which benefit to a large extent from the protected EU agricultural market and fear an erosion of their preference due to increased competition from large developing countries.

FTAs with China, India, Singapore, Nigeria and Kenya (Tralac news 27/01/2003 and 24/04/2005). So far, all these trade negotiations are led by South Africa, while the BLNS are only insufficiently involved and prepared.[62] Trade negotiations with third countries go hand in hand with the implementation of the new SACU Agreement and capture SACU countries capacities. The success or failure of the new SACU Agreement does therefore also depend on the improvement of countries' trade-related capacities.

2.7 SACU Countries' External Trade Relations and Trade Regimes with the EU

Despite their common external tariff, SACU countries had and still have different trade regimes with third countries. The SACU Agreement 1969 allowed member countries to enter into trade agreements with third parties only after having received *prior* concurrence of *all* members (Republic of South Africa 1969, Art. 19). Members were however allowed to enter into separate trade agreement, when such an agreement did not have any effect on any other member state. Thus, the 1969 Agreement did *generally* not allow member states to enter into separate trade agreements but did also not formulate any penalty when violating this clause. It could be argued that Art. 19 was superfluous since a common external tariff (CET) is the fundamental prerequisite for a CU. Once one member country changes the CET unilaterally, it infringes with the fundaments of the CU and can be excluded. However, as discussed, the distribution of power within SACU was lopsided and BLNS were (and are) neither in a position to exclude South Africa nor to leave the arrangement.

As can be obtained from Figure 7, SACU countries are members of several regional and multilateral trade arrangements.[63] Most important, all SACU countries are members of the WTO.[64] Since the multilateral obligations under the WTO Agreement predominate all other trade arrangements, any trade agreement SACU countries enter into must be in accordance to WTO provisions (WTO 1994, Chapter V, Art. 26. See Box 6).

---

[62] The issue of trade capacity building and BLNS countries' capacity constraints in regional and international trade negotiations are discussed in Chapter 6.

[63] Furthermore, all SACU countries are members of the "African Union" (AU), the successor of the Organization of African Unity (OAU). The AU wants to create a pan-African economic and political partnership and to promote integration, stabilisation, democracy and economic progress in Africa (WTO 2003:17).

[64] All SACU countries were already GATT members before the WTO entered into force. South Africa is the only SACU member that acts as observer to a WTO Agreement (WTO 2003:15).

Figure 7: Membership of SACU members in regional and multilateral trade arrangements

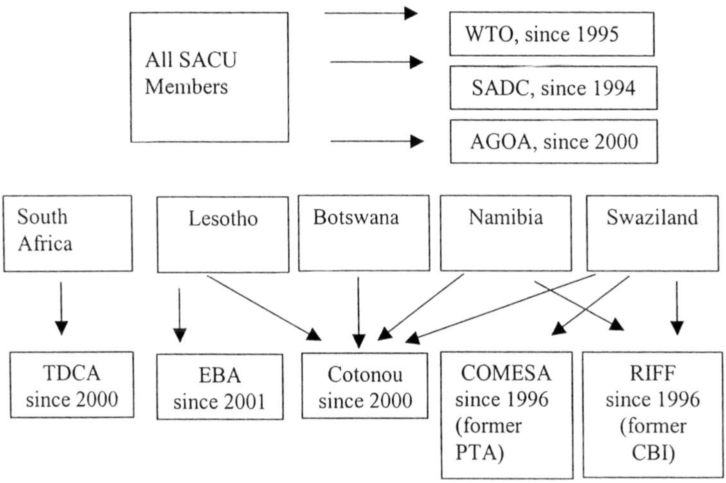

Source: Author's presentation.

All SACU countries, including South Africa, are classified as developing countries by the WTO and benefit from the "Generalised System of Preferences" (GSP), granting them preferred market access to most industrialised countries for a specific range of products. Superior market access is granted under the non-reciprocal Cotonou Agreement, where the former European colonies Botswana, Lesotho, Namibia and Swaziland enjoy free market access to the EU for all their export products. South Africa, which is not a member of the Cotonou Agreement, entered into an FTA with the EU in 2000.[65] Also the USA grant SACU countries trade preferences that exceed the GSP. Since 2000, SACU countries' trade relations with the USA are ruled by the "African Growth and Opportunity Act" (AGOA). AGOA provides 38 African countries non-reciprocal duty and quota-free market access to the USA for approximately 4,500 eligible products. As a result, SACU countries' exports to the USA have risen considerably (WTO 2003:7).[66]

[65] Lesotho, which has the status of a least developed country (LDC), is furthermore able to export under the EU "Everything But Arms" (EBA) initiative, which grants all LDCs in the world a duty and quota free access to the EU market.

[66] The contribution of AGOA, EBA and Cotonou to SACU countries' industrialisation strategies are evaluated in the Chapters 3 and 4.

Box 6: Compatibility of regional integration schemes with WTO provisions

The two principles of the WTO valid for all member countries are the Most Favoured Nation (MFN) Clause and the Non-Discrimination Clause. The MFN principle states that all member countries must get the same trading conditions. Goods have to be treated independently from their country of origin (GATT 1994, Art. 1). Thus, any form of preferential treatment to one country, discriminates against any other member country and is generally not allowed. Bilateral preferences must become multilateral in order to avoid discrimination. The second principle, the Non-Discrimination Clause, which is also called principle of reciprocity, implies the same regulations for domestic and foreign goods. Protection of domestic goods, e.g. by quantity restrictions, is forbidden. Like this, WTO regulations prove that imported goods, trade related services and trade related intellectual property rights could neither be discriminated against each other, nor against domestic goods or services.

Though economic integration schemes are not in conformity with the basic WTO provisions because of their discrimination against non-members, the WTO allows in Art. XXIV, GATT the formation of FTAs and CUs if the following conditions are fulfilled: Trade barriers (tariffs and non-tariff barriers) for "substantially all trade" have to be removed within a "reasonable length of time" (GATT 1994, Art. XXIV, § 4-10). Annex 1A, GATT on the "Understanding on the Interpretation of Art. XXIV" states that about 90% of the value of all trade must flow free within 10 years after having entered into an FTA/CU.[67] External tariff settings must be ensured on a MFN basis and shall not be higher than those existing prior the customs union (GATT 1994, Art. XXIV).[68]

In addition to these trade arrangements with their main trading partners, the SACU countries are also involved in South-South integration frameworks. All SACU countries are members of the "Southern African Development Community" (SADC). SADC was established in 1992 and is the predecessor of the "Southern African Development Co-ordination Conference" (SADCC).[69] Botswana, Lesotho and Swaziland were founding members of the SADCC; Namibia joined after its independence in 1990 and South Africa in 1994. The

[67] An extension of this period is only allowed in "exceptional cases".

[68] This clause can either be interpreted in a way that CU member chose for each commodity the lowest tariff existing in a member country or that the CU members form the average tariff for each item. Since the latter method is less restrictive, it is the one generally used for the formation of a CU in accordance to WTO provisions (Evans 2000:668-673).

[69] SADCC was established in 1980 by the frontline states Angola, Botswana, Mozambique, Tanzania, Zambia and Zimbabwe and the independent states Lesotho, Malawi and Swaziland. Its goal was to reach economic independence from its former colonies and from South Africa and to build a political counterbalance to the Apartheid regime in South Africa (Mair and Peters-Berries 2001:297-8).

SADC intends to establish an FTA by 2008 and to move towards a CU by 2010 as stated in its Regional Indicative Strategic Development Plan. However, to date the progress of implementation of the SADC Trade Protocol, leading to an FTA, is very limited and observers do not expect the FTA entering into place in time (Kalenga 2004, Hartzenberg 2004).

SACU countries' SADC membership does not infringe with the SACU 1969 Agreement since all SACU countries are SADC members and have agreed on a common liberalisation schedule in the context of the SADC FTA.[70]

Another regional trade agreement Swaziland is involved in, is the "Common Market of Eastern and Southern Africa" (COMESA), the former "Eastern and Southern African Preferential Trade Area" (PTA).[71] COMESA encompasses 19 very heterogeneous countries in southern, eastern and even northern Africa (Egypt).[72] COMESA launched its FTA, which only 9 of the 19 members joined, in 2000.[73] A CU, originally scheduled for 2004, has been postponed. Though Swaziland did not join the COMESA FTA in 2000, it still benefits from preferred market access, which is above all important for Swaziland's biggest company, Coca Cola (King 2003). Since COMESA pressures Swaziland to join the FTA, the country asked for the concurrence of the other SACU members under the condition that COMESA imports would be restricted to other SACU countries than Swaziland (Mahlinza 2003). The issue of concurrence is still pending. However, Swazi authorities are not able to guarantee the supervision of origin of products properly so that South Africa's concurrence is regarded as doubtful (Pato 2003). The logical consequence of Swaziland's inability to join the COMESA FTA would therefore be its withdrawal from the organisation.

Namibia and Swaziland are also members of the Cross Border Initiative (CBI), the predecessor of the Regional Integration Facilitation Forum (RIFF).[74] RIFF was established in 1993 by the EU, the African Development Bank, the IMF and the World Bank Group and is supposed to promote trade facilitation and liberalisation in Sub-Saharan Africa. However, so far CBI/RIFF was neither able to reduce trade barriers significantly nor to increase intra-regional trade.

---

[70] See Pallangyo (2000:76-80) for SACU's liberalisation schedule towards the rest of SADC.

[71] The PTA emerged as a project of the "United Nations Economic Commission for Africa" (UNECA) and was founded in 1981 (Foroutan 1993:246). Lesotho and Namibia, which were also PTA/COMESA members, withdrew since their obligations under COMESA were not compatible with their SACU membership (Mwase and Maasdorp 1999:242-3, Tralac news 10/06/03).

[72] Namely Angola, Burundi, Comoros, DR Congo, Djibouti, Egypt, Eritrea, Ethiopia, Kenya, Madagascar, Malawi, Mauritius, Rwanda, Seychelles, Sudan, Swaziland, Uganda, Zambia and Zimbabwe.

[73] Djibouti, Egypt, Kenya, Madagascar, Malawi, Mauritius, Sudan, Zambia and Zimbabwe are members of the COMESA FTA.

[74] The CBI has 20 member countries, which are all COMESA countries plus Namibia.

Namibia and Swaziland were granted derogation from the CBI/RIFF tariff reduction since South Africa is not a member. Overall, CBI/RIFF is regarded as an ineffective instrument that does not have any relevant influence on economic integration in Africa (AfDB 2000).[75]

African countries' overlapping memberships of often incompatible regional integration schemes are very common and often create doubts on their seriousness to form an economically integrated region. In the past, donors generally supported African countries' memberships in regional integration frameworks. Like this, the donor community contributed significantly to the contradictory obligations arising from memberships in different regional integration arrangements (Mair and Peters-Berries 2001:382-386). In southern Africa it is mainly the overlapping membership among SADC and COMESA members that is regarded as problematic (see e.g. Mair and Peters-Berries 2001, AfDB 2000, Maasdorp 1992, 1994). As will be discussed in section 3.6, the coordination problems of overlapping memberships aggravate with the restructuring of EU-African trade relations, which requires African countries to negotiate reciprocal FTAs with the EU as regional blocks.

2.8 Conclusions

The implementation of SACU's institutional arrangements, which is regarded as "extremely vital component" for deeper regional integration, is still in its infancy so that a final appraisal on the impact of the new Agreement on deeper economic integration cannot be made. It has however become clear that the limited capacities of the BLNS (e.g. in the field of tariffs and trade remedies, the collection of customs duties and the institutional set-up) as well as SACU countries' difficulties to develop common sectoral and regional policies (industry, agricultural, services, competition, investment) are the cumberstones of the agreement. If SACU fails to address the lack capacities of its weaker members and if South Africa is not ready to compromise with respect to regional policies, there is the danger of a polarised development on the expense of the BLNS countries. A *de facto* ongoing unilateralism in the name of SACU may further result in prejudices of the BLNS countries against its powerful neighbour. It is therefore unsure whether the new SACU Agreement will contribute to a more equal development within SACU.

---

[75] Additionally to their involvement in regional and multilateral trade agreements, Botswana, Namibia and South Africa also have a bilateral trade agreement with Zimbabwe. South Africa does furthermore grant Malawi and Mozambique non-reciprocal preferential treatment for a list of products (WTO 2003:5, 232). Moreover, Botswana has a 1956 signed reciprocal customs agreement with Malawi, which is however hardly used (WTO 2003:64).

In fact, the new SACU Agreement implies several challenges for all member countries. The BLNS countries have lost their "economic security" in form of a guaranteed revenue share and are pressured to formulate their economic interests vis-à-vis South Africa and the rest of the world. Common or harmonised policies in the field of industry, agriculture, competition and unfair trade practises still need to be developed so that the SACU Agreement 2002 is only regarded as "framework agreement" (McCarthy and Hansohm 2005:4) to which annexes have to be developed *"...like flesh and muscle affixed to a skeleton..."* (Ibid.). The democratic structure and the inclusion of BLNS interests complicate decision making processes within SACU, providing the risk that single countries block regional decisions because they infringe with the interests of single national interests groups. Still, the reform of the SACU Agreement towards a stronger participation of the BLNS countries was overdue and offers BLNS countries the chance to accommodate their interests' vis-à-vis their dominant neighbour more adequately. Now it is crucial that the participatory elements of the Agreement are fully implemented which requires a strong commitment towards regional integration of all parties.

Recapturing SACU countries' involvement in trade agreements with third countries, it can be summarised that none of them took the provisions of the 1969 Agreement serious. All SACU members have entered into bilateral and regional integration agreements without the concurrence of the other members. In particular Swaziland has failed to follow-up a coherent regional integration strategy as its double membership in SADC and COMESA shows. Art. 31 of the new SACU Agreement foresees that SACU creates a common negotiation mechanism and enters into external trade agreements with one voice. However, Art. 31 has not been activated yet and SACU's trade negotiations are still dominated by South Africa.

SACU countries' trade relations towards its most important external trading partner, the EU, were divided since BLNS countries' independence. The EU always differentiated between the BLNS countries and South Africa, granting the BLNS non-reciprocal trade preferences. However, EU-SACU trade relations have only become problematic when the EU entered into an FTA with South Africa in 2000. Since this time, the BLNS countries are no longer able to maintain a different import regime than South Africa towards the EU since they are locked-into the EU-South Africa FTA. The next Chapter 3 discusses the evolution of the EU's trade regimes with the SACU countries, moving from unilateral preferences to reciprocity, and its implications for regional integration and economic development in the region.

3. SACU-EU Trade Relations: From Unilateral Preferences to Reciprocal Trade

3.1 Overview of the Objectives and Instruments of the Lomé Conventions (I - IV)

With the signature of the Treaty of Rome in 1958, which led to the establishment of the European Economic Community (EEC), the EEC started a common policy towards its "colonies and overseas countries and territories" and channelled from 1958 on aid through the European Development Fund (EDF). In 1963, the EEC entered into the Yaoundé Convention with 19 newly independent African states, which were formerly colonies of France and Belgium. The African countries were granted trade preferences as well as technical and financial assistance. In countermove, they had to import European goods without tariff restrictions. The Yaoundé Convention was therefore a reciprocal trade agreement that built "the colonial bias" into the system, since pre-EEC trade patterns with its former colonies continued (Pilegaard 2005).[79]

When the United Kingdom became a member of the EEC in 1973, it claimed to include its former colonies in Africa, the Caribbean and the Pacific in the trade and aid agreement of the EEC. However, large, potentially strong economies, such as India and Pakistan, were excluded. The Lomé Convention signed in 1975 between the nine states of the EEC and 45 African, Caribbean and Pacific (ACP) states was a radical change to the Yaoundé Convention. It did not only widen and deepen the relationship between the EEC and its former colonies but also brought substantial aid and non-reciprocal trade preferences for the ACP countries. The EEC was mainly interested to secure the supply of raw materials (particularly oil and minerals) but also to build new markets for its final products (Hansohm and Schade 2001:1). Furthermore, the EEC aimed, in the view of the cold war, the promotion of a strong connection between ACP countries and European countries (Avafia and Hansohm 2004:3). However, the EEC policy towards ACP countries was not solely oriented on self-interest but did also take the destructive economic impact of Europe's colonial policy into account. The instruments of the Lomé Convention aimed to decrease ACP countries' dependency on primary commodities and to diversify their commodity structure (European Commission 1995, Art. 70). To achieve this, the LC granted the ACP countries non-reciprocal, duty free access to the EEC market for a broad product range, payments to stabilise ACP export earnings for mining and agricultural commodities, industrial cooperation and investment assistance for industrial projects, and assistance to strengthen agricultural capacities. Assis-

[79] The Yaoundé Convention II was signed in 1969 and basically extended the provisions of Yaoundé II (see Wolf 1996 and Avafia and Hansohm 2004 for a more detailed overview on the predecessor of the Lomé Conventions).

tance and aid funds were secured for five years. Between 1975 and 1989 the Lomé Agreements (I-III) were renewed every five years. Lomé IV was effective from 1990-2000 although a review with considerable changes took place in 1995 (Lomé IV *bis*).

The LC I – IV Agreement had four essential features (European Commission 1994:5):

1. Equal partners entered a binding contract.
2. Any partner was allowed to maintain his own economic systems, political regime and development model.
3. The EEC/EU provided various development instruments. The ACP countries decided on the instrument in accordance to their development priorities.
4. Permanent dialogue between the ACP-EEC/EU institutions and the European Parliament.[80]

There were two major financial instruments under the LC, namely the National Indicative Programme (NIP), and the Non-Programmable Aid (NPA). Within the BLNS countries, Botswana received the largest amount of financial support in the period 1975-200, followed by Lesotho and Namibia (see Table 12).[81]

[80] The ACP institutions consist out of the Council of Ministers that negotiates ACP-EU Agreements on the governmental level, the Committee of Ambassadors that monitors ACP-EU cooperation and the Joint Assembly, which comprises ACP and European representatives and discusses current and future EU-ACP relations (European Commission 1994:5).

[81] The NIP covers individual national development programmes based on a prior assessment of each country's needs and performance. The main areas of support are economic development and social and human development. The NPA is conditional and relates to circumstantial requirements, necessities and imperatives, and is fully grant financed. It consists of STABEX and SYSMIN and emergency humanitarian aid for refugees and returnees (ACP General Secretariat 1995a-c).

Table 12: Financial assistance of the "National Indicative Programme" (NIP) and the Non-Programmable Aid (NPA) under the Lomé Conventions (including SYSMIN and EIB Funds)

		Lomé I 1975-1980 in Mio. ECU	**Lomé II 1981-1985** in Mio. ECU	**Lomé III 1986-1990** in Mio. ECU	**Lomé IV 1991-1995** in Mio. ECU	**Lomé IV *bis* 1996-2000** in Mio. €
Botswana	NIP	19.0	23.0	30.5	32.0	38.0
	NPA	12.6	29.4	53.8	128.9	
	EC	1.6	0.8	3.3	3.1	0.7
	Budget **TOTAL**	**33.2**	**53.2**	**87.6**	**164.0**	**38.7**
Lesotho*	NIP	22	29	41.5	50.0	61.5
	NPA	2.3	6.6	10.4	52.9	
	EC		0.6	6.4	5.5	0.5
	Budget **TOTAL**	**24.3**	**36.2**	**58.3**	**108.4**	**62.0**
Na-mibia**	NIP				50.0	52.0
	NPA				102.2	
	EC	0.5	2.2	48.4	16.8	3.4
	Budget **TOTAL**	**0.5**	**2.2**	**48.4**	**169.3**	**55.4**
Swaziland	NIP	12.0	18.5	25.5	28.1	29.0
	NPA	27.8	17.5	9.3	17.5	
	EC		0.4	3.7	4.3	0.9
	Budget **TOTAL**	**39.8**	**36.4**	**38.5**	**49.9**	**29.9**

* The EU financed the *Lesotho Highland Water Project* by risk capital operations and EIB loans. Lesotho received further (outside Lomé) EU funding for the development of NGOs, democracy, environment and forestry (ACP General Secretariat 1995c:45).

** Namibia joined the ACP in 1990 but became only member of the LC IV in 1992. Namibia was granted a separate budget (1991-92) of ECU 33.5 million *plus* aid for emergencies, food, control of AIDS and co-financing of NGOs (ACP General Secretariat 1995a).

Source: Author's presentation based on data of the European Commission (1998).

In addition to financial support, which was mainly given in form of grants (European Commission 1994:5), the ACP countries also benefited from the export stabilisation systems STABEX and SYSMIN (see Box 7) supposed to mitigate the effects of export losses for agricultural and mining products due to falls of export quantities and/or deteriorating world market prices (European Commission 1997:7). Since all ACP countries were highly dependent on the export income from few primary goods, any shock of supply, such as dryness or heavy rainfalls, as well as shocks of demand, such as decreasing demand by European consumers had severe impacts on their economies (Davenport *et al.* 1995:6, Helleiner 2002:2). To moderate these negative effects, STABEX and SYSMIN were designed.

Box 7: The System for Stabilisation of Export Earnings for Mining Products (SYSMIN) and the System of Stabilisation of Export Earnings for Agricultural Products (STABEX)

SYSMIN and STABEX were in operation from 1975-1999 (Lomé I–IV *bis*) and applied only to products accounting for at least 5% of a country's export earning.[82] SYSMIN aimed to optimise mining operations towards long-term economic viability by expansion and rehabilitation of mines. Botswana and, from 1992 on, Namibia, received support from the SYSMIN system (ACP General Secretariat 1995b:26). However, two thirds of all resources were allocated to four other ACP countries, namely Zambia, DR Congo, Guinea and Guyana (Matambalya 1998:14).

STABEX covered certain agricultural and tropical goods, such as groundnuts, cocoa, coffee, cotton, palm oil, hides, skins and leather, bananas, vanilla, tea and wood. Products from temperate regions, which would potentially compete with European producers, were excluded (European Commission 1997:8, 35). STABEX underwent a number of changes with respect to product coverage, compensation conditions and derogation clauses (UNCTAD 2004a:17). Transfers were made when the actual export earnings were lower than the reference level, i.e. the average export level of the past four years (European Commission 1997:11). Swaziland was the only BLNS country that received limited support from the STABEX system.[83]

STABEX and SYSMIN were phased out with the introduction of the Cotonou Agreement since their incapability to address long-term price declines and their pro-cyclical nature were not in a position to stabilise ACP export earnings. Furthermore, STABEX ran out of resources since low prices for major ACP commodities became persistent (UNTAD 2004a:35-7).

[82] For LDCs this value was 1%. The reason that the EU stabilisation schemes were already applied at a comparably low export concentration degree was that ACP countries' diversification efforts should not be undermined (Wolf 1996:27).

[83] The list of products covered by STABEX was expanded from 26 products (Lomé I) to 44 products (Lomé IV) (European Commission 1997:8). See European Commission (1997) for an overview of the mechanism of finance and application of STABEX.

Furthermore, the EEC introduced with the LC I Commodity Protocols for sugar, rum, bananas and beef. For the first three commodities duty free market access for country specific quotas was granted. Furthermore, the EEC/EU obliged itself to purchase the quota quantities at guaranteed prices. Beef again, like sugar a product that is highly protected in the EU market, was allowed to be imported at a 90% customs reduction (92% under the successor of the LC, the Cotonou Agreement). Though an annually negotiable price guarantee existed, the EEC/EU was not obliged to purchase the whole quota (Dunlop 1999:5).[84]

In 1995, around 97% of all ACP exports entered the EU market duty free. Free market access was granted to all manufactured goods (Davenport et al. 1995:1). However, agricultural exports were hampered by restricted quantities and temporal restrictions (e.g. for grapes and strawberries) (European Commission 1995, Annex XL). In addition, ACP countries' agro-based exports that fell under the Common Agricultural Policy (CAP) faced high tariffs to enter the EU market. The Common Agricultural Policy of the EU also had negative effects on domestic agricultural production in the ACP countries (see Box 8).

Box 8: The principles of the EU's Common Agricultural Policy (CAP) and its negative effects on African countries

The principles of the CAP were established with the Treaty of Rome (1957). A common agricultural policy of the six EEC states was introduced from 1962 on. The CAP was marked by strong state intervention with respect to production, price setting and marketing. It was the goal of the CAP to increase agricultural productivity, to guarantee suitable living conditions for farmers, to stabilise markets and to secure self-sufficiency, and to provide consumers with reasonable priced agricultural products (EEC Treaty Art. 33(39) as cited in European Parliament 2000:1).

Continuation on next page.

[84] The quotas of the Sugar and Banana Protocol were partly WTO bound, while the Beef and Rum Protocol had autonomous tariff quotas for ACP countries. The EU treatment of ACP bananas and sugar exports contravened against Art. XIII, WTO stating that tariff quotas have to be non-discriminatory. However, Art. XXIII.2, WTO, confines this statement and allows import restrictions in order to reach a similar distribution of trade from a "previous representative period". In the case of bananas, a WTO panel stated that ACP suppliers were treated "far beyond their actual trade performance in the recent past" and that the Banana Protocol should be brought to an end. In 2001, the EU agreed to replace the quota system by a tariff system from 2006 on. The 12 ACP countries that benefited from the Banana Protocol received technical and financial support to comply with economic transition (European Commission 2000a:2). The Rum Protocol again was abolished because the EU liberalised its rum market on a MFN basis in 2003. Rum exporting ACP countries get financial assistance under the Cotonou Agreement (Dunlop 1999:12-6).

Continuation of Box 8 from previous page.

Since the EEC did not have comparative advantages for most agricultural goods, which would have therefore been imported in a free market situation, she created high tariff barriers to protect domestic production. Additionally, an intervention price system was introduced, which guaranteed domestic farmers a minimum price for most of their products. Since this support was coupled to production output, it resulted in considerable surpluses (Malzbender 2003:1-2, Eurostep 2000a:12). Subsidies to promote the export of these surpluses allowed European producers to export international competitive agricultural products, which had negative external effects on third countries, mainly from the developing world.

In 1997, when the "mad cow disease" (BSE) hit its high peak in Europe, Botswana and Namibia claimed that the EU "dumps" beef into their markets. The loss of income was expected higher than financial aid provided by the EU (European Research Office 2001:5, Dunlop 1999:9).

Also fruit canners from South Africa and Swaziland complained about dumping from the European fruit and vegetable canning industry, resulting in falling farm income, decreasing wages and increasing unemployment in the agricultural sector (Madonsela 2001:60-1, Eurostep 1999:3). Similar distortions are reported in various African countries with respect to tomato concentrate, milk and dairy product, wheat products, sugar and processed sugar products and poultry (Goodison 2005, ActionAid 2002, Eurostep 1999).[85]

Though the EU agreed to reform its CAP, the absolute level of subsidies has not been reduced yet. Support for the CAP accounts with € 43.2 billion p.a. (2003) for the bulk of EU financial means. However, the EU has switched from product subsidies to direct support for farmers, which has resulted in decreased intervention prices for agricultural product making the EU market less attractive for ACP exporters (preference erosion). Still, EU prices for agricultural products were in average 33% above world market prices in 2002 (WTO 2004:87).

On the other hand, the EU allowed ACP countries to export fixed quantities of their most important agricultural products at preferred conditions. The value of these preferences was considerable since all Protocol commodities were highly protected in the EU market and excluded from the General System of Preferences (GSP) granted to other developing countries (Dunlop 1999:10-1). Thus, ACP exporters enjoyed a significant competitive advantage to the tariff level paid by competitors from developed and developing countries.

[85] At the WTO Hong Kong Ministerial Meeting in December 2005 the EU agreed to abolish its agricultural export subsidies by 2013.

Botswana, Swaziland and, since 1992, Namibia, benefited from the Beef and Veal Protocol of the Lomé Conventions. Swaziland did furthermore enjoy special conditions for its sugar exports to the EU (see Table 13). These special provisions for beef and sugar did not expire with the end of the Lomé Convention IV but are also an integral part of the Cotonou Agreement.

Table 13: Special provisions to Botswana, Namibia and Swaziland granted under the LC IV and the Cotonou Agreement

Country	Product	Time frame	Quota	Provison
Botswana	Boneless Beef	1991-1995 1996-1999 since 2000	18,916 tons p.a. 18,916 tons p.a. 18,916 tons p.a	Duties reduced by 90% Duties reduced by 90% Duties reduced by 92%
Namibia	Boneless Beef	1991-1995 1996-1999 since 2000	60,000 tons p.a. 73,000 tons p.a. 13,000 tons p.a.	Duties reduced by 90% Duties reduced by 90% Duties reduced by 92%
Swaziland	Boneless Beef	1991-1995 1996-1999 since 2000	3,363 tons p.a. 3,363 tons p.a. 3,363 tons p.a.	Duties reduced by 90% Duties reduced by 90% Duties reduced by 92%
	Sugar Cane *(Sugar Protocol)*	1991-1995 1996-1999 since 2000	120,000 tons p.a. 116,400 tons p.a. 117,844 tons p.a.	Duty free at guaranteed prices
	Sugar Cane *(Sugar Preferential Scheme)*	1991-1995 1996-2000 since 2000	50,000 tons p.a. 50,000 tons p.a. 52,200 tons p.a.	Duty free at guaranteed prices

Source: European Commission 1995 and 2000, Protocols 3 and 4.

The Lomé Conventions I-IV combined preferential trade and aid instruments in order to strengthen economic development in the ACP countries, to decrease primary commodity dependence and to promote economic diversification. The generous preferences of fixed quotas for sugar, beef, rum and bananas gave ACP exporters considerable competitive advantages over producers from developed and developing countries (Kennan and Stevens 1997). However, preferential customs were only possible to be granted because of the highly protected EU agricultural market that discriminated against non-ACP developing countries as well as against processed agricultural exports from ACP countries.

3.2 Theoretical Assumptions of the Lomé Conventions

Preferential customs are import customs that favour one country or a group of countries in foreign trade. In this case, the EEC granted the group of ACP countries preferential market access, which was not given to other developing countries. This resulted in trade diversion since goods the EEC used to import from third countries were substituted by ACP imports. In theory, this increases the demand for ACP imports and *ceteris paribus* the welfare of ACP countries (at the expense of third country suppliers). In addition to trade diversion, trade creation effects occur when domestic products are substituted by competitive ACP imports. This implies positive consumer effects and results *ceteris paribus* in reduced prices for EU products. If trade creation dominates over trade diversion, ACP preference could theoretically reduce the welfare of EEC producers (since EEC products are substituted by ACP products) and increase the welfare of EEC consumers (due to reduced prices) (Feldsieper 1975:57-8). However, since the ACP countries are comparably small exporters and are only allowed to export certain quantities, their exports to the EU did not influence commodity prices. Furthermore, it has to be taken into account that EEC prices for agricultural commodities (which account together with minerals for the vast majority of ACP exports to the EU) were regulated by the market intervention forces of the CAP. The preferences given to the ACP countries were supposed to result in trade diversion benefiting ACP suppliers at the expense of third country suppliers but not at the expense of EEC suppliers.

The EEC justified the preferential treatment of ACP countries at the expense of other developing countries with ACP countries' colonial heritage, their low development degree and their high dependence on few primary commodities, which made them suffer from declining and fluctuating terms of trade.

The problem of price fluctuation and permanent price decline for agricultural products was already immanent since the 1920s and prices have deteriorated continuously. According to the so-called Prebisch-Singer theorem, export prices for primary commodity products decline over time compared to manufactured products.[86] It is therefore recommended to focus on industrialisation and reduce the dependency on primary products. However, to allow such a positive

[86] The former Secretary General of the UNCTAD, Raúl Prebisch and the economist Hans Werner Singer investigated in the early 1960s the worsening of terms of trade for primary products. They found out that the price for export-oriented tropical primary goods are continuously decreasing, while the prices for manufactured imports are increasing. Thus, the exchange relationship of goods between developing and developed countries has developed to the disadvantage of the developing world. The Prebisch-Singer theory does therefore disagree with the classical-liberal foreign trade theory of David Ricardo according to which trade is always a win-win situation when one country is in a position to produce a good more cost-effective than its trading partner (Todaro and Smith 2002:522-6).

diversification approach, it was predicted to be useful to stabilise the export revenues of commodity-dependent economies. Different UN organisations worked towards international stabilisation schemes for agricultural commodities since the late 1940ies but were not able to set through their ideas to implement an international viable stabilisation system (UNCTAD 2004a:32-4).[87] It has to be considered that the EEC/EU schemes STABEX and SYSMIN were no international commodity stabilisation schemes but compensatory finance mechanisms, introduced to accommodate temporary revenue shortfalls. Permanent price declines of primary commodities were not addressed so that the systems were of limited use for the ACP countries (UNCTAD 2004a:35-7).

The significantly more important instrument for many ACP countries was the Commodity Protocols for their main agricultural commodities beef, sugar, bananas and rum guaranteeing certain export contingents at predictable prices. The Commodity Protocols were supposed to stabilise export revenues for ACP countries' main export products and to help the countries to diversify their export range and to increase the value addition of their export products. Though this instrument was only to a very limited extent successful, ACP welcomed the reduced fluctuation of their export revenues.

Furthermore, the Lomé Conventions were of non-reciprocal nature, i.e. despite their preferred market access to the European market, ACP countries did not have to open their markets for products from the EEC/EU. This provision was made because one assumed that the import of competitive European products would have destroyed developing ACP industries. It was assumed that their infant industries needed protection to become internationally competitive.

The theory of infant industry protection goes back to the age of industrialisation, when the USA and Germany regarded their industries as underdeveloped in comparison to those of the UK. Since new firms had little chance to compete successfully against old, well-established companies that benefited from economies of scale, technology, business knowledge and contacts, they were protected from foreign competition by import duties. Like this, the national infant industry had time to adapt to international competition.[88] It was assumed

---

[87] With the emergence of the "Washington Consensus" in the early 1980s, the free-market doctrine rejecting any governmental interference was dominating. From the mid-1990ies on, the aspect of poverty alleviation of economic policies came on the agenda and international commodity stabilisation schemes were discussed again. However, WTO regulations, which forbid the discrimination of single products, have made it difficult to implement a workable international stabilisation scheme for commodity dependent countries. Nevertheless, the urgency of action however has remained and even increased for some countries (UNCTAD 2004:42-3).

[88] The founder of the idea of infant industry protection, Friedrich List (1789-1846) pleaded for global free trade but argued that countries with a lower development level needed protection to investigate their productivity source and to increase economic growth in order to

that negative short-term effects occur, such as higher consumer prices and the discouragement of the international division of labour, which would be however outweighed by increased output, improved technical knowledge and a higher productivity. In sum, infant industry protection would increase the welfare of a country. However, an important condition for successful infant industry protection is that it is only applied for a limited period and that tariffs are gradually reduced over time. Like this, the learning curve of new industries should be improved, allowing them to compete successfully against well-established domestic enterprises and to develop their own, comparative international strategy. Unlimited protection whereas, as applied for the ACP countries under the Lomé Conventions, bears the risk to create non-competitive industries that rely on subsidies (Krugman and Obsfeld 2003: 256-7, Chung 1986:7-13).[89]

Despite 25 years of preferences, the economic performance of ACP countries remained very weak and economic as well as socio-economic conditions have even worsened in most countries. ACP countries' share on total EU imports did half from 6.2% in 1976 to 3% in 1992 and their traditional trade pattern with the EU manifested. In the early 1990s, six out of 70 countries accounted for more than 50% of total ACP exports which were mainly petroleum, diamonds, coffee, sugar, copper and wood (Davenport et al. 1995:5-10).[90] Though it was also argued that ACP countries were able to expand their export for those products where Lomé margins were great and would have been even more marginalised without preferences (Goodison 2000:10), the overall estimation was that the instruments of the Lomé Conventions failed to promote economic development and prosperity in the ACP countries (European Commission 1996, Wolf 1996, Davenport *et al.* 1995).

---

benefit from the advantages of free trade. Thus, List took in difference to Ricardo the dynamic component of development into account (Chung 1986:8-9).

[89] The key arguments against infant industry protection are that it is also granted to industries, which will never become internationally competitive, that the temporary restriction is subject to political pressure and, most importantly, that import tariffs are not the best instrument to improve national welfare. Production subsidies would be more efficient since they are applied to individual industries. However, infant industry protection can be a second-best policy option if a developing countries does not have the financial means to subsidise individual industries (Krugman and Obstfeld 2003: 256-60, Suranovic 2002:6-8). Surprisingly, the WTO allows infant industry protection (WTO 1994, Art. XVIII) but no subsidies to improve a country's export performance (WTO 1994, Agreement on Subsidy and Countervailing Measures, Art. 3).

[90] The level of simple manufactured products, such as processed wood, leather and woven fabrics, remained at a level of around 30% (Davenport et al. 1995:20-1). See also European Commission (1996:21-33) for ACP countries economic, social and political performance under the LCs.

An overview of EU-BLNS trade relations should help to explain the difficulties ACP countries face when exporting to the EU. Though the Lomé Conventions provided ACP countries with generous preferences for their most important export products and helped to secure their export revenues, relevant demand- and supply-side constraints were neglected.

3.3 The Internal Reasons for the Failure of the Lomé Conventions

a. Supply-side constraints and missing ability to comply with international standards and regulations

Supply-side constraints are economic, political and social conditions that hamper ACP countries' potential benefits from accessing the EU market duty free (Liebig *et al.* 2005:2) Most ACP countries face manifold supply-side constraints, such as an unfavourable macroeconomic environment (e.g. insufficient capital supply and international non-convertible currencies), a lack of public infrastructure (deficient roads, non-reliable electricity and water supply), a low labour productivity due to lack of education, poor health and housing provisions, missing export market information, backwardness in technological services, and missing backward- and forward linkages. Since the Lomé Conventions did not take these supply-side constraints sufficiently into account, many ACP countries were not able to exploit potential export benefits (Liebig *et al.* 2005, Goodison 2002:43, Kappel 2001, Solignac Lecomte 2000:55). Though BLNS countries' infrastructure is, with exception of Lesotho's, above southern African average (see Table 14), supply-side constraints in form of limited production capacities were and are prevalent. Thus, expected scale effects did not occur since the countries were not able to expand their production capacities accordingly.

Table 14: Physical infrastructure in southern Africa

	Telephones per 1000 people 1995-2000	PC (per 1000 people)* 2000	Paved Roads (% of total)* 1999	Vehicles in use per 1000 people 1996
SADC - SACU	28	..	..	39
Botswana	41	37.0	55.0	45
Lesotho	..	...	18.3	..
Namibia	51	34.2	13.6	82
South Africa	100	55.7	20.3	121
Swaziland	..	...	...	..

Source: Africa Institute of South Africa 2002 and * World Bank 2001c

Against the original assumption of the Lomé Convention, it was less the missing demand that constrained the expansion of ACP exports but ACP producers' missing ability to expand production and to market their products. Furthermore, the ACP countries had and have problems to comply with international product standards. Health and safety standards are imposed by governments to guarantee a certain safety and quality of products for consumers. However, these standards can also be abused when requesting strict compliance with local standards in order to restrict access of imported products. In the field of agricultural products there are manifold disputes regarding the imposition of import restrictions due to health and safety concerns. EU standards and food safety regulation often pose insuperable hindrances to ACP suppliers. The increasing stringency of the EU's Sanitary and Phytosanitary Standards (SPS) implies high costs for ACP countries, thus reducing the attractiveness of preferences. (Epawatch 2002, Solignac Lecomte 2000:559). Furthermore, high standards can reduce the poverty-reducing effect of agricultural activities in Africa since mainly small-scale farmers are not able to comply with increasingly stricter SPS (Stevens 2005).

Box 9 gives some examples of BLNS countries' difficulties to comply with EU sanitary standards and health provisions.

Box 9: EU sanitary standards and health provisions – problems BLNS countries face

European standards do not only hamper southern African exports of raw commodities but also constrain the diversification of exports and the value addition of export products. The BLNS countries are for instance not allowed to export bone-in meat to the EU due to disease control provisions. As a result, the countries can only supply the low-value "pub market" in the EU that requires deboned "premium cut.[91] Another problem is that health and safety regulations become increasingly stricter, making it more difficult and costly for the BLNS countries to comply. An official from the Department of Customs and Excise in Botswana explains the difficulty:[92]

"First, we have to divide the country in quarantines to ensure that the cattle do not move from area one to area two. In early 2003, we had foot and mouth disease in the North, which had nothing to do with our products in the South. But we were not allowed to export.

Continuation on next page.

[91] On the other hand, it must be noted that poor marketing has led to the supply of a low-value market segment. Southern African meat is not branded or packaged, but sold at auction in the EU market (Molapisi 2003a).

[92] The interview was conducted personally in October 2003 in Gaborone.

Continuation of Box 9 from previous page.

Second, the meat has to be tested, for which we have to pay. Third, the EU requires new standards without informing us in a suitable way. Since 2000 they want to know where the cow has been born, to which place it moved, what it ate, etc. The beef must be of a certain quality, i.e. the cattle must have been fed with certain products. This information comes often too late so that we cannot prepare. There is no mechanism in place that informs us about the latest requirements. From the consumer side, Europe has the right to do so but it would be fair to inform us already when they are considering implementing new requirements and offering us assistance to meet them."

Furthermore, southern African countries face high market entry costs for new products they seek to introduce. Namibia for instance wants to export horticultural products such as essential oils and herbal diet pills to the EU but faces high non-tariff barriers in form of registration costs, minimum volumes and detailed packaging and labelling requirements. These manifold regulations make it very difficult to enter new market niches successfully (Bennett 2004).

Another problem the SACU countries face, is the harmonisation of product standards in the EU. Although this procedure is generally desirable, as the unification of standards raises transparency levels, the problem is that the most stringent rules are applied. The EU harmonised for instance its standard regarding the "black spot", a harmless fungus on citrus fruits. While Swaziland and South Africa were in earlier days allowed to export citrus fruits showing "black spots" to northern European countries, the stringent rules for southern Europe are now valid in the entire EU region. The Swazi Citrus Board has commissioned a study, arguing that the "black spot" does neither harm consumers nor spread in Europe since the climatic conditions are different. However, to date the EU has not indicated any intention to compromise in this respect. In Swaziland, this resulted in a decline of fruit exports, leading to the closing down of citrus fruit farmers' businesses, which have diversified into cane sugar as a result (Nϕddeboe 2003).

b. Demand-side constraints: Remaining tariff and non-tariff barriers and complex rules of origin

Nowadays, a variety of non-tariff barriers, such as quotas, export subsidies and health and safety regulations exists, aiming above all to protect sensitive products in developed countries, which are particularly located in the agricultural sector (Husted and Melvin 2004:148-212). Thus, the EU wants to import only a limited amount of unprocessed, primary products from the ACP countries but is still protecting its agricultural market comprehensively, including processed agricultural commodities. For the latter ACP countries face the problem of tariff escalation which means the increase of tariffs with each processing stage. The import of chocolate for instance, a processed sugar-based product that offers diversification options for sugar- and cocoa-exporting ACP countries, is subject to a 12.9% *ad valorem* duty[93] plus a supplementary sugar duty, as sugar is the main ingredient (USDA 2003:4-5). Though the EU's policy of tariff escalation (including the re-export of finished subsidised products into developing countries) is in contradiction to its development goals, there have not been any ambitions yet to reduce agricultural export subsidies or to improve ACP countries' market access for processed agricultural products.

Another problem is the rather complex rules of origin system of the Lomé Conventions and the Cotonou Agreement, requiring a minimum local content of 30-50%, which discourages local and regional processing and therefore the diversification of ACP countries' export range (UNCTAD 2002a:244).

c. Failure of import-substitution strategy

Only few ACP countries were able to build-up their own industries and to diversify their export range. Most ACP countries failed to increase their industrialisation degree by the policy of import substitution. The non-reciprocal approach of the Lomé Conventions was accused to result in consumer losses and ineffective industries and to discourage exports since resource were drawn towards imports (Yeats 1998).

In fact, the non-reciprocal nature of the Lomé Conventions had nothing to do with the original idea of infant industry protection since it excluded all industries from free trade and not only industries that were newly established in the ACP countries. Thus, many ACP countries established a regime of high import tariffs, not only to protect their domestic industries but also to secure income sources.[94] As a result, imported consumer and intermediary goods became expensive, which had a negative impact on consumption and manufacturing activities. Another problem was the creation of a "dual economy", characterised by an uneven development within the country with few modern capital-intensive firms but missing backward- and forward-linkages in production process and the neglection of other sectors such as agricultural activities (Krugman and Obstfeld 2003:263).[95]

---

[93] The trade tax equals to a given percentage of the selling price. Post-Uruguay tariffs on agricultural products still escalate most between semi-finished and finished products (UNCTAD 2004:58).

[94] Import tariffs are comparably easy to collect and most ACP countries are highly dependent on this income source (Davenport *et al.* 1995).

[95] To what extent this was the case in the SACU countries will be discussed in Chapter 4.

e. Complexity, Non-conditionality of aid and missing involvement of civil society

The Lomé Conventions were accused to be highly complex, leading to increased bureaucracy and inefficiencies. It was furthermore argued that the missing link of EU trade preferences and aid with ACP countries' economic, social and political performance hampered reforms in ACP countries. In 1996, the Commission claimed in its "Green Paper" to increase the conditionality of aid and to include a "political dialogue" into EU-ACP relations that also integrates non-state actors (European Commission 1996:i-xi).

Another problem was, and still is, the growing gap between the original development goals of Lomé and the availability of financial means. Thus, real per capital aid decreased by more than 40% from LC I to LC III (Gonzales 1996 as cited in Matambalya 1998:16).[96] Though the EU announced recently to increase their financial means for development cooperation in order to reach the Millennium Development Goals (MDG), the finance is still disputed.[97]

3.3.1 EU-BLNS Trade and the Impact of Lomé Preferences on BLNS Countries' Exports

The EU is, with exception of Lesotho, the second largest trading partner of the BLNS countries and receives the bulk of Botswana's and Namibia's exports. Lesotho can be described as an exception regarding its structure and location of exports. Due to its lack primary resources, Lesotho exports above all clothing and garment, mainly destined for the US market.[98]

All BLNS countries show a positive trade balance towards the EU: in 2002, exports to the EU accounted for € 2,460.5 million and were more than eight times higher than BLNS imports (see Figure 8). BLNS trade surplus towards the EU multiplied by more than 17 times in the period 1991-2002. However, these high increases, above all in the period 2000-2002, show mainly a distorted trade pattern. Thus, the raise of export values was mainly due to price increases for diamonds, the main export products of Botswana and Namibia.[99]

[96] As can be obtained from Table 11, this was not the case for the BLNS countries, which received increasing NIP and NPA funds from Lomé I to IV.

[97] The EU envisages to increase the funds for development cooperation from currently 0.28%/GDP to 0.7% in 2014 (Der Spiegel, 18/04/2005).

[98] Lesotho benefits highly from the US "African Growth and Opportunity Act" (AGOA) and delivered 74% of its total exports to the USA in 2002, which were almost exclusively garments and apparels (AGOA.info 2003).

[99] Diamond prices have roughly risen by more than 50% since 2000 (European Diamonds PLC 2005).

For the EU, BLNS were only a marginal trading partner, responsible for around 0.1% of total European imports and less than 0.05% of total European exports in 2000 (European Commission 2001).

Figure 8: BLNS trade with the EU (in Mio. €)

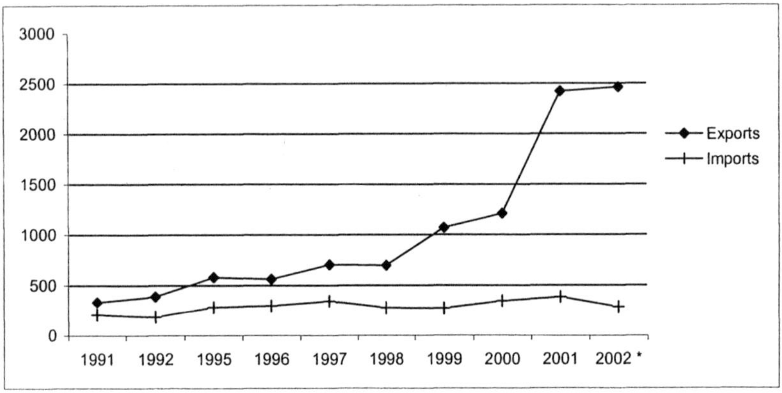

Source: Eurostat as cited in EU DG Trade (2002), * WTO 2003.

BLNS countries' exports to the EU are concentrated on precious stones and beef, mainly from Botswana and Namibia, contributing to 55% of total BLNS exports to the EU in 2000. Prepared foodstuff, vegetables and fruits, mainly delivered by Swaziland, accounted for 10% of total exports in the same year. BLNS countries' imports from the EU are highly concentrated on capital and knowledge-intensive goods, such as transport equipment, machinery and electronic products (see Figures 9 and 10).

Figure 9: BLNS exports to the EU (in % of the value of total exports 2000)

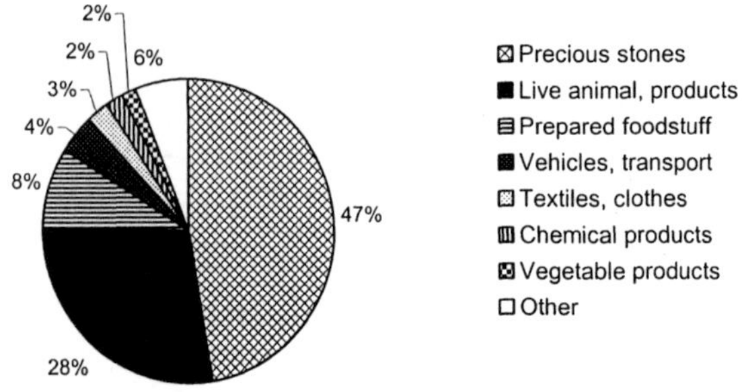

Figure 10: BLNS imports to the EU (in % of the value of total imports 2000)

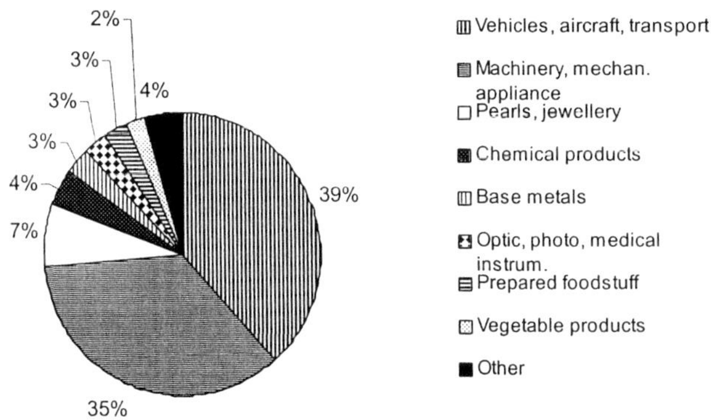

Source: European Commission 2001.

Although the official figures, as displayed in Table 15, state that the BLNS countries receive only between 1.5 - 9.2% of their total imports from the EU, it is assumed that this figure is in reality much bigger due to imperfect supervision of the rules of origin. Unrecorded imports from third countries are a problem for all BLNS countries since they receive the vast majority of their imports via South Africa (WTO 2003:A5-312).

Table 15: BLNS countries' export and import volumes and main trading products with the EU, 2001

	Export volume in million US$ and % of total exports	Export products to the EU	Import volume in million US$ and % of total imports	Import products from the EU
Botswana	1,925.0 (84.7%)	Diamonds (82.7%), Beef and beef products (8.2%), Machinery (4.3%),[100] Textiles (3.3%)	174.0 (9.2%)	Machinery (39.1%), Transport equipment (38.1%), Jewellery (8.9%), Optic instruments (2.7%)
Lesotho +	0.24 (0.8%)	-	1.1 (1.5%)	Transport equipment (62%), Machinery (34%)
Namibia	550.9 (55.1%)	Diamonds (52%), Beef and beef products (46.2%),	90.6 (6.9%)	Transport equipment (36.9%), Machinery (24.9%), Agriculture (8.6%), Jewellery (4.9%), Chemicals (4.5%)
Swaziland	151.3 (18.5%)	Prepared foodstuff (72.5%), Textiles (7.8%), Wood articles (3.5%)	17.0 (1.9%)	Machinery (22.1%), Chemical products (16.3%), Base metals (15.3%), Agriculture (11.6%), Transport equipment (8.3%), Miscellaneous manufactures (8.1%),

+ Trade figures of 2000.

Sources: European Commission (2001). Figures of trade volumes are obtained from national trade statistics as cited in WTO 2003.

In summary it can be said that trade between the BLNS countries and the EU shows a complementary pattern that is characteristic for trade relations between developing and industrialised countries. BLNS exports to the EU are dominated by primary and labour-intensive manufactured goods, while their imports are predominately capital-intensive manufactures.

[100] Until 2000, Botswana had a Hyundai car semi-knockdown plant. However, this plant closed in 2000 after the protection period elapsed. Today, the country has only one car assembly plan (Volvo Truck and Bus Botswana Pty. Ltd.), which imports pieces of trucks and buses from the EU and assembles them in Botswana. 95% of these trucks and buses are sold in Botswana and 5% are exported to other African countries (Owen 2003).

However, despite BLNS countries' high concentration on few export products, tariff preferences over competitors have to a certain extent also encouraged manufacturing exports, such as tanning activities (Botswana and Namibia) and food processing (Namibia and Swaziland). It was mainly Botswana, Namibia and Swaziland that benefited from EU preferences by secured export revenues, while Lesotho used to export garments, clothing and apparels to the EU market but has been constrained by the rules of origin.[101]

3.3.2 BNS Countries' Agro-Based Exports to the EU: Diversification Efforts and Constraints

At best, horizontal diversification moves towards more dynamic, higher valuable products, which are not directly related to a country's traditional export products in order to balance the commodity portfolio. Vertical diversification of agricultural production again means the technological upgrading, including the promotion of linkages with regional and overseas markets (UNCTAD 2004:51-4). However, considering BNS internal and external difficulties to diversify, such as the comparably narrow agricultural production base and the so far only limited manufacturing activities that are either at the first stage of processing or at the final stage of blending, BNS diversification efforts are no "radical innovations" in a Schumpeterian sense but relate first of all to the upgrading of existing products. These efforts are however inhibited by the fact that BNS are small and sparely populated respectively, show insufficient backward and forward linkages, and have - as a part of SACU - only limited options to protect their infant industries against South African competition.[102]

---

[101] Regarding textile and clothing products, specific processing requirements are formulated in order to be granted originating status. To enter the European market duty free, the clothing exports have to meet the precondition of "double transformation". This refers to two stages of production, i.e. the transformation from yarn to fabric and from fabric to clothing must take place within any ACP country (European Commission 2000b, Annex IX and XV to Protocol 1). The US-AGOA initiative provides less restrictive rules of origin: A country like Lesotho, classified as "lesser developed country", is allowed to use third country inputs for eligible exports. Thus, Lesotho's exports to the EU decreased from R 30.1 million in 1990 to R 1.2 million in 2000. Exports to the USA increased from R 41.7 million to R 736.5 million in the same period (BoL 2001:52).

[102] Infant industry protection has to be applied at the SACU Council, which grants and supervises terms and conditions of protection for a maximum period of 8 years (SACU 2002, Art. 26).

a. Meat and processed meat products

Botswana, Namibia and Swaziland (BNS) export mainly boneless beef to the EU, which is the only meat product that can be exported almost duty free (92% duty reduction).[103] Namibia is furthermore allowed to export 200 tons of boneless lamb. Though BNS comply with EU health and safety regulation, they complain that product standards are becoming continuously stricter so that the costs of compliance are increasing. As a result of some foods scandals in the early 1990ies, such as the BSE scandal, the EU has applied SPS that are above WTO standards (Wellmer 2005:27-8). In addition to high costs to comply with increasing standards, the BNS countries face falling prices for beef due to the CAP reform. Thus beef prices have dropped by almost 50% since 1999 (Mouton and Roux 2003).[104]

In 2003, Botswana exported 80% of its total beef production to the EU, Namibia 35% and Swaziland only 12% (Molapisi 2003a, Mouton and Roux 2003, Williams 2003b). None of the countries has fully utilised the quota since the Protocol has entered into force in 1975. In the period 1992-99, Namibia used in average 72% of its quota, Botswana 66% and Swaziland not even 12% (European Research Office 2001:14-16). Also in the period 1998-2002 none of the countries was able to reach its quota as illustrated in Figure 11.

Figure 11: Quota utilisation for BNS beef exports to the EU, 1998-2003 (in tons)

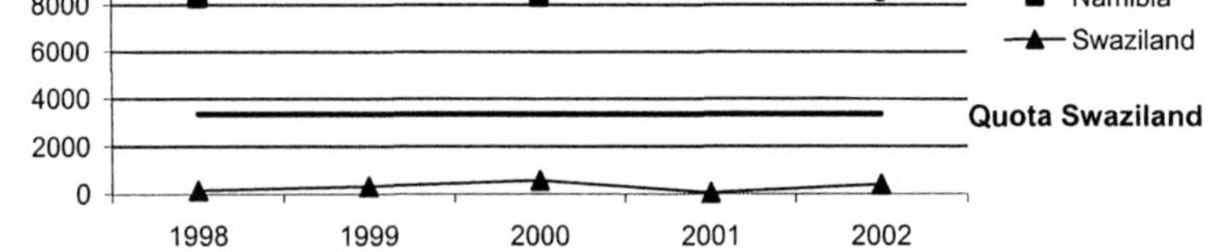

Source: Data obtained from Molapisi (2003b).

[103] The EU third country import tariff for meat of bovine animals (fresh, chilled or frozen) is 12.8% + € 141,40 - € 176,80 per 100 kilo (Expanding Exports Helpdesk 2004).

[104] In 1999, the EU paid € 3.50 for one kilo premium cut de-boned beef and in 2003 € 1.80-1.85 (Mouton and Roux 2003). In the South African market, prices have also fallen considerably due to subsidised beef exports from the EU (European Research Office 2001:8-10).

General reasons for this underutilisation are problems with sanitary and health regulations (e.g. mouth and claw disease), droughts and poor livestock. The countries did not have enough and too bad quality cattle. Since the EU allows only the import of "deboned premium cut" meat, quantities were not sufficient (Molapisi 2003a). Furthermore, the BNS have problems to comply with the rules of origin of the Cotonou Agreement, which prohibits the export of "non-originating" cattle. Most of all Swaziland struggles to meet the capacity of its abattoir and uses the bulk of its meat production for domestic sales (Williams 2003b). In addition to external shocks, such as bad weather conditions and diseases, Swaziland's low beef exports can also be explained by the fact that Swazi cattle has not been fully commercialised but is still dominated by small-scale farming where farmers own only one or two animals (Magagula and Faki 1999).

Botswana is the only of the three countries that exports processed meat products to the EU, namely corned beef and pet food. However, only 29% of Botswana's total canned beef production is destined for the EU market, while the bulk goes to the SACU market. The Botswana Meat Commission complains that health regulations are often used as NTBs. Though the country has offered to treat its meat according to the same sanitary standards applied by the EU, many EU countries would refuse canned beef from Botswana (Molapisi 2003a). The sale of diversified meat products is therefore to a large extent limited to the domestic and regional markets. The same applies to Meatco Namibia and Swaziland Meat Industry, which offer processed meat products such as sausages, burgers and prepared turkeys only for local sales. These product lines are not interesting for being exported to the EU since they are subject to a 20-30% tariff as well as to non-tariff barriers such as minimum quantity requirements and registration fees. Companies' efforts to increase their productivity by higher sales of value-added products are therefore still restricted to the SACU market (Molapisi 2003a, Mouton and Roux 2003, Williams 2003b).

However, despite its underutilisation, the BNS have benefited from the Beef and Veal Protocol. The preferential market access to the EU has helped the countries to open up alternative markets to the traditional South African market, to improve the quality of beef, to increase the level of local slaughtering and to encourage manufacturing activities in the meat industry and to develop tanning activities.[105]

---

[105] BNS export above all unprocessed hides and skins but hardly finished leather products. The EU is the main supplier of leather products worldwide and highly interested in purchasing raw skins. Around 80% of African skins and leather production is absorbed by the EU (CDI 1999:75). Generally, BNS face severe difficulties to set-up a tannery and to increase the domestic value addition of leather production. Because of their small production base and insufficient backward- and forward-linkages, they face manifold constraints "*...at every level throughout the production and marketing chain from the breeding of the animal,*

Though these diversification efforts are still in their infancies, it is doubtful whether they would have been stimulated without EU preferences (European Research Office 2001:15-8).

b. Processed sugar-based products

Swaziland, which exports above all sugar to the EU, benefits highly from the Cotonou Sugar Protocol that guarantees the purchase of around 170,000 tons of cane sugar per annum at a pre-determined price.[106] In total, Swaziland delivers around 28% of its annual sugar production to the EU (SSA 2003). Due to high protection (with tariffs up to 114%), EU prices under the Sugar Protocol are with currently € 523/t for raw sugar around three times higher than the world-market price (Rouhier 2004:4). These preferences have helped Swaziland to attract investment from large subsidiary sugar fabric producers (Cadbury and Coca Cola) and to build up a fruit-canning and jam producer (Swazican). Activities in the sugar-based industry account until today for the bulk of Swaziland's agricultural exports. To date, Swazi sugar fabric producers face only limited competition for their products since not only the EU but also the SACU market is protected. High sugar containing products are subject to high tariffs when entering the SACU market and imported chocolate and confectionary is not competitive in the moment since it is more expensive than sugar confectionary (Stock 2003). Thus, the main competitors for sugar-based products in Swaziland are informal producers that offer self-made soft-drinks at low prices (King 2003). However, this competition situation for Swazi sugar-based products is likely to change, depending on the future liberalisation of the world sugar regime.[107]

On the other hand it must be noted that the protection of sugar markets is to a certain extent also harmful for the Swazi sugar processing industry because it is held responsible to constrain the diversification efforts towards sugar-based

---

through slaughter, the leather processing up to the selling of the leather." (BEDIA 2001:11).

[106] Sugar prices under the Sugar Protocol and the Sugar Preferential Scheme are subject to annual negotiations. The Sugar Protocol runs without expiration but can be cancelled with two years' notice from 2005 on (European Commission 2000b, Protocol 3).

[107] The EU agreed to reduce its sugar prices by 36% over four years beginning in 2006/07 and to cut its production quota by 2.8 million tons to 14.6 million tons in the period 2006-09. Under this scenario, prices would fall to € 319. The EU agreed on compensation payments for ACP suppliers of € 40 million p.a., which does not cover the losses (estimated to be around € 23 million p.a. for Swaziland) but might help to restructure industries. The EU sugar regime is still under pressure from large sugar supplying developing countries, such as Brazil and Thailand, which want to bring the EU Sugar Regime to an end. It is therefore assumed that consequent steps of liberalisation are following (Agritrade 2004, INSAT 2005b:4).

manufactured products, such as chocolate éclairs, soft drink concentrate, jam, bubble gum. Thus, Swazi sugar manufacturers pay 2.4 times more for cane sugar than the world market price. The same applies to glucose and caramel, which is more than double as expensive than at the world market. Furthermore, Swaziland is not allowed to export its high sugar containing products to the EU and the US-market since it benefits from the protected regime for its cane sugar exports (Mahlinza 2003).

c. Fruits, vegetables and horticultural products

Namibia has a duty free quota of 900 tons of seedless grapes, which are however only allowed to be exported to the EU in a defined time span. In 2002, Namibia exported about 14,000 tons of seeded and seedless grapes to the EU, of which most bore an import duty of 16.3% (Hoffmann 2003). Namibia argues that these import duties constrain the expansion of its grapes exports to the EU market and do not take the country's development level sufficiently into account.[108] In fact, South Africa, which has already signed an FTA with the EU, is allowed to export its grapes duty free by 2010.

Namibia also aims to diversify its agricultural production towards horticultural products, such as melon and marula seeds, indigenous plants and organic biological products (e.g. sheep and goat cheese). Though horticultural products do not face any tariffs when entering the USA or EU market, they are subject to other trade barriers, such as volume requirements, packaging, labelling and registration costs (Bennett 2004).

Swaziland, which has three different climate zones, shows comparative advantages in a couple of agricultural products: maize, cotton, cane sugar, pineapple, grapefruit, oranges and cabbage (Magagula and Faki 1999:xi). Though the EU is an attractive market for Swazi vegetables and fruits, as it gives ACP exporters a tariff concession of up to 14% against third country suppliers, it has the disadvantage of offering only volatile prices. Thus, supermarkets determine the price and the quality of products and fix the price only after having received the product. To increase their profits it is therefore crucial for Swazi exporters to offer higher volumes of high quality products and to diversify towards higher valuable products in the medium to long-term. Since small-scale farmers in Swaziland have problems to penetrate the EU market effectively, they plan to form a vegetable network in order to manage their exports, to disseminate information about markets and producers and to acquire confidence in the suppliers. However, the establishment of such a network, which is supposed to work

---

[108] Namibia's grape industry employs currently around 10,000 full- and part-time workers. This employment is judged to be expandable when residual tariff barriers would be removed (European Research Office 2004).

comparable to the Swazi Citrus Board, was still in its infancy at the time of writing.

As mentioned above, Swaziland was able to establish a fruit canning company supported by EU preferences. The canned fruit industry is often judged as ideal for developing country to start upgrading their production and diversify their product range, since the production of canned fruits is comparably simple. However, competition in this sector is high, e.g. from southern European countries. The rents of production do therefore face a decreasing tendency, while the added value for marketing and distribution is increasing but mainly realised by big supermarket chains (Kaplinsky 2000:133-6). So far, Swazican is a niche player in the EU market. The company serves around 2% of the EU's total pineapple import, which are however 80-95% of Swaziland's total pineapple production (McConville 2003).

In total, more than 50% of BNS countries' exports to the EU (and almost all agricultural exports) enjoyed preferences exceeding 3% compared to market access under the MFN tariff in 1999 (Trades Centre 2000:27). Despite some claims over too less aid, bureaucracy and health restrictions, the BNS countries regarded the Lomé Conventions as very beneficial for their economic wellbeing, in particular the Protocols on Beef and Sugar (ACP General Secretariat 1995a, b). The Government of Swaziland (2003:40) stated that the guaranteed prices granted under Lomé have helped to improve productivity and technological innovations of sugar production and that they were a stable income resource despite adverse exchange rate movements (GoS 2003:40).

However, EU preferences are not only a blessing but also a threat as they bear the risk to manifest the dependency on few primary resources and to constrain diversification efforts. Thus, the expansion of the sugar quota in the Cotonou Agreement compared to the LC IV has resulted in increased Swazi sugar supply. Nowadays, sugar production accounts for 51% of Swaziland's agriculture production and, including sugar processing, for 24% of the country's GDP (SSA 2004). EU preferences have helped BNS only to a limited extent to diversify their exports to the EU. The bulk of their export revenue still comes from mineral exports (Botswana and Namibia) and sugar cane (Swaziland). As the discussion showed, one reason for this is that BNS countries' attempts to enter into higher valuable export niches are still hampered by EU tariffs for processed agro-based exports as well as by manifold non-tariff barriers.

In addition to internal reasons for the failure of the Lomé Convention, a rapidly changing external environment implied several challenges for EU-ACP trade relations.

3.4 The External Reasons for the Failure of Lomé

a) Limited impact of preferences and erosion of trade preference

As discussed, the extent of trade preferences is the significant factor to judge the value of preferences and thus the potential impact on a country's economic performance. In the early 1990ies, only 7% of all ACP exports to the EU enjoyed a significant preferential margin exceeding 5% compared to the GSP (Epawatch 2002:5). Since the creation of the WTO in 1994 third countries can export traditional ACP exports such as copper, wood, cotton, and aluminium at a zero or very low MNF tariffs to the EU (Wolf 1996:52-3) Thus, tariffs increasingly lose their relevance as trade barriers: the EU reduced its tariffs by almost 40% in the period 1994-99 (Hoeller *et al.* 2000:35-6). Additionally, the EU's FTAs with Eastern and Southern European countries have eroded ACP countries preferences in the EU market.[109] Furthermore, the reform of the CAP, moving away from a system of price support to a system of direct support to EU farmers, has lead to reduced EU intervention prices implying lower unit returns for ACP exporters. Though the prices for beef and sugar are still well-above world-market level, they have dropped considerably since 1999 and are expected to erode further (Agritrade 2004, 2003).

b. Changing political environment and EU enlargement

With the collapse of the Soviet Union and the end of the bi-polar world, the political relevance of ACP countries shrank. The EU focused on the economic and political integration of neighbouring eastern European countries and shifted financial and technical support to them. With the enlargement process in 2004, the EU increased its membership by 10 mainly Eastern European countries to 25. This affects the ACP countries from two sides: first, because of increased competition in the EU market and second, because of negative implications on the European Development Fund. Furthermore, the new member countries do not have any "historic bindings" to the ACP countries and do not see the necessity for special treatment (Laporte 2004:2-5, Stevens 2000:224).

c. WTO provisions

Since the banana dispute at the WTO resulted in the abolition of the ACP Banana Protocol, the EU also feared about other provisions of the LC (Stevens

---

[109] Furthermore, ACP preferences were also eroded by the EU's protectionist behaviour. Thus, the EU insisted on protection clauses, which allowed the termination of Lomé, if ACP exports cause "serious harm" to EU economies (European Commission 1995, Art. 177 following). Though this clause was never applied it resulted in increased insecurity for exporters and investors (Wolf 1996:26).

2000:233-4). It became more and more obvious that the successor of the LC had to fit into the WTO framework. There were several options to make the LC "WTO compatible":

1. *Special and Differential Treatment (GATT, Art. XVIII)*
   According to the MFN clause of the WTO any trade preference offered to one member country has to be extended to all member countries. Though exceptions for developing countries are allowed (according to GATT, Art. XVIII), special and differential treatment to a selected group of developing countries is forbidden. Thus, the LC would have been WTO compatible if its provisions would have been applied to all "developing countries" (according to WTO classification). However, such an extension was not in the interest of the EU as it would have implied extensive liberalisation and thus the *de facto* abandonment of the CAP.[110] The other option was to grant special preferences only to the world's LDCs and to treat the remaining ACP countries like other developing countries, granting them preferences under the GSP. This option, which would have also implied the abolition of Protocol preferences for non-LDC ACP countries, would have resulted in considerable economic losses and was rejected by non-LDC ACP countries (Kennan and Stevens 1997).[111] Furthermore, the GSP is of non-contractual nature and preferences could be withdrawn unilaterally. The GSP is therefore not an attractive alternative for the non-LDC ACP countries.

2. *Application of a waiver (WTO Art. IX)*
   Most waivers granted under the WTO Art. IX affect trade preference to developing countries (Stevens 2000:238). The EU applied for a waiver for the last Lomé Convention IV *bis* (1995-2000) and for the Cotonou Agreement (2000-2007). The Cotonou waiver might be extendable beyond 2008 but it has to be considered that a waiver needs to be applied on a regular basis and that its approval is costly and insecure. Moreover, the provisions can still be subject to dispute at the WTO Dispute Settlement Body. Thus, the EU rejected the maintenance of the "status quo" for all ACP countries (European Commission 1996:65-9).

---

[110] Moreover, this solution would have implied a further erosion of ACP countries' preferences.

[111] A study by Kennan and Stevens (1997) that investigated the economic impact of including non-LDC ACP countries into the GSP concluded that the countries would face deteriorated access and lose an equivalent of over 40% of EU aid. The main beneficiary of this change would be upper-middle-income and rich countries

3. *The creation of Free Trade Agreements (GATT, Art. XXIV)*

   As discussed in Box 6, FTAs and CUs are compatible with WTO provisions if they cover "substantially all trade", which has to be liberalised within "a reasonable length of time" (GATT, Art. XXIV, § 4-10). The EU proposed the creation of FTAs with ACP countries either on a bilateral or regional basis (European Commission 1996:66).

After exploring the pros and cons of these proposals, the EU decided for the creation of regional FTAs since (1) the options of a non-discriminatory application of special and differential treatment were neither in the interest of the EU nor in those of the ACP countries and (2) since the application of a WTO waiver would have been insecure and only possible for a limited period of time.

With the expiration of the last Lomé Convention the Cotonou Agreement was signed on 23 June 2000. The EU and 77 ACP countries agreed to introduce reciprocal trade arrangements after a transition period of eight years. By 31 December 2007 at the latest, the parties shall sign a reciprocal trade agreement that establishes a North-South FTA within 12 years (European Commission 2000b:8-9).

The switch from a preferential to reciprocal trade arrangements has severe impacts on ACP countries economies and their efforts on regional integration as the discussion in section 3.5 shows. For the BLNS countries the situation is even more complex since they are members of the SACU but have a different trade agreement with the EU than South Africa.

3.5 The EU-South Africa Free Trade Agreement and its Impact on the BLNS Countries and Regional Integration in Southern Africa

"Without doubt, one aspect of the FTA presented to South Africa was to test the wider application of a free trade approach to the developing world in a post-Lomé context." (Eurostep 2000a:2).

In April 1994, after the first democratic elections in South Africa, the EU decided to strengthen its cooperation with South Africa, granting the country special market access for industrial products under the GSP scheme and technical assistance to encourage regional economic integration. It was furthermore agreed to explore South Africa's options to become a member of the Lomé Convention (European Commission 1999:36). In December 1994, South Africa requested to join the LC. This request was supported by the SADC and the European Parliament. However, the European Commission and the European

Council rejected South Africa's application because of its economic weight in the region, arguing that South Africa had a much more advanced economic development than other ACP countries. Furthermore, the EU feared the damage of sensitive sectors like agriculture or textile when granting South Africa the same access than ACP countries (Eurostep 2000c:4).

In June 1995, the EU offered South Africa the so-called "twin-track approach", which was a qualified membership of the LC, including technical, social and regional cooperation and participation of the 8th Development Fund. However, participation of the general trade arrangements, special protocols and structural adjustment support was excluded. Moreover, South Africa was only allowed to become a qualified ACP member after having agreed on the immediate start of negotiations of a bilateral trade and co-operation agreement, leading to a WTO conform FTA. South Africa agreed and became the 71st ACP member in April 1997 (European Commission 1999:25).

Regarding negotiations of the proposed FTA, South Africa expressed its concerns since the formerly high protected economy was going under a comprehensive restructuring process after the end of Apartheid. Furthermore, South Africa expressed its concerns with respect to the BLNS countries and the restructuring process of the SACU (Eurostep 2000c:7). The EU assured that these concerns would be addressed and concluded its first offer of an FTA in March 1996. Negotiations proved to be very difficult. One reason was disputes regarding agricultural products, where the EU wanted to protect its market for major South African products and South Africa rejected to grant EU agricultural commodities free market access because of their high subsidy level (Eurostep 2000a:6).[112]

In January 1997, South Africa presented its offer for negotiation towards a FTA to the EU, including the following basic requests (GoSA 1997):

- Improved market access *including* improved access to the agricultural market;
- Asymmetry of FTA in *both*, coverage of goods and time schedule;
- Inclusion of a *strong development component* that acknowledges South Africa's adjustment cost and, to a bigger extent, adjustment costs of the BLNS. This includes particularly the SACU Common Revenue Pool, practical issues, like border control, rules of origin and trade and investment diversion as well as costs arising from the FTA to the sensitive sectors within the SACU, like agriculture and textiles.

[112] The EU proposed a "negative list" excluding 45% of South Africa's agricultural exports to the EU. This list included successful South African export products like apples, pears, oranges, wine and cut flowers. The EU argued that free market access for these products would not comply with the principle of the CAP and affects its agricultural market organisation negatively. However, this excessive protection was not acceptable for South Africa (Eurostep 2000a:6).

- Non-affection of the FTA to tariff concessions′ granted to SADC countries and inclusion of a trade and development framework for SADC.[113]

Since the South African offer included only duty free access for 81% of European products and claimed high protection for its motor vehicle and textile industry, it was not acceptable for the EU, which wanted free market access for 89% of its products. In 1998 the two parties started to make progress since South Africa committed to liberalise its market for 86% and the EU admitted an asymmetrical liberalisation schedule, covering contents and timing in recognition of its more advance economic development and different conditions for market access.[114]

Contents of the "Trade, Development and Co-operation Agreement"

After four nears of negotiations, including 22 rounds of talks, the TDCA was finally signed on 11th October 1999. It came provisionally into force on 01st January, 2000; without waiting for ratification of parliaments of EU member states.[115] The parties agreed on the establishment of a WTO conform FTA. By 2012, 95% of all South African exports will enter the EU market while 86% of all EU exports will enter the South African market duty free after a transitional period of 10 years (see Table 16). In 2010 the EU will have reduced its average tariffs for South African products from 2.7 in 1999 to 1.5%, while South Africa will have decreased its average tariffs for European products from 10 to 4.3% in 2012 (Eurostep 2000b:10). The parties agreed to place sensitive products, including beef and sugar, on a "reserve list". Products on the reserve list are ex-

---

[113] South Africa was concerned that SADC products would face direct competition with European products and that preferential market access granted under the SADC Trade Protocol would be undermined. Therefore, South Africa requested that its offer to SADC countries under the SADC FTA is superior to the one vis-à-vis the EU (Lowe 2000:44).

[114] Nevertheless, the parties still could not conclude a final agreement due to different objectives of the arrangements on wine and spirit and fisheries (Eurostep 2000a:7-8). South Africa rejected to grant European vessels free access to its territory due to their extensive fishing methods and because Europe refused to make other trade concessions (Yedder and Rake 2001:487). Thus, an agreement on fisheries could not be reached. Regarding the arrangement for wine and spirit, the EU claimed that South Africa had to stop labelling its products "port", "grappa" and "sherry" since these are geographical indications, protected by the WTO (Agreement on Trade Related Aspects on Intellectual Property Right (TRIPS), Art. 24.4). Finally, South Africa agreed and obtained a duty free quota of 42 million litres wine p.a. as well as financial assistance of € 15 million for restructuring its wine and spirit sector as concession (European Parliament 2002:18).

[115] This was possible because the TDCA was negotiated for such a long time. The interests of the European Commission were clear and had already been accepted by the European Council and the European Parliament (Eurostep 2000a:2). The TDCA was only ratified by all EU members in March 2004, just before the EU enlargement.

cluded from “substantially all trade” stipulated in Art. XXIV, GATT (1994).[116] However, the reserve list is subject to further liberalisation, which was first negotiated at the mid-term review in 2005.

Table 16: Liberalisation schedule of the TDCA

Duty Free market access for	Cumulative Coverage
South Africa	***In 2010***
Industrial goods	99.98%
Agricultural goods	62% (plus 11.5% partial liberalisation)
EU	***In 2012***
Industrial goods	86% (plus 3% partial liberalisation)
Agricultural goods	81%

Source: Council of the EU 1999, Annex I-V, list 1-8.

As can be obtained from Table 16, the EU is going to grant South African industrial exports almost complete free market access by 2010 but opens its market only for 62% of agricultural commodities coming from South Africa. South Africa, as lesser developed country, opens its agricultural market for 81% of all EU imports, thus, inverting the original idea of asymmetry. Considering furthermore that South African exports account for around 1.4% of the EU’s total imports, while the EU is responsible for more than 30% of South Africa’s total imports, it can be stated that the TDCA is much more challenging for South Africa than for the EU (Europstep 2000a:3).

The EU’s reserve list is large, comprehending 26% of all South African agricultural exports, including beef, sugar, some dairy products (incl. milk, butter, and whey), sweet corn, maize and maize products, rice and rice products, starches, citrus, apples, pears, grapes, bananas, tomatoes, vermouth, ethyl alcohol and fish. However, the EU has offered an additional, partial liberalisation of 11.5% of all agricultural commodities South Africa is exporting to the EU (Council of the EU, Annex IV, list 5-6). For these products, such as cheese, wine, cut flowers, strawberries, canned fruits, and fruit juices, quotas and/or reduced duties were granted.[117]

---

[116] One reason for the exclusion of these products was to avoid the preference erosion for ACP suppliers due to South African competition.

[117] See European Commission (1999:9-10) for a list of the main products and quantities offered for partial liberalisation under the TDCA. A final percentage of 0.5 of all European agricultural products is definitely excluded from the TDCA as these products are protected by geographical indications like port, sherry, parma ham etc.

Though the EU acted protective with respect to trade in agriculture, one has to appreciate that the TDCA was the first FTA where the EU did not exclude its agricultural market *a priori*. Thus, the EU included all agricultural products and EU member states drew up a list with all products they considered as highly sensitive. However, for South Africa the disadvantage was that it had to negotiate individual products with single EU member states, which was extremely time-consuming and difficult (Bertelsmann-Scott *et al.* 2000:27-8). Moreover, South Africa was not able to set through the exclusion of subsidised EU agricultural exports.[118]

In case that imported products cause "serious disturbance to the markets in the other party" or harm one or more members of the SACU, the parties agreed on the application of safeguard measures (Council of the EU 1999, Art. 16 and 24.3). In this case, a dispute settlement mechanism, called the Cooperation Council, shall decide whether protection measures are necessary. South Africa is furthermore allowed to undertake transitional safeguard measures by re-introducing customs duties of max. 20% for a maximum period of four years in case that its infant industries or BLNS infant industries are seriously affected. The BLNS countries can only apply safeguard measures by South Africa but are not part of the Cooperation Council. To date neither South Africa nor the EU has called the Cooperation Council to apply safeguard-measures.

The TDCA covers only trade in goods but the parties agreed to work together in the fields of competition policy (Council of the EU 1999, Art. 35), to liberalise trade in services, and to protect intellectual property according to WTO obligations (Ibid., Art. 29-30 and 46-47). Furthermore, the parties aim to work towards full freedom of capital movements (Ibid., Art. 32-3). All these trade-related provisions of the TDCA are endeavours of the parties without having agreed on obligatory measures how to reach them.

In addition to the trade component, the TDCA has a strong development component that also focuses on the strengthening of the political dialogue, not only on a bilateral but also on a regional level (Ibid., Art. 4, Art. 93). The EU grants South Africa technical assistance in form of grants and loans (Ibid., Art. 51-64 and 93-6). The amount granted under the "European Programme for Reconstruction and Development" (2000-06) covers an amount of € 165 million p.a., focussing on an improved trading environment, private sector development, improvement of social services and local governments, and support for democratisation (European Commission 1999a:14-5). Regional integration, which was an extra field of action of the European Indicative Programme for South Africa in the period 1995-99, is not explicitly covered (ACP General Secretariat 2002b:74-5).

---

[118] The parties only agreed that the EU should work towards *"...an accelerated timetable for ...elimination of all export refunds for (agricultural) exports to South Africa ..."* (Council of the EU 1999, Art. 17).

Motivations to enter into the TDCA

The most important economic motivation for the EU to enter into a FTA with South Africa was to secure a new market and to guarantee a competitive advantage against its main competitors, USA and Japan. Moreover, the EU was interested in a strong and steady South Africa hoping of stabilising, benevolent effects for the whole southern African region (Eurostep 2000a:10).

For South Africa, it was the competitive advantage against other developing countries that made an FTA with the EU attractive. The TDCA was concluded before a new liberalisation round under the WTO could have eroded South Africa's exclusive benefits and South Africa weighted the potential gains from duty free market access to the EU higher than potential losses by increased competition and revenue losses (Eurostep 2000a).[119] This was not only because of the improved market access and the financial dimension of the agreement but also because of the expected dynamic gains of the TDCA. South Africa pursued the strategy to tighten strategic links with its main trading and investment partners in order to increase its international reputation and to benefit from cooperation in the fields of science and technological know-how. The reciprocal character of the agreement and South Africa's success in the protracted negotiation process should strengthen its links to the "developed" world to which it sees itself belonging (van Herden 2003, Bertelsmann-Scott 2000).

Since the EU is the most important trading partner for South Africa, but South Africa accounts only for around 1.5% of EU's trade, adjustment costs, such as industrial restructuring and revenue losses, are much higher for South Africa than for the EU. The example of NAFTA, as discussed in Box 10, shows that there are not only gains from being in an FTA with an industrialised country, especially if the trading partners differ considerably regarding their economic development level.

---

[119] Several *ex ante* studies were concluded to estimate the static gains and losses of the TDCA for South Africa (see e.g. IDS 1997, Jachia and Teljeur 1999, Akinkugbe 2000). Though all studies are based on partial or general equilibrium models, which are generally used to analyse the quantitative effects of trade barrier removals, the outcome of the studies differed considerably. Thus, the IDS study, which generated seven scenarios, summarised that the TDCA will affect the level and composition of EU-South Africa trade only very limited, while Jachia and Teljeur (1999) and Akinkugbe (2000) supposed negative impacts on South Africa's trade balance. According to Bilal and Laporte (2004:20) the relevance of these impact studies is generally overestimated since they *"...rely heavily on crude assumptions about the state of an economy and possible negotiations scenarios."* while in 'real life' *"...negotiations are driven primarily by political decisions..."*

Box 10: Effects of regional integration in the case of NAFTA

The North American Free Trade Agreement (NAFTA), comprising the USA, Canada and Mexico, entered into force in 1994 liberalising trade and investment until 2009. The USA is the economic giant of NAFTA, accounting for 88.4% of its combined GDP in 2001 (Canada: 6.2%, Mexico: 5.4%) (Truman 2001:1). Since the USA and Canada have already signed an FTA in 1989, the NAFTA implies above all challenges for Mexico which had to reduce its tariffs and non-tariff barriers to trade significantly. NAFTA is not a conventional FTA but also comprises the liberalisation of investment, the non-discrimination of government procurement, and the international protection of intellectual property rights (WTO 1997).

Furthermore, NAFTA has established common regulations with respect to labour law and environmental standards in order to reduce the expected dislocation of industries from the USA and Canada to Mexico. Despite the economic and political dominance of the USA, US-interest groups were seriously concerned about job losses, which had resulted in the inclusion of labour and environmental regulations as well as the introduction of strict rules of origin into the NAFTA agreement. Labour unions and environmental groups in the USA still argue that the NAFTA is eliminating jobs, mainly in the manufacturing industry, and that the agreement has weakened collective bargaining power (Scott 2002). However, the net job effects of NAFTA were expected to be positive, with around 170,000 jobs more created than destroyed (Schott and Hufbauer as cited in Schäfer 1999:5).

With the establishment of NAFTA, most of all the Mexican economy faced increased competition. While Mexico's manufacturing sector benefited from increased investment inflows, the importing competing sector had problems to adapt to a liberalising environment. Still, NAFTA has become the cornerstone of Mexico's trade and investment policy, which is also reflected by its biased trade flows with the USA, accounting for around 80% of total trade (WTO 1997). The increase of intra-regional trade as a result of NAFTA has even increased Mexico's dependency on the US-market (Schäfer 1999). Mexico has not only benefited from NAFTA because of increased exports but was also able to improve its total factor productivity due to technological spillovers through sub-contracting and direct contact and information with its northern trading partners (Schiff and Wang 2003). The USA and Canada again improved their conditions to supply Mexico with high-tech goods and with financial services. Most of all the USA wanted to improve its position as export and investment hub in the region and aimed to establish a counterweight to regional integration in East Asia (Schäfer 1999:2)

Continuation on next page.

Continuation of Box 10 from previous page.

However, NAFTA is not fully comparable with the EU-South Africa FTA though both agreements are North-South FTAs that have established an asymmetrical liberalisation schedule. However, the TDCA liberalises only trade in goods but not trade in services and investment. What is even more important is that South Africa's trade and investment relations with the EU differ considerably from the ones Mexico has with the USA. Thus, the EU accounts for around 35% of South Africa's trade while the USA accounts for around 80% of Mexico's trade. Since Mexico is a neighbour of the USA, it is moreover recipient of outsourcing activities due to lower labour costs, more generous labour laws and more relaxed environmental legislations. Similar, European firms promote outsourcing activities in neighbouring eastern European countries but not in South Africa, which confirms the thesis that the distance to consumer markets is an important factor in explaining international trade and investment relations (Krugman 1991, Balassa 1965b). In fact, South Africa needs additional competitive advantages that outweigh its far distance from the EU in order to attract EU investment.[120]

Development of South Africa's trade and investment ties with the EU

Though the EU is by far the largest investor in South Africa (mainly the UK), accounting for almost 90% of total FDI into South Africa in 2000 (WTO 2003:A4-224), it does not seem that FDI has increased as a result of the TDCA. Only in 2001, FDI inflows into South Africa were exceptionally high (see Table 17).

Table 17: FDI in South Africa (in million US$)

	1980	1990	1995	1998	1999	2000	2001	2002	2003
Inflows	-10	-78	1241	561	1502	888	6789	757	762
Outflows	755	27	2498	1779	1580	271	-31780	-399	720
Net inflows	-765	-105	-1257	-1218	-78	617	38569	1156	42

Source: UNCTAD (2004b:276-7).

The sectors that are recipients of FDI in South Africa are finance, insurance and business services (39.3% of total FDI inflows in 2000), mining and quarrying (27.8%) and manufacturing (26.4%) (WTO 2003:A4-224). Thus, FDI inflows have been relatively diversified in terms of sectoral distribution, with more than

[120] This is also confirmed by the empirical analysis in Chapter 5.1 which discusses the determinants of EU investment in the South African automotive industry.

65% of total FDI inflows in non-mining activities. Taking into account that South Africa has large natural resources, this suggests that the South African market is also attractive for other reasons, such as access to the wider region.

Trade between the EU and South Africa has increased considerably since 2000. However, there are considerable differences between the data of Eurostat and the South African Department of Trade and Industry (DTI), accounting for € 5 billion in 2002 (DTI 2004a:16). As can be obtained from the Figures 12 and 13, these differences are large enough to change South Africa's overall trade balance vis-à-vis the EU. While DTI data indicated a trade deficit of around R 28 billion in 2003, Eurostat data showed a trade surplus in favour of South Africa of around € 2.3 billion in 2003 (DTI 2004a:106).

Figure 12: South Africa's trade with the EU in million ZAR (DTI data)

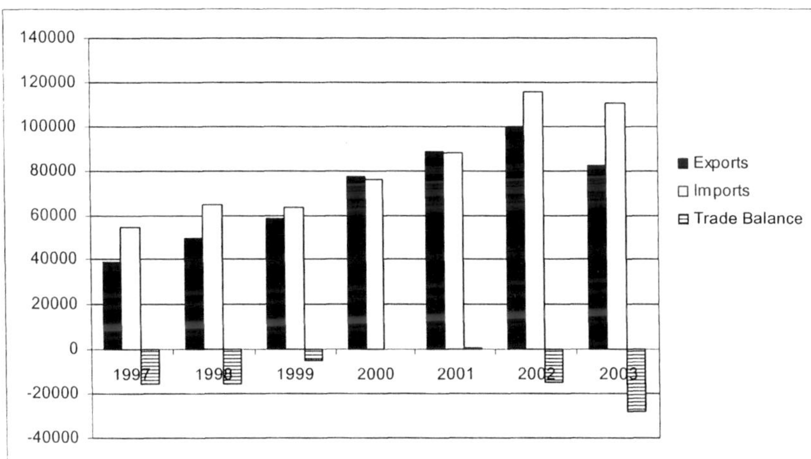

Source: DTI (2004a:9).

Figure 13: South Africa's trade with the EU in million € (Eurostat data)

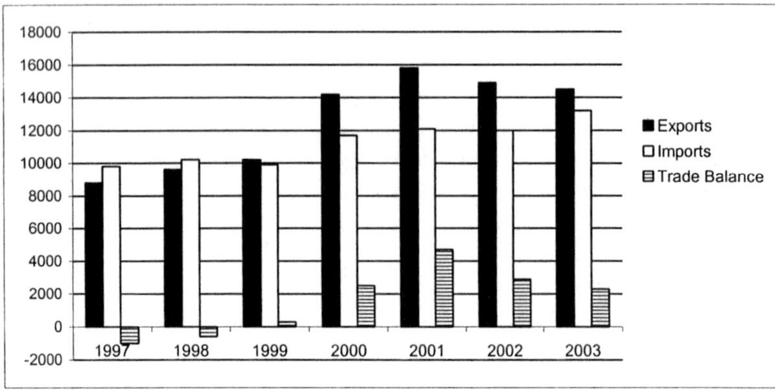

Source: Eurostat data as cited in DTI (2004a:26).

The reasons for these huge differences between EU and South African statistics can be explained as follows:

a. The total difference is reduced substantially when comparing *net* instead of *gross* differences so that different classifications at EU borders and the South African border are a possible explanation (DTI 2004:18).[121]
b. It is assumed that DTI's export values do not report the total value of South African exports to the EU. The largest gap between Eurostat and DTI occurs in the section "special classification" (mainly gold) and "vehicles". These products are often declared as final destinations of a global trading company that is not located in the EU. If for instance Toyota spare parts are shipped to their final destination in the EU they are still declared as exports to Japan (DTI 2004:21-2).[122]

It can therefore be assumed that the Eurostat data does rather reflect the flows of EU-South African trade. However, the DTI (2004:25) emphasises that the whole gap between Eurostat and DTI statistics cannot be explained completely and needs a deeper analysis for final clarification.

---

[121] Gross trade flows are defined as the sum of absolute values of 2-digit level trade, while net trade flows are the algebraic sum of 2-digit level trade. The different classifications relate mainly to mechanical goods and appliances, vehicles and special classification, which could be related to the special incentives of the MIDP (DTI 2004a:18).

[122] Another reasons that could have contributed to the trade differences is the mixture of fob and c.i.f. data in trade statistics. However, it does not become clear from the DTI report which data was used by DTI and Eurostat.

Within the EU, South Africa's trade is biased towards few countries, mainly Germany and UK, accounting for more than 65% of South Africa's imports and 57% of its exports to the EU in 2003 (DTI 2004b). South Africa's trading pattern with the EU has changed to some extent since 1994. Though South Africa's main export products were the same in 2003 than in 1994, namely pearls, precious stones and mineral fuels, which accounted for around 30% of total exports to the EU in 2003, there is trend towards more diversified exports. Further important export products to the EU are machinery and mechanical appliances (accounting for 11.4% of total exports to the EU in 2003), iron and steel (9.9%) vehicles (7.5%) and fruits and nuts (5.1%).[123] The highest growth rates in the period 1994-99 were obtained by the export of vehicles (146%), pearls and semi-precious stones (70%), and machinery and mechanical appliances (62%). Key imports from the EU are machinery and mechanical appliances (21% of total imports from the EU in 2003), electrical machinery and equipment (11%) and vehicles (11%) (DTI 2004a:33-8).

These figures show that EU-South Africa trade is, contrary to EU-BLNS trade, characterised by a certain level of intra-industrial trade, mainly in the field of electrical and non-electric machinery, vehicles and parts thereof. Intra-industrial trade (trade within one industry) reflects the relative significance of scale effects in production processes and is therefore more valuable than inter-industrial trade (trade between industries). Intra-industrial trade implies that industries stand in direct competition and that specialisation within production groups and exchange of differentiated products occur.[124] As discussed, that is the more the case the more the trading partners equal each other with respect to their industrial development.

Impact on the BLNS countries and the wider regional dimension of the TDCA

In 1995, the EU stated that the TDCA will have *"...a clear focus on the promotion of regional co-operation and integration."* and will *"...adopt policies aimed at promoting close economic co-operation in the Southern African region..."*[125] In 1996 the EU pointed out its commitment to encourage regional integration in Southern Africa again. It was confirmed that the Trade and Co-operation Agreement with South Africa should neither impede the restructuring process of the SACU nor negatively affect provisions with other preferential partners. Moreover, the negotiation mandate suggested rules of origin that in-

[123] The EU absorbs around 80% of South Africa's fresh fruit exports (DTI 2004:47).

[124] Viner (1950:51) characterised competitiveness or rivalry between countries as *"...correspondence in kind of products of the range of high costs industries between the different parts of the customs union..."*

[125] Permanent Representatives Committee of the EU Council, 14 June 1995 as cited in Eurostep (2000c:6).

clude cumulation procedures covering the use products originated from the EU, South Africa and the ACP countries.[126]

In fact, the parties took regional concerns into account when negotiating the TDCA. Thus, both, the EU and South Africa did not only protect products that are sensitive in the domestic market but also in ACP countries and SADC countries respectively, such as beef, sugar and textiles. The EU emphasised that *"In line with our general policy, which is to actively encourage economic integration at regional level, we wanted to ensure that we would not gain a better access to the South African market than the SADC countries. Concepts such as 'SADC first' or SADC preference have underpinned the negotiations..."* (Lowe 2000:44).[127] However, though South Africa's offer towards SADC was superior to its offer towards the EU, *"...the preferential market offer can only be accessed ...for a limited number of products within the three to five years. These concessions are small considering the development gap..."* (Pallangyo 2000:81). Furthermore, the SADC countries accused South Africa to protect itself from competitive SADC imports since South Africa excluded more or less the same products from the SADC FTA than from the TDCA, though *"It is highly unlikely that imports originating from SADC could pose as much threat to South Africa's industry as EU imports would."* (Pallangyo 2000:79).

Another dispute was the rules of origin. The EU envisaged to take the "regional dimension" of the TDCA into account when formulating the rules of origin. Between South Africa and the BLNS countries the so-called "full cumulation of origin" was envisaged, i.e. any value added in BLNS should have been added to the value added in South Africa and jointly the countries would meet the origin specification. The provision of full cumulation is potentially very important for the BLNS countries, as it allows them to diversify their export base by sourcing inputs from South Africa while keeping their preferential market access to the EU. However, also six years after the TDCA has entered into force South Africa has not been able to put in place the necessary customs arrangements to allow for the provision of full cumulation (see Box 11). Thus, inputs from South Africa used in the production of BLNS exports destined for the EU market are not yet allowed to enter the EU under the duty-free access provision.[128]

To link South Africa closer to the ACP countries, especially to the SADC economies, the TDCA also includes the provision of "diagonal cumulation", i.e.

[126] Permanent Representatives Committee of the EU Council, 21 March 1996 as cited in Eurostep (2000c:7).

[127] In 2000, Philip Lowe was the Director-General for Development at the European Commission.

[128] An exception has been made by the creation of a "value-tolerance rule", which allows up to 15% of the value of the final product to be originated from another country than South Africa (Council of the EU 1999, Protocol 1).

ACP products shall be considered as South African originated if they have undergone a certain working or processing process in South Africa. The goal is to promote intra-African trade by allowing SADC countries to source inputs from South Africa and to export under the Cotonou Agreement. However, to let this provision enter into force, South Africa must conclude administrative cooperation agreements with SADC countries, guaranteeing that the rules of origin are effectively supervised. This again is not feasible due to lack administrative capacities in the SADC countries. Thus, the terms of diagonal cumulation, which was regarded as incentive for the promotion of an effective intra-regional trading system, is more or less useless. The EU recognises the problem but states *"...the use of South African inputs ... was not a subject to be dealt with under the agreement with South Africa; it belongs to Lomé."* (Lowe 1999:44). However, SADC countries' problem to warrant the origin of products remains so that it is also questionable how effective cumulation provision for rules of origin could be applied under the Cotonou Agreement.

Increased competition and non-application of direct safeguard measures

The chief negotiators from the EU and the South African side agreed that BLNS concerns, such as the protection of infant industries and the exclusion of products, were sufficiently taken into account and that the positive effects of the TDCA, such as consumer benefits and competitive inputs, would outweighed possible negative effects (European Commission 1999a:33). The BLNS countries did not share this positive view and claimed that they suffer from revenue losses and increased competition without receiving anything in return. Moreover, the cost advantages of the TDCA would not be passed on to them but collected by South African transport agents and retailers.[129]

Though products that are of relevance for the BLNS are either excluded or only partially liberalised under the TDCA,[130] associated value added products, such as processed meat products, flour based products, canned fruits, jam and sugar based products (e.g. chocolate and biscuits) are not excluded from the TDCA. Thus, the inclusion of agro-processed commodities to the TDCA, which

[129] Taking into account that the South African economy has a high concentration degree (Kaplinsky *et al.* 2002:1169-72) and that South African retail stores and transport agents dominate the BLNS economies (Games 2003:34), it is indeed likely that consumers and producers in BLNS benefit only deficiently from cheaper EU imports. For Namibia, the options to benefit accordingly would increase if more goods were imported via the port of Walvis Bay, which is planned in the near future. The landlocked SACU countries can only benefit from cheaper EU imports once increased competition in the SACU market forces South African companies to pass on price advantages of cheaper imports.

[130] Such as beef, preserved meat products, sugar and high sugar content products, cereals and fish (all excluded), fresh fruits, prepared and canned fruits and fruit juices (all reduced tariffs and quotas) (European Commission 1999a:9-10).

are strongly associated to the BLNS countries' main agricultural products and are also beneficiaries of high subsidies in the EU, are likely to have an indirect detrimental effect on the BLNS economies. Taking sugar containing products such as chocolate and biscuits as example: although these products are not produced by Swaziland but by South Africa,[131] increased competition in the South African market is likely to harm Swaziland, too, since it results in a decreased purchase of Swazi sugar by South African manufacturers (Stock 2003). Since Swaziland exports more than 55% of its sugar into the (protected) SACU sugar market (Mahlinza 2003), it would face substantial income losses, when selling its SACU exports to the world market.

Furthermore, there are some products where South Africa is going to receive the same or an even more beneficial market access under the TDCA than the BLNS under Cotonou. This is e.g. the case for grapes, lamb meat, sausages and textiles and garments (see Table 18).

Table 18: BLNS and South Africa's market access to the EU for selected products

Product	Market access for BLNS	Market access for South Africa	Relevant for
Fresh, chilled, frozen de-boned meat	Quota, 92% tariff preference	MFN duty, excluded from the TDCA	Namibia, Botswana, Swaziland
Sugar	Fixed quantity and price	MFN duty, excluded from the TDCA	Swaziland
Grapes	Quota of 900 tons p.a. and only seasonal market access.	Free market access by 2010.	Namibia
Textiles and garments	Duty free market access if precondition of double transformation is fulfilled.	Free market access by 2003/2006 (depending on product). Double transformation is prerequisite.	All BLNS countries
Lamb	Quota of 600,000 tons p.a. (until 2000)	Quota of 600,000 tons applies now for southern Africa and has to be shared between BLNS and South Africa.	Namibia
Confectionery	12.9% plus a supplementary sugar duty	MFN duty, excluded from the TDCA	Swaziland

131 Cadbury Swaziland produces only high sugar content products (chewing gum and candies) that are excluded from the TDCA (Stock 2003).

Product	Market access for BLNS	Market access for South Africa	Relevant for
Sausages	65% reduction of MFN duty for a quota of 500 tons p.a.	Free market access by 2003. For other processed meat products: free market access by 2010.	Namibia, Botswana, Swaziland
Fresh and frozen fish	Free market access. All materials used must be wholly obtained. Limited cumulation options with South Africa.	15% tariff. Tariff concessions will only take effect once a fisheries agreement has been concluded.	Namibia
Canned tuna and tuna loins	Annual quota of 8,000 and 2,000 tons respectively.	Tariff concessions will only take effect once a fisheries agreement has been concluded.	Namibia

Source: European Commission (2000), Council of the EU (1999).

In sum, it can be stated that the TDCA implies increased competition for relevant agro-based BLNS products in both markets, the EU and the SACU. Additionally, BLNS countries' market access has, in contradiction South Africa's, not improved (since they continue to export under the Cotonou Agreement). The BLNS countries were also not able to increase their exports to the EU by sourcing South African inputs since the provision of full cumulation has not been implemented. Furthermore, BLNS countries are not able to apply for safeguard measures on their own but only via South Africa. Considering the negative effects (subsidised) EU imports can have on the small production bases of the BLNS, it can be stated that their ability of industrial protection is seriously affected by the TDCA.[132]

Revenue losses and re-structuring of industries

The elimination of customs duties on EU imports accounting for around 40% of SACU imports in addition to the re-structuring of the CRP under the new SACU Agreement affects BLNS revenues negatively. The revenue losses occurring from the TDCA affect the BLNS countries not to the same degree as Table 19 shows.

[132] On the other hand, BLNS might benefit from increased economic activities in South Africa resulting from expanded EU-South African trade. However, a quantification of these effects is due to the dynamics, non-distinction of origin and different motivations of economic activities not possible.

Lesotho and Swaziland lose up to 20% of their total revenue from the CRP due to the EU-South Africa FTA, Namibia around 11% and Botswana around 7%, depending on the total fall of revenue from the CRP.[133]

Table 19: BLNS dependence on SACU revenue and fall in total revenue due to the TDCA

	SACU revenue as % of total revenue	**Fall in total revenue if SACU revenue pool falls 31%**	**Fall in total revenue if SACU revenue pool falls 51%**
Botswana	17.1%	-5.3%	-8.7%
Lesotho	41.7%	-12.9%	-21.3%
Namibia	27.6%	-8.6%	-14.1%
Swaziland	44.8%	-13.9%	-22.8%

Source: BIDPA/IDS 1999:45.

Considering that the BLNS countries also lose tariff revenues because of the new SACU revenue formula, which does no longer guarantee a level of 17-23% of total revenue and takes the excise component stronger into account (see Chapter 2), BLNS countries face serious challenges to restructure their income sources. This is above all the case for Lesotho, Swaziland and Namibia whose incomes are still strongly centred on receipts from the CRP (see Table 20).

---

[133] See BIDPA/IDS (1999) for a detailed study on the economic impact of the EU-South Africa FTA on the BLNS countries and recommendations for fiscal reforms and economic restructuring processes. The effects were estimated by an analysis of tariff and trade data, a general equilibrium model and a commodity flow model. Furthermore, some interviews with big companies in the BLNS countries were compiled. The study concludes that the import competition effects of the TDCA will be rather small but that the loss of customs revenue will be a serious concern for BLNS, mainly Lesotho, Swaziland and Namibia. It is recommended to assist the BLNS countries with their public sector management, the strengthening of tax collection, and the privatisation of enterprises. Furthermore, the study recommends to investigate the impact of the TDCA on BLNS companies more detailed and to provide necessary assistance for restructuring processes.

Table 20: Source of state revenue in the SACU economies (in % of total revenues) in 2001

	SACU receipts 2000/2001	Non-SACU receipts	Domestic taxes on goods and services	Taxes on income, profit and capital gains	Aid, external grants and loans	Non-tax revenue	Other taxes
South Africa	55	n.a.	n.a.	n.a.	6.1	n.a.	n.a.
Botswana	13	67 *	n.a.	n.a.	n.a.	n.a.	n.a.
Lesotho	51.6	n.a.	n.a.	n.a.	n.a.	n.a.	n.a.
Namibia	28.4	n.a.	27	22	14	8	1
Swaziland	51	11.4	n.a.	n.a.	n.a.	1.3	1.5

n.a. = no data available.

* Mineral revenues, mainly from diamonds.

Sources: WTO 2003:7 (SACU receipts), European Commission 2002b:10 and WTO 2003:A1-89 (Botswana), BoN and Central Statistics as cited in Hansohm *et al.* 2002:60 (Namibia), Ministry of Finance and IMF projections as cited in Nowak and Ebrill 2003:27 (Swaziland).

To assist the BLNS countries to cope with the challenges of the TDCA, the EU agreed to grant technical assistance. The "Economic Integration Programme to the BLNS – Phase I", which contained a total funding of € 6 million, was designed to help the BLNS countries to conclude impact studies, to improve border efficiency procedures[134] and to support fiscal and public sector reforms (such as the introduction of VAT). Moreover, the programme should have assisted BLNS companies to increase their capacities, to improve their competitiveness, and to move their sanitary standards and licensing procedures in accordance to WTO rules (European Commission 2002b). However, the original envisaged programme had never started. The money was only released in 2005 after an almost five-year dispute regarding the "concurrence" of all BLNS countries to the TDCA (see Box 11).

[134] The EU estimates that revenue losses up to 5% of GDP could be avoided by improving the efficiency of border procedures (EU, DG Trade 2005a).

Box 11: Technical assistance under the TDCA and the problem of concurrence

In addition to the provision of technical assistance to South Africa in form of training, experts and loans, the TDCA also provides technical assistance for the BLNS countries (Council of the EU 1999, Art. 93). However, the original envisaged programme had never started since the EU argued that technical assistance as well as the provision of full cumulation could only be implemented once all BLNS countries have concurred to the TDCA, which Namibia refused to do. Namibia argued that certain issues of the TDCA that affect the BLNS countries negatively should be re-negotiated (Murangi 2003). Since the EU refused this request, it was only Botswana, Lesotho and Swaziland that concurred to the TDCA.

However, it still remains unclear what countries' "concurrence" means. The EU argued that it only implies BLNS governments' official recognition of the TDCA (Robberts 2003) However, this implies that customs arrangements cannot be facilitated since BLNS are still not part of the TDCA but have a different trade regime with the EU. If, on the other hand, the second step of BLNS countries' "concurrence" would be their official recognition of not being in a position to assess indirect EU imports, it implies BLNS countries' unilateral acceptance of the TDCA liberalisation schedule. This again would infringes upon the WTO most-favourite nation clause, as the BLNS countries would discriminate in favour of the EU without being addressor of an according FTA.[135] As a result there would be the risk that any other WTO member requested the same access to BLNS countries' markets as granted to the EU. It remains therefore doubtful that the provision of full cumulation can be implemented before the BLNS countries have their own reciprocal agreement with the EU that follows the liberalisation schedule of the TDCA.

Despite the problematic of (non-)concurrence, the EU decided in early 2004 to grant technical assistance to BLNS since the money of the 09th European Development Fund (Regional Indicative Programme) had to be released. Officially it was argued that the ratification of the new SACU Agreement would mean that all BLNS countries have accepted any trade agreement South Africa is involved in (Robberts 2003).

Continuation on next page.

[135] Botswana has acknowledged its inability to supervise indirect EU imports and has unilaterally implemented the TDCA liberalisation schedule. With this action the country infringes against both, the new SACU Agreement and the WTO Agreement. The other SACU members were only informed once Botswana has already adopted the TDCA liberalisation schedule (Otto 2003).

Continuation of Box 11 from previous page.

However, also this perception is disputed.[136] The EU did further agree to review the "Economic Integration Programme to the BLNS" and to extend its validity until 2008. Though the original objectives of the programme, namely the management of the fiscal implications of the TDCA and the restructuring of industries to cope with increased competition, should be still pertinent, the EU wants to enlarge the programme with a view to strengthening the SACU Secretariat (Tralac news, 14/01/05)

This decision provides for criticism, as formulated by an interview partner in Botswana: "*Why is the money now used to build-up the Secretariat? The Secretariat would have been established anyway! What has it to do with the TDCA?*" Still, the EU support can help to improve the management and negotiation capabilities of the SACU Secretariat, e.g. regarding the management of single development programmes in the region or with respect to competences in the field of trade negotiations (see Chapter 6). A supplement regional programme component does therefore deem to make sense. However, the focus of the programme should still be its original objectives, which still have the highest priority for the BLNS.

In addition to the problems and difficulties arising for the BLNS countries, the TDCA also has a considerable impact on the wider region and complicates both, regional integration in southern Africa and future EU-southern Africa trade relations, as the discussion in the next section shows.

3.6 The EU's Approach of "Economic Partnership Agreements" (EPAs) and its Implications for Regional Integration in Southern Africa

The Cotonou Agreement foresees the creation of reciprocal WTO compatible FTAs between the EU and regional groupings of ACP countries by 2008 (European Commission 2000b, Art. 36, 37). These so-called "Economic Partnership Agreements" (EPAs) are supposed to be asymmetrical in both, period and content, taking into account the enormous economic imbalance between the EU and

[136] The old SACU Agreement (Republic of South Africa 1969, Art. 4) allowed its members only to enter separately into trade agreements with *prior* concurrence of all members. The new SACU Agreement (2002, Art. 31) stipulates that member states are allowed to maintain existing trade arrangements with third parties but shall negotiate new agreements only with affirmation of all member countries. Thus, the new Agreement says nothing about an "automatic concurrence" of other member states to existing bilateral trade agreements but only that existing trade agreements remain valid.

the ACP countries. However, as EPAs have to be WTO compatible, they will include around 90% of total trade and allow a time frame of 10 years for liberalisation (according to the interpretation of Art. XXIV, GATT). Thus, there is only limited scope for asymmetry and ACP countries have to cope with inherent challenges, such as loss of revenue and increased competition.[137]

Though the BLNS countries are affected by the EU-South Africa FTA, they are not part of the agreement and export to the EU under the Cotonou Agreement. They must therefore, like all ACP countries, enter into an EPA with the EU. The easiest option would have been to become an official member of the TDCA. However, since the TDCA does not include any provision for the accession of BLNS countries, this would need to be jointly agreed by the EU and South Africa (European Research Office 2003). Though the EU signalled acceptance of this idea, the South African government was reluctant to open the agreement with the EU again since it feared pressure for further liberalisation of sensitive sectors, such as the automotive industry (Goodison 2004). Thus, the BLNS countries decided to negotiate an EPA with the EU in a SADC framework, which includes the BLNS countries, and the least developed countries (LDCs) Angola, Mozambique, and Tanzania.[138] South Africa has the status of an observer.

The remaining five SADC countries (DR Congo, Malawi, Mauritius, Zambia, and Zimbabwe) opted for an EPA in an "Eastern and Southern Africa" (ESA) framework, which contains most member countries of COMESA to which seven of the 14 SADC member states belong.[139] To avoid being forced to open their markets according to the EU-South Africa FTA liberalisation schedule was a major motivation for the non-LDCs Mauritius and Zimbabwe to enter into an ESA and not into a SADC EPA with the BLNS countries (Goodison 2004).

From a theoretical point of view, a South-South integration framework must have reached at least the level of a CU to allow the countries to enter commonly into a North-South FTA. Only if the countries that form an EPA have established a common external tariff and have thus harmonised their external trade relations, they are able to form a common position for trade in goods vis-à-

[137] This is not the case for trade in services. The GATS Agreement foresees for the provision of special and differential treatment (South Centre 2005:i).

[138] As discussed, the LDCs can maintain their non-reciprocal trade relations with the EU under the expanded GSP ("Everything But Arms" initiative). However, because of their contractual character, EPAs seem to be more attractive for southern African LDCs: Angola, DRC, Madagascar, Malawi, Tanzania, and Zambia opted to enter into a reciprocal FTA with the EU and hope to create a more certain trade environment.

[139] Namely Angola, DR Congo, Malawi, Madagascar, Mauritius, Zambia, Zimbabwe. With exception of Angola, DR Congo, and Swaziland these SADC countries are also members of the COMESA FTA.

vis the EU. Members of an FTA, where each country has its own external trade policy, could only negotiate as a trading block if they accept a common external tariff towards the EU, which would be however difficult to coordinate.

To date, the members of the SADC EPA are not capable of negotiating an EPA collectively, as they lack the mandate and have not agreed on common positions. Furthermore, the low level of trade integration, the divergent economic interests and the missing convergence in tariff levels as well as the perpetuation of "special and differential" treatment for LDCs complicate the formulation of a common negotiation position (Khandelwal 2004, Trades Centre 2003:43).[140]

However, if the SADC EPA differs significantly from the ESA EPA it will further complicate intra-SADC trade relations considerably, dividing the SADC countries in at least three blocks:

1) South Africa and the BLNS countries that are locked into the liberalisation schedule of the EU-South Africa FTA and have thus liberalised their markets towards the EU by 2012;
2) The rest SADC EPA countries, namely Angola, Mozambique and Tanzania, that are all LDCs and thus potentially able to retain their non-reciprocal trade relations with the EU under the EBA initiative; and
3) The remaining SADC countries (DR Congo, Madagascar, Malawi, Mauritius, Zambia and Zimbabwe) that are entering into the ESA EPA.

As illustrated in Figure 14, EPA negotiations do not, as originally envisaged by the EU, reduce southern African countries' overlapping memberships but further complicate regional integration in southern Africa, resulting in contradictory decisions that are rather motivated by political considerations than economically driven (Meyn 2004a).[141]

---

[140] Particularly for agricultural products, the high deviation of economic development within southern Africa that results in very different economic interests is problematic. Food net importing countries would for instance appreciate the import of certain (subsidised) agricultural products, as they do not have an accordant industry and hope to reap consumer benefits as well as to promote the production of locally processed value added products. The same commodities are, however, sensitive in other countries that seek to protect their agricultural sector and agro-processing industries against European competition. As neither the exclusion of single sectors nor the creation of extremely long exclusion lists would be WTO compatible, it is very difficult for the countries to find a compromise (Trades Centre 2003).

[141] Taking for example Tanzania that is bound in a CU with Kenya and Uganda, both countries, which opted for the ESA EPA configuration. Tanzania's decision to leave COMESA and to go for a SADC EPA configuration is not feasible, giving a proper implementation of the Eastern African Community (EAC) CU. However, the country wants to keep its strategic ties with South Africa. The EU has called-upon Tanzania to choose between SADC and the EAC (The East African, 16/05/05). Considering the depth of economic integration, Tanzania's interest lies in the EAC, which accounts for the bulk of Tanzania's intra-African trade (Sitta 2005). To make its regionalisation strategy coherent, Tanzania could either leave the SADC EPA and join the ESA EPA or negotiate together with Kenya and Uganda an

Figure 14: The impact of EU trade policy on regional integration in southern Africa

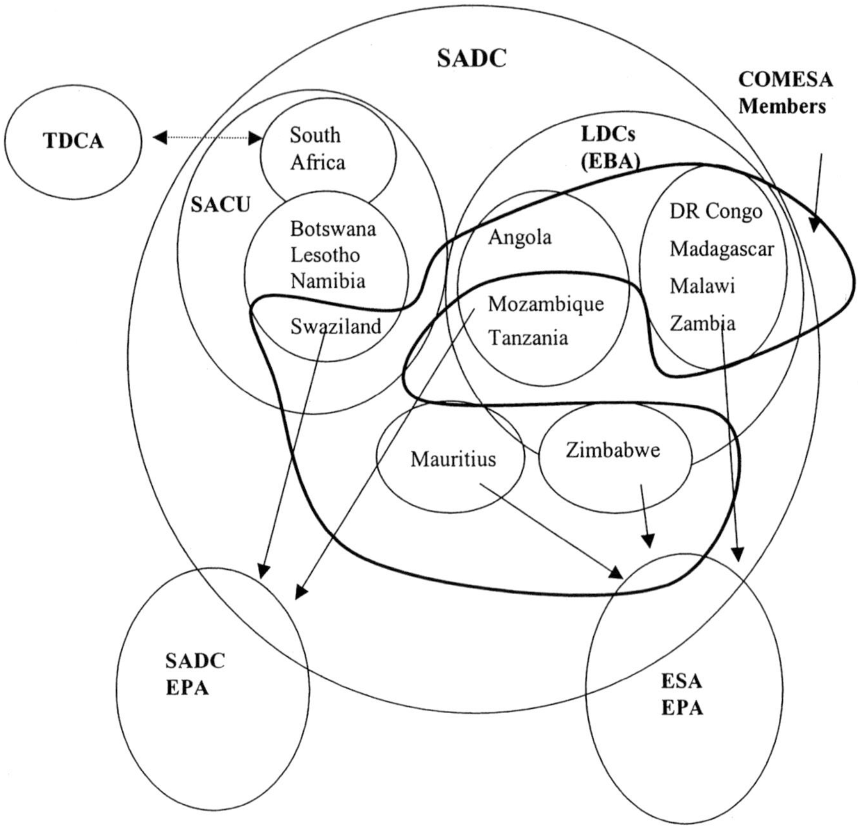

Source: Author's presentation as cited in the text.

In the (very likely) case that the SADC EPA agrees on different tariffs for EU imports than the ESA EPA, the inspection of origins of EU imports will not only be an enormous administrative burden but also hardly feasible, taking the imper-

EAC EPA (which would of course imply that Kenya and Uganda had to leave the ESA EPA). Another option would be that Tanzania opts out of EPA negotiations and goes for the maintenance of non-reciprocal trade under the EBA initiative (an option that all ACP LDCs can choose). However, considering the fact that Tanzania is locked into a CU with the non-LDC Kenya this scenario is rather unrealistic, as it would take away Tanzania's options to negotiate and influence the EPA (by which it is affected anyway) according to his interest.

fect supervision of rules of origin in southern Africa into account. The perpetuation of non-reciprocal trade relations between the EU and southern African LDCs is therefore only a theoretical but not a workable alternative. From an economic point of view, it would therefore be best if the countries of the SADC EPA and the ESA EPA agreed on a CET towards the EU. This could avoid smuggling, trade diversion and economic polarisation and promote intra-regional trade and regional integration in southern Africa. However, such a joint approach does not seem to be realistic, taking southern African countries' different economic interests in the region, their limited commitment to regional integration and the disparity of SADC countries' trade relations with the EU into account. Furthermore, the economic powers of SADC and COMESA, South Africa and Egypt, focus more on trade with industrialised countries than with the region and are not ready to compromise on their CET. Both have a bilateral FTA with their main trading partner, the EU, so that their CET is to a certain extent "locked in".

In fact, it would make sense if Angola and Swaziland drop out of COMESA and DR Congo, Malawi, Mauritius, Zambia and Zimbabwe drop either out of SADC (in case of joining the ESA EPA) or out of COMESA (in case of joining the SADC EPA). Like this, overlapping membership would be reduced and North-South and South-South integration would take place in the same regional bodies.[142] However, to date economic and political interests have not permitted the reduction of infringing regional memberships. On the contrary, countries have even increased the confusion of "regional spaghetti" as the new membership of the COMESA/ESA member Madagascar in SADC or the membership of EAC member Tanzania in the SADC EPA shows. Since the countries of the SADC EPA and the ESA EPA are still allowed to switch their EPA configuration, it remains to be seen how the issue of overlapping membership will be addressed by EPAs. However, the time frame for changing the EPA configuration is limited. Once EPAs have been concluded and a common external tariff (CET) vis-à-vis the EU has been established, southern African countries are also locked-in a certain African integration framework - given that the CET of the ESA EPA and the SADC EPA differs. Southern African countries are therefore well-advised to evaluate their long-term trade and investment interests in the region carefully before finally deciding for one EPA configuration.

Whether BLNS countries' decision for a SADC EPA makes sense remains doubtful, too. First of all, it remains problematic how to deal with the LDCs Angola, Mozambique and Tanzania within the SADC EPA since they are, with exception of Mozambique, hardly economically integrated into the SACU region (Meyn 2004a). Secondly, and that is the most critical point, South Africa is not

---

[142] However, the problem of insufficient economic integration in these frameworks and a missing negotiation body would remain – at least in the short- to medium run.

included in the EPA negotiations. How can the BLNS countries as part of SACU negotiate without South Africa? According to Art. 31 of the new Agreement, the countries have to enter into trade relations with "one voice". South Africa's observer status does hardly help: once the SADC EPA differs from the TDCA and is not in the interest of South Africa (e.g. because it includes trade-related aspects as envisaged by the EU), South Africa can block the SADC EPA by not giving its concurrence. Considering moreover the fact that the new SACU Agreement moves towards deeper integration and that the EU always formulated the promotion of South-South integration as major development goal, it can be stated that the current configuration of a SADC EPA does not make sense. South Africa's inclusion into any trade agreement the BLNS countries are involved in is a prerequisite for making SACU's regional integration and external trade relations consistent. Furthermore, the inclusion of South Africa into EPA negotiations could help to reduce the power bias the BLNS countries face when negotiating with the EU.

3.7 What Should an "Optimal" EPA for Southern African Countries Look Like?

Though the EU offered to "*examine all alternative possible in order to provide (non-LDC ACP) countries with a new framework for trade which is equivalent to their existing situation and in conformity with WTO rules*" (European Commission 2000b, Art. 37.6), such a proposal did not exist at the time of writing. In early 2006, it was still unknown how an alternative agreement could look like. In fact, alternatives are difficult to imagine. The inclusion of non-LDC ACP countries into the GSP would imply a significant erosion of preferences since other developing countries enjoy the same market access. Moreover, the GSP is a non-contractual agreement, currently valid until 2008. Any agreement that treats ACP countries better than other developing countries again would infringe with WTO provisions if no FTA exists. Under current WTO conditions it must be therefore regarded as doubtful that "alternatives" exist. The following section does therefore assume that EPAs are the only option to maintain/improve ACP countries export conditions to the EU without granting non-ACP developing countries the same market access.

An "optimal" EPA is defined as development tool that supports southern African countries to promote economic development. This means that countries' effective access to the EU market will be improved, that their supply-side constraints will be successfully tackled, that suitable financial and technical support to cope with fiscal implications will provided, and that EPAs are linked to the building of regional markets.

1. Improved market access

Today, Sub-Saharan African countries can export around 97% of their total EU exports duty free (Davenport *et al.* 1995:1). However, significant restrictions for products that fall under the EU Common Agricultural Policy, tariff escalation for agro-processed products and complex rules of origin that require a comparable high minimum local content restrict the access to the EU market. To compensate ACP countries for the erosion of preferences, the EU should open its agricultural market towards ACP suppliers for products that are still comparably protected, such as milk, wheat and meat products, as well as for processed agricultural products. Furthermore, more generous rules of origin that allow countries to source inputs from the EU and its more developed regional partners,[143] EU-wide harmonised standards that reflect not only consumer protection but also take developing countries' capacities into account as well as technical and financial support to cope with increasingly stringent standards are necessary to improve Africa's effective market access and to stimulate agro-based diversification efforts.[144]

2. Tackle supply-side constraints

As discussed, most southern African countries face manifold supply-side to expand and diversify their exports. Since these supply-side constraints were largely neglected by the development instruments of the Lomé Conventions, southern African countries were not able to exploit potential benefits from EU preferences. Effective support that helps southern African countries to overcome their individual supply-side constraints, such as the improvement of customs procedures, is crucial to improve their export capacity. However, to build-up an effective transport and telecommunication infrastructure, to provide proper financial services, and to modernise production facilities are long-term development goals that can only be supported by EPAs but not solved by them. Nevertheless, EPAs should target trade-related infrastructure projects in southern African countries, thus helping to reduce the costs and to improve the attractiveness of doing business.

---

[143] The UK Commission for Africa (2005:291) proposes that African countries should be allowed to source globally and that industrialised countries should require a minimum of only 10% value added in Africa. Research findings from the Institute for Development Studies (IDS) confirm that such a generous regulation could help to boost African exports (Stevens 2005). However, the implications of generous rules of origin on the development of domestic value addition of production processes should also be considered, as the experience of AGOA shows (see Chapter 4).

[144] In this respect, the UK Commission for Africa (2005:278) has called for a "development test" of standards, which should investigate the impact existing and new standards on African countries.

3. Limit reciprocity and build regional markets first

An important concern articulated by African negotiators is the limited option for infant industry protection. Since EPAs are supposed to liberalise around 90% of trade between the EU and southern Africa, the countries are hardly left with options to industrialise. The UK Commission for Africa (2005:279) recommends reducing the reciprocal requirements of EPAs to a minimum, thus allowing African countries to implement economic reforms in accordance to their national and regional development goals since *"Forced liberalisation will not work."* (Ibid.) It is therefore seen as necessary to review Art. XXIV, WTO, which defines the requirements of reciprocal trade agreements, as well as Art. XVIII, WTO (Special and Differential Treatment), and to make both articles more precise, effective and operational so that they better suit the development needs of African countries. It is further recommended that developed countries provide technical and financial support to African countries in order to remove internal trade barriers, to promote intra-regional trade and to build regional capacities for trade before implementing North-South FTAs (Ibid.:262).

4. Create effective safeguard-measures

It is critically highlighted that southern African countries do hardly have the capacities to implement effective safeguard measures in order to protect their industries from serious injury caused by "unfair competition", such as subsidised EU agricultural exports (Botha 2005). Due to the CAP reform, EU prices for agricultural products, such as wheat, beef and chicken are declining and EU food exports have become internationally competitive, which had already severe effects on agricultural production in certain African states (Goodison 2005, Wellmer 2005:15-6).[145]

Considering these circumstances it is proposed that EPAs should exclude *a priori* sectors that are regarded as highly sensitive as well as products that are subject to EU export subsidies (Botha 2005, Steven and Kennan 2005a). However, to date the EU's mandate on safeguards and anti-dumping does not take African countries' concerns in this respect into account. The Cotonou Agreement does even foresee the implementation of safeguard measures by the EU but not by the ACP countries (European Commission 2000b: Annex V, Art. 8).

[145] Thus, the EU intervention price for wheat shrank in the period 1992-2002 by 55%. Nevertheless, the production increased from 229 million tons to 265.5 million tons in 2004. EU chicken exports increased by 121% in the period 1996-2002 (EU DG Agriculture 2004:14 as cited in Wellmer 2005:15-6).

5. Consider the revenue implications of EPAs and assist with the restructuring of industries

The immediate costs arising from EPAs are expected to be considerable for many African countries and have resulted in a strong opposition against EPAs. Though it is to date insecure how EPAs concretely look like, they are expected to imply severe revenue losses for most African countries since they are going to liberalise their import regime towards a major trading partner. These revenue losses are expected to range between 1% for Uganda and Tanzania to 10-12% for Mauritius and Rwanda (Khandelwal 2004:32).[146] It is rather unlikely that these losses can be compensated by taxes. Most countries are not able to increase corporate taxes and income taxes accordingly since their tax base is too small. The substitution of tariff revenues by VAT is also difficult. Though VAT is regarded as economically superior since it does not discriminate against imports, it might have a negative impact on domestic consumption and on poverty alleviation. Moreover, VAT is much more complex to collect than tariff revenues and requires a sophisticated communication systems between companies and domestic authorities, which overextends the administrative capacities in most African countries (AfDB 2004:253).

To cope with increased competition from EU imports and to be able to restructure their industries, southern African countries need technical assistance. Very few companies in southern Africa have the capacity and capability to understand the potential implications of the ongoing negotiations for their business (European Research Office 2002:15-6). It would be fair if the EU released financial technical assistance for southern African countries to cope with the fiscal implications of EPAs, to assess the restructuring needs for industries and to assess the training needs for managements. Originally, the EU has planned to provide no additional funding to those provided under the Cotonou Agreement but has in the meanwhile released funding to tackle supply-side constraints and promote consultations with civil society actors.[147] It can be expected that further funds will be provided once the Commission has released its report on EPA negotiations, which is supposed to identify areas where development cooperation needs to be strengthened to support EPAs (Mandelson 2005).

---

[146] Stevens and Kennan (2005a) argue that increased imports as a result of liberalisation might compensate for revenue losses. On the other hand, it is also likely that trade diversion, i.e. the replacement of third country imports by EU imports, accelerate revenue losses. These dynamic processes make it in fact impossible to calculate the scale of revenue losses for African countries exactly.

[147] The SADC (14) region received € 61.8 million to support regional integration and trade activities. This amount includes € 7.5 million for trade capacity building of the SADC EPA (INSAT 2005a:9). The ESA EPA received € 30 million to improve the institutional capacities of its members (Liebig *et al.* 2004).

5. Limit the negotiation agenda to trade in goods and build negotiation capacities

Southern African countries are constrained by limited human capacities to negotiate EPAs, which has to be done simultaneously with multilateral trade obligations (WTO Doha Round), regional trade negotiations and the implementation of existing regional trade agreements.[148] Moreover, the countries face additional administrative costs of creating effective regional bodies to negotiate EPAs.[149]

The all-embracing EPA negotiation agenda also includes services and the "Singapore Issues" (competition policy, investment, trade facilitation and government procurement). Since the EU has not been successful to push through these issues in the WTO yet, it tries to implement them on a bilateral basis (Goodison 2005, Stevens 2003). For southern African countries this implies – in light of the enormous power imbalances - that they do not have the chance to develop their own trade-related policies but have to accept the regulations of the EU. Taking investment as example: if investment is included into EPAs on a "non-discriminatory basis" southern African countries would lose their options to protect national industries and to build-up a domestic investment policy that promotes upstream and downstream benefits. Like this, *"...a new international investment regime would benefit multinational corporations at the expense of their own industries..."* (AfDB 2004:210). As the discussion in the Chapters 4 and 5 shows, domestic policy incentives, which imply a discrimination against foreign companies in the strict sense of WTO regulations, can be very successful development tools to promote trade and investment in developing countries.[150] Moreover, national empowerment policies for formerly disadvantaged people would not be possible to apply when WTO rules on investment and government procurement would be implemented. Considering the enormous welfare disparities between the white and black population in Namibia and South Africa, black empowerment policies can act as important socio-economic policy tool, helping to include formerly disadvantaged people into the labour market (as the example of the Namibian fishing industry in Chapter 5 shows).

[148] (1) All SADC countries have to implement the SADC FTA, (2) the BLNS countries have to implement the new SACU Agreement, the recently concluded SACU-EFTA and SACU-MERCOSUR FTA and to negotiate the SACU-USA FTA, (3) Malawi, Mauritius, Zambia, and Zimbabwe negotiate the COMESA CU, and (4) Tanzania has to implement the EAC CU.

[149] The relevance of trade capacity building for improved participation in regional and international trade negotiations is discussed in Chapter 6.

[150] The same applies to government procurement, which can be an important development tool for developing countries when granting government contracts to emerging domestic companies in order to stimulate industrial development.

Table 21 summarises the steps recommended to be taken by the EU, the southern African national states, and the regional bodies to promote the developmental character of EPAs.

Table 21: Agenda for action for EPA negotiations to support economic development and regional integration in southern Africa

EPA Issue	Action EU	Action Southern African Nation State	Action Regional Body
Market Access	➢ Harmonisation of southern African countries' market access by granting all countries the same market access LDCs enjoy. ➢ Efforts to reduce protect-tion and negative external effects of the CAP.	➢ Evaluation of current and potential export products, their barriers to trade, and internal constraints of expanded exports.	➢ Reduction of intra-regional tariffs and non-tariff barriers to trade.
Rules of Origin	➢ Formulation of more generous rules of origin. ➢ Allowance of full cumulation with ACP, EU, and South Africa.	➢ Overcoming of protectionist demands of national interests groups.	➢ Implementation of more generous rules of origin to promote intra-regional trade.
Sanitary and Phytosanitary Standards (SPS)	➢ Formulation of uniform SPS measures in all EU member countries according to international standards. ➢ Provision of funds to assist southern African countries to comply with SPS measures. ➢ Securing country specific and not EPA specific check-up of imports. ➢ Establishment of an independent authority that controls the rightful application of SPS.	➢ Evaluation of problems to comply with SPS. ➢ Evaluation of technical assistance needed.	➢ Formulation of a common negotiation position vis-à-vis the EU.

EPA Issue	Action EU	Action Southern African Nation State	Action Regional Body
Administrative Arrangements	➢ Formulation of uniform administrative requirements in cooperation with southern African countries. ➢ Support to implement administrative requirements.	➢ Evaluation of administrative barriers to enter the EU market and constraints to identify the origin of imported goods. ➢ Formulation of required assistance.	➢ Creation of a CET towards the EU to minimise trade diversion. ➢ Harmonisation of trade related policies.
Import safeguard measures	➢ Exclusion of products that are regarded as highly sensitive by African countries or are subject to EU export subsidies. ➢ Implementation of transparent and uniform safeguard measures in all EU member countries. ➢ Assistance to enable southern African countries to apply safeguard measures effectively.	➢ Determination of infant industries /products that need protection. ➢ Determination of agricultural products/agro-processed products that are subject to high EU export subsidies.	➢ Mutual consent on product lists aimed to be granted infant-industry protection / to be excluded from the FTA.
Customs Losses / Industrial Restructuring	➢ Financial assistance to conclude impact studies about EPAs' effects on customs losses and industrial restructuring efforts. ➢ Financial support to diminish negative social impacts of revenue losses. ➢ Provision of technical support to assess the restructuring needs for industries, the training needs for managers and to identify new trading opportunities. ➢ Provision of technical support to implement alternative income sources.	➢ Establishment of a national trade forum to inform companies about challenges and to consider their concerns. ➢ Increased efforts to expand the tax basis and to improve the collection of taxes.	➢ Establishment of a functioning regional trade forum to promote cross-national exchange of experience.

EPA Issue	Action EU	Action Southern African Nation State	Action Regional Body
EPA Negotiations	➢ Limit negotiations to trade in goods and reconsider the EPA time schedule. ➢ Review Art. IVXX and Art. XVIII WTO and make them more suitable for developing countries. ➢ Build trade capacities to cope with regional and multilateral trade negotiations and to evaluate the EPA negotiation agenda. ➢ Grant support in trade-related areas, such as standardisation and competition and investment policy.	➢ Establish effective national consultation processes. ➢ Handing over of competences to a supra-national negotiation body.	➢ Harmonise national positions and create an effective regional negotiation mechanism. ➢ Moving towards deeper regional integration to avoid a "hub-and-spoke" trade relationship and to limit the negotiation power bias.

Source: Author's presentation as cited in the text.

Though the EU underlines that EPAs are above all development tools, supposed to integrate ACP countries into regional and international markets, there is the fear that trade liberalisation is used as a substitute for development policy. Indeed, the EU pursues to considerable extent economic and strategic interests in reciprocal trade agreements with southern African countries as the inclusion of services and the "Singapore Issues" into EPA negotiations shows. Another concern is that the different development needs of southern African countries are not sufficiently respected since the SADC EPA and the ESA EPA comprise both, developing and least developed countries. Though the LDCs keep their improved market access under the EBA initiative, they will be treated like developing countries on the import side when agreeing on a CET towards the EU together with the developing countries of the EPA. LDCs' option to switch out of EPAs and to maintain non-reciprocal trade relations under the EBA initiative is also not feasible since southern African countries are not in a position to warrant the rules of origin. EU exports to developing African countries are therefore likely to be traded in the region and not accordingly declared as EU imports when entering regional LDCs (ECA *et al.* 2005:12).

Also with respect to regional integration in southern Africa, the European approach is problematic. Though the EU states that *"...ACP regions will open their markets first of all among themselves, building larger regional markets in accordance with their own political objectives and agenda."* (European Commission 2005), the EU pursues an approach of "open regionalism" where South-South integration and North-South integration go hand in hand. However, to negotiate a North-South FTA with the EU as a region requires that a certain level of integration exists and that countries have agreed on common positions towards the EU, e.g. with respect to their external tariff structure and their strategy on how to deal with trade-related aspects. To date, most southern African countries have not even established a national position on all aspects to be negotiated in EPAs so that regional EPA negotiations with the EU do rather reflect positions of single national stakeholders than those of the region.[151] Without consistent regional bodies, support for capacity building, more time to form common regional strategies and flexible approaches that also take the development needs of the least developed countries into account, EPAs risk contributing to a further economic marginalisation of African countries.

3.8 Conclusions: Credibility and Commitment of the new EU Policy towards Southern Africa

Considering the massive development disparities between the EU and southern African countries well as their internal and external constraints to enter the European market, it is very questionable that an FTA has such a deep effect that it helps southern African countries to enter the EU market successfully. A North-South FTA can help African consumers and producers to benefit from cheaper imports by lowering countries' external tariffs. However, whether trade liberalisation in itself is beneficial for African countries as suggested by the European Commission (2005) is doubtful. Thus, trade liberalisation does not help African countries to improve their capacity to trade since their manifold supply-side constraints as well as demand-side constraints in the EU market are not tackled. It also must be doubted that a North-South FTA in form of EPAs results in increased investment, technological spillovers and increased economic and political reputation because of "locked in" trade reforms (Padoan 2001, Collier and Gunning 2000, Krugman 1990). In fact, southern African countries have not aspired to enter into EPAs with the EU but did only agree because they want to keep their market access.

The complementary trade structure and the high development disparities between the EU and southern African countries can lead to high trade imbalances, which implies the risk of further polarisation, demoting the South to the

[151] One example is the declaration of concerned SADC EPA stakeholders, which was worked out and presented by Namibian stakeholders at the launch of SADC EPA negotiations in Windhoek, 08 July 2004.

"spoke" that is supposed to deliver the "hub" with raw materials. One opportunity for southern African countries to avoid such a hub-and-spoke relationship is to integrate in a South-South framework before entering into a North-South FTA. This would offer southern African "spokes" the chance to build-up adequate negotiation capacities and limit the lopsided negotiation power of the EU (Kennes 2000:112). The EU sees regional integration schemes and processes as "key instrument" for ACP countries' integration into the world economy, which shall be "encouraged and supported." (European Commission 2000, Art. 35). South-South integration shall help small ACP countries to strengthen their competitiveness, to save resources and to increase their bargaining power vis-à-vis the EU. However, to let such a positive scenario come true, a certain degree of economic integration as well as the establishment of regional institutions that are in a position to act as a common negotiation body would be a prerequisite (Kennes 2000:120-2). It is therefore necessary to build-up regional capacities, to implement appropriate development measures and to focus on assistance to improve the competitiveness and diversification efforts of southern African countries in order to promote intra-regional integration. The EU concept of "open regionalism", promoting that South-South and North-South integration go hand in hand, is not feasible in the southern African context but has further undermined regional integration efforts. Thus, the decision of the SADC countries Malawi, Mauritius, Zambia and Zimbabwe to negotiate an EPA in an Eastern Southern Africa (ESA) framework does not necessarily mirror their long-term economic and strategic interests within the region but rather their fear of being locked into the liberalisation schedule of the EU-South Africa FTA when negotiating in a SADC EPA framework.[152]

The impact of EPAs on the SACU countries and regional integration within SACU are not predictable yet. The BLNS countries are locked-in the EU-South Africa Free Trade Agreement and are therefore already confronted with the challenges of free trade with a major trading partner, such as revenue losses and increased competition. Whether they can improve their effective access to the EU market and adequately accommodate their concerns, such the effective implementation of safeguard measures, budget support and technical assistance to identify new income sources, remains to be seen.[153] This depends to a consid-

[152] That EPAs are rather driven by political than economic considerations is also shown by the fact that not one common single product would be in the exclusion list of all member countries of any EPA configuration (Stevens and Kennan 2005b:3).

[153] Since the BLNS countries have enjoyed superior access to the EU market for most products than South Africa for three decades, it is unlikely that the SADC EPA follows the EU-South Africa FTA with respect to market access. The question is therefore rather whether the countries of the SADC EPA will be able to improve the conditions of market access they enjoy under the Cotonou Agreement, e.g. with respect to the rules of origin or EU tariffs for processed agricultural products.

erable extent on their negotiation power and on the future formation of the SADC EPA, which is currently, with the exclusion of South Africa and the inclusion of the EAC member Tanzania, not sustainable. It is therefore argued that the inclusion of South Africa into the SADC EPA negotiation is a prerequisite so as to enable the BLNS countries to set through their interests vis-à-vis the EU and to make EPAs consistent with SACU's regional integration strategy.

Another problem arising from FTAs in general and from North-South FTAs such as the TDCA or EPAs in particular is their impact on industrial policies for developing countries. The dominance of a complementary trade structure and the international competitiveness of industrial products from the North, bear the risk that domestic industrial production in developing countries is substituted by imports. Though consumer benefits and producer gains by receipt of cheaper intermediates are expected, FTAs with developed countries are likely to reduce industrial policy options in developing countries.

The next section 4 elaborates on the relationship of international trade and regional integration on SACU countries' industrialisation strategies. What are SACU countries comparative advantages and which industrialisation strategies have they pursued to date? How did their membership in SACU and their trade relations to the EU contribute to industrial development in the single countries and what are the implications of eroding preferences and the EU's approach of North-South FTAs for SACU countries' industrialisation strategies?

4 The Contribution of Free Trade Agreements to Industrialisation, Regional Integration and Economic Development in the SACU Countries

4.1 What Can Industrialisation Strategies in Developing Countries Look Like?

It is emphasised that the term "industrial policy" is not well defined and often described too narrow. The World Bank (1992:104) defines "industrial policy" as *"...government efforts to alter industrial structure to promote productivity based growth"*. According to this definition, industrial policy implies not only government's interference into market processes in order to alter industrial structures and to optimise industrial development but also the promotion of productivity based growth. Giving the structure of the SACU economies and the relevance of the agricultural sector for their economic development (mainly for the BLNS countries), the discussion of industrial policy/industrialisation strategies concentrates on the manufacturing sector but also refers to any active policy that promotes processing activities in productive capacities of the SACU countries, including agriculture,[152] mining, manufacturing and services. Giving further SACU countries' involvement in international trade and the fact that the CET can serve as instrument for industrial development, as it was the case for South Africa, the terms "industrial policy" and "trade policy" are used as substitutes since both policies are a form of public interference into market processes, aiming to promote economic development within SACU.[153]

One differentiates between the "state rationale assumption" of industrial policy according to which any decision of the state is regarded as rationale and the "plan rationale assumption", which regards a competitive market mechanism as well as government's rational planning as equally important for promoting industrial development. The first was adopted by many African countries, while Japan and the Newly Industrialised Countries (NICs) in Eastern Asia adopted the "plan rationale assumption" during the 1970s and 1980s (Edwards 1996:239-41).

There are two options to promote industrial development, the import-substituting strategy and the export-oriented approach. The import-substitution strategy bases on high tariff protection for domestic industries, supposed to produce consumer goods formerly imported and to diversify productive structures.

[152] BLNS countries' horizontal and vertical agro-based diversification efforts are discussed in section 3.3.2.

[153] The difference between trade policy and industrial policy is that the first has an impact on prices at the border while the latter impacts prices within the border of the country (McCarthy and Hansohm 2005:5).

The strategy is to start with the production of final goods and to move up steadily towards intermediate and capital goods. This inward-oriented growth strategy should reduce the dependence from industrialised countries and help to overcome traditional trade patterns (ATPC 2004:7).

The export-oriented approach pursues an outward-looking development policy, assuming that an open economy benefits from free trade and competition (Todaro and Smith 2002:556). Its instruments, such as tariff exemption for inputs or export subsidies, actively support export-oriented industries. This positive discrimination of export businesses vis-à-vis domestic industries should promote the international competitiveness of export companies and result in positive spillover effects (backward and forward linkages) for domestic industries and service providers (Edwards 1996:239-41). However, the concentration of single export products also implies the risk that domestic production and non-tradable goods, such as basic infrastructure, are disregarded. Trade policy should therefore be neutral towards domestic production and exports (Wohlmuth 2003:25-7).

The NICs combined the export-oriented approach with the idea of infant-industry protection. Thus, they promoted industrial development by protective and non-protective incentives. Over a certain period of time, the export-oriented manufacturing sector received support by high tariffs on competing imports and reduced tariffs on imported inputs necessary for production process (Perkins *et al.* 2001:689). This effective protection has enabled new industries in the NICs to develop and to compete successfully. Additionally, the export of manufactured and semi-manufactured goods was fostered by granting incentives (like tax holidays and tariff reductions on imported inputs) and by spurring private businesses with subsidies and a private-sector friendly policies.[154]

Most African countries pursued a strategy of import industrialisation after having gained independence in the early 1960s. Their economies were highly dependent on the export of few mineral and agricultural products and biased towards few (colonial) trading partners. To diversify their product range and to improve the autarky of their economies, they protected their markets by high tariffs and supported domestic industries, e.g. by overvalued exchange rates to discourage imports and by subsidised interest rates to promote domestic investment. The theoretical argument for the import-substitution strategy was not only the infant-industry argument by Friedrich List but also the Prebisch-Singer theory of long-term deteriorating terms of trade for primary goods. A switch from primary towards manufacturing exports was therefore regarded as crucial for

[154] See Bora *et al.* (1999:13) for an overview of import restrictions, export promotion and industrial policy instruments applied by South East Asian countries.

economic development. Government interventions in the areas of finance and investment was destined to support the structuring and growth of industries.

The import substitution strategy led to the development of a couple of consumer goods industries in African countries, such as flour milling industries, bakeries, breweries, sugar refineries, fruit and vegetable industries, coffee processing plants, and the textile industry. Furthermore, the countries were able to achieve high economic growth rates from the mid-1960s throughout the 1970s and increased the share of formal employment considerably (ATPC 2004:7-9). However, with the oil crisis in 1973 and the falling prices for raw materials, the problems of Africa's import substitution strategy became obvious. The focus on the production of final goods had led to high imports of intermediate and capital goods, which had resulted, together with falling terms of trade for Africa's main export products, in a worsening trade deficits and increasing external debts. Because of the high tariff protection, the economies lacked of capital-intensive inputs, necessary for vertical diversification and the creation of industrial linkages. As a result, few highly protected industries existed that were not linked to the rest of the economy. The internal consumer market was weak and failed to provide significant demand for new industries. Furthermore, agricultural production had been neglected, which resulted in low agricultural productivity and the dominance of subsistence farming, thus contributing to the weak domestic demand. Additionally, the high protection level and missing competition in domestic markets had resulted in lack market discipline, rising inefficiencies and low levels of productivity (Todaro and Smith 2002:564-7, Perkins *et al.* 2001:692-3).

Generally, import-substitution policies in Africa were characterised by discriminative incentives against investment in agriculture, capital-goods industries and exports. Another problem of the import-substitution strategy was that it neglected technological and financial support for domestic producers and exporters, especially in the field of agriculture where the countries could have benefited from comparative advantages in the export business. State interference in form of marketing boards or price controls had often discriminated against agricultural production and discouraged agricultural exports (AfDB 2004:191). Further reasons that contributed to the failure of an inward-looking industrialisation strategy in Africa were inappropriate exchange rates, high taxes on exports, low levels of investment and savings, a high concentration degree of the economies and excessive state consumption (Edwards 1996:244-6).[155]

[155] There are many other factors that are named to explain the low industrialisation degree and the poor economic growth records in African countries, such as the lack of technology and human capital, high transport costs and lack infrastructure, a low population density, natural endowment, colonial history, poor institutions, weak states, the lack of "good governance" etc. See Wohlmuth (2004) and UNIDO (2004a:21-4) for an overview.

The early 1980s were marked by a serious debt crisis for many African countries and a switch in international development economics, away from the theory of state intervention towards the traditional economics of market forces. As a result, the principles of the "Washington Consensus" gained momentum. To tackle the debt crisis and to promote economic growth, the IMF and the World Bank created Structural Adjustment Programmes (SAP) following-up two priorities: First, to create macroeconomic stability by reduced public and private demand and reduced state intervention, and second, to open the highly protected inward-looking economies towards external markets. These internal and external reforms were supposed to result in the optimal allocation of production factors and the integration of African countries into the world economy. When going under the SAP, African countries had to stop fixing their exchange rates, devaluate their currencies, reduce their external tariffs and trim down their external debts (ATPC 2004:1-2).

However, the outcome of the SAP for African countries was more than disappointing. Though some economies were able to address internal and external imbalances, overall economic growth rates remained low and external debts high. Agricultural and industrial production and productivity declined and exports decreased. Most Sub-Saharan African countries have de-industrialised since the 1970ies (UNIDO 2004a:39, UNCTAD 1998:196-8)[156]. The restrictive approach to reduce public and private demand in addition to the opening of formerly highly protected economies resulted furthermore in increased unemployment and poverty (ATPC 2004:13-4).

In the early 1990s, the Bretton Wood institutions responded to the negative social impact of their SAP in African countries and moved towards a more flexible approach that also takes social and environmental developments into account. The initiative to reduce the debts of the most indebted countries in the world (HIPC initiative),[157] the adoption of the Millennium Development Goals (MDG)[158] and the expansion of SAP by a poverty reduction component (Poverty

[156] The shares of most product groups in total manufacturing value-added decreased in most African countries in the period 1970 to 1993 (UNCTAD 1998:198).

[157] The HIPC initiative was initiated by the World Bank and the IMF in 1996, supposed to reduce the external debts of the most heavily indebted poor countries in the world. A review in 1999 enhanced the debt relief. To become HIPC-eligible indebted countries had to implement the Poverty Reduction Strategy Papers (PRSP). To date, 21 African and 4 South American countries have benefited from the HIPC initiative (World Bank 2005).

[158] The MDG comprise eight goals, namely 1. eradication of extreme poverty and hunger, 2. universal primary education, 3. promotion of gender equality and women empowerment, 4. reduction of child mortality, 5. improvement of maternal health and reduction of maternal mortality, 6. combating HIV/AIDS, malaria and other diseases, 7. ensuring environmental sustainability, and 8. develop a global partnership for development. All eight MDG have concrete targets of which most are quantified. Additionally, indicators for the monitoring

Reduction Strategy Paper – PRSP[159]) are expressions of donor countries' increased awareness about improved socio-economic conditions in developing countries.

However, despite this revival of socio-economic development goals, openness to trade and a minimum of state intervention are still seen as key elements for a successful integration of African countries into the global economy. Openness to trade is often regarded as successful development strategy *per se*, resulting in greater efficiency of resource allocation and improved access to technology and capital goods. Though it is acknowledged that state interventionist instruments, such as low interest rates and infant industry protection, were successful development tools in Asian countries' industrialisation strategy (World Bank 1992), trade policy recommendations towards African countries continue focussing on unilateral trade liberalisation; only recently supply-and demand-side constraints have also been taken into account (see e.g. policy recommendations of WTO 2003, Khandelwal 2004, AfDB 2004).

4.2 Links between Trade and Economic Development

"It is also worth remembering that, historically, no country has ever developed on the basis of free trade ... successful countries ... all adopted various means of protection at one time or another. Trade liberalization can be an ultimate goal, but the speed and manner of liberalization needs careful consideration on a country-by-country basis." (AfDB 2004:165).

The standard theory of economic convergence assumes that poor countries grow faster than rich ones as they are able to import capital and modern technologies from the advanced economies. Increased volumes of exports and imports lead to increased competition, thus, resulting in the allocation of resources according to a country's comparative advantages. Increased imports of capital- and technological intensive goods stimulate the processing of innovations and new technologies through which the labour and capital productivity is increased and economies of scale are reached. This process is supported by increased con-

process have been fixed. It is expected that most African countries fail to meet the MDG by 2015 (UNIDO 2004a:xxi-iv).

[159] PRSP were introduced by IMF and World Bank in 2000 and are supposed to bring the macro-, meso-, and micro-economic fundamentals together to reduce poverty and promote economic growth in Africa. In 2004, 28 African states had implemented PRSP running for 3-5 years. Is criticised that the development constraints identified by the PRSP are not sufficiently covered by financial means and an adequate time frame and that micro- and macroeconomic policies are not adequately linked to each other so that it comes to trade-offs between macroeconomic balances and social development objectives (UNIDO 2004a:75-7).

sumption due to competitive imports and know-how transfer from foreign cooperation. As a result, the poorer countries grow at higher rates than the developed ones, thus catching-up in economic development. Finally, the income gap between poor and rich economies closes over the time and economic convergence is reached. This implies that developing countries should open their markets for foreign trade and investment and benefit from imported goods, technology and know-how (Piazola 2001, Sachs and Warner 1996).

Though most African countries opened their economies towards external trade since the early 1980s, they have become increasingly marginalised. Their share on world's exports decreased in the period 1980-2000 from 3.8% to 1.5% and their share on world's imports shrunk from 3.2% to 1.4% (UNCTAD 2004b:14-5). According to Sachs and Warner (1996:37) the mechanism of economic convergence was not possible to be proved for African countries because of their protectionist trade regimes and the missing link to international trade. Comparing developing countries' growth from 1970-1990, Sachs and Warner found out that closed economies expanded only by 0.7% p.a. while open economies grew by 4.5%.[160] Authors like Khandelwal (2005) and Yang and Gupta (2005) confirm this theory, arguing that the reason for African countries' insufficient integration into the global economy is not their attempt towards trade liberalisation but their discriminatory liberalisation approach, which still protects uncompetitive industries. A continuing commitment towards further tariff reduction would therefore be crucial to promote economic development.

The SACU countries, which are due to their tariff level classified as "closed" by Khandelwal (2004:23), are much more open than industrialised countries. Even South Africa, the most "closed" economy within SACU (see Figure 15), with an openness degree of 25%,[161] is more open to trade than the EU or the USA, which showed an openness degree of less than 13% in 1998 (Hoeller *et al.* 2000:60-1).

---

[160] Sachs and Warner (1996:22) classify an economy as open, if the average tariff rate as well as the equivalent tariff rate of the non-tariff rate are less than 40%, the black market exchange rate takes less than 20% and the government is neither communistic nor monopolist of major export goods. In this respect, Botswana and Namibia, where diamonds account for more than 50% of total export earnings and diamond exports are controlled by the government, would be classified as closed. However, generally openness is measured simply as the ratio of average exports plus imports divided by 2 to GDP. The higher the outcome, the more open the economy is. McCulloch *et al.* (2003:14-5) emphasise that there are diverse concepts and measures of openness, which are only weakly correlated amongst each other. Thus, the validity of openness depends always on the openness measure.

[161] Measured as ratio of average exports plus imports divided by 2 to GDP.

Figure 15: The openness of SACU economies in 2000

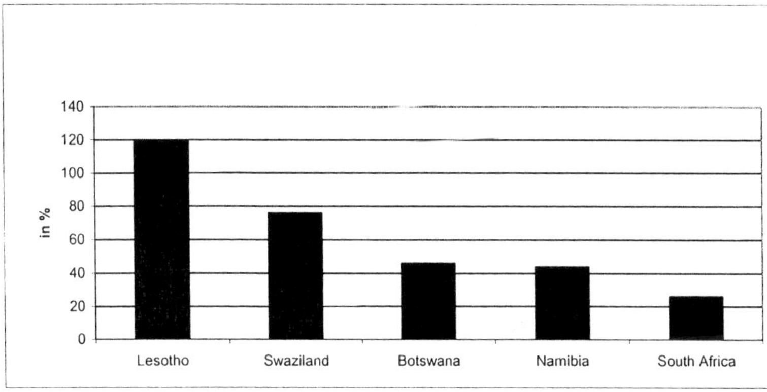

Source: World Bank 2001b, author's calculation.

This indicates that authors like Khandelwal mix-up policy instruments with policy outcome. Though SACU might be "closed" if one considers the tariff lines for single products,[162] its *de facto* openness to trade does not confirm the theory of a "restrictive trade regime". SACU's openness to trade might further indicate that tariffs have become less and less an effective instrument of protection.

Sachs' and Warner's direct relation between trade liberalisation and economic growth has received various criticisms. Thus, it is argued that an open trade regime and reasonably convertible currencies are not sufficient for economic growth and do not necessarily lead to macroeconomic stability. Sustainable economic growth and development could only be realised if institutional reforms and reforms to overcome supply-side constraints are also undertaken (Kappel 2005, AfDB 2004:162-70, Åslund 1996:97). Rodrik and Rodriguez (1999) went further in their criticism on the assumptions of Sachs and Warner (1996) and questioned the causality between an open trade regime and economic growth. Rodrik and Rodriguez rejected the indicators chosen, pointing out that they are not directly linked to trade policy. As even more problematic than the methodology they regarded the analysis itself, i.e. the direct linkage between openness and economic development. Thus, the impact of trade policy on economic growth would be difficult to isolate and must be regarded in a broader sense, considering also issues like size and specialisation degree of economies

[162] SACU's simple average tariff is 11.4%, its maximum average tariff is 60%. The total number of tariff lines is 7794 of which 98%% are bound at the WTO. For some sensitive products, such as beverages and sugar, tariffs up to 597% are applicable (WTO 2003:27).

and their access to capital and technology. Rodrik and Rodriguez (1999) concluded that it remains unclear whether countries grow because they export so much or whether they are able to export because they grew. China for instance was able to increase its trade volumes considerably although it raised substantial trade barriers against third countries while other countries have opened their market but have not been able to increase their exports because they lack a proper export base.[163] Rodrik and Rodriguez summed up that the causality between open trade and economic growth failed to be proved so far: developed and developing countries have shown in the past that there are different ways to reach economic growth and welfare; patent prescriptions do not exist. Thus, industrialised countries should allow developing countries to find their own "style of capitalism" as they have done themselves in the past.

The experience of the NICs showed that investment in production, infrastructure and institutions are key instruments for successful economic development. It is submitted that the major difference between Asian and African countries' industrialisation efforts was not how far they opened their markets but their different development dynamics and capacities to promote sustainable economic development (ATPC 2004, UNIDO 1996, Edwards 1996).[164] Another important difference between African and Asian attempts to industrialise is that African countries protected mainly their manufacturing industry, which added the highest value to the product. This resulted in the neglection of other industries so that no industrial backward- and forward linkages could have been established. The Asian approaches of a sector-by-sector bottom-upwards strategy whereas allowed Asian countries to build linkages between domestic and export-oriented industries. Moreover, Asian countries limited the negative effects of their import substitution strategy with an active export promotion policy and put considerable efforts towards learning, adaptation and imitation of imported technology and capital goods. All this has not been the case in most African countries (ATPC 2005:23). Further differences between Asian and African countries relate to the levels of investment, institution building, human capital and infrastructure, where African countries show severe constraints. UNCTAD

[163] For Africa, the African Development Bank (2004:170, 186) states that exports are much more determined by world demand, world prices and export supply constraints than by countries' trade policy.

[164] UNIDO (1996) identified the following reasons why African countries cannot follow the South East Asian development path: 1. they are not part of a cluster, i.e. no higher developed country undertakes FDI on a large scale; 2. they show serious lack of infrastructure and high transactions costs; 3. they show very low industrial and technological capacities; 4. the private sector is weak and middle-sized companies are missing; 5. the acquisition of new technology has risen in terms of costs and skills; 6. labour quality has become more important for the attraction of FDI; 7. Africa has become very dependent on expatriate technology, finance and skills.

(2000, 1999) emphasises that a new policy orientation is needed that addresses the structural constraints and institutional barriers in African economies. A strong and sustainable investment recovery in both, physical and human capital as well as supportive action for companies on the meso- and micro-level are regarded as prerequisite for an outward orientation of African economies. Moreover, industrial capabilities have to be strengthened, such as the competitive operation of plants, the production of international quality products and the guarantee of international standards as well as the introduction of new products (UNIDO 2004a:xx).[165] However, as UNIDO (2004a:58) points out: "*...there is no single, unique HPE* [High Economic Performer] *industrialization model that SSA countries can seek to emulate. Furthermore, the world has moved on...* ." In fact, the external conditions for industrialisation have changed due to an increasingly liberalised trading environment, eroding preferences and lesser options for import substitution policies. To date, trade liberalisation had not had positive effects on African countries' export performance. Research finding from UNCTAD (1999) suggests that the export-import ratio of developing countries is declining since they opened up to global trade, resulting in increased trade deficits. Only few developing countries (mainly from East Asia) have benefited from faster economic growth and greater income convergence towards industrialised countries since they were able to raise their domestic manufactured exports. However, the bulk of developing countries did not manage to diversify their export base and increased only their manufactured imports but not the domestic value addition of manufactured goods.[166] Thus, an open economy and increasing participation of developing countries in international production chains do not necessarily imply a correspondent increase in value added activities and a country's income (Wohlmuth 2003:15, 48).

Nowadays, African countries have the lowest manufacturing share of GDP in the world. All Sub-Saharan African countries, excluding South Africa, contributed to only 0.1% of the world's manufactured exports in 1998. Africa's manufactured per capita value laid nearly 30 times under the one of East Asian countries and was much higher in the 1970s than in the 1990s (UNCTAD 2000:84-8).

Most African countries are still limited to the export of minerals and few food products for their economic wellbeing and are therefore very vulnerable to external shocks. In addition to the well-known problems of fluctuating and deteriorating terms of trade and low domestic value addition of primary commodities' exports, the international constellation of supply and demand is likely to

[165] Additionally UNIDO (2004:xix) emphasises that new technologies such as information and communication technologies and biotechnology have to be adapted to upgrade industrial capabilities.

[166] See Wohlmuth *et al.* (2005, forthcoming) for an all-embracing overview of African countries' dependency on primary commodities and attempts to diversify their product range.

worsen the terms of trade even further if many developing countries with a similar factor endowment (like cheap labour) enter into the market with the same product (UNCTAD 2002b).[167] However, some authors argue that a shift from primary commodities to knowledge-intensive manufactured is likely to overextend African countries. Since "*...regions like sub-Saharan Africa should not run before they can walk...*" (Cramer 2003:31) it is proposed that African countries concentrate on horizontal and vertical diversification of primary products rather than switching towards manufactured production directly (UNCTAD 2004 and 2000, Wood and Mayer 2001, Yeats 1998, Wood and Mayer 2001).[168] In addition to this resource-based industrialisation strategy, they should build-up effective institutions, improve their human capital formation and create a stable political and macroeconomic environment. Effective policies in the field of research and development, attraction of FDI and close public-private-partnership should support the export of processed primary commodities and help to reduce the obstacles towards vertical diversification in the long run. In addition to this "resource-based" industrialisation process, it is proposed that African countries reduce their tariffs for specialised manufactured products to facilitate the establishment of backward and forward linkages (Cramer 2003, Perkins *et al.* 2001, Wood and Mayer 2001, Yeats 1998, Foroutan and Pritchett 1993).

However, the concentration on an outward-oriented industrialisation strategy based on agro-based products and simple manufacturing exports does also bear risks that go beyond the problem of fluctuating and deteriorating terms of trade. Since developing countries with large supply capacities, such as China, India or Brazil, are able to produce labour-intensive high quality products at lower costs than African countries, competition for this type of commodities is high. This can exert a downward influence on prices and the terms of trade for basic manufactured goods. If again exporters face significant and sustained declining terms of trade, their export activities may even result in "immiserizing growth" (Bhagwati 1958), which means that increased export quantities do not over-compensate terms of trade losses but contribute to a further deterioration of

[167] This "Fallacy of Composition" argument does not only apply to primary commodities but has also occurred as a result of the AGOA initiative, where African countries received superior market access to the USA for their clothing, garment and apparel exports (see discussion in section 4.2.3 and in Box 22).

[168] Diversification towards non-traditional agricultural products, such as exotic fruits, fish and seafood, has the advantage that the demand for these commodities shows a higher income and a lower price elasticity than for traditional primary commodities. Horizontal diversification towards non-traditional agricultural products also offers the advantage that these products face lower tariffs and less non-tariff barriers in industrialised countries' markets than traditional commodities, such as bananas, sugar or rice (AfDB 2004:220). Vertical diversification of agro-based products offers African countries the chance to increase their domestic value-addition of agricultural production and to become less dependent on the volatility of commodity prices (UNCTAD 2000, 2004).

terms of trade, thus increasing developing countries' dependency on exactly these export activities. It is argued that the export of simple labour-intensive manufactured goods can rather be compared with primary commodities than with technology-intensive manufactures. The Prebisch-Singer theory has therefore been expanded to low-skilled, labour-intensive manufacturing commodities, arguing that the characteristics of the supply of single components in international value added chains resemble more and more those of primary goods with respect to terms of trade, market fluctuations, learning and technology effects etc. The value added parts of the production process of manufactured goods are often concentrated in industrialised countries while developing countries contribute mainly to the labour-intensive part of production, which does not add much value to the product.[169] This "slicing of production" results in increased price pressure for producers in developing countries, leading to the displacement of production if products are not produced as cheap as possible. As a result, the producers of components or commodities that are highly exchangeable become their selves more and more exchangeable in the international production process. It is therefore important for a producer of exchangeable products to develop relevant core capabilities that aggravate the dislocation of production. The best market niches are those where the competition pressure is modest, that are difficult to copy so that the barriers of entry are comparable high, and that includes a high value addition by the producer. To enter into these market niches requires that producers upgrade either their products (introduction of new products or improvement of existing products), or their processes (increased efficiency and reliability and improved just-in-time management) (Wohlmuth 2003, UNCTAD 2002b).[170]

Ideally, African producers move from a *buyer-driven chain*, i.e. a labour-intensive industry where the critical governing role is played by the buyer (normally a global company), to a more valuable *producer-driven chain*, i.e. a capital-intensive, high-technology industry where the producer is responsible for assisting the efficiency of suppliers and customers (Kaplinsky 2000:125). Such a swift implies the extension of activities towards an all-embracing product development and –marketing. To reach this, an active industrial policy and the promotion of innovation are necessary. Although the improved inclusion of devel-

---

[169] Kaplinsky (2000:123) emphasises that the barriers to entry in production are falling with increased industrial capabilities of a country. As a result, the economic rents are falling in the field of the pure production process and are increasing in other areas, such as design, marketing and distribution.

[170] The following four forms of upgrading activities are possible: a) process upgrading by increased efficiency; b) product upgrading by introduction of new products or improvement of existing products; c) functional upgrading by increasing the complexity of products and services; and d) upgrading the value added chain by entering into new market segments (Stamm 2004, Kaplinsky *et al.* 2002).

oping countries into global value added chains requires great efforts and input from developing countries' governments (i.e. relating to the provision of infrastructure services, human capital building, regional and structural policies and support on the meso- and microeconomic level), it is seen as the only way for developing countries to benefit from the globalisation process (Wohlmuth 2003:48-55, UNCTAD 2002b).

In sum, manufacturing exports cannot be judged *per se* as key instrument for economic development. The characteristics of supply of single components in international value added chains resemble more and more those of primary goods relating to terms of trade, market fluctuations, learning and technology effects. Today, high rents are mainly obtained by exporting knowledge-based manufacturing exports or by concentrating on high-valuable product-related activities, such as marketing, branding and distribution. The best market niches are therefore those where the competition pressure is modest and the products are difficult to copy. To enter into these market niches requires that producers upgrade their products and processes. Upgrading activities should enable the producer to become more included into the global value chain in order to reduce the risk of being displaced and to increase his rents.

4.2.1 The Relevance of Manufacturing Value Added Activities for Economic Development in SACU

One option to rate the competitive industrial performance of a country is to have a look at the manufacturing value added (MVA) of production. The MVA per capita analyses the manufacturing activity of registered enterprises (excluding non-industrial service) and is deflated by the population to adjust the size of the economy. The MVA per capita is therefore a good indicator to measure a country's level of industrialisation.

As can be seen from Figure 16, South Africa's MVA per capita was declining significantly in the period 1980-90 from US$ 870 to US$ 717 (around 12% of the OECD average) (Kaplan 2003:6). In the following 12 years, South Africa maintained its 1990 value of MVA per capita. The BLNS countries show, with exception of Lesotho, a higher MVA per capita than the Sub-Saharan African average. In 2002, Swaziland had with US$ 492 the highest MVA per capita in the BLNS countries, followed by Namibia (US$ 243), Botswana (US$ 206) and Lesotho (US$ 29).

Figure 16: MVA per capita (at constant 1990 US$ prices)

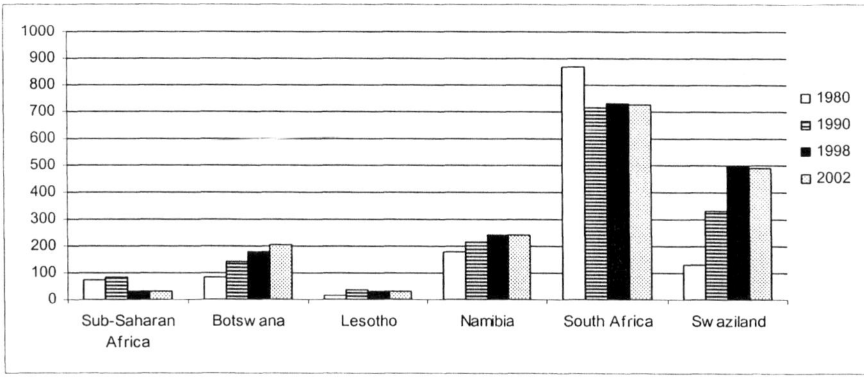

Source: UNIDO (2002a, 2004b).

Since the Swazi economy centres on sugar- and agro-processing, the high MVA per capita value is not surprising. For Botswana and Namibia, the comparable low MVA is also not surprising if one considers that minerals still account for the majority of export earning.[171] For Lesotho, however, the very low MVA per capita surprises, taking the expansion of Lesotho's clothing industry as a response to the AGOA initiative into account. Thus, manufacturing activities have expanded significantly since 2001 and around 55,000 new jobs have been created in the clothing industry (IRIN 2005b). However, as the low, stagnating MVA value shows, these expanded manufacturing activities have not contributed to increased domestic value addition.[172]

SACU countries' MVA share of GDP can be obtained from Figure 17. The share of manufacturing value added activities to a country's GDP gives an indication about its industrialisation degree. It is revealing that Swaziland has the highest MVA share within SACU. Swaziland's manufacturing value added activities contributed to more than 28% of GDP in 2002 while this figure was not even 18% in South Africa.

---

[171] Minerals accounted for 90% of total exports in Botswana and for 55% of total Namibian exports in 2001 (WTO 2003).

[172] See also discussion in Box 22.

Figure 17: SACU countries' MVA Share of GDP

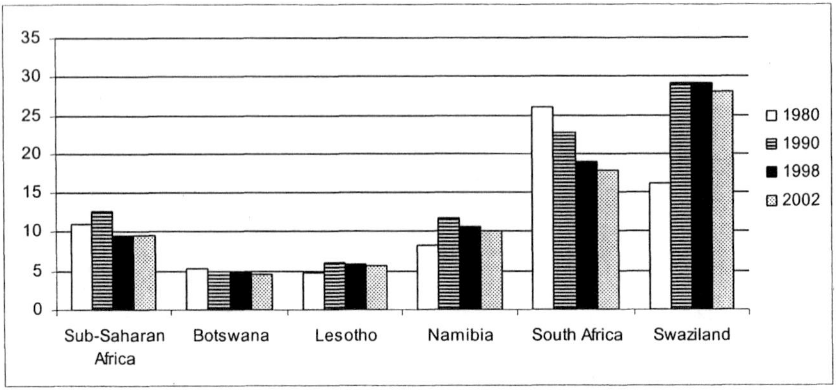

Source: UNIDO (2002a, 2004b).

All SACU countries show a lower MVA of GDP in 2002 than in 1998 though all of them showed real average annual growth rates during this period.[173] This can be explained by higher GDP growth and different deflators for GDP and MVA.[174]

As can be further obtained from Figure 17, Botswana and Lesotho have a lower MVA of GDP than the Sub-Saharan African average, which indicates that only little manufacturing activities take place (Botswana) or that the domestic value addition of manufacturing production accrues largely abroad (Lesotho). In all BLNS countries, the MVA was growing at larger scale during the 1980s than during the 1990s and thereafter. This was a result of the sanctions against Apartheid South Africa that contributed positively to BLNS countries' industrial development (UNIDO 2004a:32-5).[175]

Ranking the SACU countries according to their Competitive Industrial Performance (CIP), UNIDO (2004a:38) ranks South Africa as the most competitive industrialised African country, followed by Mauritius and Swaziland.[176] Lesotho is placed on rank 6 and Namibia and Botswana on rank 21 and 29 respec-

[173] The average annual MVA growth rate was 2% in the period 1997-2002 (UNIDO 2004b).

[174] The inflation for GDP is generally lower than for the MVA (UNIDO 2002a).

[175] In the period 1981-91 Swaziland and Lesotho were with 17.9% and 13.1% the top performers in annual MVA growth (UNIDO 2004b).

[176] The Competitiveness Industrial Performance (CIP) index combines MVA, manufactured exports per capita, the share of medium and high-tech activities and export quality of products (UNIDO 2004:194-5).

tively. Considering the global CIP, South Africa is on rank 35 (2000) in front of countries like Australia, Argentina and Indonesia. Even more important: South Africa was able to improve its position in the period 1990-2000 by nine ranks, which indicates that South Africa has managed the transition process of its economy well (Ibid.:16).

4.2.2 SACU Countries' Manufacturing Activities and Industrialisation Policies

At best, vertical product diversification, which means the technological upgrading including the promotion of linkages with regional and overseas markets, moves towards more dynamic, higher valuable products (UNCTAD 2004a:51-4). Optimal vertical diversification would be the maximisation of globally leading manufactured exports that show rising value growth rates. To realise such an optimum production portfolio is however very difficult to achieve and needs to consider the individual production base, a country's diversification strategy, its trade structure as well as the trade policy of its main trading partners. As the discussion shows, South Africa has been able to enter into some high valuable, dynamic product markets. Manufacturing activities in the BLNS countries whereas relate first of all to the upgrading of existing products and services. BLNS diversification efforts are inhibited by their size and spare population, a narrow production base with insufficient backward and forward linkages, and limited options for infant industry protection.

South Africa's manufacturing activities

Manufacturing activities are with 24.7% (2004) the second biggest contributor to national GDP after mining (SARB 2005). South Africa's main manufacturing activities are the automotive industry, food processing and beverages, mineral-based industries, textiles, machinery and equipment and pulp and paper (see Figure 18) The manufacturing sector contributed to 45% of formal employment in 2001 and to 58% of export earnings (WTO 2003:A4-273-4).

Figure 18: South Africa's manufacturing sales, 1997-2002 (in million Rand)

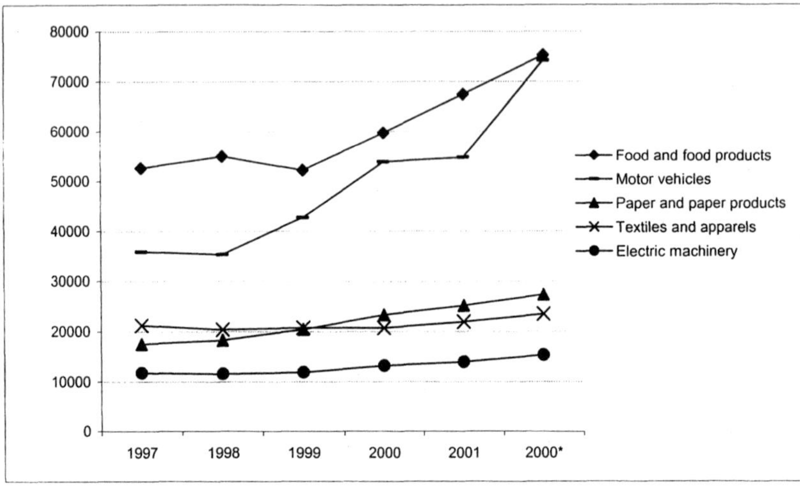

* January to November 2000.

Source: South African authorities as cited in WTO 2003:A4-273.

As discussed, manufactured exports with medium and high-skill technological intensity are the goods that grow much faster than low-skilled and labour-intensive manufactured and primary commodities. In Africa, the share of dynamic products on export is far smaller than in other regions.[177] Even South Africa, the by far most sophisticated economy on the continent, showed only a share of 4.3% of total exports of the 20-most-market-dynamic-products in the period 1991-2000. Many high-technology goods like computers, medical instruments, electricity and telecommunication distribution equipment are not produced in South Africa. There are only two of the most dynamic product groups, namely electrical machinery and beverages, where South Africa has with 1% and 1.5% respectively a noteworthy export share as measured by its total exports in the period 1991 to 2000 (UNCTAD 2002b:55, DTI 2001).

South Africa's export share for high-skilled technological goods (automotives, chemicals and pharmaceuticals) was in average 14.3% of its total exports in the period 1991-2000 (see Table 22). Moreover, the country shows high export shares of goods that grow at middle-level rates and are classified as manu-

[177] In 1995, the high dynamic goods with rising market share made out around 1/8 of Sub-Saharan Africa's total exports and the less dynamic goods with falling market share 50%, while the Eastern Asian countries exported more than 50% high competitive, growing goods and only 4% of uncompetitive goods (UNCTAD 2000:91).

facturers with medium- and low-skilled technology intensity or as labour-intensive and resource-based manufacturers as can be obtained from Table 22.

Table 22: South Africa's export shares of manufactured goods with high-, medium- and low-skilled technology intensity and in labour-intensive and resource-based manufacturers

Product (in accordance to SITC classification)	South African product group (HS2 Code)	Classification of skilled technology intensity	Share in exports from developing countries (in %) 1998	Average annual export value growth in developing countries (in %) 1980-98	Share in South Africa's total exports (in %) 1991-2000
Chemicals and pharmaceutical	28,29,30,38	high	9	13.4	4.234
Aircraft	88	high	8.7	12.7	0.563
Electrical machinery	85	medium	11.3	16.2	1.448
Road motor vehicle	87	medium	8.7	16.5	2.977
Rubber and plastic products	39+40	medium	11	13.4	1.233
Non-electrical machinery	84	medium	8.2	13.7	3.859
Share of high- and medium-skilled technological products in total exports (1991-2000)					**14.314**
Clothing	59-63	labour-intensive	11.2	11.3	0.815
Wood and paper	44, 47-49	labour-intensive	9.5	12.1	3.720
Leather	42	labour-intensive	9.2	12.3	0.065
Toys and sporting goods	95	labour-intensive	9.2	9	0.045
Textiles	52-58	labour-intensive	8.1	11.7	0.663
Non-metallic mineral products	27	labour-intensive	8	11.3	7.193
Footwear	64	labour-intensive	7.8	9.6	0.071
Fabricated metal products	74-83	low	7.6	11.5	4.422
Iron and steel	72, 73	low	6.2	11.3	9.817
Ships and boats	89	low	6	7.5	0.201
Share of low-skilled technology and labour-intensive and resource-based manufacturers in total exports (1991-2000)					**27.012**

Source: UNCTAD 2002b:69, DTI 2001.

Labour intensive and low-skilled technology products made-up for an export share of more than 27% in the period 1991-2000. South Africa's most successful export products in this category were iron and steel (9.8%), mineral products (7.2%) and fabricated metal products (4.4%). Also some crude and processed mineral and agricultural commodities showed a considerable growth dynamic: metallic ores, fertilizers, non-ferrous metals and vegetable and fruits accounted for 32.8% of South Africa's total exports in the period 1991-2000 (UNCTAD 2002b:70 and DTI 2001). However, none of these dynamic sub-sectors was able to generate new employment. Only in very few sub-sectors, such as plastic products, printing media, wood production and leather production, new employment was generated.[178] The only two sectors that showed both, a positive output and employment growth in the period 1996-2001, were the wood and the leather production industry.

South Africa's past and present industrialisation policy

South Africa started to develop its manufacturing sector in the early 20th Century when it was not able to import all inputs because of First World War. From the 1960s on, South Africa tried to diversify its exports away from minerals, mainly gold, to manufacturing goods. The manufacturing sector was able to develop successfully because of high protection, state aid and a large, cheap labour reserve. However, the high protection in addition to increasing inflation raised the prices for inputs in the 1970s so that South Africa became increasingly dependent on capital imports (Yedder and Rake 2001:471, 483). Another problem for South Africa's import substitution strategy was the decreased capital productivity and increased labour costs due to the industry's inward-looking. Moreover, the shortage of high-skilled labour prevented South Africa's move from labour-intensive manufacturing towards capital-intensive manufacturing (Black and Kahn 2002:220). From the late 1980s on, South Africa started to implement trade reforms in the textile, automotive and electronic equipment sector in order to increase international competitiveness. This pro-active industrial policy centred on support for large-scale mineral companies and associated industries but failed to downstream to increased value addition for manufacturing activities (Lewis *et al.* 2004:154).

After the end of Apartheid, South Africa went on to liberalise its economy and became a member of the WTO in 1995. Because of its high protection degree, South Africa had to restructure its economy considerably. Industrial tariffs

---

178 Formal employment in the manufacturing sector is mainly generated by SMEs. Reasons for insufficient employment growth are seen in the enormous restructuring efforts of the South African economy, which were accompanied by decreased tariff protection and increased labour productivity (plus 26% from 1994-2002). Thus, mainly economic growth in labour and resource-intensive industries, such as clothing, food, footwear and metal products remained low and employment was decreasing (WTO 2003:A4-262, 273).

were reduced by one third in the period 1995-2000, export subsidies were terminated (since 1997), the number of tariff lines was reduced significantly, an average of 98% of tariff lines were bound at the WTO, and quantitative restrictions were converted into tariffs (GoSA 2003:32-3).

In 1996, South Africa dedicated itself with advisory support from the World Bank to the "Growth, Employment And Redistribution" (GEAR) strategy, predicting fiscal restraints, privatisation measures and export promotion of manufactured goods as necessary conditions for international competitiveness and increased private investment. Moreover, the government started a supply-side programme, which aimed to support SMEs, to promote infrastructure (housing, roads, communication) and to improve working skills, mainly for the black population (Black and Kahn 2002:235). However, South Africa's growth rates remained low, with an average of 2.14% p.a. in the period 1997-2001 (World Bank 2003). To increase economic growth, improve competitiveness and generate employment, the government decided in 2001 to draw special attention to sectors with high growth potential and potential for job creation, namely agriculture, tourism,[179] the information and communication sector, and certain (export) industries: automotive, textile, chemicals, and mining (WTO 2003:A4-262).

Currently, 32 incentive schemes to which South African producers can apply exist. These include access to finance, provision of infrastructure facilities, assistance for capacity building, technology transfer and human skills, and special support for the agro-industry, the textile sector and SMEs (WTO 2003:A4-296-9).[180] For the manufacturing sector, the so-called "Six Pack" has been announced by the DTI in 2000. This initiative includes certain programmes that provide eligible manufactures with tax free grants for investment, supplements of infrastructure, and take-over of training cost. Furthermore, grant facilities for foreign investors are provided and industrial development zones offering one-stop administrative centres and duty-free import of production-related raw materials were established (WTO 2003:A4-275-6).[181]

---

[179] Tourism has become more and more important though the growth rates remained below expectations. In 2001, South Africa was the world's 24th largest tourist destination, employing almost one million people. Tourism accounts for around 2% of the country's GDP (WTO 2003:A4-284).

[180] The high income inequality and the lack of qualified workers (as a heritage of Apartheid) have hampered the development of dynamic SMEs (Lewis et al. 2004:152). To support historically disadvantaged SMEs, the "Export Marketing and Investment Assistance Scheme" (EMIA) has been created, assisting SMEs with market and FDI research, financial assistance to participate in international exhibitions, and the provision of credit facilities by the Industrial Development Corporation (IDC) (WTO 2003:A4-253).

[181] See Lewis *et al.* (2004:172-7) for an evaluation of two supply-side programmes, namely the "Spatial Development Initiative" and the "Workplace Challenge".

However, though the secondary industry responded with growing export rates positively, it shows persistent trade deficits (see Figure 19).

Figure 19: South Africa's manufactures exports and imports (in million US$)

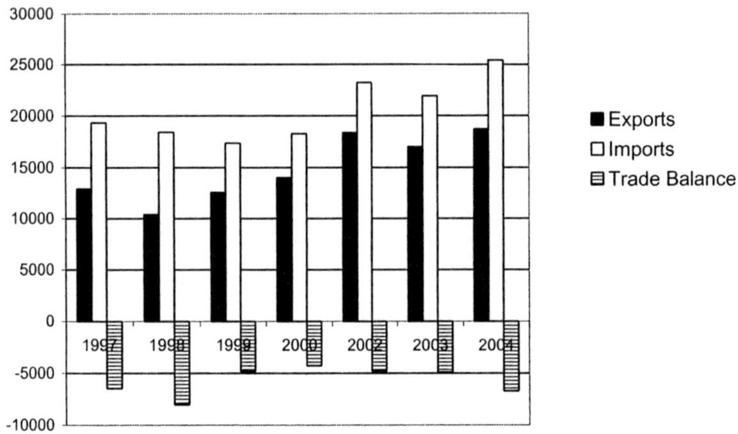

Sources: UNSD as cited in WTO 2003:A4-292-3 (1997-2000) and DTI 2005 (2002-2004).

It is criticised that the success of government's supply-side programmes to stimulate domestic manufacturing has remained limited because it has not been achieved to build backward- and forward linkages due to capacity shortages of domestic SMEs. Thus, the growth process of manufacturing exports could not be endogenised. Furthermore, the rapid tariff liberalisation had harmed labour-intensive industries and SME development (Lewis *et al.* 2004:172-4). The Department of Trade and Industry (DTI) contradicts this appraisal, arguing that tariff liberalisation had been implemented carefully and selective. However, the persistent trade deficit and high unemployment rate have resulted in increased opposition against further trade liberalisation. To date, the government got support for its comprehensive trade liberalisation policy because it has combined trade liberalisation with supply-side support. Moreover, South Africa's trade policy has been formulated in cooperation with all stakeholders concerned. For this purpose, the government established the National Economic Development and Labour Council (NEDLAC), which represents trade unions, business and community people (Lewis *et al.* 2004:158-9).[182]

[182] The role of NEDLAC in FTA negotiations is discussed in Chapter 6.

Botswana's Manufacturing activities

Botswana is highly dependent on its revenues from diamonds, which account for around 90% of its total export earning. The Minister of Natural Resources states *"...we have become almost the classic 'mono-culture' economy – even more extreme than those agricultural economies..."* (ACP General Secretariat 1995b:14). Though the country has received high capital inflows that have been used to develop its mining sector and diversify its economy towards the service sector,[183] mainly banking and tourism, linkages to the local manufacturing economy have depended weak so that *"...the second phase of diversification, "beyond diamonds", ... remains an unfinished business..."* (UNCTAD 2002a:53). Diamonds have helped Botswana to move from one of the poorest African countries at the time of independence (1966) to the one with the highest GDP per capita (2002) but the country was not able to diversify its export earnings. Botswana's dependency on diamonds has even increased since the early 1980s, while the contribution of manufacturing activities to GDP has stagnated at around 4 - 4.5% (Akinkugbe and Makepe 2005:13-5). However, the structure of the manufacturing sector has changed significantly in the past thirty years: while in 1972, beef production contributed to 78% of the manufacturing output, this share fell to 15% in 1999 (BoB 2000:100 as cited in WTO 2003:A1-93).[184] The fall of meat production was accompanied by an increase in foodstuff production (dairy and bakery products as well as beverages), clothing production and vehicle assembly.[185]

Only very few companies are involved in the export business: In 2003, six manufacturing enterprises in Botswana exported to the USA and five companies exported to the EU (Senosi 2003, Raditedu 2003).[186] Botswana's main manufacturing activities, which are also responsible for the bulk of employment in the manufacturing sector, concentrate on the domestic market: food (dairy, bakery

---

[183] Botswana has received high FDI on a stable level since 1975. With a total investment rate of 28.1% of GDP (World Bank 2001a), the country shows a higher investment level than developed countries and has been classified as "fast grower" (Berthélemy and Söderling 2002).

[184] Nevertheless, Botswana doubled its beef exports to the EU in the period 1972-84 (ACP General Secretariat 2003:70).

[185] Botswana's automotive industry suffered a setback in 2000 when, after six years, the main automobile assembly plant, Hyundai, closed after the protection period elapsed. Today, the country has only one car assembly plan (Volvo Truck and Bus Botswana Pty. Ltd.), which imports pieces of trucks and buses from the EU and assembles them in Botswana (Owen 2003).

[186] The companies that exported to the EU were Botswana Meat Commission, two textile companies, one metal processing company and one company that manufactures wiring harnesses for automobiles. The companies exporting to the USA were predominantly foreign-owned clothing companies (Senosi 2003).

and slaughtering products) and beverages account for around 50% of total manufacturing output (WTO 2003:A1-93, UNIDO 2002a, b). Employment in the manufacturing sector increased from 21,800 people in 1992 to 24,000 people in 2000, which are 11% of all employees (UNIDO 2002a, BEDIA 2001:7). Moreover, the domestic value addition of manufacturing activities has increased considerably in the last twenty years as Figure 20 shows.

Figure 20: Value added of Botswana's main manufacturing sectors (in thousand Pula)

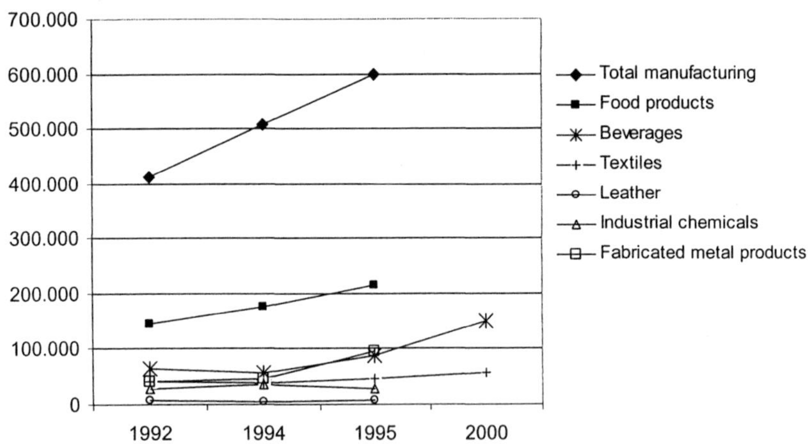

Sources: UNIDO 2002a and 2003a.

Since the early 1990ies, Botswana has further diversified its economy towards low-tech manufacturing (mainly textiles and jewellery) and tourism. Foreign firms are encouraged to engage in Botswana and are involved in many fields of the economy, like transport, wholesale trading, construction and tourism (UNCTAD 2002a:53). However, the foreign ventures into textile and motor vehicle assembly were disappointing and did not help to diversify the economy significantly (European Commission 2002b:5). The private sector in Botswana depends still heavily on public support, which is no longer seen as sustainable (Kappel 2005, ACP General Secretariat 2003:57). To make out new options for export diversification and identify market niches for competitive commodities and services, Botswana developed a National Export Strategy, which aims to expand activities in the third sector, namely tourism[187] and financial services. Moreover, Botswana wants to become an important business and banking metropolis in the region (GoB 2003:12).[188] As can be seen from Figure 21, service activities, such as banking and insurance, trade and hotels and construction activities contribute significantly more to Botswana's GDP than manufacturing activities.

Figure 21: The contribution of manufacturing and services to Botswana's GDP (in %)

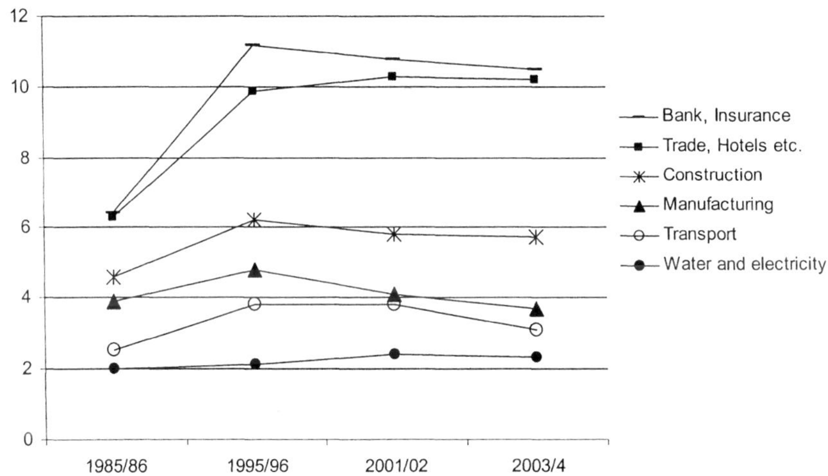

Source: BoB various issues as cited in Akinkugbe and Makepe (2005:13).

However, it is emphasised that the diversification of Botswana's economy *"... is not a choice between the two sectors; rather, it is manufacturing and services."* (ACP General Secretariat 2003:60). Since the manufacturing sector can employ more (and relatively unskilled) people than the service sector, its development is regarded as crucial for Botswana's economic diversification (Akinkugbe and Makepe 2005:18).

[187] The tourism sector has become an important income source and contributes to an estimated 5% of GDP (WTO 2003:A1-102). Although South Africa remains the most important tourist destination in Africa, Botswana's tourism has grown steadily in the last years (against the general trend), from 572,000 arrivals in 1997 to 923,000 in 2001 (ACP General Secretariat 2003:62).

[188] The income gained from banks, insurances and business services contributed for 11% of total GDP in 1999 (GoB 2003:12).

Botswana's industrialisation policy

Botswana has started its industrialisation policy in the early 1980s and pursued an import-substitution strategy though it was always considered as doubtful whether such a strategy could be successful, giving the small domestic market and the inability to determine the CET (Akinkugbe and Makepe 2005:20). As an active part of its industrialisation policy, the government funded a number of assistance schemes in order to attract investment in the manufacturing and the agriculture sector (WTO 2003:A1-77). The main instrument was the "Financial Assistance Policy", which was however abolished in 2000 since it has been reviewed that, despite almost 20 years of financial assistance, the majority of SMEs would not survive without the programme. The government runs now the "Citizen Entrepreneurial Development Agency" (CEDA) providing loans and grants to domestic businesses with the goal to establish an "entrepreneurial culture" in Botswana (ACP General Secretariat 2003:58-9).[189]

Since the early 1990s, after the end of Apartheid in South Africa and the accession of all SACU members to the WTO, the government has aimed to stimulate export-led industrialisation. Trade liberalisation and investment promotion are the key elements of Botswana's industrial policy, supported by the provision of a sound macroeconomic environment and a good infrastructure. FDI should help to diversify economic income towards textiles and clothing, apparels and engineering, leather goods, electronic products and pharmaceutical (WTO 2003:A1-62). The "Botswana Export Development and Investment Authority" (BEDIA) is responsible for the export promotion. Its duties include the sponsoring of Batswana exporters to participate in international exhibitions, promoting joint ventures, fostering FDI in the garment, textile, leather, and tannery industry, and promoting the manufacturing of jewellery and glasses. The main instruments are tariff exceptions and concessions on imported inputs used in the export to non-SACU markets and relaxed foreign exchange controls.[190] In 2002, six firms benefited from the scheme, of which all were in the clothing industry (WTO 2003:A1-77). To date, BEDIA has supported the establishment of 14 manufacturing industries in the country that created about 3,600 new jobs (BEDIA 2004 as cited in Akinkugbe and Makepe 2005:25). However, more than two third of this investment has taken place in the clothing and garment industry because of AGOA so that it remains difficult for Botswana to attract non-AGOA related FDI in the manufacturing sector. To promote manufacturing activities,

[189] See Akinkugbe and Makepe (2005:19-28) for further government incentives to promote economic diversification.

[190] Furthermore, BEDIA assist companies to exhibit their products by paying for exhibition stands and conference facilities, offers training schemes for medium and large companies (turnover > P 250,000) and promotes business contacts by its overseas offices in South Africa and London (Senosi 2003).

Botswana has also set-up an EPZ in the north-eastern part of the country, granting export companies a 15% tax rate (instead of 25%), tax on dividends exemptions and tax exemptions on imported inputs. However, to date the incentive has been hardly used and most companies close down their business after the incentive has expired (Akinkugbe and Makepe 2005:26-7).

Major constraints for a successful industrialisation of Botswana are seen in the small domestic market that makes it difficult to attract foreign investors, the landlocked location, which implies high transportation costs, underdeveloped industries, resulting in a high dependency on foreign inputs, and shortages of skilled labour and water (ACP General Secretariat 2003:56).

Lesotho's Manufacturing activities

Manufacturing sector's contribution to GDP rose from 10% in 1991 to 15% in 1994. Since then, it has remained at a level of 15 to 17% (WTO 2003:A2-115). Next to the garment and clothing industry, manufacturing activities in Lesotho take place in the fields of leather, food and beverages, consumer electronics, bricks, ceramics, television assemblies and edible oils destined for the domestic and South African market (Ibid:140-3).

Figure 22: Sectoral composition of Lesotho's GDP in 2000/2001

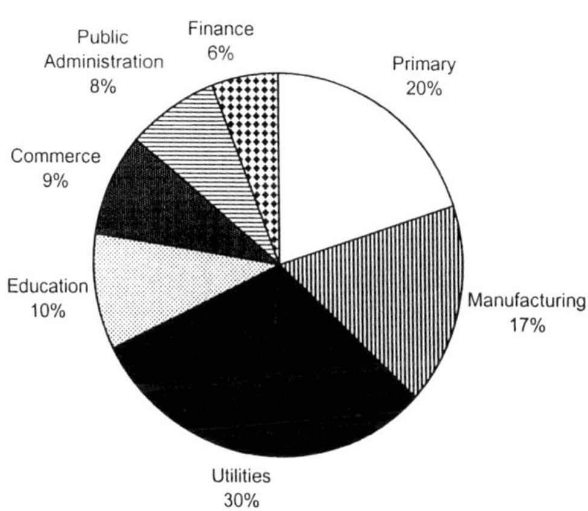

Source: IMF (2002), staff report as cited in WTO 2003:A2-115.

Industrialisation in Lesotho is almost solely based on the manufacturing of clothing and garments.[191] The lack of natural resources, the smallness of the country and the high dependency on the South African economy have contributed to the fact that Lesotho focuses its industrialisation strategy on the labour-intensive manufacturing of clothes and apparels.

Lesotho's clothing industry was established in the early 1980ies when companies, originally based in South Africa, invested in the country to avoid international sanctions. When Lesotho was exempted from the restrictive rules of origin under Lomé in the late 1980ies (until 1996), and thus allowed to use inputs from non-ACP countries, a second wave of investment from Chinese companies formerly located in South Africa's "homelands", arrived.[192] With the expiration of this derogation, many companies downsized or closed (Lall 2003:8-9, WTO 2003:A2-142). However, with the creation of the AGOA initiative, new FDI arrived and clothing companies oriented towards the US-market (see Box 22). Since the EU's EBA initiative does not allow Lesotho to use third-country inputs for clothing exports (see Box 23), its exports to the EU only accounted for 0.8% of its total exports in 2000 (WTO 2003:A2-116).

Box 22: The AGOA initiative

The non-reciprocal US-initiative AGOA ("African Growth and Opportunity Act") started in 2000 and provides duty and quota-free market access to the USA for a range of products destined from 38 eligible African countries, including all SACU countries.[193]

Continuation on next page.

[191] One has to differentiate between the textile and the clothing industry. While the textile industry is capital intensive, technologically sophisticated and often highly protected, the clothing industry is labour intensive, technologically unsophisticated and competitive (Platzky 1996:145-6). South Africa and Mauritius are the only Sub-Saharan African countries, which have a textile industry whereas the BLNS countries have only a preference-initiated clothing industry. The textile industry in South Africa is vertically integrated and covers the whole production process from the production of natural fibres over the manufacturing of intermediate inputs to the production of finished goods (Hall 2004:8).

[192] FDI in manufacturing activities other than the clothing has remained low. South African Breweries has an affiliate in the country, and a US-owned milling company exists (Lall 2003:8). As already discussed in section 2, the "Lesotho Highland Water Project" still accounts for the bulk of Lesotho's FDI. However, since the construction of the project was finalised it cannot be expected to drive further growth in Lesotho (Lall 2003:43).

[193] To become eligible, African countries have to establish a market-based economy, develop political pluralism, respect the rule of law, eliminate discriminatory barriers to the US trade and investment, protect intellectual property rights, combat corruption and protect human and workers rights (WTO 2003:17).

Continuation of Box 22 from previous page.

With AGOA, the USA expanded the list of products qualified for duty free access under the GSP to additional 1,835 product lines until the end of 2015.[194] Furthermore, an effective visa system that prevents illegal transhipment and verifies the rules of origin has to be into place (WTO 2003:17). Generally, the use of US-formed yarns, fabrics and threads must be proved and products must be wholly assembled in any eligible state in order to benefit from AGOA. Inputs from foreign origin are only accepted if the value does not exceed 25% of the assembled article. This strict interpretation of the rules of origin used to be a problem for many African states. The USA responded to African countries' concerns and classified all AGOA eligible countries with a per capita income of less than US$ 1,500 p.a. as "lesser developed countries" that are allowed to use inputs from anywhere in the world (WTO 2003:A2-121).[195] This allowance from which all BLNS countries benefit was originally restricted until 30 September 2004 but has been expanded for another three years.[196]

As a result of the AGOA initiative, the USA has become the largest singly market for Africa, purchasing around one third of African countries' total exports (which are less than 2% of total US-imports) (USTR 2002a:1). However, AGOA is still dominated by few countries and few products: Nigeria, Gabon and South Africa accounted for 92% of AGOA exports in 2002. The main export product was cruel oil, accounting for 73% of total AGOA exports (USTR 2002a:5). Clothing exports accounted for 1.6% of total US-imports from Sub-Saharan Africa in 2001 (UNIDO 2004a:65). Agricultural products, such as sugar, tobacco and cotton remain highly protected in the US-market (AfDB 2004:201).It is criticised that AGOA bears the risk that the countries promote only the clothing industry, thereby neglecting other sectors. For Lesotho, Schuler (2002, as cited in WTO 2003:A2-121) states: "*Benefits to Lesotho might ... be fairly limited if the only effect of AGOA trade preferences is that Lesotho now exports larger quantities of the same products it has always been shipping to the U.S., without any expansion of exports into new product lines...*" Like this AGOA would even increase the dependency and thus the vulnerability of African economies. The expiration of AGOA and/or the erosion of preferences in the US-market is therefore very likely to result in a collapse of Africa's clothing industry.

---

194 The Act originally covered an eight year period to September 2008 but was extended (AGOA.info 2005).

195 However, also the "lesser developed countries" have to use an "applicable percentage" of inputs from the USA. This "applicable percentage" took 2% in the period 2002-03 and raises in stages to 3.5% until 2007 (WTO 2003:A2-141).

196 Though Botswana's, Namibia's and Swaziland's GDP per capita is above US$ 1.500,00 they achieved the classification as "lesser developed country" in 2002 (WTO 2003:A2-120).

Box 23: The failure of the EU's "Everything But Arms" initiative in Africa

The EU's "Everything But Arms" (EBA) initiative exists since 2001 and grants all Least Developed Countries (LDCs) in the world duty free market access for all products except arms and weapons. For the commodities bananas, rice and sugar, tariffs are gradually reduced and will be zero by 2006 (bananas) and 2009 (rice and sugar) respectively. The EBA initiative is, like AGOA, an expanded GSP. It is not time-bound and of non-contractual nature.

To date, African countries have barely made use of the EBA initiative. This is a) because 99% of the goods African LDCs export to the EU have already free market access under the Cotonou Agreement; b) because those for the LDCs relevant products rice, sugar and bananas are still quantitatively restricted; and c) because of the strict rules of origin. EBAs rules of origin are the same applied under the GSP, which are more restrictive than those applied under the Cotonou Agreement. A study compiled by Brenton (2003:18) summarises: "*...such rules discriminate against small countries where the possibilities for local sourcing are limited or non-existent. Since most LDCs are small countries they are particularly disadvantaged by restrictive rules of origin ...*" As a result, African countries export their manufactured products, such as clothing, garments and apparels to the USA where the AGOA initiative provides more generous conditions for "lesser developed countries". The EBA initiative whereas has completely failed to increase the exports of African LDCs to the EU. Zambia has been the main African beneficiary of EBA with 0.86% of its total exports being exported under EBA in 2002. Lesotho's exports under EBA were 0% in the same year (Brenton 2003:26).

The clothing industry in Lesotho is exclusively foreign owned, mainly by Taiwanese and Chinese producers. These companies do only assemble semi-finished products in Lesotho (assembly-subcontracting) but do not source products from local producers (full package subcontracting). Thus, Lesotho's main benefit is the employment of low-skilled and low-wage workers, in particular women.

UNCTAD (2002b:99-100) emphasises that only countries that have benefited from full-package subcontracting from international textile companies have been able to go under transition. To date, these countries were mainly the first-tier NICs (Hong Kong, Korea, Singapore and Taiwan), which assembled the full package type of production and were able to switch their manufacturing sector from labour- to capital-intensive production and to outsource the labour-intensive operations to poorer, neighbouring countries. Considering Lesotho's size and development degree as well as the international competition situation it is (almost) impossible that the country establishes backward linkages in order to benefit from full-package subcontracting. Though the government promotes local producers of ancillary industries, like the production of zip fasteners, collar supports, elastic braids and buttons, the establishment of linkages between the foreign-owned clothing industry and domestic producers has proved to be very difficult (GoL 2003). There are only very few domestic firms that have the ability and capacity to supply the export-oriented clothing industry. Most companies work on a micro-base (up to three employees) and serve only the domestic market (Lall 2003:28).

In Lesotho, where most people still rely on small-scale agricultural activities and remittance from mining workers based in South Africa, the clothing sector offers, together with the public sector, the main source of formal employment. However, since the required skills are basic and Lesotho's unemployment rate is very high, workers become highly exchangeable and do not have any bargaining power.[197] Moreover, the rapid industrialisation process as a response to AGOA has resulted in a lack of water supply and the pollution of water and land.[198]

To date, AGOA has not helped Lesotho to promote economic development but contributed to "immiserizing growth". Though the country experienced stable growth rates, economic returns are decreasing. Thus, Lesotho's GNI per capita has decreased,[199] indicating that the raise in employment in the garment industry has not compensated for the income losses formerly obtained from the remittance of Basotho mining workers in South Africa. As a result, the poverty level in Lesotho persists and is even worsening (WTO 2003:A2-111-2).[200]

---

[197] Labour unions demand the government to set through the payment of minimum wages, guarantee the respect of human working conditions and basic labour rights. Though the law stipulates these rights they are very often not respected in the garment industry (Africanews 2001). An independent investigation on working conditions in the clothing industry has not yet been allowed by the owners (ACP General Secretary 2002a:90).

[198] Thus, water tariffs for the clothing industry are so low that the industry does not have any incentive to clean and recycle water. Up to now, the negative external effects are carried solely by the people, causing shortages of supply with drinking water. Requests to internalise these negative external effects by environmental regulations are becoming louder and the implementation of a corresponding World Bank programme is in progress (UNIDO 2004a:95, ACP General Secretariat 2002a:91).

[199] The GNI can be defined as GDP minus depreciation and plus net factor incomes from abroad. Lesotho's GDP per capita remained with US$ 521 static in the period 1996-2000, while its GNI per capita decreased from US$ 750 in 1996 to US$ 580 in 2000 (World Bank 2001b, 2002).

[200] Around 80% of the workforce in the clothing industry is female (Thakalekoala 2003). In 1989, these women earned in average M 5,740 p.a. compared to M 25,000 for men working in the mining industry (WBG 2003 as cited in WTO 2003:A2-113). HIV/AIDS, droughts and famines contribute to worsening poverty in Lesotho (WTO 2003:A2-111).

Lesotho's industrialisation policy

Lesotho, which is almost 100% dependent on the export of one commodity range (clothing and garments) into one market (USA) tries to diversify towards other manufacturing activities, such as the canning of beans, stone mining, clay and pottery, and towards tourism.[201] The country aims further to diversify into other markets, in particular in the region (INSAT 2005a:14). Thus, Lesotho wants to reduce its export-led industrialisation strategy and also focus its resources on the development of domestic and regional markets. Lesotho's commercial development is mainly in the hand of the 1967 established "Lesotho National Development Corporation" (LNDC), which tries to promote an industrial strategy for SMEs by using the beneficial market access to South Africa, the EU and the USA.[202] The LNDC comprehends enterprises in the clothing, brewing, and paper milling sector as well as shopping centres and hotels. In 2000, the LNDC held interest in 54 manufacturing enterprises of which 36 were in the clothing sector (WTO 2003:A2-132-3).

Lesotho practises no general export subsidy scheme. However, to support Basotho exporters, the government rebates import duties paid on inputs (raw materials or components). With the exception of diamonds, where a tax rate of 15% is levied, Basotho exporters are not subject to sales tax. Thus, the whole country is treated as an EPZ since all inputs used for export are fully rebated. Moreover, Lesotho has introduced an export finance and insurance scheme that covers commercial but also political risks for small and medium exporters. Large exporters receive only assistance if the company establishes linkages to domestic SMEs. The allowance of export financing schemes should promote export activities and compensate for domestic inefficiencies, like the poor infrastructure (GoL 2003:22). Furthermore, the government promotes the manufacturing sector, which is only subject to a corporate tax rate of 15% compared with 37% for enterprises of other sectors (WTO 2003:A2-131-2).

Namibia's manufacturing activities

In addition to the traditional fields of mining, fishing and agriculture, the young Namibian economy has started to increase its manufacturing activities in the early 1990s. However, despite some manufacturing activities in the field of

---

[201] The Government aims to promote "eco-tourism". Constraints for the expansion of tourism are seen in a low capacity and poor standard of accommodation and restaurants as well as lack of trained personnel, resulting poor services. Furthermore, the destruction of heritage sites and general poor infrastructure limit touristic activities (GoL 2003:27).

[202] The core function of the LNDC comprise promotion of manufacturing activities in the country, investment promotion, entrepreneurial development (incl. finance and technical services) and monitoring and appraisal of the national development process (WTO 2003:A2-132-3).

clothing and automotive semi-assembling, Namibia's industrial capabilities are judged as underdeveloped (AfDB 2002a:89). In the period 1991-2000, sectoral contribution to GDP changed only slightly with manufacturing activities accounting for around 11% of Namibia's GDP in 2000 (BoN 2002:6). As can be obtained from Figure 23, the manufacturing of food products and construction activities accounts for the bulk of manufacturing activities in Namibia.

Figure 23: Namibia's GDP by activity (in million N$, constant 1995 prices)

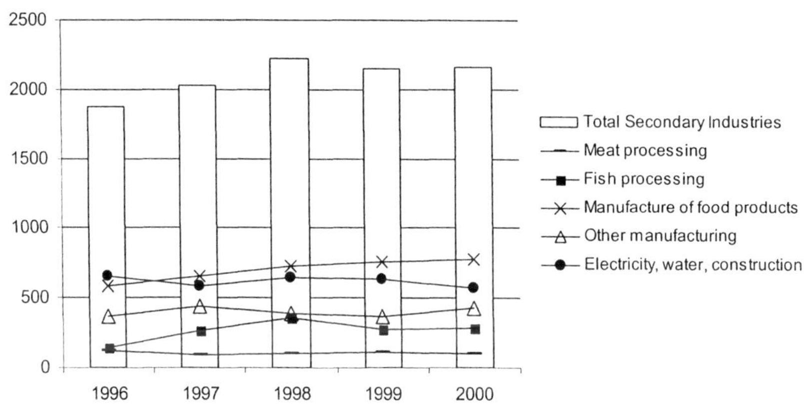

Source: Namibian Central Bureau of Statistics as cited in BoN (2002:113).

Manufacturing activities contributed to around 6% of total formal employment in 2000 (GoN 2003:20).[203] While overall employment in Namibia has decreased since 1991, it has been successfully generated in the manufacturing sector, mainly in the fishing industry. The manufacturing sector is therefore regarded as source of employment, growth and export expansion (BoN 2002:8, 25).

The manufacturing sector in Namibia is dominated by few large scale companies, mainly operating in the food sector. The food and beverage sector account together for around two third of Namibia's total manufacturing output. Other manufacturing activities take place in the fields of electricity and construction, leather, packaging materials, clothing, wood and paper, furniture, chemicals, metal components, fish cans and soaps (UNIDO 2003b:9-10). Most inputs needed for manufacturing activities are imported so that the domestic value addition is low. Namibia's manufacturing activities are either related to

[203] The government employed more than 57% of the Namibian workforce in 2001 and is the biggest contributor to the services sector (GoN 2003:20).

the first stage of processing, such as the preservation of fish, or to the final stage of blending products (UNIDO 2003b:13). The government names the lack of modern technology, skilled labour and geographical concentration as difficulties for increased diversification progress (GoN 2003:20). Namibia aims to increase its domestic value addition by increased productivity, expanded exports and an efficient import substitution policy and to diversify the economy by improved backward- and forward linkages, which should generate employment and distribute welfare more equally (UNIDO 2003b:15). The promotion of diversification activities relate to (1) horizontal diversification for agricultural products, such as table grapes, ostrich meat and horticultural products; (2) vertical diversification for manufacturing activities, such as the polishing of diamonds, development of leather production, increased value addition in the fish industry, and the expansion of assembled electronic and garment products; and (3) the expansion of the service sector, e.g. in the field of tourism (Nujoma 2003, Bank of Namibia 2002:24-5).[204]

Namibia's industrialisation policy

The government supports manufacturing activities in Namibia through indirect and direct measures. Indirect support is provided by investment in infrastructure where the expenditures for transport and communication increased by more than 160% in the period 1996-2000 (BoN 2002:114). Direct support is given by the creation of diverse investment incentives. Thus, the establishment of EPZ in Namibia is possible all over the country as long as at least 70% of production is for export purposes. Companies operating in this zone enjoy diverse preferences, like exemption from income tax, sales tax, customs duties, transfer taxes and the fee repatriation of capital and profits. In 2001, 31 companies with EPZ status acted in Namibia (UNIDO 2003b:16) but this figure shrank to 25 companies in 2003 (Nujoma 2003). Namibia wants to expand EPZ activities and intends to improve its offshore financing facilities. The fostering of activities in the manufacturing sector has also been supported by the Special Industrialisation Programme launched in 2000, which provides credit facilities and incentive programmes for entrepreneurs (European Commission 2002a:11). Moreover, the government established the Special Incentive for Manufactures in order to increase economic activities in the manufacturing sector. Manufacturers pay only taxes on 50% of their income for up to ten years, can write-off factory buildings over ten years and are exempted from paying sales taxes on imported manufacturing machineries (GoN 2003:14). However, none of these incentives has contributed to a successful promotion of industrialisation. According to UNIDO

[204] Tourism generates around 6% of Namibia's GDP, contributes to around 11% of foreign exchange earnings and has become the third important sector after mining and manufacturing (BoN 2002:25).

(2003b:15-6) this is because 1) Namibia's industrialisation policy has been only insufficiently linked to other policy objectives; 2), the Ministry of Trade and Industry shows institutional weaknesses and lacks of qualified human capital; 3) Namibia's industrialisation policy does not target specific sectors and has not taken the country's international trade obligations sufficiently into account; and 4) the policies do not sufficiently acknowledge the role of technology, labour relations and non-state actors and do not fully reflect the overall economic and socio-economic situation. Due to these weaknesses Namibia has reformulated its industrial policy since 2003, which is a still ongoing process.

Swaziland's manufacturing activities

Swaziland is the most industrialised BLNS country. The manufacturing sector accounts for around 35% of GDP and is also the main investment destination, attracting 64% of total FDI in 2000 (CBoS 2001).[205] Swaziland's industrial sector produces mainly sugar based products (soft-drinks, confectionery) and agro-processed products (canned fruits, dairy products). These products are primarily destined for the South African market, which made up for 60% of Swaziland's total export earnings in 2001 (WTO 2003:A5-312).[206]

The Swazi economy is strongly outward oriented; in fact, Swaziland's bonding into the SACU market and the since 30 years' lasting preferences for the EU market, mainly for sugar, have encouraged sugar- and agro-based industries. The preferences of the EU Sugar Protocol had helped Swaziland to attract investment from large subsidiary sugar fabric producers (Cadbury, Coca Cola) and to build up a fruit-canning and jam producer (Swazican). These activities account until today for the bulk of Swaziland's GDP (see Box 24).

Without preferences, it would be very difficult for a small, landlocked country like Swaziland to industrialise. One interview partner from a large, foreign-owned company states: *"Taking the Swazi environment into account you have no chance get into the market without preferences. ... To recruit for instance qualified labour, our competition market is not Swaziland but South Africa. We have to pay South African salaries plus a premium of 10-20% to stay in Swaziland."* To keep investors in the country, Swaziland offers special investment incentives and individual tax arrangements for its few large foreign companies (King 2003).

[205] However, since the end of Apartheid in South Africa, Swaziland has increasingly problems to attract FDI. The reinvestment inflows account for 90% of total FDI so that it is Swaziland's primarily goal to keep foreign investors that are already in the country (Basu and Srinivasan 2002:29). New FDI inflows are mainly related to AGOA (UNCTAD 2002a:54).

[206] Because of AGOA exports of clothing and garments have increased considerably from 4% in 2000 to 12% in 2002 and have overhauled forestry products as the second largest export commodity (WTO 2003:A5-312).

Box 24: The Swazi sugar industry

The Swazi sugar industry has been established in 1958 and accounts today for around 18% of GDP and 16% of private sector employment. More than 90% of Swaziland's sugar, which is to a large extent produced by large-scale enterprises, is destined for export. While the Swazi sugar industry used to be foreign-owned in the past, this has changed in the meanwhile: Today, 47% of the cane growing and 51% of the milling industry are local. The Swazi government has a keen interest in further local participation in form of "local-foreign partnerships" and tries to attract FDI in order to increase local employment and to ensure the livelihood of subsistence farmers (ACP General Secretariat 1999:47).

The Swaziland Sugar Association (SSA) is the only company that is allowed to purchase sugar from Swazi growers and to export and market it in the EU and the USA, the most valuable export markets. The quota under the EU Sugar Protocol accounted for 28% of Swaziland's total sugar exports in 2002, while 3% of total sugar exports went to the USA (SSA 2003). The bulk of Swaziland's cane sugar goes to the SACU market (56%).[207] Moreover, Swaziland exports around 11% of its production duty free to the COMESA countries Kenya, Egypt and Madagascar and 2% to the rest of the world. Thus, 98% of Swaziland's sugar exports are sold duty free and more than 85% of Swaziland's total sugar exports obtain prices that are well above the world market price (SSA 2003).

Swaziland's high dependency on sugar preferences raises concern as regional and international competition is increasing and preferences are eroding. General trade liberalisation under the WTO, the reform of the EU sugar market regime, the EBA initiative, and the insecurity about the maintenance and future worthiness of the Sugar Protocol beyond 2008 affect the Swazi sugar industry harshly (see Chapter 3). Additionally, increased regional competition under the SADC Trade Protocol[208] and Swaziland's expected pull-out from COMESA will affect the revenue from sugar exports negatively.[209]

---

207 The sales of sugar in the SACU is defined by the South African Sugar Association Agreement according to which Swaziland is allowed to supply 18.7% of SACU's total production into the market (SSA 2003).

208 The SADC Trade Protocol provides for the liberalisation of the SADC sugar market from 2013 on. Though Swaziland has ratified the SADC Trade Protocol, the country is according to the Ministry of Foreign Affairs and Trade not ready *"...to liberalise our sugar market within SADC as long as world distortions are in place."* (Pato 2003).

209 It is above all Coca Cola Swaziland, the largest company in the country that contributes to more than 25% of Swaziland's GDP that is interested in maintaining preferred market access to COMESA countries. Around 15% of Coca Cola's production goes to COMESA countries. If Swaziland is forced to pull out of COMESA, Coca Cola's prices offered in COMESA countries would increase by 15-30% due to tariffs. Because of this loss of competitiveness the COMESA market would no longer be delivered from Coca Cola Swaziland

Further industrialisation in Swaziland should be promoted through the manufacturing of clothing and garment and through improved transport and other infrastructure-related services, such as energy, rail, air, telecommunication and water.[210] With exception of the clothing and garment production, industrial development in Swaziland is based on domestic inputs, thus allowing the promotion of backward linkages to the agricultural and forestry sector (WTO 2003:A5-310).[211] As already discussed in section 3.3.2, a worldwide more liberalised sugar regime might also have some positive implications for the Swazi economy since it reduces input prices in the sugar-based manufacturing sector, which can help to increase production of chocolate éclairs, soft drink concentrate, jam, bubble gum (King 2003, Stock 2003).

Swaziland's industrialisation policy

Swaziland has not developed an industrial policy so far but is working together with UNIDO on a research study that comes up with accordant recommendations (Dlamini 2003). Up to now, the Swaziland Investment Promotion Authority (SIPA) promotes labour-intensive and export-oriented industries. Additionally, SIPA was in 2003 still promoting the cultivation of cane sugar since *"Sugar is the most valuable crop we have."*(Mkhonta and Maphalala 2003). Due to its size and its SACU membership, an industrialisation strategy for Swaziland is very difficult. Since the country has already a fruit-canning, a soft-drink and a sweets company, it would not make sense to establish new industries in these sectors. There is however the intention to promote diversification towards sugar syrup and sugar tube (Mahlinza 2003).

Swaziland does not offer any export subsidies but an export credit guarantee scheme for SMEs. However, this scheme is barely used since only few SMEs are involved in exporting and since the conditions of the programme are judged as being too strict (WTO 2003:A5-329). To promote investment and manufacturing activities in the country, Swaziland grants tax concessions on new investment or new product lines introduced in the manufacturing sector. This scheme also takes the capital stock and employment creation into account so that a reduced corporate tax rate of 10% up to ten years is possible. More-

but from the Egyptian branch, which is already supplying the Kenyan market because the strong Rand has made exports from Swaziland too expensive (King 2003).

[210] The extension of infrastructure services is supported by the trans-boarder programme of the "Maputo Development Corridor" that links the region of Gauteng (South Africa) via Swaziland to the harbour of Maputo (Swaziland) (WTO 2003:A5-321). Another service sector the government wants to promote by stronger cooperation with South Africa is tourism, which is still underdeveloped and contributed to less than 2% of GDP in 2001 (WTO 2003:A5-344-5).

[211] However, the slow economic growth rates since 1997 has affected the agricultural sector and thus, the food processing industry, negatively (WTO 2003:A5-310).

over, dividends of FDI are tax free for ten years and up to 15% of the costs spent for employees' training can be offset against tax payments (WTO 2003:A5-330).

Summarising SACU countries' manufacturing performance and industrial policy, similarities and difference become obvious. South Africa is the only SACU economy that has a sophisticated manufacturing base and also produces capital-intensive, high technological manufacturers, such as automotives and machinery. Manufacturing activities in the BLNS countries centre, with exception of Lesotho, on agro-based and food-processing products. BLNS countries' export base is very narrow and hardly linked to domestic manufacturing activities (above all in Botswana and Lesotho). Manufacturing value-addition is generally low and activities are restricted to the first stage of processing or the final stage of blending.

All SACU countries have in common that they provide indirect support (infrastructure, training facilities…) and direct support (tax exemptions, subsidised credits…) to promote manufacturing activities and to attract manufacturing-related FDI. However, none of these incentives has resulted in a boom of manufacturing activities yet, which indicates they do not outweigh investment constraints, such as lack qualified workforce, the high HIV/AIDS prevalence, institutional weakness, and a narrow domestic market. Even South Africa, which receives most investment in the manufacturing sector, has not been able to attract the investment required to promote increased growth and employment.

4.2.3 The Contribution of FDI and Trade Preference Schemes to SACU Countries' Industrialisation Strategies

It is recommended that African countries try to attract investment from multinational corporations and foster joint-ventures in order to develop linkages between export expansion and domestic investment, which are supposed to stimulate industrialisation processes through technology and skill transfers. Like this, domestic companies' position in the international value chain should be improved (AfDB 2004:267-8, UNCTAD 2002b:53-4). However, the attraction of FDI from multinational companies means to meet a challenge of complex difficulties for African countries, as it generally requires a proper infrastructure, low transport and communication costs, efficient public and private institutions, a well-skilled workforce, a sizeable domestic market and, last but not least, political and macroeconomic stability. Surveys among investors have shown that it is only "resource seeking FDI", showing the highest returns of investment that is undertaken despite the absence of political and economic stability.

South Africa, Angola and Nigeria received 50-75% of total African FDI inflows in 2003 (AfDB 2004:268). With the exception of South Africa, FDI in Sub-Saharan Africa is still determined by natural resources (oil, diamonds, gold...) and, to a much lesser extent, by preferences (AGOA/MFA, Cotonou/EBA). The BLNS countries are no exception in this respect. Though the countries provide a good investment climate with a stable macro-economic policy, a proper infrastructure, a liberal trade regime and various incentives to attract FDI (UNIDO 2004a:13), FDI is either resource-based or a result of "trade distortions", namely AGOA/MFA, Cotonou/EBA.[212] In Botswana and Namibia, FDI takes mainly place in the mining sector, particularly in the diamond sector, where joint ventures with the government have been established.[213]

South Africa is the only SACU country, which receives FDI in a broad range of sectors. FDI in non-mining activities, mainly finance and services, manufacturing and accounting, made up for more than 70% of total FDI in 2000. However, South Africa's total amount of FDI has remained very low since 1994, with an average of just below 1% of GDP. For countries with a comparable development status, this level is in average 3.5% of GDP. Moreover, manufactured-related FDI was decreasing, accounting for 26.4% of FDI in 2000, compared to 42.5% in 1997 (WTO 2003:A4-220-4).[214]

As discussed, all SACU countries have established Export Processing Zones (EPZ) to promote FDI. The idea of EPZ is that companies that produce exclusively for the export market are granted special conditions, such as tax holidays or tax free imports and/or the free repatriation of capital and profits. With such incentives, the promotion of labour-intensive manufactured activities, the attraction of domestic and foreign investment, the increase of export quantities and the promotion of linkages between the export sector and the domestic industry should be promoted. Furthermore, the import of technology and skills is supposed to stimulate domestic production and employment. Since EPZ have

---

[212] In Botswana, 79.3% of total FDI in 2000 took place in the mining sector (WTO 2003:A1-59).

[213] Botswana and Namibia aim to increase the domestic value addition of diamond production by cutting and polishing them within the country but successes are limited so that the value-added process of diamond production does still occur abroad (European Commission 2002b:13-4). Moreover, diamonds prices are very volatile and do highly respond to external shocks. The ongoing issue of "conflict diamonds" and the insufficient certification process is likely to affect Botswana and Namibia negatively. Governments have therefore decided that all diamond exports are subject to certification under the "Nation's Kimberley Process International Certification System" (WTO 2003:A1-90).

[214] The main investors in South Africa are Great Britain (74% of total FDI in 2000), the USA (6%), Germany (5.8%) and other European countries (9.3%). Only few manufacturing sectors in South Africa show a stable investment growth, which are the automotive and the automotive component industry, the leather sector, paper and paper products and basic chemicals (WTO 2003:A4-274).

supported the industrialisation strategy of East Asian countries, they were also implemented in African countries. However, the experience of EPZ in Africa has been rather negative to date. With the exception of Mauritius, EPZ have not contributed to the expansion of an industrial base in Africa. Domestic industries have not been stimulated due to a lack of vertical integration, missing qualified human capital, poor infrastructure services, and macroeconomic and political instability (UNIDO 2004a:83). In most African countries, EPZ have resulted in "export enclaves" that are not linked to the domestic industry and offer hardly option for domestic value addition.

Again, BLNS are no exception. Activities in their EPZ take mainly place in the clothing and garment industry, which is hardly linked to the domestic industry so that benefits are limited to cheap, low-skilled employment. The example of AGOA-related FDI shows that the employment effects are mixed (gender biased, low-skilled, non-sustainable) and that negative effects on the environment, on small-scale production and on people's livelihood are not incorporated into companies' costs (Madeley 2003:36-8).[215] The extensive investment incentives granted by southern African EPZ are therefore said to result into a "race to the bottom" where countries "pay more than they get". Many southern African countries compete against each other by offering the most generous investment incentive to foreign investors, including tax holiday, duty free imports, no exchange rate restrictions, subsidised wages, low social standards, no environmental restrictions and even free water and electricity. In the case of Namibia, the subsidies paid to the Malaysian textile company "Ramatex" were equivalent to the combined wages of all textile workers for three years (The Namibian, 09/08/05).[216]

In sum, the effects EPZ had on SACU countries' industrialisation process are neglectable. The effects of trade preferences under the US-AGOA initiative

---

[215] In fact, the quality of employment has to be taken into account, too. Because of high unemployment and a low organisation degree, the working force has hardly bargaining power. Thus, the increase of low-quality employment must also be seen in the light of decreasing social welfare in the single countries. The tight budgetary position makes it, moreover, increasingly difficult for developing countries to engage in necessary reforms, such as the increase of export capacities and instalment of alternative income sources (Wohlmuth 2003:25-7).

[216] Ramatex was looking for the most attractive AGOA recipient country and chose Namibia, which granted Ramatex significant labour law concession, 99 years' tax break, free land and water and free infrastructure. The total costs of these concessions were estimated to be around N$ 30 million (Namibia Economist, 28/09/01). Since Ramatex employs around 5% of the Namibian workforce, it had a very good bargaining position. However, it is criticised that Ramatex offers only poor skilled jobs and poor working conditions and pollutes the environment (Tralac news, 19/04/04). Moreover, no skill or technological transfer would take place (The Namibian 09/08/02).

were much more relevant to stimulate industrialisation in BLNS, though considerable negative side-effects have occurred. Moreover, AGOA resulted in the concentration of one export sector (clothing and apparel industry), thereby bearing the risk to neglect other manufacturing sectors, which are important for domestic and regional supply.

SACU countries' response to AGOA

South Africa and Lesotho export under AGOA since 2001 and Botswana, Namibia and Swaziland (BNS) since 2002.[217] As can be obtained from the Figures 24 and 25, Lesotho, South Africa and Swaziland experienced growing trade surpluses vis-à-vis the USA in the period 1997-2004.

Figure 24: BLNS countries' trade balance with the USA (in million US$)

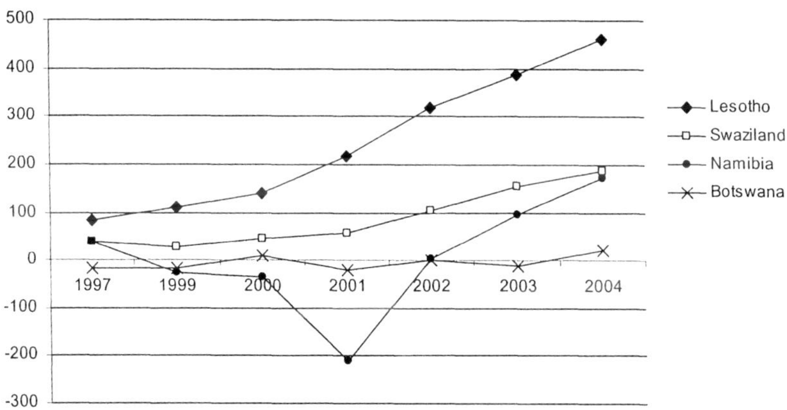

Source: AGOA.info (2005).

Namibia and Botswana whereas took comparably little advantage of the AGOA initiative and also exported lower AGOA-related volumes than Lesotho and Swaziland. With the exception of Lesotho, no SACU country experienced an "export boom" with the start of AGOA in 2001.

It is however obvious that both, exports to the USA and the export surplus vis-à-vis the USA, have developed positively for all BLNS countries since 2001.

---

217 BNS were not able to meet the rules of origin criteria valid for African countries with a GDP per capita above US$ 1.5000 (see Box 22) but reached an exemption and the classification as "lesser developed countries" in 2002 (WTO 2003:A2-120).

Figure 25: South Africa's external trade with the USA (in million US$)

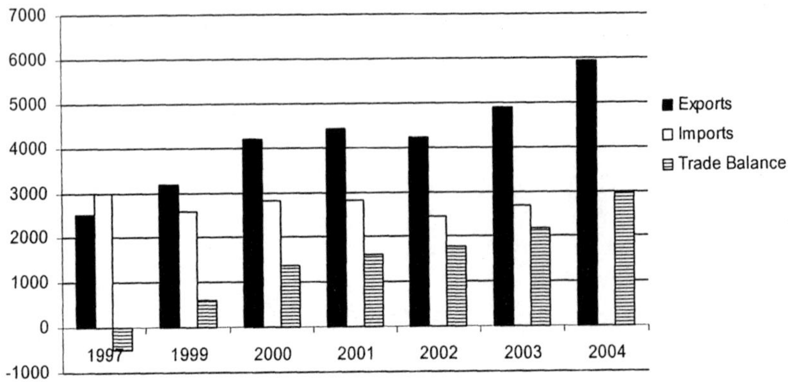

Source: AGOA.info (2005).

BLNS exports to the USA are highly biased towards minerals (Botswana and Namibia) and clothing and apparels (Lesotho and Swaziland). These two product groups account for around 90% of BLNS total exports to the USA (see Table 23).

South Africa is the only SACU country that has reached a certain diversification degree regarding its exports to the USA. Though minerals and metals are still dominating, South Africa also exports transportation equipment, vehicles (BMW), chemicals, agricultural products and machinery to the US-market.

BLNS clothing and apparel exports are highly dependent on AGOA, which considerably boosted FDI in this sector and created new employment (WTO 2003, USTR 2002a:3). South Africa again, has hardly received any AGOA-related FDI in the clothing industry (Kaplan 2004:633).[218]

[218] Reasons are the comparable high labour costs in South Africa, the highly attractive investment incentives in BLNS compared to South Africa and the fact that South Africa is not classified as "lesser developed country" under AGOA. Thus, spinning, weaving, and assembling has to take place in South Africa if clothing exports should become AGOA-eligible (Kaplan 2004:636).

Table 23: SACU countries' main export products to the USA

	Main exports (in % of total exports to the USA)	**2003**	**2004**
South Africa	Minerals and metals	55.7%	65.4%
	Transportation equipment	17.4%	14.6%
	Chemicals and related products	7.1%	6.6%
	Agricultural products	4.3%	3.8%
	Machinery	3.7%	3.2%
	Clothing and apparels	5.5%	3.0%
Botswana	Minerals and metals	44.1%	71.4%
	Clothing and apparels	52.2%	27.7%
Lesotho	Clothing and apparels	99.9%	97.6%
Namibia	Minerals and metals	40.3%	49.5%
	Clothing and apparels	34.0%	33.1%
Swaziland	Clothing and apparels	86.7%	89.9%

Source: Author's presentation based on data obtained from AGOA.info (2005).

Though it is criticised that the quality of jobs created due to AGOA is poor and that AGOA has diverted capital and jobs into favoured industries and away from others (The Economist, 16/01/03), it must be considered that the amounts of investment and the absorption of unskilled labour are very important for the BLNS countries. In Lesotho for instance, 98% of jobs in the manufacturing sector are in the clothing and apparel industry, which is estimated to offer employment for 55,000 people. In Swaziland, 45,000 jobs depend on AGOA and in Namibia around 8,000 jobs were created by the clothing factory Ramatex, contributing to around 1.5% of the annual GDP (Hall 2004:6, INRIN 2005a, b, c). The BLNS countries do therefore regard the AGOA initiative as important development instrument (WTO 2003:A1-94 and A5-319, GoL 2003:22, GoSA 2003:37).[219]

However, with the expiration of the WTO Multi-Fibre Agreement (MFA) on 1 January 2005, African countries have lost their major competitive advantage of clothing production. The end of the MFA implies that quotas for textiles and clothing in the EU and US-market were dropped so that African countries have now to compete with producers from East Asia and in particular with the new WTO member China. Though African countries still benefit from duty free market access under AGOA, while China faces an average tariff of 17.5% when entering the US-market, African countries, including South Africa, cannot compete with China (Kaplan 2004:6333, Hall, 2004:6). Foreign companies acting in

[219] AGOA is said to have attracted FDI of US$ 1.5 million in Botswana and US$ 250 million in Namibia. In Lesotho 11 textile and apparel factories were created and eight were expanded and in Swaziland around 20 factories were created (USTR 2002a:3).

the clothing and apparel industry judge the low labour productivity and the high HIV/AIDS prevalence,[220] limited capacities, lack infrastructure, government bureaucracy, high poor logistic and high transport costs as well as the missing linkages to domestic goods and services, as disadvantages of southern African countries (Hall 2004:6, UNIDO 2004a:12-3). Additionally the strength of the South African Rand and the Pula against major currencies and the poor management of the factories have contributed to a weakening of BLNS countries' competition ability (INSAT 2005a:13).[221]

The expiration of the MFA and thus, the end of the quantitative protection of the EU and US-textile and clothing market, has already resulted in de-investment in the BLNS countries. In Lesotho, eight clothing factories, which employed 12,000 workers and accounted for more than 20% of Lesotho's total clothing output, have closed since May 2004 (INSAT 2005a:12). In Namibia around 1,600 workers were retrenched in early 2005 and it is feared that the Malaysian giant Ramatex is fully closing down (The Namibian, 09/08/05).

Chances to keep investment in the clothing and textile industry would require the vertical upgrading of activities and the reduction of location disadvantages, such as weak infrastructure and lack capacities (Hall 2004:8). However, the BLNS countries are not able to build-up an integrated textile industry "out of nothing". Thus, despite manifold investment and manufacturing incentives, the prospects for the clothing and textile industry within SACU are rather weak (UNIDO 2004a:12-3).

This rather bleak picture of industrial development in the BLNS countries brings us to the question what industrial policy options southern African countries have today. As the discussion showed, export market preferences are eroding and are moreover expiring due to WTO incompatibility. Furthermore, the promotion and protection of domestic industries has been limited due to bilateral and multilateral trade liberalisation obligations. So what are the industrialisation options left in a liberalising trading environment?

---

[220] The productivity of Lesotho's workers in the clothing industry is estimated to be 30-70% lower than of its Chinese competitors. Since the clothing industry is a very labour-intensive sector and wages in Lesotho are not considerably lower than in China, Lesotho does not have comparative advantages in the clothing industry (UNIDO 2004a:13).

[221] The strength of the Rand and the Pula is generally regarded as hindering moment for the diversification of SACU countries' economies since it reduces the competitiveness of manufacturing activities compared to mining (WTO 2003:A1-56-9) As a response the Bank of Botswana devaluated the Pula in early 2004 by 7.5% against the currency basket (Akinkugbe and Makepe 2005:36).

4.2.4 SACU Countries Industrial Policy Options in a Liberalising Trading Environment

The regulations of the WTO prove that imported goods could neither be discriminated against each other nor against domestic goods or services. [222] As a result, the use of trade policy instruments to protect infant industries has shrunk considerably. The new rules on supportive trade polices have been valid since the creation of the WTO in 1994 and are fixed in the Agreement on Subsidies and Countervailing Measures (ASCM).[223] The ASCM differentiates between prohibited subsides, actionable subsidies and non-actionable subsidies. Prohibited subsidies are enterprise-, industry- or regional-specific regulations, such as minimum local content usage, export subsidies, or the public provision of goods and services others than infrastructure. Actionable and non-actionable subsidies are the funding of research activities, the promotion of disadvantaged regions, promotion of a sustainable environment, provision of market information, promotion of corporate investment, and an active exchange rate policy (Bora *et al.* 1999:12-6).

Thus, many instruments of export promotion that were successfully applied by Asian countries, such as sector-by-sector subsidies or local content regulations, are no longer allowed under WTO provisions. Also specific export incentives, such as EPZ are forbidden.[224] To sum up, any subsidy that has a direct effect on trade is explicitly forbidden and therefore, strictly interpreted, no longer a feasible instrument to promote industrial development. However, though all WTO member states obliged themselves to significant tariff reduction and to observance of the regulations of the ASCM, developed and developing countries still have sectors that are protected by tariff peaks and non-tariff barriers and that are promoted by industrial instruments. In the developed world this is above all the case in the field of agriculture.[225]

One instrument of infant industry protection that is still applicable under WTO regulations is the one of safeguard measures that are allowed to be applied when imports pose a major problem for a country's balance of payments (ATPC 2004:31-2). However, as argued in Chapter 3, African countries do hardly have the capacity to implement effective safeguard measures in order to protect their

[222] See Box 6 and the discussion in section 3.4.

[223] The successor of the GATT Code on Subsidies and Countervailing Duties of 1979 (Tokyo Round).

[224] Developing countries with a GDP of less than US$ 1.000 per capita are excluded from this provision under Art. XVIII, WTO. In the case of SACU this implies that Lesotho is the only country whose investment policy is according to WTO regulations.

[225] Thus, beef, dairy products, fresh and dried vegetables, fresh fruits, cereals and products thereof, prepared fruits and vegetables, wine, spirits and tobacco are highly protected in the EU, North America and Japan and are subject to export subsidies (AfDB 2004:220).

industries from serious injury (Botha 2005). Furthermore, the implementation of safeguard measures can only be applied *after* having realised that imports are a serious threat for domestic production. Considering the small production base of BLNS industries, there is the risks that the industry is destroyed by the time safeguard measures have been implemented (Goodison 2005, Wellmer 2005:15-6).

Another regulation of the WTO Agreement has the potential to play an important role for African countries' industrialisation strategy, namely the provision on Special and Differential Treatment (SDT) (WTO, Art. XVIII). SDT allows developing countries to maintain a flexible tariff structure in order to promote economic development. However, this provision, which was already valid but hardly used under the GATT 1947 Agreement, is criticised of being too narrow and of being applied too restrictive. Today, Art. XVIII is only used for LDCs (e.g. regarding the principle of non-reciprocity). Other developing countries are not allowed to apply for different trade regulations than developed countries but only for longer transition periods (Bora *et al.* 1999:19-20). Developing countries do therefore pursue a more comprehensive and flexible approach of SDT in the Doha Development Round allowing more policy space to promote economic development (ICTSD 2005:12).

North-South FTAs are often proposed as successful industrialisation and development tool in accordance to WTO provisions. As discussed in the Chapters 2 and 3, the theoretical gains of North-South integration lie in developing countries' options to expand and diversify their exports and to benefit from technology and learning effects when lowering their CET and strengthening cooperation with industrialised countries. On the other hand, North-South integration bears for developing countries the risk of trade diversion because of a complementary trade structure and a different factor endowment. To avoid the manifestation of a hub-and-spoke trade relationship, it is proposed to form South-South integration bodies before entering into a North-South integration framework. However, as the extensive discussion on EPAs in Chapter 3 showed, this "open regionalism" is hardly feasible in southern African since countries' economic integration interests and the geographical configurations for EPA negotiations do not match.

In the case of SACU we have the division of South Africa on the one hand and the BLNS countries on the other hand. The next section discusses how deeper regional integration by the implementation of the new SACU Agreement can promote industrial development in the region and whether the EU's approach of North-South FTAs can positively contribute to SACU countries' industrial development.

4.3 The Contribution of Deeper Regional Integration and North-South Free Trade Agreements to Economic Development in SACU

As discussed in Chapter 2, the new SACU 2002 Agreement is only regarded as "framework agreement" where annexes on substantial policies, such as in the field of competition, agriculture and unfair tradc practises, still need to be developed. This applies also to industrial policy where a common approach is envisaged but not realised yet (SACU 2002, Art. 38.2). The harmonisation of industrial policies does not necessarily mean that member states have, apart from the CET, to agree on a common industrial policy as McCarthy and Hansohm (2005:4) point out: "*If for the sake of balanced regional development the BLNS countries have incentives that encourage industrial location in these countries, it will not serve the purposes of a common industrial policy if South Africa likewise has location incentives that will neutralise the impact of the BLNS incentives.*" In other words: South Africa should promote discriminative policies in favour of BLNS in order to equalise economic development within SACU.

To date, SACU's industrial/trade policy is still solely formulated by South Africa. Though the "South African Board on Tariffs and Trade" (SABTT) has been officially replaced by the "International Trade Administration Commission" (ITAC), an institution that is supposed to work independent and serve all SACU countries by common negotiations on tariffs, import and export controls and anti-dumping measures, it is to date only the name that has changed. ITAC does therefore still act "*...as the legal entities that were mandated to implement the trade and industrial policy of the South African government*" (McCarthy and Hansohm 2005:6). Though the ITAC/SABTT is supposed to take the interests of the BLNS industries into account, namely fish, beef, milling, sugar, and clothing, South Africa has the final word on any tariff amendment. The institutions of the new SACU Agreement still need to be developed. Thus, (1) the National Bodies, which are supposed to recommend on tariff changes towards the Tariff Board, (2) the Tariff Board that proves the wishes of the National Bodies and recommends to the Council how the CET should be changed, (3) the Council that has to manage the CET, and (4) the Dispute Settlement Body that should settle any disputes also with respect to the CET, do not exist yet. Until all these institutions have been developed it will be South Africa which is responsible for SACU's CET setting and which focuses naturally on its national interests.

In order to develop a common industrial policy for SACU, it is necessary that the countries review their national industrial policy instruments in place and harmonise them, thus moving towards a common industrial policy. This does not only relate to support schemes for companies, fiscal measures and export promotion instruments, such as EPZ, but also to general policies that influence the location of production and investment, such as labour policies. It is often argued that BLNS countries have comparative advantages against South Africa since their labour costs are lower and their labour-law regulations are less strict (McCarthy and Hansohm 2005:10). However, this argument neglects that labour costs are, with exception of labour-intensive industries, only a minor factor that contributes to the investment decision of companies. Economies of scale, which can be achieved by foreign or South African firms but hardly by BLNS companies, are regarded as much more important (Ritter 2005). Assuming that a common industrial policy should promote a faster development of the BLNS in order to "catch up", the free movement of labour would therefore be an essential instrument of SACU countries' industrial policy.

Another constraint for the development of a common industrial policy is the different agricultural policies of the SACU countries. Since the BLNS industries produce mainly agro-based products, there are considerable linkages between industrial and agricultural policies so that the development of a common industrial policy without having agreed on a common agricultural policy is hardly feasible (McCarthy 2004:15). To reach a consensus in the field of industrial policy and to harmonise individual agricultural policies have proved to be very difficult due to the high development differences between South Africa on the one hand and BLNS on the other hand. To date, all SACU countries still have agricultural import protection instruments in place, which put on permit controls and non-tariff barriers to protect certain industries, such as the national pasta, broiler/chicken, stem-milk, wheat flour and maize industries in Namibia and the maize, rice, wheat, fresh fruits and vegetables and poultry industries in Swaziland.[226] However, this intra-regional trade protection is likely to diminish because of the new SACU revenue formula: since summer 2004, any restriction of imports has resulted in a loss of customs revenue because BLNS do no longer receive a guaranteed share of revenues (see Box 5 in section 2). Thus, it can be expected that BLNS are considering more carefully whether import controls should be applied or not.

Another field that needs to be harmonised when working towards a common industrial policy is the one of tax rate regimes. To date, SACU countries show different tax regimes (see Table 11 in section 2), which has resulted in divertive effect of intra-regional investment. Thus, South African firms that have branches in Namibia do not have to pay the Namibian corporate tax rate of 35% but can pay their taxes in South Africa (30%). Like this, they have a competitive advantage against Namibian firms, which contributes in addition to their economic size and market power to a disadvantaged situation for Namibian companies. Furthermore, the private sector in the BLNS countries claims that South African companies are in a position to use their power to dump products into their markets. Since South African firms profit from economies of scale, they

---

[226] See WTO 2003 (country reports) for a detailed overview of SACU countries' import levies on agricultural products.

would be in a position to sell their products below costs until domestic competitors have to give up. A national competition policy that implements remedial actions would therefore be crucial to avoid such behaviour (Ritter 2005). However, BLNS countries' national competition bills, on which the countries are currently working on, might tackle external market power but not necessarily internal market dominance. It is therefore necessary to create a regional competition body that enforces competition policy within SACU and does not represent national interests (Erasmus 2005, Hartzenberg 2005).[227]

Thus, still a lot of work needs to be done to add "flesh and muscles to the skeleton" (McCarthy and Hansohm 2005:4) and to make a common industrial policy within SACU operational. Though it was the BLNS countries that pushed forward to negotiate a new, more democratised SACU Agreement, the countries do now simply lack the capacities to implement the institutions and policies in order to gain from what they have achieved. To negotiate the detailed policies of deeper integration is hard work and the SACU 2002 Agreement is only a broad compromise that has avoided becoming concrete. The effective implementation of the new Agreement will therefore be the major challenge for SACU. Yet, South Africa has not acted as leader to push the implementation of the 2002 Agreement forward. It could be argued that the implementation of the new Agreement is not in the interest of South Africa since the perpetuation of decision power combined with lower costs arising from the CRP would be the optimal solution. However, such a point of view is too short-sighted and neglects the positive dynamics resulting from successful deeper integration. To date, the new SACU Agreement has had only negative impacts on the BLNS countries. Due to the reform of the CRP, they lose substantial revenues while at the same time being hardly involved in decision-making processes. In other words: BLNS countries' compensation for trade divertive effects of South Africa's unilateral CET setting is shrinking without benefiting from policies that promote a more equal economic development in the region. If this continues to be the outcome of the new SACU Agreement, there is the risk of increased economic disparities among member countries, which might lead to increased protectionism and BLNS countries' repel for deeper integration. The building of trade capacities in the BLNS countries is therefore crucial to enable the countries to participate in policy formulation and to make the new SACU Agreement operational in a way that benefits all parties.

Since the SACU countries have not harmonised their industrial policies yet, many different instruments exist. As the discussion has shown, all countries have policy instruments in place that promote manufacturing activities and in

---

[227] This does not necessarily imply that SACU has to establish a common competition policy. When national competition policies are enforced by an independent supra-national body, fair competition would also be ensured (Hartzenberg 2005).

particular manufacturing exports (e.g. by EPZ, import rebates etc.). Additionally, South Africa protects sectors that are regarded as sensitive (such as textiles, automotives, and certain agricultural products) by a comparably high CET (WTO 2003:27). The SACU countries do therefore apply a policy-mix of import-substitution and export-promotion to foster industrialisation.

Trade liberalisation has become an important component South Africa's industrial policy since 1995 when the SACU countries joined the WTO.[228] South Africa took active part in multilateral, regional and bilateral trade liberalisation and fought for the protection of its interest, e.g. during the negotiations of the EU-SA FTA where the EU was only able to set through the protection of geographical indications, such as parma ham or sherry, after having granted South Africa a duty free quota of 42 million litres wine p.a. and financial assistance of € 15 million for the restructuring of its wine and spirit sector (European Parliament 2002:19).

To date, South Africa has been quite successful to use selective free trade agreements with developed countries to improve its market access, expand and diversify its exports and strengthen its strategic position vis-à-vis main competitors, for instance by concluding the EU-South Africa FTA before a new liberalisation round under the WTO could erode its benefits.

Nevertheless, North-South FTAs have always been a complicated issue for South Africa and in particular for the BLNS. Taking the example of the TDCA: Though South Africa reached that the EU included its agricultural market into FTA negotiations, the EU has opened its agricultural market to a lesser extent than South Africa, thus, reversing the original principle of asymmetry. FTA negotiations with the USA, again, are highly problematic because the Americans push aggressively forward to include manifold trade-related aspects into the agreement, which bears the risk to reduce South Africa's scope for national policies, e.g. in the field of industrial policy or health policy.[229] In fact, SACU is on a tightrope walk when negotiating FTAs with developed countries. Improved market access, increased international credibility and financial and technical support make it attractive to enter into North-South FTAs but the pub-

[228] When the SACU countries joined the WTO they committed themselves to substantial tariff reductions. In 1999, SACU's average tariff unweighted tariff rate was 8.5% for all goods (and 8.6% for manufactured goods). This level was well below East Asian and South Asian countries, which showed an average unweighted tariff of 9.8% and 27.7% respectively (AfDB 2004:178).

[229] The USA aims for instance to negotiate TRIPS *plus* regulations, which enforce the rigorous protection of intellectual property rights including public health. This would imply the prohibition of generic drug imports on which US companies have licenses. Since the import of generic drugs is compulsory for the treatment of AIDS patients who cannot afford the original medication, such an agreement would have dramatic effects on South Africa's medicare (Avafia 2004).

lic is becoming increasingly aware of the possible negative impact of FTAs between very unequal partners. This is most of all the case in EPA negotiations where the European approach splits SACU into South Africa on the one hand and BLNS countries on the other hand. This does not only undermine deeper regional integration within SACU but makes it *de facto* impossible for the BLNS countries to negotiate without South Africa baring in mind that, according to the new SACU Agreement, each member country has to concur to the external relations of SACU.

4.4 Conclusions: Industrialisation Policies, Regional Integration and the Impact of North-South Free Trade Agreements on SACU countries' Industrialisation Process

Like other African countries, SACU has experienced an import-substitution strategy and is now combining export promotion with infant-industry protection. Prior 1994, South Africa was as a result of its Apartheid policy and international sanction highly protected and inward-looking and promoted the classical concept of import-substitution. This strategy contributed until the late 1980s to a broad manufacturing base, local backward- and forward linkages and the survival of some high-tech manufacturing industries, such as the automotive industry (Kaplan 2003, Kaplinsky 2000, Platzky 1996). The BLNS countries never had the chance to apply an import-substitution strategy due to their small, underdeveloped markets and their SACU membership, which makes it impossible to create effective backward- and forward linkages in autarky.

All SACU countries provide different incentives to promote manufacturing activities and to attract manufacturing-related FDI. However, none of these incentives has resulted in a boom of manufacturing activities yet and some of them bear the risk of a "race to the bottom". Another problem of different investment incentives in the SACU region is that they undermine deeper integration. From a regional economic point of view it is desirable if investment is diverted towards the less developed countries of a CU, thus allowing them to catch-up. To promote more equal economic development within SACU, a common industrialisation strategy would be necessary.

South Africa's focus was and still is on trade with developed countries, to which it sees itself belonging. Regional integration in SACU and SADC is regarded as second-rate. Thus, South Africa has not acted as "engine of integration" and promoted the implementation of the new SACU Agreement. This is however necessary if a further economic polarisation in SACU and reservations against South Africa's economic and political hegemony should be avoided. SACU's deeper integration and common policy formulations are also crucial with respect to its external trade relations, which are still ruled by South Africa.

How, if at all can free trade agreements help SACU countries to promote industrial development? This question should be discussed in detail in the next Chapter 5, presenting empirical findings from the South African automotive industry and the Namibian fishing industry. Both industries are major contributors to South Africa's and Namibia's manufacturing sector respectively and are highly export-oriented towards the EU market. Furthermore, both industries are to certain extents regulated by governments' policies and regarded as comparable successful in international terms.

It is argued in the next Chapter 5 that a successful trade policy encompasses much more than trade liberalisation. Though both sectors investigated take specific elements of trade liberalisation into account, they focus on a national development strategy. In such a context, trade liberalisation is not regarded as beneficial *per se* but used as trade policy instrument, connected to national development goals. It will be shown that the individual performance of specific industries and their connection to domestic industries and overseas market has to be taken carefully into account when formulating successful industrial policies.

5 Cases of Successful Industrial Policy and the Contribution of EU Free Trade Agreements: Evidence from the South African Automotive Industry and the Namibian Fishing Industry

5.1 Economic Relevance of the South African Automotive and the Namibian Fishing Industry and the Role of Free Trade Agreements with the EU

The South African automotive manufacturing industry is one of the fastest growing and most dynamic sectors in the South African economy with considerable further growth potential (DTI 2002b, 2003a). In 2002, the automotive manufacturing industry, which comprises vehicle manufacturers and component manufacturers, contributed 6.3% to the country's GDP and is currently the third largest economic sector (after mining and agriculture) in addition to being the largest manufacturing sector (DTI 2003a). The contribution to exports has almost doubled in the period 1997–2001 to 9.75% (DTI 2002a:18) and the sector receives high inflows of FDI. Nowadays, South Africa is the nineteenth largest automotive supplier worldwide and manufactures 0.7% of the world's automotive production (Tralac News, 09/10/03). In 2002, the automotive sector exported vehicles with a value of around R 40 billion (NZZ, 13/01/03). The component industry is responsible for over 60% of the exporting success of the automotive industry (DTI 2002a:9). The expansion of the component industry as well as the new creation of service stations created new jobs and expanded the government's income. Moreover, the automotive industry stimulated product expansion in supply industries, such as steel, paint, rubber, textile, plastic and petrochemical industries.

Like the automotive industry in South Africa, the fishing industry is tremendously important for economic development in Namibia. The fishing industry is the second largest contributor to Namibia's export earnings after mining and the country's second largest manufacturing sector after the food and beverage industry (MFMR 2004b). The fishing industry accounted for 25% of total export earnings in 2002 (Iyambo 2003b) and employs around 13,500 people (Iyambo 2004c:5). In fact, Namibia is one of the very few African countries that has been able to establish its own fishing industry and is judged as being successful in international terms (Acheampong 1997). Since Namibia's independence in 1990, the sector has attracted considerable investment and created modern processing facilities. Moreover, Namibia has achieved to invert the foreign ownership of its fishing industry and to involve formerly disadvantaged Namibian citizens stronger into the industry. To achieve this, Namibia has largely excluded foreign access to its fishing grounds and adopted a comprehensive policy framework that is strictly regulating access to the treasured resource.

Both, the South African automotive and the Namibian fishing industry are highly export-oriented, with most of their exports going to the EU. Furthermore, both industries are relatively protected from competition/foreign access and have successfully adopted national policies to promote industrial development and other national development goals (such as the improved integration of formerly disadvantaged people). Another common ground of the South African automotive and the Namibian fishing industry is that their main trading partner, the EU, seeks to improve access to these sectors. In case of the South African automotive industry, the EU largely failed to include vehicles and components into the TDCA. South Africa reached to exclude the import/export complementation scheme applied in the automotive industry from the TDCA and has only granted minor preferences to the EU compared to other trading partners hitherto. As response, the EU continues to put on pressure onto South Africa to reduce its automotive tariffs, thus improving market access for European exporters.

A similar picture appears with respect to the Namibian fishing industry where the EU has aimed to conclude an access agreement with Namibia since its independence. Namibia is reluctant to include fisheries into free trade since it fears that its national empowerment, monitoring and sustainability policies will be undermined.

Determining whether an FTA is more beneficial or harmful for a country that is whether the positive or the negative effects are more prevalent, depends on various internal and external factors, a matter already being debated in theory. It is not feasible to give a "real life analysis" about the impact of an FTA, as economic, social and political processes act simultaneously, which makes it impossible to regard influences from a free trade agreement in isolation. The following studies, based on relevant literature and face-to-face interviews with representatives from the South African automotive industry and the Namibian fishing industry as well as with government officials, trade experts and private sector support institutions in the two countries do thus not claim to quantify the impact of the TDCA on the automotive manufacturing industry or to calculate the potential impact of EPAs on the Namibian fishing industry. The analyses will, however, highlight the opportunities and risks of including these two sectors into free trade agreements, clarify how well the surveyed companies are aware of options and risks, analyse further influential factors for the industries' economic performance and discuss the strategies applied by governments and private sector support institutions to promote increased domestic value addition and an improved inclusion into the global value chain.

The EU claims that its FTAs with African countries help to integrate countries into the world economy and to manage the restructuring of uncompetitive industries. How the TDCA aims to contribute to this goal in the South African automotive industry and whether an FTA can manage this in case of the

Namibian fishing industry should be investigated in detail in the following case studies. Both analyses do not claim to be representative. However, as the discussion shows, the findings of the sample in the South African automotive industry are for the most part in accordance with recent research done in this sector and do also reflect private sector support institutions' appraisal of the current situation in the component industry. The sample of the Namibian fishing industry comprises around 75% of fishing companies that have processing plants in the country so that the study gives the reader comprehensive insights into the Namibian fishing industry. Again, expert interviews confirm that the findings of the study reflect the situation in the Namibian fishing industry well.

5.2 Main Theses and Key Questions of Case Studies

The main purpose of the two case studies presented in Chapter 5 is to investigate whether an FTA with the EU could help the companies in the South African automotive sector and the Namibian fishing industry to increase their integration into the global economy and the global value chain (GVC), which other factors determine international linkages and economic successes, and how these factors are related to free trade.

Theoretically, an FTA with a developed country helps the developing country to

a) Improve its market access to the developed country;
b) Benefit from economies of scale;
c) Diversify its exports and to upgrade product and processes by benefiting from competitive inputs and by technology and learning effects due to strong cooperation; and
d) Optimise production processes by increased competition.

The questionnaire applied to representatives of the South African automotive industry and the Namibian fishing industry aims to elaborate on these main theses by operationalising the above questions as follows:

a) 1. How is companies' current market access to the EU and what are the constraints to enter the EU market?
   2. What are the advantages and disadvantages of the EU as an export market?
b) How did companies' exports develop in the past years?
c) 1. To what extent is the EU a relevant input source?
   2. How did companies' profits develop and what are relevant factors for the development of profits?
   3. Do the companies aim to upgrade their products and processes?

4. Are the companies part of a strategic alliance and if yes, what are the benefits of such an international cooperation?

d) Where are companies' main competitors and how do they judge their competitiveness in national and international comparison?

By analysing these questions, the main theoretical considerations of North-South FTAs can be elaborated on:

a) Would an FTA with the EU really improve the (effective) market access for South African automotive component exporters and Namibian fishing exporters?
b) Would the companies be able to expand their exports?
c) To what extents are the companies already part of an international network and could an FTA with the EU strengthen cooperation with their European counterparts?
d) To what extent are the companies already exposed to international competition and how do they perform? To what extent would increased competition be stimulant/detrimental for companies' economic performance?

The interviews were conducted by means of standardised questionnaires (see Annex I and II). Findings are compared with secondary literature as well as with face-to-face interview conducted with representatives from private sector support institutions and Ministries.

For the South African automotive industry, it is further investigated how much the companies know about the TDCA and where they see opportunities and risks for their businesses. It is analysed whether businesses' individual appraisal match with the situation in the whole sector and how well businesses' responded to TDCA-related information circulated by private sector support institutions and the South African Ministry of Trade and Ministry (DTI).

5.3 Organisation of Case Studies

Both studies are organised as follows: After having given an overview of the structure of the respective case study, the economic relevance and performance of the industry and the respective national policy instruments that guide the developments are explained. In case of the Namibian fishing industry it is also the theoretical impact of free trade on the natural resource fisheries that is analysed. Thereafter, trade relations of the South African automotive and the Namibian fishing industry respectively with their European counterparts are explored. The main part of both studies is the empirical findings as discussed in section 5.4.4 and 5.5.5 respectively. The 25 interviews from the South African automotive industry and the 11 interviews from the Namibian fishing industry were conducted personally by means of a standardised questionnaire. The companies were selected in cooperation with national private sector support institutions. The methodology applied, firm profiles and the characteristics of the companies' surveyed are explained in the studies. The questions followed-up in both sectors were almost simultaneously (compare Annex I and II) but exclude the questions on the TDCA in case of the Namibian fishing industry.[232]

After having presented the empirical findings with respect to companies' features, export and import developments, competition situation, domestic value addition and companies' position in the international value added chain, the impact of an FTA with the EU is investigated. In this respect, it is mainly the effect of an FTA on the respective policy instruments applied which is analysed. In conclusion, the studies summarise whether a North-South FTA with the EU is likely to promote or constrain economic development in the South African automotive and the Namibian fishing industry.

5.4 Case Study 1: The South African Automotive Component Industry

5.4.1 Structure of Case Study 1

To give the reader a better knowledge of the South African automotive manufacturing industry, a classification of the industry within the GVC is given. Furthermore, its economic performance, its contribution to socio-economic developments, its reliance on public export assistance and its options for upgraded activities are discussed. Thereafter, the sector's trade with its European counterpart explains the linkages between South African and European firms and presents the hitherto agreed liberalisation schedule for the automotive industry. The core of the study lies in section 5.4.4, which presents in detail the empirical findings and verifies them with sector-specific research results. To gain clarity on the individual situation of the surveyed companies, their position in the value chain, and their connections to European firms and the European market, the question relates, among others, to the companies' trade relations with the EU, their strengths and weaknesses in the export business and the relevance of exporting for the total economic performance of the surveyed companies. The final sub-section of this case study will discuss the up-to-date impact of the TDCA on the South African automotive industry and what how a further inclusion into free trade would affect the sector.

[232] This was the case since Namibia is not part of the TDCA.

5.4.2 Economic Performance, Value Addition and Prospects for the South African Automotive Manufacturing Industry

When the South African automotive industry emerged in the 1960s, it was very inward looking and not internationally competitive.[233] Although demand fell in the 1980s, partially as a result of international sanctions that were imposed in the late 1970s, the import substitution policy was retained. It was the government's goal to establish an autonomous national vehicle and component industry, which had become a necessity because of the country's increasing isolation as a result of its apartheid policy. Few affiliated groups concentrated the South African economy.[234] Kaplinsky *et al.* (2002:1169–72) argue that the conglomerate structure of the South African economy has affected the upgrading capacity of firms negatively even to the present day. This is due to their large, non-specialised product range, a result of South Africa's import substitution strategy. Reliance on standardised products made many companies inflexible, thus they failed to develop their product and service portfolios along more competitive lines. The main competitive advantage of the automotive subsector was being able to offer cheap components, and this approach was aided by the depreciation of the Rand.

After the first democratic elections in 1994 and the lifting of international sanctions, the South African economy opened up. This brought massive challenges for the automotive industry. Owing to increasing worldwide liberalisation, the earlier models of import substitution, quantitative restrictions and local content requirements were no longer feasible. Furthermore, South Africa became a WTO member in 1995 and agreed to phase out GATT-inconsistent trade and investment measures, which include quantitative restrictions and local content requirements.

The production system in the automotive manufacturing industry has become increasingly globalised, and the value chain relationship between original equipment manufactures (OEMs) and component suppliers has altered, as summarised in Box 25. Since the 1980s, Western companies have lost their international competitive edge to Japanese suppliers and have started to outsource more and more parts of vehicle production. During the 1990s subcontracting companies that formerly produced in accordance with specific OEMs requirements started, in conjunction with the OEMs, to create their own design solutions by using their own technology. Thus, vehicles and automotive components became much more complex and sophisticated and also much more difficult to produce. In addition, the demands of OEMs shifted from individual components to com-

[233] The first automotive assembly plants in South Africa were established in the 1920s (see Barnes 1999 for a brief historical overview).

[234] Kaplinsky *et al.* (2002:1169) indicated that it were only five large firms that controlled more than 80% of all companies listed at the South African stock exchange in the early 1980ies.

plete function units and systems (UNIDO 2002:20). The increased demand for sophisticated component solutions of internationally standardised quality forced South African component manufacturers to restructure their production plants drastically. While South African OEMs, as well as component suppliers, used to produce many models but only in small quantities during the apartheid era, production demand was now the direct opposite: the variety of models had to be reduced and quantities had to be increased. The OEMs wanted to reduce development costs, benefit from the economies of scale and be able to source flexibly from any of their assemblers around the world. The transformation from a "broad" to a "specialised" supplier was a huge challenge for the South African automotive manufacturing industry, especially, for the component manufacturers, and not all of them survived the restructuring process.[235] However, if manufacturers want to avoid becoming dispensable they have to offer competitive prices and upgrade their production (including design and technological know-how).

It is possible to comply with global standards only if local firms show international linkages (Kaplinsky 2000:137). To cope with these manifold challenges and reduce tariffs to a level acceptable to the GATT, the government, after consultations with all stakeholders involved,[236] introduced the Motor Industry Development Programme (MIDP) in 1995. The support of the automotive industry was justified because of the massive challenges the industry was facing and also because automotives as well as components are highly sophisticated, non-traditional export products. The development of new trade and investment markets is deemed necessary to improve South Africa's international competitiveness, to increase the local value addition of production and to participate successfully in a global network (Kaplan 2003:36) The MIDP had and still has the following objectives:

1. Improve the international competitiveness of the South African automotive industry.
2. Encourage economic growth, in particular through export promotion.
3. Create new employment or at least to stabilise the employment level in the industry.
4. Improve the trade balance.
5. Improve the affordability of vehicles in the South African market (DTI 1999:1).

[235] The OEMs rationalised the models manufactured in South Africa substantially. However, despite this rationalisation, only five of the 27 models manufactured in South Africa show substantial volumes (they represent more than 45% of total production), which indicates the need for further rationalisation of models (Barnes and Black 2003: 13–14, 36).

[236] NAAMSA, NAACAM and the trade union NUMSA were involved in the MIDP formulation (Barnes 1999: 407).

With the introduction of the MIDP, South Africa switched from its infant industry approach that protected the automotive industry with quantitative restrictions, imposed tariffs of up to 115% and required a minimum local content of 50% (Barnes 1999), to an import/export complementation scheme that benefits local production but reduces external tariffs. In 2004, motor vehicle duties are at peak tariff rates of 36% and component suppliers at 28% (see Table 24). However, the real protection for both motor vehicles and components is much lower owing to the duty payback system of the MIDP. Because of the MIDP, in 2002 the average import tariff rate for vehicles was 12.5% and for components 15% (WTO 2003:A4–276). Commenting on the effective protection rate, Barnes and Black (2003:25) state: *"South African duty levels are extremely low considering the size of the domestic markets... (and) are similar to the Mercosur rates..."* Altogether, the MIDP envisages reducing import tariffs drastically to the advantage of domestically produced vehicles and to stimulate investment. Although the programme does not stipulate a local content value, it provides an incentive to source from South Africa, as the export credit granted equals the local content value of the product.[237] The programme includes light and commercial vehicles as well as medium and heavy commercial vehicles. The MIDP mechanisms are explained in Box 25.

Box 25: The Mechanisms of the MIDP

Companies that register with the MIDP can reduce payable duty through three mechanisms:

1. The *Duty Free Allowance* that grants OEMs a duty-free allowance of 27% of vehicles' wholesale value
2. The *Import/Export Complementation* scheme that allows producers to apply for a reduction of import duties according to the value exported. Producers that are registered receive Import Rebate Credit Certificates (IRCCs) that can also be traded between registered exporters and importers. For automotives, R1 of exports (calculated on South African value added) can buy R 1 of imports duty free. The value of export performance started at 94% in 2003, and declines by 4% p.a. until it reaches 70% in 2009.

Continuation on next page.

[237] Owing to the MIDP, Nissan South Africa, the leading exporter with a market share of 50%, exports around 4,600 units of its hardbody pickup truck to Europe, Singapore, Australia and New Zealand and can thus benefit from import rebates for its model 350Z (Japan Corporate News Network, 25/02/04).

Continuation of Box 25 from previous page.

Thus, in 2009, R 1 of exports that have a 100% local value buy only R 0.70 of duty free imports. For components R 1 of exports buys 75% of the value of export performance, thus 75% of 94% in 2003 and 75% of 70% in 2009 or 0.6 times of this value of automotives. over

3. *Productive Asset Allowance* that grants investors in new plants and equipment a credit certificate of up to 20% of their investment value a five-year period.

Table 24 gives an overview of the MIDP's duty reduction and its basic features.

Table 24: Basic features of the MIDP

	Cars/ light commercial vehicles	Medium and heavy commercial vehicles (> 3.5 tons)	Original equipment components
Import Duties	1995: 65% 2002: 40% } progressive 2007: 30% } reduction by 2% p.a. 2012: 25% (reduction by 1% p.a.)	1995: 40% } progressive 2000: 20% } reduction by 4% p.a. *Still to be evaluated (were not included in the 2002 MIDP Review)*	1995: 45% 2002: 30% 2007: 25% 2012: 20%
	Cars/ light commercial vehicles	Medium and heavy commercial vehicles (> 3.5 tons)	Original equipment components
Duties on complementary industries	Duty free allowance of 27% of manufacturers' factory turnover	Drive-train components are duty free. Tyres still face a duty of 6% from the EU and 10% from other countries	Import controls on pneumatic tyres
Import/Export complementation	Every Rand exported A percentage determined by the value of export performance of automotives may be imported duty free	Every Rand exported. A percentage determined by the value of export performance of automotives may be imported duty free	Every Rand exported. A percentage determined by the value of component exports or 0.6% of vehicle value can be imported duty free
Further provisions	Components must be fully disassembled by the domestic industry (only for 70% by 2009). No minimum local content required		

Source: Author's presentation based on Tradepartners (2002: 3), WTO (2003: A4–276), and NAACAM (2003).

Continuation on next page.

Continuation of Box 25 from previous page.

With the exception of harnesses, all major exporting automotive subsectors have substantial domestic raw material bases (DTI 2002: 35–6). This means that they benefit significantly from the MIDP, as the raw materials are included as local value added and therefore qualify for duty rebate. As input prices would increase further without the MIDP, the programme is essential for the vast majority of automotive subcontractors (DTI 2002a: 35–8).

The MIDP initiative is supported by internal advantages: cheap electricity, relatively cheap labour, natural resources like platinum, and expertise in component manufacturing and after-sales support. Moreover, South Africa has a favourable strategic location to supply countries in the Far East, Africa and the Australian continent (Trade Partners 2002). Another benefit for the automotive sector in South Africa is the AGOA initiative, which allows South African producers to enter the US market duty free for a broad range of automotive products. Transport equipment is currently South Africa's most important exporting sector under AGOA. Thus, South Africa is the only AGOA beneficiary country that exports a relatively diversified export range (DTI 2003a:54).[238] The Automotive Industry Export Council (AIEC) even envisages a planning and investment approach on account of AGOA (Williams 2003a).[239]

The automotive industry has developed promisingly since the introduction of the MIDP and has performed better than the manufacturing average. The manufacturing value added in the automotive industry is around three times higher than in the manufacturing industry overall and increased by 52.1% from 1993–2001 (DTI 2002a:17). The number of domestically produced cars increased from 389,400 in 1995 to 404,400 in 2002. This increase was exclusively export driven, while the number of domestically produced local sales declined by 94,000 cars. As a result, the share of exports as a percentage of domestic production increased from 4% in 1995 to 31% in 2002 (NAAMSA 2003a:3). The automotive component industry experienced an even more impressive upward trend and showed an average export growth rate of 100% p.a. in the period 1995-2001 (DTI as cited in Barnes and Black 2003:10).[240]

---

[238] BMW South Africa started to export its left-hand-drive 3-series models to the USA and DaimlerChrysler South Africa is exploring the idea to export its left-hand-drive C-class models to the USA (DTI 2003a:22).

[239] The AIEC consists of NAAMSA and NAACAM, and is part of the government's strategy to promote exports of automotive component suppliers (NAACAM 2003b).

[240] Catalytic converters, which grew more than 380% p.a., contributed significantly to this trend. However, automotive tooling, which showed the lowest growth rate, still increased by 28% p.a. (DTI as cited in Barnes and Black 2003: 10).

In addition to increased exports, the automotive as well as the automotive component industry showed increased capital investments.[241] The impact of the increased level of automatisation helped to improve the labour productivity and international competitiveness of the sector and increased the manufacturing value added by more than 50% in the period 1993–2001, compared with an increase of 19% on average of the manufacturing sector (Barnes and Black 2003: 16). However, the increased capital investment and automatisation level was double-edged, as it also led to a decrease in employment. Although automotive sales increased in the period 1994–2000 by R 30 billion (to R 42 billion), absolute employment declined from 115,000 in 1997 to 87,700 in 2003, as Figure 26 shows.[242]

Figure 26: Employment levels in the South African automotive manufacturing industry, 1997–2003

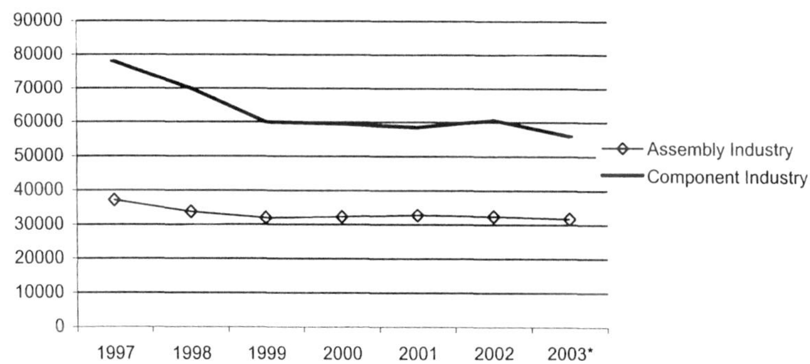

* projected figure.

Source: DTI (2002: 51), DTI (2003: 47).

However, this must also be seen in the light of the enormous restructuring process and the high increase of labour productivity (38% in the period 1993–2001).[243] Taking the general employment losses in the manufacturing sector into

---

[241] Capital investments for the eight OEMs that are based in South Africa more than doubled in the period 1996–2002, showing a total capital investment volume of R2.72 billion in 2002 (NAAMSA 2003: 5).

[242] In total, there are around 270 000 people directly and indirectly employed by the auto and the auto component industry (AIDC 2003).

[243] Labour productivity increased by 37.8% in the period 1993–2001, which was well above the manufacturing sector's average (Barnes and Black 2003: 19).

account, the automotive manufacturing industry performed above average,[244] though there were considerable employment losses, most of all in the component industry where employment decreased by almost 40% in the period 1997-2003 to 56,000 employees (NAACAM 2003).

The automotive industry was able to increase its exports drastically (see Figure 27) but shows still a considerable trade deficit (R 8 billion in 2001).

Figure 27: Trade balance and foreign exchange use in the South African automotive industry, 1995–2001 (in R billion)

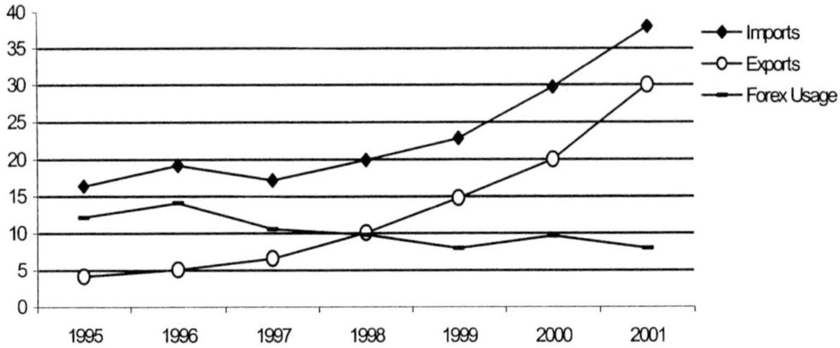

Source: DTI (2003: 29).

From 2000 to 2002, imports of passenger cars increased by more than 20% (DTI 2003:17). Reasons for this development are the reduction of external tariffs combined with the export/import complementation model of the MIDP and the vehicle model rationalisation process. Thus, models, which are no longer produced in South Africa, are imported (Barnes and Black 2003:32). As already mentioned, the automotive industry shows only a low effective protection level, which leads to increased imports of vehicles and inputs used for domestic production. The local content of production decreased from 58.1% in 1997 to 50% in 2001 (Barnes and Black 2003:12). This development seems to be alarming if one takes into account the devaluation of the Rand, which was around 20% during this period. On the other hand, the industry showed an artificially high local content before 1995 as a result of the local content requirements (Barnes 1999:404). Decreased local content usage is thus a direct result of the industry's opening up. Moreover, one has to differentiate between vehicle exporters and

244 As a result of South Africa's overall employment losses in the manufacturing industry, the share of the automotive industry employment in total manufacturing employment increased from 5.01% in 1993 to 6.21% in 2001 (DTI 2002a:1, 15).

component exporters. While vehicle exports contain in average around 50% local content, component exports contain about 90% (Williams 2004a).

In fact, the automotive industry was able to decrease its trade deficit from R 10.2 billion in 1995 to R 8 billion in 2001. Experts go so far as to project a trade surplus of around R 730 million by 2012 because of export expansion and increased usage of local contents (Barnes and Black 2003: 36, 42).[245] In summarising the performance of the automotive manufacturing industry since 1995, it can be stated that the industry was very successful in exporting, creating new value addition, improving its international competitiveness and stabilising employment. Because of the MIDP, international car producers like DaimlerChrysler, BMW, Hyundai, VW, Ford and Toyota, which were formerly thinking of leaving South Africa, not only continued their production, but expanded it significantly. Toyota, for instance, plans to double its production to 200,000 cars per annum by 2007 (Economist.com 12/02/04) and BMW, which with 8.6% enjoys the highest market share of any BMW plant in the world, is also the fastest growing BMW plant worldwide (DTI 2003a: 13). It is fair to conclude that the goals to improve the international competitiveness of the South African vehicle and component industry, to attract investment and to encourage exports have been reached with the MIDP.[246] The MIDP also ensures investment security and planning reliability for the auto sector until 2012.[247] Furthermore, the MIDP has positively contributed to productivity increases to the extent that prices for vehicles and labour costs have decreased by around 30% since 1994 (NAAMSA 2003a). However, whether this has improved the affordability of vehicles remains controversial.[248] Another achievement of the MIDP is that intra-industry

[245] The usage of local contents is expected to increase because of the reduced export performance value under the import/export complementation scheme, shrinking to 70% in 2009 (see Box 25).

[246] Compare Barnes (1999) and Barnes and Black (2003) for examples of the MIDP's positive impact on exports and investment. Kaplan (2003) contradicts Barnes and Black's positive appraisal regarding the automotive industry's competitiveness: "*Despite some productivity gains, and some improvement in its ability to compete internationally, the South African auto and auto component industry has been and remains internationally uncompetitive.*" (Kaplan 2003:21).

[247] The MIDP was reviewed in 1998, when it was extended through to 2007 and again in late 2001, when a recommendation was made to extend the MIDP until 2012 (Barnes & Black 2003: 5).

[248] NAAMSA (2003b) states that the average annual vehicle price increases were, with exception of 1999 and 2000, below the Consumer Price Index (CPI) average. Barnes *et al.* (2002 as cited in Kaplan 2003:21) who compared retail car prices in South Africa with those in the EU agree with NAAMSA. They found that South African consumers were confronted with lower product prices than their European counterparts. Kaplan 2003: 22) contradicts this appraisal and claims that auto producers were not able to increase prices enough to be compensated for currency declines. He expects further price increases in the near future. More-

trade has not been limited to transnational OEMs but has also included local component manufacturers. However, the component industry has not been sufficiently integrated into the export business of the automotive industry mainly because of limited local content use (Barnes and Black 2003: 35).

It is often argued that the continued high import bias would be a negative aspect of the industry's performance (Kaplan 2003). However, the trade deficit should not be overestimated, if one considers the abolishing of local content requirements and the enormous restructuring process the industry has successfully undergone (reduced models, increased quantities). Furthermore, the achievements that have been reached so far and the prospects the industry faces regarding the development of exports as well as the cutback of the import surpluses have to be taken into account. The fact that the South African automotive industry was able to reduce its import bias despite facing increasing worldwide competition should therefore rather be seen as a competitive advantage. However, this development was of course decisively supported by the MIDP on account of which automotive exporters are able to offer lower prices.

In this context, it might be argued that the MIDP-induced price advantage holds the risk of neglecting quality. This assumption is confirmed by findings of the UNIDO (2003) but contradicted by the DTI (2002b).[249] The firm-level data given in section 5.3.4 supports the theory that quality is becoming more and more important in the automotive component industry. Surveyed first-tier suppliers stated that the quality is predetermined by OEMs and globally standardised. However, lower tiers suppliers often have problems in meeting the required product quality (UNIDO 2003).

It is furthermore argued that the MIDP is not in conformity with the WTO, as it discriminates against imported components compared with local components and subsidises exports via input rebates. OEMs can buy duty credits from component manufacturers that export to the aftermarket. Since the trade of Import Rebate Credit Certificates (IRCCS) between component manufacturers and OEMs favours domestically produced vehicles and discriminates against OEMs that do not have manufacturing plants in South Africa, the latter feel disadvantaged. It is for this reason that the EU claims reduced import duties on totally built vehicles (Business Day, 17/10/2003).
According to Kaplan (2003), the IRCCs are essential for the competitiveness of many component suppliers, as well as for pure importers so that companies that do not export also benefit from the IRCCs. Kaplan (2003:25) comments: "*This*

over, Kaplan states that the benefits of the IRCC are not passed on to consumers but are used to subsidise local component exporters (Kaplan 2003:23–24).

[249] However, the database was very small (18 firms). These firms indicated that they improved their functional capability development in the last five years and improved their quality and their manufacturing operations. A value chain movement has not been experienced, nor is it expected (DTI 2002:54-6).

considerably dilutes the support obtained by the independent, smaller, locally owned, component exporters from the IRCC – precisely those firms that, it could be contended, should receive the highest level of support." It is thus claimed that the MIDP does not benefit smaller companies (third- and fourth-tier suppliers) but only first- and second-tier suppliers, as only these companies are linked to OEMs and the export business.[250]

The major concern regarding the MIDP is the fear that automotive exports will decrease sharply after it expires in 2012, thereby worsening the import/export bias in the industry. It is therefore seen as essential that upgrading activities in the automotive component industry continue. Confronted with increasing domestic and international competition, South African producers can only maintain their position in the value chain when they are ready to upgrade their processes (e.g. towards logistic services) and to improve the quality of their products. The DTI plans to support the upgrading activities of the sector and is considering entering into consultation with single sector representatives to identify weaknesses and implement a suitable support programme (DTI 2002a:59-61). The main goals of the DTI's policy towards the auto industry are to build stronger linkages between OEMs and local suppliers, to decrease the trade deficit, to reach a higher degree of diversification among component manufacturers and to increase the employment level in the industry (Barnes and Black 2003:43-4).

Regarding the future support of the automotive manufacturing industry when the MIDP ends in 2012, the South African government faces a dilemma. Due to reduced import duties, which will be 25% for vehicles and 20% for components in 2012, the MIDP's import rebate scheme will no longer be feasible. This again raises the question of how the industry can be supported in a WTO-compatible way. A major review of the MIDP and a suitable strategy for industry's future support will be discussed from 2005 on, involving all interested groups (Williams 2003a).

---

[250] According to Kaplan (2003:24) there is a large surplus of unused IRCCs. In 2002, only 2.6% of the total worth of R 21 billion of IRCCs were sold and a further 10–15% were traded. Thus, around 80% of IRCCs issued are not used. NAACAM counters that this statement "is completely wrong". The surplus between issued and used IRCCs was about R 1 billion in the period 2003–2004. *"With the time lag between an export being made and the IRCC being issued of about 6 months, this represents, 'Working capital' rather than, 'Excess stock'"* (Williams 2004b). The increasing value of currently unused IRCCs is also because of the considerable appreciation of the Rand (Williams 2004a).

5.4.3 Automotive Trade and Trade Liberalisation with the EU

So far it has been mainly BMW, VW, DCSA and Toyota that have expanded their overall exports significantly since 1995 (NAACAM 2003). While the first three firms produce nearly totally for the overseas market, Toyota still produces predominantly for the African market.[251] The other Japanese producers, Nissan, Mazda and Mitsubishi, have the same strategy. The main export destination for vehicles produced in South Africa is the EU, which receives around 30% of total vehicle exports and 70% of component exports (DTI 2003a: 23, NAACAM 2003).

Components account for more than 75% of South Africa's total automotive trade. In 2002, the automotive component industry exported goods of a total value of R 22.88 million of which 70.8% were destined for the EU market (Meyer 2003). The structure of this trade is shown in Figure 28. The main export components are catalytic converters and seat parts, which together make up 44% of total automotive exports to the EU in 2002 (TISA 2003).

Figure 28: Automotive trade with the EU by product group

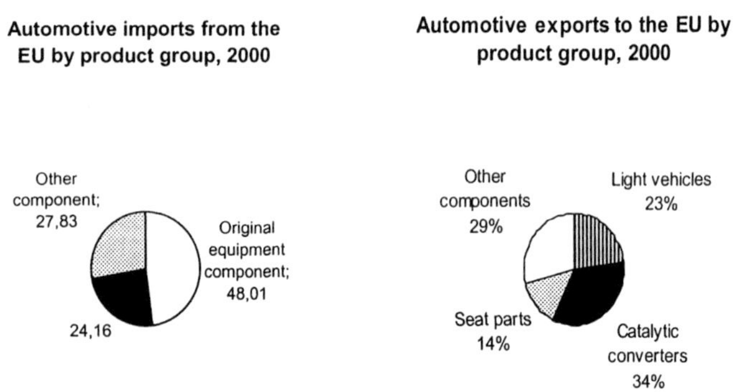

Source: DTI 2002c.

Although the EU is South Africa's main recipient for automotives, South Africa is, with the exception of catalyst converters, only a marginal supplier for the EU

[251] This is on account of export restrictions by the Japanese mother firm (compare Barnes 1999:412). However, the company plans to expand its exports to the EU owing to the TDCA (Vermeulen 2003).

and comprised only 2.01% of total European automotive imports in 2000.[252] South Africa cannot keep pace with Eastern European countries, such as the Czech Republic, Hungary and Poland (DTI 2000a:29). This indicates that, next to low production costs, proximity is a relevant factor for intra-industry trade and receipt of FDI. As the neighbouring countries of the EU (15) faced lower transport costs and were able to deliver goods faster, South Africa was not able to compete with them successfully. Furthermore, the EU has, for political reasons, adopted a strategy to integrate many of its Eastern neighbours into its production system and has expanded to EU 25 since May 2004.[253] The restructuring and integration of the Eastern European automotive industry was achieved by massive investment and reduced trade and non-trade barriers to the West-European market (UNIDO 2002b:33). Regarding the chances of the South African automotive industry becoming a major supplier for the EU, the DTI (2002a:34) states pessimistically: *"...there is no indication that South Africa is emerging as a source destination leader amongst countries economies. Eastern European countries are clearly occupying this leading position."*

Giving the harsh global competition and the limited size of the South African automotive industry in international terms, the South African government tried largely to exclude the automotive industry from the TDCA. Because of the TDCA, light commercial vehicles from the EU qualify for a 5% duty preference (see Table 25). Thus, the current South African duty for cars imported from the EU is 31% compared with 36% for the rest of the world. Heavy vehicles are subject to a 20% *ad valorem* duty but components for these products can be imported duty free (DTI 2003a:9).[254] However, parts of the automotive component industry that do not fall under the export promotion scheme, the Motor Industrial Development Programme (MIDP), are included in the TDCA. The component industry is divided into assembly (parts) and aftermarket industry (services and repairs), both of which account for around 50%. As only the assembly industry is part of the MIDP, the aftermarket industry is likely to face increasing competition (Williams 2003a).

---

[252] However, considering that EU's trade with South Africa accounts for around 1.4% of its total trade volume (European Parliament 2002:22), intra-industrial automotive trade is notably high.

[253] The new member states of the EU are Cyprus, Czech Republic, Estonia, Hungary, Latvia, Lithuania, Malta, Poland, Slovakia, and Slovenia.

[254] With the exception of tyres where European exporters face a tariff of 10% *ad valorem* compared to 15% for the rest of the world (DTI 2003a: 9). The import of motorcycles to South Africa attracts an *ad valorem* duty of 5–10% (Ibid: 19).

Table 25: Vehicle manufacturers' market access under the TDCA

	For South Africa to the EU	**For the EU to South Africa**
Current market access	Light commercial vehicles: 3.5% duty preference, i.e. 6.5% import duty	Light commercial vehicles: 5% duty preference, i.e. duty peak of 31% in 2004. Components: 5% duty preference , i.e. duty peak of 23% *Plus: Import duty reduction under the MIDP*

Source: DTI (2003a: 9).

South African vehicle exporters currently face only a 6.5% import duty when entering the EU market and can export many components duty free to the EU (DTI 2003a: 53).[255] However, this implies that South Africa receives only a 3.5% preference compared to auto manufacturers from non-EU industrialised countries. The South African vehicle and component industry has called on the EU to abolish its import duties before 2010.[256] The USA, which, for example, shows a regular import duty of 2.5% for passenger cars and 0% for South African vehicle exporters (due to AGOA) offers much better market access (Vermeulen 2003). At first glance, it appears that the automotive manufacturing industry can hardly be affected by the TDCA, as South Africa has agreed on only a 5% tariff cut hitherto. However, as discussed, South Africa's *effective* tariff with regard to European imports is much lower because of the import/export complementation scheme MIDP.

5.4.4 Empirical Findings

The purpose of the field study was to investigate automotive component manufacturers' trade relations with European companies, to gain insight into their export performance and their international competitiveness, to analyse their awareness of the TDCA and to prove whether firms see new export opportunities on account of the TDCA.

---

[255] This preferential import duty is granted under the GSP (DTI 2003a: 53).

[256] The EU has agreed to abolish its tariffs on vehicles and components until 2010 at the latest (Council of the EU 1999: Art. 11.5).

Findings will be compared with those of Barnes (1999, 2001), Barnes and Black (2003) and Kaplan (2003), who did similar firm-level research, as well as with sector-specific data published by the DTI (1999, 2002a, 2002b, 2003a), NAACAM (2003) and NAAMSA (2003a, 2003b).[257] Together with the findings from face-to-face interviews with representatives from NAACAM, NAAMSA, DTI, and CSIR/AIDC, there will be an evaluation of whether the TDCA offers new opportunities for automotive component suppliers, to what extent these are used and whether there are also risks. The DTI's, NAACAM's and NAAMSA's information policy regarding the TDCA and to what extent the information provided has been used by the companies is also discussed.[258]

The study does not claim to be representative of or to mirror the economic performance and awareness towards the TDCA of all enterprises in the automotive component industry. However, as the following discussion shows, the findings of the sample are for the most part in accordance with recent research done in this sector and also reflect NAACAM's appraisal of the current situation in the component industry (Williams 2004b).

5.4.4.1 Methodology, Firm Profiles and Characteristics

The companies were selected using the National Association of Automotive Component and Allied Manufacturers (NAACAM) 2003 Directory.[259] NAACAM represents the interests of around 30% of all companies related to the automotive component industry. In total, there are more than 600 companies that participate in the auto industry in South Africa. However, for some only a small part of their turnover comes from the auto industry and many supply only the aftermarket (NAACAM 2004e). NAACAM includes 175 member companies that represent 210 factory sites and employ 49 301 people (NAACAM 2004b).

[257] According to Barnes (1998; 2001), the manufacturing performance of the South African automotive component industry can be measured by means of the following criteria: 1) Cost, 2) Quality, 3) Lead time, 4) Flexibility, 5) Capacity to change and 6) New product development. The market demands a low cost base, an international standardised quality, the flexible adaptation to different batch sizes, the capability to respond to market changes and manage resources, such as human capital, effectively, and the ability to develop new products. Further criteria that give us an idea about the international competitiveness of the automotive component industry and that are incorporated in this analysis are 7) Development of exports, 8) Use of the MIDP, and the dependency on exchange rate developments for exporting, 9) Turnover and profit developments, and 10) Domestic and international competition situation.

[258] NAAMSA represents the interests of all vehicle producers manufacturing in South Africa (NAAMSA 2003a: 16–17). NAACAM represents the interests of the automotive component industry and incorporates 220 member companies of which around three-quarters trade with the EU (NAACAM 2003b).

[259] With exception of one company that is a vehicle manufacturer.

Thus, NAACAM member companies, which are mainly first- and second-tier suppliers, employ around 65% of the total employees in the automotive component sector in South Africa.[260]

In total, 25 companies were interviewed. With the exception of two, all companies were located in the Gauteng Province where 47% of NAACAM members' factory sites are located and which represents the largest auto component supplier cluster in South Africa. The interviews were conducted personally, on the basis of a standardised questionnaire (see Annex I). Two companies, located in Durban and Port Elizabeth, were interviewed by telephone. According to NAACAM, the sample for this study was well selected, as it covered small, medium and large companies in a range of products with a sound geographical spread (Williams 2004b). All interviews were conducted with the management of the companies. The positions of the interview partners were as follows: Managing Director/General Manager (10), Project or Technical Manager (7), Marketing Manager (4) and Plant/Operational Manager (3). With exception of one, all interview partners were male and white. This is in line with the national ratio: black South Africans control currently only 5% of the companies in the automotive component industry (Wood 2003).[261] In the quantitative breakdown only 22 interviews were analysed, namely 19 interviews from first-tier suppliers, one from a second-tier supplier and two from OEMs. The remaining three interviews were either incomplete or non-comparable[262] and were used only to verify and question results and to broaden the analysis, as were the interviews with the two automotive industry representatives (NAACAM and NAAMSA), and representatives from the DTI, TISA, and CSIR/AIDC. The interviews were mainly conducted with first-tier suppliers (19), since these suppliers are directly or indirectly involved in exporting activities, while suppliers operating lower in the value-addition chain (second to fourth-tier suppliers) are predominantly domestically engaged. However, it must be emphasised that there is no record of the level at which the companies operate. While it is known that there are in total 278 first-tier suppliers in South Africa, many of these companies also act as second- or third-tier suppliers (NAACAM 2004e).

---

[260] According to 75,000 employees in the sub-sector in 2003 (DTI 2003a:47).

[261] It is the goal of government's "Employment Equity Programme" to increase this share to 30% in 2012. However, due to the lack of human capital in the automotive industry and as the process to qualify people to become company shareholder is a long one, this goal is unlikely to be reached in time. The government proves to increase the funding to support the goal of employment equity (Wood 2003).

[262] One of the companies interviewed sold only 10% of its total production to the automotive industry, one was a service and logistic provider and one company (a vehicle manufacturer) dropped out of the interview.

Foundation: With the exception of one, all the companies already existed during the Apartheid era. It is noteworthy that the majority of companies were well established, eight of the 22 having been founded before 1960 and a further 12 before 1980. This is confirmed by Barnes (1999) who states that companies in the automotive manufacturing industry are of extensive duration and have a long tradition in South Africa.

Ownership: The majority of the surveyed companies (13) were locally owned, seven were foreign owned and two companies were joint ventures. Although five companies changed their ownership structure after 1993, there is no evidence of the dominance of foreign ownership. This finding does not accord with UNIDO (2002b) and Kaplinksy (2000:138) who state that ownership shifts in South African companies varied from having technical agreements with global component manufacturers to joint ventures or wholly owned subsidiaries of global automotive component suppliers. NAACAM supports this thesis, stating that there is a definite trend towards international ownership in the auto component industry (Williams 2004b). However, as discussed later, the surveyed companies showed other forms of international linkages, such as technical or license agreements.

Number of manufacturing plants: Most of the companies (18) had fewer than five plants. Only one firm owned more than eight plants. Nineteen of the 22 surveyed firms had their plants exclusively in South Africa; only three companies also had plants overseas. None has a branch in the BLNS countries or any other African country. This shows that the focus of South African component manufacturers, despite their international linkages, is still predominantly domestically and that the majority of companies are rather small in international terms. The fact that there are no manufacturing branches or sales offices in other African countries implies that there are neither production facilities nor a big after-sales market in Africa (see Box 26).

Box 26: Options for regional integration in the South African automotive industry

South Africa produced 83% of Africa's vehicle output in 2002. However, vehicle exports to African countries are declining: while the SADC region received 46% of South African passenger cars exports in 1997, this figure shrank to 9% in 2001. In the same period exports to the EU and NAFTA raised sharply: from 7 to 38% and from zero to 18% respectively (DTI 2003a: 12, 24). Most of the companies interviewed stated that there is neither an expandable demand in the component aftermarket nor a demand by manufacturers. Only nine of the surveyed companies are currently exporting to other African countries and seven of them intend to expand their exports to African countries. Africa seems to be an almost negligible market for the automotive component industry: four of the seven manufacturers state that they serve the aftermarket exclusively and deliver only small quantities, two suppliers are OEMs and sell small batches of their products to the African market, and one is going to supply the African market but only through the OEMs he supplies. The companies deliver all over Africa, to southern Africa (Botswana, Namibia, Zimbabwe, Angola, Zambia, Malawi, Mozambique), West Africa (Nigeria, Ghana), East Africa (Kenya, Tanzania, Uganda), and North Africa (Tunisia, Morocco, Algeria, Egypt, Mauritania). The most important reason to export to Africa is the high demand for aftermarket products, followed by low tariffs and non-tariff barriers, the high price of sale (as a result of the low volumes), proximity, and low competition. However, the result concerning the tariffs and non-tariff barriers must be cut down, as the majority of companies sell *ex works*. The product requirements seem to be largely the same for Africa and the rest of the world: five companies state that there is no difference and only one supplies lower quality products to the African market. The main reason for *not exporting* to other African countries is simply that there are no OEMs and thus a low demand for components. The supply of the aftermarket, where the African demand lies, is often not companies' business. Furthermore, the companies cite political and economical instability, bribery and payment problems as hindrances to more business. Surveyed companies that export to Africa do generally only export if payment has been received in advance or if a confirmed letter of credit has been issued.

The options of establishing an integrated regional network in the automotive industry seem to be very limited. Within SADC, it is only South Africa (and to a much lesser extent Zimbabwe and Mauritius) that show an industrial base. Botswana used to have a Hyundai vehicle assembly plant, which closed in 2000 after the tax holiday granted by the government expired. Hyundai faced the problem of very high transport and inputs costs and could not be competitive after expiration of the tax break (Williams 2003). The SADC Secretariat commissioned a study led by Dr Frank Flatters to investigate options and limits to build up a regional supply chain in the automotive manufacturing industry. A conceivable idea in this regard would be for instance the building up of tanneries for car leather seats. This very high value product could be flown out so that countries' lacks in infrastructure services would not be a problem. However, the SADC regional supply chain study has not been released yet. To date, the South African automotive industry imports only little of its leather required for seat manufacturing from Namibia and Botswana (Williams 2003).

Employment and Turnover: The companies showed high disparities regarding their number of employees and their turnover: ten companies had up to 200 employees, six 200–500, two 800–1000 and four more than 1000 employees. The average NAACAM member employs 250 people (Williams 2003a). The employees in the interviewed companies were mainly men: 21 companies indicated that at least 50% of their employees are male; more than half of the surveyed companies employ more than 70% men. The surveyed companies are a good example of the average NAACAM member, which employs almost exclusively men (around 90% of the workforce). Men work mostly in the capital-intensive manufacturing processes, while women work in the labour-intensive fields, as they would rather bypass the qualification process (Williams 2003a).

Regarding the turnover, the companies can be split into four different categories: seven generated less than R 60 million in 2002; nine earned R 100 to R 350 million per annum, three made R 400 to R 550 million a year, and two companies realised a turnover of more than R1 billion in 2002. According to the common definition the surveyed companies can be classified as small and medium-sized companies (Ayyagari *et al.* 2003:3). However, in the South African context, these companies can be regarded as large. In sum, it can be stated that the companies represent the main unit of NAACAM members very well (Williams 2004b).

Market Focus: The SACU market, or rather South Africa, was the main selling market for 20 of the 22 companies. The remaining two said that the EU was their first delivery area. With regard to their main export market, nine of the 22 companies stated that it was the EU. However, it could have been expected that the EU would be the most important export market for more companies. Eight interview partners stated that they did not know for which export market their products were mainly destined, as they supplied mainly to OEMs. In fact, only four of the interviewed firms handled their exports exclusively themselves, while nine companies exported only through OEMs and six firms exported directly as well as through OEMs. As the EU received around 70% of South Africa's automotive components (NAACAM 2003) and 30% of totally built vehicles in 2002 (DTI 2003a:23), it can be surmised that the vast majority of surveyed companies were indirectly dependent on the European market. The fact that 15 of the 22 companies (also) exported through OEMs is symptomatic of South African automotive component exporters. Barnes (1999:402,409) states that the vast majority of component suppliers in South Africa rely on OEMs for their economic survival. To export successfully, component manufacturers use either OEMs as export channels or create linkages with international companies. Domestic producers that are not linked to international producers are often not linked to the production process either (DTI 1999:5).

Table 26 summarises the characteristics of the companies surveyed.

Table 26: Summary of characteristics of surveyed South African automotive manufacturing companies

Foundation	*N* =22	
	> 1960:	36.4%
	1960–80:	54.6%
	1991–93:	4.5%
	> 1993:	4.5%
Ownership	*N* = 22	
	Domestic company:	59.0%
	Foreign company:	31.8%
	Joint venture:	9.2%
Market position	*N* = 22	
	OEMs:	2
	First-tier supplier:	19
	Second-tier supplier:	1
Number of manufacturing plants	*N* = 22	
	1 plant:	9
	2-4 plants:	9
	5-8 plants:	3
	> 8 plants:	1
Employment	*N* = 22	
	< 100:	18.2%
	100–200:	27.3%
	201–300:	13.6%
	301–500:	13.6%
	800–1000:	9.1%
	> 1000:	18.2%
Turnover (2002)	*N* = 21	
	R 15–60 million	33.3%
	R 100–170 million	23.8%
	R 200–350 million	19.0%
	R 400–550 million	14.3%
	> R 1000 million	9.6%
Market focus	*N* = 22	
	South Africa:	90.9%
	EU:	9.1%

5.4.4.2 *Exports to the EU and Development of Export Options*

The majority of the surveyed companies (12) started to export to the EU only after the end of the Apartheid era. Three companies already exported before international sanctions entered into force.[263] Three firms did not export to the EU and four exported only through OEMs and were not aware of which markets their products were destined to be exported to.

Market advantages of the EU: Only 18 of the 22 surveyed companies knew the European market well enough to be able to give the advantages and disadvantages of the EU as an export destination for their products. Six companies mentioned stable prices and quantities as important factors, whereas seven firms judged these to be partly relevant factors and five companies said that the European market did not offer stable prices and quantities. This negative appraisal relates mostly to pricing. The European market is seen as interesting because of high volumes, but it is claimed that it shows only a low profit margin (stated by 13 of the 22 companies). The majority of companies are thus able to increase their profits only when delivering high volumes. The firms are not only price but also quality takers, that is, they have to fulfil the quality requirements and to accept the prices that are given by the OEMs. Although only eight companies saw the high quality requirements of the EU as an advantage, 15 companies referred to it as a very important factor. Statements like *"We have to strive for quality all the time"* or *"The quality is the same worldwide"* confirm the theory of globally determined quality. All companies as well as NAACAM verified the theory that high quality is a precondition and competition pertains to the price only. Barnes (1999: 405–6) agrees: *"Poor performance is no longer tolerated by the OEMs, with the net result being ongoing operation pressure on the component firms by the OEMs. Failure to conform to specified performance targets results quite simply in the transfer of business from the South African company to a foreign supplier."*

Six interview partners named preferential market access to the EU as a (very) relevant factor, while nine said it was irrelevant. However, only one company referred to the TDCA in this respect. The vast majority of firms sold through European partners (licensers, OEMs) so that their market access has not changed because of the TDCA.[264]

---

[263] To deal with the sanctions, international OEMs established locally owned producers of their products in South Africa or operated through wholly owned subsidiaries (Barnes 1999: 404).

[264] Although South Africa has better market access to the European market than Brazil or China, Eastern European countries have created substantial competition (UNIDO 2003; DTI 2002a).

Long-standing cooperation, knowledge transfer and technical assistance were also named as important factors (10 and nine votes respectively). Around half the companies indicated that they benefited from cooperation with their European counterparts or with OEMs and that they received technical assistance if required. However, seven companies said that they received neither knowledge nor other assistance from their partners and had to perform their activities on their own. According to NAACAM, it is contacts rather than knowledge transfer or technical assistance that are relevant for component exporters. Because of the MIDP international OEMs have expanded their production and formed links with component manufacturers. Furthermore, the change in the international supply chain and the increasing trend to outsourcing of manufacturing activities to developing countries was also important (Williams 2003a).

When asked about other factors that promote their exports to the EU, the companies highlighted large quantities (13), the option to export standardised products (2), the usage of the MIDP (3), delivery into a stable, hard currency market (3) and the facilitation of business through cultural similarities (1) (see Figure 29).

Figure 29: Summary of surveyed firms' reasons to export to the EU (N = 18)

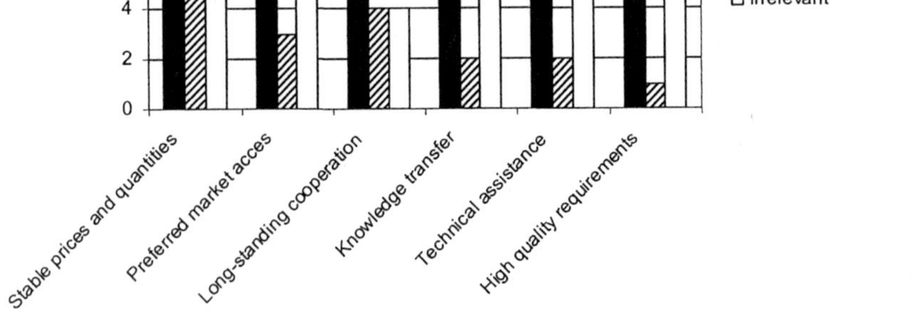

Market disadvantages of the EU: As expected, it is not a problem for the manufacturers to fulfil the Rules of Origin (16 judged it as irrelevant), as the whole manufacturing, value-adding process does generally take place in South Africa. To fulfil environmental standards and safety regulations is not a problem either:

15 of 18 companies did not have any problems in this respect; two judged it as partly relevant and only one firm had great problems meeting European standards. However, some of the interview partners emphasised the increasing importance given mainly to environmental standards and the rising costs related to compliance. With the exception of one, all companies are certified by ISO 14000 and meet international product quality standards.

Meeting the high volumes required by the European market was not a problem for 11 companies, while seven firms had or had had difficulties complying. To fulfil the quantitative requirements the companies had to adapt new technologies or run extra shifts.

Fourteen companies stated that access to finance was not a problem, while four cited it as a serious hindrance to their exports to the EU. These four companies are all domestically owned, while only five of the 14 companies for which finance was not a problem are local firms. However, four of these five companies show international linkages, which the other four local firms do not have. Thus, international connections seem to guarantee appropriate access to finance and are thus an important competitive advantage when exporting.

Only six companies saw tariffs and customs procedures as a "partial" hindrance; the other 12 did not face any tariff or non-tariff barriers when exporting to the EU. However, six of these 12 companies exported only via OEMs and did not have any first-hand experience. According to NAACAM, duties are still a problem when entering the European market, though some duties for automotive components have declined over the last years.

Twelve firms indicated that they did not face any problems meeting international technological requirements. Three companies had some problems complying and three companies showed a lack of technology. Difficulties with meeting the mechanical demands seem to be independent from ownership, but include various other reasons. One foreign-owned company stated that it had problems obtaining good quality inputs; one joint venture company stressed the point that it could not benefit from its foreign counterpart, as the companies have a dissimilar product range, and two domestically owned companies cited a lack of financial resources for realising the necessary investments.

Marketing and distributing their products in an appropriate way was not a problem for 11 companies. Six of them deliver their products to a European licenser or cooperate with a foreign logistics company: three have set up their own distribution channel or warehouse and two deliver only to regular customers within South Africa. There were seven companies that had (partial) problems distributing and marketing their products and these cited a lack of foreign warehouses and distributors or a license to market and distribute their products in the EU as the stumbling blocks. In general, the value-creating distribution and marketing activities still occur outside South Africa, in developed countries (UNIDO 2003; Williams 2003a).

Further constraints to exporting into the EU market are high transport costs and time constraints (named by six companies), exchange rate problems (4), not having a license to supply the European market as this is already done by a subsidiary company (3), the unattractiveness of the EU market because of low prices and high competition (2), and not having access to market information (2). NAACAM also cites the OEMs' high dependence on brand names for assembly products and the low credibility of South African manufacturers as constraints. People would not differentiate between individual African countries and would not believe that South Africa manufactures high quality automotive products (Williams 2003a).

Figure 30: Summary of surveyed firms' hindrances to export to the EU (N = 18)

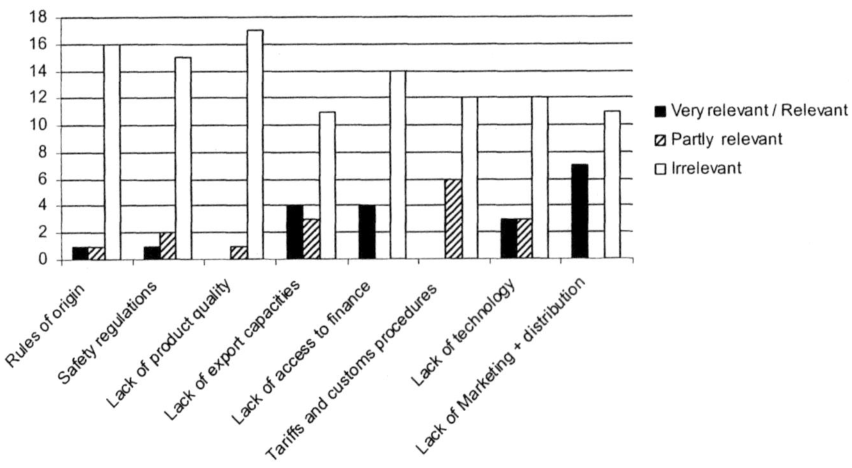

Development of exports to the EU / Sales to OEMs: Asked for the development of their exports to the EU and sales to OEMs in the last five years, 13 companies declared an increase, one a decrease, seven indicated that their exports/sales had remained stable and one company did not answer the question. In sum, a rather positive outlook can be deduced with more than half the companies showing an increase in exports/sales. Eight companies had raised their exports/sales by more than 50% (and three of them by more than 100%) in the last five years. Furthermore, four companies expected an additional increase in OEM demand in the future (see Table 27).

Table 27: Summary of firms' exports/sales development, 1998–2003

	N = 20
Increased	60.0%
Decreased	5.0%
Remained stable	35.0%
	N = 12
Increased by <10-20%	3
30-40%	1
50-75%	4
76-100%	1
>100%	3

The reasons for the boom in suppliers' exports/sales to OEMs are mainly increased demand (11) and expanded production (11). Five companies cited improved market access and cooperation with a foreign firm as important factors, while eight firms did not consider this relevant. Improved technical assistance, more generous regulations regarding quality and environmental standards, and cheaper inputs were immaterial with regard to the companies' increased exports/sales (see Figure 31).

Figure 31: Summary of surveyed firms' reasons for increased exports to the EU (N = 12)

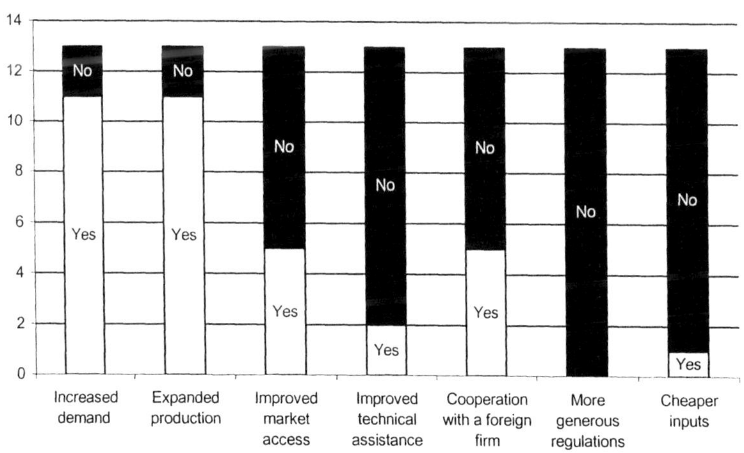

Further positive factors included the introduction of new products and an increased product range (2), improved product quality (2), the influence of the MIDP (2) and the devaluation of the rand (1). These findings are in accordance with NAACAM, which recorded a great increase in its members' exports (40% per annum.) due to increased demand from OEMs and improved OEM market access to the EU. The MIDP had also helped to create an environment for competing successfully (Williams 2003a). Tariffs are a limited factor of constraint to export to the EU and more importance is attached to this issue by NAACAM than by its members. Only three companies said that they paid tariffs to enter the European market.[265] Four companies were not aware of any duties that had to be paid and 15 companies did not pay any duties when exporting to the EU. However, as only eight of these 15 firms exported directly, the number of companies indirectly subject to tariffs may be higher.

Thus it can be stated that the surveyed companies' exports have largely developed positively and are expected to increase further. This is mainly because of the OEMs increased demand and thus expanded production. These findings are in accordance with NAACAM, which noted a great increase in its members' exports (40% per annum.) due to increased demand from OEMs (Williams 2003a).

Strengths and weaknesses in exporting: It is striking that quality was seen as main strength (20 companies out of 21).[266] As already mentioned it is obligatory to comply with the quality determined by the OEM to be competitive. Nine companies saw the price setting of their products as an advantage, six saw it as a disadvantage and six considered their prices "neutral". The scope of price negotiation with OEMs is generally limited: "*If you do not have the lowest price in the world, you do not get the business.*" (Williams 2003a). The price is predominantly determined by OEMs, so that the competitiveness of component suppliers depends very much on the exchange rate. Therefore, producers who depend to a great extent on imported inputs can often not offer a competitive price. Since the companies often have to purchase raw materials in accordance with OEMs regulations, they may not be able to source the cheapest inputs. However, the supply of locally sourced inputs can also be expensive, for example, aluminium and steel, which are still subject to a monopoly in South Africa. Thus, 15 companies saw their raw material base as a weakness, while only four perceived it as a strength. This finding does not accord with NAACAM's appraisal that South Africa is a low cost base for raw materials (Williams 2003a).

The degree of capital utilisation was very different among the surveyed companies: while 10 companies saw it as strength, eight judged it as a weakness

[265] Two companies paid only very low tariffs (1.4 and 2.2% respectively), and one OEM was charged a 6.5% tariff for bringing its light vehicles into the European market.

[266] As already mentioned, 10 of the 22 interview partners (also) exported directly to the EU, nine exclusively through OEMs and three companies did not cite the EU as an export destination. However, 21 of the 22 companies interviewed were able to state their strengths and weaknesses in exporting.

and three as neutral. The comparatively low level of automatisation in the South African automotive industry (compare Kaplan 2003) was seen as a heritage of Apartheid, when capital was substituted by (cheap) labour. The majority of companies were thus forced to engage in massive investments and to restructure their production processes when the South African economy opened up.

Most of the companies (14) felt that the labour productivity was too low: only five firms were satisfied with the productivity of their workforce. Labour costs were seen as strength by nine of the 21 companies. Seven judged labour costs to be neutral in comparison to labour productivity, and five companies felt that the wages were too high. As many companies still relied on labour-intensive production processes, the wage/productivity ratio was an important factor for them. It is emphasised that a well-trained workforce becomes more and more important for the industry (Barnes 1998:4, Meyer 2003). According to Barnes (1998) it is predominantly the low level of trust between management and workers that hinders effective working models, such as teamwork and self-directed working teams, which in turn contributes to the low level of labour productivity in the automotive industry. As the majority of management is still white, while most of the workers are black, this problem is also likely to be a heritage of Apartheid. The surveyed companies that were satisfied with the productivity level of their workforce agreed that for them worker productivity depended greatly on the performance of the management.

The majority of interview partners (12) said that the transport of goods was a weakness. Only those companies that deliver ex-works or to South African-based OEMs saw transport as an advantageous factor (6). Just-in-time delivery was either an "impossible" or a "negligible" factor. Eleven companies said that they were not able to deliver just-in-time and six stated that this was not important for them. Only four companies were strong in just-in-time delivery, but only one met the requirements of an OEM based in Europe, the other three supplying only to OEMs in South Africa.

Further strengths of the surveyed companies were the low cost base in South Africa regarding land and energy (named by four companies as a further strength), the MIDP (3), the capability to manufacture small batches (2), flexibility with regard to manufacturing processes (2), and a high capacity and technology potential that meets European requirements (2). Further weaknesses are the long distance to the European market (named as a further disadvantage by five companies) and the lack of an agent/distributor in the European market (2).

Figure 32 summarises surveyed companies' strengths and weaknesses.

Figure 32: Summary of surveyed firms' strengths and weaknesses in exporting (N = 21)

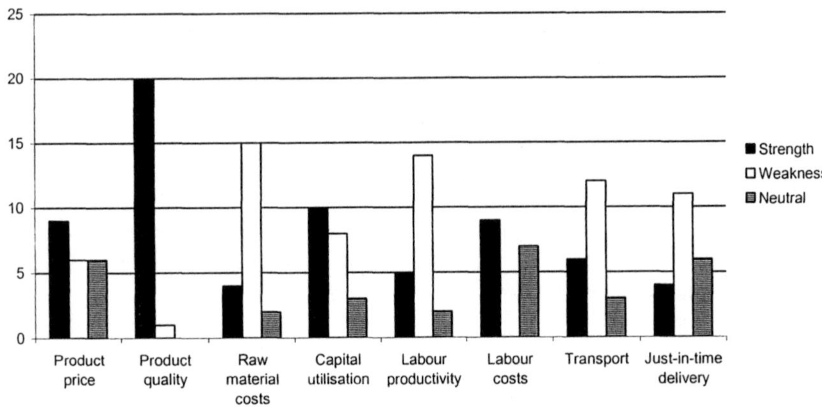

As can be seen from Figure 32, product quality and product prices are the surveyed companies' main strengths, while the cost of raw materials, the labour productivity and transport costs are their main weaknesses.

The surveyed companies' claims regarding the high cost of raw materials cannot be generalised. The majority of the South African auto component manufacturers have substantial domestic raw material bases and they do benefit significantly from the MIDP, as the raw materials are included as local value addition and therefore qualify for duty rebate (DTI 2002a: 35–38). NAACAM also states that South Africa has a low cost base for raw materials (Williams 2003a).

In contrast, the surveyed companies' assessments regarding low labour productivity and high transport costs seem to be a general problem of the South African auto sector. Although the labour productivity in the automotive industry rose well above the manufacturing average in the last 10 years, it is still judged as too low by international standards (Barnes and Black 2003:19). The high transport costs are mainly due to South Africa's unfavourable geographic location to supply its main market, the EU. However, South Africa has a comparably favourable location to supply South East Asian countries and Australia (DTI 2002a). Thus, BMW and Mercedes have invested almost R 7 million in South Africa and plan further expansion investment to serve the right-hand-drive market in the Far East (The Economist 14/02/04).

Importance of exporting for company's total performance: For the majority of companies (16) exporting was (very) important to raise the economies of scale.[267] Increased profitability and productivity owing to exporting were also cited as a (very) important factor by most of the companies (13 and 17 respectively). Those companies that had not yet been able to increase their profitability through exporting (7), claimed that it was very costly to "get a foot in the door" and become a reliable OEM supplier. Furthermore, the unstable exchange rate influenced the profitability of their exports negatively.

Exporting had helped 14 and 15 companies to increase their technology and manufacturing competences respectively. Three of the companies that did not agree with this statement said that it was not the export business but their integration into an international company that had helped them to improve their manufacturing competences.

Improved product quality as a result of exporting was confirmed by 14 of 20 interview partners. Price competitiveness, on the other hand, had only improved for 11 companies, while eight companies judged the influence of export business on their price competitiveness as limited or insignificant. The ability to develop new products, which is seen as an important factor in becoming internationally competitive (Barnes 1998), was not apparent in even half the companies.

The majority of companies (14) confirmed that their labour and management skills had improved because of the export business. Furthermore, exporting seemed to improve the e-commerce capabilities of firms, with 12 companies indicating so. Price quotations, biddings, invoicing and payments via the Internet, as well as international inquiries, are the main activities in this respect (see Figure 33).

The ability to develop new products, which is seen as important factor to become internationally competitive (Barnes 1998), is not even fulfilled by half of the companies. Only nine firms were able to improve their product development capacity, while 10 were not. This confirms the findings of Barnes (1998) and UNIDO (2003), as well as the appraisal from NAACAM (Williams 2003a), all of which state that the South African automotive industry, as part of a global network, is increasingly directed towards pure manufacturing, while high-value parts of the product chain, such as product development, design and marketing, are almost exclusively done in OEM headquarters in industrialised countries.

[267] Only 20 of the 22 companies were able to answer this question. The remaining two stated that their direct exports were currently too small to give a meaningful answer.

Figure 33: Contribution of export business to surveyed firms' economic performance (N = 20)

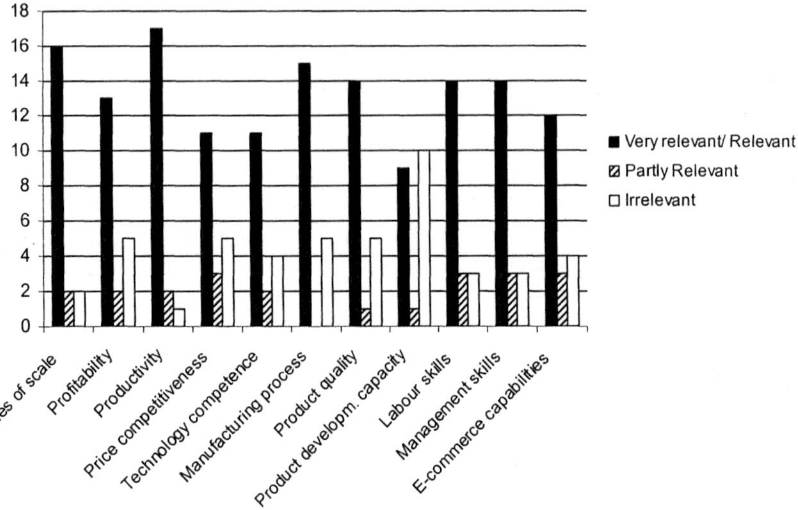

However, the fact that the surveyed companies operate successfully in an international environment already implies that they are able to develop new products and processes. Although these new products and processes are not "radical innovations", they are nevertheless innovative in the sense of Schumpeter (Sell 2000:10). New forms of organisation, improved product quality, improved labour and management skills and the introduction of new shift systems may be seen as only marginally innovative by the companies themselves, but they do show that the surveyed companies are constantly improving their performance to stay competitive.

Export assistance: With the exception of four, all companies made use of the MIDP. Of the four that did not, one is a second-tier supplier that sources exclusively local inputs and the other three deliver exclusively to domestic OEMs and do not export themselves. However, the OEMs can still rebate the local content under the MIDP so that all three suppliers benefit indirectly from the MIDP. Of the 18 companies that confirmed that they benefited from the MIDP, 12 stated that they passed the MIDP on to the OEMs to become/stay competitive; one company passed part of the MIDP to the OEMs but also used it itself, and five companies used the MIDP predominantly to rebate inputs for their own exports. Altogether, the finding shows that the companies use the MIDP to a large extent, either for direct or indirect exports. This confirms the accepted theory that the either for direct or indirect exports. This confirms the accepted theory that the MIDP is an important feature for the competitiveness of first-tier suppliers and OEMs (Barnes and Black 2003, Kaplan 2003, UNIDO 2003).[268]

However, "classical" instruments of export promotion, such as export credits or export insurance, seem hardly to exist in the South African auto component industry (see Figure 34). Though the Industrial Development Corporation (IDC) offers credits for SMEs, none of the companies surveyed used them, as the interest rates of these credits are not judged as attractive. The same applies to the export insurance offered by the IDC, which was felt to be too expensive (Williams 2003a). The DTI offers assistance for participation in international fairs through the Export Marketing and Investment Assistance Scheme (EMIA).[269] Twelve companies stated that they knew about this programme, but only five used it; the other seven said the DTI's export assistance was not of interest to them because of bureaucratic complications. Four companies were not interested in exhibiting their products and six companies did not qualify for the EMIA or were not aware of the programme..

Twenty companies stated that they did not get any assistance for training their staff. The government does not grant additional training assistance but all manufacturing industries are able to deduct 1.5% of salary expenditures for training costs (which was judged as assistance by one company). NAACAM states that public training schemes are not sufficiently promoted by the government, and that most small auto component firms are not able to make use of such programmes (Williams 2003a). Only four of the 22 companies said that they received information relevant to exporting, though all the companies are NAACAM or NAAMSA members. This either means that NAACAM/NAAMSA does not provide the companies with relevant information or that the interview partners are not sufficiently aware of the information received.

---

[268] Firm-level data of the DTI (2002: 50) also support the theory of the manufacturers' dependency on the MIDP. In a survey, 13 of 18 firms indicated that the MIDP was central to their export performance and none of the firms stated that they would be able to maintain their current success without the MIDP.

[269] EMIA is an export assistance programme run by the DTI. It is supposed to assist exporters in market and investment research and to assist in inward and outward selling of products and exhibitions and inward and outward investment. Information about EMIA is available on the Internet: http://www.thedti.gov.za/exporting/exportincentives.htm.

Figure 34: Summary of surveyed companies' export assistance (N = 22)

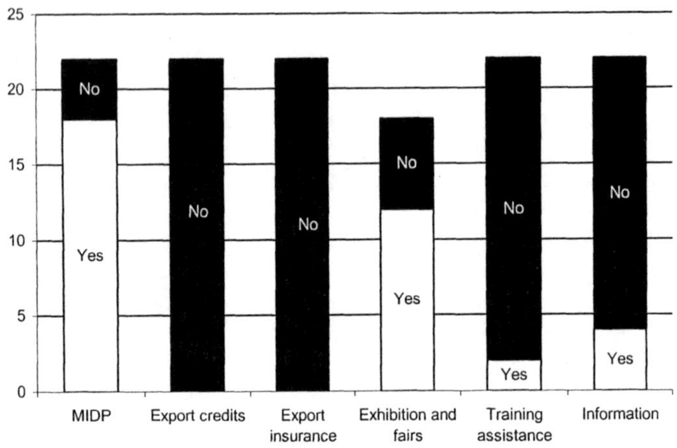

In summary it can be said that the MIDP is an important export assistance scheme for the companies surveyed, as it improves the attractiveness of South African component suppliers for OEMs in comparison to non-South African component manufacturers. Further export promotion assistance is hardly used. Since the vast majority of surveyed companies are linked to international suppliers they do not face financial constraints for their export business.

5.4.4.3 Europe's Relevance as an Input Source

Main source of inputs: The data suggest that South Africa is still the main source of inputs, despite the appreciated exchange rate since 2002. Thirteen companies sourced the majority of their inputs from South Africa, with 10 of them showing a domestic content of 71–100%.[270] These results contradict the findings of Barnes and Black (2003:12) who point out that fewer inputs have been sourced locally since the expiration of local content requirements and the introduction of the MIDP (a decline of 8% from 1997-2001). However, the surveyed firms pointed out that imported inputs are not attractive owing to high transport, packaging and warehousing costs, import duties and the volatile exchange rate. Thus, companies that rely on a high level of imported inputs find it difficult to stay competitive.

[270] One company stated that it sourced globally.

The EU was the major source of inputs for four companies, but only one obtained more than 70% of its total inputs from the EU.[271] Nationally, the EU accounts for around 75% of all imports for the auto component industry (Williams 2003a).

Development of input prices: Twenty of the 22 companies said that their prices for inputs had increased. Fourteen of them had faced price increases of more than 40% in the last five years (and 10 of more than 50%). One company registered a small price decrease for inputs (of less than 10%) and one stated that input prices had remained stable. However, the price increases were highly exchange rate driven. Twelve of the 20 companies that had faced increased prices said that prices had remained stable in €/US$ terms or had even declined (this was the case for two companies). Only two firms had noticed significant price increases in €/US$ terms owing to a shortage of input materials (see Table 28).

This finding indicates that it was mainly monetary instabilities (inflation, exchange rate) that led to price increases for inputs until 2001. The companies further claimed that the appreciation of the Rand since 2002 had not resulted in price decreases for domestic inputs.

Table 28: Summary of surveyed firms' main input source and development of input prices

Main input source		
	N = 21	
	South Africa:	62.0%
	EU:	19.0%
	Far East:	9.5%
	Other:	9.5%
Price development	*N = 22*	
Increased		91.0%
Decreased		4.5%
Remained stable		4.5%
Price development	*N = 20*	
Increased by 1–20%		10%
31-40%		20%
41-50%		20%
>50%		50%

[271] Two companies sourced their main inputs from the Far East and two from Brazil and Australia. No company interviewed received the majority of its inputs from the USA.

5.4.4.4 Competition in the Domestic and International markets

Main competitors and competition within the EU: Eight companies gave more than one answer to this question, stating that they faced stiff competition from more than only one country. European companies were the main competitors for 11 companies, seven firms faced increased competition mostly from South East Asian companies and six companies competed mainly with South African firms. For three companies the main competitor was (also) in another country and three companies stated that they faced global competition (see Figure 35).

Figure 35: "Where are your main competitors?" (N=22)[272]

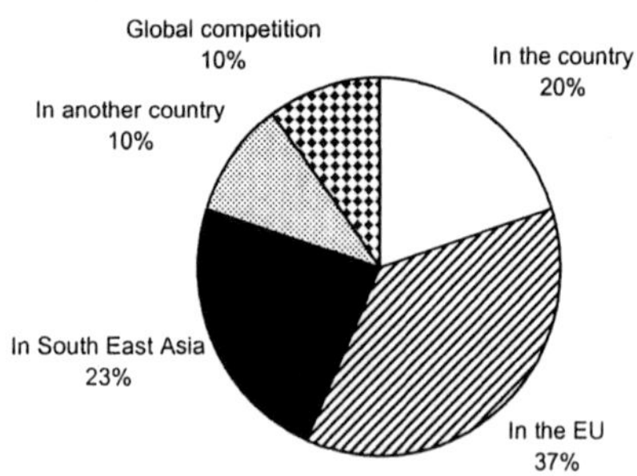

In sum, the EU seems to be the dominant competitor for the component industry. However, this relates mainly to the competitive situation in the European market and not to the South African market. Only seven of the 22 companies felt adversely affected by European imports, mainly because of high volumes (see Figure 36). The risk of replacement by European suppliers was felt to be limited since *"The EU is too expensive"* (Williams 2003a). At the time 15 of the 22 surveyed companies did not feel threatened by European competition. However, this situation is likely to change with the EU's enlargement to 25 member countries. The new EU members also offer world-class products but show higher labour productivity and lower transport costs than their South African counterparts.[273]

[272] Multiple answers possible. Eight companies said that they have more than one main competitor.

[273] The DTI (2000a:29) stated already in 2000 that South African automotive component suppliers cannot successfully compete with East European companies and that this situation is likely to worsen after the EU east enlargement.

Figure 36: "Do you feel adversely affected because of European goods imported to the country?" (N=22)

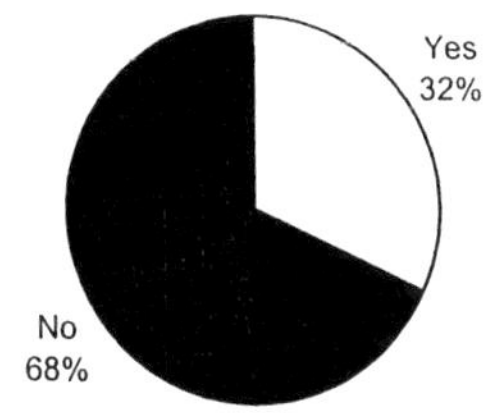

General competitive situation: According to 11 companies, competition had increased over the last five years. While three companies had noticed a decrease in competition, seven said that their competition situation had remained unchanged (see Figure 37).[274] However, those companies that registered decreased competition pointed out that this was only because they had become more competitive.

Figure 37: "How did your general competition situation develop in the last five years?" (N=21)

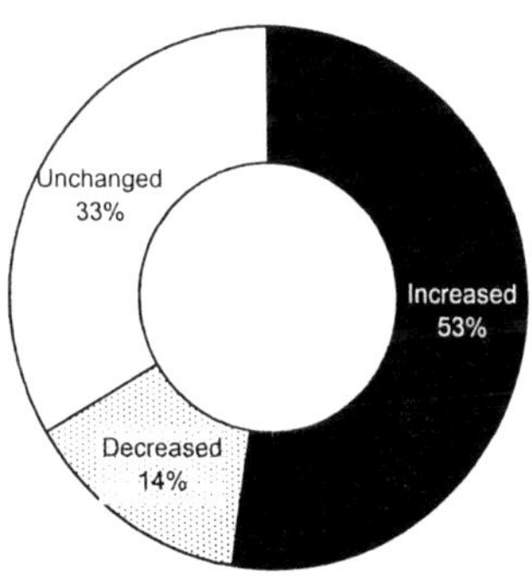

[274] One company could not state whether its competitiveness had increased, as it did not have any insight into the competitive situation of its mother company and was totally dependent on the business it got from its mother company.

The surveyed companies' answers regarding their competition situation indicate that domestic and international competition has increased for South African auto component manufacturers. As OEMs have decreased their models and increased the volumes, the chances for component manufacturers to receive a contract have decreased and the competition among component manufacturers has increased. According to NAACAM this rationalisation process is going to continue and a further increase in competition can be expected (Williams 2003a).

5.4.4.5 Value Chain and Added Value of Exports

Profit trend: Only 14 of the 22 companies answered this question in detail. However, all the companies were prepared to indicate whether their profits had increased or decreased. Regarding the general development of profits, it can be stated that the majority of companies (about 14) experienced a growth in profits during the period 1999–2003, while an average number of six companies faced declining profits.[275] About two companies showed stable profits from 1999–2003. The increase in profits was generally moderate, with seven companies showing an enhancement of less than 10%. Only two companies were able to increase their profits by more than 41% (see Table 29). In sum, the majority of companies surveyed experienced a small profit increase, which is in line with the average NAACAM member that was able to raise its profits by 2–3% per annum from 1999-2003 (Williams 2003a).

Table 29: Summary of firms' profit development, 1999–2003

		N = 22
Increased		63.6% = 14 companies
Decreased		27.3% = 6 companies
Remained stable		9.1% = 2 companies
		Detailed breakdown: N = 14
		N = 11
Increased by	<10%	63.6%
	10-20%	9.1%
	31-40%	9.1%
	41-50%	9.1%
	>50%	9.1%
		N = 3
Decreased by	<10%	66.7%
	10-20%	33.3%

[275] The decreases in profits have been moderate with less than 10% for 2 companies and only one company showing a profit decrease of 10-20%. On average one company showed stagnating profits in the period 1999-2003.

Relevant factors for profit increase/decrease: The main reasons for increased profits were lower production costs (as stated by 13 of the 14 companies that showed increased profits in this period 1999–2003), increased domestic sales (12), increased exports (11), and higher consumer prices (9). However, four companies refuted the latter statement and emphasised that consumer prices had risen only in accordance with the costs. Decreased purchasing prices, however, were not a reason for increased profits; only one of 14 companies was able to receive inputs at cheaper prices. It seems that the development of profits is greatly driven by increased volumes and the exploitation of economies of scale. When asked for further reasons that contributed to increased profits, seven companies named higher volumes. Other reasons were better cost management (4), a high return on investment (2) and the change in ownership (2) (see summary in Figure 38). Furthermore, the MIDP and the constant improvement of production processes can be seen as relevant factors for increased profits (Williams 2003a).

Figure 38: Surveyed firms' reasons for increased profits (N = 14)

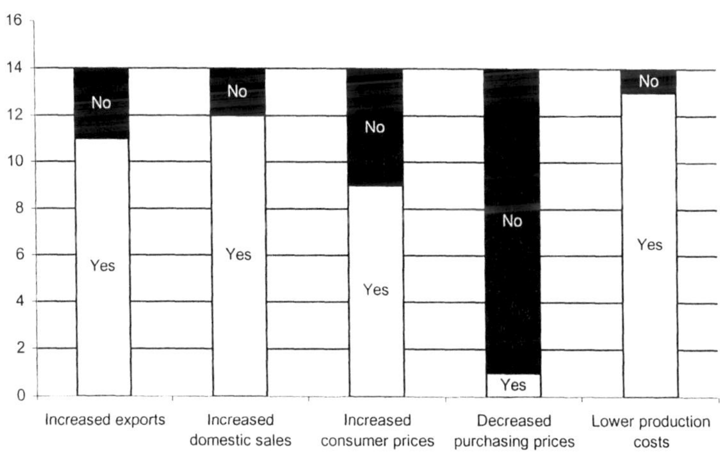

The reasons for the decreased profits as experienced by six firms (see Figure 39) were mainly increased production costs (4), decreased domestic sales (3) and increased purchasing prices (3) (multiple answers possible). The companies also named internal management constraints (2) and foreign exchange problems (2) as reasons for their profit losses. Two companies said that high expenditures on investment were the main reason for decreased profits from 1999–2003 and that they expected rising profits in the near future.

Figure 39: Surveyed firms' reasons for decreased profits (N = 6)

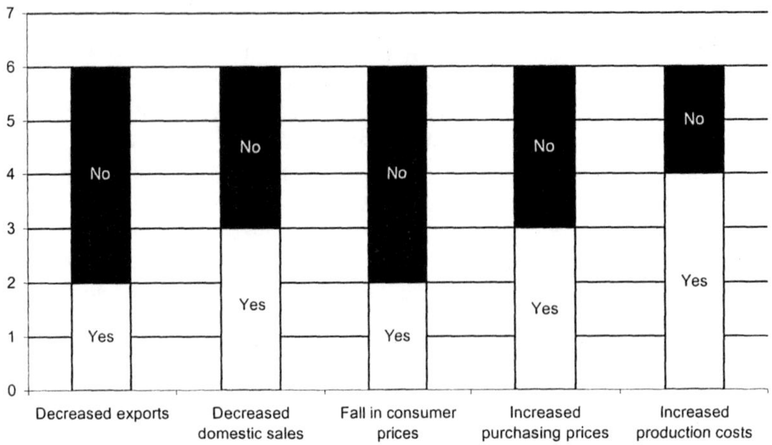

Change in unit price: Asked for changes in unit prices, 12 of the 22 companies cited slight price increases for their main products in the period 1999–2003, six companies faced slight price decreases and four indicated that their prices had remained unchanged. When one analyses product groups, 40 product groups of the 22 surveyed companies showed slight declines in sales price[276], 31 showed slight price increases[277] and 16 product groups remained stable. The price decreases were mainly enforced by OEMs, but compensated or even overcompensated for by increased volumes. However, the high inflation rate in 2000/2001 created problems for passing the cost increases to the customers (OEMs). Furthermore, owing to the unfavourable exchange rate during 2002, companies that produce products with a high imported content faced increased costs, which they were often not able to incorporate fully into their prices. Moreover, six of the companies that were able to increase their real prices also faced higher cost increases (see Table 30).

[276] Price declines were less than 5% for 34 product groups in the period 1999–2003.

[277] Price increases were less than 5% for 21 product groups in the period 1999-2003.

Table 30: Summary of firms' price development

Change in unit prices, 1999–2003 *(in real terms, inflation adjusted)*	*Per company* *N = 22* Prices increased: 54.5% Prices decreased: 27.3% Stable prices: 18.2%	*Per product group* *N = 87* Price increased: 35.6% Price decreased: 46.0% Stable prices : 18.4%
Price developments per product group, 1999–2003 *(in real terms, inflation adjusted)*	*Price increases per product group, N = 31* < 5%: 21 5-10%: 10 >10%: 0	*Price decreases per product group, N = 40* < 5%: 34 5-10%: 1 >10%: 5

It is therefore mainly high (low) volumes that are responsible for the surveyed companies' profits (losses). Since the OEMs put increasing pressure on prices, component manufacturers' profits depend very much on their ability to lower unit costs and increase their economies of scale.

Main export purchasing company: Eighteen of the 22 companies exported mainly to large transnational retailers. Only two firms exported to medium-sized buyers and two to small-scale retailers (aftermarket sales). This reflects the general structure in the South African automotive component industry where first-tier suppliers supply mainly OEMs.

Expectations of development of exports: The export prospects were generally judged as positive. Seventeen of the 22 surveyed companies expected an increase in export volumes, while only two firms expected their export volumes to decline. One company felt that the status quo would continue and two firms said that they could not project their future export developments. Regarding the extent of export gains, five companies expected a rise of more than 50% in the next five years and another five firms anticipated only a slight increase of 10–20% by 2008.

The prospect for price development was less positive. Although nine companies expected an increase in unit prices in the next five years, only five companies were able to determine the expected extent, which was rather moderate.[278] Six firms anticipated price declines, three thought their prices were likely to remain stable and four companies were not able give information about anticipated price developments. The uncertainty regarding future prices was mainly related to the exchange rate. After the sharp depreciation of the Rand during 2001, which caused problems for importers but was advantageous for

[278] Three firms expected their prices to rise by up to 20% by 2008, one firm expected price increases of 31–41% and another company anticipated a price increase of up to 100% in the next five years.

automotive exports, the component manufacturers now face the problem that the currency is too strong for their goals. This reflects once again how dependent auto component manufacturers are on high volumes for their economic well-being. However, it also shows that more than three-quarters of the companies surveyed forecast their exports positively.[279]

Figure 40: Surveyed firms' expectations of development of exports (N = 22)

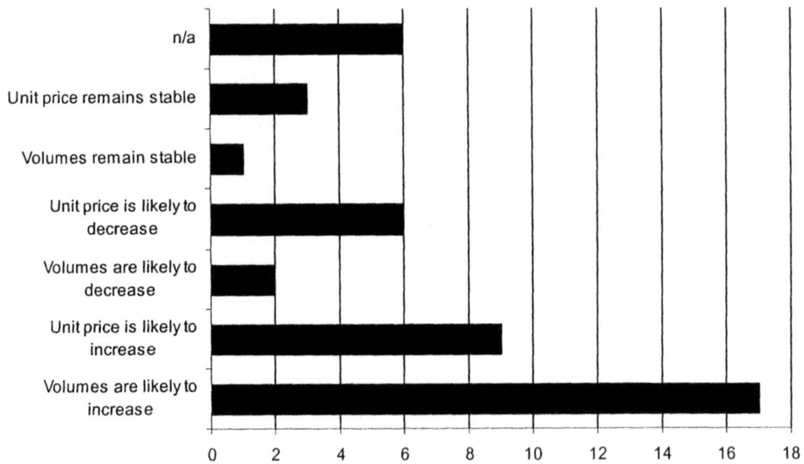

5.4.4.6 *Companies' Strategy*

Budget for product research and development: Only 10 of the 22 interviewed companies had their own budget for product research and development (R&D), while R&D was predetermined in the foreign headquarters of local firms or given by the OEMs for 12 companies.[280] This finding is in line with Barnes and Lorentzen (2003: 4) who state that the vast majority of South African auto component companies, even in so-called high-tech hubs like the Gauteng Province, are based on manufacturing activities. If at all, it would be large, domestic-owned component manufacturers that do their own R&D.

[279] This positive appraisal is supported by NAACAM, which expects auto component exports to grow because of increased demand by South African based OEMs (Williams 2004b).

[280] For those companies that had their own R&D, the budget was limited with six companies spending 0.5–1.5% of their turnover, three companies disbursing 1.6–2% and only one company expending more than 2% of its turnover on R&D.

Training of employees: All the surveyed companies invested in the training of their employees. Unfortunately, the comparability of results was limited as 14 companies indicated a percentage figure of payroll and eight gave the share of training expenditure on turnover. The bulk of the companies spent 1–2% of their payroll (12) and turnover (6) respectively to train their employees. As already mentioned, companies in the manufacturing industry are allowed to claim 1.5% of salary expenditures for training costs. It can be expected that general training expenditures are at least at this level (Williams 2003a). A cross-sectoral study in the South African manufacturing industry shows that the vehicle and auto component industry is the third most intensive skills sector that invests an average amount of R 50,000 per company into the training of its employees (Bhorat and Lundall 2001:11–12).[281] The findings seem to confirm the theory that enhancing employees' skills is an important issue for South African auto component manufacturers.

Investment in fixed assets: All of the companies did invest in fixed assets. The amount spent per company in 2002 differed considerably and varied between R 0.5 million and R 2 billion (OEM). 18 of the 22 companies invested up to R 40 million.

Upgrading of products and processes: Most of the companies planned to upgrade their products and processes. With the exception of one, all of the companies stated that they improved their products continuously. Furthermore, 17 companies planned to introduce new products, although seven of them said that they would do so only if this was required by the OEMs. It is therefore mainly the demands of the OEMs' that lead to the upgrading of products.

Almost all the companies wanted to improve their management processes and labour productivity. All the companies interviewed planned to increase capital utilisation. On the other hand, only 11 firms planned to introduce new services and activities, such as marketing and distribution, while the other 11 stated that they were "pure manufacturers" and/or that their responsibilities were "determined" by OEMs or headquarters abroad (see Figure 41). According to the DTI (2002a:58) component manufacturers' competences are largely restricted to manufacturing, as they are generally subcontractors to internationally active OEMs.

[281] The study investigated in total 325 South African firms in eight different manufacturing sectors. 34 of these companies were acting in the vehicle and auto component industry (Bhorat and Lundall 2001:2-3).

Figure 41: Surveyed companies' strategy for upgrading activities

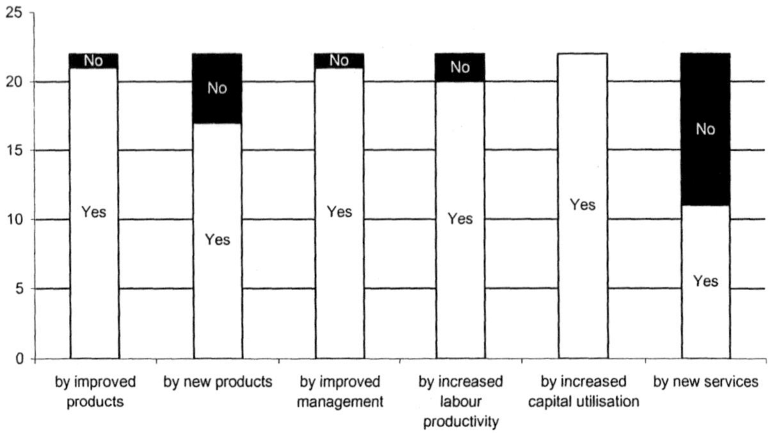

However, although South African component manufacturers' competences are largely restricted to manufacturing, as they are generally subcontractors to internationally operating OEMs (DTI 2002a:58), they are nevertheless involved in the upgrading of products and activities, as Figure 41 shows. Further upgrading activities undertaken by the companies included improved processes (6), improved management training methods (5), increased investment (5), the introduction of a new agent or marketing concept (3) and improved labour training (2).

Thus it can be stated that the companies surveyed are improving their products, services and their operating procedures continuously to comply with OEMs demand. To guarantee increased product standards, quality management and delivery requirements, the companies are forced to promote "life-long upgrading" if they want to stay competitive. Barnes and Lorentzen (2003:13) comment: *"...to pursue global niche strategies or gain world mandate, firms must possess world-class technological capability without which car makers will not even talks to them."*

Encouragement of upgrading: Fourteen companies confirmed that their main purchasing company encouraged them to upgrade activities, while seven firms did not get any support.[282] However, four of the 14 companies that were encouraged to upgrade activities said that the "support" was limited to OEM pressure to fulfil specific tasks. NAACAM confirms that the relationship between com-

[282] One company did not answer the question.

ponent suppliers and OEMs is still more dictatorial than cooperative. However, OEMs have recently realised that a cooperative approach is more fruitful for a successful, long-term business relationship and have started to cooperate with their suppliers (Williams 2003a). Interview results showed that at the time only 10 of the 22 companies received real support to upgrade their activities: four companies received technical assistance, two received support to train their staff, two got logistical and strategic support, one received information and one company was financially supported. According to Barnes & Lorentzen (2003:15) it is above all those companies involved in a global network that receive support to upgrade their activities and have superior access to advanced technologies.

Strategic alliance: With the exception of two of the companies, the rest (20) indicated that they could imagine forming a strategic alliance with a foreign enterprise or that they were already involved in one. Asked for the advantages of this, 11 answered that being part of a global network was an important benefit: their participation in networks, for instance, would allow them to stay competitive and ensure market access. Other advantages were access to the latest technology (listed by 9 companies), increased volumes (6), a wider product range (5), access to capital or financial assistance (4), and the use of a global brand name (2).

However, the companies also saw disadvantages to being in a strategic alliance with an international company. The greatest disadvantage was the loss of flexibility and decision-making authority (named by 9 companies). Further disadvantages included restrictions regarding the destination of exports (4), limitation of technical capabilities, such as the loss of R&D (2), competition with a sister company (1) and the loss of direct customer contact (1).

All in all, the advantages outweigh the disadvantages and the companies emphasised the importance of encouraging international linkages. This result is in line with empirical findings of Barnes and Lorentzen (2003) who state that subsidiary firms prefer to copy technology, design, and new production processes from their international mother company than from domestically owned firms. Moreover, they have greater financial resources as a result of their international linkages, which enable them to invest more and thus to act more innovatively. However, R&D is largely centralised in the company hub in Western Europe or North America, which determines subsidiaries' activities. It is therefore not the subsidiary company but the large, independent auto component manufacturer who is able to invest in the capital-intensive activity of R&D (Barnes and Lorentzen 2003: 10–11).[283]

[283] According to Barnes and Lorentzen (2003: 8) there is evidence that OEMs prefer to source from wholly owned subsidiary companies and not from domestic companies with licensed technology. However, since the sample is very small (five companies) this finding might not represent the whole industry.

New export markets: The majority of companies (14) were exploring new export markets, while eight companies were not interested in expanding their exports to new locations, partly because they were exporting only via OEMs and partly because of limited capacity. The North American market seemed to be the most attractive export destination, with four companies exploring it. The AGOA initiative may be contributing to this attraction. Further potential export markets for the surveyed companies were the Far East (3), other African countries (3), South America (2), European countries (2) and the Middle East (1). This finding is in contradiction to NAACAM's appraisal according to which the EU (Germany) is currently the most interesting export market, followed by the USA and Japan (Williams 2003a).

Table 31: Summary of surveyed firms' strategies

Receipt of assistance to upgrade products and processes by OEMs	*N = 21*	
	Yes:	66.7%
	No:	33.3%
Intention to enter into a strategic alliance	*N = 22*	
	Yes:	90.9%
	No:	9.1%
Exploration of new export markets	*N = 22*	
	Yes:	63.6%
	No:	36.4%

In sum, the findings about the surveyed companies' strategies as given in Table 31 show that the firms are constantly improving their manufacturing and technology performance to stay competitive. The pressure exerted by the OEMs to perform to predetermined quality standards are high. It is considered advantageous to have international links to enable compliance with the ambitious requirements and to remain competitive.

5.4.4.7 Summary of Empirical Findings thus far

The 22 companies surveyed in this analysis are old, well-established companies that are predominantly South African owned (13). They focus mainly on the South African market and have hardly any plants overseas. However, although South Africa is the main selling market for 20 of them, the EU is an important (indirect) export market: all but two surveyed companies are first-tier suppliers that are directly linked to OEMs. This is confirmed by firm-level data according to which 70% of South African component exports are destined for the EU (NAACAM 2003). The main advantages of the EU as an export market for South African component manufacturers are its high volumes, long-standing cooperation and knowledge transfer. The development of manufacturers' selling prices, however, is volatile and greatly dependent on the exchange rate. Improved market access is also a negligible advantage, as the majority of companies export through OEMs and/or their European partners. The quality requirements for exports to the EU are the same that the component manufacturers have to meet for any market, as the quality is globally determined.

The surveyed companies face hardly any hindrances when entering the European market. Owing to their size and market position they do not struggle to comply with environmental standards and safety regulations as other African companies often do. Meeting sophisticated technological requirements and the high volumes of the European market, and obtaining sufficient access to finance is difficult for only a few of the surveyed firms. Any problems with entering the European market are as a result of a lack of marketing and distribution channels, high transport costs and not having a license to supply the European market. The companies surveyed are representative of South African first- and second-tier component suppliers, most of which are competitive in supplying OEMs but limited regarding the determination of their activities. Thus, value-creating distribution and marketing activities are predominantly done by OEMs, while most companies in the South African component industry are still restricted to manufacturing activities (Williams 2003a). However, as the interviews showed, the companies are constantly engaged in improving their products and processes to remain competitive. The companies surveyed are aware that they face the risk of being replaced by the OEMs. Since producers of simple automotive components are becoming increasingly dispensable and are able to compete only on price, it is important for auto component manufacturers to upgrade their production, including design and technological know-how, to stay competitive. Once the component supplier is able to meet the required product quality at a competitive price it becomes unlikely that he will be replaced by another supplier since reliable key suppliers are becoming more and more important for the standardised automotive industry. (Kaplinsky 2000, UNIDO 2003, Williams 2003a).

The majority of companies (13) have increased their exports to the EU in the last five years and generally rate the likelihood of future export options to the EU as positive. This finding is consistent with macroeconomic projections, which estimate an increase in the export of components of 4% per annum from 2002–2012 (Barnes and Black 2003:42). However, the problems of declining export credits due to a reduction of the MIDP import/export complementation scheme should not be underestimated. If the MIDP ceases to compensate for the disadvantages of the South African market, such as high logistical costs and a small market, South Africa may become an unattractive production facility for globally operating OEMs (Barnes and Black 2003:31). In this respect it is also the renegotiation of the EU-South Africa FTA liberalisation schedule for the auto industry that is likely to affect the MIDP (see section 5.3.5).

Regarding the surveyed companies' strengths and weaknesses in the export business, it can be concluded that it is only the product quality and, to a lesser extent, product price and capital utilisation that are judged as strengths, whereas, raw material costs, labour costs, labour productivity, and timely delivery are seen as weaknesses. This rather critical self-assessment indicates that companies are very well aware of their market and competition situation. Exporting is vital for the surveyed companies' overall performance and essential for them to stay competitive. The majority of firms stated that exporting helped them to improve their economies of scale and to increase their profitability and productivity. However, as the MIDP Review Report 2003 states, volumes in the vehicle and component industry are still too small compared with international standards (Barnes and Black 2003: 28).[284]

Exporting is vital for the surveyed companies' overall performance and essential for their remaining competitive. The majority of the surveyed firms stated that exporting helped them to improve their economies of scale and to increase their profitability and productivity. However, as the MIDP Review Report 2003 states, the volumes in the vehicle and component industry are still too small compared to international standards (Barnes and Black 2003: 28).[285]
However, the export business has not only increased the surveyed companies' economies of scale, but has also positively influenced their technological competences, product quality and prices, labour and management skills, as well as their e-commerce capabilities. These responses suggest that the companies surveyed were able to benefit from learning and technology effects since the South African economy opened up. However, only a minority of surveyed firms benefited from the upgrading of processes, such as R&D. This is in line with NAACAM (Williams 2003a) and Barnes and Lorentzen (2003), both of whom state that R&D is largely centralised in the hub companies, which are mainly located in industrialised countries.

With the exception of one, all companies benefited either directly or indirectly from the MIDP. This finding confirms that the MIDP is still an important factor for the competitiveness of first-tier suppliers. It is, however, almost the only export assistance the companies receive: only very few are also assisted with participation at exhibitions and fairs, and with training their workforce.

The surveyed firms' data regarding local content usage do not accord with the sector comprehensive analysis of Barnes and Black (2003). The interviewed companies use a high level of local content, indicating that the value adding of

[284] The component manufacturers often produce different models for the domestic and the export market, which requires high outputs until unit costs are written off (Barnes and Black 2003:28).

[285] The component manufacturers often produce different models for the domestic and the export market, which requires high outputs until unit costs are written off (Barnes and Black 2003:28).

South African-based sub-assemblers is comparatively high. The surveyed firms stated that the use of local content is stimulated by the MIDP and the proximity to the production facility. The current strength of the Rand usually does not compensate for the high transport costs of imported goods.

Competition is increasing in the South African component manufacturing industry, in line with the increasing global competition in this sector. Competitors come from all over the world, from developing and industrialised countries. In the European market, South African component suppliers have to compete mainly with Eastern European manufacturers who produce higher volumes, have better market access and who do not face the constraint of a distant market. However, with regard to the development of profits, it can be stated that the companies have managed the increased competition very well: around 64% of the surveyed firms stated that they were able to increase their profits in the last five years. This was mainly due to higher volumes and thus lower production costs per unit, stimulated by increased domestic and foreign demand. Prices, on the other hand, did not increase in real terms, with the result that the increase in costs has often not been covered. Therefore, the companies rely heavily on high volumes to operate profitably.

The surveyed companies' strategy on how to deal with international challenges relates more to improving existing products and processes than to introducing new activities. Thus, new products and processes are predominantly introduced at the request of the OEMs, suggesting that the surveyed firms show a more reactive than proactive approach. On the other hand, it must also be emphasised that the windows of opportunity for upgrading activities is very narrow, as the majority of component assemblers rely on OEMs who determine the duties and responsibilities for their own economic well-being. The component manufacturers are in a difficult situation: if they do not enter into a strategic alliance with a foreign company they do not have a chance of becoming internationally competitive. However, if they agree to be part of a global network they often lose their flexibility and decision-making power.

The question that is addressed in the next section is the extent to which the (internationally linked) South African automotive component manufacturers are affected by the TDCA. Before the companies' interviews are analysed, NAAMSA and NAACAM's involvement in TDCA negotiations and the EU's plan for future trade liberalisation of the auto industry are presented.

5.4.5 The South African Automotive Manufacturing Industry and the TDCA

> *"During TDCA negotiations our trade consultants went into negotiations like lambs that were ready to be slaughtered. ... they (...) gave too much away, e.g. tariff headings, which should not have been put in and tariff reductions that were too high and too fast. So we told them that we want to get involved. Our members produce 20,000 units p.a. and cannot compete with Europeans that produce 1 million pieces p.a."* (Williams 2003a).

NAAMSA and NAACAM contacted the government in 1997 to ensure that the interests of the automotive industry were taken into account in TDCA negotiations. They monitored the development and progress of TDCA negotiations, examined the agreement and its implications for their members and reported their interests to the DTI. Furthermore, NAAMSA dealt with its French counterpart and intervened through DaimlerChrysler and BMW in Brussels (Vermeulen 2003). Through actively lobbying towards the government, the auto component industry reached agreement on fundamental interests and on being briefed after negotiations (Williams 2003a). NAAMSA and NAACAM developed a common stance and negotiated it with the DTI. Once an agreement with the government had been reached, the South African trade consultant tried to promote this position in TDCA negotiations. According to NAAMSA the South African automotive (component) industry followed a pragmatic approach: *"International trade is important but any FTA is in contradiction to the MIDP. ... Either you have national incentives or free trade. We are comparably small and cannot offer high volumes and do therefore need a national incentive programme to compete successfully, e.g. against Eastern European countries, which have huge automotive capacities."* (Vermeulen 2003) Through their active involvement, NAAMSA and NAACAM reached to exclude the MIDP and thus most sections the South African automotive and component industry from the TDCA. However, this could be achieved only because South Africa agreed to open its agricultural market to a larger extent than originally planned (Gibb 2003). Furthermore, the EU made it quite clear that it is not happy with the degree of liberalisation for the automotive and auto component industry and wants further concessions.

As already discussed in section 5.3.3, neither the South African nor the European automotive industry has noticeably opened up because of the TDCA. Thus, the current peak of South African duty for cars imported from the EU is 31% compared with 36% from the rest of the world, while South African vehicle exporters currently face a 6.5% import duty (DTI 2003a: 53).

Thus, both parties have committed themselves to investigate options for further liberalisation. Furthermore, South Africa has agreed to review its tariff structure periodically, to identify products for liberalisation and inform the EU about its policy under the MIDP (Council of the EU 1999: Art. 12.7). Since the TDCA entered into force, the EU has been putting pressure on South Africa to make further concessions with regard to vehicle and component tariffs. In 2003, South Africa offered an additional import duty preference for built-up cars of 1% per annum from 2008 to 2012. As a result, the European vehicle exporters would face a 20% import duty in 2012. Moreover, the South Africa has offered to reduce duties for a broad range of aftermarket products and tools (NAAMSA 2003c). However, the EU has not been satisfied with this offer and is seeking to secure a better deal for European exporters who do not have a manufacturing presence in South Africa (Business Day 17/10/2003). The EU has asked South Africa to liberalise its automotive sector more generously and will, in return, accelerate the agreed tariff abolishment to earlier than 2010. This could be very interesting for South African automotive manufacturers, as the industry competes on very small margins so that duty-free market access to the EU would mean having a great advantage over its competitors (Vermeulen 2003).

In more detail, the EU wants South Africa to improve its tariff reductions for cars and components and to introduce a tariff quota for vehicles, which should be increased gradually (NAAMSA 2003d). However, at the time of writing (April/May 2005), the parties have not been able to agree on a further liberalisation schedule (NAAMSA 2004; NAACAM 2004a).

From NAAMSA and NAACAM's point of view, European exporters do not have any reason to complain. If they had manufacturing bases in South Africa, owing to the MIDP, their market access would be much more favourable than those of South African manufacturers exporting to the EU. Also European car manufacturers that do not have plants in South Africa, like Renault or Peugeot, could benefit from the MIDP if they exported enough car components. However, some European car exporters argue that the MIDP discriminates against foreign producers, which is contrary to the WTO Non-Discrimination Clause that stipulates the application of the same regulations for domestic and foreign goods. South Africa, in turn, argues that its tariff reductions are already much lower than under WTO obligations, which stipulate a rate of 50% *ad valorem* on vehicles and 30% on components (DTI 2003a: 9), whereas South Africa currently (2004) has an import duty of 36% and 28% respectively. Moreover, the effective tariff reduction of the South African automotive industry is much lower owing to the MIDP. Another concern for the South African automotive industry is that, should it grant the EU preferential market access, the USA, Japan, Brazil and other countries are likely to ask for the same preferences (Vermeulen 2003). Owing to automotive industry's low effective tariffs, Barnes and Black (2003: 38) recommend that South Africa act very carefully when granting further reduced duty concessions to single trading partners.

Table 32 gives an overview over the parties' proposals for further liberalisation.

Table 32: Proposals for further liberalisation of South African - EU automotive trade

	For South Africa to the EU	**For the EU to South Africa**
Current market access	Light commercial vehicles: 3.5% duty preference, i.e. 6.5% import duty	- Light commercial vehicles: 5% duty preference, i.e. 31% import duty in 2004 - Components: 5% duty preference , i.e. duty peak of 23% *Plus: Import duty reduction under the MIDP*
South Africa's proposal	Earlier tariff abolishment than 2010.	Light commercial vehicles: additional preference to import tariff reduction agreed under the MIDP of 1% p.a. from 2008–12; i.e. 20% import duty in 2012.
EU's proposal	Abolishment of all tariffs by 2010 (agreement to earlier tariff abolishment depends on South Africa's liberalisation offer)	- Improved tariff reduction - Introduction of tariff quota, which should be increased

Source: Author's presentation as cited in the text.

Surveyed Companies' Awareness and Appraisal of the TDCA

Since the auto (component) industry has been largely excluded from the TDCA, it is not surprising that the companies surveyed are not well informed about its possible impact on their business. However, considering that the DTI as well as the private sector support institutions are continuously working on this issue and see it as a relevant factor which could influence the future performance of the industry (Williams 2003a), the lack of interest (or knowledge) of the companies surveyed is rather worrying.

Seventeen companies had heard about the EU-SA FTA and five had not. However, four of the 17 companies that had heard about the TDCA stated that they had only very limited knowledge about it. Only upon asking in more detail whether the companies felt well informed about the TDCA did the picture become clearer: only six companies knew about the possible effects of the TDCA on their business, while the rest did not. Four companies indicated that they planned to inform themselves about the TDCA in the near future. Three companies thought this was not necessary as they exported only via OEMs and relied on NAACAM or on being part of a global network to receive relevant information. However, this attitude seems to be problematic: all the surveyed companies interviewed are either NAACAM or NAAMSA members and have received information about the TDCA. However, only 12 companies remember having received relevant material from NAACAM and/or NAAMSA and the great majority have not used the information provided. In total, only eight of the 22 surveyed firms used the information provided to inform themselves about the possible impact of the TDCA. A further information source was the media (newspapers, business magazines), from which seven companies had obtained information on the TDCA.[286] However, this information source was naturally not detailed enough to evaluate the options and risks for their own businesses. Further information about the TDCA was gained from DTI or TISA by six companies. Two of these six companies stated that they were very interested in the TDCA and had collected the agreement and additional information directly from the DTI. Another company received detailed information about the TDCA during 2003 from its main customer (OEM) who intends to expand its business to the EU because of the TDCA.

The limited knowledge of the automotive component manufacturers of the TDCA suggests that they are still focusing on the local market and might not be ready to capture international markets. The surveyed component firms export predominantly through OEMs and expect the OEMs to be well aware of the agreement and to inform them accordingly if necessary. The surveyed companies often work on the principle that "If it was important for me, I would have been informed". However, this attitude does not allow for a proactive approach, which would be necessary to explore the options and risks and formulate business specific interests that could be taken into account by private sector support institutions to lobby the government and European interest groups. Members of both associations, NAAMSA and NAACAM, can participate in panel discussions and contribute actively to the formulation of the auto industry's interests in trade agreements, but only a very limited number are ready to be involved. In sum, the assessment of the government and private sector support institutions

[286] The questionnaire provided only the column "other institution". However, seven of the ten companies that received information from "other institutions" said that this was through the media.

that there is sufficient awareness of the TDCA's impact on the automotive manufacturing industry (Meyer 2003, Williams 2003a, Vermeulen 2003) cannot be confirmed. As the selected companies represent a good sample of South African auto component manufacturers (Williams 2004b), it can be expected that most South African component manufacturers are not sufficiently aware of the TDCA and its possible impact on their business.

The results of the companies' appraisal of the government's awareness of the impact of the TDCA on the private sector are quite mixed. Six of the 17 companies that knew about the TDCA said that they did not feel qualified to answer this question. This shows that they were not aware of all the information provided and/or see shortcomings in their ability to work through all the information received. Five companies thought that the government was very aware of the impact of the TDCA on the private sector. Six companies felt that the government's awareness was rather moderate or low.

Table 33 summarises surveyed companies' awareness and knowledge about the TDCA.

Table 33: Summary of surveyed firms' knowledge of the TDCA

"Have you heard about the TDCA?"	*N = 22* Yes: 77.3% No: 22.7%
"Do you feel well informed about the TDCA?"	*N = 22* Yes: 27.3% No: 72.7%
Source of information *(multiple answers possible)*	*N = 17* DTI, TISA 35.3% = 6 firms NAACAM, NAAMSA 70.6% = 12 firms Media 41.2% = 7 firms
Appraisal of government's awareness regarding the TDCA	*N = 17* Very high / high: 29.4% Moderate: 17.6% Low: 17.6% Cannot say: 35.4%

Possible impact on automotive component manufacturers' business: Only 12 of the 17 companies that had heard of the TDCA were ready to answer this question. Unfortunately their answers do not give a clear picture. Thus, five companies expected increased competition in the domestic market, while six did not and one did not know. The same ambiguous picture emerges regarding the access to competitive inputs: six companies expected such inputs, five did not. One company could not say whether its access to competitive inputs was likely to improve. These answers suggest that the companies are not sufficiently informed about the EU-South Africa FTA and to what extent the component industry has been included.

A similar picture emerges with regard to the question of input prices, which are expected to decrease by seven of 12 companies. However, taking into account that the EU is an expensive supplier (Wood 2003), it remains questionable whether the duty preference of 5% lowers the price of European inputs significantly. Again, the import duty rebate system of the MIDP has a much higher influence in this respect (Williams 2003a). Asked to elaborate on their answers, the companies referred more to the MIDP than to the TDCA in their answers. It was stated that tariffs on inputs can be reduced by using the MIDP and had already reached a low level. NAAMSA confirms that, from an automotive perspective, it is mainly the MIDP that provides an incentive for competitive imports and not the TDCA (Vermeulen 2003).

Also with regard to the competition situation, the MIDP seems to be at least as influential as the TDCA. Thus, competition from European companies is expected to increase with the reduction of the duty allowance system of the MIDP (70% of the value of export performance in 2009). However, competition may increase before that date since the EU has emphasised its demand for reduced import duties on cars and components. Although the parties have not agreed on an improved TDCA liberalisation schedule yet, the perpetuation of the status quo is very unlikely. Thus, increased competition in the South African market and increased pressure on activity upgrading can be expected in the near future. A higher competition level in the South African market will mainly affect third- and fourth-tier suppliers that are not part of a global network negatively. Around a quarter of NAACAM members (about 55 companies) are third- and fourth-tier suppliers (Meyer 2003, Wood 2003).

Seven companies felt that the TDCA offered improved opportunities for cooperation, for example through increased demand. However, it is emphasised that it depends on a case-to-case basis whether such an option can be realised. Five companies thought that there had already been opportunities for collaboration with European firms before the TDCA entered into force. As Wood (2003) states regarding the advantages of the TDCA for the private sector: "*The accessibility is given on a governmental level but to put it into practise depends often on companies' contacts.*"

Asked whether it was likely that consumer prices for cars would decrease because of the TDCA, only five companies answered in the affirmative, giving increased competition as the reason. Another five companies, however, felt that it was very unlikely that the price for such a high value consumer product was likely to fall.[287] One interview partner stated: "*This will never happen! Even if the EU has a recession we would not decrease the prices for cars. Cars have a*

[287] This appraisal is confirmed by NAAMSA Vermeulen 2003).

very long product circle and we have committed ourselves too much to decrease the prices." Then he modified his ideas: *"However, services and technical equipment could improve so that you get a better deal for the same price."* This appraisal is supported by NAAMSA (Vermeulen 2003) and NAACAM (Williams 2003a). The influence of the TDCA on prices is thus more indirectly expected.

However, another option the TDCA offers is to promote the European market as a "selling point" for non-European OEMs. Toyota and Hyundai are currently exploring the idea of expanding their South African-produced exports to the EU (Williams 2003a). In this respect, there may also be benefits from increased investment by OEMs that trickle down to South African component manufactures. Generally, the South African auto sector is going to expand and expects increasing investment (Economist 14/02/04).[288]

A concern raised by Wood (2003) is that bilateral trade agreements like the TDCA increase the complexity of trade and make it more difficult for the private sector to export. Although the DTI endeavours to harmonise regulations of South Africa's bilateral trade agreements (Smalberger 2003) this concern seems to be legitimate, considering South Africa's various obligations/intentions to enter into bilateral FTAs.

Required support to expand exports to the EU

In analysing the support the companies need to expand/initiate their exports to the EU, it seems that this is hardly necessary (see Figure 42).

Figure 42: Surveyed companies' need for export assistance (N = 20)

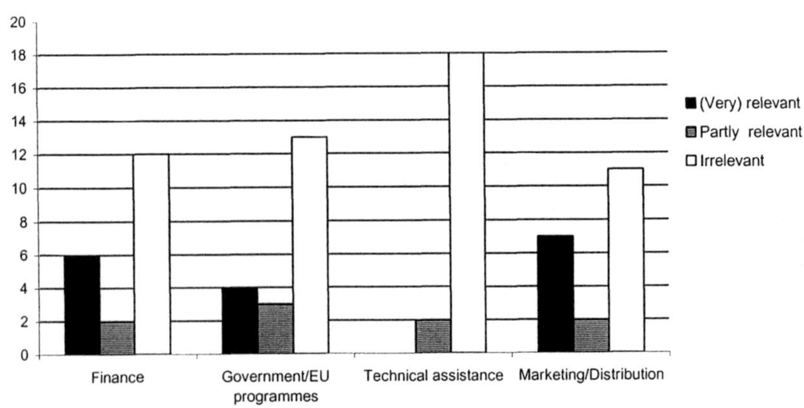

[288] However, according to the Wood (2003) investment in the automotive manufacturing industry is rather related to the MIDP than to the TDCA.

The majority of companies stated that financial support, information about government initiatives and European programmes, technical assistance and support in distributing and marketing products were not necessary (with 12, 13, 18 and 11 companies respectively indicating thus).[289] If any support is needed at all it is assistance in distributing and marketing products in the EU (cited by 7 of the 22 companies).

Furthermore, five companies are constrained by joint-venture restrictions or the lack of licenses to export to the EU. Four companies cited a lack of exposure and contacts in the EU as a drawback. Furthermore, high logistical and transport costs hindered the exports of four companies. In sum, the companies' responses to this question are similar to those given regarding their strengths and weaknesses in exporting.

The export constraints generally cited by firms in Africa, such as lack of finance, capacity and information are not those of the South African auto component industry. This shows that being part of a global network greatly facilitates the export business.

5.4.6 Conclusions: The Implications for Upgrading, Value Addition and Industrialisation Strategies when Including the South African Automotive Industry into a Free Trade Agreement with the EU

The central question of this study was whether the TDCA helps to integrate the South African automotive industry into the global economy and improve its position in the GVC. As the discussion showed, the impact of the TDCA on the South African automotive industry is somehow different than predicted by the theory of free trade and cannot be analysed in an isolated way. The strategic decisions of OEMs to invest in the South African automotive industry are determined by many factors, such as the local demand for products, export options, the MIDP, and the TDCA. The South African vehicle and component manufacturing industry is changing rapidly and becoming increasingly globalised. The transformation from broad to specialised suppliers in addition to increased competition in the domestic market and abroad has been successfully managed to a large extent. International linkages either in the form of a foreign partner or a foreign client have been essential for component manufacturers to improve their competitiveness.

It remains doubtful whether the TDCA can help South African component manufacturers to build up linkages to international companies. Why should free access to the South African market stimulate EU vehicle manufacturers to invest

[289] Seven companies, on the other hand, said information about government initiatives and European programmes was helpful. The information required relates mostly to legislation and registration requests formulated by the EU.

in the South African component industry if they are able to source from the cheapest supplier worldwide? Investment into the South African auto industry has not been attracted by free market access but by an attractive import duty reduction scheme for domestically manufactured vehicles and components. The MIDP has helped the South African automotive vehicle and component industry to cope with the enormous challenges they have faced since 1994 and to improve their competitiveness significantly. Since any free trade agreement will undermine the impact of the MIDP, the auto industry's representatives as well as governmental officials have great reservations concerning the TDCA. The current impact of the TDCA on the industry is comparatively low, as neither South Africa nor the EU was ready to grant substantial tariff preferences so that neither party has faced significantly improved market access vis-à-vis its counterpart. Thus, neither the competition situation nor the prices or technology transfer has been influenced thus far. However, whether the relationship between South African component manufacturers and their European counterparts would have developed as theoretically assumed if the industry had been included in the TDCA also remains doubtful. The majority of South African component manufacturers that are in the export business export through OEMs, therefore they would hardly have benefited from improved market access. Furthermore, better access to competitive, high technological inputs was not relevant for most NAACAM members due to their international connections.[290]

In fact, it is mainly OEM demand that determines component manufacturers' economic success or failure. Therefore, the influence of the TDCA can only be indirect, for example, by promoting the EU as "selling point" for non-European OEMs, thus offering the opportunity of increased FDI. As the examples of Hyundai and Toyota show, non-European vehicle producers that have manufacturing plants in South Africa are interested in using such opportunities. However, the inclusion of the automotive industry into the TDCA would also imply additional costs due to increased competition and its contradiction to the MIDP. As the duty rebate system of the MIDP applies only if a certain tariff level exists, any additional trade liberalisation agreed upon undermines the effectiveness of this incentive scheme. The South African auto lobby groups argue that only a few European suppliers do not have vehicle or component manufacturing plants in South Africa and therefore cannot benefit from the MIDP. Thus, Europe's economic interest in further import tariff reductions is minimal. For South Africa though, the risk of a further tariff concession is much greater, taking into account its small size, the level of international competition, and the already low effective protection rate. On the other hand, South Africa would be

[290] However, third- and fourth-tier suppliers that lack of overseas relationship might have been able to benefit accordingly. On the other hand the third- and fourth-tier suppliers are also those companies that would have the greatest problems to compete against EU imports (UNIDO 2003).

very interested to receive duty-free access to the European market before 2010. As the margins between profits and losses in the automotive business are very small, this competitive advantage would be very attractive, offering the chance to attract new investment by non-European vehicle producers.

However, the South African automotive manufacturing industry has not been able to make itself completely internationally competitive as yet. Though the industry has opened up and is rapidly transforming, it still relies to a large extent on the MIDP for its economic well-being. It must be carefully investigated whether opportunities provided by the TDCA, such as the attraction of FDI by non-European vehicle producers and receipt of competitive inputs for third- and fourth-tier suppliers, can be used or whether the risks to further opening the industry are too high. Since South Africa is negotiating FTAs with the USA, Mercosur, and the EFTA countries, which are likely to claim the same market access as the EU, the inclusion of the automotive industry into the TDCA would imply the *de facto* abandonment of the MIDP. Thus, a dedicated, controversial discussion about the pros and cons of the inclusion of the auto industry into the TDCA, involving all stakeholders, would be desirable. The knowledge the surveyed companies have regarding the TDCA and the general awareness of the impact of trade liberalising measures on the industry are rather low. The majority of firms rely on information provided by their clients (OEMs) or by private sector support institutions. However, since all the companies are NAACAM/NAAMSA members and have received a variety of information about the TDCA, it can be concluded that the surveyed companies are not adequately attentive to the changing global trading environment. Because bilateral trade agreements and governmental global liberalisation policies are rather abstract, affect businesses only temporarily delayed, and cannot be determined *ex ante*, many companies ignore the opportunities and risks that trade agreements offer. The DTI, NAACAM and NAAMSA should therefore reconsider and revise their trade information policy with regard to the private sector. Opportunities and risks of trade agreements must be specified and applied to companies. What are the opportunities the "typical" NAACAM member can expect from the EU-South Africa FTA? Can it expect increased competition and if "yes", for which products? Are further liberalisations envisaged and how and to what extent do they affect the benefits of the MIDP? These are the issues that interest and concern the companies, and private sector support institutions should do their best to address them adequately.

5.5 Case Study 2: The Namibian Fishing Industry

5.5.1 Structure of Case Study 2

The study starts with a discussion of the motivations and difficulties to manage national and global fishery resources. In this context, chances and risks of free trade in fishery products are elaborated from a developing country's perspective. Thereafter, the economic performance and management system of the Namibian fishing industry is presented. The EU is the main market for Namibian fish exports, mainly hake, 60% of which is processed onshore. However, there is scope for additional value-adding activities, which have not been sufficiently explored yet. The necessity to diversify fish exports in products and processes is elaborated at length in section 5.5.5 presenting in detail the empirical findings and verifies them with sector-specific research results. To gain clarity on the individual situation of the surveyed companies, their position in the value chain, and their connections to European firms and the European market, the question relates, among others, to the companies' trade relations with the EU, their strengths and weaknesses in the export business and the relevance of exporting for the total economic performance of the surveyed companies. Furthermore, surveyed companies' manufacturing activities and their efforts to diversify their product range are explored.

Whether and how an FTA with the EU could help the Namibian fishing industry to upgrade its products and processes is elaborated on in section 5.4.6. Thereafter, the main findings of the study are concluded and policy recommendations how a developmental oriented fishing agreement with the EU could look like are formulated.

5.5.2 Gains and Losses of Including Fisheries into Free Trade – Some Considerations from a Developing Country's Perspective

Fishery grounds are naturally an open accessible and free-of-charge resource. However, since the world-wide demand for fish exceeds the product resources, the market allocation of the resource becomes economically wasteful and ecologically unsustainable and needs to be controlled, which is tried to be done by most countries in the world.

Figure 43 illustrates the ideal level of fishery exploitation. The curve represents the total costs and the total revenue of fishing activities. An increasing effort of fishing e.g. by more vessels employed or increased efficiency, leads to an increased output that reaches its maximum at MSY. This Maximum Sustainable Yield (MSY) marks the maximum amount of fish that can be taken from a stock under existing environmental conditions without significantly affecting the reproduction process. After MSY, fishing activities can no longer be achieved on a sustainable basis. The increasing number of vessels leads to the depletion of fish stocks.

The economic target equilibrium differs from the purely biological concept, as it incorporates the costs of fishing. The Maximum Economic Yield (MEY) marks the point where the marginal benefits from the fish catches equal its marginal costs, i.e. at this point the maximum rent can be achieved.

Figure 43: The ideal level of fishery exploitation

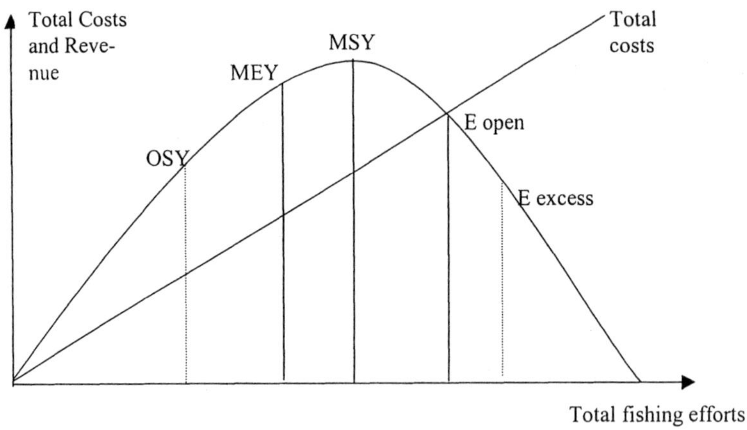

Source: Based on Gordon (1954) as cited in Costanza *et al.* (2001:65).

However, it must be kept in mind that there are long-lived and short-lived fish species as well as animals that depend on specific fish species, such as seals and sea birds. To consider these biological time lags and protect the fragile ecosystem that ensures the optimal level of biodiversity, less fish than what is economically desirable can be caught.[292] The point OSY on the curve represents therefore the Optimum Sustainable Yield, i.e. the ideal level of catches that internalises any non-market environmental effects.

If anybody who is able to goes fishing, this will result in an unsustainable exploitation of the resource, labelled by point E open on the curve. E open highlights the point where the total revenues equal the total expenses. Though total costs exceed total revenue beyond this point, it is even supposable that the fish-

[292] See Seijo *et al.* (1998) for an explanation of any externalities that have to be taken into account when managing fish stocks.

ing grounds will be more excessively exploited since the single fisherman does not know that the fishing grounds are already exploited and will keep on fishing to cover his individual costs. Thus, the personal micro-perspective differs from the macro-economic analysis of optimal fishery exploitation and the behaviour of fishermen needs to be controlled if the renewable resource is to be maintained on a sustainable level.

To manage the fish resources properly, it is therefore necessary to determine the Optimal Sustainable Yield (OSY), which corresponds to the Maximum Sustainable Yield (MSY) modified by relevant environmental, economic and social factors (FAO Glossary 2004). The OSY is therefore always subject of political pressure from different interest groups (fishermen, scientists, ecologists, investors...), which makes it difficult for the Government to set it (Cunningham *et al.* 1985:106).

Apart from the difficulty to determine and set the OSY, the Government also faces the problem of implementing a limited entry plan, which can be done by license, quota per fisherman, or taxation of catches. Moreover, the Government must provide an effective monitoring system that ensures that no unreported fishing activities take place. The right to fish must be specified to selected persons who take ownership over the resource and who know that they face penalties if they do not act as agreed. These fishing rights can be transferable among right holders as long as it is ensured that the total catches do not exceed the optimal sustainable yield (Seijo et al. 1998).

Namibia has applied a comprehensive management and surveillance system to supervise the exploitation of its fishing grounds. Catches are limited by license, non-transferable quota and taxation of catches. Namibia's monitoring system, which is judged to be effective in international terms (FAO 2001:12) as well as Namibia's fishery policy and legislation are discussed in detail in section 5.5.4.

It is not an easy task to manage fishing grounds effectively and includes several costs and required management skills. The government must ensure that scientific information on fish stocks and their development is available, has to take uncertainties, the business and investment climate and the economic and social situation of fishermen into account when fixing the limit of total allowable catches (TAC). Furthermore, it must be guaranteed that the fishery legislation is enforced and periodically evaluated and adapted if necessary (Seijo et al. 1998).

Many African countries have severe problems to manage their fish resources properly and are not even able to exploit their fishing grounds commercially as they lack of the necessary capacities. To get any revenue from their resource most African countries have agreed to sell fishing rights to foreign partners (Acheampong 1997).[293] In theory these so-called access agreements can be mutually beneficial: the industrialised country gets access to new fishing grounds and the African country receives financial compensation as well as technical assistance and other forms of aid to develop its own fishery industry. Further potential advantages are the import of capital goods and knowledge of fish catching and processing methods as well as the employment of African workers. Moreover, the fishing agreements shift the risk of stock fluctuation (e.g. by the El Niño phenomenon) to the foreign fishing nation (Stone *et al.* 2001:9-10). However, there are also negative effects of access agreements and scepticism about its net value of benefits for African countries. A severe concern is that African countries are not in a position to supervise the quotas agreed upon so that illegal fishing is taking place. The unsustainable fishing leads to the depletion of fish stocks and affects the income and nutrition of the local coastal community. Subsistence and small-scale artisanal fisheries are a major income source for coastal people in many African countries and play an important role in poverty alleviation. These small-scale fishermen are often negatively impacted by foreign access vessels that often encroach on their grounds, effectively putting them out of business (Acheampong 1997:4-5). This problem aggravates, since industrialised countries subsidise their fishing industry, which results in the overcapitalisation and thus, the overcapacity of their fleets. The subsidies reduce fishermen's cost to fish but put pressure on the fishermen to increase the number of caught fish in order to keep their vessels and factories employed.[294] Since the EU fishing stocks are largely depleted, European fishermen have to find fish somewhere else. As a result, the problem of overcapacity has shifted to developing countries in form of access agreements.

The difficulties to monitor fish catches effectively have also resulted in the claim that African countries are not sufficiently compensated for providing access to their fishing grounds. Stone *et al.* (2001:10) state: *"...it is virtually impossible, at the present level of monitoring, to confirm whether the actual catch occurred within or outside – on the high seas side – the coastal state's fisheries zone."* Though access agreements with the EU do not only include compensation payments per ton but also support that is difficult to quantify, such as technical assistance, increased aid assistance and improved market access to the EU, the price paid to African countries is claimed to be too low, not reflecting the world market price sufficiently (Ibid). Reasons are seen in the EU's lopsided negotiation power as well as in African countries' need for foreign exchange and their high economic dependency on their former colonial power.[295] Evidence for

[293] Morocco, Namibia and South Africa are the only African countries that have managed to take control over their fishing resources (Stone et al. 2001:12-13).

[294] An estimated number of 20,000 fishermen and 20,000 processing sector jobs are supported by the EU's fisheries agreement with third countries (Acheampong 1997:4).

[295] The EU is the major trading partner for most African countries (see Davenport *et al.* 1995).

the thesis of insufficient compensation is also given when analysing the single fisheries agreements African countries have negotiated with the EU. The agreements differ with respect to amount of quota allocation, agreed revenue, number of locals employed on EU vessels and financial assistance to develop a national fishery industry (European Commission 2004).

Another problem that occurs in an access agreement with a foreign fishing nation is that the local government has only little influence on the plans made by foreign investors. The options to establish an own fishing industry are very limited since domestic trawlers cannot compete with subsidised high-tech foreign fleets. Thus, the benefits for the African countries of its resource are often restricted to (limited) employment effects and increased government revenue.

For the ACP countries, the option to enter into fishery agreements with the EU was already included in the first Lomé Agreement (1975), which stressed the importance of EU-ACP cooperation regarding the optimum utilisation of ACP fishery resources. Today, the EU has 21 fishing agreements with third countries, most of them in Africa.[296] 70-85% of Sub-Saharan fish exports are destined for the EU market (Stone *et al.* 2001:16).

The EU's fishery agreements with African countries often lacked effective monitoring and control provisions and were judged to be incoherent with the EU's development goals (Acheampong 1997). The EU responded to these claims and decided to move from pure "access agreements" towards "partnership agreements" in December 2002. These "partnership agreements" do not only compensate for fishing but are also supposed to help to develop the local fishing industry in ACP countries. However, an analysis of the Institute for European Environmental Policy (IEEP 2003) summarises that this new approach is still not environmentally, socially and economically sustainable.[297]

Namibia has not entered into a fisheries agreement with the EU yet. It is argued that these agreements are incoherent with Namibia's policy objectives to increase local ownership in the fishing industry and to manage the fishing grounds in a sustainable manner.

Theoretically, free trade in fisheries can result in a win-win situation for both partners: the industrialised country imports fish and keeps its industry employed and the developing country increases its revenue by exporting fish.

---

[296] The EU has bilateral fisheries agreements with Angola, Argentina, Cape Verde, Comoros Islands, Côte D'Ivoire, Equatorial Guinea, Gabon, Greenland, Guinea Bissau, Guinea, Faeroes, Iceland, Madagascar, Mauritania, Mauritius, Morocco, Norway, Russia, Sao Tomé and Principe, Senegal, Seychelles (European Commission 2001b).

[297] It is claimed that the amount paid by the EU varies considerably among countries and does not compensate sufficiently for the value of the catch. Also the amount of development assistance to build-up an own industry varies considerably among the four countries investigated. Moreover, the fishing agreements with African countries do still lack of effective monitoring and control provisions (IEEP 2003).

Moreover, imports of capital and modern technology from advanced economies can stimulate the processing of innovations and new technologies. By this, the productivity of labour and the utilisation of capital equipment can be increased and economies of scale can successfully be exploited..

However, there are different reasons why free trade in fisheries is disputed. One argument is that existing tariffs and non-tariff barriers as well as subsidies distort free trade (FIGIS 2004). Fisheries are excluded from the WTO Agreement on Agriculture so that the main features of most favoured nation and non-discrimination (GATT 1994, Art. 1 and 2), which provide that the same regulations apply for domestic and foreign goods and services, are not applied (FAO 2004b:1).[298] Therefore, fish products, in particular some value-added fish products, are still subject to (high) tariffs. Another issue that hampers global free trade of fishery products are technical regulations, standards and safeguard measures (FIGIS 2004). Though all Sub-Saharan African countries except South Africa are classified as ACP countries and thus enjoy duty free market access for raw and processed fish products to the EU market their exports are often constrained my strict sanitary and phytosanitary standards. Moreover, EU subsidies extend the intensity of fishing and result in market distortions so that African countries' non-subsidised fleets are displaced (Acheampong 1997). The subsidies do thus result in unfair competition, undermining the comparative advantages of African fishermen, such as good quality of fish and cheap labour.

Another problem for African countries is the exchange of and the access to information. Though the FAO seeks to provide international data on fish analyses, national authorities in developing countries often lack country-specific information due to missing capacities. Companies in developing countries again, which do not show any form of international linkage have difficulties to receive up-to-date information about import market requirements. Labelling and certification have become increasingly important marketing factors in high-income import markets and many developing countries are not able to meet the determined requirements and are thus excluded from the international marketing and distribution network (FIGIS 2004).

Altogether, the options for many African countries to benefit from free trade in fisheries are constrained by their inability to manage and monitor their resource effectively as well as by non-tariff barriers of trade and high market entry costs.[299] It makes therefore a big difference whether trade in fisheries be-

[298] Though the WTO reduced the average weighted import tariff on fish products to 4.5% in industrial countries, several tariff peaks and tariff escalation for processed fish products still remained. Developing countries aim to address their concerns in the Doha Development Round (FAO 2004b:1).

[299] It is reported that illegal fishing is a big issue in many developing countries, which do not have the specific legislation and regulations and, the financial, human, material and technical capacities to patrol their coastal areas accordingly (Greenpeace 2001:3, Drammeh 2000)

tween African and industrialised countries are pure access agreements or associated with joint-ventures. While the first has above all positive effects on government's revenue, a joint-venture agreement can be also beneficial in terms of learning and technology effects (Cunningham *et al.* 1985:204-5). As the further discussion shows, joint-venture agreements have enabled businesses in the Namibian fishing industry to improve their access to markets and finance. Joint-ventures in the fishing industry have furthermore partially helped to integrate small businesses run by formerly disadvantaged Namibians.

5.5.3 Economic Performance of the Namibian Fishing Industry and Exports to the EU

The fishing industry is, after the food and beverage industry, Namibia's second largest manufacturing industry and accounted for 25% of total export earnings in 2002 (Iyambo 2003b). Employment increased by 2000 people in the period 1993-2002. Today around 13,500 people are employed in the fishing industry of which almost 80% are Namibians.[300] Most new jobs were created in the secondary sector (on-shore processing), which contributes to around 60% of total employment in the fishing industry (Iyambo 2004c:5).

According to Table 34, fisheries' contribution to GDP increased from 5.4% to 6.6% in the period 1990-2002. Though this raise of 1.2 percentage points does not seem do be much in ten years' time, one must also take the development of total GDP into account. Thus, the total value of fishing and fish processing rose by more than 36% in the period 1998-2002, which has, according to the figures in Table 34, preliminary been achieved by harvesting fish. Fish processing activities, however, grew to a lesser extent in the period.

However, the classification of fishing and fish processing has been revised by the Namibian Government and brought in line with UN definition in 2000. The term "fishing" includes now also fish processing on board (offshore processing), which was formerly (1990-99) defined as "fish processing". Now, fish processing includes, according to the definition of the UN, only processing activities on land, such as freezing, filleting and canning (MFMR 2004d:6). The figures published by the MFMR therefore show a high share of fish processing activities on total fisheries before 2000 and are not comparable with the post 2000 figures. Thus, the only statement that can be drawn from Table 34 is that the total value of fishing is increasing. Fishing contributes in average around double as much as fish processing to the total value of fisheries.

---

[300] Namibian employees accounted for 68% of sea-going employment and 98% of on-shore employment in 2002 (Iyambo 2003c:5).

Table 34: Fisheries contribution to GDP, 1990-2002

	1990	1992	1994	1996	1998	1999	2000	2001	2002*
Fishing	2.3%	3.4%	3.7%	4.0%	5%	4.7%	4.4%	5.2%	4.5%
Fish Processing	3.1%	3.2%	5.3%	3.0%	2.9%	2.2%	2.3%	1.9%	2.1%
Total	**5.4%**	**6.6%**	**9.0%**	**7.0%**	**7.9%**	**6.9%**	**6.7%**	**7.1%**	**6.6%**
Total value (in million N$)	n.a.	n.a.	n.a.	n.a.	1,476	1,422	1,592	1,922	2,016.5

* provisional figure.

Source: MFMR (2003a:4) (up to 1996) and MFMR (2004b) (1998-2002).

The main fishery in Namibia is demersal fishery that catches hake, monk, kingklip and sole, which are the most valuable species for Namibia and strictly regulated by quotas for totally allowable catches (TACs). The hake industry is the biggest sub-sector: it employs around 70% of all workers and contributes to more than 50% of the total value of the sector (Erastus 2002:5). It is also the biggest foreign currency earner and attracts most investment in the fishing industry (MFMR 2004d:4).

Further important fisheries in Namibia are the midwater fishery, which catches mainly mackerels, purse seine fishery, deep-water fishery, tuna fishery, rock lobster fishery (based in Lüderitz) and the crab fishery (MFMR 2003a:5). Commercial trawlers solely exploit Namibian fishing grounds. Because of Namibia's sparse population (around 1.8 million) lives predominantly in rural areas inland, almost no subsistence fishing takes place (FAO 2000:2. See also Box 27).

The Namibian Government is convinced that the fishing industry shows substantial growth potential. This is due to unpolluted waters, comparable rich fishing grounds, a good fish quality, and productive fishing methods (Oelofsen 2003:38). The FAO (2000:1-2) confirms that Namibia has one of the world's most productive fishing grounds with considerable development potential.

Box 27: Domestic fish consumption in Namibia

The fish consumption of the average Namibian has doubled since independence and is 8-9 kg per annum, which lies still well below world's average of 15-16 kg (FAO 2001:8). Since fish is a cheap protein source and around 50% of children in Namibia's northern region (where the majority of the population lives) are malnourished, the government further promote domestic fish consumption (FAO 2000:5). However, around 97% of Namibia's fish catches are destined for exports and only 30-40% of locally consumed fish comes from marine waters (Iyambo 2002:13). Namibian hotels and restaurants claim that they receive only over-priced domestic fish. The reason for this is that parts of the industry overprice fish for the domestic market to increase their earnings from the export business. The Minister of Fisheries and Marine Resources, Dr. Iyambo calls upon the industry: "*As a major fishing nation, we must redress this incongruity between our production and what we offer for sale to our domestic consumers! ... If fresh fish on ice can be imported, exported and sold profitably: why can't our own fishing industry sell sufficient products here? ... I want to see some workable proposals! We can do better!*" (Iyambo 2003a:7). The industry argues that a lack of cold storage and transport facilities constrains the Namibian-wide distribution of fresh fish. The Ministry promised to address this problem by building a cold storage depot in the North to supply fish to rural areas and small distributors (Iyambo 2003a:8).

As Figure 44 shows, Namibia is a bigger fish producer than South Africa and captured around 1,300 million tons fish, crustaceans and molluscs in the period 1992-2001 (FAO 2004a).

Figure 44: Capture of fish, crustacean, molluscs, etc. in Namibia's and South Africa's inland waters

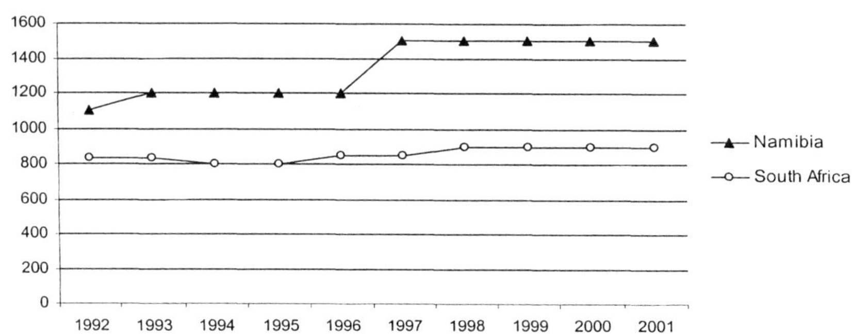

Source: FAO (2004a).

As a renewable natural resource the fishing industry is vulnerable to external shocks, such as the Benguela Niño phenomenon in 1998 that harmed Namibian stocks seriously. Moreover, the Benguela current is unpredictable as it can for instance lead to low oxygen level that damages fishing stocks. The biomass of many species was also affected by over-fishing prior independence in 1990. However, though some species, like pilchard, are still threatened, most of them have recovered. The Government was able to stabilise the TACs for most species and has even increased the TAC for hake from 60,000 tonnes in 1991 to 200,000 tonnes in 2003 (Oelofsten 2003:36).

Though fishermen's revenue is highly dependant on fluctuating fish stocks, it must be noted that fish prices are - in contradiction to many other primary commodities - not affected by the worsening of terms of trade.[301] In recent years there was even an increase in fish prices due to the scarcity of worldwide resources resulting in a considerable increase in production values of the industry in the period 1993-98 (MFMR 1999 as cited in Erastus 2002:4, 6). However, despite the depletion fishing grounds in many countries, fish prices have not increased as expected due to the development of fish farming activities, led by Asian countries (Tall 2002:4). In addition, the worldwide insecurity since 11 September 2001 and the European recession have affected the Namibian fishing industry negatively. Thus, demand and price for Namibia's largest export product, hake, have remained static (Nichols 2004a). However, in the light of increasing EU consumption and declining TACs for European fishermen, an increasing demand for fish products is expected in the near future (CBI 2003, Tall 2002).

Since the export of sea-processed fish limits the options for job creation and revenue collection, the Namibian Government promotes value adding activities on land, like the filleting and canning of fish (Iyambo 2003b). Furthermore, domestic value addition could be increased by the development of brand names, labels, and distribution and marketing activities. These value-creating activities still occur outside Namibia, in industrialised countries. The Namibian Ministry of Fisheries and Marine Resources tries to improve the communication between the fishing industry, export markets and end consumers in order to upgrade the activities in the fishing industry (Iyambo 2003b). The industry acknowledges the importance to diversify fish production towards higher valuable products. It is necessary to attract investment in order to introduce new technologies for improved catches as well as for new product and processing methods since there is still considerable scope to diversify products and markets and to move towards higher valuable activities.

[301] With exception of prices for fish meal, fish oil and canned fish, which face decreasing world market prices (WTO 2003:A3-188).

The EU is the second largest importer of fishery products in the world (Tall 2002) and the most important export market for Namibia, receiving around 70% of Namibia's total fish exports (Erastus 2002:4). The main species exported are hake and monk where 75% and 95% respectively of total production is destined for the EU market. The demand as well as the price paid by European suppliers is generally high (Nichols 2003a). Also for the EU, Namibia is an important import market for fish and was the fifth largest developing country supplier for all fish products and even the largest developing country supplier for hake in 2001 (CBI 2003:54, 59). The EU regards Namibia as reliable supplier due to its well-developed processing industry that allows Namibia to export good quality fresh and frozen fish (CBI 2003:90).[302]

As can be obtained from Figure 45, the exports of Namibia's main fish products to the EU decreased in the period 1999-2002. The quantity for hake and kingklip was reduced by almost 2.5 times and the export quantity for monk to the EU shrank by 50% (EU Export Help-Desk). However, this considerable decline in export quantities was compensated by higher prices,[303] so that Namibia's export value in 2002 remained more or less stable compared to 1999.

Figure 45: Total fish harvest and value of fish and fish products to the EU, 1999-2002

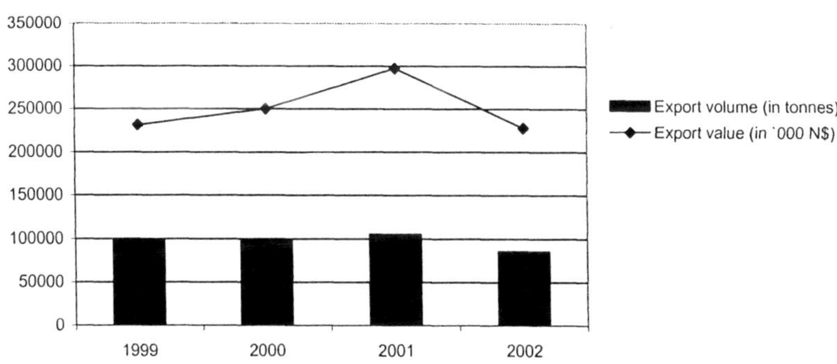

Source: CBI 2003:124, EU DG Trade (2003).

[302] The Government promotes the export of good quality fish and has adopted a national quality assurance system in accordance to international standards (MFMR 2004c:22).

[303] The value for hake increased by 9.2% to € 403 per 1000 kg and the value of monk by 23.7% to € 240 per 1000 kg. Only the price for kingklip decreased, namely by 18% (EU Export Help-Desk 2004).

Namibia is classified as an ACP country and enjoys duty free market access to the EU. This implies that Namibia currently receives a tariff advantage up to 22% for fresh fish and up to 24% for preserved fish compared to non-ACP countries (see Table 35). However, any fish product must originate in Namibia to benefit from free market access. Namibia is not allowed to import fish from South Africa, manufacture it for instance into fillets and sell it duty free to the EU. Though the Cotonou Agreement foresees that South African inputs will be handled like an ACP import product if *"... the value added there exceeds the value of the materials used originating in South Africa."* (European Commission 2000b: Protocol 1, Art. 6.4) this provision does not account for fish or fish products. These are exempt from the cumulation regulation as long as fish is still subject to tariffs under the TDCA (European Commission 2000b, Art. 6.7 and Annex XIV to Protocol I). Thus, any fish imported from South Africa and manufactured in Namibia is subject to the MFN tariff of the EU.

Table 35: Tariff structures for fish imports to Namibia and to the EU

Country	**Description of product**	**MFN Bound rate of duty (ad valorem, %)**	**GSP**	**Cotonou Agreement**
Namibia *(SACU tariff)*	Extracts or juices of meat, fish or crustaceans, molluscs or other aquatic invertebrates	37.0	-	-
EU	Fresh or chilled fish, excluding fish fillets	2-15%	2-15%	0
	Monk	15%	15%	0
	Hake	15%	8-15%	0
	Horse Mackerel	15%	15%	0
	Tuna	22%	22%	0
	Extracts or juices of meat, fish or crustaceans, molluscs or other aquatic invertebrates a) in immediate packing of a net capacity of 1 kg or less: 20% ad valorem duty b) in immediate packing of a net capacity of more than 1 kg but less than 20 kg: 4% ad valorem duty	12.8	4.4%	0
EU	Prepared or preserved fish; caviar and substitutes			
	Salmon	5.5%	2%	0
	Herrings	15-20%	15-20%	0
	Pilchard	12.5%	9%	0
	Preserved Tuna	24%	12%	0
	Hake	20%	7%	0
	Caviar	20%	7%	0

Source: EU Export Help-Desk (2004).

In addition to the restriction to cumulate with South African inputs, the Namibian fishing industry faces eroding preferences in the EU market, since the EU's motivation to protect its fishermen is declining. As discussed, TACs are always subject to political pressure and are often set higher than the scientific advice. In the EU, this has resulted in the over-capitalisation of fleets and thus to widespread exploitation of fishing grounds. Since consumers' demand for fish products is increasing and fish factories have to fully load their capacities, the EU shows a great demand for imported fish so that tariffs are expected to decline further (Payne 2003:314). For the comparable small supplier Namibia this implies increased competition in the EU market from large fish supplying nations like New Zealand, Russia or Chile (Namibia Foundation 1998).

Namibia's dependency on EU preferences raises concern about the international competitiveness of Namibian fishermen. The WTO (2003:A3-191) states: *"Continued over-reliance on ... substantial tariff preferences in foreign markets that shelter exports from international competition, can be both an indicator and a contributing cause of inefficiency."* In other words, the EU preferences might limit the efforts of Namibian fishermen to upgrade products and processes since they rely on a "secure market".

5.5.4 "Namibianisation" and other Management Policies in the Fishing Industry

"Namibianisation, simply put, is a means to peace, economic reconciliation, equity and increasing employment for Namibians, especially the previously disadvantaged." (MFMR 2004c:i).

Before independence, the Namibian fishing industry was dominated by foreign companies, from Europe, Eastern block countries and South Africa, leading to a very uneven distribution of marine resources and an over-fishing of valuable species. More than 100 vessels were fishing illegally in Namibian waters in 1990 (Nichols 2003b:3). The over-fishing by South African and international fishing fleets also resulted in the closure of fish factories. Namibia decided to drastically limit the number of foreign trawlers after its independence on 21st March 1990. The country declared 200 nautical miles as Exclusive Economic Zone (EEZ) to gain greater control over its marine resources. Moreover, a national fishery policy was created (Oelofsen 2003:33-4). Through the Fisheries Act 1992, the Ministry of Fisheries and Marine Resources (MFMR) followed up the goal to rebuild stocks and to "Namibianise" the former foreign owned fishing sector. The Act that controlled the exploitation of "internal waters, territorial sea and exclusive economic zones" pursued the following achievements (MFMR 1992):[304]

1. Sustainable use of fishing resources and establishment of a conductive maritime environment;
2. Promotion of "Nambianisation": formerly disadvantaged Namibians should be the principle beneficiaries of the fishing industry through increasing ownership of companies and vessels, new jobs, and increased training;
3. Contribution to poverty alleviation: redistribution of wealth through reasonable payments for social expenditure by the industry; and
4. Attraction of domestic and foreign investment

The Second National Development Plan (2001-2005) identifies further goals of the Namibian fishing policy as a) an increased value addition by promoting processing activities; b) the expansion of the Namibian fishing industry within the region; c) the promotion of regional integration in the fishing industry; and d) recognising the role of fish in ensuring food security (FAO 2000:6).

Companies that want to fish in Namibian territory have to apply for an exploitation right. Though the rights, given for 7, 10, 15 or 20 years, could be withdrawn by the Government if the company does not perform accordingly, there is a high confidence in the industry that the fishing rights will be renewed (Manning 2000:31).[305] If the right holder performs accordingly, the fishing rights can be extended after the maximum period has been granted. Whether and to what extent an applicant receives the right of fishing depends on the vessel and fishing methods used, to what extent Namibians are involved, their size and investment capabilities and on the socio-economic performance of the company (MFMR 2000:Art. 33).

In addition to the right of fishing, the companies have to apply annually for a quota of the fish species they want to catch. The levy system based on quotas is justified by the Government with the argument that all Namibians should have the right to benefit from their natural resources: "*As not all the "people" can participate in fishing, those awarded fishing rights are actually acting as "agents" for the people and should therefore be paying for this privilege.*" (Oelofsen 2003:37). The quota fee paid by the fishing companies is not only

[304] Ministry of Fisheries and Marine Resources (1992): "Towards the Responsible Development of the Fisheries Sector". Due to obligations resulted from the ratification of several international agreements the 1992 Act was replaced by the "Marine Resources Act" (Act. 27 of 2000).

[305] In 2002, 102 out of 163 fishing rights were granted for 10 or 15 years. In total, only four rights expired in 2002. The fishing right for 20 years is exclusively for fishing companies that employ at least 5,000 Namibians, which has not been the case at any company so far (MFMR 2004c:24).

supposed to earn revenue for the Government but is also used for research, training of Namibians and the development of the industry (Oelofsen 2003:37). The resource rent collected is further used to subsidise market entrants of newcomers and to promote the "Nambianisation" of the industry. Government's revenue from the fishing industry rose by more than 30% in the period 1998-2002 to N$ 131.8 million (MFMR 2004c:27).

The quota fee, which varies between 5 and 15% of the value of the particular fish species value, accounts for around three-quarters of the total fee amount collected in the fishing industry (MFMR 2004:14).[306] The quota fee has to be paid on the allocated quota, even if the company does not catch the fish.[307] However, the companies have the option to return the quota before the end of the season, without paying a penalty (Nichols 2004b).

To promote the engagement of Namibians in the fishing sector, reduced quota fees for Namibian owned vessels and 10 years fishing rights for Namibian owned companies (versus seven years for joint-ventures) are also part of the policy.[308] Furthermore, companies, which promote fish processing activities and training and transfer skills to Namibians, enjoy tax deductions (Erastus 2002:12). What quota is granted to a company also depends on its socio-economic contribution for poverty alleviation. Companies are called upon to engage in so-called social upliftment projects, which promote for instance the provision of improved infrastructure services in rural areas. Between 1990 and 2002 fishing right holders contributed in total N$ 33.66 million to Namibia's socio-economic development (MFMR 2004c:30).[309]

Besides the elements of fishing rights, licenses and quotas, the Namibian fishing sector is managed by the setting of TACs (totally allowed catches) for the eight main fisheries to limit their catches.[310] The TAC is distributed among

---

[306] In addition to the quota fees, registered companies have to pay a Marine Resource levy that finances research and training activities of the MFMR, license fees for licensing their fishing vessels at the MFMR, and by-catch fees. Since all caught fish must be brought to land, by-catch fees should prevent companies from catching fish for which they do not have a quota but make it still profitable to land all fish caught (FAO 2001:10-1).

[307] It is also not possible to carry the uncaught fish quota over to the next season (Iyambo 2003a:8).

[308] The rebate system differentiates between a) Namibian vessels, b) Namibian-based vessels, and c) foreign vessels. Quota fees are the lowest for Namibian companies (>51% share) that employ at least 80% Namibians off-shore. On-shore workers have to be at least 95% Namibians (WTO 2003:A3-190).

[309] Of which N$ 11.1 millions came from newcomer companies (Iyambo 2003c:6).

[310] These are hake, pilchard, orange roughy, horse mackerel, monkfish, deep-sea red crab, rock lobster and seals (FAO 2000:7). The TAC for pilchard was set at zero in 2002 (WTO 2003:A3-188).

the right holders. 25% of the TACs are allocated to new entrants, which are preferably formerly disadvantaged Namibians (Erastus 2002:13).
The Marine Resource and Advisory Council, a consortium of industry and scientific representatives, which was established in 2000, monitors the fish stocks and recommends to Government how to set the TACs (MFMR 2000, Part 4). The Government makes the final decision of TACs, trying to take not only scientific recommendations into account but also to ensure the maintenance of business activities and to promote a secure investment climate (Nichols 2004a).[311]

In addition to TACs, the Government can pronounce restrictions for fishing seasons and closed areas if the population of certain species is threatened. To observe whether companies comply with the regulations, observers are placed on board vessels. In 2003, 201 fisheries inspectors controlled the landing of fish over 1,500 km of coastline, covering between 70-85% of total landings (MFMR 2004d:2, Nichols 2004b). The Namibian monitoring and surveillance system is judged to work effectively in international terms (FAO 2001).[312]

In 2003, there were 163 right holders in the Namibian fishing industry, owing 335 vessels. All but one right holder and 71% of all registered vessels were owned by Namibians, which is defined as having at least 51% beneficial ownership and 80% of the crew comprising Namibian citizens (MFMR 2004c:25). The MFMR expects that at least 7,700 Namibians are directly and indirectly benefiting from the "Namibianisation" policy with at least 4,200 of them benefiting directly through shareholding (Iyambo 2003c:4). Foreigners are only allowed to work in the sector with a work permit granted in accordance to the Namibian immigration and labour law. This permit will be only issued if no trained Namibians are available (MFMR 2003a:5-6).

However, though more than 90% of the fishing industry is either wholly or in majority Namibian owned, the benefits of the industry are claimed to accrue only insufficiently to Namibians. Through the complex reorganisation of ownership and establishment of joint-ventures and sub-contracting agreements, companies that were formerly foreign-owned have now a 51% Namibian share, thus fulfilling the requirements of having "Namibianised" their company. However, the management would often remain the same since newcomer companies are not always adequately operationally involved into business (Erastus 2002:24,

[311] See FAO (2001:20-2) for a detailed overview of institutional and decision making arrangements in the Namibian fishing industry.

[312] Due to increasing value of landed fish, the costs for the monitoring, control and surveillance system decreased from 6% of landed value in 1991 to 3.6% in 1999 (FAO 2001:11-2). Namibian-flag fishing vessels that are engaged in unreported and unregulated fishing either in Namibia or abroad will lose their license immediately (Iyambo 2003a:9). See Nichols (2003b:3-4) for the major features of the Namibian monitoring, control and surveillance programme in the fishing industry. In the near future it is furthermore planned to introduce a satellite-based monitoring system to monitor the activities of all vessels (MFMR 2004c:16).

Manning 2000:28).[313] Though fishing quotas are officially neither transferable, nor tradable in order to avoid the market dominance of big companies, some newcomer companies rather use the financial opportunities of entering into an apparent joint-venture with a well-established company than developing technical and managerial capabilities to become a real joint-venture partner.[314]

As the discussion hitherto has shown, Namibia has established a national fishery policy with an effective control and monitoring system that ensures the sustainable exploitation of its fishing resources. The Namibian system that allocates the TACs to all registered companies according to their compliance with the goals of the national fishing policy creates stimuli for companies to perform well regarding their "Namibianisation" degree, their level of manufacturing activities, their investment levels and their socio-economic contribution. In contradiction to the EU where TACs are not bound to any company and its performance, it is not the largest company with the best fleet that catches most fish but the company that contributes to the economic and socio-economic well-being of the country.

However, despite its success, the Namibian policy model also illustrates Government's difficulty to distribute economic growth and welfare towards disadvantaged groups on the one hand and to stimulate and attract investment into the industry on the other hand. Though the industry has been officially "Namibianised" the goal of effective participation of formerly disadvantaged groups has not been reached yet. Moreover, the system is claimed to have created windfall gains for large companies that were able to reach the "Namibianisation" requirements without realising operational equity with newcomer companies. However, to enforce a more effective "Namibianisation" policy is a tightrope walk for the Government, since newcomer companies have in general only little capital, technical knowledge and business experience, it needs time to build-up technical and managerial skills to enable newcomers to succeed in the industry (Erastus 2002:24). A stricter "Nambianisation" policy does therefore bear the risk to encourage inefficient processing and to create a national industry that is not sufficiently aware of international challenges and not in a position to undertake necessary upgrading activities.

---

[313] Though almost 80% of employees are Namibian nationals, the majority of jobs was realised in relatively low positions (Erastus 2002:24).

[314] It must be noted that the joint-venture relationship between well-established firms and newcomer companies works very well in some sub-sectors such as monk and rock lobster fishery but sometimes does not work as envisaged in the small pelagic and hake sub-sector where some newcomers cannot benefit from industrial fish catches. The Government calls upon these companies to integrate newcomers more effectively and also intends to set company specific quotas in case those well-established companies do not cooperate (Iyambo 2003c:4).

5.5.5 Empirical Findings

The purpose of the field study was to investigate Namibian fishing companies' trade relations with their European counterparts and to get insights into the export performance and the international competitiveness of the Namibian fishing industry. Findings are compared with secondary literature as well as with face-to-face interviews conducted with representatives from the Food and Agriculture Organization of the United Nations (FAO), the Ministry of Trade and Industry, the Namibian Manufacturing Association, and the Walvis Bay Corridor Group (WBCG). Though the study is not representative it covers around 75% of all fishing companies with processing plants in Namibia and does therefore give comprehensive insights into the industry's structure and the challenges it faces.

5.5.5.1 Methodology, Firm Profiles and Characteristics

The interviews in the Namibian fishing industry were taken in September 2003 in Walvis Bay, Namibia's industrial centre where 90% of all fish is landed (Nichols 2004a). In total, 11 companies and grouping of companies respectively were interviewed by means of a standardised questionnaire (see Annex 2). Since a total of 30 marine resource-processing plants do currently exist in Namibia and five of the companies surveyed own more than one plant (see "Foundation and number of plants") it can be stated that the analysis comprises around three quarters of Namibian fishing companies that have processing facilities. However, the analysis does not contain any newcomer companies. Newcomer companies have been excluded from the sample since they are insufficiently involved in the export business.

The interviewed persons held the following posts in the companies: Managing Director or General Manager (8) and Product or Engineering Manager (3). With exception of two, all interview partners were male and white. This is in line with the general situation in the sector where management is highly dominated by white men. Only one company in the fishing industry is currently managed by a black Namibian man (Nichols 2004a). Additionally, interviews with officials from the Ministry of Fisheries and Marine Resources (MFMR), the Ministry of Trade and Industry, the Namibian Manufacturing Association, and the Walvis Bay Corridor Group (WBCG) were conducted.

Major products and markets: The main fishing species caught are fresh and frozen hake (caught by eight companies), monk fish (6), horse mackerel (4), and kingklip (3). Though the Namibian fishing industry catches many more species, hake and monk are primarily exported to the EU market.[315]

[315] The hake production alone accounts for 50% of the total value in the Namibian fishing sector (Erastus 2002:5).

The EU is the main market for the majority of companies surveyed (8 of 11). Seven companies deliver on average 83% of their total hake production to the EU, three companies deliver 100% of their monk production to the EU market and one company supplies the EU with 100% of its kingklip catches. The second important market is Africa (except SACU) that is predominantly supplied with low-value, high protein fish, namely horse mackerel (see Box 28). The horse mackerel is either frozen at sea or dried and salted ashore. The FAO (2000:4) states that around 70% of total Namibian production of horse mackerel is destined for African countries. The SACU market, which is the third important market for the Namibian fishermen surveyed, receives often "the rest" of fish production (10-30% of total catches of hake, horse mackerel, kingklip, and salted and dried fish). Only one company produces almost exclusively for the SACU market (pilchard, which is either canned or processed into fishmeal).

For one company each, the USA and Japan respectively are the main export markets. The products delivered are orange roughy (USA) and lobster (Japan). Orange roughy, a rather unknown fish in the EU, is very popular in the USA where the majority of Namibian orange roughy is exported to. Japan, on the other hand, is the main export market for Namibian rock lobsters and deep sea crabs (MFMR 2004c:5).

In sum it can be stated that the major products and export markets of the companies surveyed reflect the pattern of the whole sector, as discussed in section 5.5.3. Thus, the majority of surveyed companies' exports, which are mainly hake, go to the EU market.

Foundation and number of plants: With exception of one, all companies surveyed were established after independence, between 1990 and 1996.[316] Six out of 11 companies had only one plant that is located in Walvis Bay. Two companies had in total two plants,[317] two further companies owned 7 plants and one company owned 17 plants. With exception of one, all companies had exclusive plants in Namibia, which is suspected to be representative for the whole industry because of Government's "Namibianisation" policy.[318]

[316] One company was established in 1999 but had a predecessor that existed already since 1946.

[317] However, one company stated that its second plant is currently not working because of a lack of fish.

[318] One company surveyed also had a factory in Cape Town, South Africa.

Box 28: Regional exports and regional cooperation of the Namibian fishing industry

Namibian fish exported to other African countries is mainly low-value, high protein fish. Four of 11 companies surveyed export to other African countries and also want to expand their exports to Africa. The most interesting export market seems to be Angola to which all four companies want to expand their exports. Since Namibia has signed a bilateral cooperation agreement on fisheries with Angola for joint research on shared fishing grounds, in particular for pilchard and deep-sea red crab (FAO 2000:5-8), this finding is likely to be representative.

Further export markets the companies surveyed explore are Nigeria, DR Congo, Congo Brazzaville, Tanzania, Egypt and Mauritania. The companies do not only want to export to these markets but also to enter into cooperation agreements with their foreign counterparts in order to guarantee access to new resources. One company does even plan to set up factories in Mauritania and Angola in order to serve the Egyptian and Nigerian market. The expansion of Namibian fishing companies in the region could therefore be of mutual benefit and is promoted by the Namibian government, which is also working on procedures and criteria to enter into fisheries agreements with SADC member states (MFMR 2004c:15). Official agreements between Namibia and other SADC member states make sense, since the absence of any regulation implies the risk that Namibian trawlers exploit foreign resources like European and Russian trawlers did in Namibia before independence. It is therefore essential that the sustainable use of common fishing resources is regulated in a SADC framework. Namibia became the leader of the SADC "Sector Coordinating Unit for Marine Fisheries and Resource" in 1991 and provided guidance to formulate a common fishery policy (FAO 2001:23). However, efforts to implement such a policy have been limited so far. Also, the SADC Protocol on Fisheries, which was signed in 2001, has not entered into force yet.

Asked for their main reasons to export to other African countries, the companies surveyed stated that there would be a high demand for their products. Furthermore, low non-tariff barriers and low product requirements would make the African market attractive. The other issues were rather controversially discussed: the proximity of the African market was judged as advantageous by two companies, while the other two companies stated that exporting on the road would be expensive, slow and bear the risk of theft. The prices achieved in the African market were judged as insufficiently by two companies but as attractive by the other two. The same applies to the question of competition and import tariffs which were judged as low by two companies but as high by the two others.

The seven companies that do not export to Africa and/or do not intend to expand their exports to the African market gave the low price of sale as main reason. Because of the weakness of the majority of African economies, there would be a high demand but a low price so that the African market would not be attractive for high-valuable products, such as hake and monk fish.

Ownership: Four of the companies surveyed were domestically owned and six were joint-ventures. One company stated that it incorporates in total 17 companies of which eight were fully Namibian owned and seven were joint-venture companies. The contingent of shares of surveyed joint-venture companies differed, while four companies showed only a slight majority of Namibian shares (50.56-55%), two joint-venture companies were predominantly Namibian-owned (80-90%). The foreign shareholders were either South African or European citizens. This finding reflects the comprehensive re-organisation of the Namibian fishing industry after Namibia's independence. None of the companies surveyed was foreign owned and all joint-venture companies had a Namibian share of more than 50%. Since enterprises, which show a Namibian ownership of less than 50% are only entitled for 7-years fishing rights (instead of up to 20 years) and face disadvantages regarding quota allocation, the companies have a strong motivation to "Namibianise" their shares. However, foreign companies (South African and European) were involved in the majority of surveyed companies' businesses. Again, this finding presents the situation in the whole industry. There is a strong move to involve foreign companies in joint-venture cooperation since no new fishing rights have been allocated since 1997/98 (Nichols 2004a).

Turnover and Employment: The companies surveyed showed considerable differences regarding their turnovers: the smallest company showed a turnover of less than N$ 15 million and the largest company had a turnover of N$ 650 million in 2002. Seven companies showed a turnover between N$ 60-180 million.

The number of employees also differed considerably and accounted for 120 in the smallest and 850 in the largest company.[319] Five companies employed 250-600 workers. Considering the turnover and the number of employees, all companies surveyed can be classified as large companies from a Namibian perspective (UNIDO 2003b:10).[320]

The workforce of the companies surveyed was highly dominated by male workers: 10 of 11 companies employed more than 60% men.[321] The gender bias can be explained by companies' processing method: offshore processing is still dominating and the workforce on trawlers is exclusively male. Women dominate in fish fabrics where 80% of the workforce is female (Iyambo 2003c:4).

---

[319] One company stated that it employs 700 workers during the season (five months per year) but has only 48 fixed workers.

[320] According to the Namibian Policy and Programme for Small Businesses a SME in the manufacturing sector employs less than fives persons and has an annual turnover of less than N$ 250,000 and/or capital employed of less than 100,000 (UNIDO 2003b:10).

[321] For five of them this share is 90-97%. Only one (fish processing) company employed more women than men (25 vs. 75%).

Processing of products: Six of the 11 companies surveyed froze their products at sea and at land, three companies sold only sea-frozen products, one company froze exclusively on-shore and one company produced only canned fish and fish meal.

While the method of land processing is more labour intensive and favoured by the Government (which has introduced a 60% "wet-fish quota" for on-shore processing of hake) it has the disadvantage that the vessel must go on land around every eighth day (varying on vessel type). By using the capital-intensive processing method on sea, the trawler can stay at sea for up to 45 days. Furthermore, sea-frozen fish is regarded as a higher value product since the fish is frozen immediately after having being caught at sea. Thus, the returns of offshore processing are higher than of onshore production and offshore activities are still dominant in the Namibian fishing industry (MFMR 2004c:5). However, the margins between sea and land processing are narrowing. The Government strongly promotes onshore-processing, not only because this processing method is much more labour-intensive but also because it offers more options for increased value-addition. Onshore processing gives the companies a much higher flexibility to reply to the market, as they can store the fish and do not have to process it immediately (Nichols 2004a).

Summarising companies' profiles and characteristics as stated in Table 36 it can be said that all companies surveyed are large, well-established firms that contribute significantly to Namibia's employment and income from the manufacturing industry. The companies are in majority joint-ventures but Namibian shareholders are dominating. Companies' main export market is the EU, which receives the species hake, monk and kingklip. Most companies produce in both ways: offshore and onshore.

Table 36: Summary of characteristics of surveyed Namibian fishing companies

Foundation	*N =11*	
	1990-96:	10
	1999:	1
Ownership	*N = 11*	
	Domestic company:	40.0%
	Foreign company:	0%
	Joint-venture:	60%
Number of manufacturing plants	*N = 11*	
	1 plant:	6
	2 plants:	2
	7-8 plants:	2
	17 plants:	1
Employment	*N = 11*	
	100-200:	3
	250-400:	3
	450-600:	2
	700-850:	3
Turnover (2002)	*N = 21*	
	<N$ 15 Million:	9.1%
	N$ 60-90 Million:	27.2%
	N$ 130-180 Million:	45.5%
	N$ 320 Million:	9.1%
	N$ 650 Million:	9.1%
Market focus	*N = 25 (multiple answers possible)*	
	EU:	56%
	SACU:	16%
	Rest-Africa:	20%
	USA:	4%
	Japan:	4%

The landed and final value of Namibian fish increased continuously in the period 1998-2002.[322] The landed value (ex vessels price) did even increase in 2001, when the total fish harvest declined considerably (see Figure 46), which indicates that prices increased significantly and compensated fishermen for decreased volumes.

[322] The final value of fish increased by more than four times and was N$ 3,395 million in 2002 (MFMR 2004c:26).

Figure 46: Total fish harvest and value of fish and fish products, 1998-2002

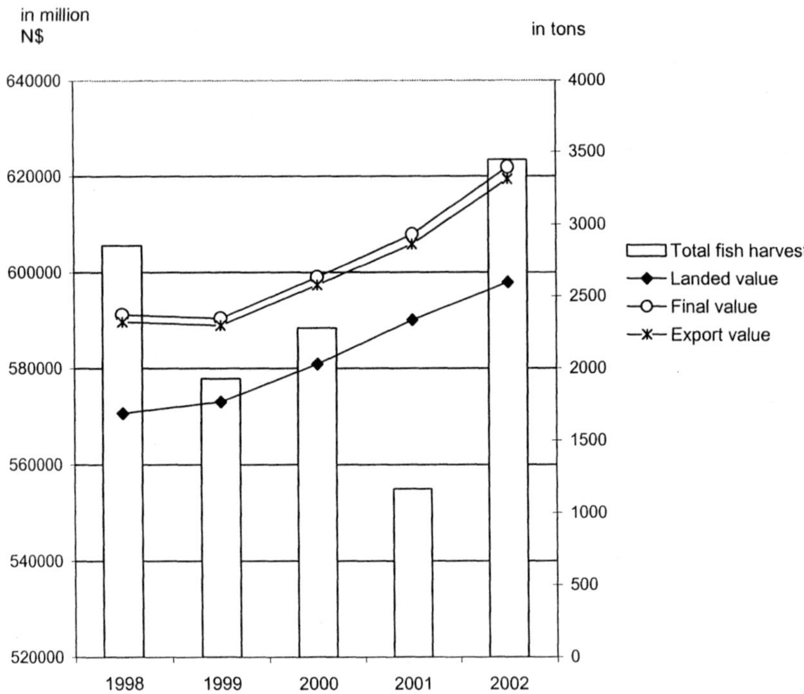

Source: Data collected from MFMR (2004b:26).

Another even more influential factor for the increased landed value is the devaluation of the N$ against major currencies. Furthermore, an improved quality of landed fish might have contributed to the increase in landed value.

However, what can also be obtained from Figure 46 is that the distance between landed value and final value increased only slightly in the period 1998-2002.[323] This again suggests that only little improvement regarding increased domestic value addition has been achieved.

Before discussing the position of the companies surveyed in the international value added chain for fishery products as well as their strategies to upgrade products and processes, the following section has a look at companies' relation-

[323] Since around 97% of total harvested fish is exported, the export value and final value of fish are almost similar (Iyambo 2003c:6).

ships to their EU counterparts, the relevance of EU inputs for manufacturing activities and the international competition situation of the companies surveyed. Special attention is given to the question where the advantages and disadvantages of the EU as export destination are and to what extent the close relationship to their European partners has helped the companies surveyed to improve their products and processing methods.

5.5.5.2 Exports to the EU and Development of Export Options

Only eight of the 11 companies surveyed export to the EU.[324] All of them have started their export business between 1992 and 2000. Since about 97% of all fish caught in Namibia's marine waters is exported, there is virtually no company in the Namibian fishing industry that produces exclusively for the domestic market (Iyambo 2002:13).

Market Advantages of the EU: All companies that export to the EU confirmed that preferred market access (15% import duty advantage compared to non-ACP suppliers for fresh or chilled fish) and long-standing cooperation with a European company are important or very important advantages. Furthermore, seven of them judged the high EU product standards as advantageous (see Figure 47). The high quality requirements of the EU market can be seen as beneficial because they offer the companies the chance to get higher prices and capture new, demanding markets (Nichols 2004a).

Asked for their appraisal about the development of EU prices, six companies stated that stable prices are a (very) important advantage of the EU market, whereas two companies said that EU prices would be rather volatile. Surveyed companies' assessment regarding knowledge transfer was also very mixed: four companies stated that this is a (very) important advantage, while the other four companies judged it as only partly relevant or irrelevant. A similar, rather mixed picture is provided by asking whether technical assistance is seen as an advantage of the EU market: five companies named it as (very) relevant factor but three companies denied the relevance of technical support.[325]

[324] The other three companies export exclusively to African countries.

[325] However, the question did not differentiate between technical assistance provided by governmental institutions (e.g. by the EU Centre for Development of Enterprises that assists some Namibian companies to attend at fairs in the EU market) and by technical support given on a company-to-company basis.

Figure 47: Summary of surveyed companies' reasons to export to the EU (N = 8)

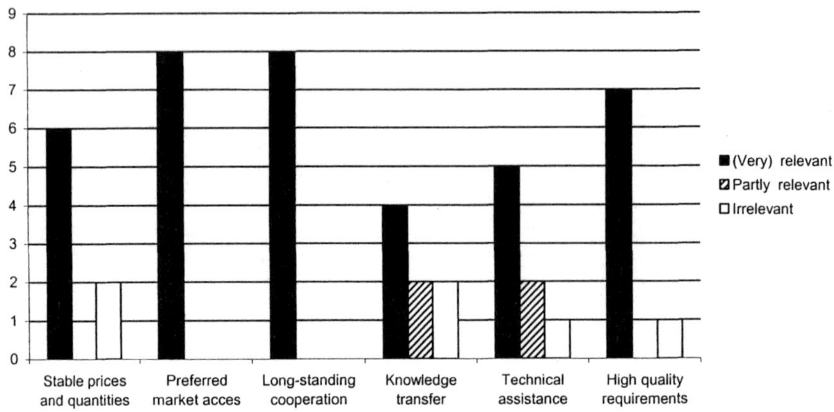

Asked for further advantages of the EU as export destination, the companies named the high demand for their products (said by four companies) and the option to supply an attractive market niche (1) as advantages. According to Nichols (2004a), The high European demand for Namibian fish, especially hake, is the driving force for Namibian fish exports. Most of all the well-organised and structured Spanish market has helped the Namibian fishing industry to bring business confidence to the sector and to improve its quality standards.

Market Disadvantages of the EU: To meet the rules of origin was not a problem for six of eight companies that export to the EU. Only two companies stated that they have had problems to meet the rules of origin when starting their export business.[326]

The product quality and health standards applied by the EU as well as the quantities required do not seem to be a hindrance for surveyed firms to enter the EU market and are rather judged as advantageous. With exception of one, none of the interviewees had any problems to comply with EU standards. To fulfil the EU's quantitative requirements is also not a problem for any company.

---

[326] As elaborated, the rules of origin under the Cotonou Agreement are very strict and do not foresee that Namibian fish products cumulate with South African inputs as long as fishery products are excluded from the TDCA (European Commission 2000b, Art. 6.7 and Annex XIV to Protocol I). Thus, Namibian fishermen are only able to export manufactured fish products originated from Namibian waters duty free.

However, three companies misunderstood the question and stated that (sometimes) quotas constrained their exports (see Figure 48).

Figure 48: Summary of surveyed firms' hindrances to export to the EU (N = 11)

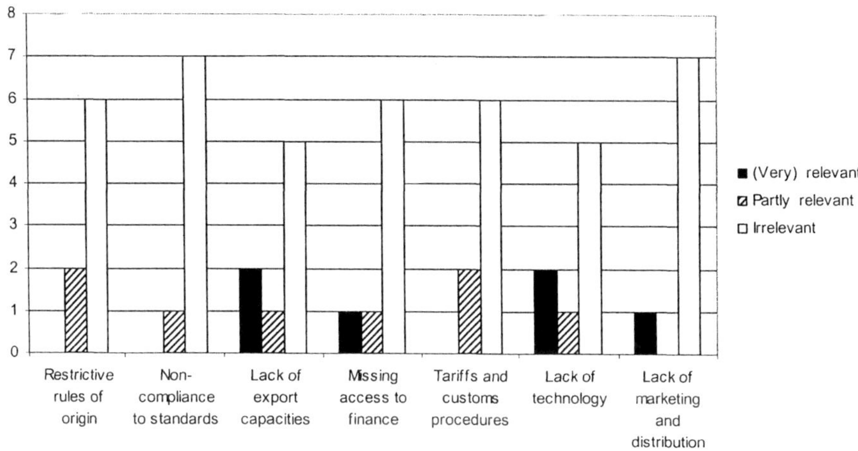

Other, almost non-existing, constraints are access to finance, tariff barriers and customs procedure as well as channels to distribute and market products successfully. Surprisingly, missing access to technology, namely of new vessels, also seemed to be only of minor relevance, with eight companies judging it as irrelevant. One company summarised the situation in the sector: *"Everybody has old vessels; we are a third world country! 95% of vessels in the fishing industry are older than 15 year. But if you have only maximum fishing rights of 15 years you will not invest in new vessels."* On average, each firm, acting in the fishing industry owns 2.1 vessels, which have a mean age of more than 30 years (Erastus 2002).

Further issues that were named as constraining factors to export to the EU were high transportation costs (said by three companies), missing business connections (1), and high credit costs due to non-existent subsidies in the industry (1). Those three companies that do not export to the EU named a missing demand for their products as reason.[327]

[327] These three companies produced predominantly frozen and salted and dried horse mackerel, and canned fish and fish meal. These products are judged as "lower valuable products" and are generally not demanded by the EU.

Altogether, the companies surveyed face few problems to enter the EU market. Nichols (2004a) confirms that rules of origins, standards, export capacities, tariff barriers and customs procedures are not a problem for Namibian fish exporters to enter the EU market. A lack of technology would only be a problem for newcomer firms. It is however surprising that the companies surveyed barely have problems to finance their business and to market their products. Generally, many fishing companies have problems to apply for local credits. Since the industry depends highly on unpredictable TACs and company specific quotas for its economic wellbeing, many banks do not grant low-priced credit (MFMR 2004d:2).[328] That the majority of companies surveyed do not have problems to obtain the money required for investment, is likely to be because most of them show international linkages.

Companies' statement that they do not face any problems to market and distribute their products in the EU does not seem to reflect the reality of dynamic changes sufficiently. The discussion in the sections 5.4.5.5 and 5.4.5.6 shows that most companies are not involved in these value added intensive activities and have not developed any strategies to improve the marketing and distribution of their products. International high value adding activities such as the creation of brands and marketing of supermarket products do still take place in industrialised countries. Considering this, surveyed companies' answers might be an indication for companies' limited awareness of their position in the global value added chain.

Development of exports to the EU: Surveyed companies' exports to the EU developed quite differently in the period 1998-2003: four companies said their exports remained stable, two companies indicated their exports increased by more than 50% and two companies experienced a decrease in exports (20-40%) in the last five years. These differences can be explained by fluctuations in catches; the EU demand for fish whereas was constantly high. Those two companies that increased their exports to the EU were able to do so because they have changed the ownership (inclusion of newcomer firms) and were therefore able to raise their quota. Those two companies that showed decreased exports to the EU had to accept a decline in quota and bad catches respectively.

These answers indicate that the expansion of exports to the EU is above all restricted by quotas and bad catches. Nichols (2004a) contradicts these complaints, which would not reflect the realities in the fishing industry sufficiently. Well-established firms could also act competitively with a declining quota if they were more innovative.[329]

[328] The Ministry does therefore plan the provision of special affordable loans by the Agricultural Bank and the Development Bank in the near future (Nichols 2004a).

[329] Newcomer firms on the other hand are often not able to use their quotas as they lack of finance and vessels (Nichols 2004a).

None of the eight companies that export to the EU face any quantitative restrictions. All their fish exports can be exported duty free because of the Cotonou Agreement. Namibia's duty free market access to the EU is judged as competitive advantage vis-à-vis competitors from other developing countries, such as South Africa. One company stated "*We hope not to lose the free market access to the EU. We see how the South African are struggling with tariffs and customs procedures.*" Though South Africa has entered into an FTA with the EU in 2000 it still faces a 15% *ad valorem* duty for most of its fish products, as fisheries were excluded from the EU-South Africa Free Trade Agreement. However, though the free market entry is judged as beneficial by the companies surveyed, the FAO (2001) and WTO (2003) point out it has been disadvantageous for the industry's willingness to upgrade products and services.

Strengths and weaknesses in exporting: The strongest advantage of the companies surveyed is obviously their product quality, which was judged to be excellent by all companies surveyed. The product price is also an advantage for the majority of companies (8); only three saw it as a disadvantage, mainly because their EU retailers would determine the price. That the majority of companies regarded their prices as strength despite the strong Rand supports the thesis that the price elasticity of demand for fish is rather low.

Raw material costs, which were defined as costs to be allowed to fish, and capital utilisation were judged very differently by the companies, with five companies seeing it as an advantage, five companies judging it as a weakness and one company judging it as neutral. Those companies that judged both, their raw material costs and their capital utilisation as strength, argued that domestic operational costs are still comparable cheap in international terms and that they invested into their fleet recently. Those five companies that saw their raw material costs and the utilisation of their capital as weakness stated that the valuation of the N$ resulted in price increases, that the costs for quota were increasing, and that their fleet would be too old. Next to the age of vessels, it is also the quota that determines the level of capital utilisation. Generally, the return rate on investment in the Namibian fishing industry is regarded as good but is currently suffering from the strengthening of the Rand (Nichols 2004a).

The labour productivity and the costs of labour were judged as disadvantages by most companies (7 each). Only three companies said that the productivity of their labour is an advantage. The labour productivity was seen as weakness because of a lack of qualified labour, high sick leave rates and too powerful labour unions. Two companies mentioned that the high HIV/AIDS infection rate among their workers would have resulted in a declining labour productivity.[330]

[330] The average HIV/AIDS infection rate in Namibia (15-49 years) was estimated to be 23% in 2002 (UNAIDS 2003). It might be even higher in the fishing industry since many fishermen are from rural areas in the North and do not live with their family.

Another reason for companies' rather negative appraisal regarding the labour productivity was that the industry suffered from illegal strikes in 2002 and 2003. The relationship between employers and employees is still bad in many companies, which is seen as a heritage of Apartheid. Some interview partners further complained that many representatives of labour unions are not sufficiently informed about companies' allocation of quota and their all-embracing economic performance, which would lead to unrealistic demands. The government has already called upon the parties to improve their communication and to establish a reliable and respectful partnership with each other (Iyambo 2003a:4).

Figure 49: Summary of surveyed firms' strengths and weaknesses in exporting (N = 11)

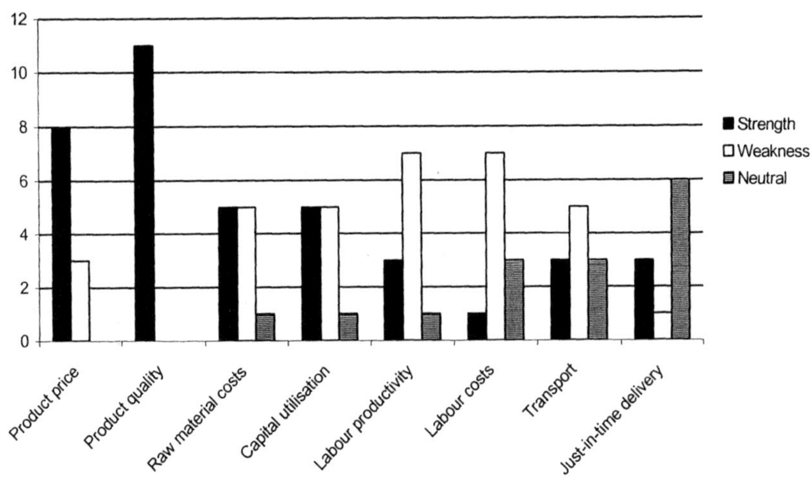

The transport of products to the EU was judged as a weakness by five of 11 companies, three companies saw it as strength (since they exported directly from Walvis Bay) and three regarded it as neutral. Reasons stated by those companies that judged transport as weakness were the unfavourable exchange rate, high costs for fuel, and the high concentration degree in the transport business. A domestic transport sector barely exists in Namibia, so that most transport agents are from South Africa from which the shipping of goods takes place. However, as discussed in Box 29, Namibia is working on the bottleneck of delivering goods via Cape Town or Durban instead of Walvis Bay.

Just-in-time delivery is not an issue for the majority of the companies surveyed (6). Three judged it as strength and only one company stated it as a disadvantage in the export business.[331] In sum, it can be stated that most companies regarded their product quality and price as advantages. Exports are not seriously constrained by the strengthening of the N$/Rand; the demand for products remained stable due to the low elasticity of demand. Companies' main weaknesses are the unfavourable labour cost/productivity ratio and the high transport costs, since most companies have to export via South Africa.

Box 29: Walvis Bay: A new port for the region?

Namibia has two ports, namely Walvis Bay and Lüderitz.[332] Walvis Bay is the industrial centre, where 91% of total landings took place in 2003 (MFMR 2004d:4). In order to upgrade its deepwater harbour in accordance to international standards and increase the trans-shipment of goods, Namibia invested around N$ 113 million in the harbour of Walvis Bay between 1994 and 2000 (Gschwender 2003a:636). As result, the port of Walvis Bay was ranked as most efficient harbour in whole Africa (World Economic Forum 2001). However, landlocked African countries like Botswana, Zambia and Zimbabwe, but also Namibia itself, still export and import via South African ports. Though Botswana, Zambia and Zimbabwe would safe considerable transit time and around 20-40% of their total transport costs when exporting from Walvis Bay instead of Durban or Cape Town, the harbour of Walvis Bay is still insufficiently used and run at 40% of its capacity in 2003. According to the Walvis Bay Corridor Group (WBCR) the situation is like the one with the chicken and the egg: the ships do not want to go over Walvis Bay since there is not enough cargo but a larger amount of cargo needs a reliable ship transport (Gschwender 2003b).

However, the bottleneck of delivering goods via South African ports instead of Walvis Bay should be overcome by the work of the WBCG, containing three projects: extension and modernisation of the Walvis Bay harbour, creation of the Trans-Caprivi-Corridor, connecting Namibia, Zambia,

Continuation on next page.

[331] When asked for further strengths and weaknesses in exporting the companies named only strength, namely (a) a stable quota and a reliable partner in the export market (said by two companies); and (b) the direct delivery to the end market, so that optimal benefit from the whole value-added chain could be reaped (2).

[332] Almost no fishing activities take place in Swakopmund, which is only 30 km distant from Walvis Bay (FAO 2001).

Continuation of Box 29 from previous page.

Zimbabwe, South of DRC and Angola) and the Trans-Kalahari Highway, connecting Namibia, Botswana and South Africa. To make the Trans-Caprivi-Corridor and the Trans-Kalahari highway work and to increase not only intra-regional but also international trade, mainly for landlocked southern African countries, the WBCG aims not only to establish an efficient infrastructure but also to smoothen trans-frontier operation, e.g. by creating a time schedule for border procedure. To improve the transition of goods on the Trans-Kalahari Highway, Namibia, Botswana and South Africa have signed a "Memorandum of Understanding" (MoU) to implement a "fast track system" that should harmonise their regulations for transport, reduce NTBs and facilitate customs and border regulations. This has been reached by a regional Public-Private Partnership (PPP), concluding an institutional component (the three Ministries of Transport, Customs and Immigration and private transport enterprises), and an operational component (e.g. longer business hours at the borders). The capacity of the Trans-Kalahari Highway increased from 15% in 2000 up to 60% in 2003 (Gschwender 2003b).

Importance of exporting for company's all-embracing performance: The majority of the companies surveyed confirmed that exporting improved their economies of scale (judged as very relevant or relevant by nine of 11 companies),[333] their profitability (9), their productivity (8), their price competitiveness (8), their technology competence (8), their manufacturing process (10), their product quality (9), their product development capacity (8), and the skills of their workforce and management (9 each). Only four companies said that their e-commerce capabilities have improved (see Figure 50).

Most companies were also able to improve technological competence and their manufacturing capabilities due to exporting. Only three companies surveyed stated that this would not be the case since one of them had already "one of the most modern plants in the world" and the other two produced only low-valuable fish (horse mackerel) where no value addition process would make sense because of the cheap image of the fish.

In sum, three quarters of the companies surveyed confirmed that the export business contributes positively to their all-embracing economic performance. Since around 90% of total catches are destined for exports, this finding is not surprising. However, the answers suggest that companies' export activities also

[333] Those two companies that were not able to improve their economies of scale and their profitability because of exporting, stated that they could not expand their production to an extent that the increasing costs and the valuation of the N$ would have been overcompensated due to a lack of quota.

contributed positively to domestic value addition. Thus, the manufacturing process of almost all companies surveyed improved, e.g. by the expansion of factories, new machinery or the re-organisation of shifts. Furthermore, the product development capacity and the skills of workforce were enhanced, e.g. by filleting activities, production of small retail packages or new management structures by entering into joint-ventures.

Figure 50: Export business' contribution to surveyed firms economic performance (N=11)

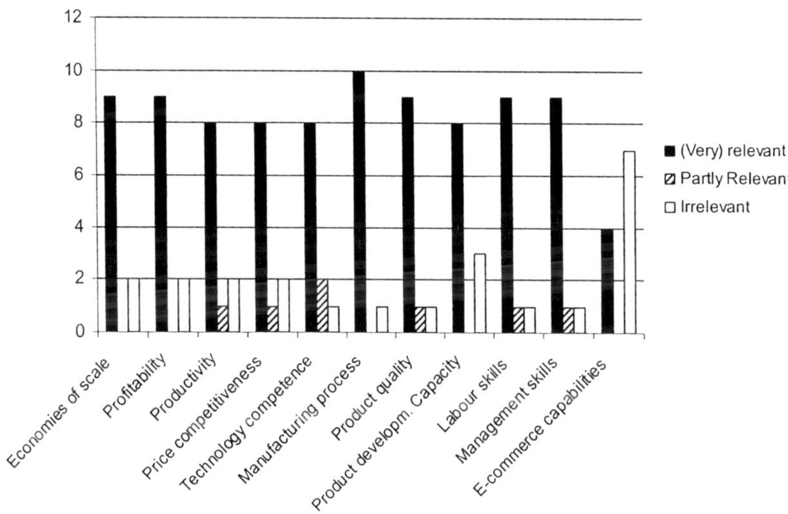

However, this positive self-estimation of the companies surveyed does not mirror the developments in the whole sector. As discussed around 60% of total exports are still offshore processed fish. Since the EU demand for unprocessed (offshore produced) fish is still high and prices are comparably stable, the incentive for upgrading activities in the whole sector is still too low. The Government tries to stimulate processing activities in the fishing industry by granting manufacturing incentives (see Box 30).

Box 30: Manufacturing incentives in the Namibian fishing industry

Namibia's corporate tax for non-mining manufacturing industries is 35%, which is the highest within the SACU region. However, as discussed, Namibia offers export-oriented companies the opportunity to act in Export-Processing Zones (EPZ) all over the country if at least 70% of total production is destined for exporting. These investment incentives, which should generate investment in labour-intensive manufactures, such as textile and garments, footwear, leather products, food and beverages, do however not apply for the fishing industry since the industry is already regarded as attractive investment destination.

After independence, the fishing industry was substantially under-capitalised and needed large amounts of new capital and new skills (Tralac News, 07/05/04). Due to government's policy to encourage fish processing activities, Namibia shows today *"some of the most advanced fish processing factories in the world."* (FAO 2000:4). The number of processing plants increased from 11 in 1991 to 30 in 2004 (MFMR 2004c:4). In total, the Namibian fishing industry attracted investment of N$ 2.08 billion in the period 1990-2002 (MFMR 2004c:30). Moreover, the industry received considerable aid amounts from various bilateral and multilateral donors since 1990 (FAO 2000:8-9).

However, processing activities in the fishing industry are still regarded as insufficient. The promotion of on-shore activities instead to capital-intensive procession at sea is one of the development goals to improve the domestic value-addition in the fishing industry. For hake production, the government has already introduced a 60% "wet-fish quota" for on-shore processing and a 40% "freezer quota" for processing the fish at sea (FAO 2001:11). The reason is that the that onshore processing employs in average one Namibian for every 70 kg fish, while the processing at sea employs one Namibian for every 450 kg fish (Iyambo 2003b). To expand processing activities in the fishing industry and to stimulate new investment, the MFMR has introduced certain incentives. Thus, fishing companies may be granted tax deductions if they use labour intensive manufacturing methods, promote the training of their employees, and invest in manufacturing activities (Manning 2000:9). Companies that employ at least 5,000 Namibians are granted maximum fishing rights of 20 instead of 15 years. Furthermore, quota fees are reduced (and fully rebated for horse mackerels) if the company undertakes on-shore processing activities, e.g. fish canning, filleting or production of fish meal (WTO 2003:A3-189).[334] The MFMR does furthermore check whether the EPZ status should be expanded to the fishing industry to encourage manufacturing activities and to attract investment (MFMR 2004c:22).

[334] However, so far the Namibian horse mackerel is fully processed off-shore (Nichols 2004).

Export assistance: The only export assistance the companies surveyed received is assistance to participate at exhibitions and fairs. Eight of 11 companies got accordant assistance from the Ministry of Trade and Industry and private sector support institutions. One company got support from the European Centre for Development of Enterprises (CDE). However, six of those eight companies that received export assistance stated that this would be irrelevant for them. Since the demand for fish is greater than the possible supply, they would not need to explore new markets. This answer indicates that the high EU demand for fish constrains the innovation and diversification efforts of Namibian fishermen. Though the sector officially recognises the need to diversify its export markets (Tralac news, 29/04/2004), most companies' surveyed did not regard their dependency on the EU as problematic.

The Government does not provide direct support for companies that train their staff but has established the Namibian Maritime and Fisheries Institute (NAMFI), which is supposed to train young Namibians for jobs in the fishing industry. However, only two of the companies surveyed stated that they recruit their staff from NAMFI. In sum, it can be stated that the Namibian fishing industry receives little assistance for exporting (see Figure 51).

Figure 51: Summary of surveyed companies' export assistance (N = 11)

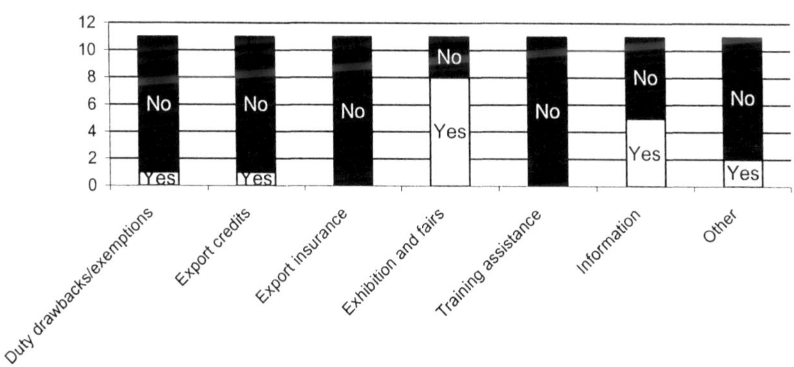

According to the interview results, most companies regarded the high requirements of the export business as advantageous. To become a successful exporter, the companies have to comply with EU market demands to be reliable and deliver high quality fish. This again motivated some companies surveyed to invest into their fleets and to improve their product quality by improved manufacturing processes and the introduction of new products. New products, such as fish fillets in retail packs, again, required better labour and management skills. High consumer demands can therefore help companies to upgrade their products and processes.

However, since the demand for offshore processed fish is still high, many companies still prefer "to take the easy way" and do not undertake sufficiently efforts to upgrade their products and processes or to diversify their markets. This again makes them vulnerable to market fluctuations and limits their options to reply to challenges.

Required support to expand exports to the EU: It can be stated that most companies surveyed needed little support to enter the EU market in form of finance, technical assistance or assistance to market and distribute their products (see Figure 52).

Figure 52: Surveyed companies' need for export assistance (N = 11)

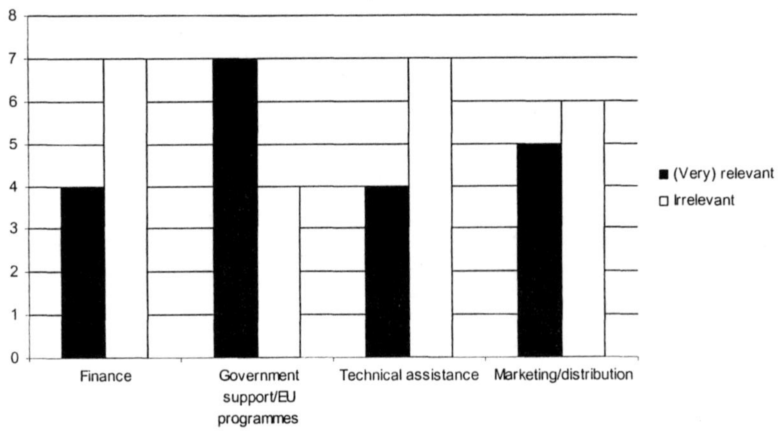

What was required was better support by the Namibian Government and the EU (said by seven of 11 companies), namely improved and updated information about joint-venture options, how one could benefit from trade agreements, latest research analysis about consumer preferences and EU standard requirements. The EU has partially responded to companies' requirements since its lack of information policy has been subject to criticism for a long time. Thus, the European Commission, General Direction Trade is publishing the "SPS newsletter" since early 2004, which is available on the Internet free of charge.[335] Mainly ex-

[335]Available at: http://trade-info.cec.eu.int/doclib/cfm/doclib_section.cfm?sec=175&lev=2&order =date, accessed 01/07/2004.

porters from developing countries should be informed about latest requirements and amendments of European food and health standards. Also the Centre for Promotion of Import from Developing Countries (CBI) offers an online information and assistance centre where exporters from developing countries receive latest information on EU import requirements for single products.[336]

5.5.5.3 Europe's Relevance as an Input Source

Main source of inputs: The majority of companies surveyed received their inputs from Namibia (8). However, those companies, which have a high processing degree, got their main inputs, such as cans, sauce, and packaging materials, but also fuel and spare parts, from South Africa. This finding suggests that Namibia lacks of effective forward and backward linkages to its industry and is in line with the appraisal of the Namibia Foundation (1998:57), which sees an investment need in fish processing related activities, such as vessel and equipment maintenance, production of packaging material and provision of services. So far, only few, well-established fishing companies are totally horizontally and vertically integrated. However, for Namibian companies it is very difficult to build-up new industries since they cannot benefit from economies of scale like established South African firms.

Development of input prices: All companies surveyed stated that the prices for inputs increased in the last five years (see Table 37).

Table 37: Summary of surveyed firms' main input source and development of input prices

Main input Source		*N = 11*
		Namibia: 8
		South Africa: 2
		Other: 1
Price Development		*N = 11*
Increased		100%
Decreased		0%
Price Development		*N = 11*
Increased by	1–10%	9.1%
	11-20%	27.3%
	21-40%	18.2%
	41-50%	36.3%
	>50%	9.1%

[336] Interested persons can register free of charge at http://www.cbi.nl.

Four companies faced price increases up to 20% and five of 30-50%. Above all, the prices for fuel, wages and spare parts increased. Price increases were aggravated by the devaluation of the N$ until the end of 2001. However, the recovery of the N$ since early 2002 has not resulted in an equivalent price reduction for domestic inputs. Since the South African economy is comparably concentrated most companies face only limited competition and were thus not forced to lower their prices (Kaplinsky *et al.* 2002 : 1169–72).

As the results showed, the companies surveyed are not connected to the EU market by imports but only by exports. Inputs used for processing activities were mainly imported from South Africa since the Namibian industry lacks of according industries. Despite being in a monetary union with South Africa, Namibian fishermen complained about exchange rate related price increases. This can be explained by indirect imports via South Africa (e.g. fuel), by price increases for inputs used for South African inputs (e.g. steel for cans) and by limited competition in the South African market.

5.5.5.4 Competition in the Domestic and International Markets

Main competitors and competition within the EU: The companies surveyed stated that their main competitors were in the country and in South Africa. Only one company said that one of its main competitors came from the EU. Three companies on the other hand stated that they do not face real competition and would compete above all with other Namibian companies for the allocation of totally allowed catches (see Figure 53).

Figure 53: "Where are your main competitors?" (N = 11)[337]

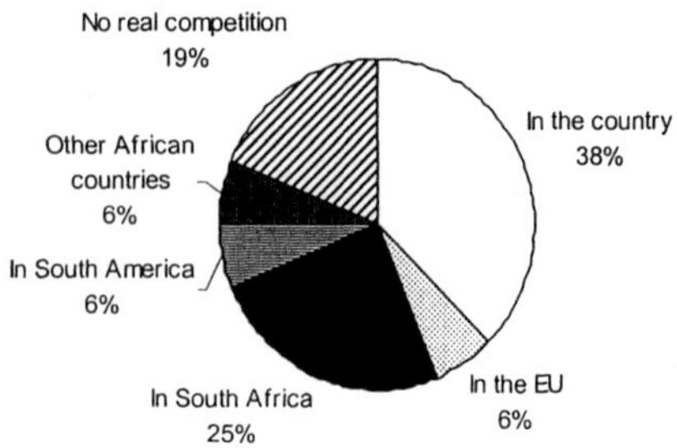

[337] Multiple answers possible.

None of the companies felt adversely affected because of European fish imported to Namibia. However, five of the eight companies that export to the EU feared South African competition in the EU market (see Figure 54).

Figure 54: "Do you feel adversely affected because of South African competition in the EU market?" (N = 11)

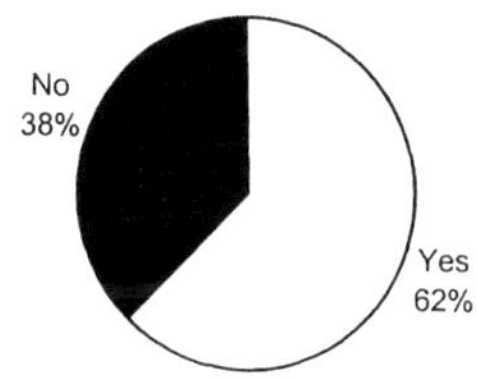

It was stated that South African exporters can compete successfully with Namibia in the EU despite the 15% import tariff rate South African fish faces. This would be the case because South African companies do not have to pay quota levies and would have a higher quota for hake. Further advantages would be the good South African hake quality (which would be preferred by European suppliers) and the proper South African infrastructure.

When asked for the development of their general competition situation in the last five years, more than half of the companies stated that it had remained unchanged or that competition had declined. Only four companies faced increased competition from South Africa or South America (see Figure 55).

Figure 55: "How did your general competition situation develop in the last five years?" (N =11)

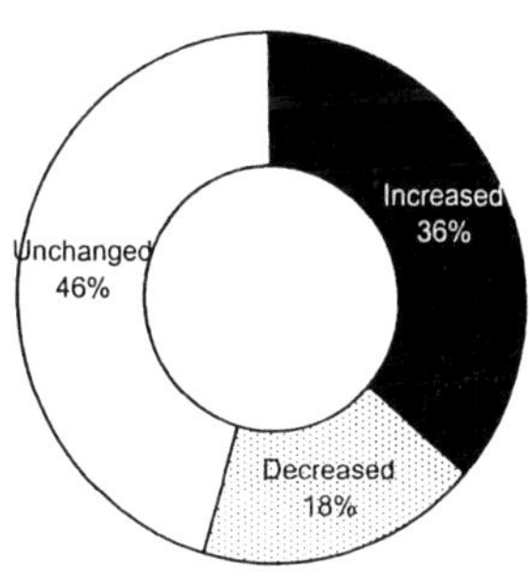

Though there are of course different market pressures for single export markets, it can be stated that most of the companies surveyed that export to the EU are not constrained by increased competition. The EU's demand for fish, in particular hake, is larger than what Namibian fishermen are able to supply. Thus, many companies state that they are rather constrained by the annual quota than by increased competition. Nichols (2004a) answers that the quantity of TACs has remained stable over the last few years for most species and that some companies do not even catch their quota. The reason for the inadequate success of some companies would rather be their unwillingness to innovate and diversify their product range as well as insufficient management capabilities.

Whether the companies surveyed are innovative or not and to what extent this finding is representative for the average fishing company in Namibia will be discussed in section 5.5.5.6, which analyses surveyed companies' strategies to cope with challenges. Before, the development of profits and the outlook for the development of exports will be discussed.

5.5.5.5 Value Chain and Value Added of Exports

Profit trend and relevant factors: 10 of 11 companies were ready to answer this question in detail. Four companies experienced an increase in profits in the period 1999-2003 (in average 40-50%), five a decline (in average 40%) and one company showed stable profits (see Table 38).

Table 38: Summary of firms' profit development, 1999-2003

	N = 10
Increased	4 companies
Decreased	5 companies
Remained Stable	1 company
	Detailed breakdown: N = 9
Profits increased by	*N = 4*
< 10%	0%
10-20%	0%
21-30%	50%
41-50%	0%
>50%	50%
Profits decreased by	*N = 5*
< 10%	20%
10-20%	0%
31-40%	20%
41-50%	40%
>50%	20%

It was the years 2002/03 during which the majority of companies experienced decreasing profits (on average nine of 10 companies), while on average six of 10 companies showed increasing profits in the period 1999-2001.

The reasons for the increase as well as for the decline in profits were mainly volume and exchange rate driven: exports increased (decreased) because of a high (low) quota and the depreciation (appreciation) of the N$ against the US$/€ (see Figures 56 and 57).

Figure 56: Surveyed firms' reasons for increased profits (N = 4)

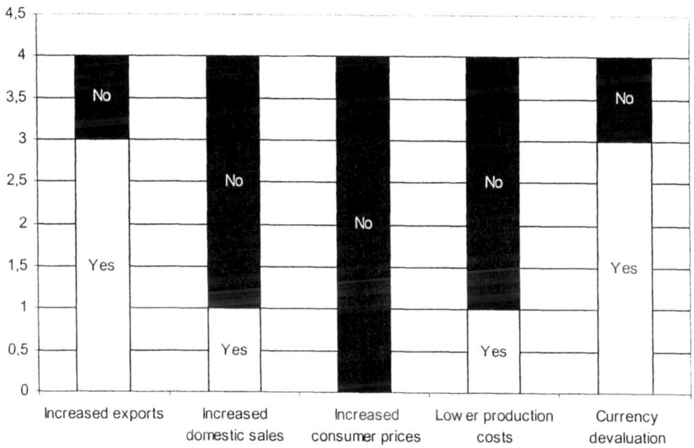

Figure 57: Surveyed firms' reasons for decreased profits (N = 5)

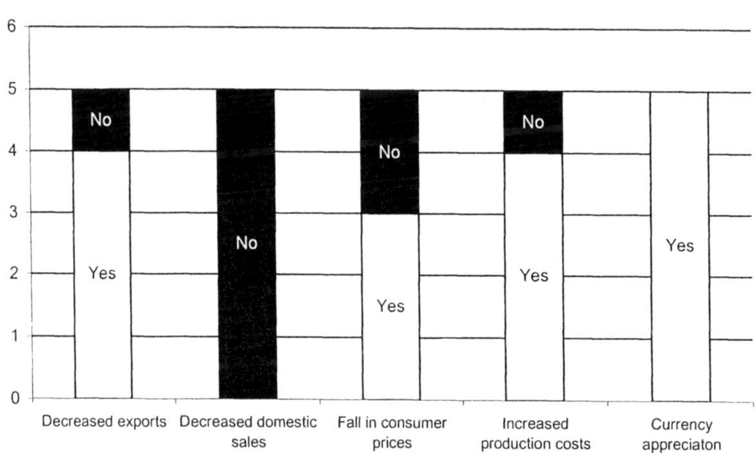

However, companies' profits depended not only on the exchange rate and the development of quota but also on their operational costs, which are judged as being too high. Many companies would not have reduced their costs and explored new markets as they could have done (MFMR 2004d:1-2). As discussed, this behaviour might be explained by limited competition in export markets and a constantly high demand for fish by industrialised countries. Thus, many companies do not see the relevance to act innovatively since their business is running. However, the concentration on traditional markets and products also bears the risk to lose market shares and to become uncompetitive. The fact that South Africa is already seen as the main competitor in the EU market, though the country still faces an import duty up to 15%, reveals that Namibian fishermen need to improve their performance.

Change in unit price: Asked for changes in unit prices, five companies said that they had faced both, increasing and declining unit prices in the period 1999-2003. Two companies stated that their prices remained stable, two companies had to accept price declines and one company was able to increase its prices. When analysing the price development per product, 11 of 28 total products remained stable, 10 showed decreasing prices and for five products the prices increased (see Table 39).

Table 39: Summary of firms' price development

Change in Unit Prices, 1999-2003 *(in real terms, inflation adjusted)*	*Per company N = 10* Prices increased: 10% Prices decreased: 20% Stable prices: 20% Prices increased and decreased: 50%	*Per product group N = 28* Price increased: 17.9% Price decreased: 35.7% Stable prices: 39.3% n/a: 7.1%
Price developments per product group, 1999-2003 *(in real terms, inflation adjusted)*	*Price increases per product group, N = 5* 5- 10%: 4 11-20%: 0 21-30%: 1 >30% 0	*Price decreases per product group, N = 10* 5-10%: 2 11-20%: 4 21-30% 1 >30%: 3

All five companies that had experienced both price increases and price decreases in the period 1999-2003 stated that their prices increased/remained stable in the period 1999-2001 but shrank in 2002-2003. This indicates that selling prices are highly exchange rate driven, a thesis, which is also supported by surveyed companies' appraisal of future price developments (see "Expectation of development of exports").

Main export purchasing company: Seven of the 11 companies surveyed supplied large, trans-national buyers and four companies exported to specialised, medium-sized buyers. Those eight companies that exported to the EU market supplied almost exclusively to large, trans-national buyers. This was judged to be attractive, because of the buy-off of large volumes. However, it must be noted that there are differences whether a company supplies a large wholesaling or retailing company: three companies surveyed exported exclusively to wholesalers, which take 5-kg catering packs and repack them at their final destination. Four companies surveyed whereas exported directly to supermarkets. These companies produced fillets in small packs for end-consumers, which is much more labour-intensive than the production of wholesaling packs. Two of these four companies had even developed their own brand, which they were trying to introduce into the EU market. It was however emphasised that the EU retail market wanted the companies to produce only their supermarket brand and did not support the development of new, company-specific brands. This finding is in line with the global value chain research of the UNCTAD (2002b), noticing a "slicing of production" in the world. Thus, value-added parts of the production process, like distribution, marketing and developing of brands would be often concentrated in industrialised countries while developing countries contribute mainly to the labour-intensive part of production.

Expectations of development of exports: Seven out of 11 companies expected stable unit prices in the next five years and three companies saw even the possibility for price increases. As can be obtained from Figure 58, no company expected price declines, which indicates that the companies did not fear according pressure from their global acting customers.

Figure 58: Surveyed firms' expectations of development of exports (N = 11)

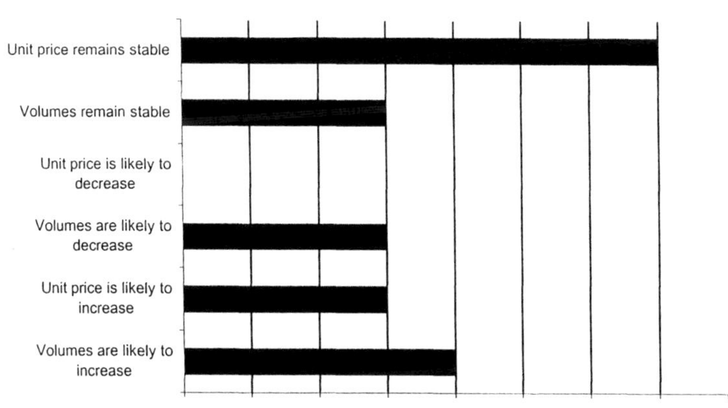

However, the companies surveyed were not so optimistic regarding the future development of volumes. Since they export a renewable natural resource, the realisable export volumes depend on the quota and the quality of fish, which can both only be influenced to a limited extent by the companies themselves. Based on the development of TACs, as stated in Table 40, one could have expected that exporters of hake appeared to be more positive than exporters of horse mackerel, considering that the TAC for hake increased by 18% in the period 1998-2002, while the one for horse mackerel decreased by almost 7%.

Table 40: Total Allowable Catches (TACs) in '000 tons

Fish species	**1991**	**1998**	**2000**	**2002**
Pilchards	60.0	65.0	25.0	0
Hake	60.0	165.0	194.0	195.0
Horse Mackerel	465.0	375.0	410.0	350.0
Crab	6.0	2.0	2.0	2.2
Rock Lobster	1.2	0.3	0.35	0.4
Orange Roughy	-	12.0	2.4	2.4
Monk	-	0	0	12.0
Total	**592.2**	**619.3**	**633.8**	**562.0**

Source: MFMR (2004b).

However, the answers given by the companies surveyed did not show a clear picture. The reasons can be twofold: first, it is conceivable that companies' representatives had rather indicators for the individual quota allocation, such as the "Nambianisation" degree of their workforce, their investment level and the amount of local value-addition in mind when answering this question, and second, companies' representatives might have also considered their difficulties to catch their quota.

The divergence between the *de facto* development of TACs and the individual expectation of the companies surveyed can also be interpreted as signs of the different policy approaches of the fishing companies on the one hand and the Government on the other hand. These differences between microeconomic and macroeconomic points of view can be summarised as follows: while the companies intend to maximise their profits with limited efforts, which can be easiest reached by more quota, the government points out that resources are limited and that sustainable profit increases are only possible if the production method is changed and new steps towards increased domestic value addition are undertaken. The Government has therefore limited the exploitation of the resource and introduced incentives to stimulate increased manufacturing activities in the fishing industry.

To what extent the companies surveyed responded to Government's incentives and how far the necessity to diversify products and markets had been adopted is discussed in the next section. The section thereupon is then going to explore to what extent a free trade agreement with the EU might help Namibian fishing companies to upgrade their products and processes.

5.5.5.6 Companies' Strategy

Budget for product research and development (R&D): Only two of 11 companies had a budget for product research and development, which was around 2% of their turnover. Both companies that were engaged in R&D were old, well-established firms and part of large holdings, which incorporated several fishing firms. In addition to these two companies, four firms had developed new products in cooperation with their partner companies or benefited from R&D of an associated company. According to this statement, more than half of the companies surveyed are directly or indirectly linked to R&D activities.

However, it remained unclear to what extent these R&D linkages improved the innovation ability of the companies surveyed. Only one company produced exclusively onshore; most companies combined on- and offshore processing. Furthermore, only four companies produced filleted retail products and only two of them had started to develop their own brand. The interview results do therefore suggest that there is still an untapped innovation potential regarding the introduction of new products, improved processes and branding activities in the Namibian fishing industry.

Training of employees: With exception of one, all companies surveyed invested into the training of their employees. The majority (7) spent 1-2% of their turnover to train their workforce. It is assumed that the companies offer enough in-house training since they have strong self-interest in having enough well-trained Namibians (Nichols 2004a).

However, the lack of skilled human capital is still a big problem to fulfil the goals of the "Namibianisation" policy. Training is therefore given high priority by the Government (Erastus 2000:19). To promote skills in the fishing industry and to integrate Namibian workers better into the industry, the Government created the Sea Fisheries Fund in 1994, which was replaced by the Marine Resources Fund in 2000. The Fund is used for research and training. The Government has developed several courses, which are undertaken by the "Namibian Maritime and Fisheries Institute" (NAMFI) in Walvis Bay, the Polytechnic of Namibia and the University of Namibia (UNAM) in Windhoek (FAO 2000:8). These three institutions are supposed to educate Namibians to be recruited by fishing companies. However, only two of the 11 companies surveyed recruited their staff at NAMFI, which might indicate the limited acceptance of NAMFI graduates by the industry. To meet the requirements of the industry, some companies recommended that training institutes devise a curriculum in cooperation with the companies, which also contain internships.

Investment in fixed assets: All companies but one answered this question. However, since four companies were not able to indicate figures of 2002 but only their total investments in the last five to ten years (mainly into vessels) the figures are not comparable.[338] It can thus only be stated the companies surveyed invest in fixed assets, mainly in their fleet.

Looking at the development in the whole industry, it can be stated that considerable investments were undertaken in the last few years. Thus, the number of licensed vessels increased by almost 30% in the period 1998-2002, as can be obtained from Table 41.[339] The largest amounts of investment were made in the demersal fisheries, which fish the most valuable species hake, monk, kingklip and sole. In the period 1990-2001 this sector contributed to more than half of the more than N$ 2 billion investment into the industry (Iyambo 2002:15).

Table 41: Number of licensed vessels 1999 and 2002

Fishery	**1998**	**2002**
Pelagic	35	25
Demersal Trawlers	85	114
Long-Liners	6	10
Midwater	25	20
Linefish	25	26
Crab	3	2
Rock Lobster	29	38
Deepwater	5	6
Large Pelagic	47	71
Monk	-	23
Total	**260** **(of which 84% were Namibian-owned)**	**335** **(of which 71% were Namibian-owned)**

Source: MFMR (2004c:25).

[338] The investment figures range from < N$ 5 Mio. (2 companies) to > N$ 60 Mio. (2 companies).

[339] The proportion of Namibian owned vessels increased from 51% in 1991 to 80% in 200 but decreased to 71% in 2002 (Iyambo 2003c:4-5).

However, the high investment into the industry is not only positive. Though fish processing plants have almost tripled since independence to 30 factories today, the considerable increase of vessels since 1998 is a reason for concern. Since the TACs remained more or less stable, competition among the single vessels has increased. The high investment into their fleets also explains why so many of the companies surveyed complained about a lack of quota: they are under pressure to keep the vessels employed in order to amortise their investment.

Upgrading of products and processes: The vast majority of companies surveyed stated that they upgraded their products and processes (see Figure 59). The companies tried to improve existing products but also introduce new products. This related less to the production of new product lines (only named by one company) than to increased value adding activities. Thus, the switch from off-shore processing to the production of hake fillets, which are packed in retail products, was named as product innovation by four companies.

Figure 59: Surveyed companies' strategy for upgraded activities (N=11)

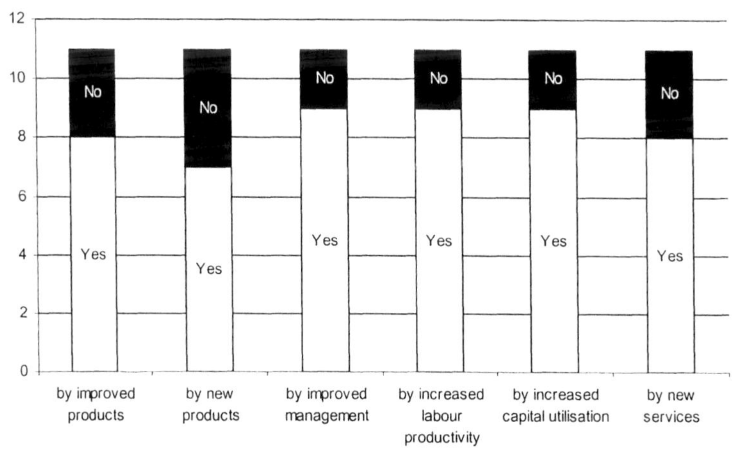

Nine of 11 companies intended to improve the productivity of their management and workers by in-house training and external workshops and to increase the efficiency of capital, e.g. by investment into their fleet or the change of factory lines. Eight companies also plan to broaden their current activities towards new services, such as the introduction of retail products (said by two companies), the engagement of a marketing agent (2), the introduction of an own label,[340] and

[340] Another company had recently introduced its own label and does currently not plan any further activities to upgrade its product.

the delivery of supermarkets outside the EU (1). Further upgrading plans related to the introduction of improved production processes and efforts to become ISO 9000 certified (named by one company each).

In sum, it can be stated that 80% of the companies surveyed stated that they were engaged in improving their products and processes. However, there is a significant difference between companies' plans and the activities that had been realised hitherto. Thus, only four of 11 companies surveyed produced fish fillets in small supermarket packs and only two companies had started to develop their own brand (and one company had planned to do so in the near future). Most companies surveyed delivered either 5-kg catering packs (4) or unprocessed fish (horse mackerel) (2).[341] One company produced canned fish and fish meal.

Considering that the sample of companies contains around three quarters of processing plants in Namibia, it can be regarded as representative, indicating that there is still scope to improve domestic value addition. Though it is undoubtedly that market entry barriers to create a good brand image and to penetrate markets in industrial countries are high and that it takes many years to get a foot into the door, the "easy way" of exporting offshore processed fish, might come to an end. Eroding preferences in the EU market, increasing competition from East Asia (by fish cultivation) and the insecurity of future development of fish stocks, require increased domestic value adding activities to stay competitive. The government states: *"Apart from the development of new resources which is deemed to be fairly limited, the real development potential for the marine resources industry lies in value adding to products, the development of new products and finding new markets for existing and new products."* (MFMR 2004c:12)

However, by far not all companies have realised the need to diversify products and markets as the dominance of offshore activities and the high investment into new trawlers show. Still, horse mackerel is exclusively frozen at sea and sold to other African countries. Asked for options to fillet this fish and sell to overseas markets the companies surveyed stated that horse mackerel is regarded as low valuable product. Value adding processes would not be rewarded by consumers. However, this statement seems to be quite sweeping since no fishing company in Namibia has tried to sell processed horse mackerel yet (Nichols 2004a). The government promotes the onshore production of horse mackerel by excluding these companies from the payment of quota fees (see Box 30).

A similar picture as with horse mackerel applies to pilchard, which is traditionally canned in a tomato-onion sauce and also only sold to the African market. Here might be product- and market-related diversification options. To in-

[341] Only three of the four companies that delivered to wholesalers exported to the EU.

crease the acceptance for Namibian pilchard in industrialised countries, the product could for instance be offered with new sauces, preserved in trendy cans, or as vacuum pack of boneless fillets. A market niche would also be pre-cooked, boneless fish dishes that can be easily prepared and are increasingly preferred by European consumers (Tall 2002:4).

Another market niche, which some Namibian fishing companies tried to explore, was the creation of an eco-label, which promotes their fish as caught in clean waters in a sustainable way. However, the MFMR, which is generally supporting the idea of eco-labelling, is concerned whether each company in the Namibian fishing industry is in a position to provide the detailed biological, economic and technical data and whether the provision of this data, which is necessary to receive the eco-label, can be monitored by Government authorities (Iyambo 2003b). Another concern is the international acceptance of a Namibian eco-label. Globally, there are already several eco-labels but no standardised label exists so far. It would, however, be desirable to agree on global guidelines for a fishery eco-label in order to increase certification transparency and consumers acceptance.[342] The Government could support endeavours in this respect by offering Namibian companies assistance to provide the necessary data and to create guidelines on how a Namibian label should look and how the compliance with these obligatory regulations could be monitored.

Next to the diversification of products and markets, there is also some scope for the development of fish processing support industries, such as gear manufacture and repairs, provision of processing equipment, the creation of storage facilities, and a distribution and marketing network (MFMR 2004c:12).

Encouragement of upgrading: Seven of 11 companies were encouraged by their main purchasers to upgrade their activities. The assistance granted related mainly to technical support to produce supermarket brands (said by five companies). For the development of their own brand, the companies did not receive any assistance. One company also received financial support from its customer to create a supermarket brand. Two companies, on the other hand, stated that their customers formulated only action tasks and did not grant any support at all.

In sum, the technical assistance provided was largely restricted to processing activities and not granted for highly valuable activities, such as branding or marketing. It is therefore judged as important for the Namibian fishing industry to go abroad and to establish its own distribution and marketing network (Nichols 2004a). However, the European fish market is characterised by many distributors so competition is very high. The CBI (2003) expects a further centralisation of the management of trade channels, which makes it very difficult for

[342] For this reason, the WTO Doha Round promotes the creation of an international certified eco-label for fisheries products (FAO 2004b:2).

comparable small Namibian suppliers to get a foot into the door. On the other hand cooperation with European partners is likely to offer new chances to break down barriers to distribute and market products (CBI 2003:2-4).

Strategic alliances: Nine of 11 companies wanted to enter or had already entered into a strategic alliance with a foreign producer.[343] Only two companies said that they want to stay "100% Namibian". Asked for the advantages of cooperating with a foreign firm, the surveyed companies named the following:

a) Improved access to markets and distribution channels by valuable contacts (said by 7 companies);
b) Improved access to finance and modern vessels (4);
c) Inclusion into international value added chains and thus, higher profitability of business activities (2),
d) Exchange of skills (1); and
e) A higher quota that would allow for a higher capital utilisation (1).[344]

Altogether, the companies surveyed saw few disadvantages in a partnership with a foreign firm. Only two interview partners were strictly against any foreign involvement into their company and named the sharing of power and resources as reasons.

New export markets: Most companies surveyed (8) investigated new export markets; only three companies stated that their capacities would be overloaded so that they did not see any reasons to analyse new export options. The main markets the companies surveyed explored were the USA (said by five companies), EU countries (5), African countries (3), Japan and Australia (2 each).[345] Since most of the companies said that they would investigate new export markets despite their constraints to supply them, they seemed to be well aware of the problems that can result of one-sided market dependency (see Table 42).

Most companies surveyed planned to undertake considerable efforts to upgrade their activities and to explore new markets. Cooperation with a foreign partner was desirable for all but two companies surveyed. In cases where companies delivered to retailers, most of them encouraged Namibian fishermen to upgrade their products towards supermarket brands.

---

[343] Six of the companies surveyed were in a joint-venture with a foreign company.

[344] N = 9. Multiple answers possible.

[345] N = 8. Multiple answers possible.

Table 42: Summary of surveyed firms' strategies

Receipt of assistance to upgrade products and processes	*N = 11*	
	Yes:	63.6%
	No:	36.4%
Intention to enter into a strategic alliance	*N = 11*	
	Yes:	81.8%
	No:	18.2%
Exploration of new export markets	*N = 11*	
	Yes:	72.7%
	No:	27.3%

However, as discussed the realisation of upgrading activities for the whole industry has not been sufficient yet. In addition to the limited effort of some companies to leave "the easy way", the dualism between well-established companies and newcomer firms is also a reason for the deficient manufacturing performance of the industry. Though newcomer companies are connected to well-established companies by joint-venture agreements, they are not always well integrated into business operations. To reach the integration of newcomers into the international value chain, it is important that they benefit from international business experiences.

According to the interview results, all companies that have diversified their product range successfully were in a joint-venture agreement, which linked them to an international company group. These international linkages were judged as essential to upgrade products and services and to stay competitive. To enter into a strategic alliance with a foreign company was attractive for all but two of the 11 companies surveyed. The interview partners hoped that international linkages would help them to improve their access to markets, finance and distribution channels, and to receive support to upgrade their activities. In fact, examples from other countries have shown that the cooperation with a foreign counterpart might help the fishing industry to improve its access to inputs and to break down barriers to distribute and market products in overseas markets (CBI 2003:2-4).

The question is whether a fisheries agreement with the EU has the potential to help the Namibian fishing industry to enter into multi-beneficial cooperation with European firms. As yet, all EU fishery agreements with African countries are *de facto* FTAs that grant European vessels access to resources and compensate the countries for fishing rights (European Commission 2004). Thus, it should be discussed how the inclusion of fisheries into free trade could help the Namibian fishing industry to benefit from cheap capital goods and knowledge transfer and what are the consequences for national policies in the fishing industry.

5.5.6 Chances and Risks for Namibia of Entering into a Fishery Agreement with the EU

Soon after Namibia's independence and its accession to the Lomé Convention, the EU wanted to negotiate a fishery agreement with the country. However, the two parties could not agree on a common position and talks broke down. Since that time the EU has tried several times to negotiate a fishery agreement with Namibia but the Namibian side is not ready to enter into an agreement that provides quota allocations to the EU. Namibia has largely restricted foreign access to its fishing grounds, as experiences of other African countries, where foreign trawlers exploit fish resources, leaving only very limited value added in the country, have been put off Namibia. The Namibian side emphasises that there are, however, existing options of joint-venture or franchise arrangements, which have not been sufficiently exploited by EU fishermen. However, these arrangements do not go far enough for the EU that is highly interested in negotiating an access agreement with Namibia the only southern African coastal state with South Africa, which has not signed a fishery agreement with the EU yet.

To enter into a fishery agreement with the EU would imply several chances and risks for Namibia. Possible advantages the Namibian fishing industry could obtain would be improved and cheaper access to modern European fishing vessels. As discussed the EU has an (subsidised) overcapacity of vessels and Namibia would – as an ACP country that has successfully negotiated a fishery agreement with the EU – be allowed to buy these vessels at reduced prices.[346] Currently EU fishermen are not allowed to sell their vessels to Namibian fishermen. One of the companies interviewed states: *"Our average fleet age is 36.24 years. In the EU fishermen receive subsidies when they scrap their vessels. They receive the more money the newer the vessels are. As a result new vessels are scrapped but fishermen still trawl with their old vessels. We offered them to by their vessel because we urgently need them but it is forbidden; they must be destroyed."* Thus, a fishery agreement with the EU would offer the industry the chance to modernise its old fleet at substantially reduced costs. It would therefore be of special interest for newcomer companies that lack capital. As a result of a modernised fleet, the profitability of fishing activities per company would be likely to increase. However, as discussed, companies' investment into their fleet, which was substantial in the last few years, would also bear the risks of overcapitalisation since it increases the pressure on companies to amortise their investment. Another concern is that an "oversupply" of vessels results in increased fishing activities and illegal fishing, which would be detrimental for the sustainability of fishing grounds. Increased supply of minor quality fish could further result in price declines.

---

[346] As stipulated in the Cotonou Agreement, Art. 3.3 (European Commission 2000b).

In fact, the Namibian fishing industry needs modern processing facilities rather than modern vessels, which would offer the sector the chance to increase the value addition of catches. However, the EU is interested in keeping its own factories busy and seeks to increase the import of unprocessed fish. It is therefore doubtful that entering into a fishery agreement with the EU would result in increased investment in Namibian fish factories. Moreover, a fishery agreement with the EU is likely to oblige Namibia to "reserve" a certain quota for EU vessels, largely independent from the development of stocks. For Namibian fishing companies such a regulation would imply decreased quotas, if the fishing grounds do not develop as predicted. As a result, the "Namibianisation" policy could be slowed down since only a smaller quota could be redistributed to newcomer companies.

On the other hand, a fishery agreement with the EU would increase Government's revenue from the sector, thus offering the chance to stimulate investment and manufacturing activities by public kick-off finance in the sector. Furthermore, higher revenue could be used to improve the effectiveness of "Namibianisation" policies, e.g. by improving the training of Namibians to be recruited by the fishing companies as well as the communication and cooperation between companies and trade unions. Though the experience of other African countries showed that the revenue paid does often not cover the full costs of foreign access, such as unreported fishing activities, it must be considered that Namibia shows excellent monitoring and surveillance methods to supervise foreign fishing activities. It can therefore be expected that the price negotiated for access would reflect world market prices.

Namibia emphasises the importance that any agreement with the EU is in line with the principle of its national fishing policy, namely the "Namibianisation" policy and the promotion of sustainable fishing. The Minister of Fisheries and Marine Resources, Dr Abraham Iyambo, states *"... 'too many fishermen chasing too few fish'... This is because gross fishing overcapacity has been allowed to develop. The inescapable fact is that it is the industrialised nations that have created this mess. ... Reducing over-capacity through a real reduction in vessel numbers is the only way to reduce pressure on stocks ... Moving excess capacity to the developing world through destructive access arrangement is not a solution."* (Iyambo 2003b). Since Namibia complains that its companies face increased competition as well as decreasing prices in their main export markets due to industrialised countries' subsidies, indirect promotion of the trade distorting effects of subsidies by entering into a fishing agreement with the EU would - from the Government's point of view - undermine Namibia's political credibility.

5.5.7 Conclusions: The Implications for Upgrading, Value Addition and Industrialisation Strategies when Including the Namibian Fishing Industry into a Free Trade Agreement with the EU

At present, it is increasingly difficult for African countries to compete successfully in the global market, which is highly dominated by trans-national companies. There must be a stern examination of how, if at all, African countries can be integrated into the global value-added chain. So far, African countries export mainly unprocessed fish to the EU and have to a large extent not been able to manage their resources effectively (Tall 2002, Acheampong 1997). The Namibian fishing industry must be seen as a positive exemption in this respect, which has been able to manage its domestic fisheries in a responsible manner and develop it to be sustainable in the long-term.

However, despite the successful management and the attraction of considerable investment, the industry has not increased its manufacturing activities as envisaged and has not been able to diversify towards new activities, such as the marketing and distribution of its products. It is therefore challenging whether Namibia can perpetuate, enlarge and upgrade its domestic fishing industry. Thus, the allocation of quota and the quality of catches are, together with the exchange rate, still the decisive factors for the development of profits. The appreciated exchange rate in the years 2002/03 resulted in declining profits since fishermen were not able negotiate higher Euro prices though the demand for their products was high. This can, on the one hand, be explained by the fact that their EU counterparts were mainly large, trans-national retailers and wholesalers. On the other hand it was also the exchangeability of their products (frozen fish), which decreased their bargaining power. Thus, producers of commodities that are highly exchangeable become themselves increasingly exchangeable in the international production process. It is therefore important for a producer of exchangeable products to develop relevant core capabilities that aggravate the dislocation of production, including the extension of activities towards an all-embracing product development and –marketing (Wohlmuth 2003:48-9). Namibian fish is a high valuable product, which is shown by the low price elasticity of demand. However, so far many Namibian fishermen have not taken the natural limitation of their resource sufficiently into account but relied on the export of offshore processed goods. To limit their dependency on fluctuations of stocks and EU preferences, to reduce the lopsided negotiation power of their EU counterpart, and to increase domestic value addition, it is important to increase manufacturing activities in the industry.

Though most of the companies' representatives interviewed in this sample said that they are dedicated to upgrade their products and processes, the discussion showed, there is still a considerable potential for Namibian fishing companies to upgrade their activities. Only four companies surveyed sold retail products and only two of them had introduced their own brand.

By moving strongly towards retail products the companies would not only employ more people, improve their manufacturing capabilities and create increased domestic value addition but would in the long run also be enabled to create their own product brand and become engaged into marketing and distribution activities. The Namibian fishing industry has few problems to enter the EU market, as it offers admittedly good quality fish, which is increasingly demanded and cannot be satisfied by the EU. Since the EU requirements for quality and health standards but also environmental and social aspects become more and more important, Namibian fishing companies should use the chance and market their fish actively. However, it is very difficult for the Namibian fishing industry, which is tiny in international terms, to diversify its product range and activities since the trade channels in the EU market are centralised and difficult to enter. Moreover, the industry has to import the majority of inputs for processing activities, struggles with high investment costs and missing backward- and forward linkages, a low level of labour productivity and a worker-employer relationship that is often stamped by mistrust. The Government intends to promote manufacturing activities in the fishing industry and has introduced a "60% onshore quota" for hake production as well as several manufacturing incentives. However, so far these attempts have not satisfactorily helped to diversify the fishing exports.

According to the sample it was those companies that are part of an international network, which have successfully upgraded their activities towards the production of retail products, the development of an own label and efforts to market and distribute their products. Though the Government acknowledges the positive contribution of joint-venture agreements to the overall economic performance of Namibian fishing companies, it still favours Namibian owned enterprises in comparison to joint-ventures. This policy, which aims to improve the "Namibianisation" of the industry, should however be evaluated and discussed controversially. So far, it is not clear whether newcomer companies are suitably operationally involved in domestic-owned companies than in joint-ventures. If joint-ventures contribute more to employment, investment and product diversification, as this study suggest, it would be recommendable to promote joint-venture cooperation in order to boost the international competitiveness of the Namibian fishing industry.

In theory, it is also a fishery agreement with the EU could help the Namibian fishing industry to benefit from technical assistance and knowledge transfer with an advanced partner. However, so far it is not sufficiently ensured that these agreements are also beneficial for the developing country. The sustainable exploitation of natural resources that benefits Namibian fishermen, the Government, and, most of all, the people, is only possible if the EU shows a long-term commitment. This is not the case with current access agreements (though they are now called "partnership agreements"), which do not regulate the modalities of cooperation sufficiently. The present concept of EU fishery agreements does not help Namibia to expand its processing facilities, since the EU is not interested in processing the fish in Namibia but in keeping its own processing facilities engaged. For Namibia, the benefits of such an agreement would be limited to increased revenue and employed labour but would not offer the chance to improve companies' management capabilities, to diversify the product range and to enter into new product-related activities.

Still, the well-established management of the Namibian fishing industry as well as the EU's high interest in entering into a fisheries agreement with Namibia might offer the chance for negotiating a fisheries agreement that sufficiently accommodates Namibia's concerns. Considering that the EU is increasingly under pressure to resolve the development inconsistencies of its fishery agreements with developing countries, Namibia should keep open the options to negotiate a sustainable fishery agreement with the EU.

5.6 Overall Conclusions: Economic Performance, Industrial Policy and the Impact of Free Trade with the EU: Common Grounds and Differences of the South African Automotive Industry and the Namibian Fishing Industry

From a classical trade theory point of view, an FTA with an industrialised country offers the South African automotive and the Namibian fishing industry better access to competitive inputs and the latest technology, allows producers to exploit economies of scale due to a larger market, promotes cooperation with foreign firms and helps to attract FDI. Competitive regional producers replace domestic ones so that production is shifted to the most competitive suppliers (trade creation) and resources are optimally allocated. Furthermore, protected access to a large market and cooperation with European firms may offer African producers the chance to improve their industrial capacities and increase their international competitiveness.

However, as the discussion in the two case studies showed, the export performance and investment behaviour in the South African automotive and the Namibian fishing industry are somehow different. Whether an FTA with the EU can help these two industries to improve the economic performance and to stimulate the creation of international linkages remains doubtful. Why should free access to the South African market stimulate EU vehicle manufacturers to invest in the South African component industry if they are able to source from the cheapest supplier worldwide? And why should free access to Namibian waters stimulate joint-ventures in the fishing industry if overcapitalised European trawlers can catch fish themselves and process it in European factories, which have to be kept busy? In fact, foreign and domestic investment in the South African automotive industry and the Namibian fishing industry as well the creation of international linkages have been supported by domestic incentives and a certain level of protection from international competition.

The South African automotive industry was very successful in exporting, creating new value addition, improving its international competitiveness and stabilising employment since 1994. Because of the import/export complementation scheme MIDP, international car producers, which were formerly thinking of leaving South Africa, have not only continued production but expanded it significantly. Thus, the MIDP contributed to the improvement of the automotive industry's international competitiveness, helped to increase and stabilise international and domestic investment, and improved the productivity level and the export performance of the sector. Furthermore, the MIDP has helped to include domestic component manufacturers into the global value added chain since it promoted local content usage, thus supporting local sourcing from international OEMs. Since South African component manufacturers export hardly themselves but via international OEMs of which most are either European firms or have subsidiaries in the EU, South African automotive manufacturers have already preferred market access to the EU. Thus, investment into the South African auto industry has not been attracted by the TDCA, which guarantees free market access for South African automotive exports to the EU by 2010, but by an attractive import duty reduction scheme for domestically manufactured vehicles and components. Since any tariff reduction vis-à-vis trading partners undermines the effectiveness of the MIDP (because its duty rebate system applies only if a certain tariff level exists) South Africa is reluctant to include the automotive sector into free trade. Though South Africa would be interested to improve its market access to the EU market before the original envisaged liberalisation schedule, it fears the negative effects of a more comprehensive tariff liberalisation and thus the de facto abandonment of the MIDP. It should not be forgotten that South Africa is only a minor player in international terms and shows already a very low effective rate of protection. Considering the international level of competition for automotives and the concentration degree of global OEMs, it is doubtful that developing countries like South Africa have a chance to compete successfully without domestic incentive schemes. It is an open secret that South Africa needs ongoing support after the expiration of the MIDP in 2012. However, how this support looks like is insecure. In times of low tariff protection and the strict regulations of the WTO Agreement on Subsidies and Countervailing Measures (ASCM) there is hardly scope for developing countries to promote their industries. Since the MIDP is moreover "self-financing", does not included local contents requirements and lowers the tariffs below WTO obligations, it can be regarded as very clever industry promotion incentive. South Africa's interest in keeping this successful instrument and emphasising that the inclusion of the automotive industry into free trade is in contradiction to national policy goals, is therefore understandable.

In case of the Namibian fishing industry, the inclusion of fisheries into free trade implies several risks for the Namibian fishing industry and might even deprive its basic principles, thus risking the end of a national fisheries policy. Since independence, Namibia has successfully developed its own fishing industry, which is today the second largest manufacturing industry and a major contributor to Namibia's export earnings. Namibia has applied a comprehensive management and surveillance system to supervise the exploitation of its fishing grounds. Catches are limited by license, non-transferable quota and taxation of catches. As the discussion showed, it is not an easy task to manage an open access resource and most African countries lack of the capability to do so. Namibian is one of the few developing countries that have implemented a monitoring and surveillance system which is judged to be effective in international terms.

The EU's interest in concluding a fisheries agreement with Namibia does not follow up developmental interests but is solely economically driven. Since European waters are empty, the overcapitalisation of European fleets is more and more shifted towards developing countries. In theory, an access agreement is mutually beneficial since the industrialised country gets access to new fishing grounds and the African country receives financial compensation as well as technical assistance and other forms of aid to develop its own fishery industry. In practise however these access agreements as well as their successors, the so-called "partnership agreements" failed to be environmentally, socially and economically sustainable. As a result, Namibia continues to reject to enter into a fisheries agreement with the EU, emphasising that EU fishermen have not sufficiently exploited the option to enter into joint-venture or franchise arrangements with Namibian fishermen. Though a fisheries agreement with the EU might offer Namibia the chance to modernise its fleet at reduced costs and would therefore offer the chance to improve the inclusion of formerly disadvantaged Namibian into the sector, it bears on the other hand the risk of slowing down the "Namibianisation" policy since limited quotas have to be shared with EU trawlers. Moreover, increased competition in the sector might result in increased illegal fishing so that the costs of entering into a fisheries agreement with the EU are judged to be higher than the benefits in form of financial compensation and increased technical support.

Talking about the South African automotive and the Namibian fishing industry and their inclusion into an FTA with the EU, similarities but also differences appear. Both industries have in common that they are successful in national but also international terms and that they contribute significantly to the overall performance of the manufacturing sector and to employment creation. Both industries had to implement national policy instruments that guide economic and, in case of the fishing industry, also social developments. However, both industries are neither subsidised nor do they enjoy governmental support in a traditional way.

In case of the Namibian fishing industry government's intervention is direct giving guidelines who are allowed to fish what, thus connecting economic performance with social and environmental aspects. Considering the nature of the good (open accessible resource) and the historic rooted economic inequality within Namibia, this intervention might be justified. It is however a tight trope walk for the government: as the discussion showed, the promotion of an increased "Namibianisation" level bears the risk to encourage inefficient processing and to create a national industry that is neither sufficiently aware of international challenges nor in a position to undertake necessary upgrading activities.

In contradiction to the Namibian fishing industry, the intervention of the South African government into the automotive industry is indirect, offering export-oriented companies that produce in South Africa the option to deduct import duties on automotives according to the value exported.

Though governments' interventions in both sectors are disputed and shortcomings have appeared, such as the inadequate transfer of automotive import duty reductions to South African consumers or the insufficient inclusion of Namibian newcomer firms into the management of fishing companies, the overall policy approach of the South African automotive industry and the Namibian fishing industry has been successful. The inclusion of these sectors into a free trade agreement would bereave governments to apply individual policies, which promote domestic value addition and industrial development. This does not imply that the South African automotive industry and the Namibian fishing industry should not be exposed to international competition. In fact, both sectors are linked to global markets. In case of the South African automotive industry, international linkages are tremendously important for domestic manufacturers' economic performance and their success in exporting. The inclusion into a global manufacturing network has helped domestic manufacturers to improve their product quality, their international competitiveness and their economies of scale, and is crucial for their economic success. A similar picture, though not to this extent, applies to the Namibian fishing industry, where cooperation with foreign firms and the inclusion of the Namibian management into multi-beneficial joint-ventures have contributed to companies' improved economic performances.

However, the examples of the South African automotive industry and the Namibian fishing industry also show that there is an important difference between selective openness to foreign investment and multi-beneficial cooperation on the one hand and an overall openness to free trade on the other hand. In fact, the two case studies show that "policy matters" (Rodrik 1999) and that government's guidance cannot be substituted by free trade agreements. Since the inclusion of the South African automotive industry and the Namibian fishing industry into free trade agreements bears the risk that only few international competitive domestic companies survive while the inclusion of small, formerly disadvantaged domestic companies would be made impossible, such a policy would be counterproductive from an economic development point of view. Thus, the resistance of the South African and the Namibian government to include successful manufacturing sectors into free trade and their insistence to apply national, "individual" policies that are best for economic development and overall socio-economic performances seem to be appropriate from an economic development perspective.

However, how can the SACU countries set through their national interests if negotiating FTAs with developed countries? What are governments' capacities in international trade negotiations and to what extent are national stakeholders involved? To what extent are public officials and companies aware of the chances and risks North-South FTAs offer and what strategies do they pursue to set through their interests? These are the questions that should be elaborated in Chapter 6. Since an FTA with the EU does not only imply challenges for SACU countries' industries but also for their institutional capacities to negotiate and implement the agreement effectively, Chapter 6 highlights the importance of trade capacity building and formulates policy recommendations what needs to be done to improve SACU countries' trade capacities in order to allow their effective participation in trade negotiations.

6 Trade Capacity Building in the SACU countries and its Relevance for Development Oriented Trade Relations with the EU

6.1 Free Trade Agreements and Economic Development: Why is Trade Capacity Building Crucial?

The concept of trade capacity building is comparably new and only came on the agenda in the mid-1990s. Before, donors' trade support concentrated on export promotion (1960s and 1970s) and trade liberalisation (since the 1980s). With trade capacity, the focus has been broadened, realising that functioning institutions and human and institutional capacities are crucial to participate effectively in international trade (Jensen 2005:2). The OECD Development Assistance Committee defines trade capacity building in a very broad manner. Trade capacity building should not only a) enable developing countries to identify trade objectives and to formulate their trade policy by integrating all relevant stakeholders, but also b) support countries' export expansion and diversification strategy, and c) assist to strengthen national and regional trade-related institutions in order to participate best at regional and international trade negotiations (OECD 2003:2 and 2001:22). Jensen (2005:2) emphasises that this broad definition comprises two components of trade capacity building, namely *trade policy* and *trade development*. Trade policy addresses countries' ability to analyse, negotiate and implement trade agreement while trade development investigates how supply-side constraints could be overcome.

The discussion in this chapter focuses on trade policy and thus, SACU countries' trade capacities to be optimally involved in international trade.[349] In this context, the relevance for SACU countries' governments to formulate a national trade strategy and to build national and regional capacities in order to work towards a regional trade strategy is discussed.[350] Furthermore, the involvement of SACU businesses, private sector support institutions and research institutions in trade negotiations is evaluated. As the discussion shows, an inclusive approach, involving all stakeholders, is crucial for successful trade negotiations.

Given the world-wide policy towards trade liberalisation – on a multilateral, bilateral and regional level, and the increasing pressure on developing

[349] The question of trade development has already been extensively dealt with in the Chapters 3 and 4 where SACU countries' diversification strategies and how to tackle supply-side constraints were discussed. Moreover, the case studies in Chapter 5 discussed the relevance of technical support and incentive for companies' export success.

[350] It needs to be considered that SACU countries' trade-related needs are less weighted towards areas that are problematic in other African countries, such as macroeconomic stability or infrastructure services.

countries to participate accordingly, the strengthening of trade-related capacities is regarded as crucial for enabling developing countries to benefit from the opportunities arising from trade liberalisation and for defending their interests (Bonaglia and Fukasaku 2002). To use international trade as successful development strategy, a county needs to identify its trade interests clearly and translate these interests into policies and negotiation strategies. Furthermore, resources have to be set free to implement trade policies and the role of the single actors needs to be defined. Critical elements for such a successful trade policy are a) government leadership, i.e. government's commitment to the official trade strategy, b) institutional capacity at all levels from trade analysis to the implementation of existing agreements, and c) the inclusion of all state and non-state actors involved (Solignac Lecomte 2001:6).

As can be obtained from Figure 60, an effective trade policy framework needs to be in place, including:

1) A consistent trade strategy that fits into the country's overall development strategy and SACU's regional development strategy;
2) An effective consultation mechanism, including all relevant stakeholder (private sector, research institutions, trade unions, parliament, other civil society members);
3) An effective communication among the relevant Ministries (e.g. Ministry of Trade with the Ministry of Agriculture, the Ministry of Customs and Excise, and the Ministry of Foreign Affairs);
4) A trade supportive network, providing decision makers with relevant inputs (e.g. inputs from indigenous research institutions and private sector support institutions) (OECD 2001:14).

To allow the creation of an effective trade policy, the SACU countries need capacities

a) *At the policy-making level:* Analytical capacities for trade analyses, the formulation of a coherent strategy and the negotiation capacity to set through identified interests;
b) *At the institutional level:* The effective implementation of a trade agreement requires the knowledge, capacity and equipment of according institutions, such as customs and excise services, standard agencies or anti-dumping proceedings.
c) *At the marketing and management level:* It is important to build a platform where all relevant actors (private sector, trade unions, research institutions, other civil society actors) can articulate their interests, which are translated in a national trade policy. The implications of trade agreements must in turn be made public towards the different national interest groups.

This policy approach of "inclusiveness" ensures that the trade policy is in accordance to the overall national development strategy and "owned" by the country (Bilal and Laporte 2004).

Figure 60: The process of trade policy

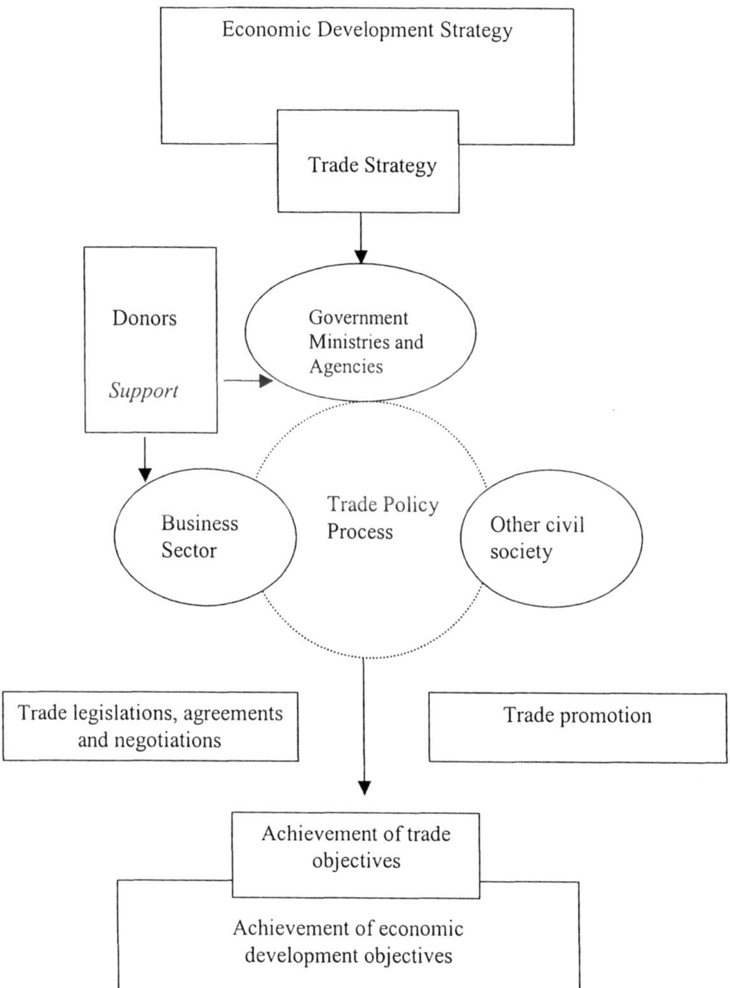

Source: Solignac-Lecomte 2001:7.

Donor countries' ability to support this trade policy process is generally judged as limited since the "ownership" of trade reforms is regarded as crucial. Donors can however assist developing countries to define their trade strategy in accordance to national development goals and in cooperation with the business sector and other civil society actors. Technical and financial support should focus on institutions rather than on individuals so that structures can be improved and the process of trade policy can be smoothened (Solignac Lecomte 2001:13-8).

6.2 The Capacity of SACU Countries' Public and Private Sectors to Participate in Regional and International Trade Negotiations

The requirements for active participation in regional and international forums are constantly increasing. Small, developing countries like the BLNS are supposed to participate in the multilateral trading system through the WTO, which means that they have to implement agreements and obligations with respect to import licensing, customs valuation, intellectual property law, sanitary and phytosanitary standards etc. Additionally, bilateral agreements and regulations have to be negotiated and implemented, which also stresses SACU countries' limited capacities. Another problem arising from different regulations with different trading partners under different trade agreements is that it adds to the complexity of SACU's trade regime, bearing the risk of making it unmanageable for the private sector and to contribute to the inconsistency of countries' trade policy.

National Capacities and Duties

South Africa is the only SACU country that has due to its involvement in the WTO and the negotiations of the TDCA already gained experience in international trade negotiations. However, also for South Africa, which employed 11 officials to negotiate the TDCA, while the EU had a staff of over 250 people, the multiplicity and complexity of trade agreements is demanding. For the BLNS countries again, the complexity of international trade negotiations is a completely new experience and poses severe challenges on their capacities. Like most African countries (OECD 2001:34), BLNS have only a handful trade experts who are working on *all* trade agreements the countries are involved in, namely the SACU-USA FTA, the SACU-EFTA FTA, and EPA negotiations.

1. The SACU-USA FTA

Negotiations started in June 2003 and were supposed to be finalised by the end of 2004. The US-side aims to conclude a comprehensive FTA, including trade in goods, trade in services, protection of intellectual property rights, regulations for competition, investment, government procurement, and trade facilitation. SACU countries however want to negotiate on market access for goods and services before discussing any other issues. Since all SACU countries are beneficiary of AGOA, which is particularly important for Lesotho and Swaziland, SACU is interested in the maintenance of its preferences vis-à-vis the USA. However, after six rounds of talks, negotiations were stalled for more than nine months from December 2004 on. The reason was that the USA insisted to include the Singapore Issues on a broad basis, which South Africa was not ready to accept.[351] Though the (official) positions have remained the same, negotiations have started again in September 2005, focussing on uncontroversial aspects such as industrial tariff reductions (Tralac news, 23/08/05).

2. The SACU-EFTA FTA

To harmonise trade relations with European countries, SACU negotiates an FTA with the EFTA countries Switzerland, Norway, Iceland and Liechtenstein since 2003. The SACU-EFTA FTA is supposed to follow in large parts the TDCA (Smalberger 2004).[352] However, the EFTA countries also aim to include the protection of intellectual property rights for medicine and agriculture into the FTA, which is rejected by SACU. Because of the dispute on the inclusion of trade-related aspects, an agreement has not been reached yet (Bilaterals 07/03/2005).

3. EPA Negotiations (BLNS)

As discussed in Chapter 3, the BLNS countries negotiate an EPA with the EU in a SADC framework, which comprises the BLNS countries, Angola, Mozambique and Tanzania. South Africa, which is not part of the EPA, supervises the negotiations and has offered to provide technical assistance.[353] The Ministry of Trade and Industry in Botswana coordinates EPA negotiations. Technical working groups meetings regarding barriers to trade, SPS and customs issues were held in early 2005, with discussion focussing on how to improve market access (ECDPM 2005a). A second meeting between officials of the SADC EPA and the EU were held in April 2005 where the parties agreed to launch a study on multiple memberships, reciprocity, SDT, market access and technical barriers to trade (ECDPM 2005b). However, to date no details on how the SADC EPA is

[351] The USA favours a "negative list" for service and investment, which would require the SACU countries to open their markets for all sectors except those that are excluded *a priori*. SACU again insists on a "positive list", which names explicitly the sectors included into the FTA. SACU's trade negotiators argue that a "negative list" which requires the identification of excluded product lines would be an enormous administrative burden for the SACU countries (INSAT 2005a:3).

[352] SACU will receive immediate access for industrial goods, market access for agricultural products is negotiated through bilateral FTAs (Smalberger 2004).

[353] South Africa's possible role in EPA negotiations in discussed in section 6.5.

supposed to look like are known.[354] Moreover, it is doubtful whether the current configuration of the SADC EPA will come into force due to the incoherence with regional integration frameworks and South Africa's veto right (see discussion in section 3.6 and 3.8).

Additionally, to these current trade negotiations, the countries have to implement the new SACU Agreement, the SADC FTA,[355] and a PTA with the trading block MERCOSUR,[356] and elicit options to enter into trade negotiations with China, Japan, Singapore, India, Kenya, Egypt and Nigeria (Bilaterals 2005). South Africa is furthermore busy to negotiate the mid-term review of the TDCA,[357] which also includes a discussion on how the TDCA and EPA negotiations can be coordinated (EU DG Trade 2005b).

International Representation

Besides all these bilateral obligations, the SACU countries have as founding members of the WTO also multilateral obligations but are only insufficiently represented in Geneva.[358] South Africa and Botswana are the only SACU coun-

---

[354] The Commission plans to release a report on EPA negotiations in autumn 2005, supposed to identify areas where development cooperation needs to be strengthened (Mandelson 2005). To date, the SADC EPA has received € 7.5 million from the EU to support the ongoing negotiations and build trade capacity in the SADC EPA configuration (INSAT 2005a:9).

[355] The SADC Trade Protocol was signed in 2000 by 11 member countries and aims to liberalise 85% of intra-SADC trade in goods by 2008; the remaining 15% is regarded as sensitive and supposed to be liberalised by 2012. The SACU members front-loaded their offer, i.e. they made a single offer to the rest of SADC to reduce tariffs to zero by 2005 (except for sensitive products). However, the implementation of the SADC FTA is still in its infancy and insecure to be fulfilled by 2012 (Kalenga 2004).

[356] SACU signed a preferential trade agreement with the South-American trading block MERCOSUR countries in April 2005. To date, the PTA covers only 1,000 products (Bilaterals 12/04/05). SACU is also exploring the option of a "triangle trade alliance" including MERCOSUR, SACU and India (INSAT 2005a:4).

[357] The review of the TDCA has started in November 2004 and involves the implementation process, additional liberalisation (such as diverse agricultural products for the EU and automotives and textiles for South Africa), implications of the EU enlargement, and improvements of consultation processes (Bilaterals, 01/09/05).

[358] The SACU countries are also supposed to articulate their interests in the following international organisations, based in Geneva: UN High Commission for Human Rights, UN High Commission for Refugee, World Health Organisation (WHO), International Labour Organisation (ILO), International Standardisation Organisation (ISO), World Intellectual Property Organisation (WIPO), International Telecommunication Union (ITU), World Meteorological Organisation (WMO), United Nations Conference on Trade and Development (UNCTAD), International Trade Center (ITC).

tries that have a permanent mission based in Geneva.[359] Namibia is not represented in Geneva but has a one-man mission to WTO since 2004. Lesotho has a permanent mission in Geneva (6 staff member including the Ambassador), which is however based in Brussels. Swaziland is not represented in Geneva but has like all SACU countries a diplomatic representation in Brussels.

Four experts of South Africa's permanent mission to Geneva are working in the field of trade and industry and represent the country at the WTO. In comparison: Germany has around 550 people at the WTO. Moreover, all EU countries are not only represented by their national trade experts but also by the EU, represented by the Commission's Directorate for Trade and the Liaison Office of the Council of Ministers (Swiss Mission in Geneva 2005).

The BLNS countries, of which only Botswana and Namibia have a one and two men mission to WTO, are highly overextended with representing their interests in the manifold forums, including the negotiations of preferences, waivers, extensions, SDT etc. in the fields of trade, services and intellectual property rights. Furthermore, the complexity of the WTO Agreements puts constraints on BLNS countries' capacities. Lesotho's Minister of Trade and Industry states: *"...we still have a problem with implementing some of the obligations that we have and it's not through lack of trying, it's through lack of resources, financial, technical, you name it."* (INSAT 2005a:15). In fact, apart from the scarceness of qualified staff, effective participation at WTO is also a financial problem – above all for the BLNS countries. Thus, the implementation of the WTO obligations in the fields of customs valuation, SPS and the TRIPS Agreement is expected to cost a country around US$ 150 million (Finger 2001).[360]

Participation of the private sector, parliamentarians and civil society in trade negotiations

South Africa established the "National Economic and Development and Labour Council" (NEDLAC) during TDCA negotiations, comprising government officials, mainly from the Department of Labour, organised business (represented by two business representative organisations), organised labour (represented by three trade unions) and civil society actors (represented by different councils) (Bilal and Laporte 2004:16-7). In addition to NEDLAC, large industries lobbied

[359] South Africa, which is represented by 16 staff members, has the biggest mission in Geneva, working in five main fields, namely human rights, disarmanent, health, trade and industry and labour relations (Swiss Mission in Geneva 2005).

[360] The SDT provision of the WTO Agreement provides for technical assistance to help developing countries to implement sanitary and phytosanitary standards, the agreement on technical barriers to trade, customs valuation, and the provisions of GATS and TRIPS. WTO and OECD are running all sorts of trade capacity-related projects and try to coordinate donor countries' efforts. See the Doha Development Agenda Database at http://tcbdb.wto.org/index.asp?lang=ENG.

for their interests directly to DTI. While South Africa has large industries, such as the automotive, steal, textile, chemical and agricultural industry, which are represented by well-functioning private sector support institutions (such as NAAMSA and NAACAM in the case of automotives), the private sector in the BLNS countries is rather weak and only insufficiently organised. Only few companies have enough knowledge and experience to defend their interests and the national chambers of commerce and industry provide only few services for their members and are less demand-driven but more donor-driven (Meyn 2004b, c).[361]

However, few approaches of "private sector lobbying" exist in the BLNS countries. In Namibia, the "Agricultural Trade Forum" (ATF)[362], representing the interests of commercial farmers and agro-based industries and the "Namibian Manufacturing Association" (NMA), representing mainly the interests of the biggest holding in the country (Olthaver & List)[363] have jointly worked on the impact of North-South FTAs on the Namibian economy and informed their members about expected challenges. The ATF and NMA took further lead when the SADC EPA negotiation were launched on 8 July, 2004 and initiated "A declaration of concerned stakeholders", which was published in the "Namibian Economist", "The Namibian" and the Afrikaans speaking newspaper "Republikein".[364] In Swaziland, the Swazi Sugar Association (SSA) is defending Swaziland's interests in cane sugar exports and in Botswana the Botswana Meat Commission is lobbying for its interests. However, a joint-approach of national and regional businesses does not exist. There are endeavours within the BLNS countries to create similar interdisciplinary forums like NEDLAC but to date the

[361] The interviews with representative of the private sector support institutions in Botswana (BOCCIM, EAOB), Namibia (NCCI) and Swaziland (SCCI) revealed that they did not provide any information on the TDCA among their members. The few large companies in BLNS contacted government officials directly and received according information (see discussion in section 6.3).

[362] The Namibian Agricultural Trade Forum consists of the Meat Board of Namibia and the Namibian Agronomic Board.

[363] The General Manager of the Olthaver & List Company Group is also the Chairman of the Namibian Manufacturing Association (NAM). The Olthaver & List Company Group owns 13 companies in Namibia, employs 4,200-4,500 people and contributes around 4% to the annual GDP. Olthaver & List is involved in the Namibian fishing industry (Hangana Fishing), the beer business (Namibian Breweries), the milk and dairy production (Nammilk, Namibian Dairies), meat production (Windhoek Schlachterei), the hotel management, farming operations, marine engineering, banking and IT support (Reissner 2003).

[364] The article is titled "EU market access – first steps to new deal" and available at http://www.economist.com.na/2004/2july/07-02-03.htm. A detailed version of the views of SADC EPA stakeholders presented at the launch of negotiations can be obtained from the Epawatch website: http://www.epawatch.net/general/text.php?itemID=220&menuID=61, accessed 24/08/2004.

success is rather limited. In 2002, Swaziland has created the "National Consultative Network on Trade and Industry", which contains representatives from the Ministry of Trade, public enterprises, the chamber of commerce, and trade unions. However, this network has not produced any output and has hardly been recognized in public (Pato 2003).

In sum it can be stated that the private sector in the BLNS countries is comparably weak and that only few companies have the ability to lobby for their interests at the governments. However, even these companies, which are big in the context of the BLNS countries but tiny in international terms, lack the capacity to set through their interests in the EU market. As discussed in Chapter 3 and in Chapter 5.5 (Namibian fishing industry), BLNS companies have not able to build-up distribution and marketing networks in the EU and to disseminate information accordingly. Since BLNS companies are small and only insufficiently involved into international networks they are not represented in the EU market and are thus, in contradiction to large corporations in South Africa (such as the automotive sector) not able to lobby for their interest in the EU market.[365]

Another problem of the BLNS countries is their lack of domestic research capacities and a broad critical civil society providing valuable inputs to the debate. In 1998, the Batswana think-tank BIDPA has in cooperation with the British Institute for Development Studies (IDS) compiled an extensive study on the impact of the TDCA on the BLNS countries. It was mainly this study and subsequent seminars that informed the public in the BLNS countries about the challenges due to the TDCA. However, the research institutions in Botswana (BIDPA) and Namibia (NEPRU, IPPR) do not have the capacities to compile comprehensive trade analyses for all trade negotiations the countries are involved in. Lesotho and Swaziland do not have a national economic research institute and have also not received any input from national Universities.

Furthermore, BLNS parliamentarians are only insufficiently involved in FTA negotiations, since the economic sub-committee is very weak and the subcommittee of foreign affairs is not involved in trade negotiations. Thus, BLNS trade negotiators receive neither from the private sector nor from parliament or the civil society substantial inputs. In South Africa, trade negotiators briefed during TDCA negotiations the national parliament as well as the provincial parliaments, which were again able to influence trade negotiations via according requests (Bilal and Laporte 2004:14).

[365] In case of the EU-South Africa FTA, South African representatives from large businesses met regularly with key government officials as well as with EU trade negotiators (Bilal and Laporte 2004:15).

6.3 Case Study 3: Trade Capacity in Botswana and Namibia

The third case study aims to give a more detailed picture on Botswana's and Namibia's trade capacity gaps and countries' needs for technical assistance. Countries' constraints for effective participation in current trade negotiations and problems regarding the implementation of trade obligation are discussed with special reference to EPA negotiations and the implementation of the new SACU Agreement. Furthermore, interview partners' appraisal of the TDCA and its effect on BLNS economies are analysed, which in turn shall allow a perception of the knowledge and awareness of the institutions surveyed.[366]

6.3.1 Methodology and Characteristics of Interview Partners

The interviews were concluded in September and October 2003 in Windhoek and Gaborone by the means of a standardised questionnaire (see Annex III). In total, 17 interviews with public and private organisations were made in each country. In Botswana, standardised interviews were concluded with representatives from the Ministry of Agriculture, the Department of Trade and Consumer Affairs, the Botswana Institute for Development and Policy Analysis (BIDPA) (2), the Exporter's Association of Botswana (EAOB), the University of Botswana, the SADC Secretariat and a trade capacity building agency (2). In addition to these nine interviews, interviews with the Ministry of Finance, the Department of Customs and Excise, the Botswana Confederation of Commerce, Industry and Manpower (BOCCIM), Botswana Export Development and Investment Authority (BEDIA), the Bureau of Standards, a trade capacity agency, and the EU Delegation in Botswana were concluded. However, these interviews contain individual question modules and are not part of the following analysis but are used for the verification of theses and quoted accordingly.

In Namibia, standardised interviews (see Annex III) were compiled with representatives from the Ministry of Trade and Industry (3), the Ministry of Finance, Customs and Excise, the Bank of Namibia (2), the Namibia Manufacturing Association, the Namibia Chamber of Commerce and Industry (NCCI), the Namibian Investment Centre, the Namibian Economic Policy Research Unit (NEPRU), the Institute for Private Public Research (IPPR), and the Meat Board of Namibia/the Namibian Agronomic Board.

---

[366] However, since the focus of this section is on SACU countries' trade negotiation capacities, the results on the expected impact of the TDCA on national economies, competition situation and regional integration will only be presented briefly. The detailed analysis can be obtained from the author.

In addition to this, individual interviews were concluded with the Ministry of Agriculture, Water and Rural Development (2), the EU Delegation in Namibia, the Walvis Bay Corridor Group (WBCG), and a political foundation.[367]

Table 43 gives an overview of all interviews concluded in Botswana and Namibia.

Table 43: Overview of interviews conducted in Botswana and Namibia

	Companies	Ministries / Central Bank	Export Assistance Agencies	Private sector support institutions	Research Institutions/ University	SADC Secretariat / Donors	*Total*
Botswana	8	4	2	2	3	5	*24*
Namibia	13	8	1	2	4	2	*30*

All interviews in Botswana and Namibia were conducted with the management of the respective organisations and/or with experts who were working on the TDCA. With exception of four, all interview partners in Botswana were Africans. In Namibia, nine interviewees were black Namibians, six were white Namibians and four interview partners were European expatriates. None of the interviewees in Botswana and Namibia was female.

6.3.2 Awareness and Appraisal of the EU-South Africa Free Trade Agreement in Botswana and Namibia

Appraisal on the advantages and disadvantage of the TDCA: It is very difficult to assign the questioned effects to the TDCA in practise but the surveyed institutions tried to bring the theoretical assumptions of a North-South FTA into the right context for Botswana and Namibia. Though the appraisals of advantages of the TDCA were rather different among the interviewees, it became obvious, that there is no automatism to benefit from cheaper inputs, economies of scale and learning effects. It was pointed out that the dominance of South Africa firms in the SACU region, the non-provision of technical assistance by the EU, and the missing implementation of full cumulation with South African inputs is likely to hamper BLNS countries' benefit from the TDCA.[368] Respondents argued that it is not expected that South African companies pass on price advantages to the

[367] Two interviews, namely with the EU Delegation in Namibia and with the Ministry of Agriculture were made in June 2004.

[368] See Box 11 in section 3.

BLNS due to their market dominance. Taking into account that the South African economy has a high concentration degree (Kaplinsky et al. 2002:1169-72) and that South African retail stores and transport agents dominate the BLNS economies (Games 2003:34), this assumption can be regarded as valid. For Namibia, the options to benefit from cheaper EU imports due to the TDCA would increase if more goods were imported via the port of Walvis Bay, which is planned in the near future. Botswana on the other hand, benefits only if increased competition in the SACU market forces South African companies to pass on price advantages of cheaper imports.

The main disadvantages of the TDCA for BLNS were seen in increased competition by (subsidised) European goods, while the risk of trade diversion was only partly rated as relevant. Revenue losses seemed to be much more relevant for Namibia than for Botswana since Botswana has to a large extent already diversified its income base away from import tariffs towards indirect taxation. A similar picture of divergent opinions in Botswana and Namibia applied regarding the issue of competition, where most interviewees in Botswana highlighted consumer benefits while in Namibia producer losses were weighted much more importance. This might be explained by the fact that Namibia has a broader production range than Botswana and is rather negatively affected by competition from European firms.

The view prevalent in both countries regarding the impact of the TDCA on regional integration was negative. It was argued that the TDCA further complicates regional integration and had resulted in complex rules of origin for the SADC FTA. It was furthermore judged as disadvantageous that neither the provision of "full cumulation" with South Africa nor the provision of "diagonal cumulation" with other SADC countries has entered into force yet.

Generally, the interviewees in Botswana judged the impact of the TDCA on their economy less negative than the interview partners in Namibia. While most Namibian respondents referred to SADC when asking for the impact of the TDCA on regional integration, the interviewees from Botswana focussed on SACU, which was regarded as the "only regional integration framework that makes sense" by the majority.

Awareness of the TDCA: There was large conformity concerning institutions' appraisal on the awareness of national stakeholders on the TDCA (see Figures 61 and 62). In both countries, the awareness of the possible impact of the TDCA seems to be rather limited. Research institutions and the public sector are the only ones, which are regarded as well informed by the interviewees. In Botswana, some officials in the Ministry of Trade, Agriculture and Finance, who were involved in the re-negotiations of the SACU, were briefed on the TDCA by their South African counterparts. Moreover, certain researchers at BIDPA and some persons at the University of Botswana were working on the TDCA. In

Namibia, the SACU negotiators from the Ministries and from the Central Bank were also informed by their South African counterparts.

Figure 61: Awareness of the TDCA in Botswana (N=9)

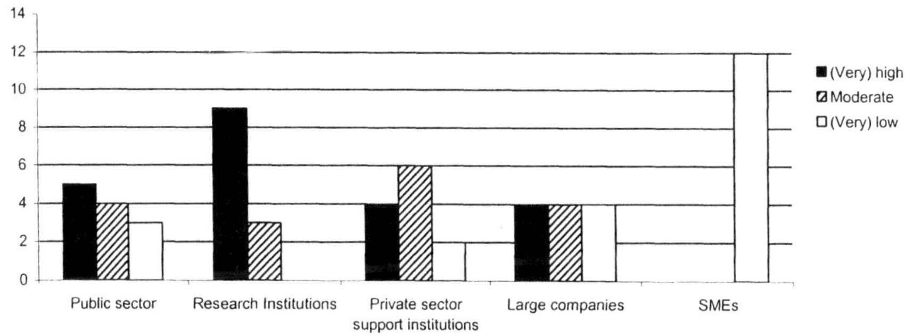

According to the interviewees, SMEs are not aware of the TDCA. Considering large companies' deficient knowledge in the South African automotive industry and the Namibian fishing industry, this appraisal is expected to be representative. However, since SMEs in the BLNS countries are hardly involved in manufacturing activities but in services (hairdressing, phone services, packaging of sugar, flour…), they are also not expected to be affected by the TDCA.[369]

Figure 62: Awareness of the TDCA in Namibia (N=12)

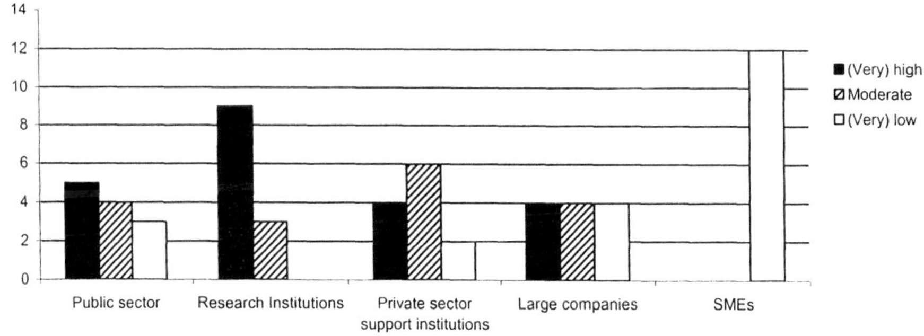

[369] If at all, manufacturing activities take place on a very small-scale, such as production of wedding dresses and fleece-nappies (Handschuh 2003).

Appraisal on the impact of the TDCA on diversification processes: The institutions surveyed saw only limited options how the TDCA could help Botswana and Namibia to diversify their export base. Two important advantages would be cheaper inputs and technical assistance. Once BLNS were able to benefit from these two factors, there would be options for companies' improved innovation capability, which could in turn offer the chance to stimulate investment. However, it was emphasised that it remains uncertain whether reduced price of European imports are passed on by South African retailers and transport agents and whether any technical assistance will be provided for industrial restructuring processes.

The options for stronger cooperation with European firms were judged more positive in Namibia than in Botswana. However, some interview partners demurred, arguing that that improved business contacts are rather unlikely since the TDCA is an agreement between governments that would not take private sector interests into account.

Companies' innovation capability, which might be stimulated by increased competition, was rated as limited by most interviewees. There would be only few large companies, which are neither innovative nor internationally competitive. The creation of market niches was rather expected to be survival strategies for SMEs than a contribution to the countries' product diversification process. In this context some institutions in Botswana also emphasised that European technical assistance – once it has been released – should be directed to the private sector. Specific funds given to SMEs might help the private sector to improve its ability to cope with the challenges inherent to the TDCA

Whether Botswana and Namibia will benefit from increased FDI because of the TDCA was disputed among the institutions surveyed. Around half of the interview partners in both countries argued that the TDCA would offer options to reap FDI since it helped to create a conductive environment, thus increasing the attractiveness of Botswana and Namibia as investment destination. The other half of respondents whereas argued that the TDCA is not linked to investment and that there are many other factors that decide about investment behaviours. As summed-up by one government official from Namibia: "*There is no evidence so far that there are linkages between the TDCA and expanded investment from the EU. Our major investors come from Asia. So is the TDCA really working?*"

Appraisal on the impact of the TDCA on the competition situation: As discussed in Chapter 3, most products that are of relevance for the BLNS are either excluded from the TDCA or only partially liberalised. However, the inclusion of agro-processed value added products, which are strongly associated to BLNS main agro-based products, such as processed meat products, flour based products, and canned fruits, might be detrimental for the BLNS.

The number of companies that are likely to be negatively affected by the TDCA is limited. As discussed, micro and small enterprises are mainly resident in the service sector. Medium enterprises again produce above all low-quality products for the domestic market, which are not exported to the EU (BIDPA/IDS 1998:64). It is therefore above few large food processing companies that are going to face increased competition.

In addition to increased competition in the domestic market, those companies that are involved in the export business to the EU are likely to face increased competition from South Africa. Since the preferences granted by industrialised countries are crucial for BLNS export companies, any agreement that contributes to the erosion of preferences is likely to affect the economy's export performance negatively. As one interview partner from a research institution in Botswana said: *"All industries that are sitting in this country do so because of our preferred market access under Cotonou and AGOA. If you take this away, they will remove immediately."*

Institutions' appraisals on the competition situation of the BLNS countries due to the TDCA reveal that the interview partners were only limited aware which products are likely to face increased competition. This again is problematic since it hampers an adequate information policy towards the private sector and is likely to result in a defensive attitude against the TDCA without considering important lesson that can be drawn, e.g. with respect to EPA negotiations. The OECD (2001:32) highlights the problem of limited knowledge of regional and multilateral trade agreements that is prevalent in many developing countries. This hampers effective participation and negotiation as well as the meeting of ongoing obligations resulting from the implementation of the agreement.

6.3.3 Technical Assistance and Training Needs

Technical assistance: The interview partners in Botswana and Namibia agreed that the countries need technical assistance in various fields to cope with the challenges of the TDCA. The training of customs official for instance is seen as crucial to improve the supervision of origin of imports. An official from the Department of Customs and Excise in Botswana summarises:

> *"There is a huge need to train our customs. They need computer literacy and the automatisation process has to be improved. Moreover, the attitude has to change: the customs are often more interested in the collection of duties than in the smoothening of trade flows. ... We need more knowledgeable custom officials and modern equipment."*

Customs also need to be trained to apply the regulations of the new SACU Agreement accordingly. A start was made with a joint seminar for customs from Botswana, Namibia and South Africa in 2003 (Valashia 2003).

Another relevant lack of capacity is judged to be the number of trade experts. In 2003 Botswana had two persons who represented the country in regional and international trade negotiations plus handful experts that dealt with these topics. Namibia also lacked of qualified staff to negotiate and evaluate the manifold trade agreements the country is involved in. The EU has started a € 3 million support programme in Namibia (2004-2007) to improve the policy formulation, coordination and execution of Namibia's trade policy. One major problem for the SACU countries is to build-up domestic trade negotiators. A high official from the Ministry of Trade and Industry in Namibia states:

> *"A person who is representing Namibia in trade negotiation must be able to perform in law and trade issues and link his knowledge to the social dimensions of these issues, which have to be discussed with the civil society. These people are very rare."*

However, it is not sufficient to enhance the capacities of individuals in trade negotiations and trade-related areas. As the evaluation of according projects has revealed, improved training for individuals in a given environment is likely to result in the leave of civil servants who are looking for better paid jobs as consultants in the private sector or at donor agencies. It is therefore important that institutional capacities are also improved (Solignac Lecomte 2001:19, 37).

Surprisingly, almost all institutions surveyed in Botswana stated that the country needs to improve its infrastructure and communication services to cope with the challenges of the TDCA though the country is ranked as most competitive African country by the World Economic Forum (2003).[370] According to the interviewees, Botswana needs an improved cargo air transport, better roads and more efficient transport services, improved railway services and a bridge over the Zambezi to connect the country with Zambia and to accelerate and facilitate intra-regional trade. Moreover, the interview partners named improved telecommunication and IT services, which are currently run by the state-owned telecommunication provider, as relevant to cope with an altered trading environment (See Figure 63).

[370] The competitiveness report of the World Economic Forum assesses the macroeconomic environment, the quality of public institutions and technology among 102 countries in the world. Overall, Botswana took the 36th place in 2003 (WEF 2003).

Figure 63: Surveyed institutions' appraisal about technical assistance required in Botswana (N=9)

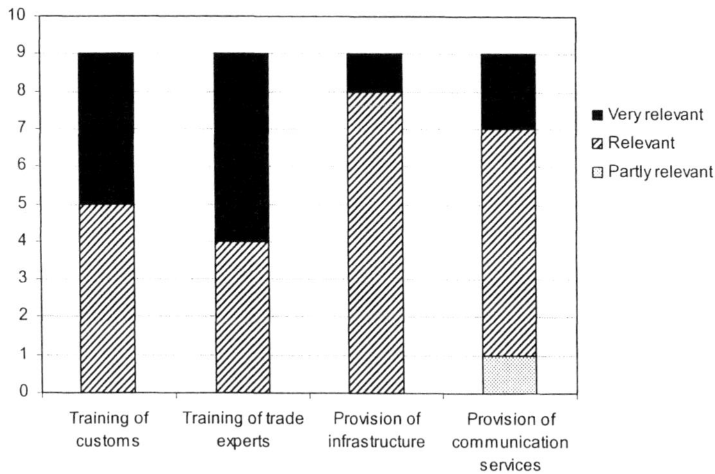

Figure 64: Surveyed institutions' appraisal about technical assistance required in Namibia (N=12)

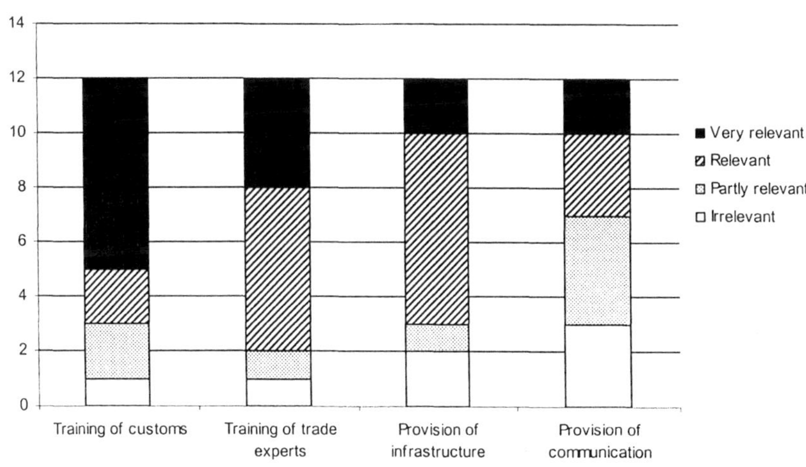

The Namibian institutions surveyed also judged a better infrastructure as crucial. This would be most of all necessary in rural areas, where basic infrastructure services like roads, schools, banks and communication services needed to be enhanced. Moreover, the expansion and advanced completion of intra-regional transport and service corridors, such as the Trans-Caprivi and Trans-Kalahari Highway were regarded as necessary to expand and diversify Namibia's trade with neighbouring countries. The provision of improved communication services would be necessary in rural but not in urban areas. Additionally, courses to improve citizens' computer literacy would be needed.

Training needs of the private sector: There was large accordance among the institutions that companies in Botswana and Namibia need to improve the quality and availability of their products, to increase capacities, and to upgrade their activities (see Figure 65 and 66).

To meet international standards is also regarded as important by the majority of institutions surveyed though both countries have according institutions since the late 1990ies. The Botswana Bureau of Standards (BOBS) and the Namibia Standards Information and Quality Office (NSIQO) are responsible to supervise that products made in their countries meet international standards. Moreover, the institutions serve as the countries' focal point on the WTO Agreement on Technical Barriers to Trade.[371]

Despite Botswana's and Namibia's efforts to comply with international standards there are still difficulties to serve all markets in industrialised countries. Thus, the USA goes beyond ISO standards and has called upon the SACU countries to harmonise their standards according to US-requirements. Namibia, South Africa and Botswana are currently working on the harmonisation of standards within SACU (Segomelo and Mbaiwa 2003). Many of the institutions surveyed complained that standards and health regulations would often act as non-tariff barriers and should be internationally codified.

Though nearly all institutions surveyed admitted the need to enhance production capacities, they also highlighted the difficulties for their countries: since Botswana and Namibia export above all unprocessed agricultural commodities and simple manufactured goods, it would also depend on market access and more generous rules of origin (i.e. the implementation of the provision of full cumulation provided under the TDCA) whether companies are able to expand production. There is also wide agreement among the institutions surveyed that

[371] The services provided by the BOBS and NSIQO are product and system certification, testing of health and safety provision, training for laboratories in quality and environment management, trade metrology and standardisation. Both countries have adopted ISO standards so that any company acting in the country can be ISO certified. It is most of all domestic, non-export-oriented companies that ask for assistance to meet the country's health and safety standards (Segomelo and Mbaiwa 2003).

the companies in Botswana and Namibia have to improve the availability of products and endeavour to upgrade products and services. Named options for upgraded activities were related to both, production and services, e.g. leather and processed beef production, improved marketing for meat, beer and fish products, polishing of diamonds, double transformation of clothing products, as well as improved transport and financial services, higher involvement of Batswana and Namibian citizens in the tourism industry, and the creation of a national or a SACU label to create a positive image and to make the country/region known overseas. The Namibian interviewees did further highlight the importance for Namibia to overcome the high dependency from the South African economy and to establish an own production and service base. However, concrete proposals how these upgrading processes can be managed were rare.

All interview partners in Botswana and Namibia regarded improved services by private sector support institutions as (very) relevant. Core competences like the promotion of SMEs and trade facilitation would be only insufficiently developed and the services provided would be often of limited use for the private sector. The Chief Executive Officer of the Namibia Chamber of Commerce and Industry (NCCI) stated self-critical: *"We need to collect and disseminate data, facilitate business linkages and export options, and improve the access to finance for some companies. However, the NCCI lacks of capacity. We do not have enough qualified people and do not pay enough to get good people."*

Figure 65: Technical assistance needs of the private sector in Botswana (N=9)[372]

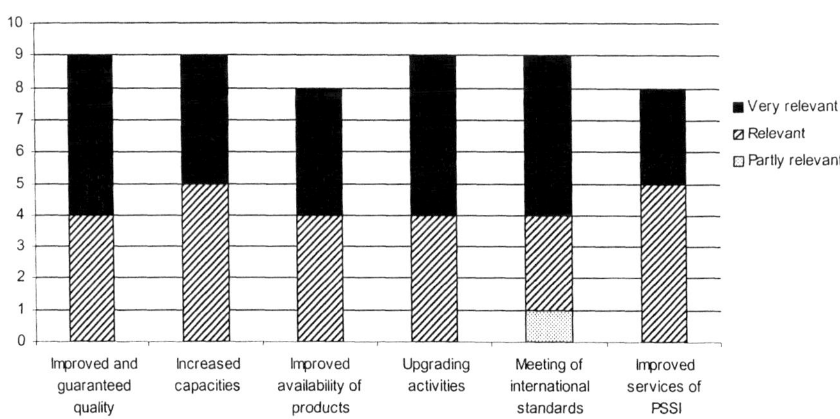

[372] The questions that relate to the international standards and service provision of private sector support institutions were only answered by eight of the institutions surveyed.

Figure 66: Technical assistance needs of the private sector in Namibia (N=12)

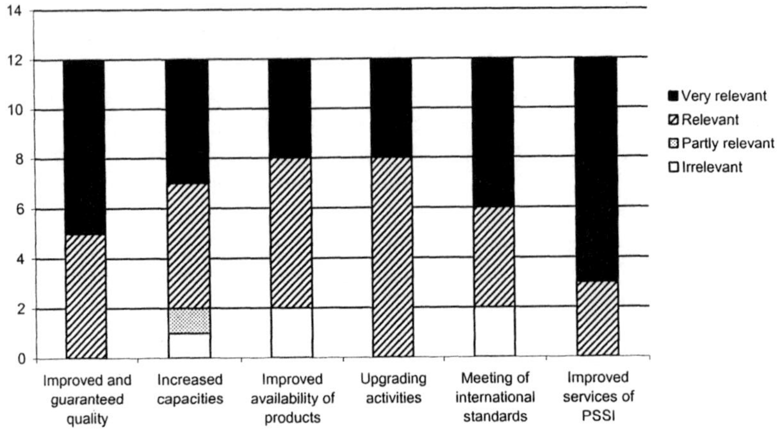

The interview results of companies' needs for technical assistance suggest that the private sector in Botswana and Namibia is not fully prepared to cope with the challenges of reciprocal trade relations with the EU. Thus, many companies would have difficulties to comply with qualitative and quantitative requirements in international terms and to diversify their product and service range towards higher value activities. Assistance provided by private sector support institutions was judged to be limited.

6.3.4 Information and Participation Policy

As can be obtained from Table 44, most interview partners were informed about the TDCA in 1997 or even earlier, either by their Governments or directly from South African Ministries (Trade, Finance or Agriculture). Some interview partners were informed at SACU institutional meetings or from their Permanent Mission in Brussels. Only few interviewees (two in Botswana and three in Namibia) were not officially informed but obtained information from the media.

Table 44: Summary of TDCA information policy in Botswana and Namibia

	Botswana *N=9*		**Namibia** *N=12*	
"When did you first hear about the TDCA?"	< 1997	2	< 1997	2
	1997	4	1997	5
	1998	2	1998	1
	1999	1	1999	4
Information source	Government:	2	Government:	2
	DTI/SA Ministries:	4	DTI /SA Ministries:	3
	Media/Internet:	2	Media/Internet:	3
	Embassy/Mission :	1	Embassy/Mission :	2
			SACU Forum	2
"Do you feel well informed about the TDCA and its impact on SACU?"	Yes:	4	Yes:	8
	No:	5	No:	3
			Partially:	1

Only three of twelve interview partners in Namibia but five of nine in Botswana stated that they do not feel well informed about the TDCA and its impact on their country. Statements about the information policy differed among the institutions surveyed: while those respondents who fell well informed regarded South Africa's information policy as good though no formal consultation took place, the other respondents criticised that information sessions were not on a regular basis and took often only place after South Africa had already negotiated with the EU.[373] Thus, BLNS concerns would not have taken sufficiently into account.

With exception of two interview partners in Botswana, who were involved in a TDCA impact study, none of the interview partners or their institutions provided any input to negotiations. The national business community did also not make any official input but the few large enterprises lobbied accordingly to reach the exclusion of their products. In Namibia it was in particular the Namibian Agricultural Trade Forum (ATF), which represents mainly commercial farmers, and the largest company group in the country, Olthaver & List, which lobbied for their interests when the TDCA was negotiated. In Botswana, no company was involved concerning this matter.

[373] Since the BLNS countries are not part of the TDCA, South Africa was not obliged to accommodate BLNS concerns though the South African authorities feel that they did their very best to do so (Smalberger 2003).

6.3.5 Appraisal on the Impact of the EU-South Africa Free Trade Agreement on Regional Integration and SACU's External Trade Relations

In a SADC context: Surveyed institutions' view on the TDCA's impact on regional integration in southern Africa was very similar. Around 90% of all interviewees stated that the TDCA would raise the need to integrate and increases the pressure on SADC to agree on common policies. Thus, the TDCA would have accelerated the process to agree on the liberalisation schedule of the SADC FTA.

The majority of interviewees did furthermore agree on the statement that the TDCA would lead to a higher level of trade liberalisation within the region since it would press ahead the implementation of the SADC FTA. The other respondents disagreed with this statement and claimed that the TDCA would rather force trade liberalisation by increased competition but not promoting it. Moreover, the TDCA would have resulted in complex rules of origin for the SADC FTA, which would have slowed down and not accelerated the implementation of the SADC Trade Protocol.[374]

Most respondents agreed that the TDCA has lead to a fragmentation of interests within SADC since it would constrain both, intra-regional trade and SADC's future trade relations with the EU.

In a SADC-EU context: When the interviews were taken, in October 2003, southern African countries had not finally decided in which framework(s) they are negotiating an EPA with the EU. Officially, SADC member countries decided at a summit in summer 2003 to negotiate in a SADC framework. However, DR Congo, Mauritius, Malawi, Zambia and Zimbabwe also opted for a "Eastern Southern Eastern Africa" (ESA) EPA at a COMESA summit in 2003. In fact, there was a lot of confusion and many speculations about EPA configurations before southern African countries finally announced their organisation in a SADC EPA and ESA EPA framework in early 2004.

Before this still alterable decision of EPA configurations was made, there were several options for BLNS to negotiate a WTO compatible trade arrangement with the EU, namely a) the accession of the BLNS countries to the TDCA, b) within a SACU EPA, or c) within a SADC EPA including all SADC countries (SADC-14 EPA).

Though the accession of BLNS countries to the TDCA might sound pragmatic, hardly any interviewee opted for such a configuration. It was emphasised that the TDCA has been negotiated between South Africa and the EU and does not foresee any accession. However, around 80% of interviewees in both countries shared the opinion that any EPA should include South Africa. Thus,

---

[374] This statement is confirmed by Akinkugbe (2000), Pallangyo (2000), and Kalenga (2004).

they proposed to re-negotiate the TDCA or at least those provisions that are in the interest of BLNS countries (Protocol preferences, safeguard measures...) and to create a SACU EPA. Only a minority of institutions (3 of 9 in Botswana and 4 of 11 in Namibia) opted for EPA negotiations in a SADC-14 framework. It was argued that the SADC countries would be economically too different to negotiate a common agreement with the EU.

The interview partners in Namibia were much more sceptical regarding the potential positive impact of EPAs on regional integration than those in Botswana. Thus, half of the interviewees in Botswana but only one in Namibia said that EPAs would promote regional integration. There was however scepticism whether the accommodation of different countries' concerns can appropriately be addressed appropriately.

Further free trade negotiations: In addition to EPA negotiations, the SACU countries were in late 2003 employed with negotiating FTAs with the USA, EFTA and MERCOSUR and by exploring options to negotiate FTAs with China, India, and Nigeria. When asking the institutions surveyed about their opinion on additional free trade agreements, namely with the USA and EFTA, a rather positive attitude appeared. The vast majority of interviewees in both countries shared the opinion that SACU countries' market access will improve or at least maintained when entering into an FTA with the USA and EFTA countries. BLNS membership in SACU would help them to "get a good deal" since the USA and EFTA countries are economically interested in South Africa. There were however also few respondents who argued that improved market access would mainly benefit South Africa, the only SACU country, which has identified market opportunities and which is leading negotiations with third countries. Thus, South Africa would formulate negotiation positions on behalf of all SACU countries while the BLNS countries largely follow the track.

In fact, in late 2003, when negotiations were already underway, Lesotho, Namibia and Swaziland had not analysed their trade flows and formulated a coherent negotiation strategy vis-à-vis the USA or the EFTA countries. Only the research institution BIDPA in Botswana was working on study identifying Botswana's interests in a SACU-USA FTA.[375]

Whether North-South FTAs are *per se* beneficial for SACU is disputed. Five of nine interviewees in Botswana and four of 12 in Namibia said that positive effects are likely to dominate in the long run. FTAs with industrialised countries would help the SACU countries to restructure their industries and to diversify their product range, reap FDI, generate new employment opportunities and to increase their competitiveness. Furthermore, FTAs with the USA and

---

[375] See Ndzinge (2003) for an analysis about chances and risks of a SACU-USA FTA on Botswana.

EFTA would help to reduce the dependency on the EU market, to minimize trade diversion in the southern African market and to benefit from cheaper consumer prices.

Four interview partners in Botswana and five in Namibia, on the other hand, shared a rather negative attitude regarding the impact of North-South FTAs on SACU and pointed out that the BLNS countries lack of production capacities so that improved market access would rather result in a shift of exports from the EU to the USA than to the expansion of exports. Thus, it would depend on the specific design of any agreement whether it is beneficial for development or not. On the other hand, it was also emphasised by most respondents that the maintenance of the status quo (AGOA, GSP) would not be a viable option for BLNS. Though AGOA has been extended until the end of 2015, it can be withdrawn at any time. Since a considerable amount of jobs depends on AGOA, the BLNS countries are highly interested in maintaining their preferential market access. However, "hidden" and complicate issues, such as a broad negotiation agenda that forces SACU countries to negotiate common regulations vis-à-vis their trading partners before having agreed on these issues in a SACU context, would make negotiations with industrialised countries very difficult.[376] Also detrimental competition, e.g. by subsidised products could harm SACU countries. Easy applicable safeguard measures as well as infant industry protection would therefore be crucial. Furthermore, the "support component" of a North-South FTA (technical assistance to comply with standards, increase product capacities etc.) should be formulated generous to *"allow us to swim"*.

Almost all respondents agree that SACU is "terribly" overextended with FTA negotiations. Considering the lack of appropriate human capital within SACU countries, the overloaded negotiation agenda, the time pressure, as well the relevance to coordinate overlapping arrangements, this appraisal does not take wonder. Nevertheless, most institutions surveyed in Botswana and half of all interviewees in Namibia prefer bilateral trade negotiations to multilateral trade liberalisation. It was argued that small countries interests could be more appropriate accommodated in bilateral or regional trade negotiations since *"your voice is not heard in the WTO forum"*. Thus, not only trade liberalisation but also issues like technical assistance and financial support could be negotiated. Moreover, the lack of progress in the WTO Doha Round would make it important to negotiate individual trade agreements. Contrary, six institutions in Namibia and two in Botswana shared the opinion that multilateral negotiations are superior to bilateral because of the limited capacities and negotiation power of the BLNS countries.

---

[376] As discussed in the Chapters 2 and 4, the development divergences and the non-harmonisation of industrial, agricultural and other trade-related policies, are major constraints for the SACU countries to develop a common negotiation strategy.

Figure 67: Expected impact of future SACU FTA negotiations on Botswana (N=9)

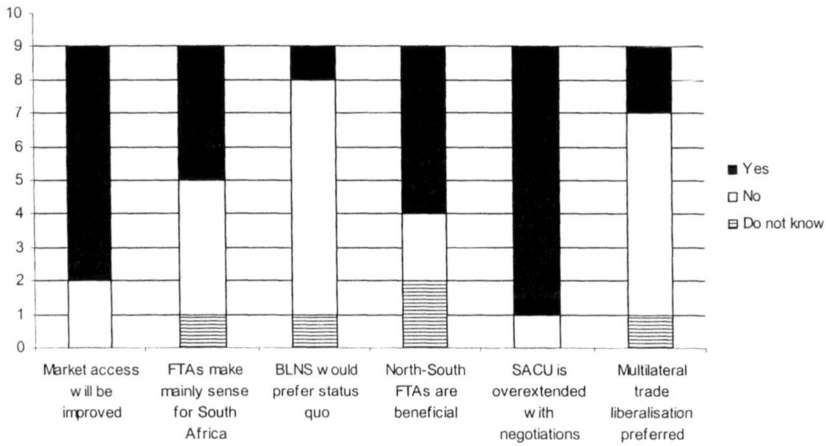

Figure 68: Expected impact of future SACU FTA negotiations on Namibia (N=12)

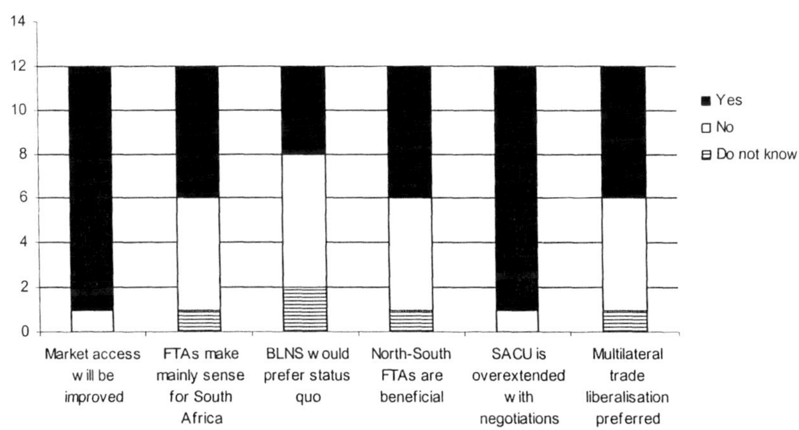

Whether SACU's manifold FTA negotiations are beneficial for the development of BLNS countries was discussed controversially among the institutions surveyed in Botswana and Namibia. Though there are chances like improved market access, the maintenance of preferential treatment and increased technical assistance, FTAs with developing countries also imply several risks for the SACU economies, such as revenue losses and detrimental competition. Moreover, missing preparations within the BLNS countries impede an optimal outcome of negotiations since market opportunities and export constraints are not identified.

6.4 Summary of Empirical Findings

The discussion showed that most interview partners in Botswana had a more positive attitude towards the TDCA than those in Namibia. The chances in form of cheaper inputs and consumer goods, trade creation, learning effects and (certain) diversification options were judged to dominate over the negative effects, such as harmful competition and revenue losses. Though the Namibian institutions did also emphasise the chances of the TDCA, they were more critical regarding the potential negative effects, such as detrimental competition and revenue losses. This critical appraisal of the Namibian interview partners might be explained by the fact that Namibia has a broader production base than Botswana, which is more likely to be negatively affected by increased competition. Furthermore, the country is much more dependent on tariff revenues than Botswana. In fact, Botswana is in a much better situation than the other BLNS countries: it has already diversified its income base towards indirect taxation and is expecting only small revenue losses due the restructuring of the CRP and trade liberalisation. Harmful effects of increased competition are likely to be limited since most of the products relevant for Botswana are excluded from the TDCA.

Botswana has chosen a very pragmatic approach and even adopted the TDCA liberalisation schedule though it is not part of the agreement.[377] The Namibian government whereas has not accepted that it is a *de facto* member of the TDCA and has refused its concurrence to the agreement. Though this policy is understandable since the EU refused to include the BLNS countries into TDCA negotiations, it remains doubtful that anything had been gained by this attitude. If Namibia would have been more cooperative, this might have helped to release technical assistance in time and to implement the provision of full cumulation.

Though it remains speculative to what extent the provision of full cumulation with South African inputs and company-related technical assistance would have contributed to BLNS countries' diversification efforts, it must be emphasised that both components offer at least some options to support diversification and industrialisation processes within the BLNS countries. It is therefore argued that the BLNS countries gave away chances to benefit from the TDCA. Namibia's

[377] As discussed in Chapter 3 (Box 11) Botswana's unilateral acknowledgement of the TDCA infringes against new SACU Agreement and the WTO Agreement.

argument, that its concurrence to the TDCA would have left the country without any forfeit in EPA negotiations does not convince: first of all, the EU has already *de facto* preferential market access to Namibia, and secondly, the country is of neglectable economic importance for the EU.

However, in the meanwhile BLNS countries' "concurrence" to the TDCA is not a topic anymore, since BLNS plus Angola, Mozambique and Tanzania decided to negotiate an EPA with the EU. This again is not only problematic from a regional integration point of view as discussed in Chapter 3 but also implies severe challenges for BLNS countries' trade-related capacities.

6.5 The Relevance of Trade Capacity Building for EU-SACU Trade Relations - What Needs to be Done to Improve BLNS Countries' Capabilities to Participate Effectively in Trade Negotiations?

When negotiating an EPA with the EU, the BLNS countries are supposed to formulate and set through their trade interests as well as their interests in trade related aspects, such as competition policy and government procurement. As the discussion in this Chapter has shown, the BLNS countries are heavily overextended with all aspects of negotiating effectively with the EU: the analysis of their trade flows, the formulation of trade interests, and the negotiation and lobbying power to set through their interest.

The lack of trade capacity at various levels is also confirmed by the empirical results from Botswana and Namibia, showing that the switch from preferential to reciprocal trade relations with the EU in addition to the admission of trade-related aspects that have not been harmonised within SACU yet, are an enormous burden for the BLNS countries. Additionally, BLNS capacities are strained by the negotiation of further FTAs and the implementation of existing agreements, above all the new SACU Agreement.

The overextension of BLNS countries to negotiate an EPA with the EU as well as the observer status of South Africa rise the question what support South Africa can provide to improve BLNS countries' trade capacity in EPA negotiations. As discussed, South Africa has offered technical assistance to the BLNS countries, which has been however not specified yet. Due to the experience South Africa gained during TDCA negotiations it could provide BLNS with valuable tips and establish important connections within the relevant stakeholders in the EU.

Having however a closer look at the SADC EPA, its inconsistency with regional integration within SACU and SADC and the problems it implies for deeper integration within SACU, it must be regarded as doubtful that South Africa is ready to support SADC EPA negotiations in the current configuration. Why should South Africa support the BLNS countries to negotiate an Agreement with the EU that undermines regional integration and incorporates trade-related aspects that are not part of the EU-South Africa FTA without getting anything in return?

It is rather likely that South Africa asks the EU "to stop the train" and to negotiate an EPA within a SACU framework. Since the EU needs, according to the new SACU Agreement, South Africa's concurrence for any arrangement with the BLNS countries, it can be assumed that the EU has a vital interest in an "acceptable" EPA, too. How such a SACU EPA could look like, how far it follows the EU-South Africa FTA, whether it incorporates trade-related aspects and whether special preferences for the BLNS countries will be included, remains speculative. What is however clear, is that the BLNS countries have a much better bargaining position once South Africa is "on board".

To date, all FTA negotiations SACU countries are involved in are still leaded by South Africa with only little input from BLNS. It is therefore necessary for the BLNS countries to evaluate the chances and risks of the single FTAs for their economies, to determine their interests and to formulate, together with South Africa, a common negotiation position to ensure that regional integration within SACU is not undermined. To achieve this, an inclusive trade negotiation strategy should be adopted, like South Africa did when negotiating the TDCA. To date, neither the public sector nor other relevant actors in the BLNS countries, such as trade unions and civil society organisation are sufficiently aware or included into trade negotiations. The involvement of domestic academics in providing relevant research and analysis is limited and the coöperation of government institutions at both, the national and regional level is not formalised but on *ad hoc* basis. To improve BLNS countries' trade capacities and to create an inclusive trade strategy in order to allow their effective participation in trade negotiations cannot be achieved in the short run but requires increased human and institutional capacities as highlighted in the following discussion.

Cost-benefit analysis

With exception of South Africa (TDCA) and Botswana (SACU-USA FTA), none of the SACU countries has undertaken a cost-benefit analysis of any of the forthcoming FTAs, investigated its trade flows with the USA, EFTA, Mercosur, SADC, identified niche products, and formulated chances and problems to tackle new export markets.[378] Swaziland, for instance was in late 2003, when negotiations with the USA were already underway for half a year, still busy to

[378] Though Namibia has not undertaken a cost-benefit-analysis, the Ministry of Agriculture has identified potential export products to the USA and its hindrances to enter the US-market, such as minimum quantities and labelling requirements (Bennett 2004). USAID is currently undertaking an impact study to evaluate the impact of SACU's FTAs with third countries. The study was requested by the SACU Secretariat (USAID 2005:5).

compile a list of its export products to the USA and to identify potentially new export products. If BLNS have already difficulties to identify their interests for trade in goods, it is not difficult to imagine how the situation looks like for trade in services, investment, intellectual property, government procurement, and trade facilitation. An analysis of potential costs and benefits of an FTA as well as the identification of interests are however indispensable to formulae a coherent national negotiation strategy. Giving the low production capacities within the BLNS countries it is insecure whether improved market access really results in expanded production and diversified export products or whether traditional exports are just shifted to another market.[379] It is therefore essential for the BLNS countries to investigate the options for expanded capacities and to identify niche products into new markets when entering into an FTA.

Build-up human capital and expertise in trade negotiations and strengthen institutional capacities

The interview results revealed the scarcity of resources in some fields, such as trade analyses, capacity of trade negotiators and institutional settings for effective implementation of trade agreements, such as customs administration and trade facilitation. These results do not surprise considering that BLNS countries were as members of the 1969 SACU Agreement not responsible for tariff policy, collection of excise and customs duties or trade policy formulation. In fact, BLNS countries current experience is similar to the one of post-Apartheid South Africa, which had to negotiate an FTA with its main trading partner while at the same time restructuring its economic policy and to formulate a new regional and bilateral trade policy that is consistence with its multilateral obligations.[380] Now the BLNS countries must, for the first time in their history, contribute to SACU's trade policy and identify and set through their interests vis-à-vis major trading partners. Considering that BLNS countries lack capacity at almost every level, this implies that their national and regional trade policy formulation is to a considerable extent dependent on international research and technical support of donors. To develop national capacities to identify their interests in trade negotiations and to formulate a strategy which mirrors the awareness of all aspects and challenges of a trade agreement as well as its coherence with national and regional trade policy and the overall development strategy, BLNS need technical

---

[379] Moreover, it must be analysed, whether the FTA results in an *effective* improvement for BLNS countries' market access or whether NTBs continue to hamper their exports. This is for instance feared for agro-based exports in case of the SACU-USA FTA (Bennett 2004).

[380] A South African trade negotiator summarised the challenges for the new South Africa as follows: *"Not many people appreciate the difficulties encountered in trade negotiations when time is of the essence and one's own national policy framework is not finalised. The new South Africa was forced to think anew about almost every aspect of society and the economy."* (Smalberger 2000:48).

assistance.[381] Thus, national administration and analytical capacities need to be improved and all stakeholders, from Ministries over standard agencies to private sector representatives, need to be included. However, the consultancy process can only be successful is strong political commitment towards an inclusive trade strategy is given (Dunlop *et al.* 2004:11). The relevance of well-prepared trade flow analyses and a coherent negotiation strategy cannot be overestimated as a South African negotiator of the TDCA emphasises: *"There is no substitute during tough negotiations for a good argument and proper preparation."* (Smalberger 2000:49).

In this context it is also the communication, coordination and cooperation among national Ministries that needs to be improved, e.g. between the Ministry of Agriculture and the Ministry of Trade and Industry in Namibia. Formal information mechanisms between Ministries need to be developed and responsibilities must be clearly defined. Furthermore, effective linkages to the national business sector and to the other SACU Ministries need to be expanded to allow a sort of regional trade strategy before the new SACU Agreement has been implemented. As the experience of South Africa during TDCA negotiations showed, the leading roles of the Department of Trade and Industry (DTI), high political commitment and government leadership, and a strong involvement of all relevant stakeholders into negotiation processes was key for success (Bilal and Laporte 2004:10-3).[382]

Effective participation of the private sector, parliamentarians and civil society in trade negotiations

For southern African countries, it is crucial to establish an international trade forum when negotiating EPAs like South Africa did when negotiating the EU-South Africa FTA. Like this, the private sector would be (indirectly) involved in discussions, influence the agenda, and formulate requirements for technical assistance without biasing negotiations towards the protectionist demands of few

[381] The United States Agency for International Development (USAID) is providing trade capacity support in the SADC region since 2002 when the Trade Hub was established in Gaborone, Botswana. The Trade Hub is organising trade capacity workshops, undertaking research and providing trade seminars for private sector representatives and Parliamentarians (USAID 2005).

[382] The DTI lead negotiations but worked closely with the Ministry of Agriculture and the Department of Foreign Affairs. The Ministry of Agriculture established the Agricultural Trade Forum, where the private sector made his voice heard – from large exporters to small farmers. Like this, close consultation not only with key industries but also the agricultural sector was guaranteed. The Department of Foreign Affairs coordinated the international negotiations, e.g. by linking with the Embassy in Brussels (Bilal and Laporte 2004:13-7).

large companies.[383] A joint approach, including all (formal) businesses and all other relevant actors, such as trade unions, research institutions and government officials would also offer the chance to channel information on trade negotiations to the public and avoid a "closed-shop". Moreover, it helps to save time and to bundle different interests in one forum (Bilal and Laporte 2004:17).

However, to get involved, a strong commitment of the according interest groups is crucial. As discussed, the private sector in the BLNS countries is weak and only to a limited extent organised. Demand-driven private sector support institutions that are capable to fund and manage themselves are however a prerequisite for effective partnering. To date, the ATF/MFA in Namibia and the Sugar Association in Swaziland are the only private sector support institutions that got involved in trade policy formulation.

In addition to the private sector, it is also important that the BLNS countries include parliamentarians and other parts of the civil society (such as research institutions, trade unions and NGOs) into their trade policy. Though participants in trade policy formulation within the BLNS countries are only few compared with developed countries, where well-organised private sector support, research institutions and parliaments exists, an inclusive approach is nonetheless relevant. Otherwise, governments' trade policy bears the risk that it does not fit into the country's overall development strategy and is not carried by the population. As discussed, South Africa applied an inclusive approach when negotiating the TDCA, including all Ministries concerned, private sector representatives, national and federal parliaments, social and economic stakeholders (such as trade unions and research institutions), and foreign expatriates. Lewis et al. (2004 :163) judge:

> *"Indeed it appears that the South African government has been unique in the space that it has given to civil society, notably business and labour, in the preparation and conduct of trade negotiations. This effective extension of tripartism to the international arena has undoubtedly contributed to the consistency of South Africa's trade policy and is a ringing endorsement of the benefits of participatory governance of trade policy formulation."*

Obtain knowledge about EU negotiation mechanisms

To obtain knowledge about the EU's trade strategy, to lobby for BLNS interests and to gain public sympathy in the EU, as well as to understand the complex decision-making process of the EU, are regarded as crucial factors for the successful outcome of trade negotiations.

---

[383] In this respect, Bilal and Laporte (2004:20) point out the relevance that the private sector presents the expected impact of an FTA well-founded and in written form so as to provide trade negotiators with relevant insights to be used during negotiation process.

Again, BLNS can learn from South Africa, which created a comprehensive network of formal and informal contacts in the EU and experienced the complexity of the EU's decision-making process (Bilal and Laporte 2004:23-4). Moreover, expertise from EU-based NGOs can help the BLNS countries to gain important insights into negotiation mechanisms.

Implementation of the new SACU Agreement and harmonisation of trade-related policy fields

Though the new SACU Agreement has not been implemented yet, SACU is negotiating as "block" with the USA and EFTA and has already concluded an FTA with MERCOSUR.

As discussed extensively in the Chapters 2 and 4 it is crucial for SACU to move towards deeper regional integration and to develop common trade negotiation machinery that does not only represent South Africa's interest in trade negotiations. Considering the limited resources in all SACU countries, a regional approach can further help to pool capacities and resources in the most effective way and improve the representation of the region's interests. The example of the CARICOM regional negotiation mechanism shows that a clear mandate and defined responsibilities can help small countries to negotiate effectively in behalf of the region though it does not substitute for national preparations (Dunlop *et al.* 2004). However, the creation of a regional negotiation mechanism requires a strong commitment towards deeper regional integration of all member countries since *"In the end, a regional process can only be as strong and as fast as the national member countries want to go."* (Dunlop *et al.* 2004:22).

Summarising SACU countries experiences and deficiencies of trade capacities it can be stated that the creation of an effective trade policy framework is a long-term goal, which requires major investments in institutional and human capacities and a strong private sector – prerequisites which are to a certain extent given in South Africa but not within the BLNS countries. Donor agencies can support the process of trade capacity building. It is however important that the recipient's national sovereignty with respect to its trade policy formulation is accepted and that the trade and development interests of a donor country do not infringe. Thus, it is mainly the developing country's ability to make independent decisions regarding its trade policy that should be strengthened. Such an approach is however often not given since most trade reforms in African countries are donor-driven and lack "ownership".[384] The EU's technical assistance for EPA ne-

[384] See Solignac Lecomte (2001:21-44 and 2003) and Prowse (2002) for an evaluation of successive and limitative factors of effective trade capacity building and the problems of donor activities' coordination. In 2002/02 donor countries' trade-related technical assistances accounted for 4.8% of total development aid (OECD 2003:4).

gotiations is no exemption in this respect. Prowse (2002:1244-5) defines the prerequisites for successful trade capacity building as follows:

> *"The success of ...* [trade capacity building] *can only be determined over the medium-term taking into account the extent to which the trade agenda including the policy recommendations are meaningfully included into the country's development process, and the extent to which bilateral and multilateral agencies continue to respond to the capacity building needs ... Ultimately, success can only be defined on the basis that realised trade improvements will promote growth and contribute to welfare gains."*

At the end of the day, the lack of trade capacity is only part of the overall problem of economic underdevelopment. It cannot be tackled in isolation and small, sparely populated developing countries like the BLNS that fight with limited resources against numerous problems, such as widespread poverty and high income inequality, low production capacities and high dependency on few export products, high HIV/AIDS incidence and poor public services, have to focus on the most urgent needs (Rodrik 2001). Though trade capacity building becomes more and more important and should not be neglected because of more urgent policy fields, it needs to fit into the overall development strategy of the SACU countries. Nevertheless, trade capacity support is important for the BLNS countries, in the light of current SACU-EU trade relations and with respect to deeper regional integration within SACU. The BLNS countries do not only need to identify and articulate their interests but must in cooperation with South Africa also formulate a coherent trade strategy that is in accordance with SACU's trade and development policy. This requires that BLNS governments' are fully committed to the successful implementation of the new SACU Agreement and the formulation of a common SACU trade strategy vis-à-vis the EU. As already discussed in Chapter 3 and as revealed by the interview results with institutions in Botswana and Namibia, any trade agreement with the EU needs to incorporate *all* SACU countries. However, to let the SACU countries negotiate with "one voice", the institutional framework of the new SACU Agreement needs to be implemented. For this, the BLNS countries require external support to expand their institutional and human capacities, to improve the inclusion of non-state actors and the communication between national Ministries as well as between the single SACU member states.

7 Syntheses, Recommendations and Outlook of the Study

7.1 Analytical and Strategic Syntheses

The synopsis drawn in Figure 69 gives an overview of the theoretical and empirical development chain of EU free trade agreements with southern African countries as discussed throughout the study. The different external and internal factors, such as a rapidly altering trading environment, WTO regulations, the end of the bi-polar world but also the worsening socio-economic conditions in most ACP countries had resulted in the end of unilateral preferences and had contributed to the dominance of the theory of free market forces according to which an open trading environment is a successful development tool *per se*. According to the EU's concept of North-South FTAs reciprocal trade agreements should benefit African countries as an FTA with their main trading partner enables them to benefit from competitive inputs, technology and learning effects. The different factor endowment is supposed to stimulate the division of labour and a competitive environment should promote an optimal factor allocation and innovation. Revenue losses are supposed to be compensated by alternative income sources and increased economic activities while safeguard measures can be applied in the event destructive competition. To avoid a hub- and spoke trade relationship and to reduce the dominance of EU bargaining power, the EU promotes its concept of "open regionalism" according to which southern African "spokes" integrate, thus, building-up a counterweight to their Northern trading partner.

The study showed on the example of the SACU countries that this simple theory of causality between North-South FTAs and economic development is unlikely to become realised because the effects of an EU FTA on regional integration and industrial development within SACU are much more complex.

Figure 69: Synopsis I - The impact of EU free trade agreements on economic development and regional integration in southern Africa

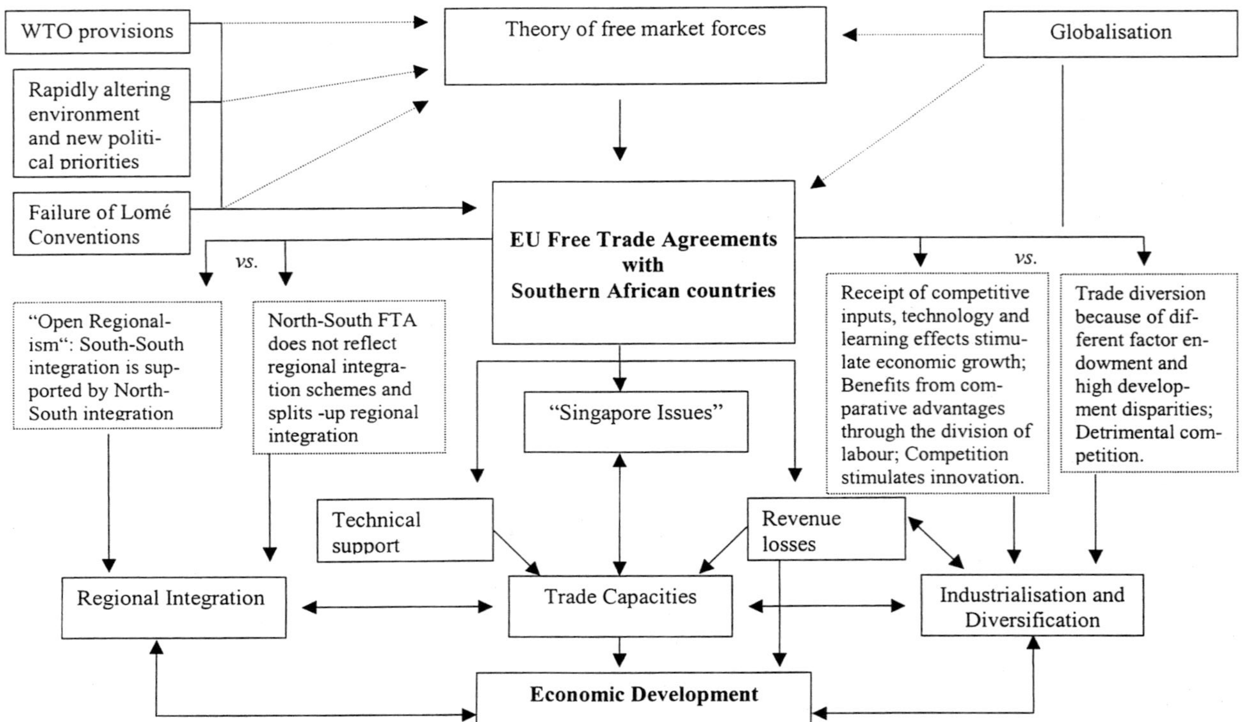

SACU countries' motivations for regional integration can be only partly explained by the theoretical assumptions of regional integration and are also a result of South Africa's economic and political dominance in the region. Due to the different development degrees and economic imbalances, SACU is more likely characterised as a North-South integration scheme than a South-South integration scheme. The polarisation between South Africa and BLNS has been aggravated by EU trade policies characterised by preferential treatment for the BLNS countries and reciprocity towards South Africa. With its different approaches of FTAs towards southern African countries, the EU has split-up regional integration within SADC and has seriously undermined deeper regional integration within SACU. Southern African countries are not in a position to avoid the perpetuation of a hub- and spoke relationship by integrating in a South-South framework before entering into a North-South trade agreement since regional integration has been hardly driven by economic considerations and is still in its infancy. Whether the assumed positive effects of North-South FTAs on industrial development and countries' diversification efforts are realised is doubtful, too. The immediate effects of revenue losses and increased competition from EU imports on the few BLNS industries were underestimated. Thus, the restructuring of the CRP and SACU's trade liberalisation approaches have resulted in diminishing revenues for the BLNS countries for which customs are still the major income source. Furthermore, some products that are of relevance for the BLNS countries, such as processed food products, will face increased competition in the SACU market. This is worrying if one considers BLNS countries' small manufacturing production base and their difficulties for economic diversification in a customs union that involves South Africa. Here, the interdependent relationship between revenues and economic development becomes apparent. Revenues can help to stimulate industrial development (e.g. by public investment) and economic development (e.g. by social expenditures), while economic development enables an economy to increase and diversify its income sources. A similar interdependency exists between trade capacities and economic development (see Figure 69). The capacity to analyse its trade flows, to formulate trade interests, to set through these interests in regional and international negotiations, and to implement trade obligations, are crucial for a country's ability to benefit from trade agreements, which in turn are supposed to stimulate economic development. As the discussion in Chapter 6 showed, the BLNS countries lack as a result of their economic underdevelopment the capacity to trade at the institutional, administrative and human capital level. Revenue losses, complex trade agreements, and strict time schedules for the negotiation and implementation of agreements aggravate this lack of trade capacity and avoid that BLNS benefit optimally from the trade agreements they are involved in. It is therefore argued that technical assistance and trade capacity support is a prerequisite but not a sufficient condition to build-up trade capacity in the BLNS countries. Only a long-term development process that takes SACU countries' interdependent processes of deeper and wider regional integration, external trade relations, industrial development and diversification efforts, as well as countries' capacities to cope with challenges of an altering trading environment into account, and which links these processes to the countries' economic development strategy, can be successful. This requires a development-oriented state which regulates market processes without undermining their positive effects on economic development. The policy tools applied in the South African automotive industry and the Namibian fishing industry are examples of what successful industrial policies destined to support economic development in the SACU countries can look like. The characteristics of these two manufacturing industries, their international linkages, and the different national policies in place, show that a country's trade policy that is supposed to support economic development encompasses much more than trade liberalisation and also has to take national development strategies and the embedding of key sectors into their socio-economic environment and international value-chains into account. The synopsis drawn in Figure 70 illustrates the contradictory impacts an FTA with the EU has on the South African automotive and the Namibian fishing industry. Though sectors' export orientation to the EU offers some chances, such as the attraction of FDI, which would for instance allow the modernisation of the Namibian fishing fleet, the inclusion of these sectors into an FTA with the EU affects the industrial development policies in place negatively. Moreover, a North-South FTA does not necessarily improve companies' international linkages and their position in the global value chain. Thus, its net effects on economic development remain insecure.

Figure 70: The impact of an EU free trade agreement on the South African automotive and the Namibian fishing industry

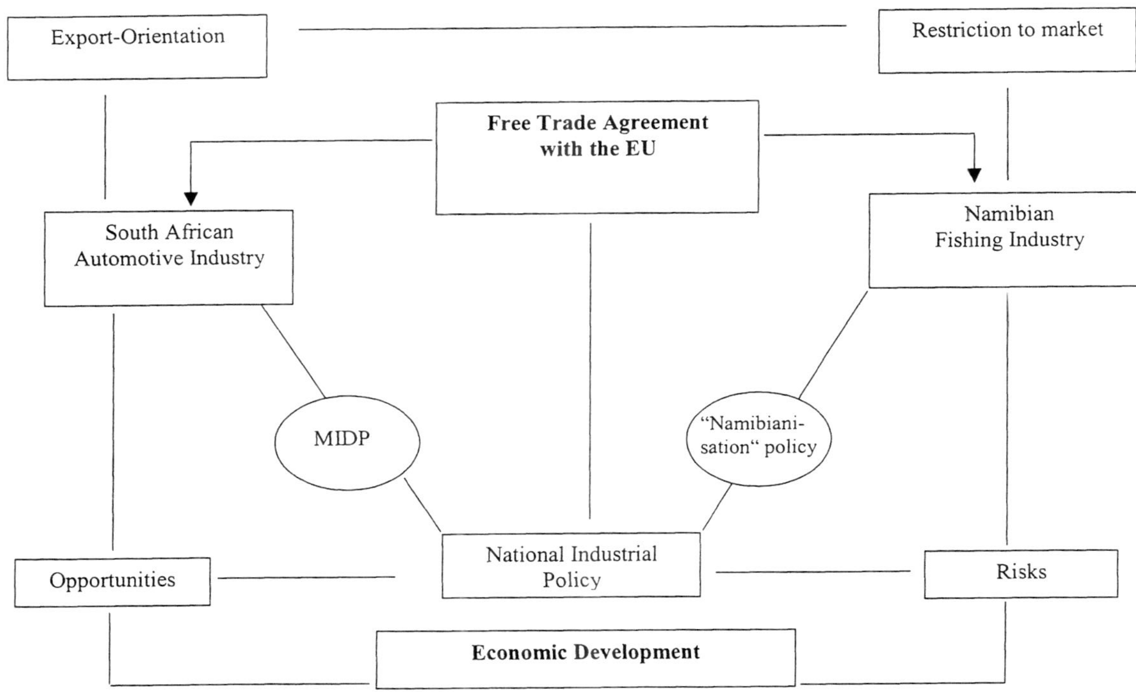

7.2 Appraisal of the effects of EU Free Trade Agreements

7.2.1. On Regional Integration within SACU

With the ratification of the new SACU Agreement, member states have reformed the CU considerably. The democratised SACU Agreement emphasises member countries' commitment to work towards deeper regional integration and their willingness to establish common institutions that rule in the interest of all member countries and speak with one voice towards third parties. However, to date, the new SACU Agreement is not much more than a framework. For its proper implementation, the parties have to move towards a common trade-related agenda, for instance in the fields of technical cooperation, agricultural policy, competition law and industrial policy. Despite the expected gains to be derived from deeper integration, such as higher trade volumes and investment flows, improved distribution and marketing systems, simplified procedures and, in the end, higher growth rates and improved economic development, it must be remembered that it is hard work to achieve deeper integration. This is much more the case in an integration framework like SACU, which covers two very different economy types with respect to size and levels of development. Due to their different economic development levels, South Africa and BLNS have also different policy focuses and development strategies, which make the agreement on common policies very difficult. Furthermore, the BLNS countries lack capacities in the fields of customs administration, documentation, and statistical compilation as well as in their missing expertise to conduct tariffs and investigate trade remedies. This raises concerns regarding the effective implementation of the new Agreement including the revenue formula and BLNS countries' ability to manage the Common Revenue Pool (CRP) effectively.

It became clear that the new SACU Agreement offers the BLNS countries improved options to set through their interests but also implies disadvantages and challenges for them. They have lost "economic security" in form of secure tariff revenues from the Customs Revenue Pool and have to build administrative capacities to participate in the democratised regional body. If this fails, the whole integration process in SACU is likely to fail, leading to the continuation of South Africa's political dominance. However, it is also in South Africa's self-interest to promote the implementation process and to help the BLNS countries to build-up institutional and administrative capacities. Regional integration can only work if *all* parties feel that they gain from the integration scheme. In case that the new SACU Agreement implies only revenue losses for the BLNS countries without accommodating their interests and without reducing the political dominance of South Africa, SACU faces the risk that its integration process will not be driven further. In fact, the driving forces and stumbling blocks for deeper regional integration within SACU are both, internal and external. The motivation for deeper integration and more equal participation of regional decision-making was internally driven - by the BLNS countries who wanted to overcome the *de facto* unilateralism of South Africa within SACU. The lack of progress in implementing the new Agreement is a result of internal capacity problems but also of missing political will of all parties to set the new institutions effectively into place. However, the need for deeper economic integration and the successful implementation of common policies will become more and more important for SACU countries' external trade relations. SACU is already negotiating several bilateral trade agreements as a "block" but is far away from speaking with "one voice". It is still South Africa that leads negotiations while the BLNS countries largely follow the track without having formulated a negotiation strategy consistent with national development goals or harmonised with their CU partners. South Africa's focus on trade with developed countries and its focus on selective FTAs, which mirror only insufficiently the trade interests of the BLNS countries, complicate regional integration in SACU. To date, South Africa has not acted as "engine of integration" and promoted the implementation of the new SACU Agreement. This is however necessary if a further economic polarisation in SACU and reservations against South Africa's economic and political hegemony is to be avoided. Deeper regional integration within SACU is however not only constrained by the different development degrees of member countries and the lack capacities but also by SACU countries' different trade agreements with the EU. When the EU entered into an FTA with South Africa in 2000 it took South Africa's SACU membership and thus, the direct affection of the FTA on the BLNS countries only insufficiently into account. By the time the agreement was negotiated, it became more and more obvious that non-reciprocal trade arrangements with developing countries have come to an end and that the ACP countries are no homogenous group, which would allow a common positive discrimination under WTO regulations. However, since there was also a lot of opposition against North-South FTAs and since the EU-South Africa FTA was the first North-South FTA with an African country, it was politically easier to deal only with South Africa and to leave the BLNS countries to the Cotonou Agreement. What was however neglected, was the negative impact the TDCA has on regional integration in southern Africa – on both, SACU and SADC. This detrimental effect first became apparent when negotiating the SADC FTA, where South Africa excluded sectors and insisted on complex rules of origin, thus following in large parts the TDCA. From 2002 on, when African countries had to announce in which configuration they were going to negotiate an EPA with the EU, the counterproductive effects of the TDCA on regional integration in southern Africa became very evident. The TDCA has resulted in SADC's split-up, dividing the integration framework into South Africa, the SADC EPA, and the ESA EPA. Actually, southern African countries are the only ACP countries that are not negotiating within their original regional integration schemes but within the political constructs of a SADC EPA and an ESA EPA, hardly mirroring their economic and strategic long-term interests in regional integration. Taking as example the SADC EPA: it comprises four of five members of a functioning customs union and three least developed countries. The countries of the SADC EPA hardly trade with each other, have not reached any degree of economic integration and are thus not able to create a common negotiation body. Moreover, they have as LDCs and non-LDCs, different interests when negotiating with the EU and do, in contradiction to SACU, not share the same legal and administrative traditions. Nevertheless, these individual countries of the SADC EPA are requested to a) form a common external tariff vis-à-vis a major trading partner and b) to negotiate trade-related aspect, such as regulations for competition policy and intellectual property rights with this trading partner as a block. It has become obvious that this approach which the EU calls "open regionalism" is not working in southern Africa. Apart from the non-existent level of economic integration within the SADC EPA, the BLNS countries are according to Art. 31 of the new SACU Agreement not allowed to entering into external trade relations without South Africa's concurrence. Though South Africa is attending the EPA negotiations as observer it remains doubtful that it will agree if the SADC EPA differs considerably from the TDCA. To date, South Africa has only liberalised trade in goods vis-à-vis the EU. Trade in services, the protection of intellectual property rights, competition policy, investment policies, and government procurement whereas are not part of the agreement and have also not been harmonised in a SACU context. Nevertheless, the BLNS countries are as part of the SADC EPA supposed to comprise various trade related aspects at stricter standards than hitherto agreed in the WTO framework. South Africa's concurrence to such an arrangement must be regarded as very unlikely.

7.2.2 On the Development Aspects of Future Trade Relations with the BLNS Countries

Trade between the BLNS countries and the EU shows a complementary pattern that is characteristic for trade relations between developing and industrialised countries. BLNS exports to the EU are dominated by primary and labour-intensive manufactured goods, while their imports are predominately capital-intensive manufactures. This trade structure and the high development disparities between the EU and southern African countries can lead to high trade imbalances. Whether such a "hub-and-spoke" trade relationship could be avoided by EPAs, as envisaged by the EU, remains doubtful since no integrated "spokes" exist that could form a counterweight against their powerful trading partner. South Africa locked the BLNS countries into the TDCA which had the effect that SACU's trade relations with the EU are determined. For the BLNS countries this implies a) increased competition for relevant agro-based products of in both markets, the EU and the SACU, without having improved their market access to the EU; b) significant revenue losses; and c) severe challenges for regional integration and their trade related capacities. Though the EU underlines that EPAs are above all development tools, supposed to integrate ACP countries into regional and international markets, there is the fear that trade liberalisation is being used as substitute for development policy. One indication is that EPAs are negotiated by the European Commission's Directorate-General (DG) Trade while the TDCA was negotiated by DG Development emphasising that it is only part of South Africa's overall trade and development strategy with development cooperation being an important component.

The major problem of free trade agreements in form of EPAs is that they fail to address structural obstacles to trade. Thus, it has not become clear yet how supply-side constraints that hamper BLNS countries exports, such as high transit and communication costs, low production capacities, and lack of export market information should be addressed. Furthermore, it is insecure to what extent BLNS countries' access to the EU market will be improved. Quantitative and timely restrictions for exports, tariff escalation for processed agricultural products, complex rules of origin that hamper diversification efforts and restrictive Sanitary and Phytosanitary Standards (SPS) exceeding those of the WTO are severe barriers for BLNS exporters. Additionally, the EU market is becoming less and less attractive because of eroding preferences as a result of market liberalisation and the CAP reform. However, the CAP reform has not reduced its negative external effects on the BLNS countries. On the contrary, the switch from product support to direct farmers' support while maintaining the total level of subsidies has resulted in reduced prices of commodities and has increased the international competitiveness of agricultural and simple agro-processed EU exports. The situation for southern African countries has therefore worsened: reduced EU intervention prices and increased costs to comply with EU standards on the one hand and increased competition in domestic markets by competitive EU products, such as wheat, beef and poultry, on the other hand. Another concern of EPAs is that the different development needs of southern African countries are not sufficiently respected since the SADC EPA and the ESA EPA comprise both developing and least developed countries. Though the LDCs keep their "improved" market access under the EBA initiative (which is hardly used and regarded as inadequate due to restrictive rules of origin) they will be treated like developing countries on the import side when agreeing on a CET with the EU in one EPA group. The decision of LDCs to opt out of EPAs and to maintain non-reciprocal trade relations under the EBA initiative is also not feasible since southern African countries are not in a position to warrant the rules of origin. A further worry regarding the development dimension of EPAs is that the EU pursues to a considerable extent economic and strategic interests such as the inclusion of services and the "Singapore Issues" (competition, intellectual property rights, government procurement, and trade facilitation). The BLNS countries have not even developed/fully implemented a national competition policy, let alone a harmonised regional position. How should they negotiate on this issue towards an external trading partner? Furthermore, the EU failed to convince African countries on the positive development impacts when including trade-related aspects into EPA negotiations. In light of the enormous power imbalances there is the fear of African countries that they will not have the chance to develop their own trade-related policies but have to accept the WTO *plus* regulations the EU wants to set through.

How EPAs concretely look like is still unknown but it is evident that they are not part of southern African countries' development strategy. In fact, no "regional development strategy" that matches with EPA configurations exists and southern African countries only agreed to negotiate EPAs because of their lop-sided dependency on EU preferences. A viable alternative to EPAs as announced by the EU for all those non-LDC ACP countries that do not want to enter into EPA negotiations does not exist. The inclusion of ACP countries into the GSP would imply a significant erosion of preferences, most of all for those countries that benefit from the Commodity Protocols, and any agreement that treats ACP countries better than other developing countries would infringe with WTO provisions if no FTA exists. It is therefore still unknown how an alternative agreement to EPAs that offers ACP countries similar market access than under Cotonou could look like.

7.2.3 On SACU Countries' Industrialisation Strategies and Industrial Policy Options

Ideally, African producers move from a buyer-driven chain, i.e. a labour-intensive industry where the critical governing role is played by the buyer (generally a global company) to a more valuable producer-driven chain, i.e. a capital-intensive, high-technology industry where the producer is responsible for assisting the efficiency of suppliers and customers. However, such a shift implies the extension of activities towards an all-embracing product development and marketing, which requires an active industrial policy, the promotion of innovation, and great efforts with respect to infrastructure services, human capital building, structural policies and effective support schemes on the firm level. As the discussion in Chapter 4 showed, South Africa is the only SACU country which has been able to enter into some high valuable, dynamic product markets, such as beverages, chemicals and automotives. Manufacturing activities in the BLNS countries on the other hand relate first of all to the upgrading of existing products and services. BLNS diversification efforts are inhibited by their size and low population, a narrow production base with insufficient backward and forward linkages that makes it difficult to attract foreign investors, high transportation costs, shortage of skilled labour, and limited protection options for infant industries due to their SACU membership. The BLNS countries show a dualistic industry: the non-mineral export-oriented sector is highly dependent on foreign inputs and hardly linked to domestic industries.[386] Manufacturing export activities are either related to the first stage of processing, such as the preservation of fish, or to the final stage of blending products, such as the single transformation of clothing products. Domestic manufacturing activities again are mainly centred on the food industry and hardly linked to export activities.

All SACU countries provide indirect and direct support to promote manufacturing activities and to attract manufacturing-related FDI. However, these strategies have not resulted in a boom of manufacturing activities and some incentive schemes have even resulted in a "race to the bottom" where the subsidies paid by FDI recipient countries exceeded the benefits to the economy. For the BLNS countries, such negative experiences were felt when attracting FDI to the clothing and garment industry. Comparative disadvantages such as water and power shortages, low labour productivity, insufficient backward and forward linkages, institutional weakness, and narrow markets became prevalent once competitive (artificial) advantages, namely the exemption from the WTO Multi Fibre Agreement (MFA) expired and preferences eroded.

Preferences over competing developing countries were supporting factors to BLNS industrialisation efforts but were hardly able to establish sustainable industries linked to the rest of the economy. None of the BLNS countries' domestic incentives has contributed to sustainable industrialisation processes. To date, BLNS industrialisation policies have been only insufficiently linked to other policy objectives, such as poverty reduction and sustainable development, which is mirrored by the heavy promotion of export-oriented industries, such as the clothing and garment industry, without sufficiently considering the net benefits. The reasons for this might also be explained by the weaknesses of government institutions and SACU countries' inability to harmonise their industrial policies yet. Thus, many different instruments exist, applying a policy-mix of import substitution and export promotion.

Prior to 1994, South Africa promoted the classical concept of import-substitution, which contributed to the country's broad manufacturing base, local backward- and forward linkages and the survival of some high-tech manufacturing industries, such as the automotive industry. The BLNS countries never had the chance to apply an import-substitution strategy due to their small, underdeveloped markets and their SACU membership. After 1994, the South African

[386] An exception is the sugar industry in Swaziland, which managed due to attractive preference in the EU market to establish a sugar-based industry serving the domestic market and regional markets.

economy has undergone a comprehensive transformation process during which trade liberalisation became one of the pillars of South Africa's industrial policy. The country took an active part in multilateral, regional and bilateral trade liberalisation and has used FTAs with its main trading partners, such as the EU, to improve its market access, to expand and diversify its exports and to strengthen its strategic position vis-à-vis main competitors. South Africa argues that tariff liberalisation had been implemented carefully and selectively but the persistent trade deficit and high unemployment rate have increased the opposition against further trade liberalisation. In fact, North-South FTAs are a tightrope walk for the SACU countries, particularly for the BLNS. Improved market access, increased international credibility and financial and technical support make it attractive to enter into North-South FTAs but limited production capacities, insufficient market knowledge, and existing non-tariff barriers make it difficult to reap these potential benefits. Furthermore, revenue losses and strained capacities as well as "hidden" and complicated issues such as a broad negotiation agenda, contribute to the limited attractiveness of North-South FTAs for the BLNS countries.

In fact, the BLNS countries are like most African countries disadvantaged by international trade because of their small size, their geographical location, poor infrastructure, high transaction costs, low labour and capital productivity, lack of effective institutions and competitive companies. Because of the erosion of preferences in their main markets, persisting barriers for agriculture and labour-intensive export products, and pressure to open their markets towards industrial countries, the countries are "squeezed" (AfDB 2004:206) and hardly left with industrialisation options. African countries cannot follow the path of South East Asian countries, which combined strategic and selective industrial trade policy with selective trade liberalisation. Today, African countries are much more dependent on external policy formulation, mainly by the EU, USA and WTO. In addition to the changes in the international arena, African countries have to focus on national development priorities.

The example of the BLNS countries showed that it is very difficult for small, sparsely populated countries that face high competition from its customs union member to diversify. Though thirty years of preferences to the EU market have to a certain extent encouraged manufacturing activities, such as tanning activities (Botswana and Namibia) and food processing (Swaziland, Namibia and Botswana), these activities concentrate on the domestic market while BLNS exports are still highly concentrated.

However, the problems of successful diversification relate not only to supply-side constraints but also to the manifold demand-side constraints in the EU market. Thus, the BLNS countries have comparative advantages for several agricultural and agro-based products and try to tackle EU niche markets by combining horizontal and vertical agro-based diversification.

However, quantitative restrictions, labelling requirements, and WTO plus standards, as well as the protective nature of the EU Common Agricultural Policy constrain BLNS agro-based exports.

7.2.4 On the South African Automotive and the Namibian Fishing Industry

The examples of the South African automotive industry and the Namibian fishing industry, important manufacturing sectors in both countries, have shown that trade policies need to differentiate between the needs of the single sectors to promote economic development. Flexible and individual instruments that suit the needs of national industries can support the economic development process and improve the international competitiveness of industries. The right mix of politics, effective institutions and ownership matters, taking development constraints of sectors into account and creating a supportive framework, thus considering that trade liberalisation and supply-side measures are crucial. Though there is no simple causality between trade policy and economic development, a successful trade policy that also takes the domestic market into account is likely to influence economic development positively.

The sector studies investigated whether an FTA with the EU would a) improve the effective market access for the companies surveyed; b) help to expand and diversify their exports; c) strengthen the cooperation with their European counterparts; and d) improve their international competitiveness. Both studies confirmed the thesis that the complexity of the national industries prevents the simple logic of textbook analyses of free trade agreements. Thus, the individual economic situation of the respective manufacturing sector, the management and policy tools in place, its national and international linkages, and its inclusion into international value chains need to be considered.

In fact, hardly any of the companies surveyed in the South African automotive and the Namibian fishing industry faced any hindrances when entering the EU market. South African automotive component producers hardly export directly into the EU but mainly indirectly via global vehicle manufacturers, which are all also based within the EU. Namibian fishermen again can as ACP country exporters already sell their fish duty free to the EU. The interview results also revealed that the diversification of exports and upgrading of products and services was mainly determined by being part of an international network. Because of their international connections, the companies in the South African automotive industry already had access to high technological inputs. In the Namibian fishing industry it was also those companies that were part of a joint-venture that performed best. An FTA with the EU would not have the same effects since the EU is not interested in the expansion of Namibian processing facilities but in the receipt of the unprocessed resource.

Regarding the international competitiveness of the two sectors investigated it can be stated that both of them have undergone significant transformation processes in the past 15 years. The South African automotive component industry went from a highly protected broad manufacturing base to a specialised high-tech exporter. In fact, exporting is vital for surveyed companies' overall performance and essential for them to stay competitive, to improve their economies of scale and to increase their profitability and productivity. Nevertheless, the industry is not able to be internationally competitive without the export-import complementation scheme MIDP.

The Namibian fishing industry, which was almost completely in foreign hands when the country became independent, has been successfully nationalised and set in place effective monitoring and management systems – a scarcity for a developing country. Namibia has become a very successful fish exporting developing country but still faces the problem of how to increase value to its products and to market and distribute it in the export markets, mainly the EU.

The two sector studies from South Africa and Namibia showed that there are chances but also relevant risks when being included into an FTA with the EU. For the South African automotive industry the most important opportunities of an FTA with the EU is to promote the EU as selling point for non-European vehicle manufacturers. For the Namibian fishing industry an FTA with the EU would offer the industry the chance to modernise its old fleet at substantially reduced costs and increase government's revenue, which would be a welcome support considering Namibia's revenue losses due to the restructuring of the SACU Common Revenue Pool and the TDCA.

However, the chances of entering into an FTA with the EU do not necessarily outweigh the risks. The inclusion of the South African automotive industry into an FTA with the EU would undermine the effects of the export promotion programme MIDP, leaving the industry more vulnerable to international competition. Moreover, it remains doubtful that new investment can be attracted by the South African automotive industry only by having free market access to the EU – giving the erosion of tariffs and the favourable conditions for main competitors from Eastern Europe. For the Namibian fishing industry the risks are even greater. European investment into domestic fleets would bear the risk of overcapitalisation and thus illegal fishing to amortise the investment. Moreover, a shared quota for European and domestic fishermen bears the risk of slowing down the "Namibianisation" policy, to reduce domestic fish processing due to limited inputs, and to strain the effective monitoring and management of the fishing industry.

Both sector studies made it apparent that successful trade policy differs from country to country, from sector to sector and even within a sector over time, taking the internal constraints and the external challenges into account. Successful trade policy is not only linked to international competitiveness but also takes national development strategies into account, following-up a holistic and sustainable approach towards economic development. A general approach towards free trade agreements on the other hand does not take the specific needs of sectors into account and can be counterproductive. Openness to international trade does not automatically lead to optimal factor allocation and increased efficiency but has different effects on different sectors. National trade policies, such as an import-duty reduction scheme, export market information, support on human capital formation, and access to finance were regarded as more supportive instruments by the companies' surveyed than pure trade liberalisation.

The empirical analyses also revealed that effective participation in international trade depends not only on countries' trade policy but also on strategic decisions of global lead companies. This decision again can be influenced by trade policy as the example of the South African automotive industry shows. Because of the MIDP, global automotive assemblers have used South Africa as a production platform, which boosted demand for South African automotive components. To improve their access to finance and technical know-how many component suppliers became part of an international network, which enabled them to meet the high product standards and to transform from specialised to broad suppliers and to benefit from economies of scale. In fact, strong linkages to global suppliers and being part of a global network has helped significantly to transform the formerly inward-looking and specialised South African automotive component industry to become internationally competitive and well-integrated in the global value chain.

Therefore, developing countries need a strategy of structural transformation that takes both, domestic market development and export expansion and diversification into account. It must therefore be the goal of every successful trade policy to search for the optimum of trade liberalisation and control, of export promotion and import substitution in order to optimise economic development. In this understanding, trade policy is integrated in a coherent and sustainable overall development strategy, taking the dynamic needs of single sectors into account. Economic development is not left to market forces but also needs a "developmental state". State intervention has to be reasonable, help to support industrial capacities and to strengthen international competitiveness. However, the SACU countries find themselves more and more caught in political interest conflicts between national industrial policies and international and bilateral trade obligations.

7.2.5 On SACU Countries Trade-Related Capacities

Given the world-wide policy towards trade liberalisation and the increasing pressure on the SACU countries to participate in bilateral, regional and multilateral trade agreements, the strengthening of trade-related capacities is most of all for the BLNS countries crucial in order to reap benefits and to protect their interests. To use international trade as successful development strategy, the BLNS countries need to identify their offensive and defensive trade interests clearly and translate these interests into policies and negotiation strategies. Therefore, they need support to expand their human and institutional capacities and to include all state and non-state actors involved into their trade strategy, which is crucial for successful trade negotiations and a trade policy that is coherent with articulated development goals.

When negotiating an FTA with an industrialised country as part of SACU, the BLNS countries need to evaluate the chances and risks for their economies, to determine their interests and to formulate, together with South Africa, a common negotiation position to ensure that regional integration within SACU is not undermined. To achieve this, an inclusive trade negotiation strategy needs be adopted, like South Africa did when negotiating the TDCA. To date, neither the public sector nor other relevant actors in the BLNS countries, such as trade unions and civil society organisations, are sufficiently aware or included into trade negotiations. The involvement of domestic academics in providing relevant research and analysis is limited and the cooperation of government institutions at both, the national and regional level, is not formalised but on an *ad hoc* basis. The challenge of improving BLNS countries' trade capacities and to create an inclusive trade strategy in order to allow their effective participation in trade negotiations cannot be achieved in the short run but requires increased human and institutional capacities so as to allow the countries a) to undertake necessary cost-benefits analyses including the identification of niche products and capacities on the one hand and the protection of interests on the other hand; b) to build-up expertise in the fields of administrative and analytical capacities; c) to strengthen the effective participation of private sector representatives, parliamentarians and other civil society actors; and d) to improve their knowledge about EU negotiation mechanisms and decision-making processes and to create an EU contact network. South Africa could assist the BLNS countries regarding all these points since it has collected valuable experience in international trade negotiations with the EU and the USA. To allow the BLNS countries to benefit from South Africa's trade experience without being dominated, a common SACU trade negotiations machinery needs to be developed. A regional approach can help the BLNS countries to pool capacities and resources in the most effective way and to improve the representation of their interests. Donors can support the process of trade capacity building but have to respect SACU countries' sovereignty with respect to its trade policy formulation. Since the EU follows-up its own agenda when negotiating EPAs for instance with respect to the inclusion of trade-related aspects, its trade-related support is not without problems. It is therefore important to make sure that any trade-related technical assistance is demand driven and coordinated between all national actors involved.

Table 45 summarises the key messages that have come up from the analyses in the Chapters 2-6.

Table 45: The Impact of EU Free Trade Agreements on Economic Development and Regional Integration in Southern Africa – Key Messages

Policy Field	Promoting Factors	Constraining Factors	Policy Recommendations
Deeper Regional Integration within SACU	➢ Agreement on the necessity to restructure SACU, to democratise decision-making processes, and to formulate common policies was reached by all member countries.	➢ Different economic structures and development degrees result in different interests. ➢ The new Agreement is only a framework, critical issues have not been agreed on yet. ➢ BLNS countries lack the capacity to implement the Agreement. ➢ Missing political priority of all countries. ➢ TDCA and EPA negotiations undermine deeper regional integration.	➢ For all parties, including the EU, the view must prevail that SACU is important for further economic integration in the region and can act as engine for successful regional integration in southern Africa, building-up a stable region. SACU, and most of all South Africa, cannot survive in a "sea of poverty". Political priorities of all member countries should be re-adjusted towards deeper integration within SACU, and, in the longer term, its expansion.
WTO - compatible Trade Agreement with the EU	➢ BLNS have as part of SACU a strong bargaining position since South Africa has to agree to any EPA.	➢ BLNS are locked in the TDCA without benefits. ➢ EPAs are not consistent with existing regional integration schemes in southern Africa. ➢ No sufficient funding for the implementation of EPAs. ➢ Development concept of EPAs remains unclear, negative effects such as revenue losses, and risks of WTO *plus* provisions are not sufficiently considered.	➢ South Africa, BLNS, EU: Include BLNS into a revised TDCA, taking BLNS defensive and offensive trade interests better into account. ➢ EU: Provide financial and technical support to address budget losses and supply-side constraints. ➢ EU: Make the provision of full and diagonal cumulation applicable and the rules of origin less restrictive. ➢ EU: Leave the negotiation of trade-related aspects to the WTO. ➢ EU: Make trade policy consistent with development goals. ➢ BLNS: Evaluate trade interests and build capacities.

Policy Field	Promoting Factors	Constraining Factors	Policy Recommendations
Industrial Development	➢ For BLNS: Preference regimes from the EU and USA have to a certain extent stimulated industrial development.	➢ SACU (price rising effects, South African competition), TDCA (revenue losses, trade diversion, harmful competition for some sectors). ➢ Preferences were not able to initiate sustainable industrial development and economic diversification, export concentration and dependencies have partly increased (sugar, beef, garment and clothing). ➢ FTAs with developed countries serve South Africa's trade interests.	➢ Reduce the focus on export-orientation and improve domestic backward- and forward linkages to ensure sustainable industrial development. ➢ Explore new export markets and alternative export products (such as horticultural and agro-processed products). ➢ Work on the reduction of domestic weaknesses for FDI such as shortages of skilled labour, poor communication facilities, and high transport costs (e.g. through the promotion of the harbour of Walvis Bay and intra-regional corridors). ➢ Review the industrial policy instruments and investment incentives in place critically and ensure that they are coherent with national development goals. ➢ Link the industrial strategy to the overall national development strategy.
	➢ For South Africa: Policy mix of import-substitution, export-promotion and free trade agreements (SACU's CET, export incentives, selective asymmetric FTAs with developed countries).	➢ TDCA: Reversion of asymmetry in the case of agriculture. ➢ Risk that FTAs with industrialised countries reduce the scope for national policies, e.g. by the inclusion of trade-related aspects.	➢ Promote discriminative policies in favour of BLNS in order to equalise economic development within SACU. ➢ Allow free movement of labour within SACU to promote the "catch-up" process of BLNS. ➢ Broader focus on regional development by opening-up for SADC imports.

Policy Field	Promoting Factors	Constraining Factors	Policy Recommendations
Industrial Development	➢ For all SACU countries: The new SACU Agreement offers options for a more equal industrial development within SACU.	➢ Having two different trade agreements with the EU ➢ New SACU Agreements has not been operationalised yet.	➢ Work on a regional competition bill to reduce the dominance of South African firms but also the concentration of few companies in the BLNS countries. ➢ Implement the provisions of the new SACU Agreement and work on a coherent regional industrial policy that is linked to SACU's trade policy, to member countries' agricultural policy, and to SACU's overall development strategy. ➢ Establish a common negotiation body to enter into external trade relations.
Industrial Development in the South African Automotive Industry	➢ The EU has offered to accelerate the agreed tariff abolishment in the auto industry before 2010 if South Africa liberalises more generously. ➢ Second- and third-tier suppliers might benefit from competitive inputs. ➢ Consumer effects. ➢ Option to attract FDI from non-European vehicle producers.	➢ Market access will be hardly improved due to component manufacturers' indirect exports via OEMs. ➢ Strong linkages to European production networks exist already. ➢ Any FTA undermines the effects of the import-export complementation scheme MIDP and thus, the sector's international competitiveness. ➢ Risk that other trading partners claim the same market access resulting in the abandonment of the MIDP.	➢ Component manufacturers: Increase value-creating distribution and marketing activities. ➢ PSSI: Improve information policy regarding the implications of including the sector into an FTA. ➢ Government and PSSI: Explore options and risks of the sector's opening-up for first-, second- and third-tier suppliers. ➢ Government: Explore chances and risks to use the liberalisation of the automotive industry as pledge for ongoing trade negotiations with the EU (TDCA Mid-Term, Review, EPAs).

Policy Field	Promoting Factors	Constraining Factors	Policy Recommendations
Industrial Development in the Namibian Fishing Industry	➢ Increased revenue offers the chance to stimulate investment and manufacturing activities by public kick-off finance. ➢ Improved and cheaper access to European vessels could modernise the comparably old Namibian fleet at reduced costs. ➢ Profitability of fishing activities per company would be likely to increase. ➢ Increased employment in the fishing industry due to more economic activities.	➢ The inclusion of fisheries into an FTA with the EU would not promote fish processing activities in Namibia but the export of unprocessed fish caught by European trawlers. ➢ Risk that overcapitalisation of the Namibian fleet results in illegal fishing. ➢ Increased supply of minor quality fish could reduce prices. ➢ A reserved quota for the EU could slow down the "Namibianisation" policy and fish processing activities and affect the sustainability of fishing activities negatively. ➢ The revenue obtained from a fisheries agreement is not linked to the sector's development.	➢ Avoid entering into an access agreement with the EU. ➢ Government and PSSI: Promotion of joint-ventures. ➢ Companies: Improved efforts to upgrade products and processes and to diversify towards new activities, such as marketing and distribution. To limit the dependency on quotas and price fluctuations, to reduce the international exchangeability of products and to enter into higher valuable market segments core capabilities need to be developed. ➢ Government: Promote linkages to other industries, such as the canning and food-processing industry.

Policy Field	Promoting Factors	Constraining Factors	Policy Recommendations
Trade Capacity	➢ South Africa gained relevant trade experience when negotiating the TDCA from which BLNS can benefit. ➢ Trade capacity has become an important policy field for donors. The SACU countries' can expect financial support when they endeavour to improve their trade capacity.	➢ BLNS: Institutional, administrative, and human capital weaknesses. ➢ BLNS: No consisting trade strategy exists. Existing trade strategy is not coherent with national development goals. ➢ BLNS: Trade interests have only been only insufficiently identified. ➢ BLNS: Cooperation among national and regional Ministries is insufficient ➢ SACU: No regional trade strategy exists yet.	➢ The BLNS countries need to work on improved human and institutional capacities in order to build-up expertise and to strengthen effective participation in trade agreements. This process can be supported by donor countries and South African experts. ➢ BLNS: Identify defensive and offensive trade interests with single trading partners. ➢ BLNS: Translate trade interests into policies and negotiations strategies. ➢ BLNS: Adapt an inclusive approach by involving civil society actors (research institutions, PSSI, labour unions, parliamentarians…). ➢ BLNS: Improve and formalise the cooperation of national Ministries (Trade, Agriculture, Customs, Foreign Affairs). ➢ SACU: Improve and formalise the cooperation of regional Ministries and work towards a regional trade strategy. ➢ BLNS: Improve the networking in the EU by benefiting from South Africa's experience. ➢ South Africa and EU: Provide technical and financial support to improve BLNS countries capacity to trade. Respect countries' sovereignty with respect to trade policy formulation and coordinate instruments between all SACU countries.

7.3 Conclusions and Outlook

What can the single actors do to make SACU's regional integration strategy consistent with members' trade relations towards the EU? To begin with, SACU should negotiate an EPA/FTA with the EU as one block. Any EPA including the BLNS countries also has to include South Africa. This docs not only help the SACU countries to promote deeper economic integration but is also the only feasible alternative. Such an approach requires however flexibilities from all partners. First of all, the EU needs to accept that the scope of EPAs is limited to trade in goods, which is sufficient to be WTO compatible. Trade-related aspects have to be negotiated in a WTO forum where negotiation power is less biased towards the EU than in bilateral/regional negotiations. Secondly, South Africa needs to open the TDCA again in order to incorporate the interests of the BLNS countries, e.g. with respect to the Commodity Protocols. This would imply that a) South Africa and the BLNS countries keep on having different export regimes towards the EU, mirroring the difference of their development levels and b) South Africa might have to re-negotiate certain sectors that are of particular interest for the EU, such as the automotive industry or the fishing sector. Last but not least, the negotiation of a SACU-EU EPA would require that the BLNS countries finally accept that they are locked-into the EU-South Africa FTA and that they formally adopt its liberalisation schedule.

However, there is also something to win: If all parties involved work constructively on a SACU-EU EPA, the EU would have finally made its external trade relations with SACU coherent and the SACU countries could work towards deeper regional integration and might one day also be able to expand their successful integration scheme towards new member countries. Moreover, an EPA that includes South Africa would certainly improve BLNS countries' options to set through their interests in negotiations with the EU since South Africa has the economic power and the negotiation experience. Another point that needs to be considered when talking about future EU-SACU trade relations is that politics are highly dynamic and thus subject to permanent change. Indeed, the coalition of very different countries in the WTO claiming for a "real" Development Round have shown that there is scope for negotiations. Even within the World Bank and the WTO the view prevails that openness to trade is not a development tool *per se* and has to be applied individually. Despite the membership of 148 countries in a rules-based multilateral trade regime, developed and developing countries still apply measures to support and protect their industries directly or indirectly. Though these policies are to date mainly used by the powerful nations of the WTO (as the example of the EU's CAP shows), the Ministerial meeting in Cancún in 2003 showed that developing countries have increased their power and shape the rules to their advantage. However, one has to distinguish between large developing countries that are aggressively tackling foreign markets, such as South Africa, Brazil or India and small developing countries, such as the BLNS countries that are highly dependent on few export commodities into a few markets. Since the WTO allows only non-reciprocal trade for least developed countries and limits the special and differential treatment for developing countries to longer transition periods, the trade needs of small developing countries are not adequately considered.

Even if African countries have determined a sectoral trade policy in line with national development priorities and successful in international terms, the policy approach still has to comply with WTO principles. The principles of the WTO do not discriminate but equalise: imports and domestic production, developed and developing countries. If however, unequal partners are treated equally, inequality can increase. The EU is the largest trading block in the world with a well developed institutional mechanism, many highly-educated trade experts and much experience in multilateral and bilateral trade negotiations. The SACU countries on the other hand are a group of very heterogeneous developing countries – with the middle-income developing country South Africa showing a comparably diversified product range on the one side of the scale and the tiny landlocked LDC Lesotho that is highly dependent on one commodity on the other side of the scale. Considering that South Africa faced already major challenges when it had to negotiate an FTA with the EU while being in the middle of an economic and social restructuring process and having hardly any experience in international trade negotiations, the challenges for the BLNS countries are even more extreme: after having enjoyed preferential access to a major trading partner for thirty years and after having relied on South Africa for external policy formulation for decades, the BLNS countries are now requested to formulate a national trade policy and bring it into a regional context, consistent with multilateral obligations. The formulation of such a comprehensive trade policy is hardly feasible giving the BLNS countries' lack of trade-related capacities and inexperience in trade relations. Longer transition periods are therefore useless if no according assistance to tackle demand- and supply-side constraints and to build capacity to trade is applied. Only if the BLNS countries have the capacity to trade, to implement existing agreements and to understand the challenges and development impacts of all agreements they are involved in, can they participate effectively in international trade. The interview results reveal that most companies and many institutions surveyed have a limited knowledge of the effects of free trade agreements. Such a limited knowledge does however hamper the effective participation as well as the meeting of ongoing obligations resulting from the implementation of the agreement. It is therefore important that the capacity to trade is built before the BLNS countries have to implement all-embracing bilateral and multilateral agreements that are not limited to trade in goods and services but also include other trade-related aspects. Only this can allow them to determine a trade policy that fits into their development strategy. There is therefore the urgent need to address the lack capacities of the BLNS countries and support them to implement the provisions of the new SACU Agreement accordingly. South Africa should provide support in this respect and be also ready to compromise with respect to common/harmonised regional policies to help accommodating BLNS interests in the regional agreement accordingly and to move successfully towards deeper regional integration.

Finally it can be concluded that North-South free trade agreements (FTAs) are no substitute for development policy. An FTA that does not take individual sectoral needs and their settings into the national development strategy into account is more detrimental than helpful for economic development. The effects of the EU's approach of North-South FTAs on SACU countries' options for industrial development, export diversification, and a move towards deeper regional integration failed to be proved development-oriented. The EU is therefore called on to harmonise its different trade policies towards the SACU countries and to bring them into line with the expressed development goals.

References

Acheampong, Anthony (1997): *Coherence between EU Fisheries Agreements and EU Development Cooperation: The Case of West Africa.* ECDPM Working Paper No. 52, December.

ACP General Secretariat (2003): *Country Report Botswana.* In: The Courier. The magazine of ACP-EU development cooperation, no. 198, May/June, pp. 52-72.

ACP General Secretariat (2002a): *Country Report Lesotho.* In: The Courier. The magazine of ACP-EU development cooperation, no. 194, September/October, pp. 70-92.

ACP General Secretariat (2002b): *Country Report South Africa.* In: The Courier. The magazine of the ACP-EU development cooperation, no. 195, pp. 62-83.

ACP General Secretariat (1999): *Country Report Swaziland.* In: The Courier. The magazine of the ACP-EU development cooperation, no. 174, March/April 1999, pp. 37-56.

ACP General Secretariat (1995a): *Country Report Namibia.* In: The Courier. The magazine the ACP-EU development cooperation, no. 153, September/October, pp. 32-46.

ACP General Secretariat (1995b): *Country Report Botswana.* In: The Courier. The magazine of the ACP-EU development cooperation, No. 154, November/December, pp. 12-28.

ACP General Secretariat (1995c): *Country Report Lesotho.* In: The Courier. The magazine of the ACP-EU development cooperation, No. 154, November/December, pp. 29-47.

ActionAid (2002): *Farmgate: The development impact of agriculture subsidies.* (online) http://www.ukfg.org.uk/docs/AAFarmgate%20briefing.pdf, accessed 12/06/03.

AfDB (African Development Bank) (2004): *African Development Report 2004: Africa in the Global Trading System.* Oxford: Oxford University Press.

AfDB (2003): *African Development Report 2003: Globalization and Africa's Development.* Oxford: Oxford University Press.

AfDB (2002a): *African Development Report 2002: Africa in the world economy, rural development for poverty reduction in Africa, economic and social statistics on Africa.* Oxford: Oxford University Press.

AfDB (2002b): *Report by the Boards of Directors of the African Development Bank and African Development Fund covering the period 1 January to 31 December 2001*. Addis Ababa: African Development Bank.

AfDB (2000): *African Development Report 2000: Africa in the world economy. Regional integration in Africa, economic and social statistics on Africa.* New York: Oxford University Press.

AfDB (1993): *Economic Integration in Southern Africa vol. 2: integrating regional markets and infrastructure.* Biddles: African Development Bank.

Africa Institute of South Africa (AISA) (2002): *Africa at a Glance: Facts and Figures 2001/02*. Pretoria: Africa Institute of South Africa.

Africanews (2001): Motlamelle, Thabo: *Lesotho: Slavery in Lesotho's textile industry.* Issue 59, February.

AGOA.Info (2005): *Information and resource webpage on the African Growth and Opportunity Act.* (online): http://www.agoa.info/, accessed 26/05/2003 and 22/06/2005.

Agritrade (2004): *Commission proposed price cuts "first step"*. Agritrade Monthly News Update, Issue 33, December.

Agritrade (2003): *Sugar sector. A report on the internal background to reform is released.* Agritrade Monthly News Update, Issue 21, December.

AIDC (Automotive Industrial Development Council) (2003): *AIDC helps to improve competitiveness.* Brochure published by the DTI, Pretoria: Government Printer.

Ailola, David A. (2000): *Investment Codes as a Restraint: The Experience of Southern Africa.* In: Collier, Paul / Pattillo, Catherine (Eds.): Investment and Risk in Africa, pp. 246-71, Basingstoke *et al.*: Macmillan Press.

Akinkugbe, Oluyele (2000): *The European Union and South Africa Free Trade Agreements. An Exploratory Partial Equilibrium Analysis of Potential Effect on ACP – EU Trade Flows.* In: Journal of World Trade vol. 34:3, pp. 95-109.

Akinkugbe, Oluyele / Makepe, Patricia (2005): *Botswana: An Examination of Recent Economic Redirection Strategies.* In: Wohlmuth, Karl et al. (Eds.): African Development Perspectives Yearbook vol. 11-2005/06: "Africa – Escaping the Primary Commodities Dilemma", Hamburg and Münster: Lit-Verlag (forthcoming).

Åslund, Anders (1996): *Comments and Discussion.* In: Development Discussion Paper No. 552, Reprint Series, pp. 96-100.

ATPC (African Trade Policy Centre) (2004): *Trade Liberalization and Development: Lessons for Africa.* (online): http://www.uneca.org/atcp/trade%20Lib%20and%20Dev_Lessons%20for%20Africa. pdf, accessed 16/06/2005.

Avafia, Tenu (2004): *The potential impact of US-SACU FTA negotiations on public health in southern Africa.* tralac Working Paper No 6/2004 (online): http://www.tralac.org/pdf/WP_6-04_-_sacu-us_public_health.doc, accessed 03/02/05.

Avafia, Tenu / Hansohm, Dirk (2004): *Political Conditions in the Cotonou Agreement: Economic and Legal Implications.* Windhoek: Nepru Working Paper No. 93.

Balassa, Bela (1965a): *The Theory of Economic Integration.* Second impression, London: Allen & Unwin.

Balassa, Bela (1965b): *Economic Development and Integration.* Mexico: Centro de Estudios Monetarios Latinoamericanos.

Balassa, Bela / Bauwens, Luc (1988): *Changing Trade Patterns in Manufactured Goods: an Econometric Investigation,* Amsterdam-New York: North-Holland.

Baldwin, Richard (1992): *Measurable Dynamic Gains from Trade*, The Journal of Political Economy, vol. 100:1, pp. 162-74.

Baldwin, Richard / Venables, Anthony (1994): *Regional Economic Integration.* In: Grossman, Gene / Rogoff, Kenneth (Ed.): Handbook of International Economics, Vol. 3, pp. 1597-1644, Amsterdam et al: North-Holland.

Barnes, Justin (2001) *Final report on broad sectoral trends of the past five years in the auto component sector. DTI policy support programme: International competitiveness and value chains in selected manufacturing sectors study* (Code: A.1.006), Durban: Government Printer.

Barnes, Justin (1999): *Changing lanes: the political economy of the South African automotive value chain.* In: Development Southern Africa. 17(3), p. 401–415.

Barnes, Justin (1998) *The competitiveness challenges facing the domestic automotive components industry.* In: Trade & Industry Monitor. 8, Dec., p. 1-5.

Barnes, Justin / Black, Anthony (2003): *Motor industry development programme. Review report.* 13 May. Durban, University Press.

Barnes, Justin / Lorentzen, Jochen (2003): *Learning, Upgrading, and Innovation in the South African Automotive Industry.* Paper (2nd draft) prepared for the workshop on Understanding FDI-Assisted Economic Development. TIK Centre, University of Oslo, 22-24 May, 2003.

Basu, Anupam / Srinivasan, Krishna (2002): *Foreign Direct Investment in Africa – Some case studies.* IMF Working Paper 61, Washington D.C.: IMF.

Baßeler, Ulrich / Heinrich, Jürgen / Koch, Walter (1995): Grundlagen und Probleme der Volkswirtschaft. 14th Edition, Cologne: Wirtschaftsverlag Bachem.

BEDIA (Botswana Export Development and Investment Authority) (2001a): *Botswana. The right location for the right investor.* Brochure printed by Horizon Ogilvy & Mather, Gaborone.

BEDIA (Botswana Export Development and Investment Authority) (2001b): *Opportunity Study for the implementation of a Tannery in Botswana.* Study undertaken by Aloy, M. / Fioreti, F. / Lecomte, P. / Poncet, T., Gaborone: Government Publication.

Bennett, Ben (2004): Senior Economist: International Trade Negotiations and Marketing, Ministry of Agriculture, Water and Rural Development. Interview with Bennett, 15/06/2004, Windhoek.

Bertelsmann-Scott, Talitha / Mills, Greg / Gibb, Richard (2000): *The EU-SA Agreement in a global context.* In: Bertelsmann-Scott, T. / Mills, G. / Sidiropoulos, E. (Eds.): The EU-SA Agreement. South Africa, Southern Africa and the European Union, pp. 17-30, Johannesburg: SAIIA.

Berthélemy, Jean-Claude / Söderling, Ludvig (2002): *Emerging Africa.* OECD Development Centre Studies. Paris: OECD.

Bhagwati, J. (1958), *Immiserizing Growth: A Geometric Note.* In: Review of Economic Studies vol. 25, pp. 201-205.

Bhorat, Haroon / Lundall, Paul (2001): *Employment, Wages & Skills Development: Firm-Specific Effects. Evidence from two firm surveys in South Africa.* Paper presented at the TIPS 2001 Annual Forum, 10-12 September, 2001.

BIDPA (Botswana Institute for Development and Policy Analysis) and IDS (Institute for Development Studies) (1998): *Study to Assess the Economic Impact of the Proposed European Union – South Africa Free Trade Agreement on Botswana, Lesotho, Namibia and Swaziland Final Report.* Gaborone and Sussex: BIDPA/IDS.

Bilal, San / Laporte, Geert (2004): *How did David prepare to talk to Goliath? South Africa's experience of trade negotiating with the EU.* ECDPM Discussion Paper No. 53, September.

Bilaterals (12/04/05): *SA union signs trade agreement with Mercosur.* (online) http://www.bilaterals.org/article.php3?id_article=2158&var_recherche=sacu+ mercosur, accessed 08/08/05.

Bilaterals (07/03/05): *Southern African countries have taken firm stand against EFTA demands on intellectual property rights in free trade agreement.* (online): http://www.bilaterals.org/article.php3?id_article=1407&var_recherche=sacu+efta, accessed 08/08/05.

Bilaterals (01/09/04): *EU-SA trade deal set for a tune-up.* (online): http://www.bilaterals.org/article.php3?id_article=517&var_recherche=south+africa +eu, accessed 08/08/05.

Black, Anthony / Kahn, Brian (2002): *Growing without Gold? South Africa's non-traditional export experience since 1980.* In: G.K. Helleiner (Ed.): Non-traditional export promotion in Africa. Experiences and Issues. pp. 217-52, Basingstoke *et al.*: Palgrave.

Blank, Jürgen E. / Clausen, Hartmut / Wacker, Holger (1998): *Internationale ökonomische Integration: von der Freihandelszone zur Wirtschafts- und Währungsunion.* WISO-Kurzlehrbücher, Munich: Vahlen.

BoL (Central Bank of Lesotho) (2001): *Annual Report for 2000.* Maseru: Government Printer.

BoN (Bank of Namibia) (2003): *Challenges and Implications of the 2002 SACU Agreement.* Windhoek: Government Printer.

BoN (2002): *Annual Report 2001.* Windhoek: Government Printer.

Bonaglia, Federico / Fukasaku, K. (2002): *Trade Competitively: Trade Capacity Building in Sub-Saharan Africa.* Paris: OECD.

Bora, Bijit / Lloyd, Peter / Pangestu, Mari (1999): *Industrial Policy and the WTO.* UNCTAD Policy Issues in International Trade and Commodities Study Series No. 6. (online): http://www.unctad.org/en/docs/itcdtab7_en.pdf, accessed 18/06/2005

Botha, Lambert (2005): *Guidelines for the Negotiations of the SADC EPA: Appropriate Legal Provisions dealing with Safeguard Measures in the proposed Economic Partnership Agreements.* Study for the project "Trade Advisor at the SADC Secretariat" funded by GTZ, Eschborn.

van Brabant, Jozef M. (2001): *Regional Economic Integration and Africa – Towards a New Paradigma.* In: Wohlmuth, Karl *et al.* (Eds.): African Development Perspectives Yearbook vol. 8 (2000/2001): Africa's reintegration into the world economy, pp. 375-406, Hamburg and Münster: Lit-Verlag.

Brenton, Paul (2003): *Integrating the Least Developed Countries into the World Trading System: The Current Impact of EU Preferences under Everything But Arms.* World Bank Policy Research Working Paper 3018, Washington D.C.: World Bank Publication.

Business Day (17/10/2003): N.N.: *EU looks to SA for new trade deal for vehicles.* (available online) http://www.bday.co.za/, accessed 15/01/04.

CBI (Centre for Promotion of Import from Developing Countries) (2003): *EU Market Survey Fishery Products 2003.* Available at: http://www.cbi.nl/show.php?file=show_summary.html&id=2261, accessed 30/06/2004.

CBoS (Central Bank of Swaziland) (2001): *Annual Report 2000/2001.* Mbabane: Government Printer.

CDI (Centre for the Development of Industry) (1999): *Leather and hides – how can Euro-African collaboration be enhanced?* In: ACP General Secretariat: The Courier. The magazine of the ACP-EU development cooperation, no. 176, July/August 1999, pp. 74-77.

Central Bank of Lesotho (2001): *Annual Report for 2000.* Maseru: Government Printer.

Chung, Yung-Sup (1986): *Die Erziehungszollidee als Instrument der Entwicklungspolitik.* Pfaffenweiler: Centaurus-Verlagsgesellschaft.

Collier, Paul / Gunning, Jan W. (2000): *The Potential for Restraint through International Trade Agreements.* In: Collier, Paul / Pattillo, Catherine (Eds.): Investment and Risk in Africa, pp. 338-51, Basingstoke *et al.*: Macmillan Press.

Collier, Paul / Gunning, Jan, W. (1999): *Restraint, Cooperation and Conditionality in Africa Trade Policy.* In: Oyejide, A. / Elbadawi, I. / Collier, P. (Eds.): Regional integration and trade liberalization in Sub-Saharan Africa. Volume 4, pp. 74-99, Basingstoke *et al.*: Macmillan Press.

Costanza, Robert / Cumberland, John / Daly, Herman / Goodland, Robert / Norgaard, Richard (2001): *Einführung in die Ökologische Ökonomik.* Lucius & Lucius, Stuttgart.

Council of the European Union (1999): *Agreement on Trade, Development and Cooperation between the European Community and its Member States, of the one part, and the Re-public of South Africa, of the other part.* Doc. 8731/99, 09 July 1999, Brussels.

Cramer, Christopher (2003): *Should developing country industrialisation policies encourage processing of primary commodities?* In: The Courier. The magazine of ACP-EU development cooperation, no. 196, January/February, pp. 30-32.

CSO (Botswana Central Statistics Office) (2001): Statistical Bulletin: Gaborone: CSO.

Cunningham, Stephen / Dunn, Michael / Whitmarsh, David (1984): *Fisheries Economics. An Introduction.* St. Martin's Press, New York.

Davenport, Michael / Hewitt, Adrian / Koning, Antonique (1995): *Europe's preferred partners? The Lomé countries in world trade.* Overseas Development Institute, ODI Special Report, London: Chameleon Press Ltd.

Davis, Robert (1994): *Creating an appropriate institutional framework.* In: Venter, Minnie (Ed.): Prospects for Progress. Critical Choices for Southern Africa. Johannesburg: Maskew Miller Longman, pp. 2-13.

Der Spiegel (18/04/05): N.N.: *Erhöhte Entwicklungshilfe. Eichel will Flugbenzin besteuern.* (online): http://www.spiegel.de/politik/deutschland/0,1518,351910,00.html, accessed 20/04/05.

Dlamini, Phumlele (2003): Industrial Officer, Ministry of Enterprise and Employment. Interview with Dlamini, 21 November 2003, Mbabane.

Drammeh, Ousman K. L. (2000): *Illegal, Unreported & Unregulated Fishing In Small-Scale Marine And Inland Capture Fisheries.* Document AUS:IUU/2000/7. Available at : http://www.fao.org/DOCREP/005/Y3274E/y3274e09.htm, accessed 13/09/2004

DTI (Department of Trade and Industry of the Republic of South Africa) (2005): *South African Trade by SIC codes: Manufacturing (ranking order)* (online) http://www.thedti.gov.za/econdb/raportt/rapsimacurrent.html, accessed 17/07/05.

DTI (2004a): *Study into the evolving trade patterns between South Africa and the EU following introduction of TDCA.* Final Report V.1, December 3, 2004. Pretoria: DTI.

DTI (2004b): *South Africa's Trade Data.* (online): http://www.thedti.gov.za/econdb/raportt/rap100c2.html, accessed 26/01/2005.

DTI (2003a): *South Africa. Current developments in the automotive industry. Seventh report on the state of the South African automotive industry to be published by the DTI since the introduction of the Motor Industry Development Programme.* Pretoria: Government Printer.

DTI (2003b): *Incentives Fact Sheets.* Pretoria: Government Printer.

DTI (Eds) (2002a): *Industrial sector's policy support project code A.1.008. D6. Final report – automotive sector.* Submitted by Industrial Restructuring Project School of Development Studies. Pretoria: Government Printer.

DTI (2002b): *South Africa. Current developments in the automotive industry. Sixth report on the state of the South African automotive industry to be published by the DTI since the introduction of the Motor Industry Development Programme.* Pretoria: Government Printer.

DTI (2002c): *Customs and excise statistics.* Pretoria: Government Printer.

DTI (2001): *South Africa's Foreign Trade,* 2001 Edition, Pretoria: Government Publication.

DTI (Ed.) (1999): *International competitiveness and value chains in selected manufacturing sectors.* Study Code A.1.001: Automotive textile study, submitted by Justin Barnes (University of Natal: Industrial Restructuring Project). Pretoria: Government Printer.

Dunlop, Adam (1999): *What future for Lomés Commodity Protocols?* ECDPM Discussion Paper 5, Maastricht: ECDPM (online): http://www.ecdpm.org

Dunlop, Adam / Szepesi, Stefan / van Hove, Kathleen (2004): *Organising trade negotiating capacity at regional level. A Caribbean case study.* ECDPM Discussion Paper No. 54, September.

Economist (19/02/2004): N.N.: Emerging deals. Seeking a friend in South Africa. (online): http://www.economist.com/PrinterFriendly.cfm?Story_ID=2451759, accessed 04/06/2004.

Economist.com (2004): N.N.: *Reviving up. South Africa's car industry roars ahead.* (online) http://www.economist.com/PrinterFriendly.cfm?Story_ID=2430012 accessed 05/03/2004.

Edwards, Chris (1996): *East Asia and Industrial Policy in Malaysia: Lessons for Africa?* In: Stein, Howard (Ed.): Asian Industrialization and Africa. Studies in Policy Alternatives to Structural Adjustment, pp. 239-58, New York: Palgrave Macmillan.

El-Agraa, Ali M. (1997a): *The Theory of Economic Integration.* In: El-Agraa, Ali M. (Ed.): Economic Integration Worldwide, pp. 34-73, Basingstoke *et al.*: Macmillan Press.

El-Agraa, Ali M. (1997b): *Policy Directives, Pertinent Questions, Overall Conclusions and Prognostications.* In: El-Agraa, Ali M. (Ed.): Economic Integration Worldwide, pp. 379-86, Basingstoke *et al.*: Macmillan Press.

ECA (Economic Commission for Africa) / AfDB (African Development Bank) / UNDP (United Nations Development Programme) / SADC (Southern African Development Community (2005): *The Ad-Hoc Group Meeting and Workshop on Economic Partnership Agreements and WTO Issues for Southern African Countries. Final Report and Recommendations.* ECA/SA/WS/EPA/2005, April.

ECDPM (European Centre for Development Policy Management) (2005a): *EPA negotiation update.* Trade Negotiations Insight, vol. 4:2, April.

ECDPM (2005b): *EPA negotiation update.* Trade Negotiations Insight, vol. 4:3, June. Epawatch (2002): Market access and making use of Trade Preferences. (online) http://www.epawatch.net/documents/doc10_1.doc, accessed 15/07/02.

Erasmus, Gerhard (2005): *The Consequences of Regional Integration in Southern Africa of Overlapping Trade Arrangements with Third Parties.* Paper presented at the NEPRU workshop on "Monitoring Regional Integration in Southern Africa", Windhoek, June 11-12.

Erasmus, Gerhard (2004): *The New SACU Structures Get Underway.* (online): http://www.tralac.org/scripts/content_print.php?id=2943, accessed 28/09/2004.

Erastus, Anna N. (2002): *The Development of the Namibianisation Policy in the Hake Subsector, 1994-1999.* NEPRU Working Paper No. 82, June, Windhoek.

EU, DG Trade (2005a) : *The Doha Development Agenda.* (online): http://europa.eu.int/comm/trade/issues/newround/doha_da/pr080605_en.htm, accessed 14/06/2005.

EU, DG Trade (2005b): *EU Trade News.* EPA Newsletter N 7, Brussels, May 2005.

EU, DG Trade (2003): 2002 EU *imports. Main traded products with Namibia.* (online): http://tradeinfo.cec.eu.int/doclib/docs/2003/june/tradoc_113164.pdf#zoom =100 &page=47, accessed 30/06/04

EU DG Trade (2002): *External Trade: EU – Botswana, Lesotho, Namibia, Swaziland*, 07 May 2002. (online): http://europa.eu.int/comm/trade/pdf/bilstat/vol1part2.pdf, accessed 30/05/2003.

EU Export Help-Desk (2004): http://export-help.cec.eu.int. data accessed 22/05/2004.

European Commission (2005): *Economic Partnership Agreements: putting a rigorous priority on development.* Memo, 20 January 2005, European Commission: Brussels.

European Commission (2004): *The international dimensions of European fisheries.* http://europa.eu.int/comm/fisheries/doc_et_publ/factsheets/facts/en/pcp4_1.htm, accessed 01/07/2004.

European Commission (2002a): *Republic of Namibia and European Commu nity: Strategy Paper and Indicative Programme for 2002 – 2007.* (online): http://europa.eu.int/comm/development/strat_papers/docs/na_csp.pdf, accessed 24/06/02.

European Commission (2002b): *Republic of Botswana and European Commu nity: Strategy Paper and Indicative Programme for the period 2002 – 2007.* (online): http://europa.eu.int./comm/development/strat_papers/docs/ bw_csp.pdf, accessed 24/06/02.

European Commission (2001a): ACP Statistical Analysis. Imports and Exports by TDC Section 2000/2001, (online) : http://europa.eu.int/comm/trade/bilateral/acp/acp.htm, accessed 02/12/02.

European Commission (2001b): *Some principles and some data. European distant fishing water fleets.* (online): http://europa.eu.int/comm/fisheries/doc_et_publ/liste_publi/facts/peche_en.pdf, accessed 10/09/2004.

European Commission (2000a): *Communication from the Commission to the Council and the European Parliament. Special Framework of Assistance for Traditional ACP Suppliers of Bananas.* Brussels: Council Regulation No. 856/1999.

European Commission (2000b): *ACP-EU Partnership Agreement signed in Cotonou on 23rd June, 2000*. Supplement to the Courier, September 2000, Brussels.

European Commission (1999): Partners in Progress: *The EU/South Africa Trade, Development and Co-operation Agreement for the 21st Century*. Brussels: European Commission, De Series.

European Commission (1998): *Annual Reports 1998: Botswana, Lesotho, Namibia, Swaziland,* http://europa.eu.int/comm/development/publicat/rep98/pdf/, accessed 29/11/02.

European Commission (1997): *The Stabex System and export revenues in ACP countries*. Brussels: Office for Official Publications of the European Communities.

European Commission (1996): *Green Paper on relations between the European Union and the ACP countries on the eve of the 21st century. Challenges and options for a new partnership*. Brussels: European Commission.

European Commission (1995): *Agreement. Amending the Fourth ACP-EC Convention of Lomé, signed in Mauritius on 4 November 1995*. ACP-CE 2163/95, Brussels. (online): http://www.acpsec.org/gb/lome/lome4_e.htm, accessed 05/12/2002.

European Commission (1994): *Southern Africa and the European Union.* Europe Information Development No. 78, Brussels: European Commission.

European Community (1999): *Support to African countries in implementation of the UN Convention to Combat Desertification (Report to the Third Conference of the Parties), June 1999.* (online): www.unccd.int/cop/reports/igo/1999/ec-eng.pdf, accessed 29/11/02.

European Diamonds PLC (2005): *Press Release: Highlights of Operations, 31 March 2005* (online): http://www.europeandiamondsplc.com/QwikReport, accessed 17/05/2005.

European Parliament (2002): *Generaldirektion Wissenschaft: Mitteilung zur politischen und wirtschaftlichen Lage in Südafrika (aktualisiert).* Document NT/454611DE.doc. (available online): http://europarl.eut.in/.

European Parliament (2000): *Der Vertrag von Rom und das grüne Europa.* Kurzdarstellung des Europäischen Parlaments, 28/06/2000 (online): http://www.europarl.eu.int/factsheets/4_1_1_de.htm, accessed 11/03/2005.

European Research Office (2004): *Residual Tariff Barriers to African Exports to the EU.* (online): http://www.epawatch.net/general/text.php?itemID=245&menuID=33, accessed 28/11/2004.

European Research Office (2003): *Agriculture and Fisheries Issues.* Unpublished Document.

European Research Office (2002): *EPAs: What's in it for the BLNS? Getting to Grips with Regional Realities.* (online): http://www.epawatch.net/documents/doc126_1.doc, accessed 13/12/2003.

European Research Office (2001): *Implications of the Reform of the EU Beef Regime for Southern African Countries. Part Two. The Impact of the EU Beef Regime on Southern Africa: A review of the experience and issues arising.* (online): http://www.fos-socsol.be/nl/ero/documenten/cap/Beef%202.PDF, accessed 02./12/03.

Eurostep (2000a): *The EU-South Africa Trade, Development and Co-operation Agreement: Analysis of the Negotiating Process, the Agreement and the Economic Impact.* Eurostep Briefing Paper, March.

Eurostep (2000b): *The new ACP-EU Agreement – An assessment and recommendations for Implementation.* Eurostep Briefing Paper, May.

Eurostep (2000c): *The EU-South Africa Trade Development and Co-operation Agreement: An analysis of its implications in Southern Africa.* Eurostep Briefing Paper, June.

Eurostep (1999): *CAP reforms will hit South's poor farmers.* (online): http://www.twnside.org.sg/title/farm-cn.htm, accessed 14/08/2002.

Evans, H.D. (2000): *Options for regional integration in Southern Africa.* In: The South African Journal of Economics, vol. 68:4, pp. 662-692.

FAS (Foreign Agriculture Service of the US Department of Agriculture) (2004): *Most-Favoured-Nation Tariff. Section 1 Agricultural Products.* (online): http://www.fas.usda.gov/scriptsw/wtopdf/wtopdf_lout.asp, accessed 10/05/2004.

FAO (Food and Agriculture Organization of the United Nations) (2004a): *Fish, crustaceans, molluscs, etc. Capture production by countries or areas. Africa – Inland waters.* (online): ftp://ftp.fao.org/fi/stat/by_fishArea_00/c01b.pdf, accessed 05/05/04.

FAO (Food and Agriculture Organization of the United Nations) (2004b): *The WTO Doha Round and Fisheries; what is at stake?* FAO Fact Sheet for WTO Ministerial Conference in Cancun, Mexico. (online): http://www.globefish.org/dynamisk.php4?id=2112, accessed 13/09/2004.

FAO (Food and Agriculture Organization of the United Nations) (2001): *Information on Namibia's Fisheries Management System for the FAO Digital Atlas*, Version 1, (unpublished document)

FAO (Food and Agriculture Organization of the United Nations) (2000): *Fisheries country profile for Namibia.* http://www.fao.org/fi/fcp/en/NAM/profile.htm, accessed 10/09/03.

FAO Glossary (2004): http://www.fao.org/glossary/, accessed 14/09/2004.

Feldsieper, Manfred (1975): *Zollpräferenzen für Entwicklungsländer.* Bochumer Schriften zur Entwicklungsforschung und Entwicklungspolitik, vol. 20, Tübingen und Basel: Horst Erdmann Verlag.

FIGIS (Fisheries Global Information System) (2004): *Fisheries and Aquaculture Issues Fact Sheet.* (online): http://www.fao.org/figis/servlet/FiRefServlet?ds=topic&fid=2004, accessed 01/07/04.

Finger, J.M. (2001): *Implementing the Uruguay Round Agreements: Problems for Developing Countries.* In: The World Economy vol. 24:9, pp. 1097-1108.

Foroutan, Faezeh (1993): *Regional integration in Sub-Saharan Africa: past experience and future prospects.* In: De Melo, Jaime / Panagariya, Arvind (Eds.): New dimensions in regional integration, pp. 234-71, Cambridge: Cambridge University Press.

Foroutan, Faezeh / Pritchett, Lant (1993): *Intra-Sub-Saharan African Trade: is it too little?* In: Journal of African economies, vol. 2:1, pp. 74-105.

Games, Diana (2003): *The experience of South African firms doing business in Africa. A preliminary survey and analysis.* SAIIA Reports no. 37, Johannesburg.

GATT (1994): Benedek, Wolfgang (Ed.) (1998): *Die Welthandelsorganisation (WTO): alle Texte einschließlich GATT (1994), GATS und TRIPS. Textausgabe.* Munich: Beck.

Gibb, Richard (2003): *Globalisation and Africa's economic recovery: a case study of the European Union-South Africa post-apartheid trading regime.* In: Journal of Southern African Studies. 29 (4), p. 885–901.

GoB (Government of Botswana) (2003): *Report by the Government of the Republic of Botswana.* In: WTO (Ed). Trade Policy Review. Southern African Customs Union. Report by the Governments. Doc.WT/TPR/G/114, pp.1-12, Geneva: WTO.

GoL (Government of Lesotho) (2003): *Report by the Government of the King dom of Lesotho.* In: WTO (Ed). Trade Policy Review. Southern African Customs Union. Report by the Governments. Doc. WT/TPR/G/114, pp. 22-29, Geneva: WTO.

Goldstein, Andrea / Quenan, Carlos (2002): *Regionalism and Development in Latin America: What Implications for Sub-Saharan Africa?* In: OECD and AfDB: Regional Integration in Africa. OECD Development Centre Seminars, pp. 47-76, Paris: OECD Publication.

GoN (Government of Namibia) (2003): *Report by the Government of the Republic of Namibia.* In: WTO (Ed). Trade Policy Review. Southern African Customs Union. Report by the Governments. Doc. WT/TPR/G/114, pp. 13-21, Geneva: WTO.

Goodison, Paul (2005): *Making EPAs work for Development. The Regional Integration and Agricultural Dimension.* Presentation held at the Trade Mondays Seminar Series of the Danish Institute for International Studies, 07 March 2005, Copenhagen.

Goodison, Paul (2004): *Economic Partnership Agreements with the EU: an independent assessment.* Presentation held at the Namibian Agricultural Boards, 11 June 2004, Windhoek.

Goodison, Paul (2002): *To sign or not to sign? EPAs and alternative options for EU-ACP negotiations.* In: FES, terre des hommes, Weed (Eds.): The Cotonou Agreement – New Perspective for European Trade Policy? June 2002, pp. 38-45, Berlin and Bonn: FES publication.

Goodison, Paul (2000): *SADC and the Future of the Lomé Trade arrangements.* In: Hartzenberg, Trudi (Ed.): SADC-EU Trade Relations, pp. 5-31, Oxford: African Books Collective.

Goodison, Paul (1999): *Marginalisation or Integration? Implications for South Africa's Customs Union Partners of the South Africa – European Union Trade Deal.* The Institute for Global Dialogue (Ed): Occasional Paper, IGD: Braamfontein.

GoS (Government of the Kingdom of Swaziland) (2003): *Report by the Government of the Kingdom of Swaziland.* In: WTO (Ed). Trade Policy Review. Southern African Customs Union. Report by the Governments, pp. 30-40, Geneva: Doc. WT/TPR/G/114.

GoSA (Government of the Republic of South Africa) (2003): *Report by the Government of the Republic of South Africa.* In: WTO (Ed). Trade Policy Review. Southern African Customs Union. Report by the Governments. Doc. WT/TPR/G/114, pp. 30-38, Geneva: WTO.

GoSA (Government of the Republic of South Africa) (1997): *Basis for Negotiations for a Trade and Development Agreement between the Republic of South Africa and the EU.* 23 January 1997, Pretoria: Government Printer.

Greenpeace (2001): *Pirate Fishing: Plundering West Africa. Greenpeace Publication, September.*(online): http://archive.greenpeace.org/oceans/reports/wafricapiratefish.pdf, accessed 13/09/2001.

Grinspun, Ricardo / Cameron, Maxwell A. (1994): *Restructuring North America: The Impact of Unequal Integration.* In: Georgakopoulos, T. / Paraskevopoulos, C. / Smithin, J. (Eds.): Economic Integration between Unequal Partners, pp. 23-34, Hants: Edward Elgar.

Grossman, Gene / Helpman, Elhanan (1991): *New Growth Theory: Innovation and Growth in the Global Economy*, Cambridge *et al.*: MIT Press.

Gschwender, Frank (2003a): *A Corridor Development Approach – the Walvis Bay Case Study.* In: Wohlmuth, Karl et al. (Eds.): African Development Perspectives Yearbook 2002/03, vol. 9, Lit-Verlag, Hamburg, pp. 634-9.

Gschwender, Frank (2003b): Business Development Executive Walvis Bay Corridor Group. Interview with Gschwender. 25 September 2003, Windhoek.

Hall, James (2004): *The impact of negating AGOA trade advantages on sub-Saharan Africa's textile industry.* In: Traders African Business Journal, Issue 18, May-August, pp. 6-8.

Handschuh, Klaus D. (2003): Trade and Investment Development Programme Coordinator. Interview with Handschuh. 04 September 2003, Windhoek.

Hansohm, Dirk / Schade, Klaus / Nepembe, Maano (2002): *Taxation, Expendi ture and Accountability: Lessons from Namibia.* In: IDS Bulletin vol. 33:3, July.

Hansohm, Dirk / Schade, Klaus (2001): *The Lomé Convention, the Cotonou Convention and Namibia.* A NEPRU Viewpoint. NEPRU Quarterly Commentary on the Economy No. 34, Windhoek: NEPRU.

Hartzenberg, Trudi (2004): *South Africa's Trade Policy and Southern and Eastern Africa: Focus on SACU and SADC.* Commonwealth Trade Hot Topics, Issue No. 31 (online): http://www.commonwealth.int, accessed 03/11/2004.

Hashiyana, André / Einarsson, Olafur V. (1998): *Towards Regional Integration in the Marine Fisheries Sector*. In: Namibia Brief. Focus on Fisheries and Research, Windhoek, p. 85-8.

Helleiner, Gerald K. (Ed.) (2002): *Non-traditional export promotion in Africa. Experiences and Issues*. Basingstoke *et al.:* Palgrave.

van Herden, Neil (2003): Executive Director, South Africa Foundation. Inter view with van Herden, 06 November 2003, Johannesburg.

Hoeller, Peter / Girouard, Nathalie / Colecchia, Alessandra (2000): *The Europe an Union's trade policies and their economic effects*. Paris: OECD Publication.

Hoffmann, Jürgen A.H. (2003): Trade Advisor. Meat Board of Namibia/Namibian Agronomic Board. Interview with Hoffmann. Windhoek, 15 September.

Husted, Steven / Melvin, Michael (2004): *International Economics*. Sixth Edition, Pearson Education: Boston et al.

ICTSD (International Centre for Trade and Sustainable Development) (2005): *S&D Talks Held Up Over Work Plan Disagreement*. In: Bridges vol. 4, p. 12.

IDS (Institute of Development Studies) (1997): *Economic Assessment of the proposed free trade area between the European Union and South Africa*. Final Report. Trade Policy Monitoring Project, University of Sussex.

IEEP (Institute for European Environmental Policy) (2003): *Fisheries Agreements with third countries – is the EU moving towards sustainable development?* (online): http://www.wwf.org.uk/filelibrary/pdf/eufishdeals.pdf, accessed 29/06/2004.

IFSC (International Financial Service Centre (2003): *Botswana's tax rates*. (online): http://www.ifsc.co.bw/country_profile.htm, accessed 05/03/2003.

IMF (International Monetary Fund) (2002): *Botswana: Selected issues and statistical appendix*. Study prepared by Mzwanele Mfunwa. (online) http://www.imf.org/external/pubs/cat/longres.cfm?sk=161620, accessed 15/11/2002.

INSAT (Inside Southern African Trade) (2005): Newsletter from the Southern Africa Global Competitiveness Hub, Issue 01, May. www.satradehub.org

IRIN (UN Office for the Coordination of Humanitarian Aid) (2005a): *Namibia: Textile industry faces multiple challenges*. (available online): http://www.irinnews.org/, accessed 09/02/2005.

IRIN (2005b): *Southern Africa: Clothing and textile industries need a rethink, say economists.* (available online): http://www.irinnews.org/, accessed 09/02/2005.

IRIN (2005c): *Swaziland: Huge job losses feared in garment industry.* (available online): http://www.irinnews.org/, accessed 09/02/2005.

INSAT (Inside Southern African Trade) (2005a): *Newsletter from the Southern Africa Global Competitiveness Hub*, Issue 01, May. (available online): www.satradehub.org

INSAT (2005b): *Newsletter from the Southern Africa global Competitiveness Hub*, Issue 2 (available online): http://www.irinnews.org/ accessed 12/10/05.

Iyambo, Abraham (2003a): *Annual Address Namibian Fisheries Sector*, 3 February 2003, Swakopmund.

Iyambo, Abraham (2003b): *Fishing, Trade and Development.* A short address by Dr. Abraham Iyambo, Minister for Fisheries and marine Resources, Republic of Namibia at the Fisheries Ministers' Conference, Vigo, Spain, 15-17 September 2003.

Iyambo, Abraham (2003c): *Progress in broad-based empowerment in the Fisheries and Marine Resource Sector.* Paper presented at the Socio-Economic Empowerment Workshop, 4-5 December 2003, Swakopmund.

Iyambo, Abraham (2002): *Annual statement on the status of the Namibian fisheries sectors by Dr. Abraham Iyambo. Minister for Fisheries and Marine Resources*, January 2002, Windhoek.

Iyambo, A.P. / Shiimi, I.W. / Rukoro, L. / Kalenga, P. / Ndalikokule, V. (2001): *Assessing the Impact of the EU-SA FTA on Namibia's Public Revenue.* In Bank of Namibia Working Paper No. 04/2001, Windhoek.

Jachia, Lorenza / Teljeur, Ethél (1999): *Free trade between South Africa and the European Union. A quantitative analysis.* UNCTAD Discussion Paper No. 141, Geneva.

Japan Corporate News Network (2004): *Nissan to export hardbody pickup truck manufactured in South Africa. Destinations including Europe.* (online): http://www.japancorp.net/Article.Asp?Art_ID=6632, accessed 05/03/2004.

Jenkins, Carolyn (2000): *Compensatory Mechanism.* In: Jenkins, C. / Leape, J. / Thomas, L. (Eds.): Gaining from Trade in Southern Africa, pp. 140-62, Basingstoke et al.: Macmillan Press.

Jensen, Michael Friis (2005): *Capacity Building for Pro-Poor Trade: Learning from the Limitations in Current Models*. Human Development Report Office. Occasional Paper. (online): http://hdr.undp.org/docs/publications/background_papers/2005/HDR2005_Jensen_Michael_Friis_15.pdf, accessed 27/09(05.

Jilberto, Alex E. F. / Mommen, André (1999): *Globalization versus Regionalization*. In: Jilberto, Alex E. F. / Mommen, André (Eds.): Regionalization and Globalization in the Modern World Economy, pp. 1-26, London et al.: Routledge.

Kalenga, Paul (2004): *Implementation of the SADC Trade Protocol: Some Reflections*. (online): http://www.tralc/scripts/content.php?id=3045, accessed 03/11/2004.

Kamidza, Richard (2004): *ESA-EPA negotiations still lack substance and direction*. (online): http://www.seatini.org/publications/articles/2004/esa-epa.htm, accessed 01/02/2005.

Kaplan, David (2004): *Manufacturing in South Africa over the last decade: a review of industrial performance and policy*. In: Development Southern Africa vol. 21:4, pp. 623-44, Carfax Publishing.

Kaplan, David (2003): *Manufacturing performance and policy in South Africa: a review*. Paper prepared for the TIPS/DPRU Forum 2003, September.

Kaplinsky, Raphael (2000): *Globalisation and Unequalisation: What can be learned from value chain analysis?* In: The Journal of Development Studies, vol. 37:2, pp. 117-145.

Kaplinsky, Raphael / Morris, Mike (2001): *A handbook for value chain analysis. Prepared for the IRDC* (online): http://www.ids.ac.uk/ids/global/pdfs/VchNov01.pdf, accessed 10/06/2003.

Kaplinsky, Raphael / Morris, Mike / Readman, Jeff (2002): *The Globalization of Product Markets and Immiserizing Growth: Lessons from the South African Furniture Industry*. In: World Development vol. 30:7, pp. 1159-1177.

Kappel, Robert (2005): *Wirtschaftsreformen und Armutsbekämpfung in Afrika*. Bundeszentrale für politische Bildung: Aus Politik und Zeitgeschichte 04/2005.

Kappel, Robert (2001): *Entwicklung durch Handel? Was bringen geöffnete Industrieländer-Märkte den armen Ländern?* In Entwicklung und Zusammenarbeit No. 9, pp. 248-9.

Kennan, Jane / Stevens, Christopher (2005): *Preparing for Economic Partnership Agreements.* Institute for Development Studies Briefing Paper, March, Sussex: IDS.

Kennan, Jane / Stevens, Christopher (1997): *From Lomé to the GSP: Implications for the ACP of Losing Lomé Trade Preferences.* Sussex: Institute of Development Studies.

Kennes, Walter (2000): *Small Developing Countries and Global Markets. Competing in the Big League.* MacMillan Press Ltd., Houndsmill et al.

Khandelwal, Padamja (2004): *COMESA and SADC: Prospects and Challenges for Regional Trade Integration.* IMF WP/04/227, IMF: Washington D.C.

King, Ian (2003): General Manager, Coca Cola Swaziland. Interview with King, 25 November 2003, Matsapha.

Kirk, Robert / Stern, Matthew (2003): *The New Southern African Customs Union Agreement.* Africa Region Working Paper Series No. 57, Washington D.C.: World Bank Publication.

Konings, Piet / Meilink, Henk (1999): *Regional Economic Integration in Sub-Saharan Africa.* In: Jilberto, Alex E. F. / Mommen, André (Eds.): Regionalization and Globalization in the modern World Economy, pp. 128-45, London *et al.*: Routledge.

Kreinin, Mordechai E. / Plummer, Michael G. (2002): *Economic Integration and Development. Has regionalism delivered for developing countries?* Cheltenham et. al.: Edward Elgar.

Krugman, Paul (1991): *Geography and Trade.* Leuven: Leuven University Press.

Krugman, Paul (1990): *Rethinking International Trade*, Cambridge *et al.*: MIT Press.

Krugman, Paul R. / Obstfeld, Maurice (2003): *International Economics. Theory and Policy.* Sixth Edition, Boston *et al.*: Addison-Wesley.

Laletsang, K. (2003): Assistant Director (Foreign Trade) of the Department of Trade and Consumer Affairs, Ministry Commerce of the Republic of Botswana. Interview with Laletsang, 06 October 2003, Gaborone.

Lall, Sanjaya (2003): *Lesotho investment policy review. Paper presented at the UNIDO expert group meeting: The Role of Industrialization in Achieving the MDGs – The Case of the sub-Saharan Countries"*, Vienna, 14-15 August.

Laporte, Geert (2004): *Changes in EU Foreign Policy. Implications for Southern Africa and the ACP.* Paper presented at the SAIA-ECDPM conference on the Trade and Development Cooperation Agreement: Impacts, Lessons and Perspectives for EU-South and Southern Africa Relations. (available online): http://www.ecdpm.org/

Laurent, H.E. Edwin (2005): *Commodity Protocols, the WTO and EPAs.* In: ECDPM: Trade Negotiations Insight vol. 4:3, May-June, pp. 4-7.

Leith, J.C. (1992): *The static welfare economics of a small developing country's membership in a customs union: Botswana in the Southern African Customs Union.* In: World Development, vol. 20:7, pp. 1021-1028.

Lewis, David / Reed, Kabelo / Teljeur, Ethel (2004): *South Africa: Economic Policy-Making and Implementation in Africa: A Study of Strategic Trade and Selective Industrial Policies.* In: Soludo, C. / Ogbu, O. / Chang, H.-J. (Eds.): The Politics of Trade and Industrial Policy in Africa. Forced Consensus?, pp. 151-78, New Jersey: Africa World Press.

Lewis, Jeffrey, D. / Robinson, Sherman / Thierfelder, Karen (2002): *Free Trade Agreements and the SADC Economies*, World Bank Group (Ed.): Africa Region Working Paper Series No. 27, February, Washington D.C.: World Bank Publication.

Liebig, Stefan / Niemann, Arne / von Uexküll, Erik / Vogt, Florian: *Putting Liberalization on the right track – the case of supply side constraints in the EU-ESA negotiations for an Economic Partnership Agreement.* European Analysis Research Paper Series, No. 1, January (online): http://www.europeananalysis.org.uk, accessed 03/03/2005.

Lovasz, Juergen (2004): Round-table discussion on EU-SA Relations into the Future: Reviewing development and Cooperation Agreement. South African Institute of International Affairs, 26 August. (online): http://www.saiia.org.za/modules.php?op=modload&name=News&file=article&sid=3, accessed 09/08/05.

Lowe, Philip (2000): *Main Parameters of the EU-SA Partnership.* In: Bertelsmann-Scott, Talitha / Mills, Greg / Sidiropoulos, Elizabeth (Eds.): The EU-SA Agreement. South Africa, Southern Africa and European Union, pp. 39-46, Johannesburg: SAIIA.

Maasdorp, Gavin (1994): *Models of co-operation in southern Africa.* In: Venter, Minnie (Ed): Prospects for Progress. Critical Choices for Southern Africa, pp. 14-27, Johannesburg: Maskew Miller Longman.

Maasdorp, Gavin (1992): *Economic Co-operation in Southern Africa: Prospects for Regional Integration.* In: Research Institute for the Study of Conflict and Terrorism (Ed.): Revised version of G. Maasdorp "Regional Economic Groupings: Co-operation or Integration", RISCT, London.

Maasdorp, Gavin / Whiteside, A. (Eds.): *Rethinking Economic Co-operation in Southern Africa: Trade and Investment.* Johannesburg: Konrad Adenauer Foundation.

Madeley, John (2003): *Transnational corporations and developing countries: big business, poor people.* In: The Courier. The magazine of ACP-EU development cooperation, no. 196, January/February 2003, pp. 36-38.

Madonsela, Winnie S. (2001): *CAP and CAP reform: What's in it for Southern Africa?* In: Danmarks Naturfredningsforening (Eds.): Closing the Gap. North-South views on a reform of the European Common Agricultural Policy and the need for a new global deal, pp. 59-66. (online) http://www.gem.org.za/html/documents/closingthegap.pdf, accessed 14/04/03.

Magagula, Glenn T. / Faki, Harmid H.M. (1999): *Comparative Economic Advantage of alternative agricultural production options in Swaziland.* USAID Technical Paper No. 103, December, USAID: The Mitchell Group, Inc.

Mahlinza, Duminsani (2003), Economist, Swaziland Sugar Association. Interview with Mahlinza, 17 November 2003, Mbabane.

Mair, Stefan / Peters-Berries, Christian (2001): *Regionale Integration und Kooperation in Afrika südlich der Sahara. EAC, ECOWAS und SADC im Vergleich*, Bonn: Weltforum-Verlag.

Malzbender, Daniel (2003): *Reforming the EU sugar regime: will Southern Africa still feature?* Tralac Working Paper No. 12/2003, October.

Mandelson, Peter (2005): Open Letter to F. Polman, President Concord, Cab24/PM/RL/kr/D(2005)D 1224, Brussels.

Manning, Peter (2000): *Review of the Distributive Aspects of Namibia's Fisheries Policy.* NEPRU Research Report No. 21, July, Windhoek.

Mansfield, Edward (1993): *Effects of international politics on regionalism in international trades*, In: Anderson, Kym / Blackhurst, Richard (Eds.): Regional Integration and the Global Trading System, pp. 199-217, New York and London: Harvester Wheatsheaf.

Matambalya, Francis A.S.T. (1998): *Future Perspectives of EU-ACP Relationship. The Case of the Southern African ACP-States*. Friedrich Ebert Stiftung (Eds.): Arbeitspapiere zur EU-Entwicklungspolitik, No. 7, Bonn: FES.

Matthee, M. / Naudé, W.A. / Viviers, W. (2005): *Challenges for developing country suppliers in the global floriculture chain: A South African perspective.* Paper presented at the Biennial Conference of the Economic Society of South Africa (ESSA), 7-9 September, Durban.

Mayer, Marina / Zarenda, Harry (1994): *The Southern African Customs Union. A review of costs and benefits.* Development Bank of Southern Africa Policy Working Paper No. 19, Thorold's Africana Books: Johannesburg.

Mbekeani, Kennedy (2003): Senior Research Fellow, Botswana Institute for Development and Policy Analysis (BIDPA). Interview with Mbekeani, 15 October 2003, Gaborone.

McCarthy, C.L. (2004): *The new Southern African Customs Union Agreement (SACUA) – challenges and prospects.* Paper presented at the NEPRU Workshop "Monitoring Regional Integration in Southern Africa", 12-13 June 2004, Midgard/Namibia.

McCarthy, C.L. (1994): *Revenue Distribution and Economic Development in the Southern African Customs Union.* In: The South African Journal of Economics, vol. 62:3, pp. 167-187.

McCarthy, C.L. (1992): *The Southern African Customs Union in a Changing Economic and Political Environment.* In: Journal of World Trade, vol. 26:4, pp. 5-24.

McCarthy, Colin / Hansohm, Dirk (2005): *Common Industrial Policies for SACU Member States* Paper presented at the NEPRU workshop on "Monitoring Regional Integration in Southern Africa", Windhoek, June 11-12.

McConville, Will (2003): Managing Director Swaziland Fruit Canners (Pty.) Ltd. Interview with McConville, 24 November 2003, Malkerns.

McCulloch, Neil / Winters, L. Alan / Cirera, Xavier (2003): *Trade Liberalization and Poverty: A Handbook.* London: Centre for Economic Policy Research.

de Melo, Jaime / Panagariya, Arvind / Rodrik, Dani (1993): *The new regionalism: a country perspective.* In: de Melo, J. / Panagariy, A. (Eds.): New Dimensions in regional integration, pp. 159-93, Camebridge et al.: Cambridge University Press.

Meyer, Gustav (2003): Director Automotive TISA. Interview with Meyer, 22 October 2003, Midrand.

Meyn, Mareike (2005): *The Export Potential of Southern African Countries Agro-based Products and the Impact of Challenged Trade Relations with the EU.* In: Wohlmuth, Karl et al. (Eds.): African Development Perspectives Yearbook vol. 11: Africa – Escaping the Primary Commodities Dilemma, pp. 211-43.

Meyn, Mareike (2004a): *Are Economic Partnership Agreements likely to Promote or Constrain Regional Integration in Southern Africa? Options, Limits and Challenges Botswana, Mauritius and Mozambique are Facing.* NEPRU Working Paper No. 96, July 2004, Windhoek.

Meyn, Mareike (2004b): *Struggling without Support. Private Sector Support Institutions in SADC.* In: SADC Barometer Issue No. 4, January 2004, S. 10-11.

Meyn, Mareike (2004c): *Private Sector Support Institutions in the Southern African Development Community: objectives, achievements and limits.* In: Wohlmuth, Karl *et al.* (Eds.): African Development Perspectives Yearbook vol. 10: Private and Public Sectors: towards a balance, Lit-Verlag: Münster and Hamburg.

MFMR (Ministry of Fisheries and Marine Resources of the Republic of Namibia) (2004a): *Namibia's Marine Resources Policy. Towards Responsible Development and Management of the Marine Resources Sector.* August 2004, Windhoek: Government Printer.

MFMR (2004b): *Annual Report 2002*, Windhoek: Government Printer.

MFMR (2004c): *Namibia's Marine Resources Policy. Towards Responsible Development and Management of the Marine Resources Sector.* Windhoek: Government Printer.

MFMR (2004d): *Industry Review.* No. 1. January - June. Windhoek: Government Printer.

MFMR (2003a): Ministry of Fisheries and Marine Resources. Introduction. http://www.op.gov.na/Decade_peace/mfmr.htm, accessed 05/07/2003

MFMR (2003b): *Annual Report 2002*, Windhoek: Government Printer.

MFMR (2000): *Marine Resources Act 2000.* Government Notice No. 292. Windhoek: Government Gazette No. 2458.

MFMR (1992): *Towards the Responsible Development of the Fisheries Sector.* Windhoek: Government Printer.

Michaely, Michael (2004): *Trade Liberalization and Trade Preferences.* Burlington: Ashgate.

Mkhonta, Funekile / Maphalala, Welcome M. (2003): Deputy Director - SME / Deputy Director – FDI. Swaziland Investment Promotion Authority (SIPA). Interview with Mkhonta and Maphalala. 19 November 2003, Mbabane.

Molapisi, Sonny (2003a): General Manager Marketing, Botswana Meat Commission (BMC). Interview with Molapisi, 16/10/2003, Gaborone.

Molapisi, Sonny (2003b): *Presentation of the Botswana Meat Commission (BMC),* Internal document.

Mouton, André / Roux, Wallie (2003): Marketing Manager and Market Research Officer, Meatco Namibia. Interview with Mouton and Roux, 29 September 2003, Windhoek.

Murangi, Noko (2003): Deputy Director: Trade Policy and External Relations. Directorate of International Trade. Ministry of Trade and Industry of the Republic of Namibia. Interview with Murangi. Windhoek, 29 September.

Mwase, Ngila / Maasdorp, Gavin (1999): *The Southern African Customs Union (SACU).* In: Oyejide, A. / Elbadawi, I. / Yeo, Stephen (Eds.): Regional Integration and Trade Liberalization in SubSaharan Africa. Vol. 3: Regional Case-Studies, pp. 197-249. London: McMillan Press.

NAACAM (National Association of Automotive Component and Allied Manufacturers) (2004a): *NAACAM 2004 Directory.* Official Directory of the National Association of Automotive Component and Allied Manufacturers. (online) http://www.naacam.co.za, accessed 14/05/2004.

NAACAM (2004b): Employment Figures. (Internal, unpublished document).

NAACAM (2003): *NAACAM 2003 Directory. Official Directory of the National Association of Automotive Component and Allied Manufacturers.* CD-Rom.

NAAMSA (National Association of Automobile Manufacturers of South Africa) (2003a): *Annual Report 2003.* Pretoria: NAAMSA.

NAAMSA (2003b): *Annual average new vehicle price rises versus consumer price index (CPI) movements: 1980–2003.* August (Internal, unpublished document).

NAAMSA (2003c): *South Africa – European Union Free Trade Agreement negotiations.* October (Internal, unpublished document).

NAAMSA (2003d): *Further update on the SA-EU Free Trade Agreement* negotiations relating to automotive products. October (internal, unpublished document).

Namibia Economist (28/08/2001): Graig, Augetto: *Windhoek to pay N$ 30 million for Ramatex.*

Namibia Foundation (Ed.) (1998b): *Business Opportunities in the Fishing Industry.* In: Namibia Brief. Focus on Fisheries and Research, Windhoek, p. 57.

Ndzinge, Victoria (2003): *The SACU-USA Free Trade Agreement Negotiations: What is the Benefit for Botswana? A Preliminary Analysis.* Unpublished Draft Paper. October 2003, BIDPA: Gaborone.

Nichols, Paul (2004a): FAO Special Advisor to the Minister. Interview with Nichols. 14 June and 17 June 2004, Windhoek.

Nichols, Paul (2004b): Comments on draft paper. E-mail from Nichols. Received 02 September, 2004.

Nichols, Paul (2003a): FAO Special Advisor to the Minister. Interview with Nichols. 24 September 2003, Windhoek.

Nichols, Paul (2003b): *A Developing Country Puts a Halt to Foreign Overfishing.* In: Economic Perspectives, vol. 8, no. 1, January. (online) http://usinfo.state.gov/journals/ites/0103/ijee/nichols.htm, accessed 01/06/2004.

Nielson, Poul (2004): Opening of SADC/EU negotiations for the Economic Partnership Agreement, Windhoek, 8th July 2004. EU Press Release, 09/07/04.

Nϕddeboe, Hans (2003): Chairman, Swaziland Citrus Board. Interview with Nϕddeboe, 17 November 2003, Mbabane,

Nowak, Michael / Ebrill, Liam P. (2003): Swaziland. *IMF Staff Report for the 2002 Article IV Consultation.* In: IMF Country Report No. 03/21, Washington D.C.: IMF Publication.

Nujoma, David (2003): Director Namibian Investment Centre. Interview with Nujoma. 24 September 2003, Windhoek.

NZZ (Neue Zürcher Zeitung, 13/01/2003): N.N.: *Autos als wichtige Exportartikel Südafrikas. Besonders starke Stellung bei Fahrzeugkomponenten.*

OECD (Organisation for Economic Co-operation and Development) (2004): *African Economic Outlook.* Paris: OECD Publication.

OECD (2003): *Trade Capacity Building: Critical for Development.* OECD Pol icy Brief August.

OECD (2001): *The DAC Guidelines. Strengthening Trade Capacity for Development.* OECD: Paris.

Oelofsen, Burger (2003): *A Political Will and Management Transparency.* In: Namibia Trade Directory 2003, Windhoek, pp. 33-38.

Oshikoya W.T. / Hussain, Nureldin M. (2002): *Infrastructure for Economic Development in Africa.* In: OECD and AfDB Development Centre Seminars: Regional Integration in Africa, pp. 77-114, Paris: OECD Publication.

Otto, Rolf (2003): Deputy Director: Bilateral Trade Negotiation. Directorate International Trade. National Department of Agriculture of the Republic of South Africa. Interview with Otto. 14 November 2003, Pretoria.

Owen, G.W. (2003): General Manager, Volvo Truck and Bus (Botswana) (Pty.) Ltd. Interview with G.W. Owen, 16 October 2003, Gaborone.

Padoan, Pier Carlo (2001): *Political Economy of New Regionalism and World Governance.* In: Telò, Mario (Ed.): European Union and New Regionalism, pp. 39-58, Aldershot *et al.*: Ashgate.

Pallangyo, Abraham (2000): *The Impact of the EU-SA Agreement on SADC.* In: Bertelsmann-Scott, Talitha / Mills, Greg / Sidiropoulos, Elizabeth (Eds.): The EU-SA Agreement. South Africa, Southern Africa and European Union, pp. 71-82, Johannesburg: SAIIA.

Pato, Sandile: Director of International Trade Department, Ministry of Foreign Affairs and Trade of the Kingdom of Swaziland, Interview with Pato, 18 November 2003, Mbabane.

Payne, Dexter C. (2000): *Policy-making in Nested Institutions: Explaining the Conservation Failure of the EU's Common Fisheries Policy.* In: Journal of Common Market Studies, vol. 38, no. 2, pp. 303-24.

Perkins, D. / Radelet, S. / Snodgrass, D. / Gillis, M. / Roemer, M. (2001): *Economics of Development.* Fifth Edition, W.W. Norton & Company, Inc.: New York.

Piazolo, Marc (2001): *Regional Integration in Southern Africa: Motor of Economic Development?* Conference Paper prepared for Economic Society of South Africa (ESSA), (online): http://www.essa.org.za/download/papers/reginteg.pdf, accessed 27/01/2004.

Pilegaard, Jess (2005): *EU-ACP Trade Relations. The Regional Economic Partnership Agreements.* Presentation held at the Trade Mondays Seminar Series of the Danish Institute for International Studies, 07 March 2005, Copenhagen.

Platzky, Laurine (1996): *The Development Impact of South Africa's Industrial Location Policies: An Unforeseen Legacy.* PhD thesis, The Hague.

Prowse, Susan (2002): *The Role of International and National Agencies in Trade-related Capacity Building.* In: The World Economy vol. 25:9, pp. 1235-61.

Puga, Diego/Venables, Anthony (1997): *Preferential Trading Arrangements and Industrial Locations.* In: Journal of international Economics, vol. 43:3, pp. 347-68.

Raditedu, Loago (2003): Executive Director EAOB. Interview with Raditedu. 14 October 2003, Gaborone.

Reissner, Douglas (2003): General Manager. Olthaver & List Company Group. Interview with Reissner. 23 September 2003, Windhoek.

Republic of South Africa (1969): *Government Notice Department of Commerce R. 3914 – 12 December 1969: Customs Union Agreement between the Governments of The Republic of South Africa, The Republic of Botswana, The Kingdom of Lesotho and the Kingdom of Swaziland.* (online): http://www.tralac.org/documents/sacu_1969.htm, accessed 04/07/02.

Ritter, Rainer (2005): Ritter Consulting, Member of the Standing Committee of the Namibian Chamber of Commerce and Industry (NCCI). Comments of Ritter at the NEPRU workshop on "Monitoring Regional Integration in Southern Africa", Windhoek, 11-12 June.

Robberts, Tom (2003): Councellor. Delegation of the European Commission in Botswana. Interview with Robberts, 10 October 2003, Gaborone.

Robson, Peter (1998): *The Economics of International Integration.* 14th Edition, London *et al.*: George Allen & Unwin.

Robson, Peter (1997): *Integration in Sub-Saharan Africa.* In: El-Agraa, Ali M. (Ed.): Economic Integration Worldwide, pp. 348-67, Basingstoke *et al.*: Macmillan Press.

Rodrik, Dani (2001): *Trading in Illusions.* Foreign Policy, March/April. (online):http://www.foreinpolicy.com/issue/marapr_2001/rodrick.html, accessed 12/04/03.

Rodrik, Dani (1999): *The new global economy and developing countries: making openness work,* Washington D.C.: Overseas Development Council.

Rodrik, Dani / Rodriguez, Francisco (1999): *Trade policy and economic growth:*

a sceptic's guide to the cross-national evidence. National Bureau of Economic Research WP 7081, April.

Rouhier, Pascale (2004): *WTO case on EU Sugar: Implications for Africa on Preferential Access.* Tralac Trade Brief Agri Conference, September. (online): www.tralac.org.

Sachs, Jeffrey D. / Warner, Andrew (1996): *Economic Reform and the Process of Global Integration.* Development Discussion Paper No. 552, Reprint Series.

SACU (2002): *The Southern African Customs Union Agreement – Draft Final between the Governments of the Republic of Botswana, the Kingdom of Lesotho, the Republic of Namibia, the Republic of South Africa and the Kingdom of Swaziland.* (online): http://www.tralac.org/documents/sacu_2002.htm, accessed 05/07/2002.

SARB (South African Reserve Bank) (2005): *Online Statistic.* (online): http://www.reservebank.co.za/, accessed 04/07/2005.

Schäfer, Alexander (1999): *Ein amerikanischer Wirtschafts(t)raum von Alaska bis Feuerland?: NAFTA und die Integrationsperspektiven.* FES Electronic Library (online): http://www.fes.de/fulltext/stabsabteilung/00503toc.htm, accessed 26/05/2005.

Schiff, Maurice / Wang, Yanling (2003): *Regional Integration and Technology Diffusion. The Case of the North American Free Trade Agreement.* World Bank Policy Research WP 3132. World Bank: Washington D.C.

Schiff, Maurice / Winters, Alan (1998): *Dynamics and Politics in Regional Integration Arrangements: An Introduction*, In: World Bank Economic Review, vol 12.:2, pp. 177-95

Scott, Robert E. (2001): *NAFTA's Hidden Costs.* Economic Policy Institute (EPI) Briefing Paper, April. (available online): http://epint.org/

Segomelo, Keolebogile and Mbaiwa, Sophie (2003): Standards Officers BOBS. Interview with Keolebogile and Mbaiwa. 08 October 2003, Gaborone.

Seijo, J.C. / Defeo, O. / Salas, S. (1998): Fisheries bioeconomics. Theory, modelling and management. FAO Fisheries Technical Paper 368, Rome.

Sell, Axel (2000): *Innovationen und weltwirtschaftliche Dynamik - Der Beitrag der Innovationsforschung nach Schumpeter.* Knorr, A. / Lemper, A. / Sell, A. / Wohlmuth K. (Eds.): Berichte aus dem Weltwirtschaftlichen Colloquium der Universität Bremen, Nr. 67, Universität Bremen.

Senosi, Omphitlhetse Bobo (2003), Export Promotion Officer BEDIA. Interview Senosi. 02 October 2003, Gaborone.

Simataa, Stanley (1998): *Developing Training for the Namibian Fishing Industry*. In: Namibia Brief. Focus on Fisheries and Research, Windhoek, p. 62.

Sitta, Samuel (2005): *Quitting Comesa: Implications for Tanzania*. SADC Barometer, Issue 8, SADCs future, March 2005. SAIIA: Johannesburg.

Smalberger, Wilhelm (2004): Round-table discussion on EU-SA Relations into the Future: Reviewing development and Cooperation Agreement. South African Institute of International Affairs, 26 August. (online): http://www.saiia.org.za/modules.php?op=modload&name=News&file=art cle&sid=3, accessed 09/08/05.

Smalberger, William (2003): Head of EU and EFTA Desk, DTI. Interview with Smalberger. 12 November 2003, Pretoria.

Smalberger, Wilhelm (2000): *Lessons Learnt by South Africa during Negotiations*. In: Bertelsmann-Scott, T. / Mills, G. / Sidiropoulos, E. (Eds.): The EU-SA Agreement. South Africa, Southern Africa and the European Union, pp. 47-52, Johannesburg: SAIIA.

Solignac Lecomte, Henri-Bernard (2003): *Building Capacity to Trade: What are the Priorities?* OECD Development Centre Working Paper No. 223, November.

Solignac Lecomte, Henri-Bernard (2001): *Building Capacity to Trade: A Road Map for Development Partners. Insights from Africa and the Caribbean.* Overseas Development Institute (ODI) Working Paper, July.

Solignac Lecomte, Henri-Bernard (2000): *The impact of the EU-SA Agreement on Lomé*. In: Bertelsmann-Scott, T. / Mills, G. / Sidiropoulos, E. (Eds.): The EU-SA Agreement. South Africa, Southern Africa and the European Union, pp. 53-69, Johannesburg: SAIIA.

South Centre (2005): *Revisiting EPAs and WTO Compatibility*. South Centre Analytical Note, July 2005, SC/TADP/AN/DS/2.

Southern-African German Chamber of Commerce and Industry (SAGC) (2001): *SADC country info*, http://www.germanchamber.co.za/files/countries, accessed 01/07/02.

SSA (Swaziland Sugar Association) (2004): *The Swaziland Sugar Association – Fact Sheet*. (online): http://www.swazibusiness.com/swazisugar/facts.html, accessed 29/06.2005.

SSA (2003): *Annual Report 2002/03*. Mbabane: SSA.

Stamm, Andreas (2003): *Value Chains for Development Policy: Challenges for Trade Policy and the Promotion of Economic Development.* Concept Study for the BMZ and the GTZ, Eschborn: DIE. (online): http://www2.gtz.de/trade/download/stamm2004en.pdf, accessed 01/02/04.

Stern, Matthew (2003): *The New SACU Revenue Sharing Formula.* Unpublished document received from Stern via e-mail, 11 November 2003.

Stevens, Christopher (2005): *Commission for Africa Report Response. The Africa Commission on trade.* (online): www.ids.ac.uk/ids/news/CFA%20Response/StevensResponse.pdf, accessed 10/05/05.

Stevens, Christopher (2000): *The EU-ACP Relationship after Lomé.* In: van Dijck, Pitou / Faber, Gerrit (Eds.): The External Economic Dimension of the European Union, pp. 223-43, The Hague *et al.*: Kluwer Law International.

Stevens, Christopher / Kennan, Jane (2005a): *Preparing for Economic Partnership Agreements.* Institute for Development Studies Briefing Paper, March, Sussex: IDS.

Stevens, Christopher / Kennan, Jane (2005b): *EU-ACP Economic Partnership Agreements: The Effects of Reciprocity.* Institute for Development Studies Briefing Paper, July, Sussex: IDS.

Stock, Greg (2003): General Manager, Cadbury Swaziland (Pty.) Ltd. Interview with Stock, 21 November 2003, Matsapha.

Stone, Christopher / Downes, David / de Fontaubert, Charlotte (2001): *Biodiversity, Trade, and the Fishing Sector. Case Study: West Africa.* (online): http://biodiversityeconomics.org/pdf/topics-20-01.pdf, accessed 01/07/2004.

Suranovic, Steven (2002): *The Infant Industry Argument and Dynamic Comparative Advantage. International Trade Theory and Policy Lecture Notes* (online): http://internationalecon.com/v1.0/ch100/100c050.html, accessed 11/03/2005.

Swiss Mission in Geneva (2005): *Foreign States represented in Geneva.* (online): http://www.eda.admin.ch/geneva_miss/e/home/numbe/etatchi.html, accessed 05/08/2005.

Tall, Amadou (2002): *World Trade Trends for Fishery Products and the Share of Africa.* Infopeche Trade. (online). http://r0.unctad.org/infocomm/comm_docs/docs/projectp/docsgamb/gambiapaper2.pdf, accessed 30/06/2004.

Thakalekoala, Thabo (2003): *New M/Hoek industrial expansion to create 18,000 jobs, thanks to AGOA*. (online) http://www.sahims.net/doclibrary/les/les_creating_jobs.doc, accessed 13/08/03.

The East African (16/05/05), Stanley Kamana: *Now EU Advises Tanzania to Choose EAC Or SADC.* (online): http://allafrica.com/stories/200505180677.html, accessed 23/05/05.

The Economist (16/01/2003): N.N.: *No silver bullets. But cutting American tariffs on African goods has helped a bit.*

The Namibian (09/08/05): Jauch, Herbert: *The global textile industry, the WTO and Namibia* (online): http://www.namibian.com.na/2005/August/national/05CC117B4D.html, accessed 17/08/05.

TISA (Trade and Investment South Africa) (2003): *TISA MIDP Export Data for main automotive components – fob values – R million.* (Internal Document, unpublished).

Todaro, Michael P. / Stephen C. Smith (2002): *Economic Development*, 8th Edition. Harlow: Pearson Education.

Tradepartners (2002): Automotive industry market in South Africa. (online) http://www.tradepartners.gov.uk/automotive/south_africa/profile/ accessed 13/01/03.

Trades Centre (Trade and Development Study Centre) (2003): *Study of the Compatibility of Trade Policies in the Context of Current Regional Economic Integration Processes: the Case of SADC.* Prepared by Tekere, Moses and Ndlela, Daniel, Harare: Trades Centre.

UK Commission for Africa: *Report on TRIPS and FTAs. Chapter 8. More Trade and Fairer Trade* (online): http://www.commissiononafrica.org/english/report/thereport/15chap8.pdf, accessed 29/03/05.

UNAIDS (2003): *Epidemiological Fact Sheets on HIV/AIDS and Sexual Transmitted Infections,* http://www.unaids.org/hivaidsinfo/statistics/fact_sheets/index_en.htm, accessed 03/06/2004.

UNCTAD (United Nations Conference on Trade and Development) (2004a): *Economic Development in Africa. Trade Performance and Commodity Dependence.* New York and Geneva: United Nations.

UNCTAD (2004b): *UNCTAD Handbook of Statistics*. New York and Geneva: UNCTAD.

UNCTAD (2003): *Trade and Development Report 2003.* New York: United Nations

UNCTAD (2002a): *World Investment Report 2001.* UN Publication: Geneva and New York.

UNCTAD (2002b): *Trade and Development Report 2002.* UN Publication: Geneva and New York.

UNCTAD (2000): *African Development in a Comparative Perspective.* Asmara: Africa World Press.

UNCTAD (1999): *Trade and Development Report 1999.* Geneva and New York.

UNCTAD (1998): *Trade and Development Report 1998.* Geneva and New York.

UNECA (United Nations Economic Commission for Africa) (2005): *Economics and Welfare Impacts of the EU-Africa Economic Partnership Agreements* (online): http://www.uneca.org/eca_programmes/trade_and_regional_integration/documents/ Karingi.pdf, accessed 02/04/2005.

UNIDO (United Nations Industrial Development Organisation) (2004a): *Industrial Development Report 2004: Industrialization, Environment and the Millennium Development Goals in Sub-Saharan Africa. The new frontier in the fight against poverty.* Vienna: UNIDO Publication.

UNIDO (2004b): *International Comparisons of Industrial Performance: Country-specific statistical information.* (online): http://www.unido.org/data/country/stats/, accessed 16/06/2005.

UNIDO (2003a): *International Yearbook of Industrial Statistics 2003.* Vienna: UNIDO.

UNIDO (2003b): *Integrated Industrial Development Programme Namibia. Fostering Initiatives for Agro-industry based SME Development in Northern Regions.* Non-officially edited document, Vienna: UNIDO Publication.

UNIDO (2002a): *UNIDO Country Industrial Statistics. Value added (at current prices, in national currency) and Employment by manufacturing branch.* CD-Rom, Vienna: UNIDO.

UNIDO (2002b): *Industrial Statistics Database. 3-and 4-digit level of ISIC Code (Rev.3)*, CD-ROM, Vienna: UNIDO.

UNIDO (1996): *The Globalization of Industry: Implications for Developing Countries Beyond 2000.* Vienna: UNDO Publication.

US Department of State (2004): *Background Note: Botswana.* (online): http://www.state.gov/r/pa/ei/bgn/1830.htm, accessed 19/08/2004.

USAID (United States Agency for International Development) (2005): *Trade Hub Happenings,* August (available online): http://ww.satradehub.org.

USTR (United States Trades Representatives) (2002a): *Comprehensive report of the President on U.S. trade and investment policy toward sub-Saharan Africa and implementation of the African Growth and Opportunity Act.* In: http://www.ustr.gov/regions.african/growth.shtml, accessed 13/01/03.

USTR (2002b): *Foreign Trade Barriers: South Africa.* (online): http://www.ustr.gov/reports/nte/2002/southafrica.pdf, accessed 10/03/03.

Valashia, Phodiso Philiso (2003): Customs Administrator I (International Customs Matters), Department of Customs and Excise. Interview with Valashia. 07 October 2003, Gaborone.

Venables, Anthony J. (1999): *Regional Integration Agreements: a force for convergence or divergence?* World Bank Policy Research Working Paper 2260

Vermeulen, Nico (2004): Director of NAAMSA. E-mail from Vermeulen, 10 March 2004.

Vermeulen, Nico (2003): Director of NAAMSA and Director of the AIEC. Interview with Vermeulen. 12 November 2003, Johannesburg.

Viner, Jacob (1950): *The Customs Union Issue.* New York: Carnegie Endowment for International Peace.

Weed/Urgewald (2002): *Internationale Firma in Lesotho wegen Korruption verurteilt. Verfahren gegen deutsche Unternehmen läuft.* Press release (online): http://www.weed.org, accessed 29/10/2002.

WEF (World Economic Forum) (2003): *Africa Competitiveness Report 2002/2003.* WEF: Geneva.

Wellmer, Gottfried (2005): *Tragen wirtschaftliche Partnerschaftsabkommen (EPAs) zur Beseitigung der Armut bei? Die Handelspolitik der Europäischen Union mit den AKP-Staaten am Beispiel der Entwicklungsgemeinschaft des Südlichen Afrikas (SADC).* Bielefeld: KOSA e.V. / InWent (Eds.).

Williams, Clive (2004a): Executive Director of NAACAM. E-mail from Williams, 31 March 2004.

Williams, Clive (2004b): Executive Director of NAACAM. E-mail from Williams, 17 May 2004.

Williams, Clive (2003a): Executive Director of NAACAM. Interview with Williams. 13 October 2003, Johannesburg.

Williams, Jon (2003b): Managing Director, Swaziland Meat Industries. Interview with Williams, 20 November 2003, Matsapha.

Wohlmuth, Karl (2004): *The African Growth Tragedy. Comments and an Agenda for Action.* Knorr, A. / Lemper, A. / Sell, A. / Wohlmuth K. (Eds.): Berichte aus dem Weltwirtschaftlichen Colloquium der Universität Bremen, Nr. 91, Universität Bremen.

Wohlmuth, Karl (2003): *Chancen der Globalisierung – für wen?* Knorr, A. / Lemper, A. / Sell, A. / Wohlmuth K. (Eds.): Berichte aus dem Weltwirtschaftlichen Colloquium der Universität Bremen, Nr. 81, Universität Bremen.

Wohlmuth, Karl / Gutowski, Achim / Knedlik, Tobias / Meyn, Mareike (Eds.) (2005): *Africa – Escaping the Primary Commodities Dilemma.* African Development Perspectives Yearbook vol. 11/2005, Hamburg: Lit-Verlag (forthcoming).

Wolf, Susanna (1996): *Begrenzter Erfolg der Lomé-Abkommen. Eine empirische Untersuchung der Wirkungen der EU-Zollpräferenzen auf den Handel der AKP-Staaten.* Diss., Frankfurt a.M.: Europäische Hochschulschriften.

Wood, Nick (2003): Director of CSIR Enterprise Development Centre and former Executive Director of the AIDC (until May 2003). Interview with Wood, 22 October 2003, Midrand.

Wood, Adrian / Mayer, Jörg (2001): *Africa's export structure in a comparative perspective.* In: Cambridge Journal of Economics, vol. 25, pp. 369-394.

World Bank (2005): The HIPC Initiative: Background and Progress Through December 2001. (online): http://www.worldbank.org/hipc/progress-to-date/May99v3/may99v3.htm, accessed 03/07/2005.

World Bank (2004): *Country Data Profile: South Africa, Botswana, Lesotho, Namibia and Swaziland Country Data.* (online) http://devdata.worldbank.org/data-query/, accessed 14/10/04.

World Bank (2003): *African Development Indicators 2002.* Washington D.C: The World Bank.

World Bank Group (2001a): *Country Profile Table: South Africa, Botswana, Lesotho, Namibia and Swaziland Data Profile* ,(online): http://devdata.worldbank.org/external/CPProfile.asp?, accessed 14/06/02.

World Bank (2001b): *Countries at a Glance: South Africa, Botswana, Lesotho, Namibia and Swaziland at a Glance*, (online) http://www.worldbank.org/data/, accessed 14/06/02.

World Bank (1993): *World Development Report.* Washington D.C.: World Bank Publication.

World Bank (1992): *The East Asian Miracle: Economic Growth and Public Policy.* Washington D.C.: The World Bank.

WTO (World Trade Organization) (2004) (Ed.): *Trade Policy Review. Report by the European Communities,* Doc.WT/TPR/G/136, Geneva.

WTO (2003) (Ed.): *Trade Policy Review. Southern African Customs Union.* Doc.WT/TPR/G/114, Geneva: WTO.

WTO (1997): *Trade Policy Review. Mexico. Press Release and Summary* (online): http://www.wto.org/english/tratop_e/tpr_e/tp63_e.htm, accessed 20/05/2005:

WTO (1994): Benedek, Wolfgang (Ed.) (1998): *Die Welthandelsorganisation (WTO): alle Texte einschließlich GATT (1994), GATS und TRIPS. Textausgabe.* Munich: Beck.

Yang, Yongzheng / Gupta, Sanjeev (2005): *Regional Trade Arrangements in Africa: Past Performance and the Way Forward.* IMF Working Paper (WP/05/36), Washington D.C.: IMF.

Yeats, Alexander J. (1998): *What can be expected from African Regional Trade Arrangements? Some Empirical Evidence.* World Bank Policy Research Working Paper 2004, Washington D.C.: World Bank Publication.

Yedder, Afif Ben / Rake, Alan (2001): *New African Yearbook 2001.* 13th Edition, London: IC Publication.

Tralac News (available online): http://www.tralac.org/
23/08/2005: SACU and the US will resume trade negotiations in September.
26/04/2005: Free trade talks to begin between Singapore and SACU.
22/09/2004: Namibian suppliers struggling to import dairy products from SA.
19/07/2004: SACU agreement comes into effect on July 15.
11/05/2004: Namibia one step closer to being a gateway to the EU and US.
07/05/2004: Namibian fishing industry growing despite setbacks
29/04/2004: Namibian fishing industry need to look outside of EU.
19/04/2004: Trade influencing labour laws in Africa.
10/06/2003: Namibia's exit from Comesa won't harm.
27/01/2003: SACU negotiators face mammoth talks.
10/12/2002: Swazi blunder causes AGOA trouble.

Appendix I : Company Questionnaire (South African Automotive Industry)

Company : ________________________

Date : ________________________

Name of respondent: ________________________

Position in company: ________________________

I. General questions

- When was your company established? ________

- Describe the ownership structure of your company?
    a. Owner managed by domestic company ________
    b. Owner managed by foreign company (Subsidiary company) ________
    c. Joint venture with foreign company ________

- How many branches do you have in the SACU and where are they situated?

- What are the 5 major products (that) you manufacture and where are the main markets for these products? (Please indicate in % of total)

Product	SACU market	European market	US market	Other market ______	Other market ______
a)					
b)					
c)					
d)					

- What was your annual turnover in 2002? ________

- How many employees (including contractees on payroll) do you have in total? ________

    - Number (percentage) of men? ________

    - Number (percentage) of women? ________

II. Exports to the EU and development of export options

1. When did you start to export to the EU? _______

2a. What are the main advantages of the EU as an export destination for your products? *[Please mark 1) very relevant, 2) relevant, 3) partly relevant, 4) irrelevant]*

a. Stable prices and quantities ________
b. Preferred market access ________
c. Long-standing cooperation ________
d. Knowledge transfer ________
e. Technical assistance ________
f. High quality requirements ________
g. Other, please name

____

2b. What are the main hindrances regarding export to the EU? *[Please mark 1) very relevant, 2) relevant, 3) partly relevant, 4) irrelevant]*

a. Restrictive rules of origin ________
b. Safety regulations ________
c. Lack of product quality and standardisation (i.e. ISO) ________
d. Lack of export capacities ________
e. Lack of access to finance ________
f. Tariff barriers and customs procedures ________
g. Lack of technology ________
h. Lack of marketing and distribution channels ________
i. Other, please name ____________________________________

3a. How did your exports to the EU /sales to OEMs develop in the last five years?

a. Increased by <10, 10-20, 21-30, 31-40, 41-50, 51-75, 76-100, >100%
b. Decreased by <10, 10-20, 21-30, 31-40, 41-50, 51-75, 76-100, >100%
c. Remained stable ______

3b. What were the relevant factors for this development?
(Please mark yes or no)

I. Increase: 1) Increased demand _______, 2) Expanded production _______, 3) Improved market access _______, 4) Improved technical assistance ______, 5) Cooperation with a foreign firm _______, 6) More generous regulations relating to quality and safety regulations ______, 7) Cheaper inputs _______,
8) Others, please name ___________________

II. Decrease: 1) Factor(s) mentioned in question 3bI _______, 2) Increased competition in the EU market _______, 3) Increased competition in the SACU market _______, 4) Internal constraints _______, 5) Increase in input prices _______,
6) Others, please name ________________________

4. Do you face any tariffs or quantitative restrictions for your exports to the EU?

a. No _______
b. Yes, which is _______ % of the product value.
c. Yes, a quota, which is ____________ p.a.

5. What are your strengths (+) and weaknesses (-) in exporting?

a. Product price ________
b. Product quality ________
c. Raw material costs ________
d. Capital utilisation ________
e. Labour productivity ________
f. Labour costs ________
g. Transport ________
h. Just-in-time delivery ________
i. Other, please name ________________________________

6. How important has exporting been for your firm over the last three years regarding the following issues? *[Please mark 1) very relevant, 2) relevant, 3) partly relevant, 4) irrelevant]*

   a. Improved economies of scale ________
   b. Increased profitability ________
   c. Increased productivity ________
   d. Improved price competitiveness ________
   e. Increased technology competence ________
   f. Improved manufacturing processes ________
   g. Improved product quality ________
   h. Increased product development capacity ________
   i. Enhanced labour skills ________
   j. Enhanced management skills ________
   k. Enhanced e-commerce capabilities ________

7. What kind of assistance do you receive for exporting?
   a. Duty drawbacks (MIDP) ________
   b. Export credits ________
   c. Export insurance ________
   d. Exhibition and fairs ________
   e. Training in the field of ________
   f. Information __________________________
      (Please specify by whom and kind of information)
   g. Other assistance, please name __________________
   h. None ________

8a. Do you think of expanding your exports to other African countries?
   a. Yes, to ____________________________________
   b. No _____

8b. Please state the main reasons for exporting / not exporting to other African countries. *(Please indicate yes or no).*
   a. Proximity / High transport costs ________
   b. High / Low demand for products ________
   c. High / Low price of sale ________
   d. Low / High tariffs ________
   e. Low / High non-tariff barriers ________
   f. Low / High competition ________
   g. Low / High product requirements ________
   h. Other, please name __________________________

III. Usage of European inputs for production and development of competition situation

1a. From wherc do you source your main input materials needed for production? *(Please indicate the % of total volume)*

a. Domestically produced _______%
b. From the EU _______%
c. From the USA _______%
d. From Far East _______%
e. From ___________ _______%

1b. How did the prices of your inputs develop in the last five years?

a. Increased by <10, 10-20, 21-30, 31-40, 41-50, >50%
b. Decreased by <10, 10-20, 21-30, 31-40, 41-50, >50%
c. Remained stable ______

2. Where are your main competitors?

a. In the country _______
b. In the EU _______
c. In South East Asia _______
d. Global competition _______
e. In ______________________________

3. Do you feel adversely affected because of European goods imported into the country?

a. Yes _______
b. No _______

4. How did your general competition situation develop in the last five years?

a. Competition increased _______
b. Competition decreased _______
c. Unchanged _______

IV. Value chain and added value of exports

1. Please indicate your real profit trends for the period 1999 to 2003.
   (Please indicate: <10, 10-20, 21-30, 31-40, 41-50, >50%)

Year	Increased	Unchanged	Decreased
1999			
2000			
2001			
2002			
2003			

2. What were the relevant factors for this development?
   (Please mark yes or no)

   a. Increased: 1) Increase in exports_____, 2) Increased domestic sales _____, 3) Increased consumer prices _____, 4) Decreased purchasing prices _____, 5) Lower production costs______, 6) Other, please name ________________

   b. Decreased: 1) Decrease in exports _____, 2) Decreased domestic sales _____ ,3) Fall in consumer prices _____, 4) Increased purchasing prices _____, 5) Increased production costs _____, 6) Other, please name ______________

3. Please indicate the change in unit prices for your main export products (in real terms, inflation adjusted. Base year 2000).

Product	**1999**	**2000**	**2001**	**2002**	**2003**
a)		100			
b)		100			
c)		100			
d)		100			

4. How would you classify your main export purchasing company?
   a. Large, transnational retailer _______
   b. Specialised medium-sized buyer _______
   c. Small-scale retailer _______

5. How do you expect your exports to develop in the next five years?
   (Please indicate: <10, 10-20, 21-30, 31-40, 41-50, >50%)

   a. Volume of exports is likely to increase by ________%
   b. Unit price of exports is likely to increase by ________%
   c. Volume of exports is likely to decrease by ________%
   d. Unit price of exports is likely to decrease by ________%
   e. Volume are likely to remain stable ________
   f. Unit price is likely to remain stable ________

V. Companies strategies

1. Do you have a budget for new product research and development?
   a. Yes, which is around ________% of turnover.
   b. No ______

2. Do you invest in the training of your employees?
   a. Yes, which is around ________% of turnover/payroll.
   b. No ______

3. Do you invest in fixed assets?
   a) Yes, which was __________ in 2002.
   b) No ______

4. Do you plan to upgrade your products or processes?
   a. Yes, by improved products ________
   b. Yes, by the introduction of new products ________
   c. Yes, by increasing the efficiency of management processes ________
   d. Yes, by increasing labour productivity ________
   e. Yes, by increasing capital utilisation ________
   f. Yes, by increasing firms' services towards new activities (e.g. towards marketing, distribution) ________
   g. Yes, by ____

5. Do your main purchasers encourage you to upgrade activities?
   a. If yes, what kind of assistance do they grant?
      ____
   b. No ______

6a. Could you imagine forming a strategic alliance (i.e. a joint-venture) with foreign producer?
   a. Yes _____
   b. No ______

6b. If yes: what kind of benefits do you expect from such cooperation and where do you see the disadvantages?

____

7. Are you investigating new export markets?
   a. Yes, which are ______________________________
   b. No ______

VI. Information / support

1. Have you heard about the EU-SA Free Trade Agreement? _______

2. From whom did you receive information about the EU-SA Free Trade Agreement? _______
   a. From government authorities _______
   b. From private sector support institutions _______
   c. From another institution, please specify ________________
   d. I have not received any information about the EU-SA FTA _______

3. Do you feel well informed about the EU-SA FTA?
   a. Yes ______
   b. No ______

4. How would you judge the government's awareness of the impact of the EU-South Africa FTA on the private sector?
   a. Very high ______
   b. High ______
   c. Moderate ______
   d. Low ______
   e. Very low ______

5. To what extent do you think will the EU-SA FTA affect your business?
   (Please indicate yes or no)
   a. By increased competition in the European market ______
   b. By increased competition in the SACU market ______
   c. Access to competitive inputs will improve ______
   d. Prices for inputs will decrease ______
   e. Prices for consumer goods will decrease ______
   f. It offers cooperation chances with European firms ______
   g. Other, please specify

   ____

6. What kind of support would you need to expand your exports to the EU?
   [Please mark 1) very relevant, 2) relevant,3) partly relevant, 4) irrelevant]
   a. Financial support (credits, export credits) ______
   b. Information about government initiatives and European
   c. programmes ______
   d. Technical assistance to meet European standards ______
   e. Support regarding distribution and marketing of products ______
   f. Other, please specify ______________________________

Appendix II : Company Questionnaire (Namibian Fishing Industry)

Company : ________________________

Date : ________________________

Name of respondent: ________________________

Position in company: ________________________

I. General questions

- When was your company established? ________

- Describe the ownership structure of your company?
    a. Owner managed by domestic company ________
    b. Owner managed by foreign company (Subsidiary company) ________
    c. Joint venture with foreign company ________

- How many branches do you have in the SACU and where are they situated?

- What are the 5 major products (that) you manufacture and where are the main markets for these products? (Please indicate in % of total)

Product	SACU market	European market	US market	Other market ______	Other market ______
a)					
b)					
c)					
d)					

- What was your annual turnover in 2002? ________

- How many employees (including contractees on payroll) do you have in total? ________

    - Number (percentage) of men? ________

    - Number (percentage) of women? ________

II. Exports to the EU and development of export options

1. When did you start to export to the EU? ________

2a. What are the main advantages of the EU as an export destination for your products? *[Please mark 1) very relevant, 2) relevant, 3) partly relevant, 4) irrelevant]*

a. Stable prices and quantities ________
b. Preferred market access ________
c. Long-standing cooperation ________
d. Knowledge transfer ________
e. Technical assistance ________
f. High quality requirements ________
g. Other, please name

____

2b. What are the main hindrances regarding export to the EU? *[Please mark 1) very relevant, 2) relevant, 3) partly relevant, 4) irrelevant]*

a. Restrictive rules of origin ________
b. Safety regulations ________
c. Lack of product quality and standardisation ________
d. Lack of export capacities ________
e. Lack of access to finance ________
f. Tariff barriers and customs procedures ________
g. Lack of technology ________
h. Lack of marketing and distribution channels ________
i. Other, please name ________________________________

3a. How did your exports to the EU /sales to OEMs develop in the last five years?

a. Increased by <10, 10-20, 21-30, 31-40, 41-50, 51-75, 76-100, >100%
b. Decreased by <10, 10-20, 21-30, 31-40, 41-50, 51-75, 76-100, >100%
c. Remained stable ______

3b. What were the relevant factors for this development?
(Please mark yes or no)

I. Increase: 1) Increased demand _______, 2) Expanded production _______, 3) Improved market access _______, 4) Improved technical assistance ______, 5) Cooperation with a foreign firm _______, 6) More generous regulations relating to quality and safety regulations ______, 7) Cheaper inputs _______,
8) Others, please name __________________

II. Decrease: 1) Factor(s) mentioned in question 3bI _______, 2) Increased competition in the EU market _______, 3) Increased competition in the SACU market _______, 4) Internal constraints _______, 5) Increase in input prices _______,
6) Others, please name ______________________

4. Do you face any tariffs or quantitative restrictions for your exports to the EU?

a. No _______
b. Yes, which is _______ % of the product value.
c. Yes, a quota, which is ___________ p.a.

5. What are your strengths (+) and weaknesses (-) in exporting?

a. Product price ________
b. Product quality ________
c. Raw material costs ________
d. Capital utilisation ________
e. Labour productivity ________
f. Labour costs ________
g. Transport ________
h. Just-in-time delivery ________
i. Other, please name ______________________________

6. How important has exporting been for your firm over the last three years regarding the following issues? *[Please mark 1) very relevant, 2) relevant, 3) partly relevant, 4) irrelevant]*

   a. Improved economies of scale ________
   b. Increased profitability ________
   c. Increased productivity ________
   d. Improved price competitiveness ________
   e. Increased technology competence ________
   f. Improved manufacturing processes ________
   g. Improved product quality ________
   h. Increased product development capacity ________
   i. Enhanced labour skills ________
   j. Enhanced management skills ________
   k. Enhanced e-commerce capabilities ________

7. What kind of assistance do you receive for exporting?
   a. Duty drawbacks/exemptions on inputs ________
   b. Export credits ________
   c. Export insurance ________
   d. Exhibition and fairs ________
   e. Training in the field of ________
   f. Information ________________________________
      (Please specify by whom and kind of information)
   g. Other assistance, please name ____________________
   h. None ________

8a. Do you think of expanding your exports to other African countries?
   a. Yes, to ____
   b. No _____

8b. Please state the main reasons for exporting / not exporting to other African countries. *(Please indicate yes or no).*
   a. Proximity / High transport costs ________
   b. High / Low demand for products ________
   c. High / Low price of sale ________
   d. Low / High tariffs ________
   e. Low / High non-tariff barriers ________
   f. Low / High competition ________
   g. Low / High product requirements ________
   h. Other, please name ____________________________

III. Usage of European inputs for production and development of competition situation

1a. From where do you source your main input materials needed for production? *(Please indicate the % of total volume)*

a. Domestically produced _______%
b. From the EU _______%
c. From the USA _______%
d. From Far East _______%
e. From ___________ _______%

1b. How did the prices of your inputs develop in the last five years?

a. Increased by <10, 10-20, 21-30, 31-40, 41-50, >50%
b. Decreased by <10, 10-20, 21-30, 31-40, 41-50, >50%
c. Remained stable ______

2. Where are your main competitors?

a. In the country _______
b. In the EU _______
c. In South East Asia _______
d. Global competition _______
e. In ___________________________________

3. Do you feel adversely affected because of European goods imported into the country?

a. Yes _______
b. No _______

4. How did your general competition situation develop in the last five years?

a. Competition increased _______
b. Competition decreased _______
c. Unchanged _______

IV. Value chain and added value of exports

1. Please indicate your real profit trends for the period 1999 to 2003.
   (Please indicate: <10, 10-20, 21-30, 31-40, 41-50, >50%)

Year	Increased	Unchanged	Decreased
1999			
2000			
2001			
2002			
2003			

2. What were the relevant factors for this development?
   (Please mark yes or no)

   a. Increased: 1) Increase in exports_____, 2) Increased domestic sales _____, 3) Increased consumer prices _____, 4) Decreased purchasing prices _____, 5) Lower production costs______, 6) Other, please name _______________

   b. Decreased: 1) Decrease in exports _____, 2) Decreased domestic sales _____ ,3) Fall in consumer prices _____, 4) Increased purchasing prices _____, 5) Increased production costs _____, 6) Other, please name _______________

3. Please indicate the change in unit prices for your main export products (in real terms, inflation adjusted. Base year 2000).

Product	**1999**	**2000**	**2001**	**2002**	**2003**
a)		100			
b)		100			
c)		100			
d)		100			

4. How would you classify your main export purchasing company?
   a. Large, transnational retailer _______
   b. Specialised medium-sized buyer _______
   c. Small-scale retailer _______

5. How do you expect your exports to develop in the next five years?
(Please indicate: <10, 10-20, 21-30, 31-40, 41-50, >50%)

a. Volume of exports is likely to increase by _______%
b. Unit price of exports is likely to increase by _______%
c. Volume of exports is likely to decrease by _______%
d. Unit price of exports is likely to decrease by _______%
e. Volume are likely to remain stable _______
f. Unit price is likely to remain stable _______

V. Companies strategies

1. Do you have a budget for new product research and development?
   a. Yes, which is around _______% of turnover.
   b. No _____

2. Do you invest in the training of your employees?
   a. Yes, which is around _______% of turnover/payroll.
   b. No _____

3. Do you invest in fixed assets?
   a) Yes, which was _________ in 2002.
   b) No _____

4. Do you plan to upgrade your products or processes?
   a. Yes, by improved products _______
   b. Yes, by the introduction of new products _______
   c. Yes, by increasing the efficiency of management processes _______
   d. Yes, by increasing labour productivity _______
   e. Yes, by increasing capital utilisation _______
   f. Yes, by increasing firms' services towards new activities (e.g. towards marketing, distribution) _______
   g. Yes, by ____

5. Do your main purchasers encourage you to upgrade activities?
   a. If yes, what kind of assistance do they grant?
   ____
   b. No _____

6a. Could you imagine forming a strategic alliance (i.e. a joint-venture) with foreign producer?

a. Yes _____
b. No ______

6b. If yes: what kind of benefits do you expect from such cooperation and where do you see the disadvantages?

____

7. Are you investigating new export markets?

a. Yes, which are ____
b. No ______

Appendix III : Questionnaire for Public and Private Sector Organisations in Botswana and Namibia

Organisation: ______________________

Date: ______________________

Name of Respondent: ______________________

Position: ______________________

I. General questions

1. What are the main advantages of the TDCA for your country? *(Please indicate 1) very relevant, 2) relevant, 3) partly relevant, 4) irrelevant)*
   a. Preferred market access ______
   b. Cheap, high quality inputs ______
   c. Reciprocal contractual arrangement with the main trading partner ______
   d. Technical assistance ______
   e. Learning effects and upgrading of products and processes ______
   f. Attraction of FDI ______
   g. Exploitation of economies of scale ______
   h. Reorganisation of income sources ______
   i. Increase of political stability ______
   j. Others, please name ______________________

2. What are the main disadvantages of the TDCA for your country? *(Please indicate 1) very relevant, 2) relevant, 3) partly relevant, 4) irrelevant)*
   a. Increased competition in the SACU market ______
   b. Increased competition in the European market ______
   c. Trade diversion ______
   d. Revenue losses ______
   e. Direct competition with subsidised European agricultural products ______
   f. Loss of non-reciprocal trade relations ______

g. Negative impact on regional integration ______
h. Other, please name ______________________________

3. How would you judge the awareness of the impact of the EU-South Africa FTA on the private sector in your country?
(Please indicate 1) very high, 2) high, 3) moderate, 4) low
   a. By the public sector ______
   b. By research institutions ______
   c. By private sector support institutions ______
   d. By large companies ______
   e. By SMEs ______

4. Does the TDCA help to realise diversify the export base?
(Please indicate Yes or No)
   a. By stronger cooperation with European firms ______
   b. By technical assistance from by the EU ______
   c. By cheaper inputs ______
   d. By increased competition, leading to increased innovation ______
   e. By increased investment from European firms ______
   f. By improved market access to the EU ______
   g. By ______________________________________

II. Competition situation and technical assistance

1. Have you already noticed increased competition due to the TDCA ______
2. In which sectors do you expect increased competition due to the TDCA? *(multiple answers possible)*

   ____

3. In which of the following areas does your country need technical assistance to cope with the challenges of the TDCA?
(Please indicate 1) very relevant, 2) relevant, 3) partly relevant, 4) irrelevant)
   a. Training of customs officials ______
   b. Training of trade experts in government and research institutions ______
   c. Provision of infrastructure ______
   d. Provision of communication services ______
   e. Other, please specify ______________________________

4. Which are the training needs for the private sector?
   (Please indicate 1) very relevant, 2) relevant, 3) partly relevant, 4) irrelevant)
   a. Improvement and assurance of quality ______
   b. Increase of capacities ______
   c. Improved the availability of products ______
   d. Upgrading activities ______
   e. Meeting of international standards ______
   f. Improved services of private sector support institutions ______

III. Information and participation policy

1. When did you first hear about the TDCA? ______
2. Who informed you about the TDCA? ______________
3. Do you feel well informed about the TDCA and its impact on SACU? ______

4a. Did the national business community influence the TDCA?
   a. No ______
   b. Yes ______

4b. If yes, to what extent? ______________________________

5. Which provisions of the TDCA are in the interest of the national business community?

   ____

6. Which provisions are not in the interest of the national business community?

   ____

IV. Regional integration and capacity constraints

1. How does the TDCA affect regional integration within the SADC?
   (Please indicate a) yes, b) no, c) do not know)
   a. It increases the pressure to agree on common policies ______
   b. It promotes trade liberalisation within SADC ______
   c. It promotes "Good Governance" in SADC ______

   d. It raises prejudices against South Africa ______
   e. It leads to a fragmentation of interests ______
   f. It increases the competition within SADC ______
   g. Additional remarks ____________________________

2. What is your opinion on the "Economic Partnership Agreements" (EPAs) between the ACP countries and the EU?
   (Please indicate a) yes, b) no, c) do not know)
   a. The BLNS countries should accede to the TDCA ______
   b. Any EPA has to include South Africa ______
   c. The whole SADC should negotiate an EPA with the EU ______
   d. Other proposal for negotiation ________________________
   e. EPAs promote regional integration in southern Africa
      (Please explain)

      ____

   f. EPAs undermine regional integration in southern Africa
      (Please explain)

      ____

3. What is you opinion about the forthcoming SACU-USA and the SACU-EFTA FTA?
   (Please indicate a) yes, b) no, c) do not know)
   a. Further FTAs will improve SACU's market access ______
   b. Further FTAs are mainly in the interest of South Africa ______
   c. BLNS countries would prefer the maintenance of the status quo ______
   d. FTAs with industrialised countries are beneficial for SACU ______
      (Please explain)

      ____

   e. FTAs with industrialised countries are harmful for SACU _____
      (Please explain)

      ____

   f. The SACU countries are overextended with negotiating further FTAs ______
   g. Any trade liberalisation should be negotiated at WTO ______
   h. Additional remarks

      ____

Development Economics and Policy

Series edited by Franz Heidhues and Joachim von Braun

Band 1 Andrea Fadani: Agricultural Price Policy and Export and Food Production in Cameroon. A Farming Systems Analysis of Pricing Policies. The Case of Coffee-Based Farming Systems. 1999.

Band 2 Heike Michelsen: Auswirkungen der Währungsunion auf den Strukturanpassungsprozeß der Länder der afrikanischen Franc-Zone. 1995.

Band 3 Stephan Bea: Direktinvestitionen in Entwicklungsländern. Auswirkungen von Stabilisierungsmaßnahmen und Strukturreformen in Mexiko. 1995.

Band 4 Franz Heidhues / François Kamajou: Agricultural Policy Analysis – Proceedings of an International Seminar, held at the University of Dschang, Cameroon on May 26 and 27 1994, funded by the European Union under the Science and Technology Program (STD). 1996.

Band 5 Elke M. Förster: Protection or Liberalization? A Policy Analysis of the Korean Beef Sector. 1996.

Band 6 Gertrud Schrieder: The Role of Rural Finance for Food Security of the Poor in Cameroon. 1996.

Band 7 Nestor R. Ahoyo Adjovi: Economie des Systèmes de Production intégrant la Culture de Riz au Sud du Bénin: Potentialités, Contraintes et Perspectives. 1996.

Band 8 Jenny Müller: Income Distribution in the Agricultural Sector of Thailand. Empirical Analysis and Policy Options. 1996.

Band 9 Michael Brüntrup: Agricultural Price Policy and its Impact on Production, Income, Employment and the Adoption of Innovations. A Farming Systems Based Analysis of Cotton Policy in Northern Benin. 1997.

Band 10 Justin Bomda: Déterminants de l'Epargne et du Crédit, et leurs Implications pour le Développement du Système Financier Rural au Cameroun. 1998.

Band 11 John M. Msuya: Nutrition Improvement Projects in Tanzania: Implementation, Determinants of Performance, and Policy Implications. 1998.

Band 12 Andreas Neef: Auswirkungen von Bodenrechtswandel auf Ressourcennutzung und wirtschaftliches Verhalten von Kleinbauern in Niger und Benin. 1999.

Band 13 Susanna Wolf (ed.): The Future of EU-ACP Relations. 1999.

Band 14 Franz Heidhues / Gertrud Schrieder (eds.): Romania – Rural Finance in Transition Economies. 2000.

Band 15 Katinka Weinberger: Women's Participation. An Economic Analysis in Rural Chad and Pakistan. 2000.

Band 16 Christof Batzlen: Migration and Economic Development. Remittances and Investments in South Asia: A Case Study of Pakistan. 2000.

Band 17 Matin Qaim: Potential Impacts of Crop Biotechnology in Developing Countries. 2000.

Band 18 Jean Senahoun: Programmes d'ajustement structurel, sécurité alimentaire et durabilité agricole. Une approche d'analyse intégrée, appliquée au Bénin. 2001.

Band 19 Torsten Feldbrügge: Economics of Emergency Relief Management in Developing Countries. With Case Studies on Food Relief in Angola and Mozambique. 2001.

Band 20 Claudia Ringler: Optimal Allocation and Use of Water Resources in the Mekong River Basin: Multi-Country and Intersectoral Analyses. 2001.

Band 21 Arnim Kuhn: Handelskosten und regionale (Des-)Integration. Russlands Agrarmärkte in der Transformation. 2001.

Band 22 Ortrun Anne Gronski: Stock Markets and Economic Growth. Evidence from South Africa. 2001.

Band 23 Patrick Webb / Katinka Weinberger (eds.): Women Farmers. Enhancing Rights, Recognition and Productivity. 2001.

Band 24 Mingzhi Sheng: Lebensmittelkonsum und -konsumtrends in China. Eine empirische Analyse auf der Basis ökonometrischer Nachfragemodelle. 2002.

Band 25 Maria Iskandarani: Economics of Household Water Security in Jordan. 2002.

Band 26 Romeo Bertolini: Telecommunication Services in Sub-Saharan Africa. An Analysis of Access and Use in the Southern Volta Region in Ghana. 2002.

Band 27 Dietrich Müller-Falcke: Use and Impact of Information and Communication Technologies in Developing Countries' Small Businesses. Evidence from Indian Small Scale Industry. 2002.

Band 28 Wolfram Erhardt: Financial Markets for Small Enterprises in Urban and Rural Northern Thailand. Empirical Analysis on the Demand for and Supply of Financial Services, with Particular Emphasis on the Determinants of Credit Access and Borrower Transaction Costs. 2002.

Band 29 Wensheng Wang: The Impact of Information and Communication Technologies on Farm Households in China. 2002.

Band 30 Shyamal K. Chowdhury: Institutional and Welfare Aspects of the Provision and Use of Information and Communication Technologies in the Rural Areas of Bangladesh and Peru. 2002.

Band 31 Annette Luibrand: Transition in Vietnam. Impact of the Rural Reform Process on an Ethnic Minority. 2002.

Band 32 Felix Ankomah Asante: Economic Analysis of Decentralisation in Rural Ghana. 2003.

Band 33 Chodechai Suwanaporn: Determinants of Bank Lending in Thailand: An Empirical Examination for the Years 1992 to 1996. 2003.

Band 34 Abay Asfaw: Costs of Illness, Demand for Medical Care, and the Prospect of Community Health Insurance Schemes in the Rural Areas of Ethiopia. 2003.

Band 35 Gi-Soon Song: The Impact of Information and Communication Technologies (ICTs) on Rural Households. A Holistic Approach Applied to the Case of Lao People's Democratic Republic. 2003.

Band 36 Daniela Lohlein: An Economic Analysis of Public Good Provision in Rural Russia. The Case of Education and Health Care. 2003.

Band 37 Johannes Woelcke. Bio-Economics of Sustainable Land Management in Uganda. 2003.

Band 38 Susanne M. Ziemek: The Economics of Volunteer Labor Supply. An Application to Countries of a Different Development Level. 2003.

Band 39 Doris Wiesmann: An International Nutrition Index. Concept and Analyses of Food Insecurity and Undernutrition at Country Levels. 2004.

Band 40 Isaac Osei-Akoto: The Economics of Rural Health Insurance. The Effects of Formal and Informal Risk-Sharing Schemes in Ghana. 2004.

Band 41 Yuansheng Jiang: Health Insurance Demand and Health Risk Management in Rural China. 2004.

Band 42 Roukayatou Zimmermann: Biotechnology and Value-added Traits in Food Crops: Relevance for Developing Countries and Economic Analyses. 2004.

Band 43 F. Markus Kaiser: Incentives in Community-based Health Insurance Schemes. 2004.

Band 44 Thomas Herzfeld: *Corruption begets Corruption.* Zur Dynamik und Persistenz der Korruption. 2004.

Band 45 Edilegnaw Wale Zegeye: The Economics of On-Farm Conservation of Crop Diversity in Ethiopia: Incentives, Attribute Preferences and Opportunity Costs of Maintaining Local Varieties of Crops. 2004.

Band 46 Adama Konseiga: Regional Integration Beyond the Traditional Trade Benefits: Labor Mobility contribution. The Case of Burkina Faso and Côte d'Ivoire. 2005.

Band 47 Beyene Tadesse Ferenji: The Impact of Policy Reform and Institutional Transformation on Agricultural Performance. An Economic Study of Ethiopian Agriculture. 2005.

Band 48 Sabine Daude: Agricultural Trade Liberalization in the WTO and Its Poverty Implications. A Study of Rural Households in Northern Vietnam. 2005.

Band 49 Kadir Osman Gyasi: Determinants of Success of Collective Action on Local Commons. An Empirical Analysis of Community-Based Irrigation Management in Northern Ghana. 2005.

Band 50 Borbala E. Balint: Determinants of Commercial Orientation and Sustainability of Agricultural Production of the Individual Farms in Romania. 2006.

Band 51 Pamela Marinda: Effects of Gender Inequality in Resource Ownership and Access on Household Welfare and Food Security in Kenya. A Case Study of West Pokot District. 2006.

Band 52 Charles Palmer: The Outcomes and their Determinants from Community-Company Contracting over Forest Use in Post-Decentralization Indonesia. 2006.

Band 53 Hardwick Tchale: Agricultural Policy and Soil Fertility Management in the Maize-based Smallholder Farming System in Malawi. 2006.

Band 54 John Kedi Mduma: Rural Off-Form Employment and its Effects on Adoption of Labor Intensive Soil Conserving Measures in Tanzania. 2006.

Band 55 Mareike Meyn: The Impact of EU Free Trade Agreements on Economic Development and Regional Integration in Southern Africa. The Example of EU-SACU Trade Relations. 2006.

www.peterlang.de